Toyota Corolla

Owners Workshop Manual

Peter T. Gill

Models covered (4791 - 336)

Saloon, Hatchback & Estate, including special/limited editions
Petrol: 1.4 litre (1398cc) & 1.6 litre (1598cc)
Diesel: 2.0 litre (1995cc)

Does NOT cover models with 1.8 litre (1796cc) petrol engines or 1.4 litre (1364cc) diesel engines

A book in the **Haynes Owners Workshop Manual Series**

ISBN **978 1 78521 393 9**

British Library Cataloguing in Publication Data
A catalogue record for this book is available from the British Library.

Haynes Group Limited
Haynes North America, Inc

www.haynes.com

The manufacturer's authorised representative in the EU for product safety is:

HaynesPro BV
Stationsstraat 79 F, 3811MH Amersfoort, The Netherlands
gpsr@haynes.co.uk

Disclaimer

There are risks associated with automotive repairs. The ability to make repairs depends on the individual's skill, experience and proper tools. Individuals should act with due care and acknowledge and assume the risk of performing automotive repairs.

The purpose of this manual is to provide comprehensive, useful and accessible automotive repair information, to help you get the best value from your vehicle. However, this manual is not a substitute for a professional certified technician or mechanic.

This repair manual is produced by a third party and is not associated with an individual vehicle manufacturer. If there is any doubt or discrepancy between this manual and the owner's manual or the factory service manual, please refer to the factory service manual or seek assistance from a professional certified technician or mechanic.

Even though we have prepared this manual with extreme care and every attempt is made to ensure that the information in this manual is correct, neither the publisher nor the author can accept responsibility for loss, damage or injury caused by any errors in, or omissions from, the information given.

Contents

LIVING WITH YOUR TOYOTA COROLLA

Roadside repairs

Weekly checks

MAINTENANCE

Routine maintenance and servicing

Contents

REPAIRS & OVERHAUL

Continuing the tradition of the 'World's best-selling car', the range of Corolla models covered by this manual offers a wide range of body styles and engines, with the emphasis on proven, solid engineering, further reinforcing Toyota's deserved reputation for outstanding reliability.

This manual covers models from 2002; the Corolla was completely redeveloped and restyled, to give us a completely new Corolla. In 2004 this underwent a facelift, with cosmetic revisions to the front bumper, headlights, bonnet and front grille.

All petrol engines covered in this manual are normally-aspirated, and incorporate a hydraulically-controlled mechanism on the inlet camshaft which varies the valve timing. This facility improves the driveability, efficiency and emissions of the engines. All engines feature a comprehensive engine management system with extensive emission control equipment. Although two diesel engines were available for this model, only the 2.0 litre diesel engine is covered in this manual.

5-speed manual transmissions were available, along with a 4-speed automatic option. Although a four-wheel-drive model was available in some markets, only the front-wheel-drive versions are covered by this manual.

Braking is by discs at the front and at the rear, with ABS as standard on all models. Electrically-operated power-assisted steering is standard on all models.

A wide range of standard and optional equipment is available within the range to suit virtually all tastes. Both a driver's and passenger's airbag were fitted as standard, with side airbags incorporated into the front seats, and front seat belt pretensioners.

Provided that regular servicing is carried out in accordance with the manufacturer's recommendations, the Toyota Corolla will provide the enviable reliability for which this marque is famous. The engine compartment is relatively spacious, and most of the items requiring frequent attention are easily accessible.

Your Toyota manual

The aim of this manual is to help you get the best value from your vehicle. It can do so in several ways. It can help you decide what work must be done (even should you choose to get it done by a garage). It will also provide information on routine maintenance and servicing, and give a logical course of action and diagnosis when random faults occur. However, it is hoped that you will use the manual by tackling the work yourself. On simpler jobs it may even be quicker than booking the car into a garage and going there twice, to leave and collect it. Perhaps most important, a lot of money can be saved by avoiding the costs a garage must charge to cover its labour and overheads.

The manual has drawings and descriptions to show the function of the various components so that their layout can be understood. Tasks are described and photographed in a clear step-by-step sequence. The illustrations are numbered by the Section number and paragraph number to which they relate – if there is more than one illustration per paragraph, the sequence is denoted alphabetically.

References to the 'left' or 'right' of the vehicle are in the sense of a person in the driver's seat, facing forwards.

Acknowledgements

Thanks are due to Draper Tools Limited, who provided some of the workshop tools, and to all those people at Sparkford who helped in the production of this manual.

We take great pride in the accuracy of information given in this manual, but vehicle manufacturers make alterations and design changes during the production run of a particular vehicle of which they do not inform us. No liability can be accepted by the authors or publishers for loss, damage or injury caused by any errors in, or omissions from the information given.

Working on your car can be dangerous. This page shows just some of the potential risks and hazards, with the aim of creating a safety-conscious attitude.

General hazards

Scalding

• Don't remove the radiator or expansion tank cap while the engine is hot.
• Engine oil, automatic transmission fluid or power steering fluid may also be dangerously hot if the engine has recently been running.

Burning

• Beware of burns from the exhaust system and from any part of the engine. Brake discs and drums can also be extremely hot immediately after use.

Crushing

• When working under or near a raised vehicle, always supplement the jack with axle stands, or use drive-on ramps. ***Never venture under a car which is only supported by a jack.***
• Take care if loosening or tightening high-torque nuts when the vehicle is on stands. Initial loosening and final tightening should be done with the wheels on the ground.

Fire

• Fuel is highly flammable; fuel vapour is explosive.
• Don't let fuel spill onto a hot engine.
• Do not smoke or allow naked lights (including pilot lights) anywhere near a vehicle being worked on. Also beware of creating sparks (electrically or by use of tools).
• Fuel vapour is heavier than air, so don't work on the fuel system with the vehicle over an inspection pit.
• Another cause of fire is an electrical overload or short-circuit. Take care when repairing or modifying the vehicle wiring.
• Keep a fire extinguisher handy, of a type suitable for use on fuel and electrical fires.

Electric shock

• Ignition HT voltage can be dangerous, especially to people with heart problems or a pacemaker. Don't work on or near the ignition system with the engine running or the ignition switched on.
• Mains voltage is also dangerous. Make sure that any mains-operated equipment is correctly earthed. Mains power points should be protected by a residual current device (RCD) circuit breaker.

Fume or gas intoxication

• Exhaust fumes are poisonous; they often contain carbon monoxide, which is rapidly fatal if inhaled. Never run the engine in a confined space such as a garage with the doors shut.
• Fuel vapour is also poisonous, as are the vapours from some cleaning solvents and paint thinners.

Poisonous or irritant substances

• Avoid skin contact with battery acid and with any fuel, fluid or lubricant, especially antifreeze, brake hydraulic fluid and Diesel fuel. Don't syphon them by mouth. If such a substance is swallowed or gets into the eyes, seek medical advice.
• Prolonged contact with used engine oil can cause skin cancer. Wear gloves or use a barrier cream if necessary. Change out of oil-soaked clothes and do not keep oily rags in your pocket.
• Air conditioning refrigerant forms a poisonous gas if exposed to a naked flame (including a cigarette). It can also cause skin burns on contact.

Asbestos

• Asbestos dust can cause cancer if inhaled or swallowed. Asbestos may be found in gaskets and in brake and clutch linings. When dealing with such components it is safest to assume that they contain asbestos.

Special hazards

Hydrofluoric acid

• This extremely corrosive acid is formed when certain types of synthetic rubber, found in some O-rings, oil seals, fuel hoses etc, are exposed to temperatures above 400ºC. The rubber changes into a charred or sticky substance containing the acid. *Once formed, the acid remains dangerous for years. If it gets onto the skin, it may be necessary to amputate the limb concerned.*
• When dealing with a vehicle which has suffered a fire, or with components salvaged from such a vehicle, wear protective gloves and discard them after use.

The battery

• Batteries contain sulphuric acid, which attacks clothing, eyes and skin. Take care when topping-up or carrying the battery.
• The hydrogen gas given off by the battery is highly explosive. Never cause a spark or allow a naked light nearby. Be careful when connecting and disconnecting battery chargers or jump leads.

Air bags

• Air bags can cause injury if they go off accidentally. Take care when removing the steering wheel and/or facia. Special storage instructions may apply.

Diesel injection equipment

• Diesel injection pumps supply fuel at very high pressure. Take care when working on the fuel injectors and fuel pipes.

Warning: Never expose the hands, face or any other part of the body to injector spray; the fuel can penetrate the skin with potentially fatal results.

Remember...

DO

• Do use eye protection when using power tools, and when working under the vehicle.

• Do wear gloves or use barrier cream to protect your hands when necessary.

• Do get someone to check periodically that all is well when working alone on the vehicle.

• Do keep loose clothing and long hair well out of the way of moving mechanical parts.

• Do remove rings, wristwatch etc, before working on the vehicle – especially the electrical system.

• Do ensure that any lifting or jacking equipment has a safe working load rating adequate for the job.

DON'T

• Don't attempt to lift a heavy component which may be beyond your capability – get assistance.

• Don't rush to finish a job, or take unverified short cuts.

• Don't use ill-fitting tools which may slip and cause injury.

• Don't leave tools or parts lying around where someone can trip over them. Mop up oil and fuel spills at once.

• Don't allow children or pets to play in or near a vehicle being worked on.

The following pages are intended to help in dealing with common roadside emergencies and breakdowns. You will find more detailed fault finding information at the back of the manual, and repair information in the main chapters.

If your car won't start and the starter motor doesn't turn

- ☐ If it's a model with automatic transmission, make sure the selector is in P or N.
- ☐ Remove the battery cover and make sure that the battery terminals are clean and tight.
- ☐ Switch on the headlights and try to start the engine. If the headlights go very dim when you're trying to start, the battery is probably flat. Get out of trouble by jump starting (see next page) using a friend's car.

If your car won't start even though the starter motor turns as normal

- ☐ Is there fuel in the tank?
- ☐ Is there moisture on electrical components under the bonnet? Switch off the ignition, and then wipe off any obvious dampness with a dry cloth. Spray a water-repellent aerosol product (WD-40 or equivalent) on ignition and fuel system electrical connectors like those shown in the photos. (Note that diesel engines don't usually suffer from damp.)

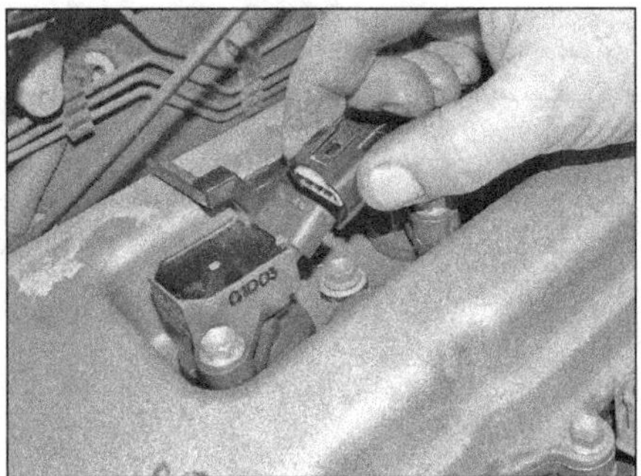

A Check the security of the wiring to the ignition coils (petrol models only).

B Check the condition and security of the connections to the starter motor.

C Check the fuses in the fusebox located in the engine compartment.

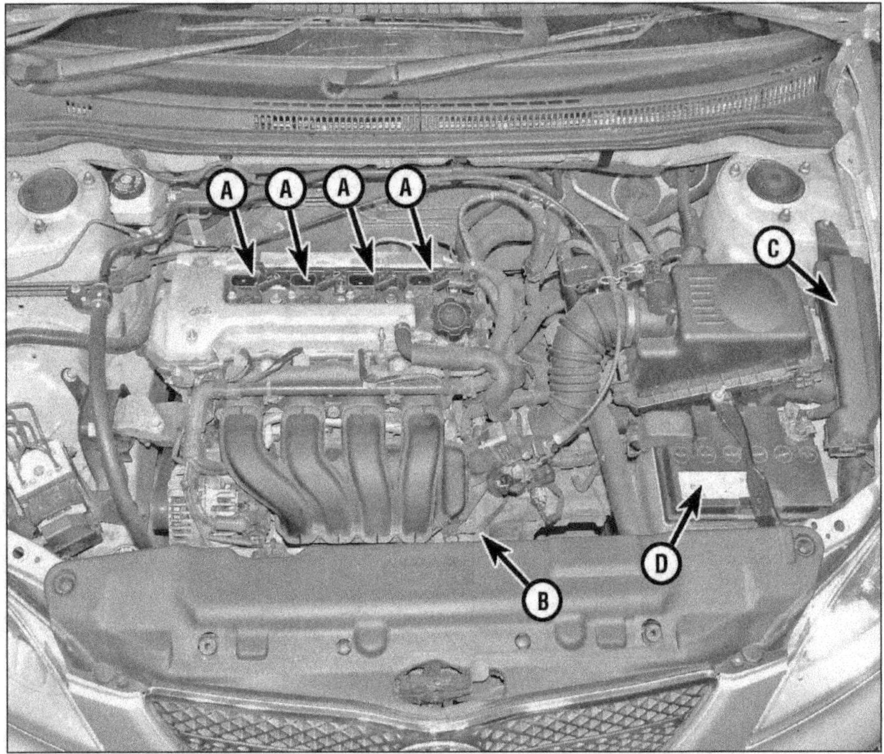

Check that electrical connections are secure (with the ignition switched off) and spray them with a water-dispersant spray like WD-40 if you suspect a problem due to damp.

D Check the condition and security of the battery connections.

E Check that the fuel filter and fuel lines are secure and no air in the system (diesel model shown).

Jump starting

When jump-starting a car using a booster battery, observe the following precautions:

- ✔ Before connecting the booster battery, make sure that the ignition is switched off.
- ✔ Ensure that all electrical equipment (lights, heater, wipers, etc) is switched off.
- ✔ Take note of any special precautions printed on the battery case.
- ✔ Make sure that the booster battery is the same voltage as the discharged one in the vehicle.
- ✔ If the battery is being jump-started from the battery in another vehicle, the two vehicles MUST NOT TOUCH each other.
- ✔ Make sure that the transmission is in neutral (or PARK, in the case of automatic transmission).

Jump starting will get you out of trouble, but you must correct whatever made the battery go flat in the first place. There are three possibilities:

1 The battery has been drained by repeated attempts to start, or by leaving the lights on.

2 The charging system is not working properly (alternator drivebelt slack or broken, alternator wiring fault or alternator itself faulty).

3 The battery itself is at fault (electrolyte low, or battery worn out).

1 Connect one end of the red jump lead to the positive (+) terminal of the flat battery

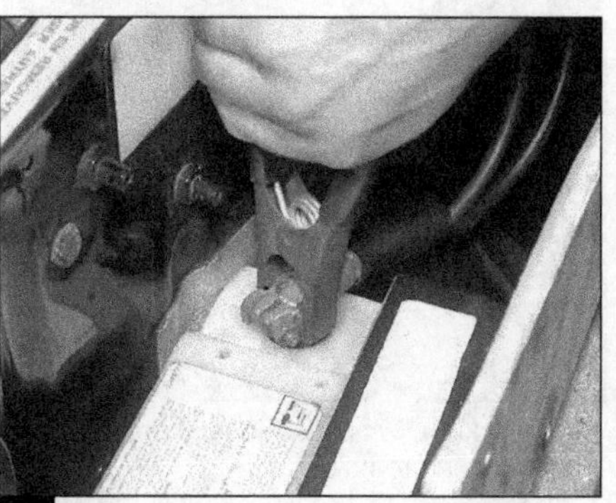

2 Connect the other end of the red lead to the positive (+) terminal of the booster battery.

3 Connect one end of the black jump lead to the negative (-) terminal of the booster battery

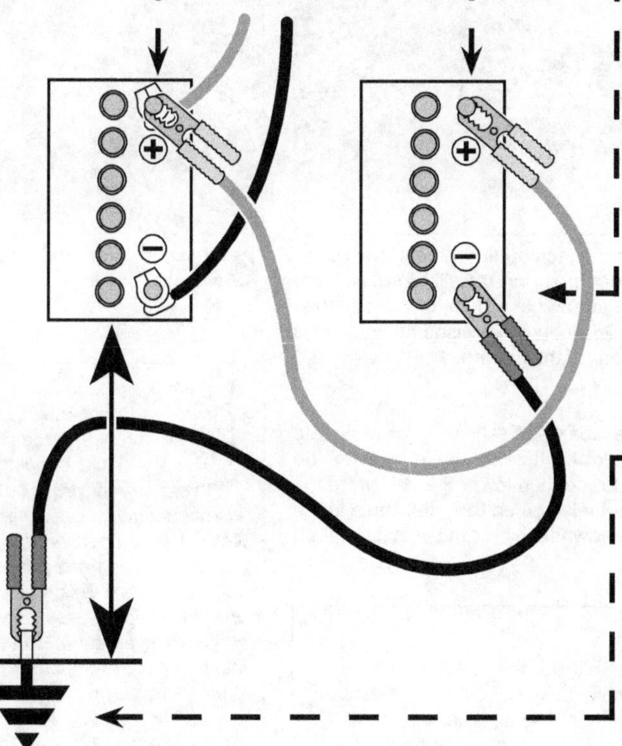

4 Connect the other end of the black jump lead to a bolt or bracket on the engine block, well away from the battery, on the vehicle to be started.

5 Make sure that the jump leads will not come into contact with the fan, drive-belts or other moving parts of the engine.

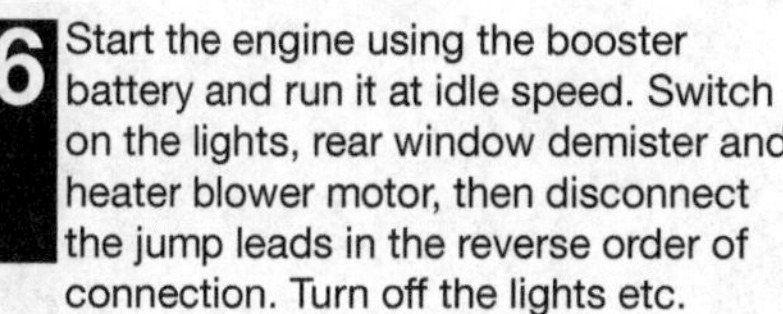

6 Start the engine using the booster battery and run it at idle speed. Switch on the lights, rear window demister and heater blower motor, then disconnect the jump leads in the reverse order of connection. Turn off the lights etc.

Wheel changing

Some of the details shown here will vary according to model

Warning: Do not change a wheel in a situation where you risk being hit by other traffic. On busy roads, try to stop in a lay-by or a gateway. Be wary of passing traffic while changing the wheel – it is easy to become distracted by the job in hand.

Preparation

- ☐ When a puncture occurs, stop as soon as it is safe to do so.
- ☐ Park on firm level ground, if possible, and well out of the way of other traffic.
- ☐ Use hazard warning lights if necessary.
- ☐ If you have one, use a warning triangle to alert other drivers of your presence.
- ☐ Apply the handbrake and engage first or reverse gear (or P on models with automatic transmission).
- ☐ Chock the wheel diagonally opposite the one being removed – a couple of large stones will do for this.
- ☐ If the ground is soft, use a flat piece of wood to spread the load under the jack.

Changing the wheel

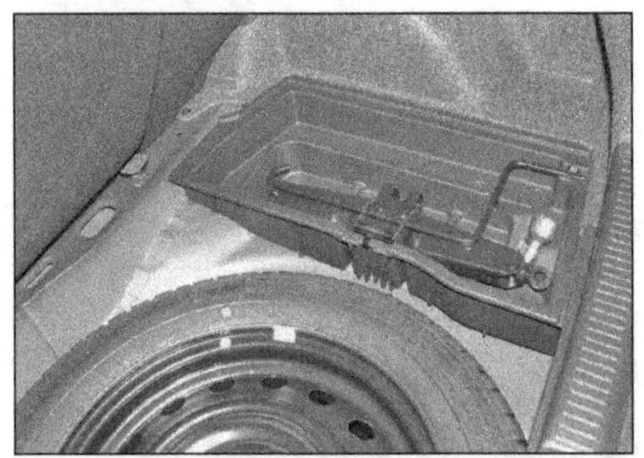

1 The spare wheel and tools are stored in the luggage compartment. Raise the floor covering, and lift out the jack and wheel changing tools.

2 Chock the wheel diagonally opposite the one being removed.

3 Use the wheel brace to prise off the wheel trim (where fitted).

4 Using the wheel brace, slacken each wheel nut by half a turn. On models with alloy wheels, a Toyota socket may be needed to remove the security nut – the socket should be in the glovebox or toolkit.

5 Locate the jack on firm ground below the reinforced point on the sill (don't jack the vehicle at any other point of the sill), then turn the jack handle clockwise until the wheel is raised clear of the ground.

6 Unscrew the wheel nuts and remove the wheel.

7 Fit the spare wheel, and screw in the nuts. Lightly tighten the nuts with the wheel brace then lower the vehicle to the ground. Securely tighten the wheel nuts in the sequence shown then refit the wheel trim/hub cap.

Finally . . .

- ☐ Remove the wheel chocks.
- ☐ Stow the jack and tools with the spare wheel in the luggage compartment.
- ☐ Check the tyre pressure on the wheel just fitted. If it is low, or if you don't have a pressure gauge with you, drive slowly to the nearest garage and inflate the tyre to the correct pressure.
- ☐ The wheel nuts should be tightened to the specified torque (103 Nm/76 lbf ft) at the earliest possible opportunity.

Note: *If a temporary 'space-saver' spare wheel has been fitted, special conditions apply to its use. This type of spare wheel is only intended for use in an emergency, and should not remain fitted any longer than it takes to get the punctured wheel repaired. While the temporary wheel is in use, ensure it is inflated to the correct pressure, do not exceed 50 mph, and avoid harsh acceleration, braking or cornering.*

Identifying leaks

Puddles on the garage floor or drive, or obvious wetness under the bonnet or underneath the car, suggest a leak that needs investigating. It can sometimes be difficult to decide where the leak is coming from, especially if the engine bay is very dirty already. Leaking oil or fluid can also be blown rearwards by the passage of air under the car, giving a false impression of where the problem lies.

Warning: Most automotive oils and fluids are poisonous. Wash them off skin, and change out of contaminated clothing, without delay.

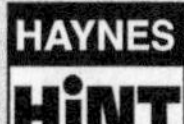

The smell of a fluid leaking from the car may provide a clue to what's leaking. Some fluids are distinctively coloured.
It may help to clean the car carefully and to park it over some clean paper overnight as an aid to locating the source of the leak.
Remember that some leaks may only occur while the engine is running.

Sump oil

Engine oil may leak from the drain plug...

Oil from filter

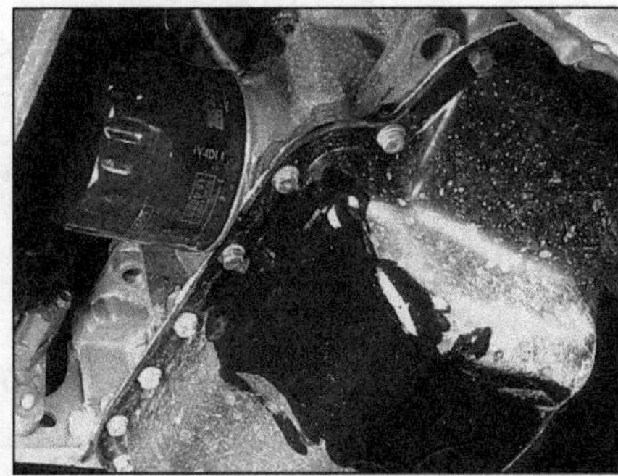

...or from the base of the oil filter.

Gearbox oil

Gearbox oil can leak from the seals at the inboard ends of the driveshafts.

Antifreeze

Leaking antifreeze often leaves a crystalline deposit like this.

Brake fluid

A leak occurring at a wheel is almost certainly brake fluid.

Towing

When all else fails, you may find yourself having to get a tow home – or of course you may be helping somebody else. Long-distance recovery should only be done by a garage or breakdown service. For shorter distances, DIY towing using another car is easy enough, but observe the following points:

- ☐ Use a proper tow-rope – they are not expensive. The vehicle being towed must display an ON TOW sign in its rear window.
- ☐ Always turn the ignition key to the 'On' position when the vehicle is being towed, so that the steering lock is released, and the direction indicator and brake lights work.
- ☐ Only attach the tow-rope to the towing eyes provided. The towing eye is supplied as part of the toolkit stored in the luggage compartment. To fit the eye, remove the vent/cover from the bumper. Screw the eye into position, and tighten using the wheel brace handle.
- ☐ Before being towed, release the handbrake and select neutral on the transmission. On models with automatic transmission, do not exceed 30 mph and do not tow for more than 30 miles. If in doubt, do not tow, or transmission damage may result.
- ☐ The driver of the car being towed must keep the tow-rope taut at all times to avoid snatching.
- ☐ Note that greater-than-usual pedal pressure will be required to operate the brakes, since the vacuum servo unit is only operational with the engine running.
- ☐ Because the power steering will not be operational, greater-than-usual steering effort will be required.
- ☐ Make sure that both drivers know the route before setting off.
- ☐ Only drive at moderate speeds and keep the distance towed to a minimum. Drive smoothly and allow plenty of time for slowing down at junctions.

Introduction

There are some very simple checks which need only take a few minutes to carry out, but which could save you a lot of inconvenience and expense.

These *Weekly checks* require no great skill or special tools, and the small amount of time they take to perform could prove to be very well spent, for example:

☐ Keeping an eye on tyre condition and pressures, will not only help to stop them wearing out prematurely, but could also save your life.

☐ Many breakdowns are caused by electrical problems. Battery-related faults are particularly common, and a quick check on a regular basis will often prevent the majority of these.

☐ If your car develops a brake fluid leak, the first time you might know about it is when your brakes don't work properly. Checking the level regularly will give advance warning of this kind of problem.

☐ If the oil or coolant levels run low, the cost of repairing any engine damage will be far greater than fixing the leak, for example.

Underbonnet check points

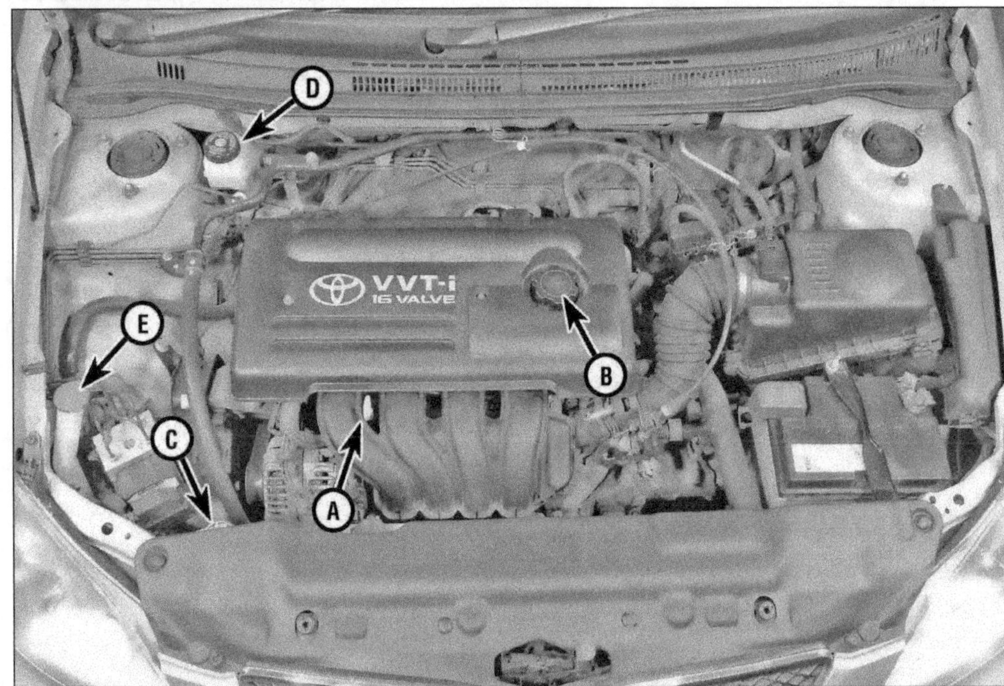

◀ 1.6 litre petrol engine

A *Engine oil level dipstick*
B *Engine oil filler cap*
C *Coolant expansion tank*
D *Brake/clutch fluid reservoir*
E *Screen washer fluid reservoir*

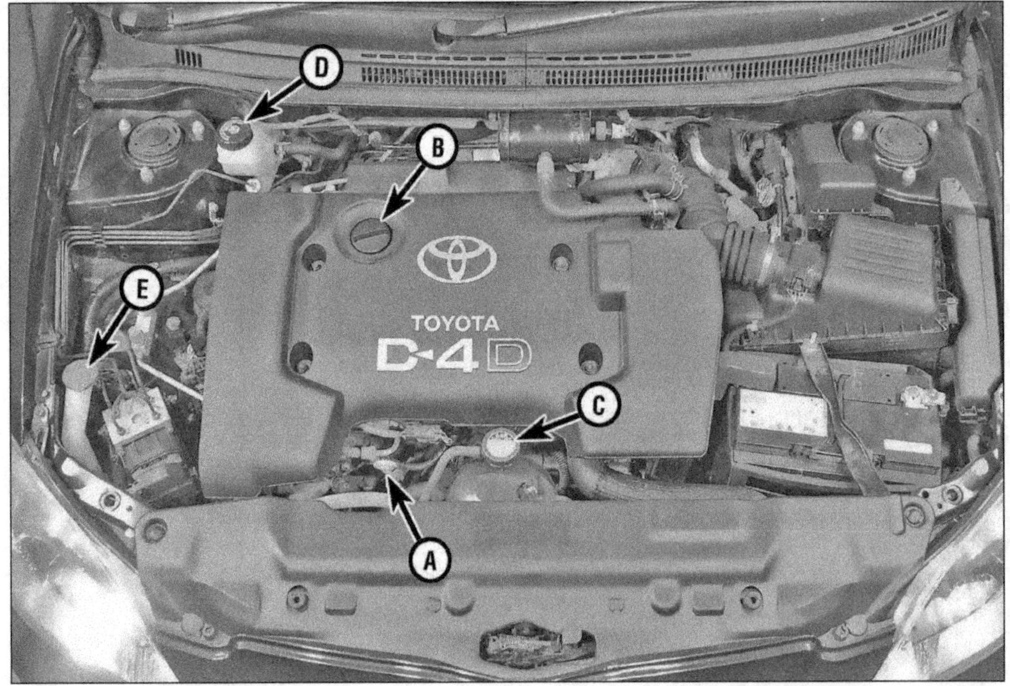

◀ 2.0 litre diesel engine

A *Engine oil level dipstick*
B *Engine oil filler cap*
C *Coolant expansion tank*
D *Brake/clutch fluid reservoir*
E *Screen washer fluid reservoir*

Engine oil level

Before you start

✔ Make sure that the car is on level ground.

✔ Check the oil level before the car is driven, or at least 5 minutes after the engine has been switched off.

If the oil is checked immediately after driving the vehicle, some of the oil will remain in the upper engine components, resulting in an inaccurate reading on the dipstick.

The correct oil

Modern engines place great demands on their oil. It is very important that the correct oil for your car is used (see *Lubricants and fluids*).

Car care

● If you have to add oil frequently, you should check whether you have any oil leaks. Place some clean paper under the car overnight, and check for stains in the morning. If there are no leaks, then the engine may be burning oil.

● Always maintain the level between the upper and lower dipstick marks. If the level is too low, severe engine damage may occur. Oil seal failure may result if the engine is overfilled by adding too much oil.

1 The dipsticks top is brightly coloured for easy identification (see *Underbonnet check points* for exact location). Withdraw the dipstick, and then use a clean rag or paper towel to wipe the oil from it. Insert the clean dipstick into the tube as far as it will go, then withdraw it again.

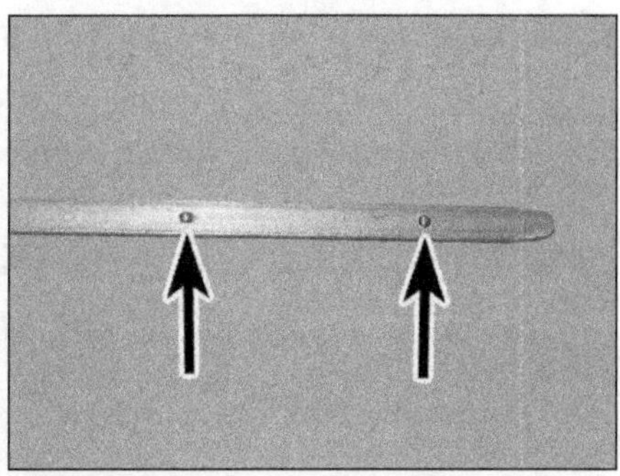

2 Note the level on the end of the dipstick, which should be between the upper (MAX) and lower (MIN) mark (arrowed) . . .

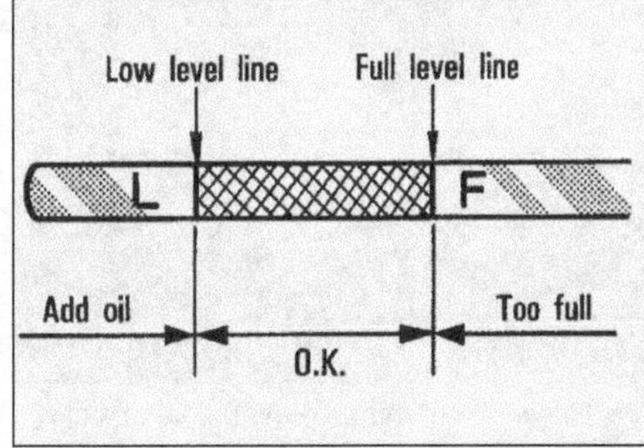

3 . . . or on some models, in the hatched area indicating MAX and MIN between the upper (F) mark and the lower (L) mark. Approximately 1.0 litre of oil will raise the level from the lower mark to the upper mark

4 Oil is added through the filler cap aperture. Unscrew the cap, place some cloth rags around the filler cap aperture, then top-up the level. A funnel may help to reduce spillage. Add the oil slowly, checking the level on the dipstick frequently. Avoid overfilling (see *Car care*).

Coolant level

Warning: Do not attempt to remove the expansion tank pressure cap when the engine is hot, as there is a very great risk of scalding. Do not leave open containers of coolant about, as it is poisonous.

Car care

● With a sealed-type cooling system, adding coolant should not be necessary on a regular basis. If frequent topping-up is required, it is likely there is a leak. Check the radiator, all hoses and joint faces for signs of staining or wetness, and rectify as necessary.

● It is important that antifreeze is used in the cooling system all year round, not just during the winter months. Don't top-up with water alone, as the antifreeze will become diluted.

1 The coolant level varies with the temperature of the engine. If topping-up is necessary, wait until the engine is cold. Slowly unscrew the cap to release any pressure present in the cooling system, and remove the cap.

2 Add the specified antifreeze (see *Lubricants and fluids*) to the expansion tank until the coolant level is halfway between the level marks. Refit the cap and tighten it securely (diesel model shown).

Brake (and clutch) fluid level

Note: *On manual transmission models, the fluid reservoir also supplies the clutch master cylinder with fluid.*

Before you start

✔ Make sure that the car is on level ground.

✔ Cleanliness is of great importance when dealing with the braking system; so take care to clean around the reservoir cap before topping-up. Use only clean brake fluid.

Safety first!

● If the reservoir requires repeated topping-up, this is an indication of a fluid leak somewhere in the system, which should be investigated immediately. Note that the level will drop naturally as the brake pad linings wear, but must never be allowed to fall below the MIN mark.

● If a leak is suspected, the car should not be driven until the braking system has been checked. Never take any risks where brakes are concerned.

Warning: Brake fluid can harm your eyes and damage painted surfaces, so use extreme caution when handling and pouring it. Do not use fluid that has been standing open for some time, as it absorbs moisture from the air, which can cause a dangerous loss of braking effectiveness.

1 The MAX mark is indicated on the side of the reservoir. The fluid level must be kept up to this mark at all times.

2 If topping-up is necessary, first wipe clean the area around the filler cap to prevent dirt entering the hydraulic system.

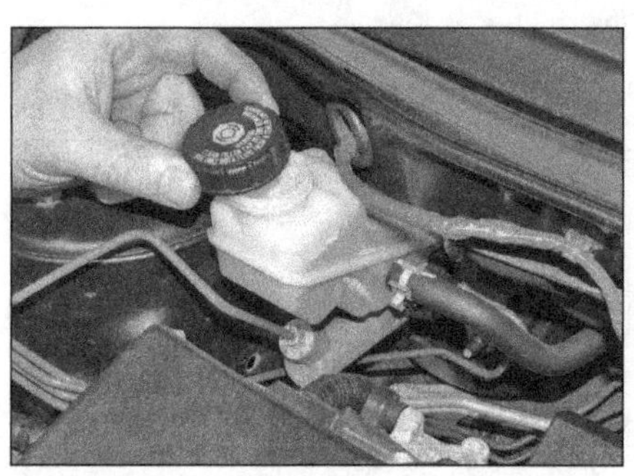

3 Unscrew and remove the reservoir's cap. Carefully add fluid, taking care not to spill it onto the surrounding components (use a funnel).

4 Use only the specified fluid (see *Lubricants and fluids*); mixing different types can cause damage to the system. On completion, securely refit the cap and wipe away any spilt fluid.

Washer fluid level

● Screenwash additives not only keep the windscreen clean during bad weather, they also prevent the washer system freezing in cold weather – which is when you are likely to need it most. Don't top-up using plain water, as the screenwash will become diluted, and will freeze in cold weather.

Warning: On no account use engine coolant antifreeze in the screen washer system – this may damage the paintwork.

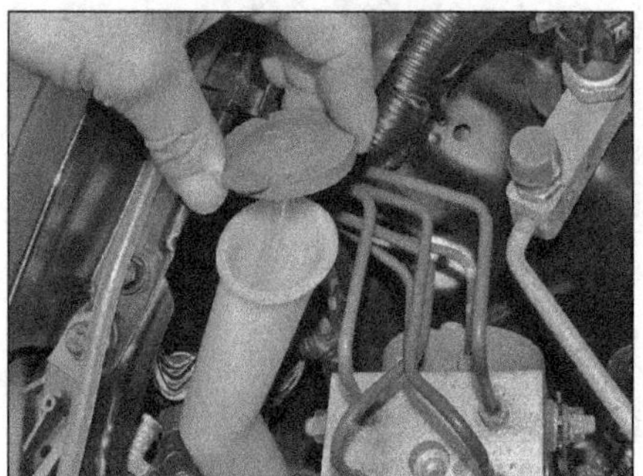

1 The screenwash fluid reservoir is located on the right-hand side (as seen from the driver's seat) of the engine compartment, behind the headlight. Pull up the filler cap to release it from the reservoir.

2 When topping-up the reservoir, a screenwash additive should be added in the quantities recommended on the bottle.

Tyre condition and pressure

It is very important that tyres are in good condition, and at the correct pressure - having a tyre failure at any speed is highly dangerous. Tyre wear is influenced by driving style - harsh braking and acceleration, or fast cornering, will all produce more rapid tyre wear. As a general rule, the front tyres wear out faster than the rears. Interchanging the tyres from front to rear ("rotating" the tyres) may result in more even wear. However, if this is completely effective, you may have the expense of replacing all four tyres at once!

Remove any nails or stones embedded in the tread before they penetrate the tyre to cause deflation. If removal of a nail does reveal that the tyre has been punctured, refit the nail so that its point of penetration is marked. Then immediately change the wheel, and have the tyre repaired by a tyre dealer.

Regularly check the tyres for damage in the form of cuts or bulges, especially in the sidewalls. Periodically remove the wheels, and clean any dirt or mud from the inside and outside surfaces. Examine the wheel rims for signs of rusting, corrosion or other damage. Light alloy wheels are easily damaged by "kerbing" whilst parking; steel wheels may also become dented or buckled. A new wheel is very often the only way to overcome severe damage.

New tyres should be balanced when they are fitted, but it may become necessary to re-balance them as they wear, or if the balance weights fitted to the wheel rim should fall off. Unbalanced tyres will wear more quickly, as will the steering and suspension components. Wheel imbalance is normally signified by vibration, particularly at a certain speed (typically around 50 mph). If this vibration is felt only through the steering, then it is likely that just the front wheels need balancing. If, however, the vibration is felt through the whole car, the rear wheels could be out of balance. Wheel balancing should be carried out by a tyre dealer or garage.

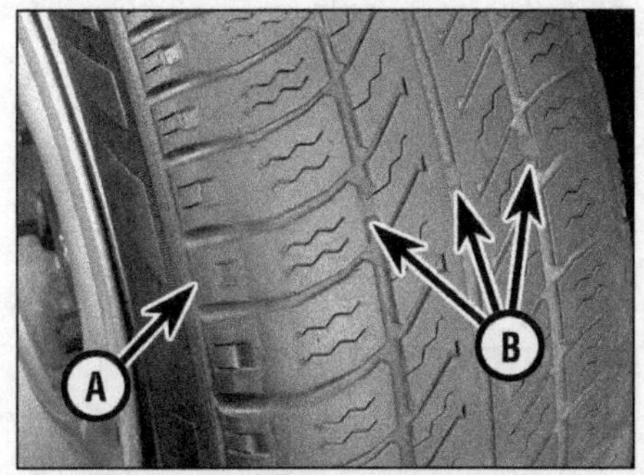

1 ***Tread Depth - visual check***
The original tyres have tread wear safety bands (B), which will appear when the tread depth reaches approximately 1.6 mm. The band positions are indicated by a triangular mark on the tyre sidewall (A).

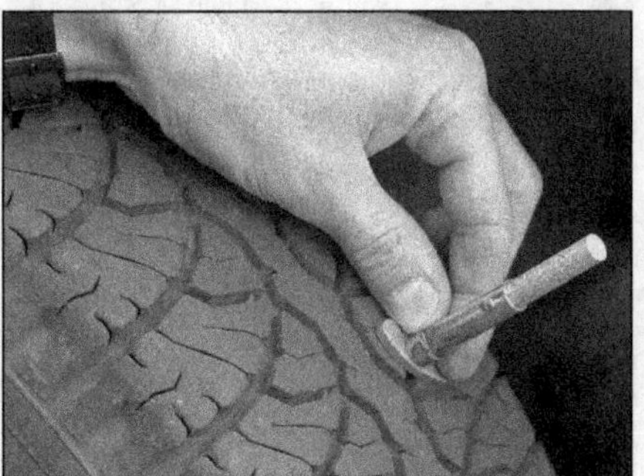

2 ***Tread Depth - manual check***
Alternatively, tread wear can be monitored with a simple, inexpensive device known as a tread depth indicator gauge.

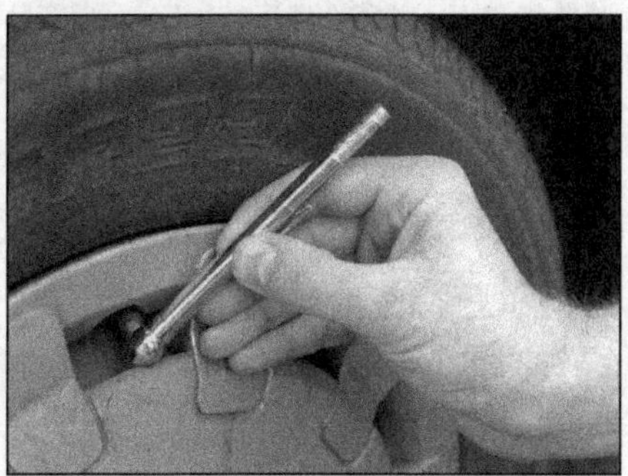

3 ***Tyre Pressure Check***
Check the tyre pressures regularly with the tyres cold. Do not adjust the tyre pressures immediately after the vehicle has been used, or an inaccurate setting will result.

Tyre tread wear patterns

Shoulder Wear

Underinflation (wear on both sides)
Under-inflation will cause overheating of the tyre, because the tyre will flex too much, and the tread will not sit correctly on the road surface. This will cause a loss of grip and excessive wear, not to mention the danger of sudden tyre failure due to heat build-up.
Check and adjust pressures
Incorrect wheel camber (wear on one side)
Repair or renew suspension parts
Hard cornering
Reduce speed!

Centre Wear

Overinflation
Over-inflation will cause rapid wear of the centre part of the tyre tread, coupled with reduced grip, harsher ride, and the danger of shock damage occurring in the tyre casing.
Check and adjust pressures

If you sometimes have to inflate your car's tyres to the higher pressures specified for maximum load or sustained high speed, don't forget to reduce the pressures to normal afterwards.

Uneven Wear

Front tyres may wear unevenly as a result of wheel misalignment. Most tyre dealers and garages can check and adjust the wheel alignment (or "tracking") for a modest charge.
Incorrect camber or castor
Repair or renew suspension parts
Malfunctioning suspension
Repair or renew suspension parts
Unbalanced wheel
Balance tyres
Incorrect toe setting
Adjust front wheel alignment
Note: *The feathered edge of the tread which typifies toe wear is best checked by feel.*

Wiper blades

Note: *Fitting details for wiper blades vary according to model, and according to whether genuine Toyota wiper blades have been fitted. Use the following procedures and illustrations shown as a guide for your car.*

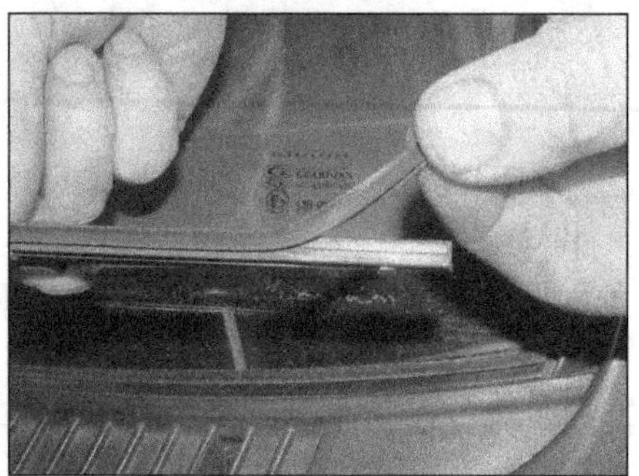

1 Check the condition of the wiper blades; if they are cracked or show any signs of deterioration, or if the glass swept area is smeared, renew them. For maximum clarity of vision, wiper blades should be renewed annually as a matter of course.

2 To remove a windscreen wiper blade, pull the arm fully away from the screen until it locks. Swivel the blade through 90°, and press the locking tab with your fingers

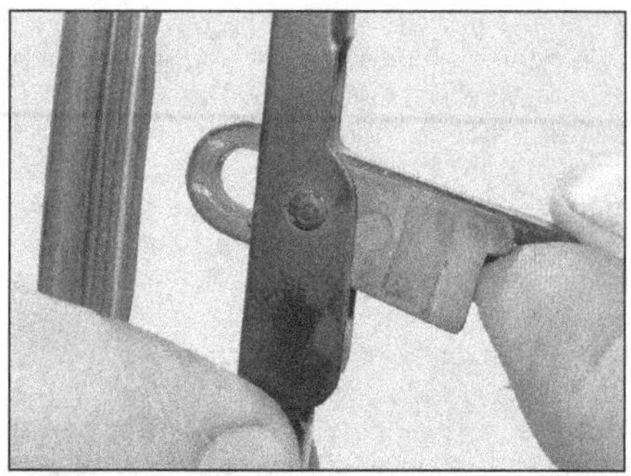

3 To remove the blade, depress the retaining tab and slide the blade out of the hooked end of the arm. Where applicable, don't forget to check the tailgate wiper blade as well.

Battery

Caution: Before carrying out any work on the vehicle battery, read the precautions given in 'Safety first!' at the start of this manual.

✔ Make sure that the battery tray is in good condition, and that the clamp is tight. Corrosion on the tray, retaining clamp and the battery itself can be removed with a solution of water and baking soda, after removing the affected components from the car (see Chapter 5A). Thoroughly rinse all cleaned areas with water. Any metal parts damaged by corrosion should be covered with a zinc-based primer, then painted.

✔ Periodically (approximately every three months), check the charge condition of the battery as described in Chapter 5A. A 'magic eye' charge indicator is fitted to the standard battery – if the indicator is green in colour, the battery is fully-charged, however, if it is colourless, it should be recharged. If it is yellow in colour, the battery should be renewed.

✔ If the battery is flat, and you need to jump start your vehicle, see *Roadside Repairs*.

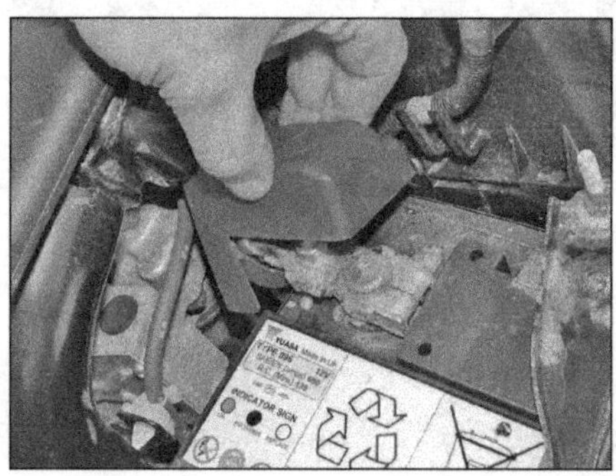

1 Open the bonnet and lift the small cover over the battery positive terminal. The exterior of the battery should be inspected periodically for damage such as a cracked case or cover.

2 Check the tightness of the battery clamps to ensure good electrical connections. You should not be able to move them. Also check each cable for cracks and frayed conductors.

Battery corrosion can be kept to a minimum by applying a layer of petroleum jelly to the clamps and terminals after they are reconnected.

3 If corrosion (white, fluffy deposits) is evident, remove the cables from the battery terminals, clean them with a small wire brush, then refit them. Automotive stores sell a tool for cleaning the battery post . . .

4 . . . as well as the battery cable clamps.

Electrical systems

✔ Check all external lights and the horn. Refer to the appropriate Sections of Chapter 12 for details if any of the circuits are found to be inoperative.

✔ Visually check all accessible wiring connectors, harnesses and retaining clips for security, and for signs of chafing or damage.

If you need to check your brake lights and indicators unaided, back up to a wall or garage door and operate the lights. The reflected light should show if they are working properly.

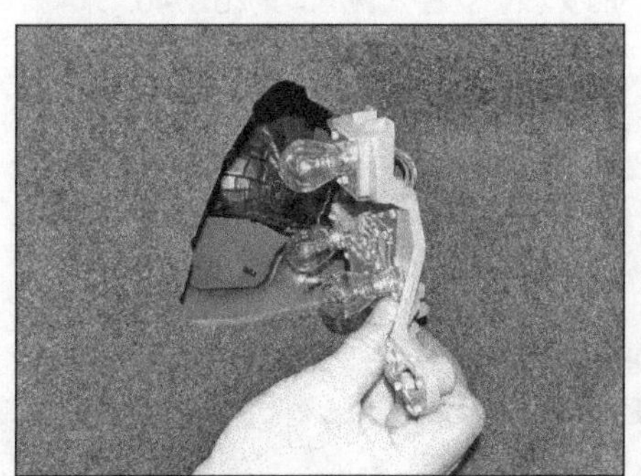

1 If a single indicator light, brake light or headlight has failed, it is likely that a bulb has blown and will need to be renewed. Refer to Chapter 12 for details. If both brake lights have failed, it is possible that the brake light switch operated by the brake pedal has failed. Refer to Chapter 9 for details.

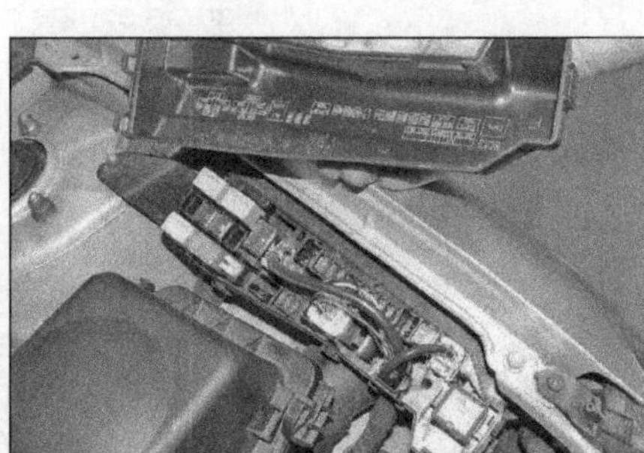

2 If more than one indicator light or headlight has failed, it is likely that either a fuse has blown or that there is a fault in the circuit (see *Electrical fault finding* in Chapter 12). The lighting circuit fuses are in the fusebox in the engine comaprtment. Unclip the cover. The circuits protected by the fuses are shown on the inside of the cover. Additional fuses and fusible links are in the fusebox located behind the glovebox inside the vehicle.

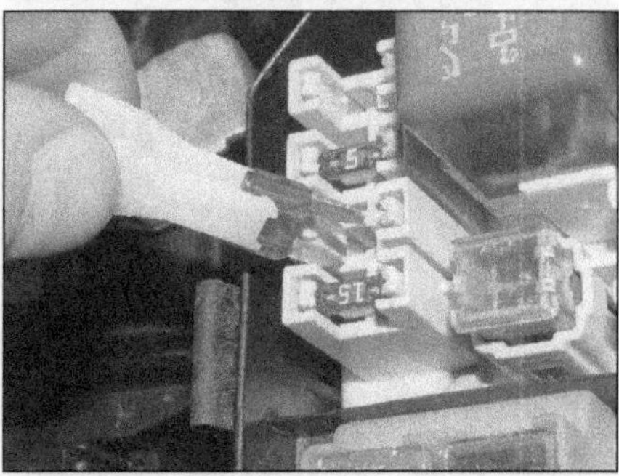

3 To renew a blown fuse, pull it from its location in the fusebox, using the plastic pliers provided. Fit a new fuse of the same rating, available from car accessory shops. It is important that you find the reason that the fuse blew (see *Electrical fault finding* in Chapter 12).

Lubricants and fluids

Engine	
Petrol engines	Multigrade engine oil, viscosity SAE 20W/50 or 15W/40. API grade SL or SM Multigrade engine oil, viscosity SAE 10W/30 or 5W/30. API grade SL 'energy saving' or SM 'energy saving'
Diesel engines	Multigrade engine oil, viscosity SAE 5W/30 to 20W/50. API CF-4 or CF (also CE or CD). ACEA B1
Cooling system	Toyota Super Long Life Coolant or a 50/50 mixture of high quality ethylene glycol-based antifreeze and distilled water
Manual transmission	Gear oil viscosity SAE 75W/90 GL4 or GL5
Automatic transmission	ATF Dexron II or III
Braking system	Hydraulic fluid to SAE J1703F or DOT 4
Clutch system	Hydraulic fluid to SAE J1703F or DOT 4

Tyre pressures

Note: *The pressures given are for the original equipment tyres under normal conditions – the recommended pressures may vary if any other make or type of tyre is fitted; check with the tyre manufacturer or supplier for latest recommendations. The following pressures are typical.*

	Front	**Rear**
Petrol models		
175/70R14 84H	2.3 bars (33 psi)	2.3 bars (33 psi)
195/60R15 88V	2.2 bars (32 psi)	2.2 bars (32 psi)
195/55R16 87V	2.2 bars (32 psi)	2.2 bars (32 psi)
Diesel models		
195/60R15 88V	2.4 bars (35 psi)	2.4 bars (35 psi)
195/55R16 87V	2.4 bars (35 psi)	2.4 bars (35 psi)

Chapter 1 Part A: Routine maintenance and servicing – petrol models

Contents

Degrees of difficulty

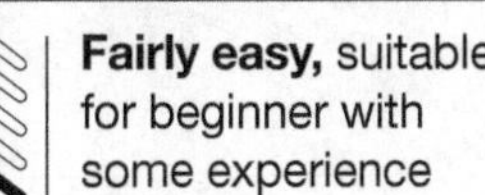

Easy, suitable for novice with little experience	**Fairly easy,** suitable for beginner with some experience	**Fairly difficult,** suitable for competent DIY mechanic	**Difficult,** suitable for experienced DIY mechanic	**Very difficult,** suitable for expert DIY or professional

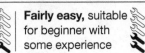

Lubricants and fluids . . . . Refer to *Weekly checks* on page 0•16

Capacities*

Engine oil (including filter):	
Up to 2004	3.7 litres
From 2004	4.2 litres
Transmission:	
Manual	1.9 litres
Automatic (drain and refill)	3.0 litres
Cooling system (approximate)	6.5 litres
Fuel tank	55 litres

** All capacities approximate. Add as necessary to bring up to appropriate level.*

Cooling system

Frost and corrosion protection	Refer to antifreeze manufacturer's concentration recommendations

Engine

Engine codes:	
1.4 litre (1398 cc) VVT-i engine	4ZZ-FE
1.6 litre (1598 cc) VVT-i engine	3ZZ-FE
Valve clearances (engine cold):	
Inlet valve	0.15 to 0.25 mm
Exhaust valve	0.25 to 0.35 mm

Ignition system

Spark plugs:	
1.4 litre 4ZZ-FE engine	Bosch FR8KCU
Electrode gap	1.0 mm
1.6 litre 3ZZ-FE engine	NGK BKR5EYA11
Electrode gap	1.1 mm

Brakes

Brake pad friction material minimum thickness	1.0 mm
Brake shoe lining minimum thickness	1.0 mm
Parking brake adjustment (when pulled with a force of 196 N)	6 to 9 clicks

Torque wrench settings

	Nm	lbf ft
Automatic transmission drain plug	17	13
Cylinder block drain plug	25	18
Ignition coil to cylinder head	7	5
Manual transmission filler/level and drain plugs	39	29
Roadwheel nuts	103	76
Spark plugs	25	18
Sump drain plug	37	27

The maintenance intervals in this manual are provided with the assumption that you, not the dealer, will be doing the work. These are the minimum maintenance intervals recommended by the factory for vehicles that are driven daily. If you wish to keep your vehicle in peak condition at all times, you may wish to perform some of these procedures even more often. Because frequent maintenance enhances the efficiency, performance and resale value of your car, we encourage you to do so. If you drive in dusty areas, tow a trailer, idle or drive at low speeds for extended periods or drive for short distances (less than four miles) in below freezing temperatures, shorter intervals are also recommended.

When the vehicle is new, it should be serviced by a dealer service department (or other workshop recognised by the vehicle manufacturer as providing the same standard of service) in order to preserve the warranty. The vehicle manufacturer may reject warranty claims if you are unable to prove that servicing has been carried out as and when specified, using only original equipment parts or parts certified to be of equivalent quality.

Caution: These models are equipped with an anti-theft radio. Before performing a procedure that requires disconnecting the battery, make sure you have the proper activation code.

Every 250 miles or weekly

- ☐ Refer to Weekly checks

Every 5000 miles or 6 months – whichever comes first

- ☐ Renew the engine oil and filter (Section 3).

Note: *Frequent oil and filter changes are good for the engine. We recommend changing the oil at the mileage specified here, or at least twice a year if the mileage covered is less.*

Every 10 000 miles or 12 months – whichever comes first

- ☐ Check all underbonnet components or fluid leaks (Section 4).
- ☐ Check the condition of the driveshaft rubber gaiters and CV joints (Section 5).
- ☐ Lubricate all hinges and locks (Section 6).
- ☐ Check the automatic transmission fluid level* (Section 7).
- ☐ Check the condition of the auxiliary drivebelt (Section 8).
- ☐ Check the condition of the air filter element (Section 9).
- ☐ Check the operation of the handbrake (Section 10).
- ☐ Check the condition of the brake pads (Section 11).
- ☐ Check the condition of the exhaust system and mountings (Section 12).
- ☐ Inspect the suspension and steering components (Section 13).
- ☐ Check the clutch pedal adjustment (Section 14).
- ☐ Check the condition of the pollen filter (Section 15).
- ☐ Carry out a road test (Section 16).

* **Note:** *Toyota do not specify an interval for checking the **manual** transmission fluid level.*

Every 20 000 miles or 2 years – whichever comes first

- ☐ Check the condition of the brake drums and shoes (Section 17).
- ☐ Renew remote alarm/locking handset battery (Section 18).
- ☐ Renew the brake fluid (Section 19).

Every 40 000 miles or 3 years – whichever comes first

- ☐ Renew the coolant (Section 20).

Note: *Coolant renewal at this interval applies to standard coolant (red/green only) and not to Toyota Super Long Life Coolant (pink) which is 'filled-for-life'.*

Every 40 000 miles or 4 years – whichever comes first

- ☐ Renew the manual transmission fluid* (Section 21).
- ☐ Renew the air filter element (Section 9).
- ☐ Renew the spark plugs (Section 22).

* **Note:** *Toyota do not specify an interval for renewing the **automatic** transmission fluid.*

Every 60 000 miles or 6 years – whichever comes first

- ☐ Renew the auxiliary drivebelt (Section 8).
- ☐ Check and adjust the valve clearances (Section 23).

Front underbonnet view

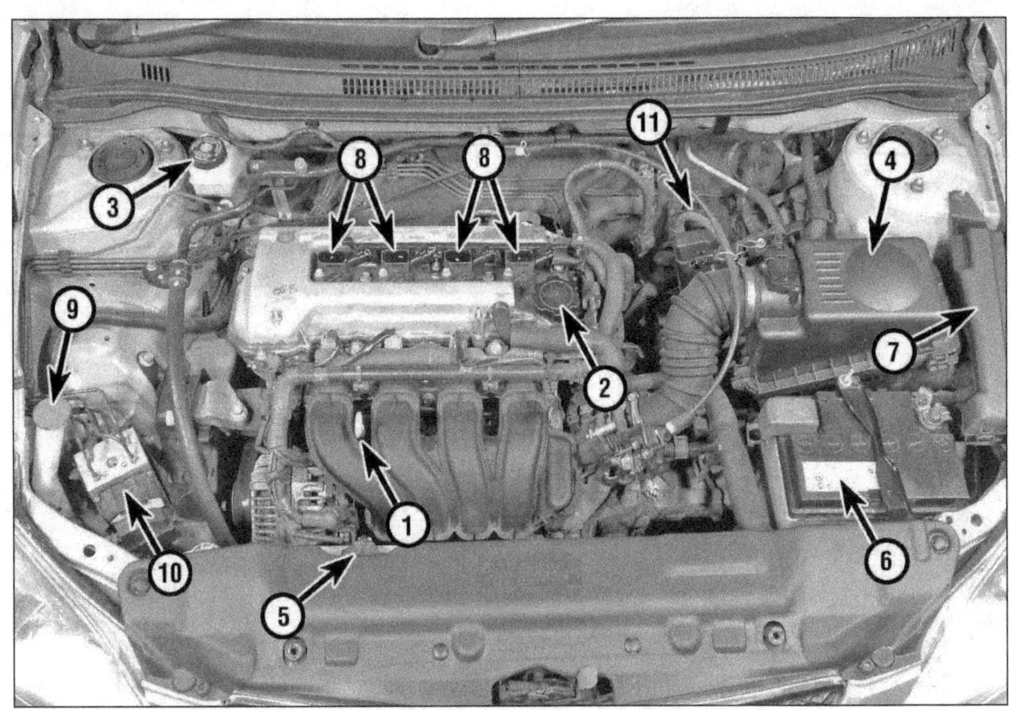

1 *Oil level dipstick*
2 *Engine oil filler cap*
3 *Brake/clutch fluid reservoir*
4 *Air cleaner housing*
5 *Coolant reservoir*
6 *Battery*
7 *Fuse/relay box*
8 *Ignition coils*
9 *Washer fluid reservoir*
10 *Brake ABS hydraulic unit*
11 *Charcoal canister*

Front underbody view

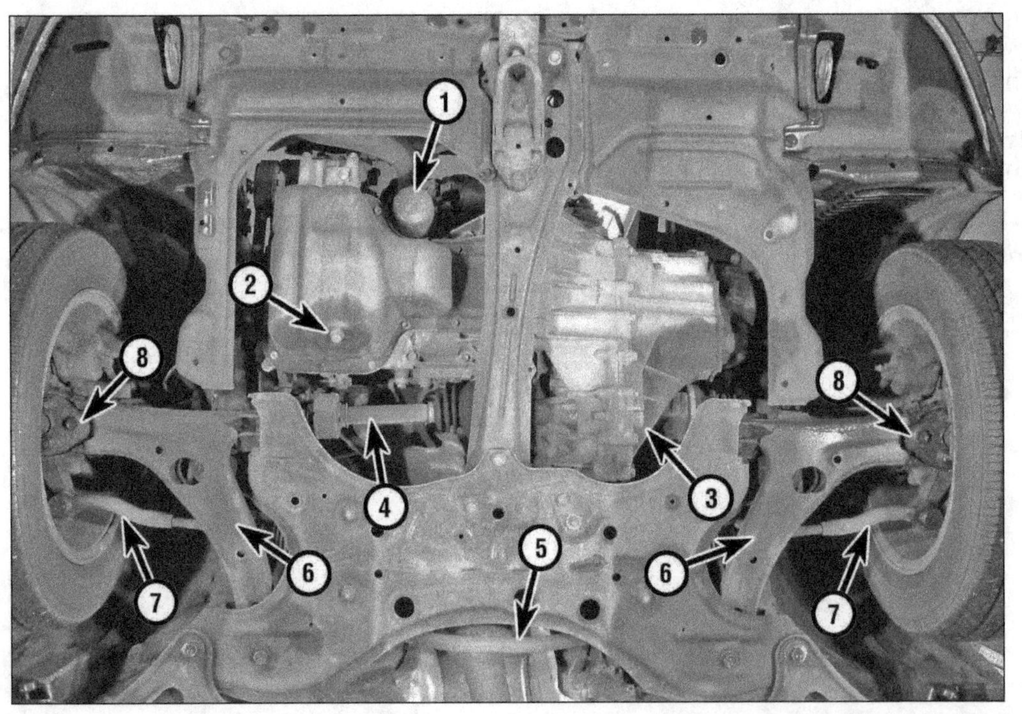

1 *Oil filter*
2 *Engine oil drain plug*
3 *Transmission drain plug*
4 *Right-hand driveshaft*
5 *Anti-roll bar*
6 *Lower suspension control arm*
7 *Track rod end*
8 *Lower balljoint*

Rear underbody view

1 *Fuel tank*
2 *Exhaust rear silencer*
3 *Suspension strut*
4 *Rear jacking point*
5 *Rear beam axle*
6 *Handbrake cable*

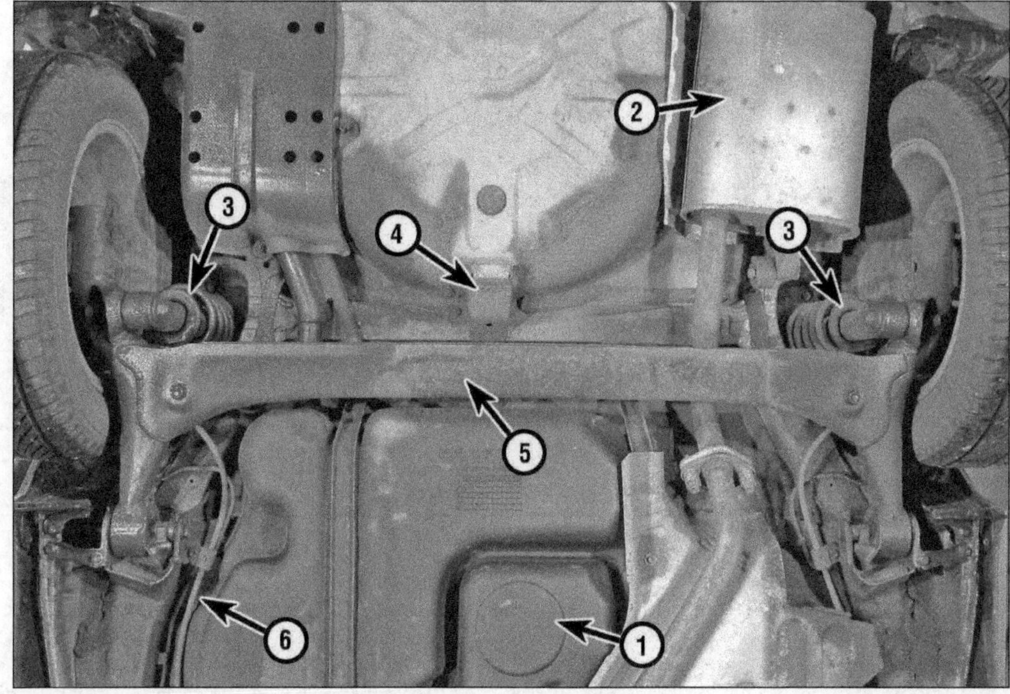

Maintenance procedures

1 General information

1 This Chapter is designed to help the home mechanic maintain his/her vehicle for safety, economy, long life and peak performance.

2 The Chapter contains master maintenance schedules, followed by Sections dealing specifically with each task in the schedule. Visual checks, adjustments, component renewal and other helpful items are included. Refer to the accompanying illustrations of the engine compartment and the underside of the vehicle for the locations of the various components.

3 Servicing your vehicle in accordance with the mileage/time maintenance schedule and the following Sections will provide a planned maintenance programme, which should result in a long and reliable service life. This is a comprehensive plan, so maintaining some items but not others at the specified service intervals will not produce the same results.

4 As you service your vehicle, you will discover that many of the procedures can – and should – be grouped together, because of the particular procedure being performed, or because of the close proximity of two otherwise-unrelated components to one another. For example, if the vehicle is raised for any reason, the exhaust can be inspected at the same time as the suspension and steering components.

5 The first step in this maintenance programme is to prepare yourself before the actual work begins. Read through all the Sections relevant to the work to be carried out, then make a list and gather together all the parts and tools required. If a problem is encountered, seek advice from a parts specialist, or a dealer service department.

2 Routine maintenance

1 If, from the time the vehicle is new, the routine maintenance schedule is followed closely, and frequent checks are made of fluid levels and high-wear items, as suggested throughout this manual, the engine will be kept in relatively good running condition, and the need for additional work will be minimised.

2 It is possible that there will be times when the engine is running poorly due to the lack of regular maintenance. This is even more likely if a used vehicle, which has not received regular and frequent maintenance checks, is purchased. In such cases, additional work may need to be carried out, outside of the regular maintenance intervals.

3 If engine wear is suspected, a compression test (refer to Chapter 2A) will provide valuable information regarding the overall performance of the main internal components. Such a test can be used as a basis to decide on the extent of the work to be carried out. If, for example, a compression test indicates serious internal engine wear, conventional maintenance as described in this Chapter will not greatly improve the performance of the engine, and may prove a waste of time and money, unless extensive overhaul work (Chapter 2C) is carried out first.

4 The following series of operations are those often required to improve the performance of a generally poor-running engine:

Primary operations

a) Clean, inspect and test the battery (See 'Weekly checks').
b) Check all the engine-related fluids (See 'Weekly checks').
c) Check the condition and tension of the auxiliary drivebelt (Section 8).
d) Renew the spark plugs (Section 22).
e) Check the condition of the air cleaner filter element, and renew if necessary (Section 9).
f) Check the condition of all hoses, and check for fluid leaks (Section 4).

5 If the above operations do not prove fully effective, carry out the following operations:

Secondary operations

All items listed under *Primary operations*, plus the following:

a) Check the charging system (Chapter 5A).
b) Check the ignition system (Chapter 5B).
c) Check the fuel system (Chapter 4A).

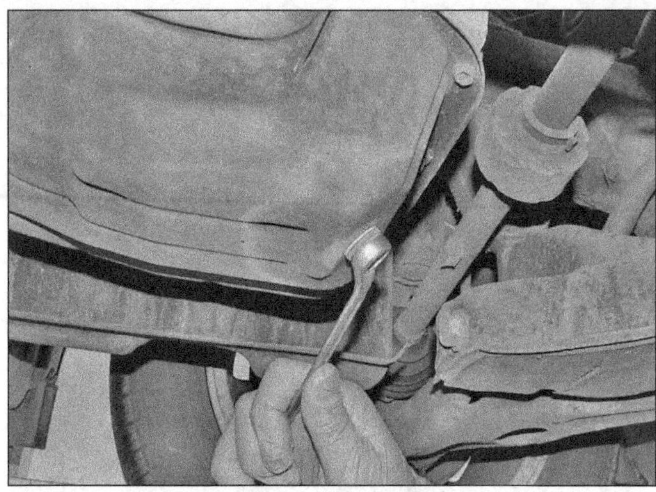
3.4a Slacken the engine oil drain plug . . .

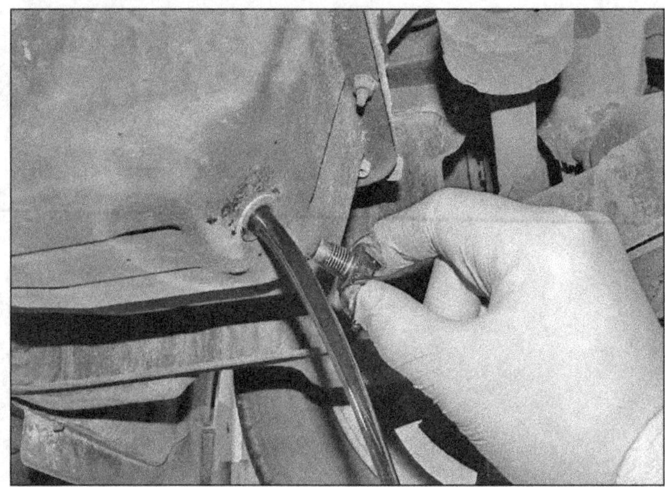
3.4b . . . and slowly withdraw it from the sump

Every 5000 miles or 6 months

3 Engine oil and filter renewal

1 Frequent oil and filter changes are the most important preventative maintenance procedures, which can be undertaken by the DIY owner. As engine oil ages, it becomes diluted and contaminated, which leads to premature engine wear.

HAYNES HiNT

As the drain plug releases from the sump threads, move it away sharply, so the stream of oil issuing from the sump runs into the container, not up your sleeve.

2 Before starting this procedure, gather together all the necessary tools and materials. Also make sure that you have plenty of clean rags and newspapers handy, to mop-up any spills. Ideally, the engine oil should be warm, as it will drain better, and more built-up sludge will be removed with it. Take care, however, not to touch the exhaust or any other hot parts of the engine when working under the vehicle. To avoid any possibility of scalding, and to protect yourself from possible skin irritants and other harmful contaminants in used engine oils, it is advisable to wear gloves when carrying out this work. Access to the underside of the vehicle will be greatly improved if it can be raised on a lift, driven onto ramps, or jacked up and supported on axle stands (see *Jacking and vehicle support*). Whichever method is chosen, make sure that the vehicle remains level, or if it is at an angle, that the drain plug is at the lowest point.

3 If required, undo the retaining screws and remove the engine undertray, where fitted.

4 Slacken the drain plug about half a turn **(see illustrations)**. Position the draining container under the drain plug, and then remove the plug completely. If possible, try to keep the plug pressed into the sump while unscrewing it by hand the last couple of turns **(see Haynes Hint)**. Recover the old sealing ring from the drain plug or sump.

5 Allow some time for the old oil to drain, noting that it may be necessary to reposition the container as the oil flow slows to a trickle.

6 After all the oil has drained, wipe off the drain plug with a clean rag, and fit a new sealing washer **(see illustration)**. Clean the area around the drain plug opening in the sump, and refit the plug, tightening it to the specified torque.

7 Move the container into position under the oil filter, which is located on the front of the cylinder block.

8 Using an oil filter removal tool if necessary, slacken the filter initially, then unscrew it by hand the rest of the way **(see illustrations)**. Empty the oil in the old filter into the container.

9 Use a clean rag to remove all oil, dirt and sludge from the filter sealing area on the engine. Check the old filter to make sure that the rubber sealing ring hasn't stuck to the engine. If it has, carefully remove it.

10 Apply a light coating of clean engine oil to the sealing ring on the new filter (note that some oil filters come with the seal already

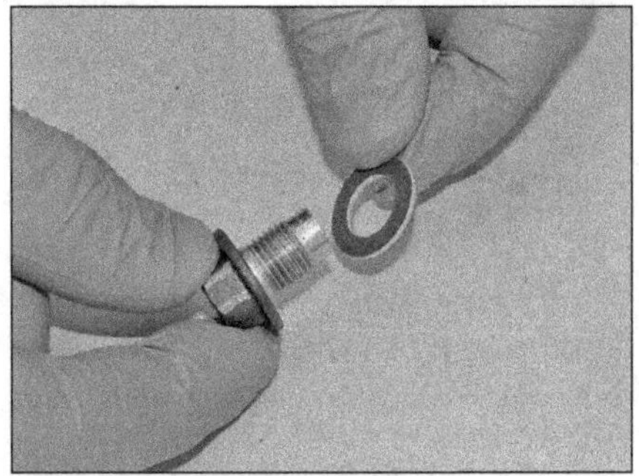
3.6 Fit a new sealing washer to the drain plug

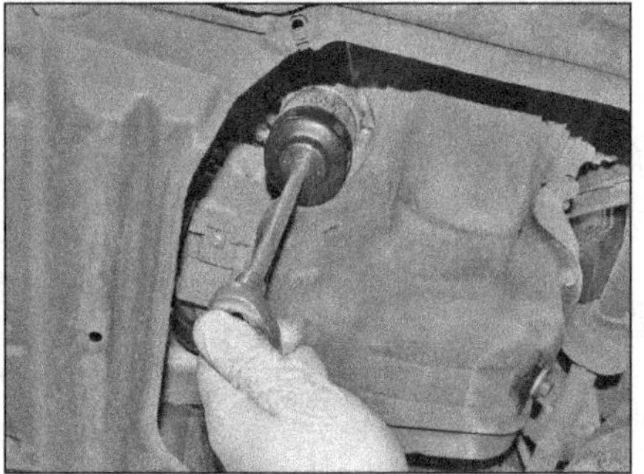
3.8a Use a filter removal tool to slacken . . .

3.8b . . . and then remove the oil filter

lubricated, ready for fitting), and then screw it into position on the engine **(see illustration)**. Tighten the filter firmly by hand only – **do not** use any tools.

11 Remove the old oil and all tools from under the car, then lower the car to the ground (if applicable).

12 Remove the dipstick, and then unscrew the oil filler cap from the cylinder head cover **(see illustrations)**. Fill the engine, using the correct grade and type of oil (see *Weekly checks*). An oil can spout or funnel may help to reduce spillage. Pour in half the specified quantity of oil first, and then wait a few minutes for the oil to run to the sump. Continue adding oil a small quantity at a time until the level is up to the lower mark on the dipstick. Adding approximately 1 litre will bring the level up to the upper mark on the dipstick. Refit the filler cap.

13 Start the engine and run it for a few minutes; check for leaks around the oil filter seal and the sump drain plug. Note that there may be a delay of a few seconds before the oil pressure warning light goes out when the engine is first started, as the oil circulates through the engine oil galleries and the new oil filter before the pressure builds-up.

14 Refit the engine undertray (where applicable), and secure it in place with the screw fasteners.

15 Switch off the engine, and wait a few minutes for the oil to settle in the sump once more. With the new oil circulated and the filter completely full, recheck the level on the dipstick, and add more oil as necessary.

16 Dispose of the used engine oil safely, with reference to *General repair procedures*.

3.10 Apply a little clean oil to the filter sealing ring

3.12a Withdraw the dipstick . . .

3.12b . . . and remove the oil filler cap . . .

3.12c . . . and pour the oil into the engine

Every 10 000 miles or 12 months

4 Hose and fluid leak check

1 Visually inspect the engine joint faces, gaskets and seals for any signs of water or oil leaks. Pay particular attention to the areas around the cylinder head cover, cylinder head, oil filter and sump joint faces. Bear in mind that, over a period of time, some very slight seepage from these areas is to be expected – what you are really looking for is any indication of a serious leak. Should a leak be found, renew the offending gasket or oil seal by referring to the appropriate Chapters in this manual.

2 Also check the security and condition of all the engine-related pipes and hoses. Ensure that all cable ties or securing clips are in place, and in good condition. Clips that are broken or missing can lead to chafing of the hoses, pipes or wiring, which could cause more serious problems in the future.

3 Carefully check the radiator hoses and heater hoses along their entire length. Renew any hose which is cracked, swollen or deteriorated. Cracks will show up better if the hose is squeezed. Pay close attention to the hose clips that secure the hoses to the cooling system components. Hose clips can pinch and puncture hoses, resulting in cooling system leaks. If crimped-type hose clips are used, it may be a good idea to use standard worm-drive clips.

4 Inspect all the cooling system components (hoses, joint faces, etc) for leaks **(see illustration and Haynes Hint)**.

5 Where any problems are found on system components, renew the component or gasket with reference to Chapter 3.

Check for a chafed area that could fail prematurely.

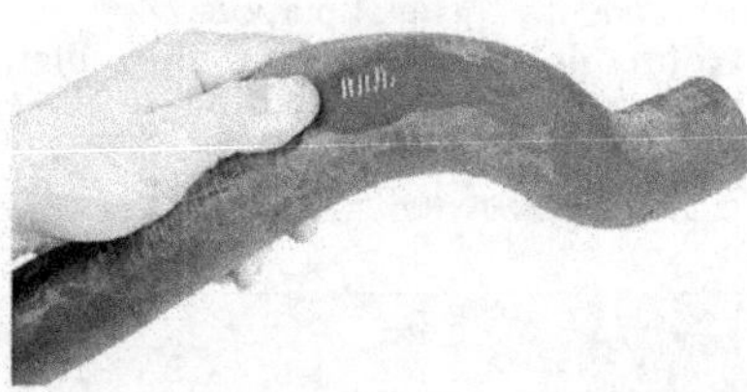

Check for a soft area indicating the hose has deteriorated inside.

Overtightening the clamp on a hardened hose will damage the hose and cause a leak.

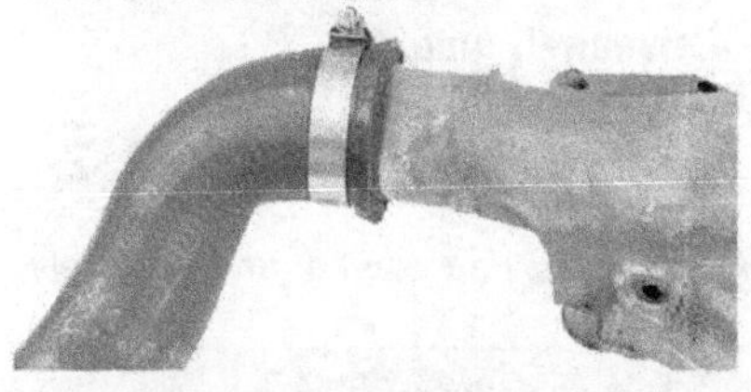

Check each hose for swelling and oil-soaked ends. Cracks and breaks can be located by squeezing the hose.

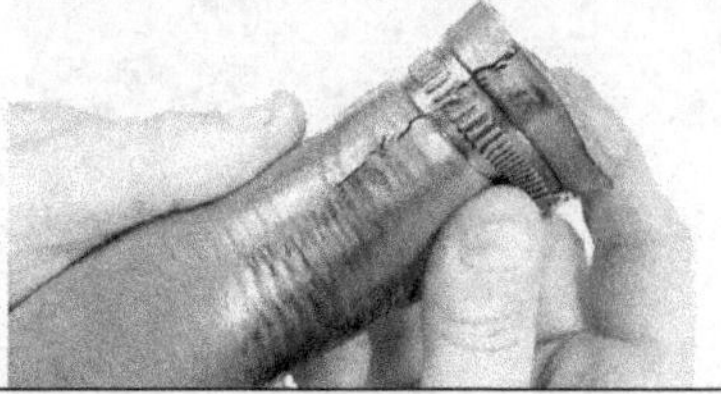

4.4 To prevent the inconvenience of a blown radiator or heater hose, inspect them carefully as shown

A leak in the cooling system will usually show up as white- or antifreeze-coloured deposits on the area adjoining the leak.

6 Where applicable, inspect the automatic transmission fluid cooler hoses for leaks or deterioration.

7 With the vehicle raised, inspect the petrol tank and filler neck for punctures, cracks and other damage. The connection between the filler neck and tank is especially critical. Sometimes a rubber filler neck or connecting hose will leak due to loose retaining clamps or deteriorated rubber.

8 Carefully check all rubber hoses and fuel pipes leading away from the petrol tank. Check for loose connections, deteriorated hoses, crimped lines, and other damage. Pay particular attention to the vent pipes and hoses, which often loop up around the filler neck and can become blocked or crimped. Follow the pipes to the front of the vehicle, carefully inspecting them all the way. Renew damaged sections as necessary.

9 From within the engine compartment, check the security of all fuel pipe attachments and unions, and inspect the fuel pipes and vacuum hoses for kinks, chafing and deterioration.

10 Where applicable, check the condition of the power steering fluid hoses and pipes.

5 Driveshaft gaiter and CV joints check

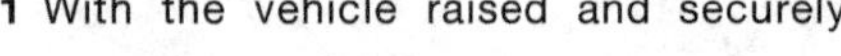

1 With the vehicle raised and securely

5.1 Check the driveshaft gaiters for signs of damage or deterioration

supported on stands (see *Jacking and vehicle support*), turn the steering onto full lock, then slowly rotate the roadwheel. Inspect the condition of the outer constant velocity (CV) joint gaiters, squeezing the gaiters to open out the folds **(see illustration)**. Check for signs of cracking, splits or deterioration of the gaiter, which may allow the grease to escape, and lead to water and grit entry into the joint. Also check the security and condition of the retaining clips. Repeat these checks on the inner CV joints. If any damage or deterioration is found, the gaiters should be renewed (see Chapter 8).

2 At the same time, check the general condition of the CV joints themselves by first holding the driveshaft and attempting to rotate the wheel. Repeat this check by holding the inner joint and attempting to rotate the driveshaft. Any appreciable movement indicates wear in the joints, wear in the driveshaft splines, or a loose driveshaft retaining nut.

6 Hinge and lock lubrication

1 Work around the vehicle, and lubricate the hinges of the bonnet, doors and tailgate with a small amount of general-purpose oil.

2 Lightly lubricate the bonnet release mechanism and exposed section of inner cable with a smear of grease.

3 Check carefully the security and operation of all hinges, latches and locks, adjusting them where required. Check the operation of the central locking system (if fitted).

4 Check the condition and operation of the tailgate struts, renewing them if either is leaking or no longer able to support the tailgate securely when raised.

7 Automatic transmission fluid level check and renewal

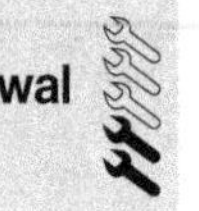

Note: *Toyota do not specify an interval for **renewing** the automatic transmission fluid.*

Level check

1 The transmission should be at normal operating temperature (fluid temperature 70 to 80°C). Set the selector lever in the Park position, making sure the vehicle is parked on a level surface.

2 Start the engine and allow it to idle. With your foot on the brake pedal, move the selector lever through all the positions, and then return it to Park.

3 Pull out the transmission oil level dipstick, and wipe it clean **(see illustration)**.

4 Fully insert the dipstick, and then pull it out again. The level should be within the two notches either side of the HOT mark on the dipstick **(see illustration)**. If not, add fluid and check again.

5 Check the condition of the fluid. If it smells burnt or is blackened, the fluid must be renewed as follows.

Fluid renewal

6 Stop the engine, jack up the front of the vehicle and support it securely on axle stands (see *Jacking and vehicle support*). Place a suitable container under the transmission drain plug.

7 Using an Allen (hexagonal) key, unscrew the drain plug and allow the fluid to drain into the container **(see illustration)**. When all the fluid has drained, refit the plug, tightening it to the specified torque.

8 Fill the transmission through the dipstick aperture with the correct quantity of specified fluid, and check the level as previously described.

7.3 Automatic transmission oil level dipstick (arrowed)

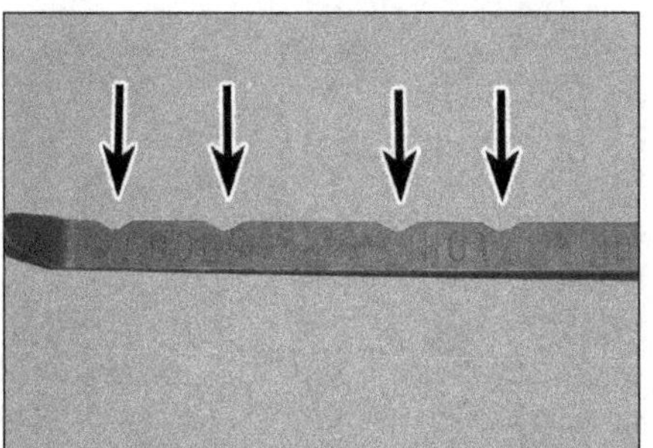

7.4 HOT max and min marks are the right-hand arrows, the COOL max and min marks are on the left

7.7 Automatic transmission drain plug (arrowed)

8 Auxiliary drivebelt check and renewal

Check

1 The alternator, coolant pump and air conditioning compressor drivebelt, also referred to as simply a 'fan' belt, is located at the right end of the engine. The good condition and proper adjustment of the belts is critical to the operation of the engine. Because of their composition and the high stresses to which they are subjected, drivebelts stretch and deteriorate, as they get older. They must therefore be periodically inspected. One belt is used to drive all the pulleys.

2 With the engine stopped, open the bonnet and locate the drivebelt. With an electric torch, check the belt for separation of the adhesive rubber on both sides of the core, core separation from the belt side, a severed core, separation of the ribs from the adhesive rubber, cracking or separation of the ribs, and torn or worn ribs or cracks in the inner ridges of the ribs **(see illustration)**. Also check for fraying and glazing, which gives the belt a shiny appearance. Both sides of the belt should be inspected, which means you will have to twist the belt to check the underside. Use your fingers to feel the belt where you can't see it. If any of the above conditions are evident, renew the belt. The tension of the belt is maintained by an automatic tensioner mechanism.

Renewal

3 Using a spanner on the hexagonal section, rotate the tensioner clockwise to relieve the tension on the belt **(see illustration)**.

4 Lift the belt from the pulleys.

5 Fit the new belt to the pulleys, and then, holding the tensioner clockwise, fit the belt around the tensioner pulley, and gently release the tensioner **(see illustration)**. If better access is required, undo the screws and remove the right-hand side engine undertray.

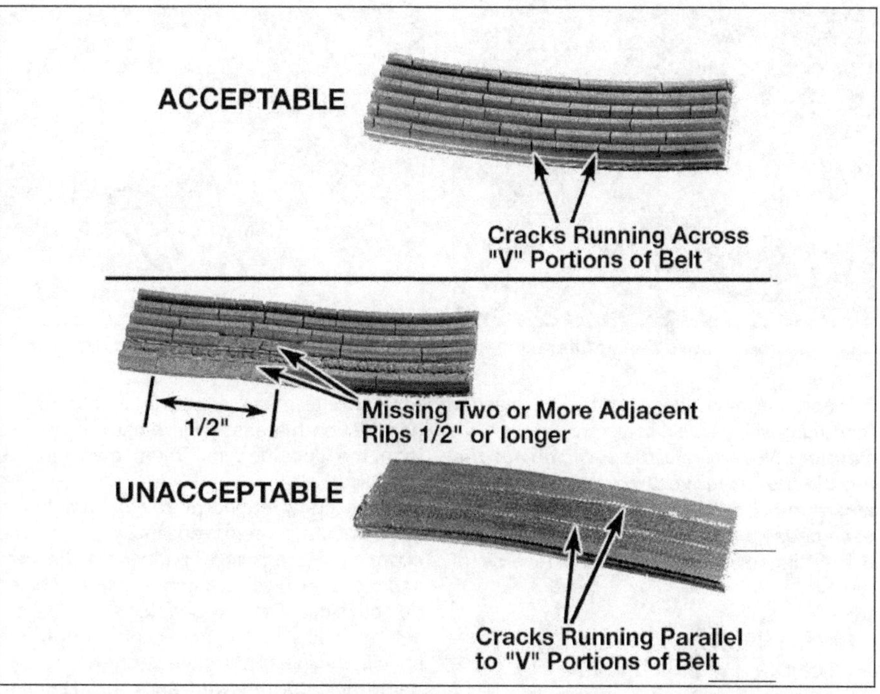

8.2 Check the belt for signs of wear like these – if the belt looks worn, renew it

8.3 Use a spanner on the hexagonal section (arrowed) of the auxiliary drivebelt tensioner

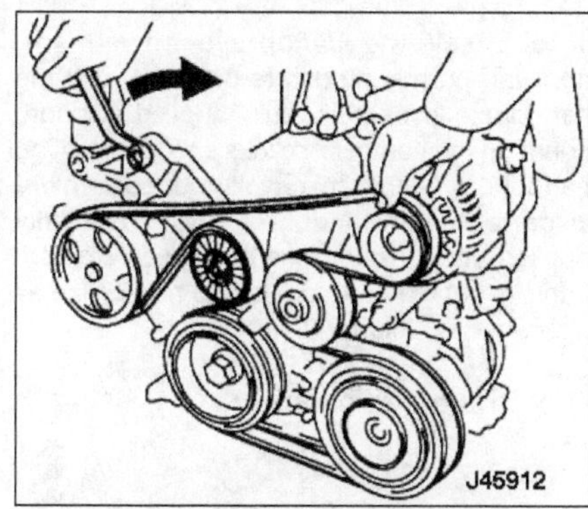

8.5 Fit the new belt to the pulleys

9 Air filter element check and renewal

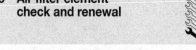

1 The air filter is located inside a housing at the left side of the engine compartment.

2 To remove the air filter, release the two plastic levers on the outer edge of the air cleaner housing, then lift the cover up and withdraw it from the lower part of the housing. Remove the air filter element, noting the fitted position **(see illustrations)**.

3 Inspect the outer surface of the filter element. If it is dirty, renew it. If it is only moderately dusty, it can be re-used by blowing it clean from the back to the front surface with compressed air. Because it is a pleated paper type filter, it cannot be washed or oiled. If it cannot be cleaned satisfactorily with compressed air, discard and renew it. While the cover is off, be careful not to drop anything down into the housing.

Warning: Wear eye protection when using compressed air.

4 Wipe out the inside of the air cleaner housing.

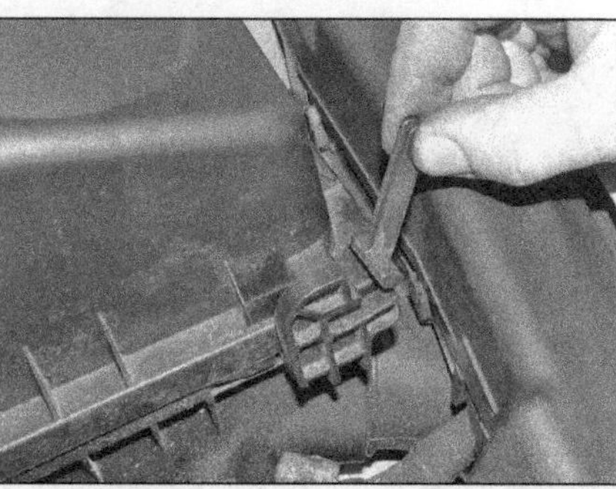

9.2a Release the plastic securing clips . . .

9.2b . . . withdraw the upper cover . . .

9.2c . . . and remove the air filter element

5 Place the new filter into the air cleaner housing, making sure it seats properly.

Caution: Never drive the vehicle with the air cleaner removed. Excessive engine wear could result and backfiring could even cause a fire under the bonnet.

6 Refitting of the cover is the reverse of removal.

10 Handbrake check and adjustment

1 To check the handbrake adjustment, applying normal moderate pressure, pull the handbrake lever to the fully-applied position, counting the number of clicks emitted from the handbrake ratchet mechanism. If adjustment is correct, the handbrake should be fully applied after 6 to 9 clicks have been emitted. If this is not the case, adjust the handbrake as described in Chapter 9.

11 Brake pad check

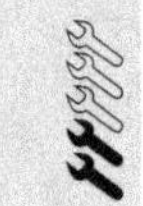

1 Slacken the front roadwheel nuts. Firmly apply the handbrake, and then jack up the front of the car and support it securely on axle stands (see *Jacking and vehicle support*). Remove the front roadwheels.

2 For a quick check, the pad thickness can be carried out via the inspection hole on the front caliper **(see illustration)**. Using a steel rule, measure the thickness of the pad friction material. This must not be less than the specified minimum given in the Specifications.

11.2 Check the brake pad thickness

3 For a comprehensive check, the brake pads should be removed and cleaned. The operation of the caliper can then be checked, and the brake disc itself can be fully examined on both sides. Refer to Chapter 9 for details.

4 If any pad's friction material is worn to the specified minimum thickness or less; all four pads must be renewed as a set. Refer to Chapter 9 for details.

5 On completion, refit the roadwheels then lower the vehicle to the ground and tighten the wheel nuts to the specified torque.

6 Slacken the rear roadwheel nuts. Jack up the rear of the car and support it securely on axle stands. Remove the rear roadwheels. Repeat the procedure described in paragraphs 2 to 5 on the rear brake pads.

12 Exhaust system and mountings check

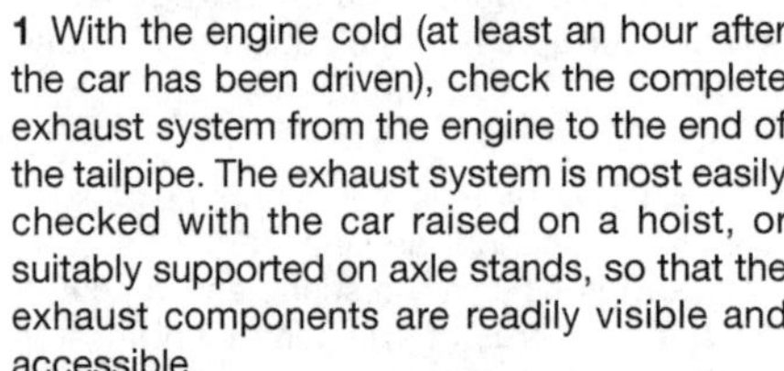

1 With the engine cold (at least an hour after the car has been driven), check the complete exhaust system from the engine to the end of the tailpipe. The exhaust system is most easily checked with the car raised on a hoist, or suitably supported on axle stands, so that the exhaust components are readily visible and accessible.

2 Check the exhaust pipes and connections for evidence of leaks, severe corrosion and damage. Make sure that all brackets and mountings are in good condition, and that all relevant nuts and bolts are tight **(see illustration)**. Leakage at any of the joints or in other parts of the system will usually show up as a black sooty stain in the vicinity of the leak.

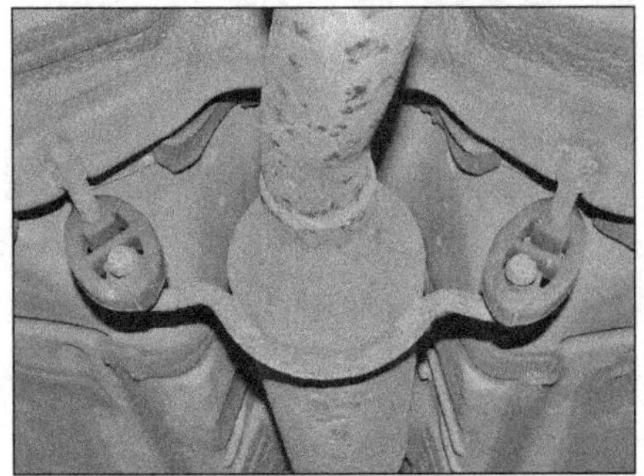

12.2 Check the condition of the exhaust rubber mountings

3 Rattles and other noises can often be traced to the exhaust system, especially the brackets and mountings. Try to move the pipes and silencers. If the components are able to come into contact with the body or suspension parts, secure the system with new mountings. Otherwise separate the joints (if possible) and twist the pipes as necessary to provide additional clearance.

13 Steering and suspension check

Front suspension and steering

1 Raise the front of the vehicle, and securely support it on axle stands (see *Jacking and vehicle support*).

2 Visually inspect the balljoint dust covers and the steering gear gaiters for splits, chafing or deterioration. Any wear of these components will cause loss of lubricant, together with dirt and water entry, resulting in rapid deterioration of the balljoints or steering gear.

3 Check the power steering fluid pipes/hoses for chafing or deterioration, and the pipe and hose unions for fluid leaks. Also check for signs of fluid leakage under pressure from the steering gear rubber gaiters, which would indicate failed fluid seals within the steering gear.

4 Grasp the roadwheel at the 12 o'clock and 6 o'clock positions, and try to rock it **(see illustration)**. Very slight free play may be felt, but if the movement is appreciable, further investigation is necessary to determine the source. Continue rocking the wheel while an assistant depresses the footbrake. If the movement is now eliminated or significantly reduced, it is likely that the hub bearings are at fault. If the free play is still evident with the footbrake depressed, then there is wear in the suspension joints or mountings.

13.4 Check for wear in the hub bearings by grasping the wheel and trying to rock it

5 Now grasp the wheel at the 9 o'clock and 3 o'clock positions, and try to rock it as before. Any movement felt now may again be caused by wear in the hub bearings or the steering track rod balljoints. If the inner or outer balljoint is worn, the visual movement will be obvious.

6 Using a large screwdriver or flat bar, check for wear in the suspension mounting bushes by levering between the relevant suspension component and its attachment point. Some movement is to be expected as the mountings are made of rubber, but excessive wear should be obvious. Also check the condition of any visible rubber bushes, looking for splits, cracks or contamination of the rubber.

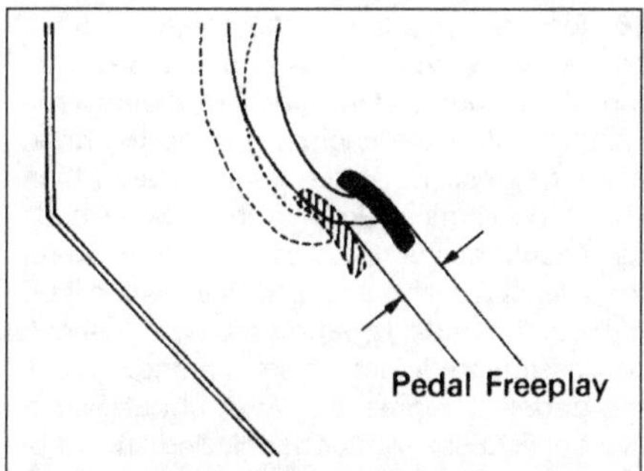

14.1 To check the clutch pedal free play, measure the distance between the natural resting place of the pedal and point where you encounter resistance

7 With the car standing on its wheels, have an assistant turn the steering wheel back-and-forth about an eighth of a turn each way. There should be very little, if any, lost movement between the steering wheel and roadwheels. If this is not the case, closely observe the joints and mountings previously described, but in addition, check the steering column universal joints for wear, and the steering gear itself.

Strut/shock absorber

8 Check for any signs of fluid leakage around the suspension strut/shock absorber body, or from the rubber gaiter around the piston rod. Should any fluid be noticed, the suspension strut/shock absorber is defective internally, and should be renewed. **Note:** *Suspension struts/shock absorbers should always be renewed in pairs on the same axle, or the handling of the vehicle will be adversely affected.*

9 The efficiency of the suspension strut/shock absorber may be checked by bouncing the vehicle at each corner. Generally speaking, the body will return to its normal position and stop after being depressed. If it rises and returns on a rebound, the suspension strut/shock absorber is probably suspect. Examine also the suspension strut/shock absorber upper and lower mountings for any signs of wear.

14 Clutch pedal check and adjustment

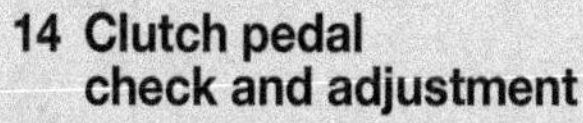
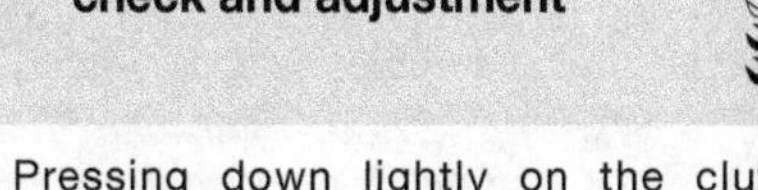

1 Pressing down lightly on the clutch pedal, measure the distance that it moves freely before the clutch resistance is felt **(see illustration)**. The freeplay should be approximately 5.0 mm. If it isn't proceed as follows:

2 Slacken the locknut on the pedal end of the clutch pushrod.

3 Turn the pushrod until the pedal freeplay is correct, and then tighten the locknut.

4 After adjusting the freeplay, check the pedal height from the centre of the pedal pad to the footwell metal floor. The distance should be 142.0 to 152.0 mm.

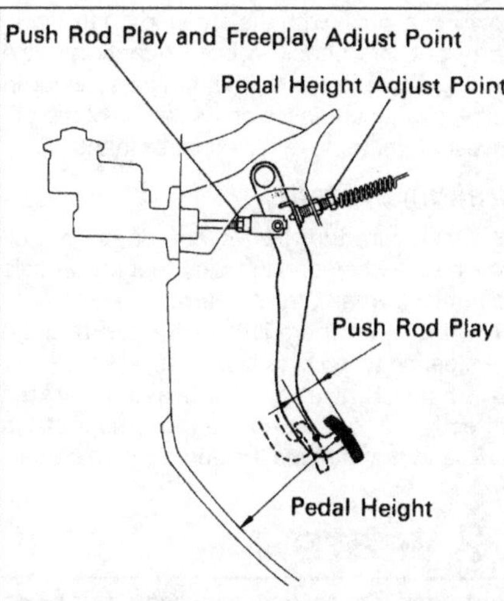

14.5a The clutch pedal pushrod play, pedal height and free play adjustments are made by slackening the locknut and turning the threaded adjuster

5 If the pedal height is incorrect, slacken the locknut and turn the stop bolt until the height is correct **(see illustrations)**. Tighten the locknut.

15 Pollen filter check

1 Remove the glovebox as described in Chapter 11.

2 Reach inside the glovebox aperture, release the retaining clips and remove the cover from the filter housing **(see illustration)**.

3 Withdraw the filter from the housing, noting the position of the arrow on the front of the filter **(see illustration)**. Check the condition of the filter, and renew it if dirty.

4 Wipe clean the inside of the housing and fit the pollen filter element, making sure that it is correctly fitted, as noted on removal.

5 Refit the pollen filter cover; making sure it is securely fitted.

6 Refit the glovebox as described in Chapter 11.

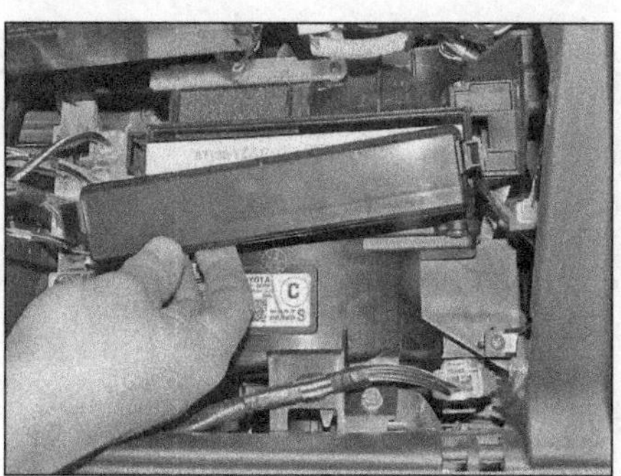

15.2 unclip the pollen filter cover

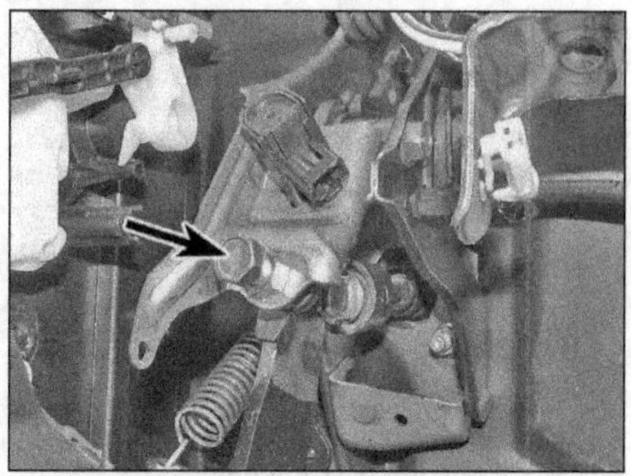

14.5b Pedal adjustment bolt (arrowed)

16 Road test

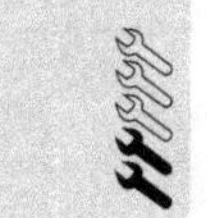

Instruments and electrical equipment

1 Check the operation of all instruments and electrical equipment.

2 Make sure that all instruments read correctly, and switch on all electrical equipment in turn to check it functions properly.

Steering and suspension

3 Check for any abnormalities in the steering, suspension, handling or road 'feel'.

4 Drive the vehicle, and check that there are no unusual vibrations or noises.

5 Check that the steering feels positive, with no excessive 'sloppiness', or roughness, and check for any suspension noises when cornering, or when driving over bumps.

Drivetrain

6 Check the performance of the engine, clutch, transmission and driveshafts.

7 Listen for any unusual noises from the engine, clutch and transmission.

8 Make sure the engine idles smoothly, and that there is no hesitation when accelerating.

9 Check that the clutch action is smooth and progressive, that the drive is taken up smoothly, and that the pedal travel is not

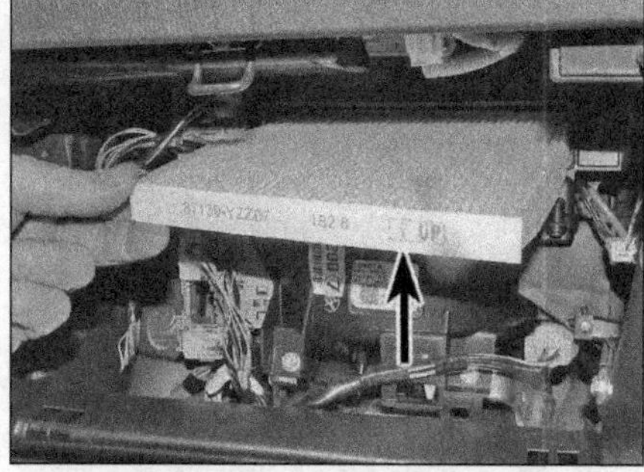

15.3 Withdraw the filter, noting its fitted position (arrowed)

excessive. Also listen for any noises when the clutch pedal is depressed.

10 Check that all gears can be engaged smoothly, without noise, and that the gear lever action is smooth and not vague or 'notchy'.

11 On automatic transmission models, make sure that all gearchanges occur smoothly, without snatching, and without an increase in engine speed between changes. Check that all the gear positions can be selected with the vehicle at rest. If any problems are found, they should be referred to a Toyota dealer.

12 Listen for a metallic clicking sound from the front of the vehicle, as the vehicle is driven slowly in a circle with the steering on full lock. Carry out this check in both directions. If a clicking noise is heard, this indicates wear in a driveshaft joint; in which case, the complete driveshaft must be renewed (see Chapter 8).

Braking system

13 Make sure that the vehicle does not pull to one side when braking, and that the wheels do not lock when braking hard.

14 Check that there is no vibration through the steering when braking.

15 Check that the handbrake operates correctly, without excessive movement of the lever, and that it holds the vehicle on a slope.

16 Test the operation of the brake servo unit as follows. With the engine off, depress the footbrake four or five times to exhaust the vacuum. Start the engine, holding the brake pedal depressed. As the engine starts, there should be a noticeable 'give' in the brake pedal as vacuum builds-up. Allow the engine to run for at least two minutes, and then switch it off. If the brake pedal is depressed now, it should be possible to detect a hiss from the servo as the pedal is depressed. After about four or five applications, no further hissing should be heard, and the pedal should feel considerably firmer.

Every 20 000 miles or 2 years

17 Handbrake shoe check

Warning: Brake dust produced by lining wear and deposited on brake components may contain asbestos, which is hazardous to your health. DO NOT blow it out with compressed air and DO NOT inhale it. DO NOT use petrol or solvents to remove the dust. Brake system cleaner should be used to flush the dust into a drain pan. After the brake components are wiped clean with a damp rag, dispose of the contaminated rag(s) and solvent in a covered and labeled container. Try to use non-asbestos parts whenever possible.

1 Refer to Chapter 9 and remove the rear brake discs.

2 Note the thickness of the lining material on the handbrake shoes **(see illustration)** and look for signs of contamination by brake fluid and grease.

3 If the lining material is within 1.0 mm of the recessed rivets or metal shoes, renew the brake shoes. The shoes should also be renewed if they are cracked, glazed (shiny lining surfaces) or contaminated with brake fluid or grease. See Chapter 9 for the renewal procedure.

4 Check the shoe return and hold-down springs and the adjusting mechanism to make sure they're installed correctly and in good condition. Deteriorated or distorted springs, if not renewed, could allow the linings to drag and wear prematurely.

5 Check the disc/drums for cracks, score marks, deep scratches and hard spots, which will appear as small discoloured areas. If imperfections cannot be removed with emery cloth, the discs/drums must be resurfaced by an automotive engineering workshop (see Chapter 9 for more detailed information).

6 Refit the brake discs (see Chapter 9).

7 Refit the wheels and nuts.

8 Remove the axle stands and lower the vehicle.

9 Tighten the wheel nuts to the specified torque.

17.2 Measure the thickness of the brake shoe friction material

18 Remote control battery renewal

1 Undo the small screw and lift the cover from the remote control unit **(see illustration)**.

2 Lift the module from the unit, then remove the battery case cover **(see illustration)**.

3 Note how it's fitted (positive side upwards) and remove the battery **(see illustration)**.

4 Refitting is a reversal of removal.

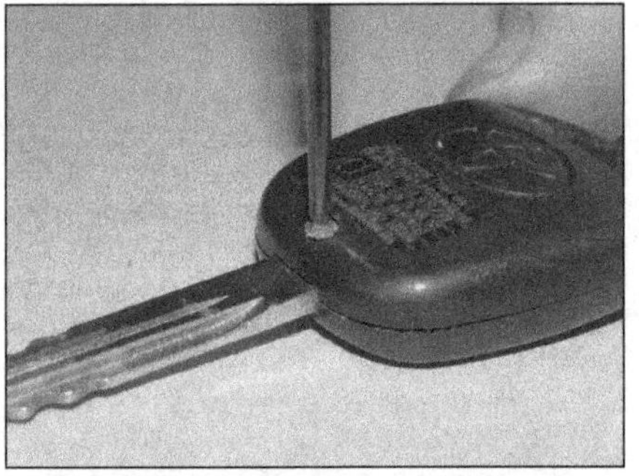

18.1 Undo the small screw and lift the remote control cover . . .

18.2 . . . prise open the battery case cover . . .

18.3 . . . note the positive side of the battery is upwards

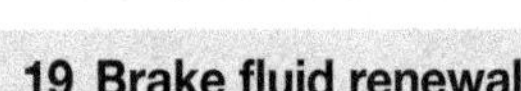

19 Brake fluid renewal

Warning: Brake hydraulic fluid can harm your eyes and damage painted surfaces, so use extreme caution when handling and pouring it. Do not use fluid that has been standing open for some time, as it absorbs moisture from the air. Excess moisture can cause a dangerous loss of braking effectiveness.

Caution: Ensure the ignition is switched off before starting the bleeding procedure to avoid any possibility of voltage being applied to the hydraulic modulator (see Chapter 9, Section 2).

1 The procedure is similar to that for the bleeding of the hydraulic system as described in

Chapter 9, except that the brake fluid reservoir should be emptied by syphoning, using a clean poultry baster or similar before starting, and allowance should be made for the old fluid to be expelled when bleeding a section of the circuit.

2 Working as described in Chapter 9, open the first bleed screw in the sequence, and pump the brake pedal gently until nearly all the old fluid has been emptied from the master cylinder reservoir.

3 Top-up to the MAX level with new fluid, and continue pumping until only the new fluid remains in the reservoir, and new fluid can be seen emerging from the bleed screw. Tighten the screw, and top the reservoir level up to the MAX level line.

4 Work through all the remaining bleed screws in the sequence until new fluid can be seen at all of them. Be careful to keep the master cylinder reservoir topped-up to above the MIN level at all times, or air may enter the system and increase the length of the task.

5 When the operation is complete, check that all bleed screws are securely tightened, and that their dust caps are refitted. Wash off all traces of spilt fluid, and recheck the master cylinder reservoir fluid level.

6 Check the operation of the brakes before taking the car on the road.

Every 40 000 miles or 3 years

20 Coolant renewal

Warning: Wait until the engine is cold before starting this procedure. Do not allow antifreeze to come in contact with your skin, or with the painted surfaces of the vehicle. Rinse off spills immediately with plenty of water. Never leave antifreeze lying around in an open container, or in a puddle in the driveway or on the garage floor. Children and pets are attracted by its sweet smell, but antifreeze can be fatal if ingested. Check with local authorities on disposing of used antifreeze. Many communities have collection centres, which will see that antifreeze is disposed of safely. Antifreeze is flammable under certain conditions – be sure to read the precautions on the container.

Note: *Coolant renewal at this interval applies to standard coolant (red/green only) and not to Long Life Coolant (pink).*

Cooling system draining

1 With the engine completely cold, unscrew the radiator pressure cap.

2 Undo the screws and remove the right-hand engine undertray (where fitted).

3 Position a suitable container beneath the coolant drain tap at the lower left-hand side of the radiator, then open the drain tap, and allow the coolant to drain into the container **(see illustration)**. When the coolant has finished draining, close the tap.

4 Move the container to under the rear of the engine block, then open the block drain tap and drain the coolant into the container **(see illustration)**. Once the coolant has finished draining, close the tap.

Cooling system flushing

5 If coolant renewal has been neglected, or if the antifreeze mixture has become diluted, then in time, the cooling system may gradually lose efficiency as the coolant passages become restricted due to rust, scale deposits, and other sediment. The cooling system efficiency can be restored by flushing the system clean.

6 The radiator should be flushed separately from the engine, to avoid excess contamination.

Radiator flushing

7 Disconnect the top and bottom hoses and any other relevant hoses from the radiator (see Chapter 3).

8 Insert a garden hose into the radiator top inlet. Direct a flow of clean water through the radiator, and continue flushing until clean water emerges from the radiator bottom outlet.

9 If after a reasonable period, the water still does not run clear, the radiator can be flushed with a good proprietary cleaning agent. It is important that their manufacturer's instructions are followed carefully. If the contamination is particularly bad, insert the hose in the radiator bottom outlet, and reverse-flush the radiator.

Engine flushing

10 To flush the engine, remove the thermostat (see Chapter 3).

11 With the bottom hose disconnected from the radiator, insert a garden hose into the coolant housing. Direct a clean flow of water through the engine, and continue flushing until clean water emerges from the radiator bottom hose.

12 When flushing is complete, refit the thermostat and reconnect the hoses (see Chapter 3).

Cooling system filling

13 Before attempting to fill the cooling system, make sure that all hoses and clips are in good condition, and that the clips are tight. Note that an antifreeze mixture must be used all year round, to prevent corrosion of the engine components (see following sub-Section).

14 Remove the radiator pressure cap, and ensure all drain taps/plugs are secured.

15 Place the heater temperature control in the maximum heat position.

16 Slowly add new coolant (50/50 mix of antifreeze and coolant. Note that Toyota antifreeze is normally supplied premixed) to the radiator until it's full. Add coolant to the reservoir up to the lower mark.

17 Leave the radiator cap off, and run the engine in a well-ventilated area until the thermostat opens (coolant will begin flowing through the radiator and the upper hose will become hot).

18 Turn the engine off and let it cool. Add more coolant mixture to bring the level back to the lip of the radiator filler neck.

19 Squeeze the upper radiator hose to expel air, then add more coolant mixture if necessary. Refit the filler cap.

20 Start the engine, allow it to reach normal operating temperature and check for leaks.

Antifreeze mixture

21 The antifreeze should always be renewed at the specified intervals. This is necessary not only to maintain the anti-freeze properties, but also to prevent corrosion, which would otherwise occur as the corrosion inhibitors become progressively less effective.

22 Always use an ethylene glycol-based antifreeze, which is suitable for use in mixed-metal cooling systems.

23 Before adding antifreeze, the cooling system should be completely drained, preferably flushed, and all hoses checked for condition and security.

20.3 Radiator drain tap (arrowed)

20.4 On some models, there is a coolant drain tap on the rear of the engine block

24 After filling with antifreeze, a label should be attached to the expansion tank, stating the type and concentration of antifreeze used, and the date installed. Any subsequent topping-up should be made with the same type and concentration of antifreeze.

Caution: Do not use engine antifreeze in the windscreen/tailgate washer system, as it will damage the vehicle paintwork. A screen wash additive should be added to the washer system in the quantities stated on the bottle.

Every 40 000 miles or 4 years

21 Manual transmission fluid level check and renewal

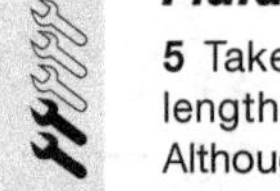

Note: *Toyota do not specify an interval for* ***checking*** *the manual transmission fluid level.*

Level check

1 The manual transmission does not have a dipstick. To check the fluid level, raise the vehicle and support it securely on axle stands (see *Jacking and vehicle support*). Undo the screws and remove the left-hand side engine undertray (where fitted).

2 On the front side of the transmission housing, you will see a plug **(see illustration)**. Remove it. If the lubricant level is correct, it should be up to the lower edge of the hole.

3 If the transmission needs more lubricant (if the level is not up to the hole), use a syringe or a gear oil pump to add more. Stop filling the transmission when the lubricant begins to run out the hole.

4 Refit the plug and tighten it to the specified torque. Drive the vehicle a short distance, and then check for leaks.

Fluid renewal

5 Take the vehicle for a drive of sufficient length to warm-up the transmission fluid. Although this is not essential, it does help to ensure all the fluid is drained, along with any contaminants.

6 Raise the vehicle, and remove the left-hand engine undertray as described in paragraph 1.

7 The fluid drain plug is located on the underside of the transmission casing **(see illustration)**. Position a suitable container, and undo the drain plug. Recover the drain plug sealing washer. Renew it if it shows any sign of damage, wear, or deformity.

8 Once the fluid has finished draining, refit the drain plug (with a new washer where necessary), and tighten it to the specified torque.

9 Remove the filler plug and refill the transmission as described in paragraphs 2, 3 and 4.

22 Spark plug renewal

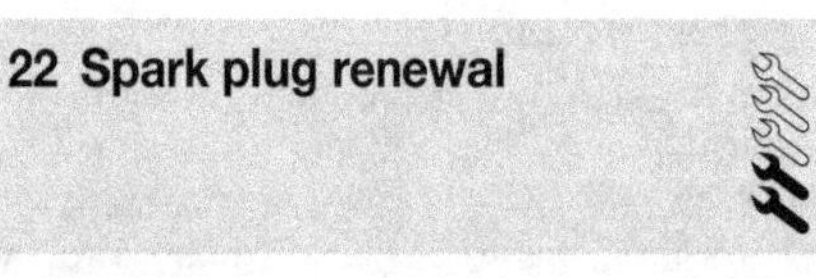

1 Spark plug renewal requires a spark plug socket which fits onto a ratchet. This socket is lined with a rubber grommet to protect the porcelain insulator of the spark plug and to hold the plug while you insert it into the spark plug hole. You will also need a feeler gauge to check and adjust the spark plug gap and a torque wrench to tighten the new plugs to the specified torque **(see illustration)**.

2 If you are renewing the plugs, purchase the new plugs, adjust them to the proper gap and then fit each plug one at a time. **Note:** *When buying new spark plugs, it's essential that you obtain the correct plugs for your vehicle. This information can be found in the Specifications Section at the beginning of this Chapter, or in the owner's handbook.*

3 Inspect each of the new plugs for defects. If there are any signs of cracks in the porcelain insulator of a plug, don't use it.

4 Check the electrode gaps of the new plugs. Check the gap by inserting the feeler gauge of the proper thickness between the electrodes at the tip of the plug **(see illustration)**. The gap between the electrodes should be identical to that listed in this Chapter's Specifications. If the gap is incorrect, carefully bend the curved side electrode slightly.

Caution: Some plugs are supplied with the gap preset. There is no need to adjust them.

5 If the side electrode is not exactly over the centre electrode, align them.

Removal

6 Undo the two nuts at the center of the cover, prise out the two plastic fasteners at the rear, and then lift off the plastic cover on top of the engine **(see illustrations)**.

7 Disconnect the wiring plugs from the ignition coils **(see illustration)**.

8 Undo the bolts and pull the ignition coils from the top of the spark plugs **(see illustrations)**. Recover the dust seal (where fitted).

21.2 Manual transmission fluid level plug (arrowed)

21.7 Manual transmission fluid drain plug (arrowed)

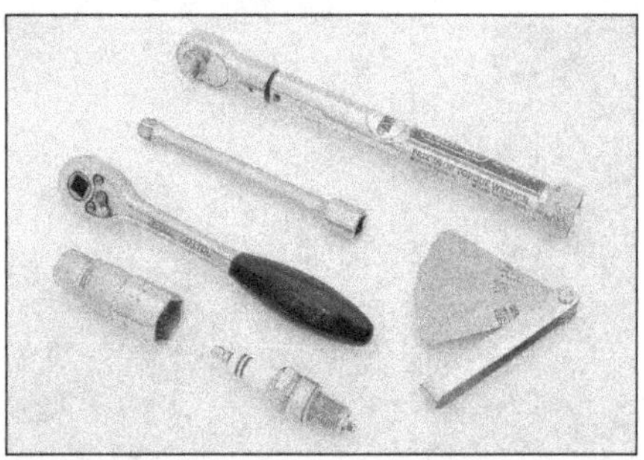

22.1 To change the spark plugs you'll need a torque wrench, extension, ratchet, socket and a set of feeler gauges

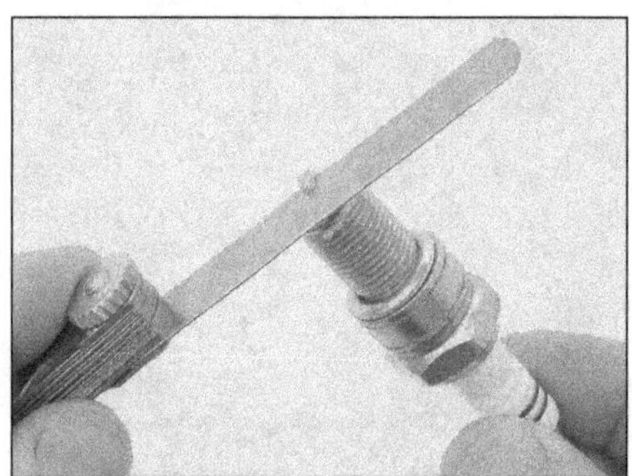

22.4 Measure the spark plug electrode gap with a feeler gauge

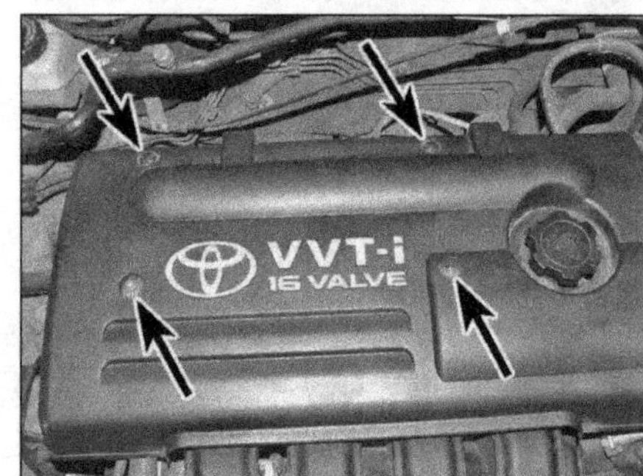

22.6a Undo the retaining nuts . . .

22.6b . . . release the securing clips . . .

22.6c . . . and remove the engine upper cover

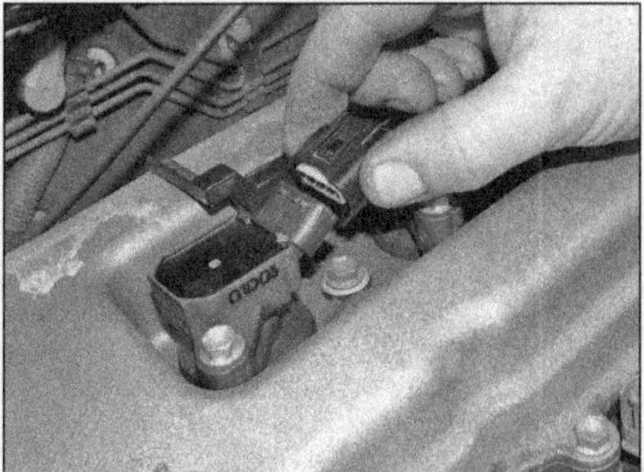
22.7 Disconnect the wiring connector

22.8a Undo the securing bolt . . .

22.8b . . . and lift out the ignition coil

22.10 Remove the spark plug

9 If compressed air is available, blow any dirt or foreign material away from the spark plug area before proceeding (a common bicycle pump will also work).

10 Remove the spark plug **(see illustration)**. Examination of the spark plugs will give a good indication of the condition of the engine. If the insulator nose of the spark plug is clean and white, with no deposits, this is indicative of a weak mixture or too hot a plug (a hot plug transfers heat away from the electrode slowly, a cold plug transfers heat away quickly).

11 If the tip and insulator nose are covered with hard black-looking deposits, then this is indicative that the mixture is too rich. Should the plug be black and oily, and then it is likely that the engine is fairly worn, as well as the mixture being too rich. If the insulator nose is covered with light tan to greyish-brown deposits, then the mixture is correct and it is likely that the engine is in good condition.

Refitting

12 Prior to installation, it's a good idea to coat the spark plug threads with anti-seize compound **(see illustration)**. Also, it's often difficult to insert spark plugs into their holes without cross-threading them. To avoid this possibility, fit a short piece of 8 mm internal diameter rubber hose over the end of the spark plug **(see illustration)**. The flexible hose acts as a universal joint to help align the plug with the plug hole. Should the plug begin to cross-thread, the hose will slip on the spark plug, preventing thread damage. Tighten the plug to the torque listed in this Chapter's Specifications.

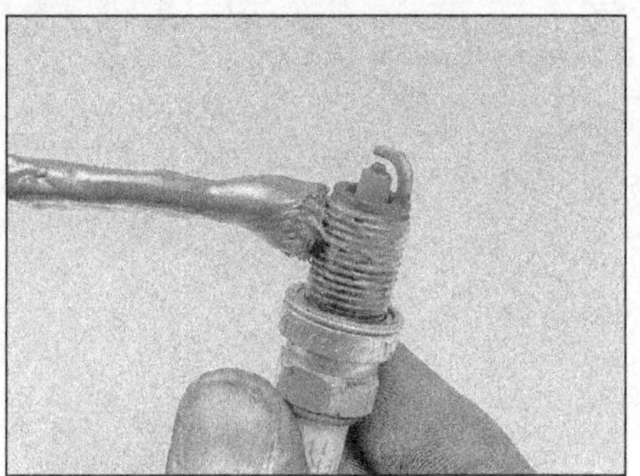
22.12a Apply a thin coat of anti-seize compound to the spark plug threads

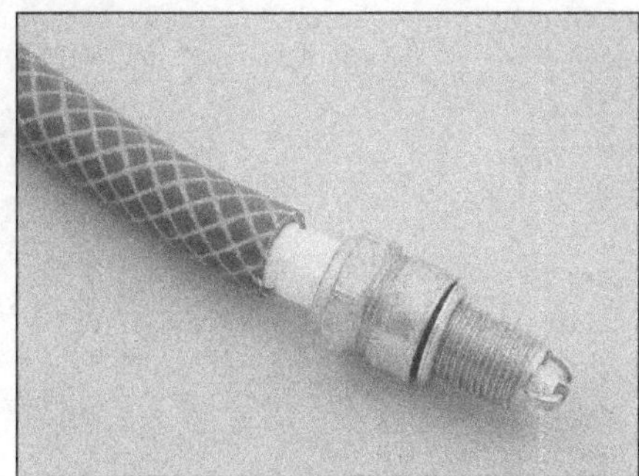
22.12b A length of 8 mm ID rubber hose will save time and prevent damaged threads when installing the spark plugs

13 Refit the coils to the top of each spark plug; ensuring the dust seal (where fitted) is correctly located. Tighten the ignition coil bolts to the specified torque,

Every 60 000 miles or 6 years

23 Valve clearance check and adjustment

1 Remove the cylinder head cover and position the engine at TDC for No 1 cylinder, as described in Chapter 2A.

2 Using feeler gauges, measure the clearance between the camshaft lobes and the cam followers of the inlet valves for cylinders 1 and 2, and the exhaust valves for cylinders 1 and 3. No 1 cylinder is at the timing chain end of the engine. Record the measurements obtained **(see illustration)**.

3 Turn the crankshaft *one* complete revolution (360°).

4 Using feeler gauges, measure the clearance

23.2 Measure the clearance between the camshaft lobe and the cam follower

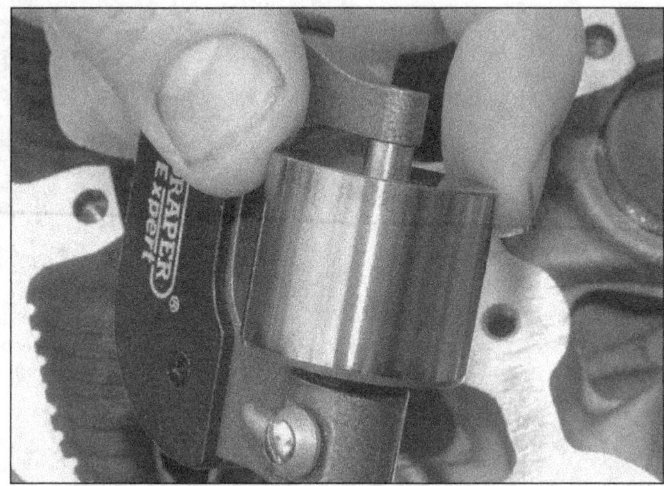

23.6 Measure the thickness of the cam follower using a micrometer

between the camshaft lobes and the cam followers of the inlet valves for cylinders 3 and 4, and the exhaust valves for cylinders 2 and 4. Record the measurements obtained.

5 Compare the measurements obtained with those given in the Specifications. If any measure is outside the specified range, remove the camshafts as described in Chapter 2A.

6 With the camshafts removed, use a magnet to lift the relevant cam follower(s) from place, then measure and record the thickness of the follower using a micrometer **(see illustration)**.

7 Determine the required thickness of the new follower using the following formula:

Inlet followers: N = T + (A – 0.20 mm).
Exhaust followers: N = T + (A – 0.30 mm).
A = Measured valve clearance.
N = Thickness of new follower.
T = Thickness of the used follower.

8 Select a follower with a thickness as close as possible to the valve clearance calculated. Followers, which are available in 35 sizes in increments of 0.020 mm, range in size from 5.060 mm to 5.740 mm.

9 With all the followers in their correct locations, refit the camshafts as described in Chapter 2A. Before refitting the cylinder head cover, recheck the valve clearances as previously described, and, if necessary, remove the camshafts again and change followers as necessary.

Chapter 1 Part B:
Routine maintenance and servicing – diesel models

Contents

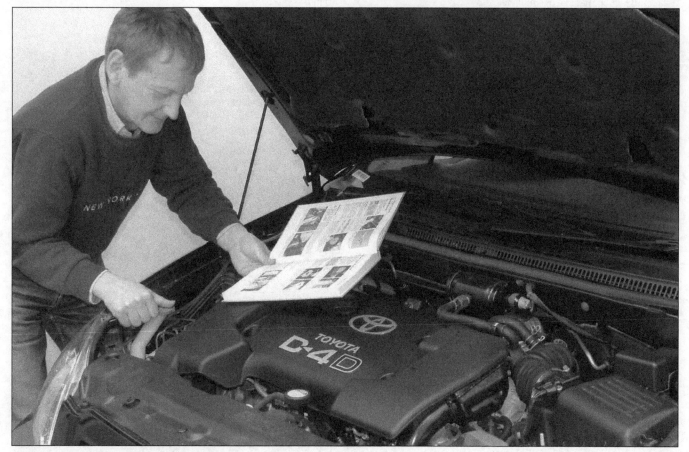

Degrees of difficulty

Easy, suitable for novice with little experience 	**Fairly easy,** suitable for beginner with some experience	**Fairly difficult,** suitable for competent DIY mechanic	**Difficult,** suitable for experienced DIY mechanic	**Very difficult,** suitable for expert DIY or professional 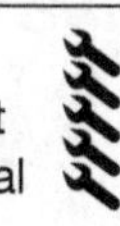

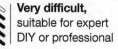

Lubricants and fluids	Refer to *Weekly checks* on page 0•16

Capacities*

Engine oil (including filter)	5.9 litres
Manual transmission	2.5 litres
Cooling system (approximate)	7.5 litres
Fuel tank	55 litres

* *All capacities approximate. Add as necessary to bring up to appropriate level*

Cooling system

Frost and corrosion protection	Refer to antifreeze manufacturer's concentration recommendations

Engine

Engine code	1CD-FTV
Valve clearances (engine cold):	
Intake valve	0.20 to 0.30 mm
Exhaust valve	0.35 to 0.45 mm

Brakes

Brake pad friction material minimum thickness	1.0 mm
Brake shoe lining minimum thickness	1.0 mm
Parking brake adjustment (when pulled with a force of 196 N)	6 to 9 clicks

Auxiliary drivebelt tension

Using a Burroughs or Nippondenso tension gauge:	
Used belt (a belt which has been used more than 5 minutes)	519 to 755 N (equivalent to approximately 10.0 mm deflection)
New belt (a belt that has been used less than 5 minutes)	196 to 392 N (equivalent to approximately 14.0 mm deflection)

Note: *The alternator drivebelt is fitted with an automatic tensioner, however, the power steering pump/air conditioning compressor drivebelt has manual adjustment.*

Torque wrench settings	**Nm**	**lbf ft**
Auxiliary drivebelt tensioner	60	44
Cylinder block drain plug	25	18
Ignition coil to cylinder head	7	5
Manual transmission:		
Filler/level plug	39	29
Drain plug	39	29
Roadwheel nuts	103	76
Spark plugs	25	18
Sump drain plug	37	27

The maintenance intervals in this manual are provided with the assumption that you, not the dealer, will be doing the work. These are the minimum maintenance intervals recommended by the factory for vehicles that are driven daily. If you wish to keep your vehicle in peak condition at all times, you may wish to perform some of these procedures even more often. Because frequent maintenance enhances the efficiency, performance and resale value of your car, we encourage you to do so. If you drive in dusty areas, tow a trailer, idle or drive at low speeds for extended periods or drive for short distances (less than four miles) in below freezing temperatures, shorter intervals are also recommended.

When the vehicle is new, it should be serviced by a dealer service department (or other workshop recognised by the vehicle manufacturer as providing the same standard of service) in order to preserve the warranty. The vehicle manufacturer may reject warranty claims if you are unable to prove that servicing has been carried out as and when specified, using only original equipment parts or parts certified to be of equivalent quality.

Every 250 miles or weekly

- ☐ Refer to Weekly checks

Every 5000 miles or 6 months – whichever comes first

- ☐ Renew the engine oil and filter (Section 3).

Note: *Frequent oil and filter changes are good for the engine. We recommend changing the oil at the mileage specified here, or at least twice a year if the mileage covered is a less.*

Every 10 000 miles or 12 months – whichever comes first

- ☐ Check all underbonnet components or fluid leaks (Section 4).
- ☐ Check the condition of the driveshaft rubber gaiters and CV joints (Section 5).
- ☐ Lubricate all hinges and locks (Section 6).
- ☐ Check the transmission oil level* (Section 7).
- ☐ Check the condition of the auxiliary drivebelt (Section 8).
- ☐ Check the condition of the air filter element (Section 9).
- ☐ Check the operation of the handbrake (Section 10).
- ☐ Check the condition of the brake pads (Section 11).
- ☐ Check the condition of the exhaust system and mountings (Section 12).
- ☐ Inspect the suspension and steering components (Section 13).
- ☐ Check the clutch pedal adjustment (Section 14).
- ☐ Check the condition of the pollen filter (Section 15).
- ☐ Carry out a road test (Section 16).

*** Note:** *Toyota do not specify an interval for checking the transmission fluid level.*

Every 20 000 miles or 2 years – whichever comes first

- ☐ Renew the fuel filter element (Section 17).
- ☐ Check the condition of the handbrake shoes (Section 18).
- ☐ Renew remote alarm/locking handset battery (Section 19).
- ☐ Renew the brake fluid (Section 20).

Every 40 000 miles or 3 years – whichever comes first

- ☐ Renew the coolant (Section 21).

Note: *Coolant renewal at this interval applies to standard coolant (red/green only) and not to Toyota Super Long Life Coolant (pink) which is 'filled-for-life'.*

Every 40 000 miles or 4 years – whichever comes first

- ☐ Renew the transmission oil (Section 7).
- ☐ Renew the air filter element (Section 9).
- ☐ Check and renew if necessary the PCV hoses (Section 22).

Every 60 000 miles or 6 years – whichever comes first

- ☐ Renew the auxiliary drivebelt (Section 8).
- ☐ Check and adjust the valve clearances (Section 23).
- ☐ Renew the timing belt (Section 24).

Front underbonnet view

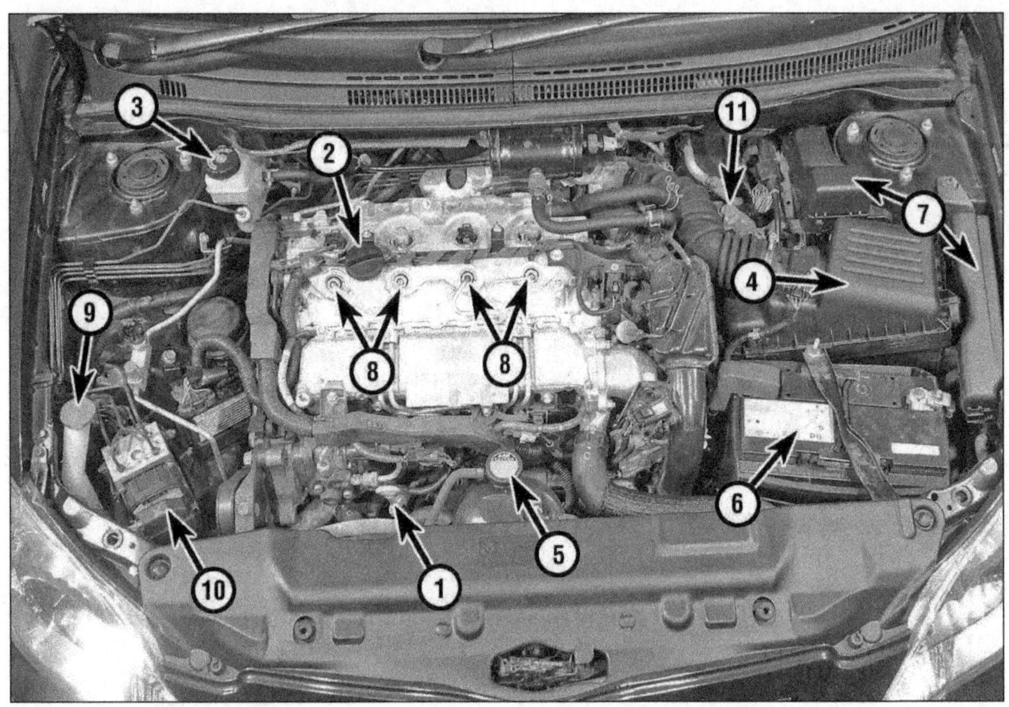

1. Oil level dipstick
2. Engine oil filler cap
3. Brake fluid reservoir
4. Air cleaner housing
5. Coolant reservoir
6. Battery
7. Fuse/relay box
8. Ignition coils
9. Washer fluid reservoir
10. Brake ABS hydraulic unit
11. Fuel filter

Front underbody view

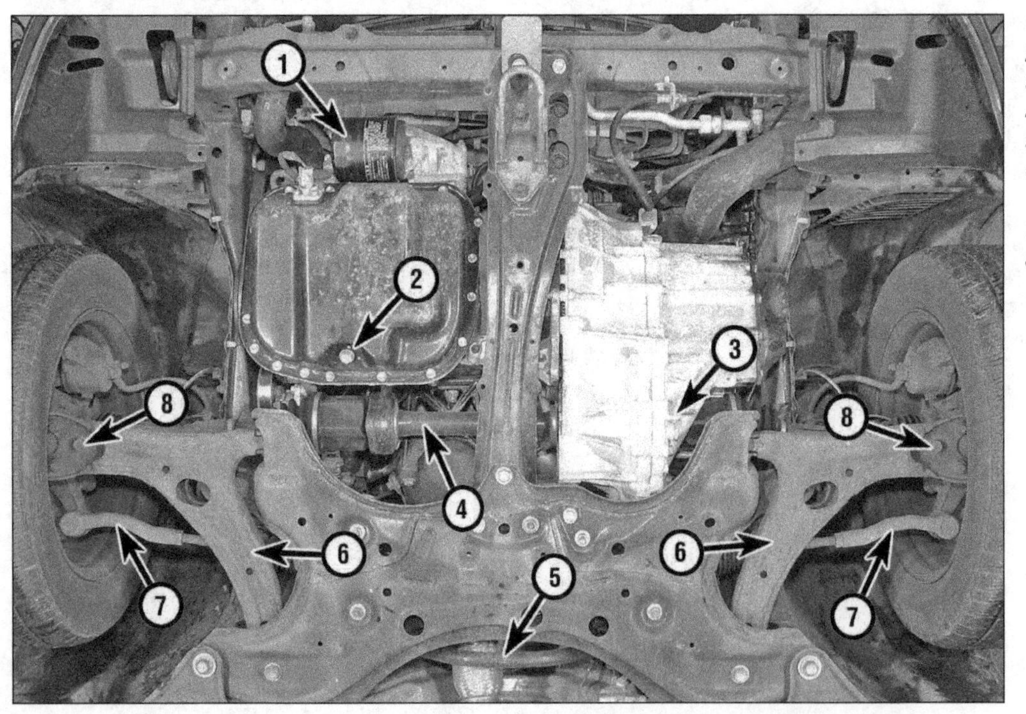

1. Oil filter
2. Engine oil drain plug
3. Transmission drain plug
4. Right-hand driveshaft
5. Anti-roll bar
6. Lower suspension control arm
7. Track rod end
8. Lower balljoint

Rear underbody view

1 *Fuel tank*
2 *Exhaust rear silencer*
3 *Suspension strut*
4 *Rear jacking point*
5 *Rear beam axle*
6 *Handbrake cable*

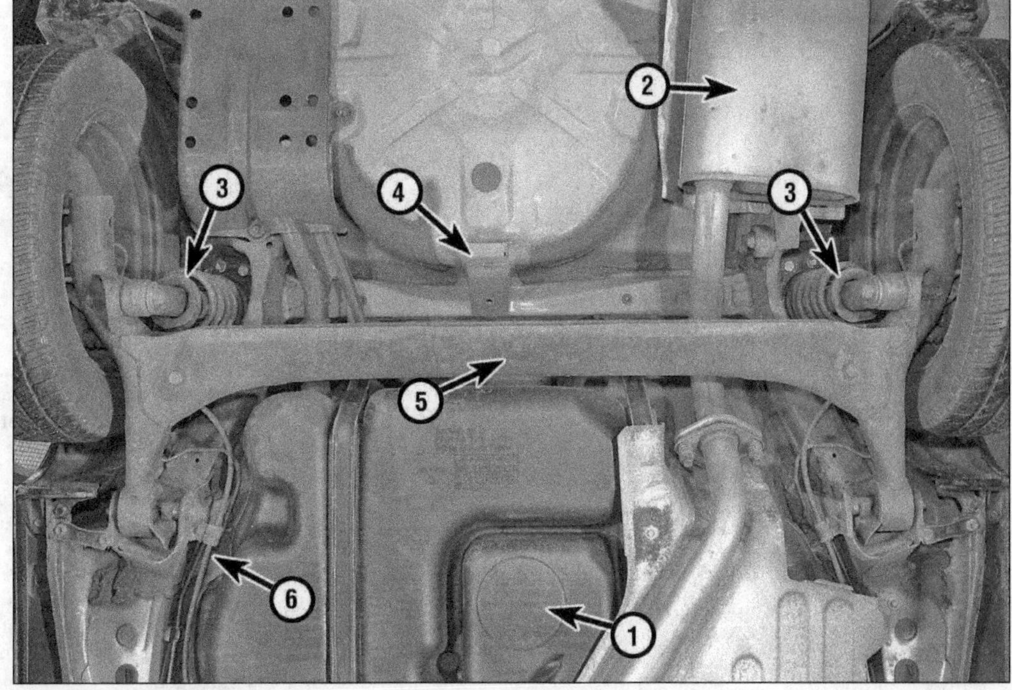

Maintenance procedures

1 General information

1 This Chapter is designed to help the home mechanic maintain his/her vehicle for safety, economy, long life and peak performance.

2 The Chapter contains master maintenance schedules, followed by Sections dealing specifically with each task in the schedule. Visual checks, adjustments, component renewal and other helpful items are included. Refer to the accompanying illustrations of the engine compartment and the underside of the vehicle for the locations of the various components.

3 Servicing your vehicle in accordance with the mileage/time maintenance schedule and the following Sections will provide a planned maintenance programme, which should result in a long and reliable service life. This is a comprehensive plan, so maintaining some items but not others at the specified service intervals will not produce the same results.

4 As you service your vehicle, you will discover that many of the procedures can – and should – be grouped together, because of the particular procedure being performed, or because of the close proximity of two otherwise-unrelated components to one another. For example, if the vehicle is raised for any reason, the exhaust can be inspected at the same time as the suspension and steering components.

5 The first step in this maintenance programme is to prepare yourself before the actual work begins. Read through all the Sections relevant to the work to be carried out, then make a list and gather together all the parts and tools required. If a problem is encountered, seek advice from a parts specialist, or a dealer service department.

2 Routine maintenance

1 If, from the time the vehicle is new, the routine maintenance schedule is followed closely, and frequent checks are made of fluid levels and high-wear items, as suggested throughout this manual, the engine will be kept in relatively good running condition, and the need for additional work will be minimised.

2 It is possible that there will be times when the engine is running poorly due to the lack of regular maintenance. This is even more likely if a used vehicle, which has not received regular and frequent maintenance checks, is purchased. In such cases, additional work may need to be carried out, outside of the regular maintenance intervals.

3 If engine wear is suspected, a compression test (refer to Chapter 2A, although note that testing with oil injected into the cylinders isn't an effective test with diesel engines) will provide valuable information regarding the overall performance of the main internal components. Such a test can be used as a basis to decide on the extent of the work to be carried out. If, for example, a compression test indicates serious internal engine wear, conventional maintenance as described in this Chapter will not greatly improve the performance of the engine, and may prove a waste of time and money, unless extensive overhaul work (Chapter 2C) is carried out first.

4 The following series of operations are those often required to improve the performance of a generally poor-running engine:

Primary operations

a) Clean, inspect and test the battery (See 'Weekly checks').
b) Check all the engine-related fluids (See 'Weekly checks').
c) Check the condition and tension of the auxiliary drivebelt (Section 8).
d) Drain water from the fuel filter (Section 17).
e) Check the condition of the air cleaner filter element, and renew if necessary (Section 9).
f) Check the condition of all hoses, and check for fluid leaks (Section 4).

5 If the above operations do not prove fully effective, carry out the following operations:

Secondary operations

All items listed under *Primary operations*, plus the following:

a) Check the charging system (Chapter 5A).
b) Check the preheating/glow plug system (Chapter 5A).
c) Check the fuel filter and fuel system (Chapter 4B).

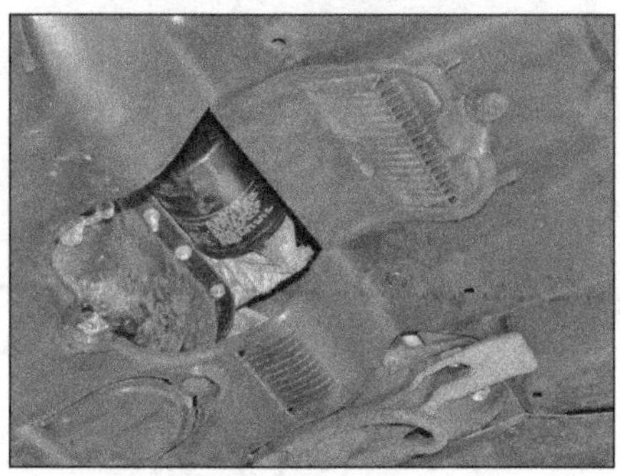
3.3 Open the access panel in the undertray

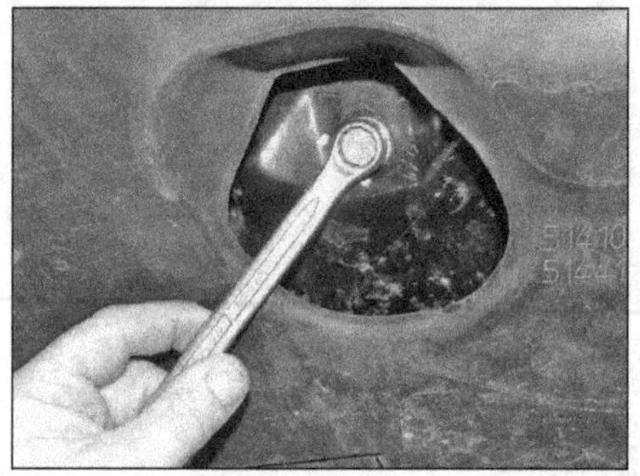
3.4a Slacken the drain plug . . .

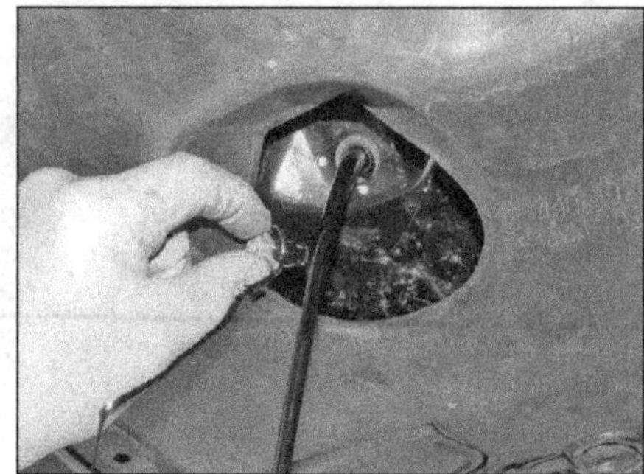
3.4b . . . and slowly withdraw the drain plug

Every 5000 miles or 6 months

3 Engine oil and filter renewal

1 Frequent oil and filter changes are the most important preventative maintenance procedures, which can be undertaken by the DIY owner. As engine oil ages, it becomes diluted and contaminated, which leads to premature engine wear.

2 Before starting this procedure, gather together all the necessary tools and materials. Also make sure that you have plenty of clean rags and newspapers handy, to mop-up any spills. Ideally, the engine oil should be warm, as it will drain better, and more built-up sludge will be removed with it. Take care, however, not to touch the exhaust or any other hot parts of the engine when working under the vehicle. To avoid any possibility of scalding, and to protect yourself from possible skin irritants and other harmful contaminants in used engine oils, it is advisable to wear gloves when carrying out this work. Access to the underside of the vehicle will be greatly improved if it can be raised on a lift, driven onto ramps, or jacked up and supported on axle stands (see *Jacking and vehicle support*). Whichever method is chosen, make sure that the vehicle remains level, or if it is at an angle, that the drain plug is at the lowest point.

3 Although not strictly necessary, to improve access, undo the screws and remove the engine undertray – or undo the retaining bolt and open the oil filter access panel **(see illustration)**.

HAYNES HiNT

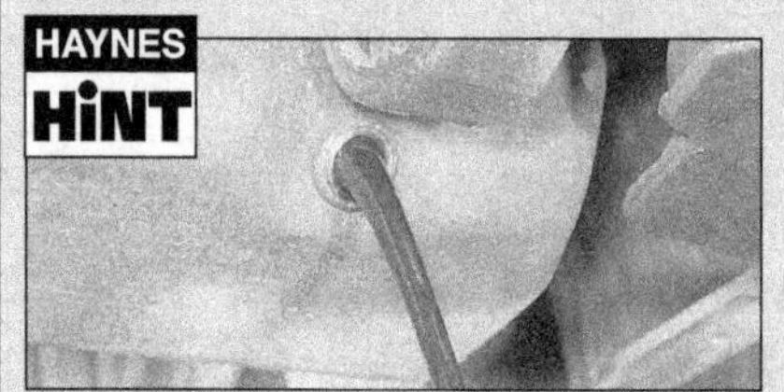

As the drain plug releases from the sump threads, move it away sharply, so the stream of oil issuing from the sump runs into the container, not up your sleeve.

3.6 Fit a new sealing washer to the drain plug

4 Slacken the drain plug about half a turn **(see illustration)**. Position the draining container under the drain plug, and then remove the plug completely **(see illustration)**. If possible, try to keep the plug pressed into the sump while unscrewing it by hand the last couple of turns **(see Haynes Hint)**. Recover the sealing ring from the drain plug.

5 Allow some time for the old oil to drain, noting that it may be necessary to reposition the container as the oil flow slows to a trickle.

6 After all the oil has drained, wipe off the drain plug with a clean rag, and fit a new sealing washer **(see illustration)**. Clean the area around the drain plug opening, and refit the plug, tightening it to the specified torque.

7 Move the container into position under the oil filter, which is located on the front of the cylinder block.

8 Using an oil filter removal tool if necessary, slacken the filter initially, then unscrew it by hand the rest of the way **(see illustrations)**. Empty the oil in the old filter into the container.

9 Use a clean rag to remove all oil, dirt and sludge from the filter sealing area on the engine. Check the old filter to make sure that the rubber sealing ring hasn't stuck to the engine. If it has, carefully remove it.

10 Apply a light coating of clean engine oil to the sealing ring on the new filter, then screw it into position on the engine **(see illustration)**. Tighten the filter firmly by hand only – **do not** use any tools.

11 Remove the old oil and all tools from

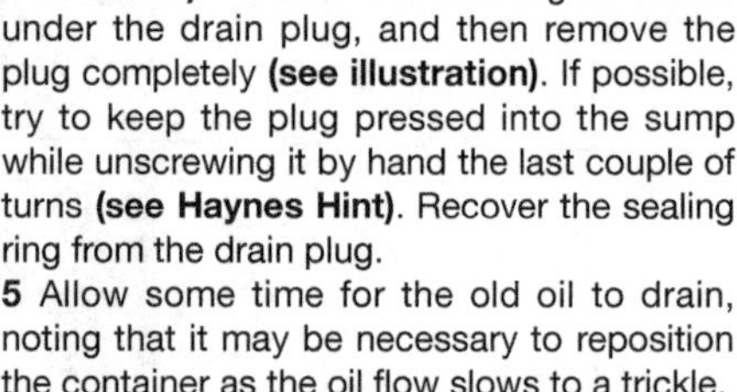

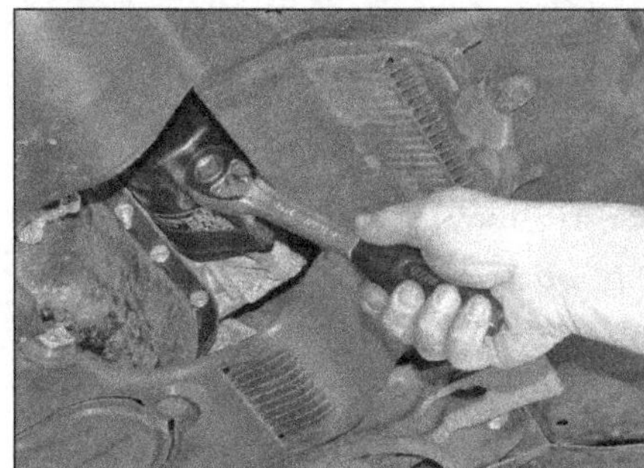
3.8a Use a filter removal tool to slacken . . .

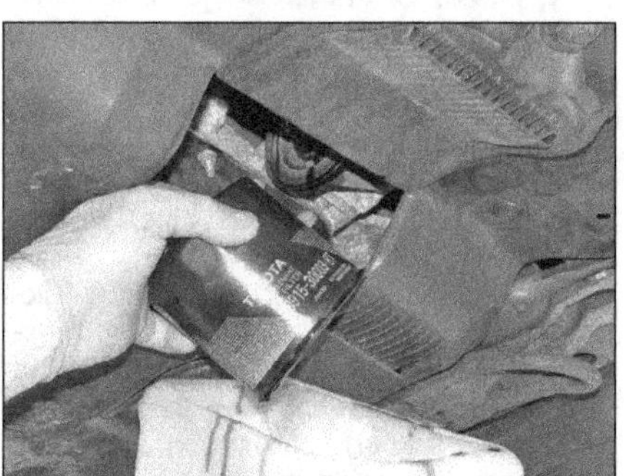
3.8b . . . and then remove the oil filter

3.10 Apply a little clean oil to the filter sealing ring

under the car, then lower the car to the ground (if applicable).

12 Remove the dipstick, and then unscrew the oil filler cap from the cylinder head cover. Fill the engine, using the correct grade and type of oil (see *Weekly checks*). An oil can spout or funnel may help to reduce spillage. Pour in half the specified quantity of oil first, and then wait a few minutes for the oil to run to the sump. Continue adding oil a small quantity at a time until the level is up to the lower mark on the dipstick. Adding approximately 1 litre will bring the level up to the upper mark on the dipstick. Refit the filler cap.

13 Start the engine and run it for a few minutes; check for leaks around the oil filter seal and the sump drain plug. Note that there may be a delay of a few seconds before the oil pressure warning light goes out when the engine is first started, as the oil circulates through the engine oil galleries and the new oil filter before the pressure builds-up.

14 Refit the engine undertray (where applicable), and secure it in place with the screw fasteners.

15 Switch off the engine, and wait a few minutes for the oil to settle in the sump once more. With the new oil circulated and the filter completely full, recheck the level on the dipstick, and add more oil as necessary.

16 Dispose of the used engine oil safely, with reference to *General repair procedures*.

Every 10 000 miles or 12 months

4 Hose and fluid leak check

1 Visually inspect the engine joint faces, gaskets and seals for any signs of water or oil leaks. Pay particular attention to the areas around the cylinder head cover, cylinder head, oil filter and sump joint faces. Bear in mind that, over a period of time, some very slight seepage from these areas is to be expected – what you are really looking for is any indication of a serious leak. Should a leak be found, renew the offending gasket or oil seal by referring to the appropriate Chapters in this manual.

2 Also check the security and condition of all the engine-related pipes and hoses. Ensure that all cable ties or securing clips are in place, and in good condition. Clips, which are broken or missing, can lead to chafing of the hoses, pipes or wiring, which could cause more serious problems in the future.

3 Carefully check the radiator hoses and heater hoses along their entire length. Renew any hose, which is cracked, swollen or deteriorated. Cracks will show up better if the hose is squeezed. Pay close attention to the hose clips that secure the hoses to the cooling system components. Hose clips can pinch and puncture hoses, resulting in cooling system leaks. If crimped-type hose clips are used, it may be a good idea to use standard worm-drive clips.

4 Inspect all the cooling system components (hoses, joint faces, etc) for leaks **(see illustration and Haynes Hint)**.

5 Where any problems are found on system components, renew the component or gasket with reference to Chapter 3.

6 With the vehicle raised, inspect the petrol tank and filler neck for punctures, cracks and other damage. The connection between the filler neck and tank is especially critical. Sometimes a rubber filler neck or connecting hose will leak due to loose retaining clamps or deteriorated rubber.

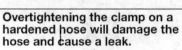

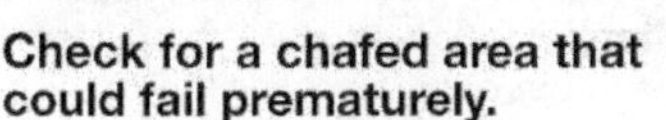
Check for a chafed area that could fail prematurely.

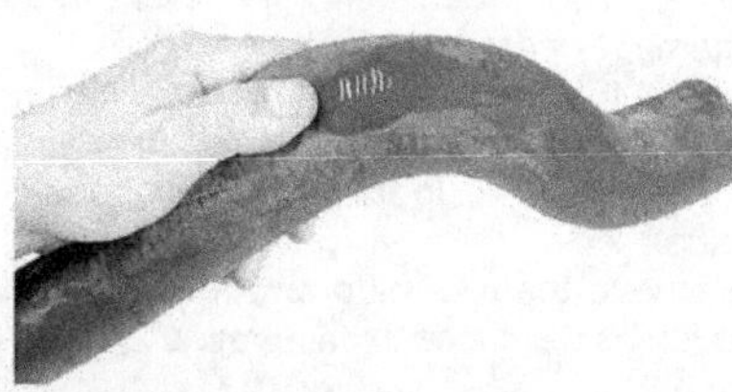

Check for a soft area indicating the hose has deteriorated inside.

Overtightening the clamp on a hardened hose will damage the hose and cause a leak.

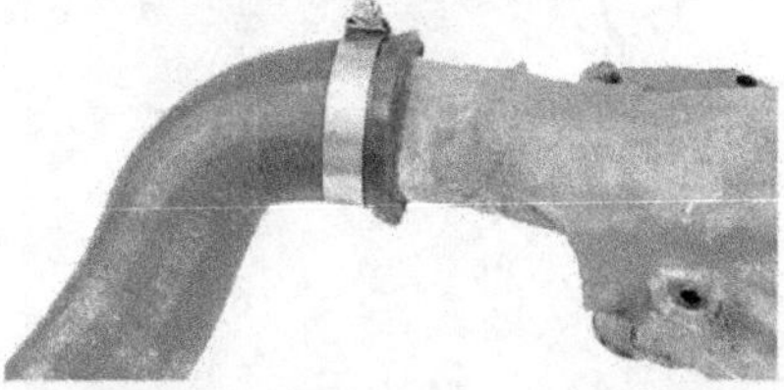

Check each hose for swelling and oil-soaked ends. Cracks and breaks can be located by squeezing the hose.

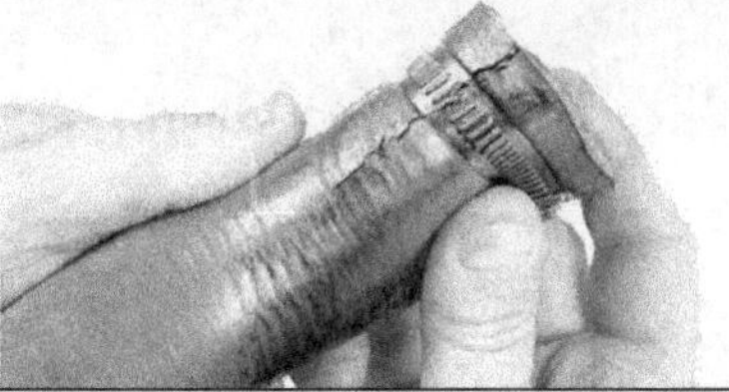

4.4 To prevent the inconvenience of a blown radiator or heater hose, inspect them carefully as shown

7 Carefully check all rubber hoses and fuel pipes leading away from the petrol tank. Check for loose connections, deteriorated hoses, crimped lines, and other damage. Pay particular attention to the vent pipes and hoses, which often loop up around the filler neck and can become blocked or crimped. Follow the pipes to the front of the vehicle, carefully inspecting them all the way. Renew damaged sections as necessary.

8 From within the engine compartment, check the security of all fuel pipe attachments and unions, and inspect the fuel pipes and vacuum hoses for kinks, chafing and deterioration.

9 Where applicable, check the condition of the power steering fluid hoses and pipes.

5 Driveshaft gaiter and CV joints check

1 With the vehicle raised and securely supported on stands (see *Jacking and vehicle support*), turn the steering onto full lock, then slowly rotate the roadwheel. Inspect the condition of the outer constant velocity (CV) joint gaiters, squeezing the gaiters to open out the folds **(see illustration)**. Check for signs of cracking, splits or deterioration of the

A leak in the cooling system will usually show up as white- or antifreeze-coloured deposits on the area adjoining the leak.

5.1 Check the driveshaft gaiters for signs of damage or deterioration

gaiter, which may allow the grease to escape, and lead to water and grit entry into the joint. Also check the security and condition of the retaining clips. Repeat these checks on the inner CV joints. If any damage or deterioration is found, the gaiters should be renewed (see Chapter 8).

2 At the same time, check the general condition of the CV joints themselves by first holding the driveshaft and attempting to rotate the wheel. Repeat this check by holding the inner joint and attempting to rotate the driveshaft. Any appreciable movement indicates wear in the joints, wear in the driveshaft splines, or a loose driveshaft retaining nut.

6 Hinge and lock lubrication

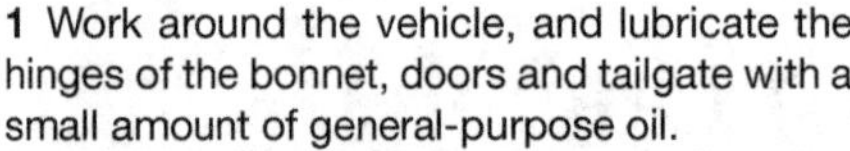

1 Work around the vehicle, and lubricate the hinges of the bonnet, doors and tailgate with a small amount of general-purpose oil.

2 Lightly lubricate the bonnet release mechanism and exposed section of inner cable with a smear of grease.

3 Check carefully the security and operation of all hinges, latches and locks, adjusting them where required. Check the operation of the central locking system (if fitted).

4 Check the condition and operation of the tailgate struts, renewing them if either is leaking or no longer able to support the tailgate securely when raised.

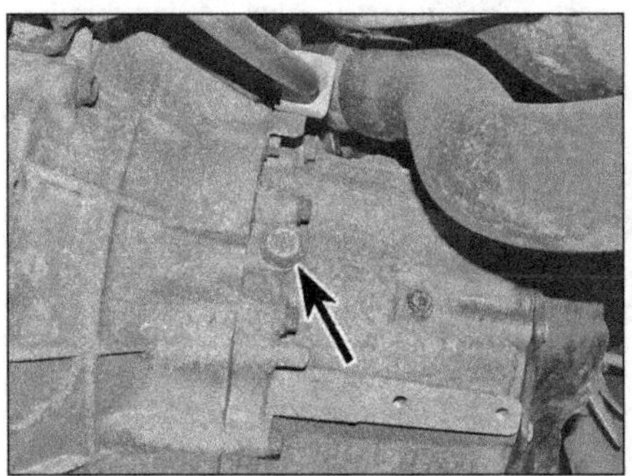
7.2 Manual transmission fluid level plug (arrowed)

7.7 Manual transmission fluid drain plug (arrowed)

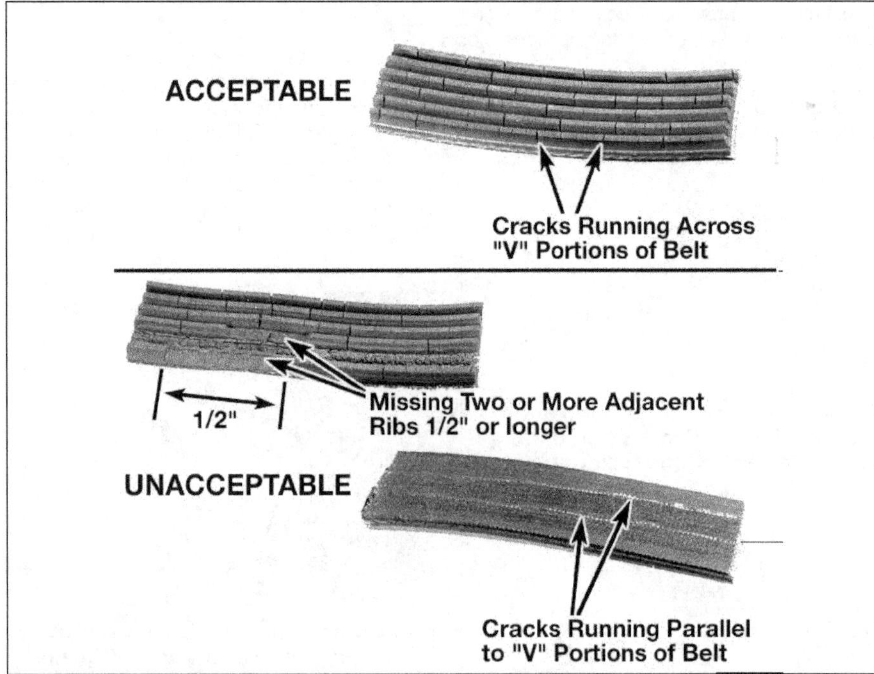

8.3 Check the multi-ribbed belt for signs of wear like these – if the belt looks worn, renew it

7 Manual transmission fluid level check and renewal

Note: *Toyota do not specify an interval for* ***checking*** *the manual transmission fluid level.*

Level check

1 The manual transmission does not have a dipstick. To check the fluid level, raise the vehicle and support it securely on axle stands (see *Jacking and vehicle support*). Undo the screws and remove the left-hand side engine undertray (where fitted).

2 On the lower front side of the transmission housing, you will see a plug **(see illustration)**. Remove it. If the lubricant level is correct, it should be up to the lower edge of the hole.

3 If the transmission needs more lubricant (if the level is not up to the hole), use a syringe or a gear oil pump to add more. Stop filling the transmission when the lubricant begins to run out the hole.

4 Refit the plug and tighten it to the specified torque. Drive the vehicle a short distance, and then check for leaks.

Fluid renewal

5 Take the vehicle for a drive of sufficient length to warm-up the transmission fluid. Although this is not essential, it does help to ensure all the fluid is drained, along with any contaminants.

6 Raise the vehicle, and remove the left-hand engine undertray as described in paragraph 1.

7 The fluid drain plug is located on the underside of the transmission casing **(see illustration)**. Position a suitable container, and undo the drain plug. Recover the drain plug sealing washer. Renew it if it shows any sign of damage, wear, or deformity.

8 Once the fluid has finished draining, refit the drain plug (with a new washer where necessary), and tighten it to the specified torque.

9 Remove the filler plug and refill the transmission as described in paragraphs 2, 3 and 4.

8 Auxiliary drivebelt check and renewal

Check

1 The alternator, power steering pump and air conditioning compressor auxiliary drivebelts, also referred to as simply 'fan' belts, are located at the right end of the engine. The good condition and proper adjustment of the alternator belt is critical to the operation of the engine. Because of their composition and the high stresses to which they are subjected, auxiliary drivebelts stretch and deteriorate as they get older. They must therefore be periodically inspected.

2 Two belts are used; one belt transmits power from the crankshaft to the alternator, and the other drives the air conditioning compressor.

3 With the engine off, open the bonnet and locate the auxiliary drivebelt(s). With an electric torch, check each belt for separation of the adhesive rubber on both sides of the core, core separation from the belt side, a severed core, separation of the ribs from the adhesive rubber, cracking or separation of the ribs, and torn or worn ribs or cracks in the inner ridges of the ribs **(see illustration)**. Also check for fraying and glazing, which gives the belt a shiny appearance. Both sides of the belt should be inspected, which means you will have to twist the belt to check the underside. Use your fingers to feel the belt where you can't see it. If any of the above conditions are evident, renew the belt (go to Paragraph 7).

4 The alternator drivebelt is fitted with an automatic tensioner, however, the air conditioning compressor drivebelt has manual adjustment. To check the tension of the compressor belt in accordance with factory specifications, use either a Nippondenso or Burroughs belt tension gauge on the belt **(see illustration)**. Measure the tension in accordance with the manufacturer's instructions and compare your measurement to the specified auxiliary drivebelt tension for either a used or new belt. **Note:** *A 'used' belt is defined as any belt, which has been operated more than five minutes on the engine; a 'new' belt is one that has been used for less than five minutes.*

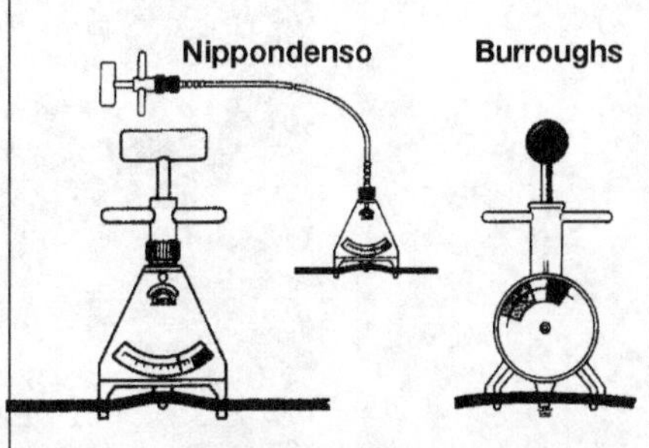

8.4 If you use a Nippondenso or Burroughs belt tension gauge, this is how it's installed on the belt – compare the reading on the scale with the specified drivebelt tension

5 If you don't have either of the above tools, and cannot borrow one, the following method is recommended: push firmly on the belt with your thumb at a distance halfway between the pulleys and note how far the belt can be pushed (deflected). See Specifications for recommended deflections.

Adjustment

6 To adjust the air conditioning compressor drivebelt, first loosen the locknut in the centre of the idler pulley, and then turn the adjustment bolt located at the top of the adjustment pulley bracket **(see illustrations)**. On completion of the adjustment, tighten the locknut.

Drivebelt renewal

7 To renew the air conditioning compressor drivebelt, follow the procedures for adjustment as described above, then slip the belt from the pulleys **(see illustration)**. Fit the new belt, and adjust as described previously.

8 To renew the alternator drivebelt, working from under the front wheel arch, rotate the belt tensioner clockwise to release the tension, and then slip the belt off the pulleys **(see illustrations)**. Slowly release the tensioner. Fit the new belt, again rotating the tensioner to allow the belt to be fitted, and then release the belt tensioner.

9 Make sure the belt is properly centred in the pulleys **(see illustration)**.

Automatic tensioner renewal

Warning: Disconnect the cable from the negative terminal of the battery before performing this procedure.

10 To renew a tensioner that does not properly tension the belt, or one that exhibits binding or a worn-out bearing/pulley, remove the auxiliary drivebelt then unscrew the mounting bolt and nut.

11 Refitting is the reverse of the removal procedure. Tighten the nuts and bolts to the torque values listed in this Chapter's Specifications.

12 Refit the auxiliary drivebelt as previously described.

8.6a Loosen the locknut (arrowed) in the centre of the idler pulley . . .

8.6b . . . then turn the adjustment bolt (arrowed) as required

8.7 Removing the air conditioning drivebelt

8.8a Rotate the tensioner clockwise . . .

8.8b . . . and remove the alternator drivebelt

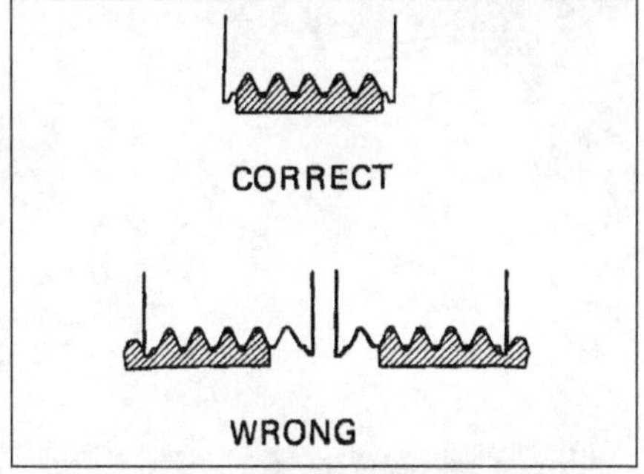

8.9 When installing a multi-ribbed belt, make sure that it is centred – it must not overlap either edge of the pulley

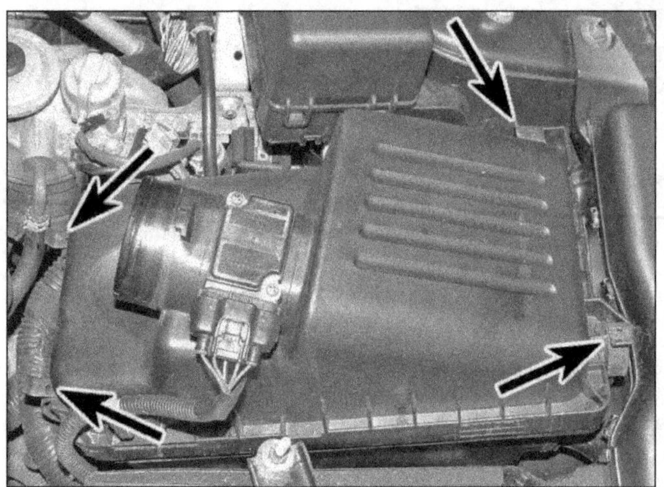

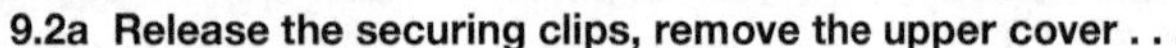

9.2a Release the securing clips, remove the upper cover . . .

9.2b . . . and withdraw the air filter element

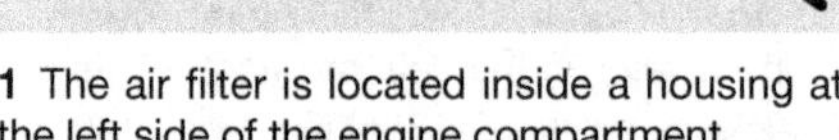

9 Air filter element check and renewal

1 The air filter is located inside a housing at the left side of the engine compartment.

2 To remove the air filter, release the spring clips that keep the two halves of the air cleaner housing together, then lift the cover up and remove the air filter element, noting the fitted position **(see illustration)**.

3 Inspect the outer surface of the filter element. If it is dirty, renew it. If it is only moderately dusty, it can be re-used by blowing it clean from the back to the front surface with compressed air. Because it is a pleated paper type filter, it cannot be washed or oiled. If it cannot be cleaned satisfactorily with compressed air, discard and renew it.

Warning: Wear eye protection when using compressed air.

4 Wipe out the inside of the air cleaner housing.

5 Place the new filter into the air cleaner housing, making sure it seats properly **(see illustration)**.

Caution: Never drive the vehicle with the air cleaner removed. Excessive engine wear could result and backfiring could even cause a fire under the bonnet. While the cover is off, be careful not to drop anything down into the filter housing.

6 Refitting of the cover is the reverse of removal.

10 Handbrake check and adjustment

1 To check the handbrake adjustment, applying normal moderate pressure, pull the handbrake lever to the fully-applied position, counting the number of clicks emitted from the handbrake ratchet mechanism. If adjustment is correct, the handbrake should be fully applied after 6 to 9 clicks have been emitted. If this is not the case, adjust the handbrake as described in Chapter 9.

11 Brake pad check

1 Slacken the front roadwheel nuts. Firmly apply the handbrake, and then jack up the front of the car and support it securely on axle stands (see *Jacking and vehicle support*). Remove the front roadwheels.

2 For a quick check, the pad thickness can be carried out via the inspection hole on the front caliper **(see illustration)**. Using a steel rule, measure the thickness of the pad friction material. This must not be less than the specified minimum given in the Specifications.

3 For a comprehensive check, the brake pads should be removed and cleaned. The operation of the caliper can then be checked, and the brake disc itself can be fully examined on both sides. Refer to Chapter 9 for details.

4 If any pad's friction material is worn to the specified minimum thickness or less; all four pads must be renewed as a set. Refer to Chapter 9 for details.

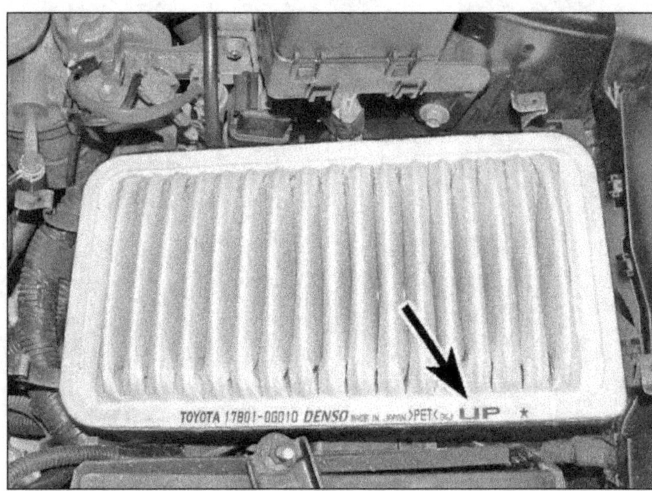

9.5 Note the fitted position of the air filter element

11.2 Check the brake pad thickness

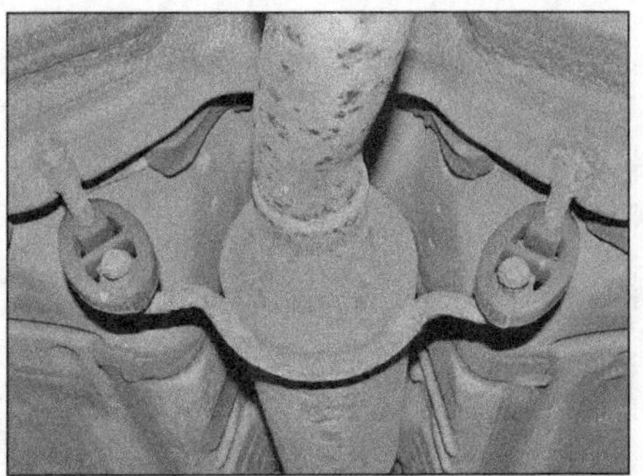
12.2a Check the condition of the exhaust rubber mountings

12.2b Check the condition of the exhaust joints

13.4 Check for wear in the hub bearings by grasping the wheel and trying to rock it

5 On completion, refit the roadwheels then lower the vehicle to the ground and tighten the wheel nuts to the specified torque.
6 Slacken the rear roadwheel nuts. Jack up the rear of the car and support it securely on axle stands. Remove the rear roadwheels. Repeat the procedure described in paragraphs 2 to 5 on the rear brake pads.

12 Exhaust system and mountings check

1 With the engine cold (at least an hour after the car has been driven), check the complete exhaust system from the engine to the end of the tailpipe. The exhaust system is most easily checked with the car raised on a hoist, or suitably-supported on axle stands, so that the exhaust components are readily visible and accessible.
2 Check the exhaust pipes and connections for evidence of leaks, severe corrosion and damage. Make sure that all brackets and mountings are in good condition, and that all relevant nuts and bolts are tight **(see illustrations)**. Leakage at any of the joints or in other parts of the system will usually show up as a black sooty stain in the vicinity of the leak.
3 Rattles and other noises can often be traced to the exhaust system, especially the brackets and mountings. Try to move the pipes and silencers. If the components are able to come into contact with the body or suspension parts, secure the system with new mountings. Otherwise separate the joints (if possible) and twist the pipes as necessary to provide additional clearance.

13 Steering and suspension check

Front suspension and steering

1 Raise the front of the vehicle, and securely support it on axle stands (see *Jacking and vehicle support*).
2 Visually inspect the balljoint dust covers and the steering gear gaiters for splits, chafing or deterioration. Any wear of these components will cause loss of lubricant, together with dirt and water entry, resulting in rapid deterioration of the balljoints or steering gear.
3 Check the power steering fluid pipes/hoses for chafing or deterioration, and the pipe and hose unions for fluid leaks. Also check for signs of fluid leakage under pressure from the steering gear rubber gaiters, which would indicate failed fluid seals within the steering gear.
4 Grasp the roadwheel at the 12 o'clock and 6 o'clock positions, and try to rock it **(see illustration)**. Very slight free play may be felt, but if the movement is appreciable, further investigation is necessary to determine the source. Continue rocking the wheel while an assistant depresses the footbrake. If the movement is now eliminated or significantly reduced, it is likely that the hub bearings are at fault. If the free play is still evident with the footbrake depressed, then there is wear in the suspension joints or mountings.
5 Now grasp the wheel at the 9 o'clock and 3 o'clock positions, and try to rock it as before. Any movement felt now may again be caused by wear in the hub bearings or the steering track rod balljoints. If the inner or outer balljoint is worn, the visual movement will be obvious.
6 Using a large screwdriver or flat bar, check for wear in the suspension mounting bushes by levering between the relevant suspension component and its attachment point. Some movement is to be expected as the mountings are made of rubber, but excessive wear should be obvious. Also check the condition of any visible rubber bushes, looking for splits, cracks or contamination of the rubber.
7 With the car standing on its wheels, have an assistant turn the steering wheel back-and-forth about an eighth of a turn each way. There should be very little, if any, lost movement between the steering wheel and roadwheels. If this is not the case, closely observe the joints and mountings previously described, but in addition, check the steering column universal joints for wear, and the steering gear itself.

Strut/shock absorber

8 Check for any signs of fluid leakage around the suspension strut/shock absorber body, or from the rubber gaiter around the piston rod. Should any fluid be noticed, the suspension strut/shock absorber is defective internally, and should be renewed. **Note:** *Suspension struts/shock absorbers should always be renewed in pairs on the same axle, or the handling of the vehicle will be adversely affected.*
9 The efficiency of the suspension strut/shock absorber may be checked by bouncing the vehicle at each corner. Generally speaking, the body will return to its normal position and stop after being depressed. If it rises and returns on a rebound, the suspension strut/shock absorber is probably suspect. Examine also the suspension strut/shock absorber upper and lower mountings for any signs of wear.

14 Clutch pedal check and adjustment

1 Press down lightly on the clutch pedal and, with a small steel ruler, measure the distance that it moves freely before the clutch resistance is felt **(see illustration)**. The freeplay should be approximately 5.0 to 15.0 mm. If it isn't proceed as follows:
2 Slacken the locknut on the pedal end of the clutch pushrod.
3 Turn the pushrod until the pedal freeplay is correct, and then tighten the locknut.
4 After adjusting the freeplay, check the pedal height from the centre of the pedal pad to the footwell metal floor. The distance should be 146.0 to 156.0 mm.

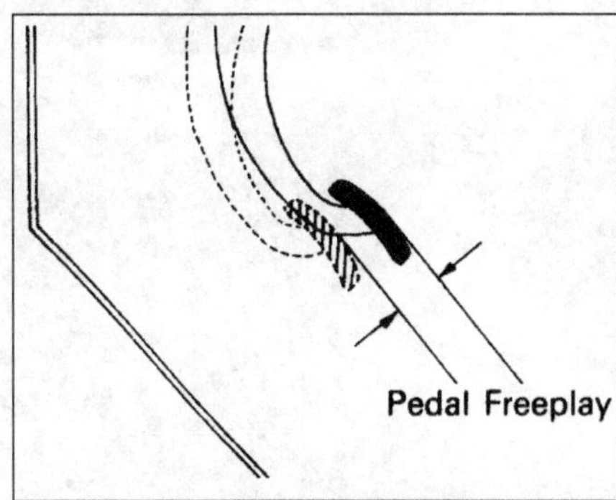

14.1 To check the clutch pedal free play, measure the distance between the natural resting place of the pedal and point where you encounter resistance

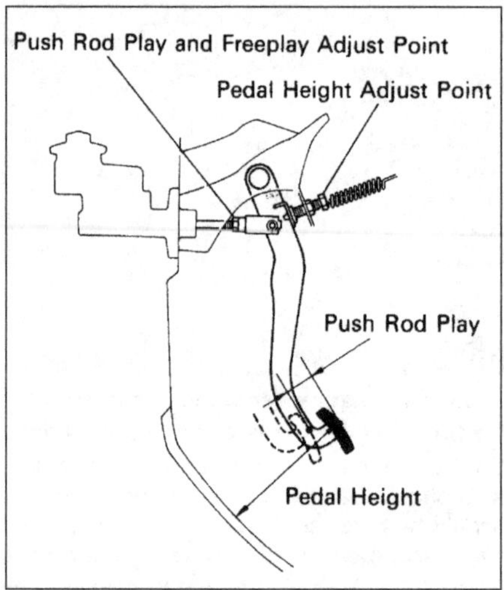

14.5a **The clutch pedal pushrod play, pedal height and free play adjustments are made by slackening the locknut and turning the threaded adjuster**

5 If the pedal height is incorrect, slacken the locknut and turn the stop bolt until the height is correct **(see illustrations)**. Tighten the locknut.

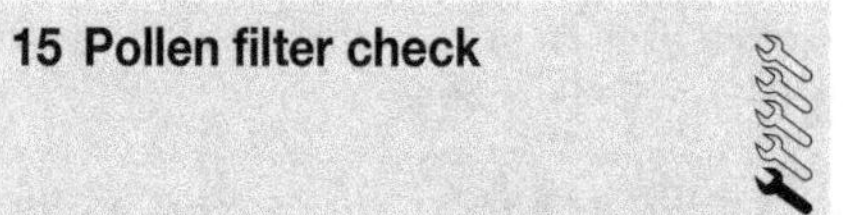

15 Pollen filter check

1 Remove the glovebox as described in Chapter 11.

2 Reach inside the glovebox aperture, release the retaining clips and remove the cover from the filter housing **(see illustration)**.

3 Withdraw the filter from the housing, noting the position of the arrow on the front of the filter **(see illustration)**. Check the condition of the filter, and renew it if dirty.

4 Wipe clean the inside of the housing and fit the pollen filter element, making sure that it is correctly fitted, as noted on removal.

5 Refit the pollen filter cover; making sure it is securely fitted.

6 Refit the glovebox as described in Chapter 11.

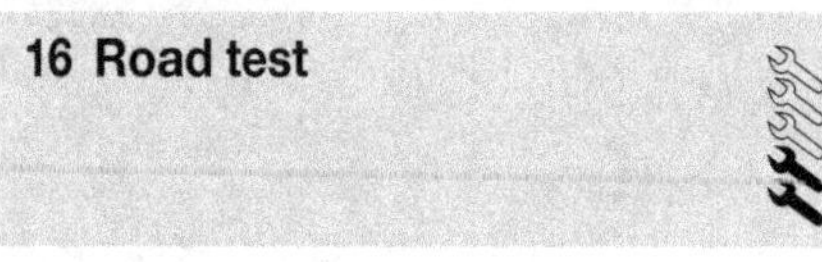

16 Road test

Instruments and electrical equipment

1 Check the operation of all instruments and electrical equipment.

2 Make sure that all instruments read correctly, and switch on all electrical equipment in turn to check it functions properly.

Steering and suspension

3 Check for any abnormalities in the steering, suspension, handling or road 'feel'.

4 Drive the vehicle, and check that there are no unusual vibrations or noises.

5 Check that the steering feels positive, with no excessive 'sloppiness', or roughness, and check for any suspension noises when cornering, or when driving over bumps.

Drivetrain

6 Check the performance of the engine, clutch, transmission and driveshafts.

7 Listen for any unusual noises from the engine, clutch and transmission.

8 Make sure the engine idles smoothly, and that there is no hesitation when accelerating.

9 Check that the clutch action is smooth and progressive, that the drive is taken up smoothly, and that the pedal travel is not excessive. Also listen for any noises when the clutch pedal is depressed.

10 Check that all gears can be engaged smoothly, without noise, and that the gear lever action is smooth and not vague or 'notchy'.

11 Listen for a metallic clicking sound from the front of the vehicle, as the vehicle is driven slowly in a circle with the steering on full lock. Carry out this check in both directions. If a clicking noise is heard, this indicates wear in a driveshaft joint; in which case, the complete driveshaft must be renewed (see Chapter 8).

14.5b Pedal adjustment bolt (arrowed)

Braking system

12 Make sure that the vehicle does not pull to one side when braking, and that the wheels do not lock when braking hard.

13 Check that there is no vibration through the steering when braking.

14 Check that the handbrake operates correctly, without excessive movement of the lever, and that it holds the vehicle on a slope.

15 Test the operation of the brake servo unit as follows. With the engine off, depress the footbrake four or five times to exhaust the vacuum. Start the engine, holding the brake pedal depressed. As the engine starts, there should be a noticeable 'give' in the brake pedal as vacuum builds-up. Allow the engine to run for at least two minutes, and then switch it off. If the brake pedal is depressed now, it should be possible to detect a hiss from the servo as the pedal is depressed. After about four or five applications, no further hissing should be heard, and the pedal should feel considerably firmer.

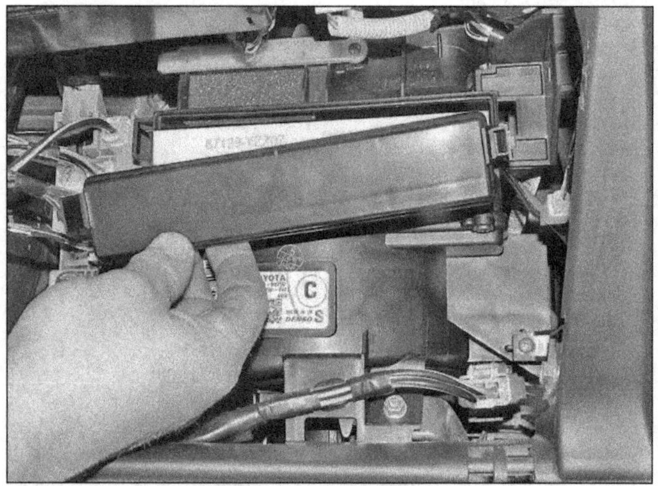

15.2 unclip the pollen filter cover

15.3 Withdraw the filter, noting its fitted position (arrowed)

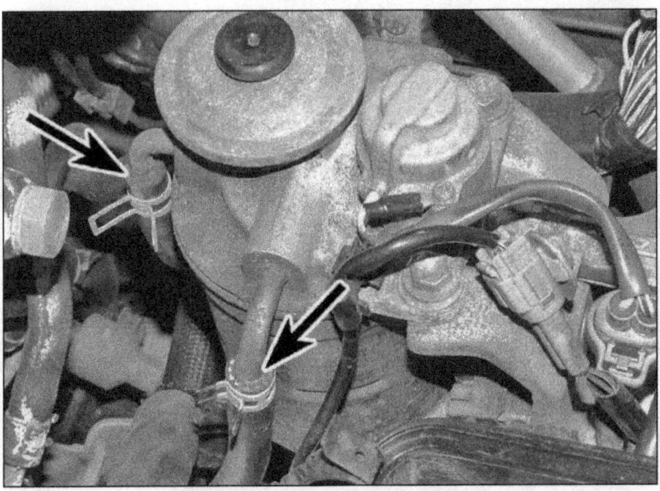

17.2a Disconnect the hoses . . .

17.2b . . . and plug the ends

Every 20 000 miles or 2 years

17 Fuel filter renewal

1 Access to the fuel filter is gained by removing the air cleaner assembly as described in Chapter 4B.

2 Position a container beneath the fuel filter to catch spilt fuel, then disconnect the supply and return hoses **(see illustrations)**. Plug the ends of the fuel pipe to prevent dirt ingress.

3 Disconnect the wiring connectors for the fuel heater on top of the filter assembly and the fuel level warning switch on the bottom of the filter assembly **(see illustration)**.

4 Unscrew the mounting bolts and lift the filter assembly from the support bracket **(see illustrations)**. Loosen the drain plug at the bottom of the filter and drain the fuel into the container. Tighten the plug on completion.

5 Holding the filter securely, unscrew the fuel level warning switch from the bottom of the filter canister. Recover the O-ring seal **(see illustrations)**.

6 Unscrew the filter canister and discard. Toyota technicians use a special ring spanner, which engages the multi-flats on the canister perimeter, however, an oil filter removal strap can be used instead **(see illustrations)**.

7 Clean the contact surfaces of the new filter

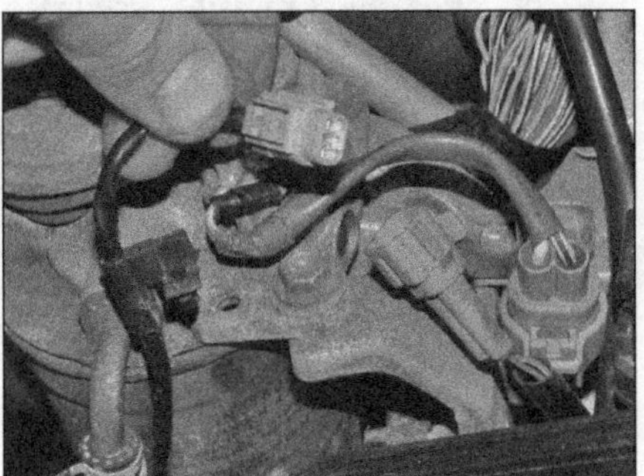

17.3 Disconnect the wiring connector

17.4a undo the retaining bolts (arrowed) . . .

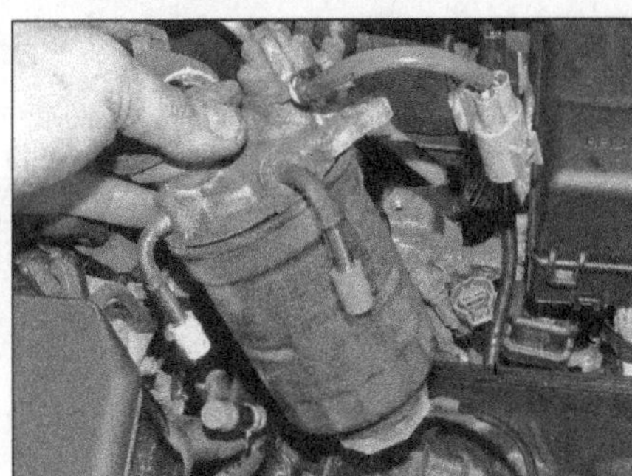

17.4b . . . and withdraw the fuel filter

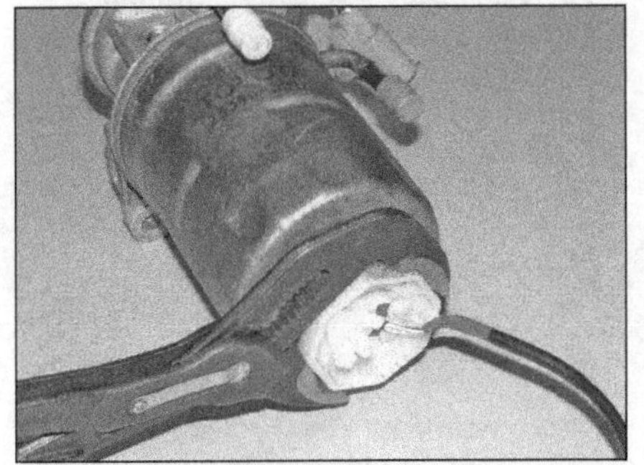

17.5a Use a pair of grips to unscrew the fuel level warning switch . . .

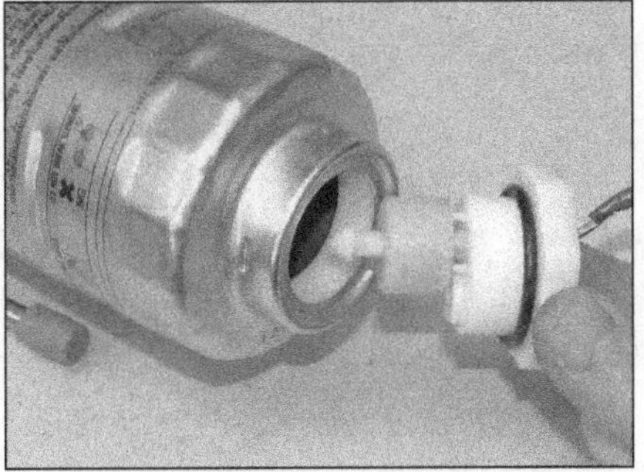

17.5b . . . and remove it from the bottom of the filter canister

17.6a Use an oil filter removal strap to unscrew the canister . . .

17.6b . . . and remove it from the filter body

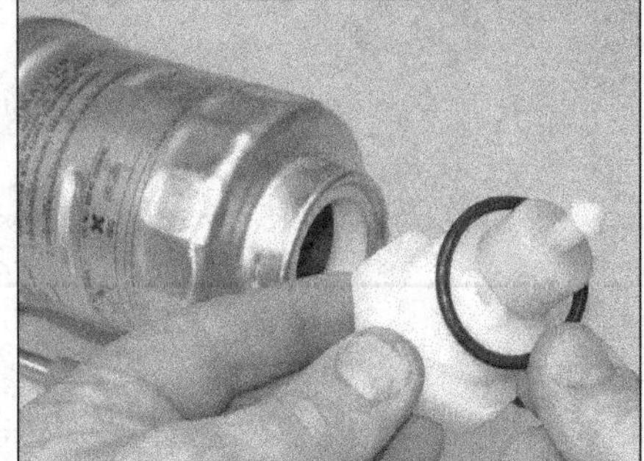
17.9 Fit new O-ring seal to level switch

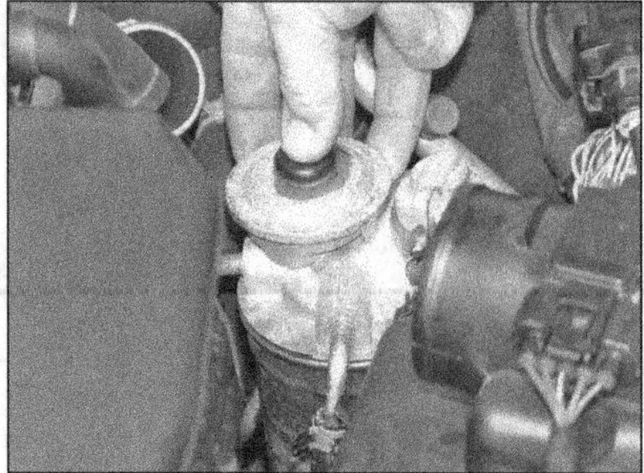
17.14 Operate pump to prime filter

canister and body, and smear a little fuel oil onto them.

8 Screw on the canister until it contacts the body, then tighten it an additional ¾ turn by hand only.

9 Apply a little fuel oil to a new O-ring seal **(see illustration)**, and locate it on the fuel level warning switch. Screw the switch into the filter canister and tighten securely.

10 Fit the filter assembly to the support bracket and tighten the mounting nuts.

11 Reconnect the wiring to the level warning switch and heater.

12 Reconnect the feed and supply hoses.

13 Refit the air cleaner assembly.

14 Operate the hand pump on top of the fuel filter until resistance is felt indicating that the filter is primed **(see illustration)**.

15 Run the engine and check for leaks.

18 Handbrake shoe check

Warning: Brake dust produced by lining wear and deposited on brake components may contain asbestos, which is hazardous to your health. DO NOT blow it out with compressed air and DO NOT inhale it. DO NOT use petrol or solvents to remove the dust. Brake system cleaner should be used to flush the dust into a drain pan. After the brake components are wiped clean with a damp rag, dispose of the contaminated rag(s) and solvent in a covered and labeled container. Try to use non-asbestos parts whenever possible.

1 Refer to Chapter 9 and remove the rear brake discs.

2 Note the thickness of the lining material on the handbrake shoes **(see illustration)** and look for signs of contamination by brake fluid and grease.

3 If the lining material is within 1.0 mm of the recessed rivets or metal shoes, renew the brake shoes. The shoes should also be renewed if they are cracked, glazed (shiny lining surfaces) or contaminated with brake fluid or grease. See Chapter 9 for the renewal procedure.

4 Check the shoe return and hold-down springs and the adjusting mechanism to make sure they're installed correctly and in good condition. Deteriorated or distorted springs, if not renewed, could allow the linings to drag and wear prematurely.

5 Check the disc/drums for cracks, score marks, deep scratches and hard spots, which will appear as small discoloured areas. If imperfections cannot be removed with emery cloth, the discs/drums must be resurfaced by an automotive engineering workshop (see Chapter 9 for more detailed information).

6 Refit the brake discs (see Chapter 9).

7 Refit the wheels and nuts.

8 Remove the axle stands and lower the vehicle.

9 Tighten the wheel nuts to the specified torque.

18.2 Measure the thickness of the brake shoe friction material

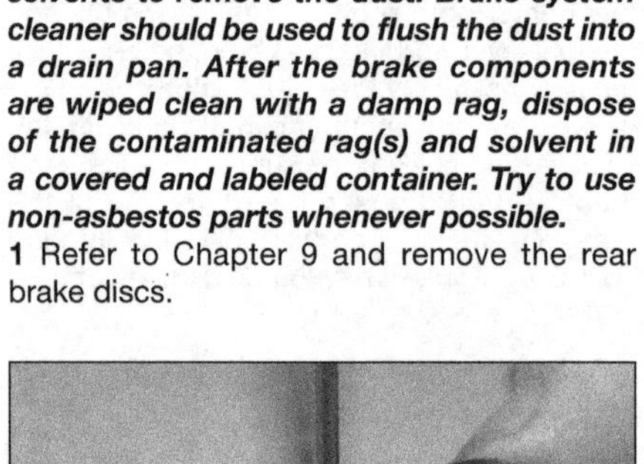
19.1 Undo the small screw and lift the remote control cover . . .

19 Remote control battery renewal

1 Undo the small screw and lift the cover from the remote control unit **(see illustration)**.

2 Lift the module from the unit, then remove the battery case cover **(see illustration)**.

3 Note how it's fitted (positive side upwards) and remove the battery **(see illustration)**.

4 Refitting is a reversal of removal.

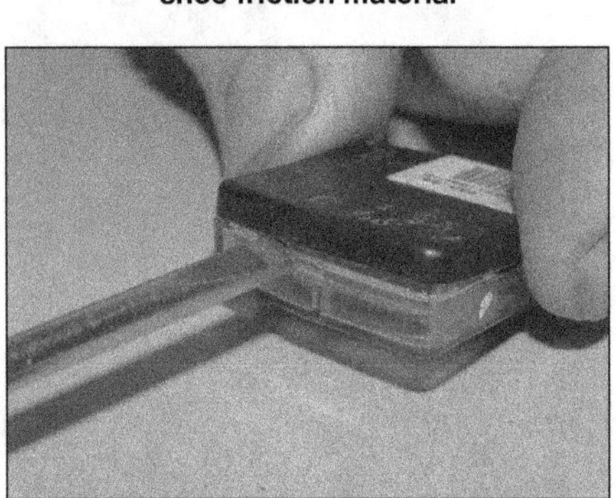
19.2 . . . prise open the battery case cover . . .

19.3 . . . note the positive side of the battery is upwards

20 Brake fluid renewal

Warning: Brake hydraulic fluid can harm your eyes and damage painted surfaces, so use extreme caution when handling and pouring it. Do

not use fluid that has been standing open for some time, as it absorbs moisture from the air. Excess moisture can cause a dangerous loss of braking effectiveness.

Caution: Ensure the ignition is switched off before starting the bleeding procedure to avoid any possibility of voltage being applied to the hydraulic modulator (see Chapter 9, Section 2).

1 The procedure is similar to that for the bleeding of the hydraulic system as described in Chapter 9, except that the brake fluid reservoir should be emptied by syphoning, using a clean poultry baster or similar before starting, and allowance should be made for the old fluid to be expelled when bleeding a section of the circuit.

2 Working as described in Chapter 9, open the first bleed screw in the sequence, and pump the brake pedal gently until nearly all the old fluid has been emptied from the master cylinder reservoir.

3 Top-up to the MAX level with new fluid, and continue pumping until only the new fluid remains in the reservoir, and new fluid can be seen emerging from the bleed screw. Tighten the screw, and top the reservoir level up to the MAX level line.

4 Work through all the remaining bleed screws in the sequence until new fluid can be seen at all of them. Be careful to keep the master cylinder reservoir topped-up to above the MIN level at all times, or air may enter the system and increase the length of the task.

5 When the operation is complete, check that all bleed screws are securely tightened, and that their dust caps are refitted. Wash off all traces of spilt fluid, and recheck the master cylinder reservoir fluid level.

6 Check the operation of the brakes before taking the car on the road.

Every 40 000 miles or 3 years

21 Coolant renewal

Warning: Wait until the engine is cold before starting this procedure. Do not allow antifreeze to come in contact with your skin, or with the painted surfaces of the vehicle. Rinse off spills immediately with plenty of water. Never leave antifreeze lying around in an open container, or in a puddle in the driveway or on the garage floor. Children and pets are attracted by its sweet smell, but antifreeze can be fatal if ingested. Check with local authorities on disposing of used antifreeze. Many communities have collection centres, which will see that antifreeze is disposed of safely. Antifreeze is flammable under certain conditions – be sure to read the precautions on the container.

Note: *Coolant renewal at this interval applies to standard coolant (red/green only) and not to Long Life Coolant (pink).*

Cooling system draining

1 With the engine completely cold, unscrew the radiator pressure cap.

2 Undo the screws and remove the right-hand engine undertray (where fitted).

3 Position a suitable container beneath the coolant drain tap at the lower right-hand side of the radiator, then open the drain tap, and allow the coolant to drain into the container **(see illustration)**. When the coolant has finished draining, close the tap.

4 Move the container to under the rear of the engine block, then open the block drain tap (where applicable) and drain the coolant into the container. Once the coolant has finished draining, close the tap.

Cooling system flushing

5 If coolant renewal has been neglected, or if the antifreeze mixture has become diluted, then in time, the cooling system may gradually lose efficiency, as the coolant passages become restricted due to rust, scale deposits, and other sediment. The cooling system efficiency can be restored by flushing the system clean.

6 The radiator should be flushed separately from the engine, to avoid excess contamination.

Radiator flushing

7 Disconnect the top and bottom hoses and any other relevant hoses from the radiator (see Chapter 3).

8 Insert a garden hose into the radiator top inlet. Direct a flow of clean water through the radiator, and continue flushing until clean water emerges from the radiator bottom outlet.

9 If after a reasonable period, the water still does not run clear, the radiator can be flushed with a good proprietary cleaning agent. It is important that their manufacturer's instructions are followed carefully. If the contamination is particularly bad, insert the hose in the radiator bottom outlet, and reverse-flush the radiator.

Engine flushing

10 To flush the engine, remove the thermostat (see Chapter 3).

11 With the bottom hose disconnected from the radiator, insert a garden hose into the coolant housing. Direct a clean flow of water through the engine, and continue flushing until clean water emerges from the radiator bottom hose.

12 When flushing is complete, refit the thermostat and reconnect the hoses (see Chapter 3).

Cooling system filling

13 Before attempting to fill the cooling system, make sure that all hoses and clips are in good condition, and that the clips are tight. Note that an antifreeze mixture must be used all year round, to prevent corrosion of the engine components (see following sub-Section).

14 Remove the radiator pressure cap, and ensure all drain taps/plugs are secured.

15 Place the heater temperature control in the maximum heat position.

16 Slowly add new coolant (50/50 mix of antifreeze and coolant. Note that Toyota genuine antifreeze is normally supplied premixed) to the radiator until it's full. Add coolant to the reservoir up to the lower mark.

17 Leave the radiator cap off, and run the engine in a well-ventilated area until the thermostat opens (coolant will begin flowing through the radiator and the upper hose will become hot).

18 Turn the engine off and let it cool. Add more coolant mixture to bring the level back to the lip of the radiator filler neck.

19 Squeeze the upper radiator hose to expel air, then add more coolant mixture if necessary. Refit the filler cap.

20 Start the engine, allow it to reach normal operating temperature and check for leaks.

Antifreeze mixture

21 The antifreeze should always be renewed at the specified intervals. This is necessary not only to maintain the antifreeze properties, but also to prevent corrosion, which would otherwise occur as the corrosion inhibitors become progressively less effective.

22 Always use an ethylene glycol-based antifreeze, which is suitable for use in mixed-metal cooling systems.

23 Before adding antifreeze, the cooling system should be completely drained, preferably flushed, and all hoses checked for condition and security.

24 After filling with antifreeze, a label should be attached to the expansion tank, stating the type and concentration of antifreeze used, and the date installed. Any subsequent topping-up

21.3 Radiator drain tap (arrowed)

should be made with the same type and concentration of antifreeze.

Caution: Do not use engine antifreeze in the windscreen/tailgate washer system, as it will damage the vehicle paintwork. A screen wash additive should be added to the washer system in the quantities stated on the bottle.

Every 40 000 miles or 4 years

22 Positive Crankcase Ventilation (PCV) valve and hose check and renewal

1 The PCV valve and hose is located in the valve cover.

2 Disconnect the hose, and then unscrew the PCV valve from the cover. Reattach the hose.

3 With the engine idling at normal operating temperature, place your finger over the end of the valve. If there's no vacuum at the valve, check for a plugged hose or valve. Renew any plugged or deteriorated hoses.

4 Turn off the engine. Remove the PCV valve from the hose. Connect a clean piece of hose and blow through the valve from the valve cover (cylinder head) end. If air will not pass through the valve in this direction, renew it.

5 When purchasing a new PCV valve, make sure it's for your particular vehicle. Compare the old valve with the new one to make sure they're the same.

Every 60 000 miles or 6 years

23 Valve clearance check and adjustment

Warning: These models are equipped with airbags. Always disable the airbag system before working in the vicinity of any airbag system component to avoid the possibility of accidental deployment of the airbag(s), which could cause personal injury (see Chapter 12).

Note: *To carry out the following procedure leaving the camshafts in position requires the use of a special valve lifter tool. The alternative is to remove the camshafts after making the following check.*

Check

1 Disconnect the negative cable from the battery.

2 Remove the valve cover as described in Chapter 2B.

3 Turn the crankshaft so that the inlet camshaft lobes of No 1 cylinder are pointing upwards, then use feeler blades to measure the clearances between the lobes and follower shims. Record the measurements which are out of specification. Turn the crankshaft so that the exhaust camshaft lobes of No 1 cylinder are pointing upwards, and record the clearances. Measure the remaining valve clearances in the same manner.

Adjustment

Note: *All diesel models use renewable adjustment shims that ride on top of the followers.*

4 If any of the valve clearances were out of specification and you have the special valve lifter tool, turn the crankshaft pulley until the camshaft lobe above the first valve, which you intend to adjust, is pointing upward, away from the shim. If you do not have the special tool proceed to paragraph 6.

5 Position the notch in the valve follower toward the centre. Then depress the valve follower with the special valve lifter tools **(see illustration)**. Place the special valve lifter tool in position as shown, with the longer jaw of the tool gripping the lower edge of the cast follower boss and the upper, shorter jaw gripping the upper edge of the follower itself. Depress the valve follower by squeezing the handles of the valve lifter tool together, then hold the follower down with the smaller tool and remove the larger one. Remove the adjusting shim with a small screwdriver or a pair of tweezers **(see illustrations)**. Note that the wire hook on the end of some valve lifter tool handles can be used to clamp both handles together to keep the follower depressed while the shim is removed.

6 If any of the valve clearances were out of adjustment and you don't have the special valve lifter tool, remove the camshaft(s) from over the follower(s) that was/were out of the specified clearance range (see Chapter 2B).

23.5a Install the valve lifter tool as shown and squeeze the handles together to depress the valve follower, then hold the follower down with the smaller tool so the shim can be removed

23.5b Keep pressure on the follower with the smaller tool and remove the shim with a small screwdriver . . .

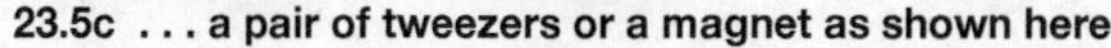

23.5c . . . a pair of tweezers or a magnet as shown here

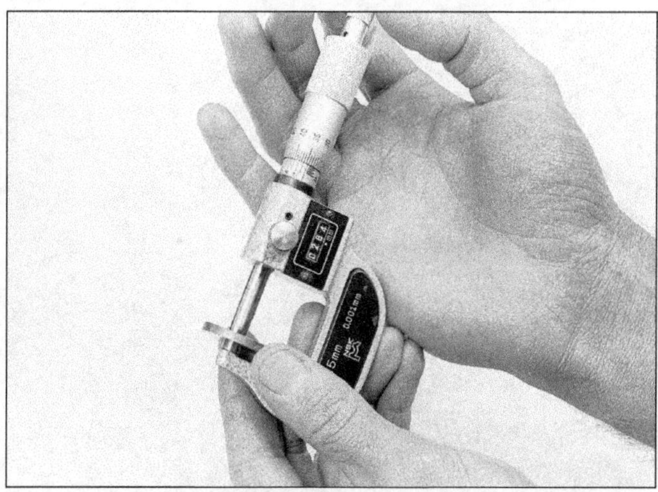

23.7 Measure the shim thickness with a micrometer

7 Measure the thickness of the shim with a micrometer **(see illustration)**. To calculate the correct thickness of a new shim that will place the valve clearance within the specified value, use the following formula:

N = T + (A – V)

T =Thickness of the old shim.

A = Valve clearance measured.

N = Thickness of the new shim.

V = Desired valve clearance (see this Chapter's Specifications).

8 Select a shim with a thickness as close as possible to the valve clearance calculated. The shims are available in several sizes. **Note:** *Through careful analysis of the shim sizes needed to bring the out-of-specification valve clearance within specification, it is often possible to simply move a shim that has to come out anyway to another location requiring a shim of that particular size, thereby reducing the number of new shims that must be purchased.*

9 If you are using the special lifter tool, place it in position, with the longer jaw of the tool gripping the lower edge of the cast follower boss and the upper, shorter jaw gripping the upper edge of the follower itself, press down the valve lifter by squeezing the handles of the valve lifter tool together and fit the new adjusting shim (note that the wire hook on the end of one valve lifter tool handle can be used to clamp the handles together to keep the follower depressed while the shim is inserted. Measure the clearance with a feeler gauge to make sure that your calculations are correct. If you are not using the special tool, proceed to paragraph 11.

10 Repeat this procedure until all the valves which are out of clearance, have been corrected.

11 Fit the proper thickness follower(s) in position, making sure to lubricate them with camshaft installation grease first. **Note:** *Apply the lubricant to the underside of the follower where it contacts the valve stem, the walls of the follower and the face of the follower.*

12 Where removed, refit the camshaft(s) (see Chapter 2B).

13 Refit the valve cover and remaining components using a reversal of the removal procedure.

24 Timing belt renewal

1 Refer to Chapter 2B.

Notes

Chapter 2 Part A:
Petrol engine in-car repair procedures

Contents

Section number

Degrees of difficulty

Easy, suitable for novice with little experience	**Fairly easy,** suitable for beginner with some experience	**Fairly difficult,** suitable for competent DIY mechanic	**Difficult,** suitable for experienced DIY mechanic	**Very difficult,** suitable for expert DIY or professional

Specifications

General

Engine type	DOHC, in-line four-cylinder, four valves per cylinder	
Cylinder numbers (timing chain end to transmission end)	1-2-3-4	
Firing order	1-3-4-2	
Engine codes:		
1.4 litre (1398 cc) VVT-i engine	4ZZ-FE	
1.6 litre (1598 cc) VVT-i engine	3ZZ-FE	
Compression pressure:		
Minimum	10.0 bar	
Difference between cylinders (maximum)	1.0 bar	

Oil pump

	Standard	Service limit
Rotor-to-body clearance	0.260 to 0.325 mm	0.325 mm
Rotor tip clearance	0.040 to 0.160 mm	0.160 mm
Rotor-to-cover clearance	0.025 to 0.071 mm	0.071 mm
Oil pressure:		
At idle speed	0.29 bar min	
At 3000 rpm	2.94 to 5.39 bar	

Timing chain and sprockets

Maximum chain length at 16 pins (see text)	122.7 mm
Crankshaft sprocket minimum diameter (with chain)	51.6 mm
Camshaft sprocket minimum diameter (with chain)	97.3 mm

Camshaft thrust clearance (endfloat)

	Inlet	Exhaust
Standard	0.040 to 0.095 mm	0.040 to 0.095 mm
Service limit, maximum	0.11 mm	0.11 mm

Cylinder head bolt length

Standard	156.0 mm to 159.0 mm
Maximum	159.5 mm

Torque wrench settings

	Nm	lbf ft
Auxiliary belt tensioner:		
Bolt	69	51
Nut	29	21
Camshaft bearing cap:		
No 1 (right-hand) bearing cap	23	17
All other bearing caps	13	10
Camshaft position sensor	9	7
Camshaft sprocket bolts	54	40
Connecting rod (big-end) bolts:*		
Stage 1	20	15
Stage 2	Angle tighten a further 90°	
Coolant pump	10	7
Crankshaft pulley bolt	138	102
Cylinder head bolts:		
Stage 1	49	36
Stage 2	Angle tighten a further 90°	
Cylinder head cover	10	7
Driveplate	83	61
Flywheel:		
Stage 1	49	36
Stage 2	Angle tighten a further 90°	
Ignition coil to cylinder head	9	7
Main bearing ladder bolts:		
M8	19	14
M10:		
Stage 1	44	32
Stage 2	Angle tighten a further 90°	
Oil control valve	9	7
Oil control valve filter	30	22
Oil drain plug	37	27
Oil pick-up strainer	9	7
Oil pressure relief valve plug	37	27
Oil pressure switch	15	11
Oil pump	10	7
Oil pump cover screws	10	7
Oil sump	9	7
Timing chain cover:		
10 mm head	13	10
12 mm head	19	14
Timing chain guide bolts	9	7
Timing chain tensioner housing	9	7
Timing chain tensioner slipper bolts	19	14

** Do not re-use*

1 General information

How to use this Chapter

This Part of Chapter 2 is devoted to in-vehicle engine repair procedures. All information concerning engine removal and refitting, and engine block and cylinder head overhaul can be found in Part C of this Chapter.

The following repair procedures are based on the assumption that the engine is installed in the vehicle. If the engine has been removed from the vehicle and mounted on a stand, many of the steps outlined in this Part of Chapter 2 will not apply.

The Specifications included in this Part of Chapter 2 apply only to the procedures contained in this Part. Part C of Chapter 2 contains the Specifications necessary for cylinder head and engine block rebuilding.

Engine description

The engines covered by this manual are four cylinders, double overhead camshaft (DOHC) 16-valve units with variable valve timing (VVT-i).

The 1.4 litre 4ZZ-FE and 1.6 litre 3ZZ-FE engines have a variable valve timing unit fitted to the inlet camshaft sprocket, and a timing chain driving both the camshafts. The engine management system adjusts the timing of the camshaft via a hydraulic control system (using engine oil as the hydraulic fluid). The timing is varied according to engine speed and load – retarding the timing at low and high engine speeds to improve low speed driveability and maximum power respectively. At medium engine speeds, the timings are advanced (the valves open earlier) to increase mid-range torque and to improve exhaust emissions.

No shims are fitted, and to adjust the clearances the camshaft followers themselves must be changed, necessitating the removal of the camshafts.

At the lower end of the engine, a cast main bearing 'ladder' fitted between the engine block and the oil sump supports the one-piece crankshaft. A rotor-type oil pump is fitted directly over the end of and driven directly by the crankshaft.

Operations with engine in car

The following operations can be carried out without having to remove the engine from the vehicle:

a) Removal and refitting of the cylinder head.

b) Removal and refitting of the timing chain and sprockets.
c) Removal and refitting of the camshafts.
d) Removal and refitting of the oil sump.
e) Removal and refitting of the oil pump.
f) Renewal of the engine/transmission mountings.
g) Removal and refitting of the flywheel/driveplate.

Although in theory, it is possible to remove the big-end bearings, connecting rods and pistons with the engine in place, for reasons of access and cleanliness it is recommended that the engine is removed.

2 Cylinder compression check

1 When engine performance is down, or if misfiring occurs which cannot be attributed to the ignition or fuel systems, a compression test can provide diagnostic clues as to the engine's condition. If the test is performed regularly, it can give warning of trouble before any other symptoms become apparent.

2 The engine must be fully warmed-up to normal operating temperature, the battery must be fully-charged. The aid of an assistant will also be required.

3 Remove the fuel pump fuse (No 10 from the engine compartment fusebox), and if possible, start the engine and allow it to run until the residual fuel in the system is exhausted. Failure to do so could result in damage to the catalytic converter.

4 Remove the spark plugs as described in Chapter 1A.

5 Fit a compression tester to the No 1 cylinder spark plug hole – the type of tester which screws into the plug thread is to be preferred.

6 Have the assistant hold the throttle wide open, and crank the engine on the starter motor. After one or two revolutions, the compression pressure should build-up to a maximum figure, and then stabilise. Record the highest reading obtained.

7 Repeat the test on the remaining cylinders, recording the pressure in each.

8 All cylinders should produce very similar pressures; a difference of more than 1 bar between any two cylinders may indicate a fault. Note that the compression should build-up quickly in a healthy engine; low compression on the first stroke, followed by gradually increasing pressure on successive strokes, indicates worn piston rings. A low compression reading on the first stroke, which does not build-up during successive strokes, indicates leaking valves or a blown head gasket (a cracked head could also be the cause). Deposits on the undersides of the valve heads can also cause low compression.

9 Toyota minimum values for compression pressures are given in the Specifications.

10 If the pressure in any cylinder is low, carry out the following test to isolate the cause. Introduce a teaspoonful of clean oil into that cylinder through its spark plug hole, and repeat the test.

11 If the addition of oil temporarily improves the compression pressure, this indicates that bore or piston wear is responsible for the pressure loss. No improvement suggests that leaking or burnt valves, or a blown head gasket, may be to blame.

12 A low reading from two adjacent cylinders is almost certainly due to the head gasket having blown between them; the presence of coolant in the engine oil will confirm this.

13 If one cylinder is about 20 percent lower than the others and the engine has a slightly rough idle; a worn camshaft lobe could be the cause.

14 If the compression reading is unusually high, the combustion chambers are probably coated with carbon deposits. If this is the case, the cylinder head should be removed and decarbonised.

15 On completion of the test, refit the spark plugs (see Chapter 1A) and refit the fuel pump fuse.

3 Top Dead Centre (TDC) for number one piston – locating

1 Top Dead Centre (TDC) is the highest point in the cylinder that each piston reaches as it travels up the cylinder bore. Each piston reaches TDC on the compression stroke and again on the exhaust stroke, but TDC generally refers to piston position on the compression stroke.

2 Positioning the piston(s) at TDC is an essential part of many procedures such as camshaft and timing chain removal.

3 Before beginning this procedure, be sure to place the transmission in Neutral and apply the handbrake or block the rear wheels. Remove the spark plugs (see Chapter 1A).

4 In order to bring any piston to TDC, the crankshaft must be turned using the method outlined below. When looking at the timing chain end of the engine, normal crankshaft rotation is clockwise. Turn the crankshaft with a socket and ratchet attached to the bolt threaded into the front of the crankshaft. Apply pressure on the bolt in a clockwise direction only. Never turn the bolt anti-clockwise.

5 Remove the cylinder head cover as described in Section 4.

6 Turn the crankshaft until the notch in the crankshaft pulley is aligned with the 0 on the timing cover **(see illustration)**.

7 Look at the camshaft lobes for No 1 cylinder. Both the inlet and exhaust camshaft lobes should be pointing away from the camshaft followers. If they are not, use the socket/spanner to rotate the crankshaft one complete revolution (360°) – now the lobes should be pointing away from the followers. Additionally, the reference marks on the inlet and exhaust camshaft sprockets should be aligned with the top of the cylinder head **(see illustration)**.

8 After the number one piston has been positioned at TDC on the compression stroke, TDC for any of the remaining pistons can be located by turning the crankshaft 180° and following the firing order.

3.6 Align the crankshaft drivebelt pulley notch (arrowed) with the 0 (zero) on the timing cover

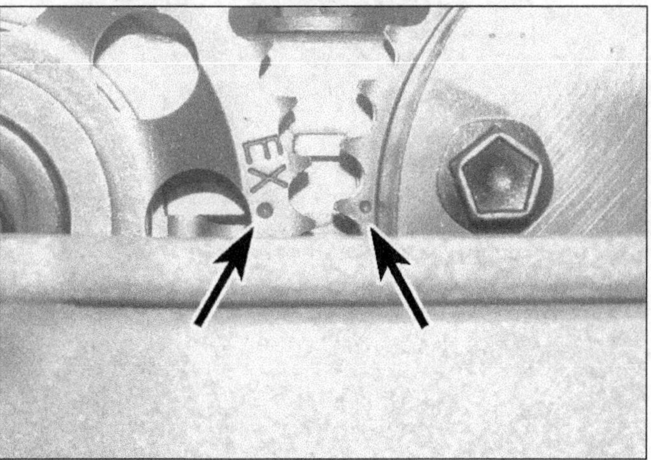

3.7 The marks on the camshaft sprockets (arrowed) should align with the top edge of the cylinder head

4.1a Undo the fasteners . . .

4.1b . . . prise out the plastic fasteners at the rear of the engine cover . . .

4.1c . . . then lift it from place

4 Cylinder head cover – removal and refitting

Removal

1 Undo the two nuts at the center of the cover, prise out the two plastic fasteners at the rear, and then lift off the plastic cover on top of the engine **(see illustrations)**.

2 Detach the two breather (PCV) hoses from the cylinder head cover.

3 Remove the ignition coils as described in Chapter 5B.

4 Remove the cylinder head cover mounting nuts/bolts, and then detach the cylinder head cover and gasket from the cylinder head **(see illustration)**. If the cylinder head cover is stuck to the cylinder head, bump the end with a wood block and a hammer to jar it loose. If that doesn't work, try to slip a flexible putty knife between the cylinder head and cylinder head cover to break the seal.

Caution: Don't lever at the cylinder head cover-to-cylinder head joint or damage to the sealing surfaces may occur, leading to oil leaks after the valve cover is refitted.

Refitting

5 The mating surfaces of the housing or cylinder head and cylinder head cover must be clean when the cylinder head cover is refitted. The rubber sealing gasket can be re-used unless it has seen high mileage and the rubber has hardened or cracked, then pull out the rubber seal and clean the mating surfaces with brake cleaner. Install a new rubber gasket, pressing it evenly into the groove around the underside of the cylinder head cover. If there's residue or oil on the mating surfaces when the cylinder head cover is installed, oil leaks may develop. **Note:** *Make sure that the spark plug tube gaskets are in place on the underside of the valve cover before refitting it* ***(see illustration)***.

6 Apply sealant (Toyota No 08826-00080 or equivalent) to the area where the timing chain cover abuts the cylinder head.

7 Refit the cylinder head cover and tighten the nuts/bolts evenly to the specified torque.

8 Refit the remaining parts, run the engine and check for oil leaks.

4.4 Cylinder head cover bolts/nuts/studs

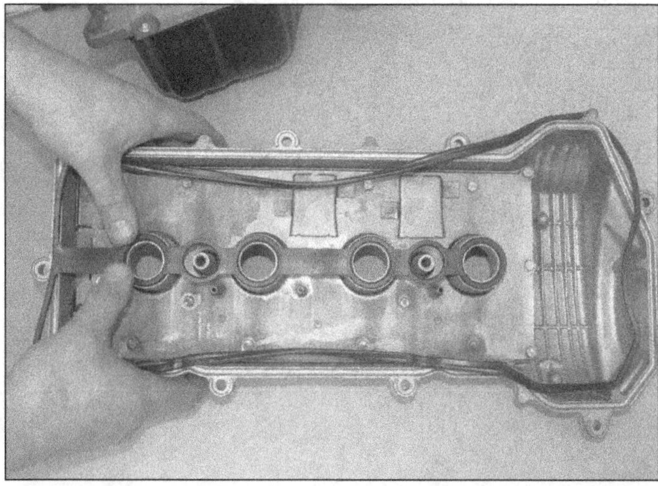

4.5 Ensure the one-piece cylinder head cover gasket is fitted to the spark plug tube grooves

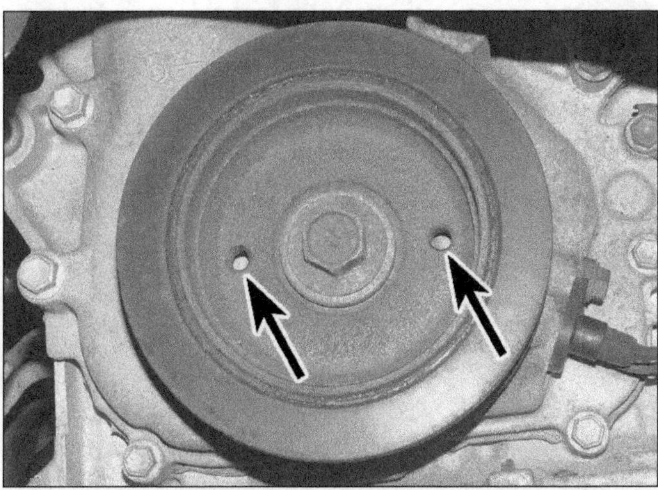

5.7 **If the crankshaft pulley is stuck, screw two 8 mm bolts into the threaded holes (arrowed) and push the pulley from place**

5.8 **Undo the nut and bolt (arrowed) and remove the auxiliary belt tensioner assembly**

5 Timing chain and sprockets – removal, inspection and refitting

Removal

1 Drain the coolant as described in Chapter 1A.

2 Remove the auxiliary drivebelt as described in Chapter 1A.

3 Remove the alternator (Chapter 5A).

4 Set the engine to TDC on No 1 cylinder as described in Section 3.

5 To prevent the crankshaft from rotating whilst the crankshaft pulley central bolt is slackened, engage top gear and have an assistant press the brake pedal firmly. Slacken the pulley bolt.

6 On automatic transmission models, it will be necessary to remove the starter motor (Chapter 5A) and have an assistant wedge a large flat-bladed screwdriver between the driveplate teeth and the transmission casing – ensure the screwdriver doesn't slip.

7 Check the timing marks are still aligned as described in Section 3, and then slide the crankshaft pulley from the crankshaft **(see illustration)**.

8 Undo the bolt/nut and remove the auxiliary drivebelt tensioner assembly **(see illustration)**.

9 Support the engine from underneath with a jack (use a wood block on the jack, but don't place the block under the oil sump drain plug). **Note:** *If you're planning on removing the oil sump in addition to the timing chain, support the engine with a hoist from above.*

10 Undo the bolts and remove the right-hand engine mounting bracket from the engine block **(see illustration)**. Where applicable, disconnect the earth lead from the mounting bracket.

11 Undo the two nuts and withdraw the chain tensioner assembly **(see illustration)**.

12 Undo the 6 bolts and remove the coolant pump **(see illustration)**. Discard the coolant pump O-ring seal; a new one must be fitted.

13 Undo the bolt and remove the crankshaft position sensor from the timing cover, then undo the bolt securing the wiring loom bracket clip and move the sensor to one side.

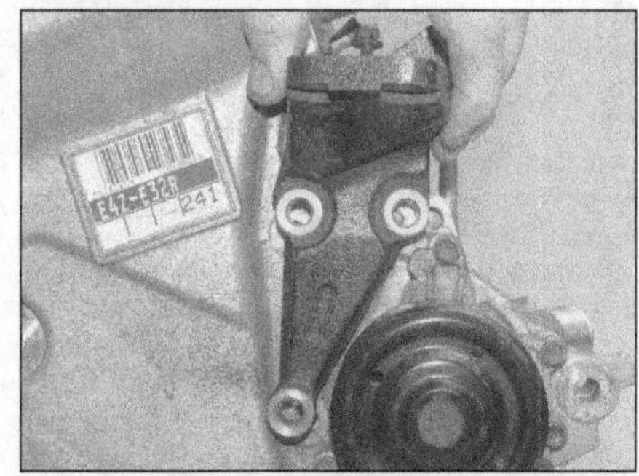

5.10 **Undo the bolts/nuts and remove the right-hand engine mounting bracket from the engine block**

14 Undo the bolts/nuts securing the timing cover to the engine, then use a Torx socket to remove the stud in the upper left-hand corner.

15 Use a flat-bladed screwdriver to carefully

5.11 **Undo the two nuts and remove the chain tensioner assembly**

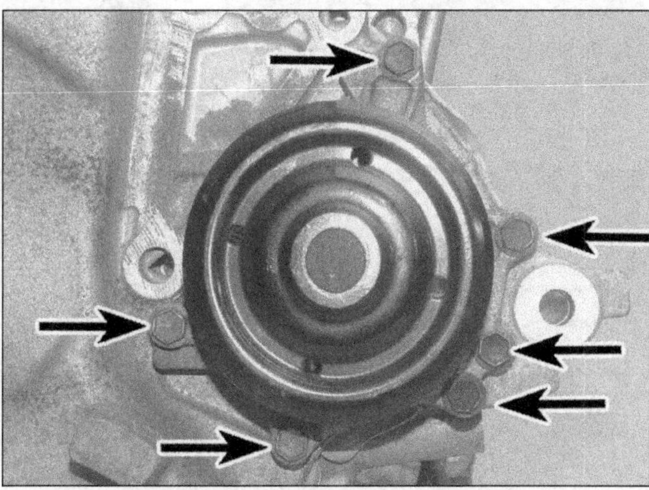

5.12 **Undo the 6 bolts (arrowed) and remove the coolant pump**

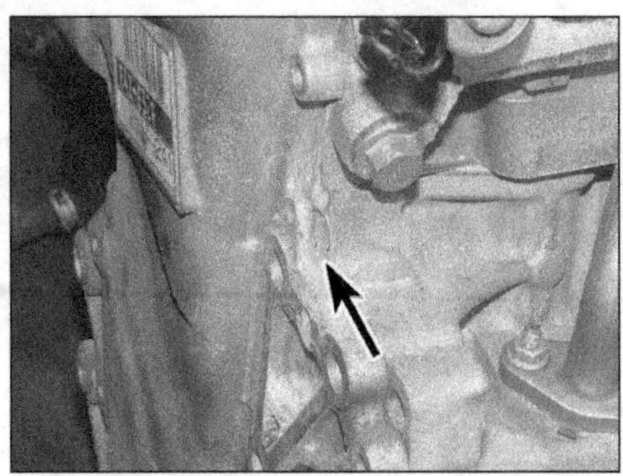

5.15 Insert a flat-bladed screwdriver into the leverage point provided (arrowed)

5.17 Undo the bolt (arrowed) and remove the tensioner slipper

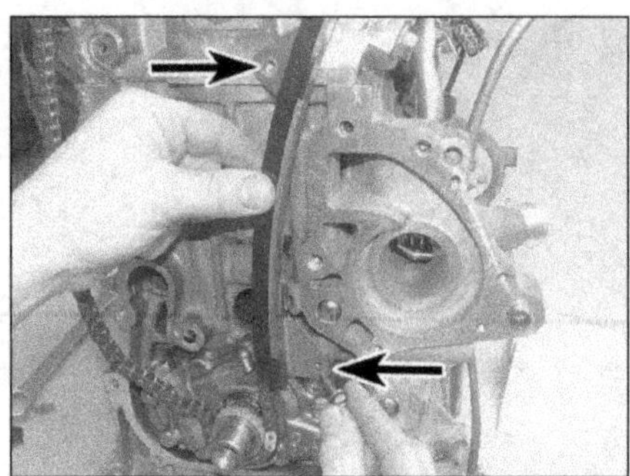

5.19 Undo the bolts (arrowed) and remove the chain guide

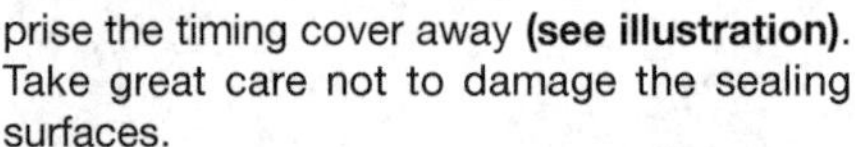

prise the timing cover away **(see illustration)**. Take great care not to damage the sealing surfaces.

16 Note which way round it's fitted, and then pull the crankshaft angle sensor plate from place.

17 Undo the bolt and remove the chain tensioner slipper **(see illustration)**.

18 Slide the sprocket (with the chain still fitted) from the crankshaft. If it's tight, use two flat-bladed screwdrivers to ease the sprocket from place, then lift the chain from the camshaft sprockets.

19 Undo the bolts and remove the chain guide **(see illustration)**.

20 Undo the centre bolt and remove the inlet camshaft sprocket. Use a spanner on the hexagonal section of the camshaft to prevent it from rotating **(see illustration)**. Repeat this procedure on the exhaust camshaft sprocket. **Note:** *The inlet sprocket with the VVT-i mechanism will be locked in the 'retarded' position.*

Inspection

21 Pull the timing chain taut by hand, and measure the length of 16 pins **(see illustration)**. Repeat this procedure at 3 or more sections of the chain. If any of the measurements obtained exceed that given in the Specifications, the chain must be renewed.

22 Wrap the chain around the crankshaft sprocket and use a pair of vernier calipers to measure the diameter of the assembly **(see illustration)**. If the measurement obtained is less than that given in the Specifications, renew the chain and *all* the sprockets. Repeat this procedure on both camshaft sprockets.

23 Check the condition of the chain guide and tensioner slipper. There should be no sign of cracking or damage. As the chain runs along the guide/slipper it will create two grooves along the slipper/guide length. The maximum depth of these grooves is 1.0 mm. If their depth exceeds this, renew the slipper/guide.

24 Press the top of the locking pawl on the tensioner assembly to disengage the pawl from the plunger, and check that the plunger moves smoothly in and out of the housing **(see illustration)**. Release the pawl and check that the plunger cannot be pushed into the housing with your finger.

Refitting

25 Align the locating hole on the VVT-i unit/sprocket with the locating pin on the inlet camshaft, then hold the camshaft in position with a spanner on the hexagonal section, and attempt to rotate the sprocket anti-clockwise whilst gently pushing it against the camshaft. This is to ensure it's locked in the 'retarded' position. If the VVT-i unit is already in the 'retarded' position (as it should be) the sprocket will not move. If it's not, the sprocket will rotate anti-clockwise slightly until the locating pin on the end of the camshaft aligns with a further locating slot inside the VVT-i assembly **(see illustration)**. Fit the sprocket retaining bolt and tighten it to the specified torque, using a spanner on the hexagonal section of the camshaft to prevent it from rotating.

26 Align the locating hole in the exhaust sprocket with the locating pin on the exhaust camshaft, then fit the bolt and tighten it to the specified torque, using a spanner on the camshaft hexagonal section to prevent it from rotating. Note that the sprocket must be

5.20 With a spanner on the hexagonal section, slacken the sprocket bolt

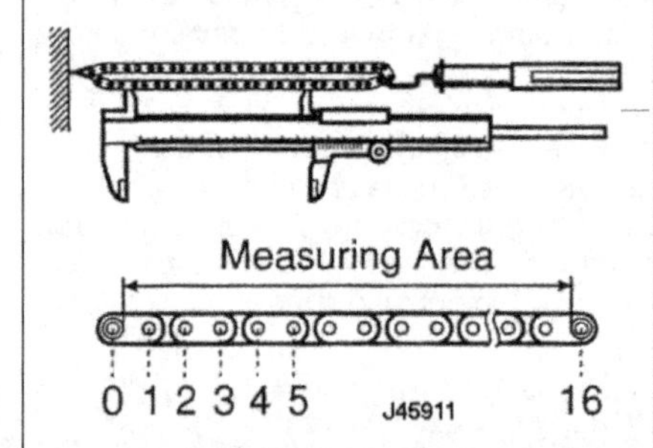

5.21 Pull the chain taut, and measure the length over 16 pins as shown

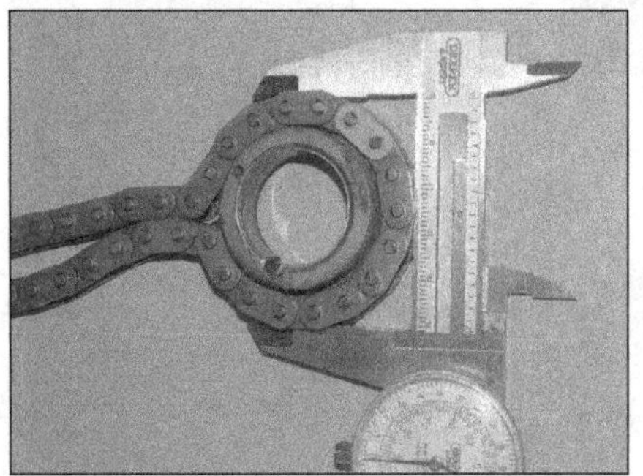

5.22 Wrap the chain around the sprocket and measure the diameter

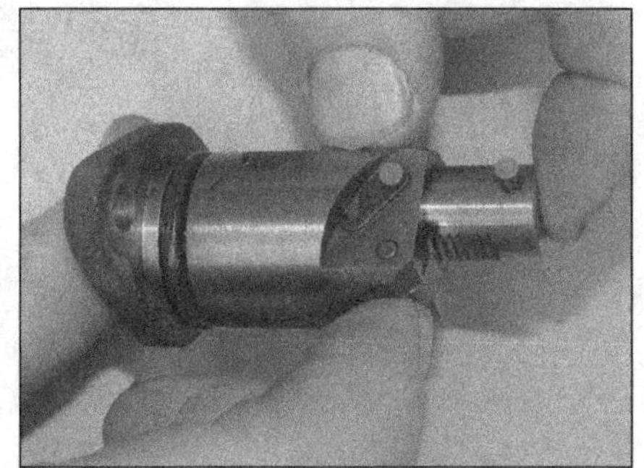

5.24 Press in the top of the locking pawl and check the plunger moves freely

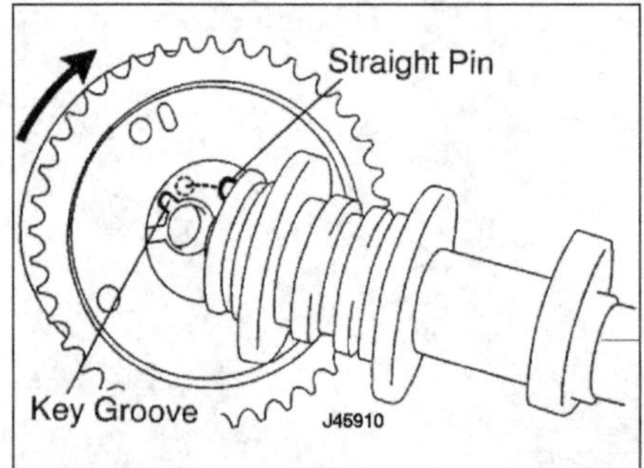

5.25 Align the pin on the camshaft with the locating hole in the VVT-i unit

5.26a Fit the exhaust camshaft sprocket with the timing marks facing outwards . . .

5.26b . . . then tighten the bolt whilst holding the camshaft with a spanner at its hexagonal section

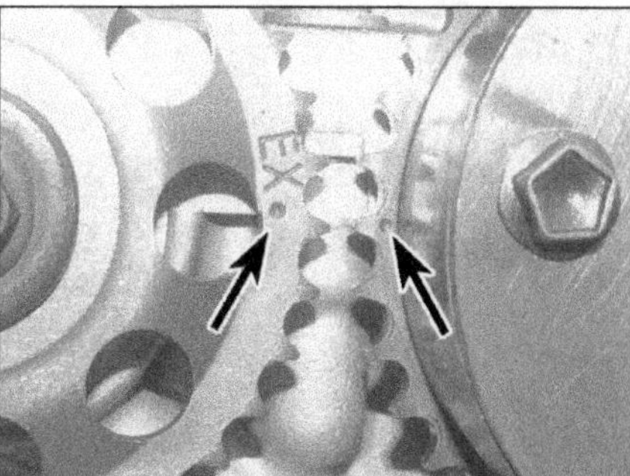

5.27 Align the camshaft sprocket marks (arrowed) with the top surface of the cylinder head

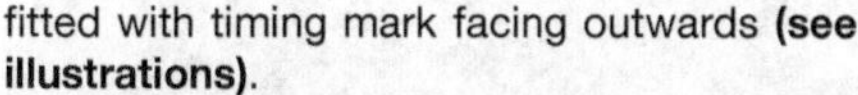

fitted with timing mark facing outwards **(see illustrations)**.

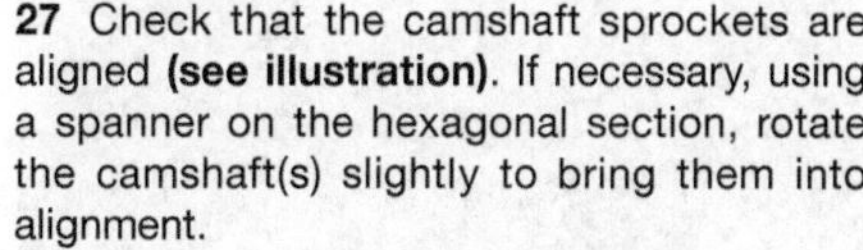

27 Check that the camshaft sprockets are aligned **(see illustration)**. If necessary, using a spanner on the hexagonal section, rotate the camshaft(s) slightly to bring them into alignment.

28 Check that the locating key in the end of the crankshaft is in the 12 o'clock position (upright). If necessary, temporarily insert the crankshaft pulley bolt and turn the crankshaft slightly to this position **(see illustration)**.

29 There are three yellow-coloured links on the timing chain – two close together that correspond with the camshaft sprockets, and one that corresponds with the crankshaft sprocket. Engage the crankshaft sprocket with the timing chain, aligning the mark on the sprocket with the yellow-coloured link, then slide the sprocket over the end of the crankshaft, ensuring the locating key in the crankshaft aligns with the corresponding slot in the sprocket **(see illustration)**. If necessary, using a tubular spacer (deep socket) and a hammer, tap the sprocket fully into position.

30 Engage the timing chain with the camshaft sprockets, ensuring the yellow-coloured links align with the marks on the sprockets **(see illustration)**.

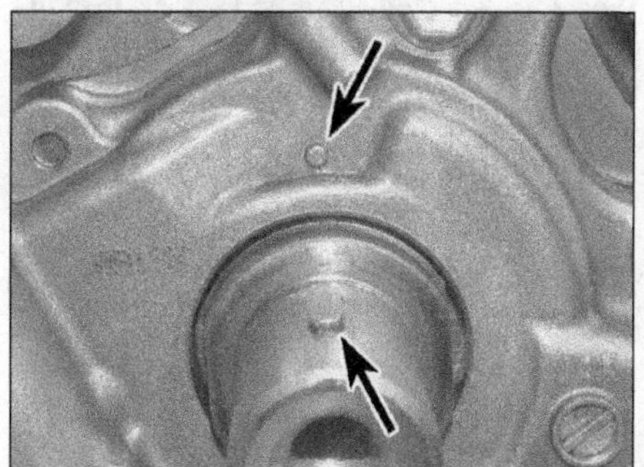

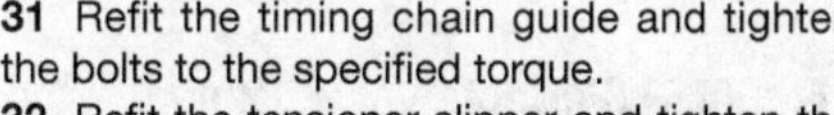

5.28 Set the crankshaft key in the 12 o'clock position (the key aligns with the mark on the oil pump body – arrowed)

5.29 Align the yellow link of the timing chain with the mark on the crankshaft sprocket (arrowed)

31 Refit the timing chain guide and tighten the bolts to the specified torque.

32 Refit the tensioner slipper and tighten the retaining bolt to the specified torque.

33 Refit the crankshaft angle sensor plate with the B mark (4ZZ-FE) or F mark (3ZZ-FE) facing outwards **(see illustration)**.

34 Thoroughly clean the timing chain cover and engine block/cylinder gasket surfaces, removing all traces of the old sealant. Take the opportunity to renew the crankshaft oil seal in the timing chain cover as described in Section 7.

35 Apply a thin bead of sealant (Toyota part no 08826-00080 or equivalent) to the timing cover gasket surfaces as shown, then fit the timing chain cover, and tighten the bolts/nuts to the specified torques **(see illustration)**.

36 Press in the top of the locking pawl to disengage it from the chain tensioner plunger, then use a finger to press the plunger fully into the tensioner housing, and retain it in place with the hook **(see illustrations)**.

37 Check the condition of the tensioner housing O-ring seal and renew if necessary. Fit the housing to the timing chain cover, taking

5.30 Align the marks on the sprockets (arrowed) with the yellow links on the timing chain

5.33 Fit the crankshaft angle sensor plate with the B mark (4ZZ-FE) or F mark (3ZZ-FE) facing outwards (arrowed)

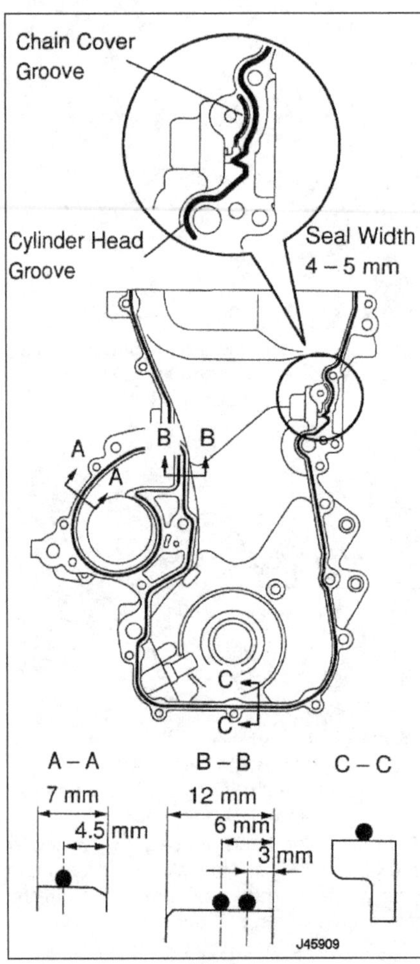

5.35 Apply a bead of sealant to the timing chain cover

care not to disturb the plunger hook. If the hook is disturbed and the plunger released, remove the housing and reset the plunger as previously described. Tighten the housing retaining bolts to the specified torque.

38 Refit the crankshaft pulley and tighten the retaining bolt to the specified torque. Prevent the crankshaft from rotating using the same method employed during removal.

39 Rotate the crankshaft anti-clockwise a few degrees to release the hook retaining the tensioner plunger **(see illustration 5.36b)**, and

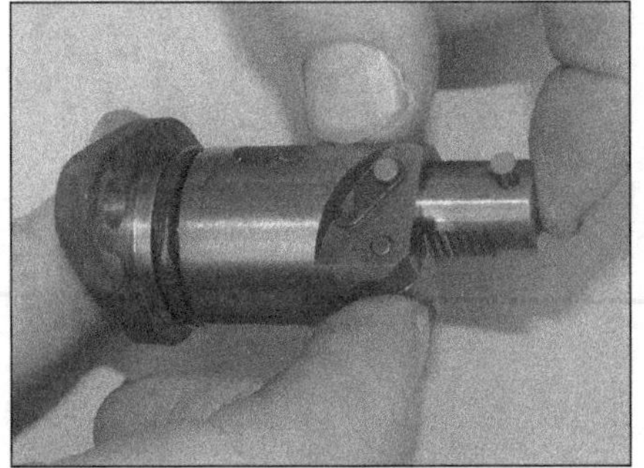

5.36a Disengage the locking pawl and press in the plunger . . .

5.36b . . . then retain it with the hook

then rotate it clockwise and check that the tensioner slipper is pushed against the chain by the plunger. If it isn't, use your finger or a screwdriver to push the slipper against the tensioner plunger and release the hook **(see illustration)**.

40 Turn the crankshaft clockwise until the notch in the crankshaft pulley is aligned with the 0 on the timing plate located at the front of the engine, and check that the marks on the camshaft sprockets align with the top of the cylinder head **(see illustrations 3.6 and 3.7)**.

41 Fit a new O-ring seal to the coolant pump and refit it, tightening the bolts to the specified torque.

42 The remainder of refitting is a reversal of removal.

5.39 If necessary, use a screwdriver to push the chain against the slipper to release the tensioner plunger

Oil control valve filter

4 The filter is located at the timing chain end of the cylinder head. Undo the plug and pull the filter from place **(see illustration)**.

6 VVT-i (Variable Valve Timing) components – removal, inspection and refitting

Removal

Camshaft VVT-i unit

1 The VVT-i unit is integral with the inlet sprocket (see Section 5) – no dismantling is recommended.

Oil control valve

2 Unplug the wiring connector from the oil control valve at the timing chain end of the cylinder head.

3 Undo the bolt and withdraw the valve from the cylinder head **(see illustration)**. Be prepared for oil spillage.

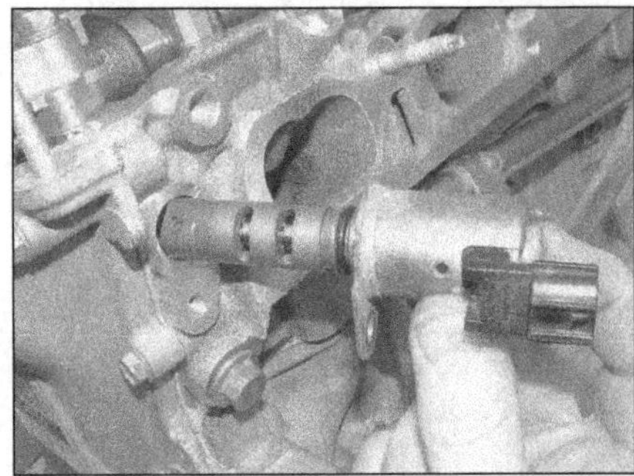

6.3 Undo the bolt and withdrawn the oil control valve from the cylinder head

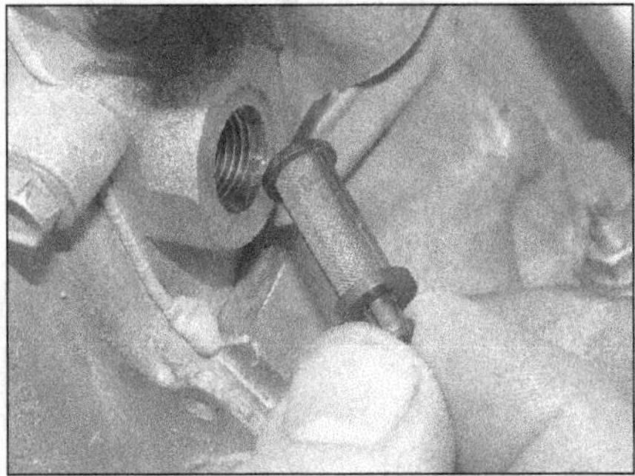

6.4 Pull the oil control valve filter from the cylinder head

Inspection

Camshaft VVT-i unit

5 Testing the VVT-i unit is beyond the scope of the DIY mechanic. If the unit is faulty, the engine management ECM should store a relevant fault code. Have the system's self-diagnosis system interrogated by a Toyota dealer or suitably-equipped repairer.

Oil control valve

6 Disconnect the wiring plug from the control valve, and connect an ohmmeter to the valve terminals. The resistance should be 6.9 to 7.9Ω. If the resistance is not as specified the valve may be defective.

Oil control valve filter

7 Clean the filter and ensure it's free from debris and damage.

Refitting

Camshaft VVT-i unit

8 As the VVT-i unit is integral with the inlet camshaft sprocket, refitting is described in Section 5.

Oil control valve

9 Check the condition of the O-ring seal on the valve and renew if necessary.

10 Insert the valve into the cylinder head

and tighten the retaining bolt to the specified torque. Reconnect the wiring plug.

Oil control valve filter

11 Insert the filter into the cylinder head.
12 Check the condition of the plug sealing washer and renew if necessary. Refit the plug and tighten it to the specified torque.

7 Crankshaft right-hand oil seal – renewal

1 If the timing chain cover has been removed (part of the timing chain removal procedure), the seal can simply be driven from the cover using a hammer and punch. The new seal can then be fitted into place (spring towards the engine internals) using a block of wood and a hammer. The seal should be fitted with its outside edge flush with the timing cover **(see illustrations)**.

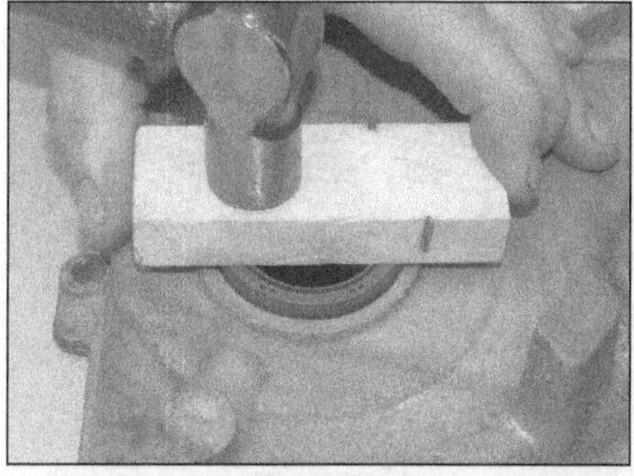

7.1a Use a block of wood and a hammer to drive the new seal squarely into position

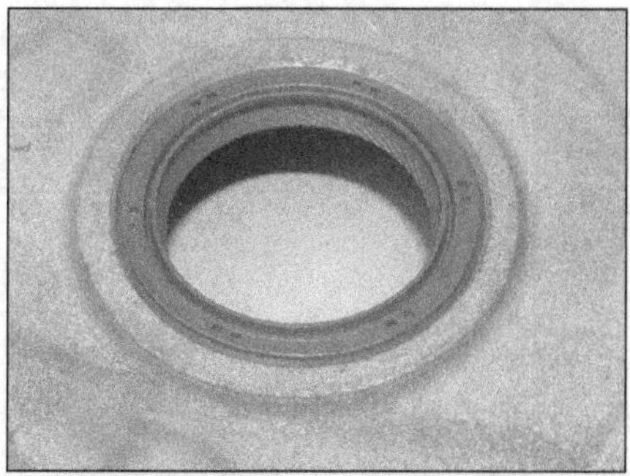

7.1b The new seal's outer edge should be flush with the timing cover

2 If the timing cover is still in place, remove the auxiliary drivebelt as described in Chapter 1A.
3 Remove the crankshaft pulley. To prevent the crankshaft from rotating whilst the crankshaft pulley central bolt is slackened, engage top gear and have an assistant press the brake pedal firmly. Slacken the pulley bolt. On automatic transmission models, it will be necessary to remove the starter motor (Chapter 5A) and have an assistant wedge a large flat-bladed screwdriver between the driveplate teeth and the transmission casing – ensure the screwdriver doesn't slip.
4 Carefully prise the seal from the timing cover with a screwdriver or seal removal tool **(see illustration)**. Take great care not to scratch the cover bore or the surface of the crankshaft in the process.

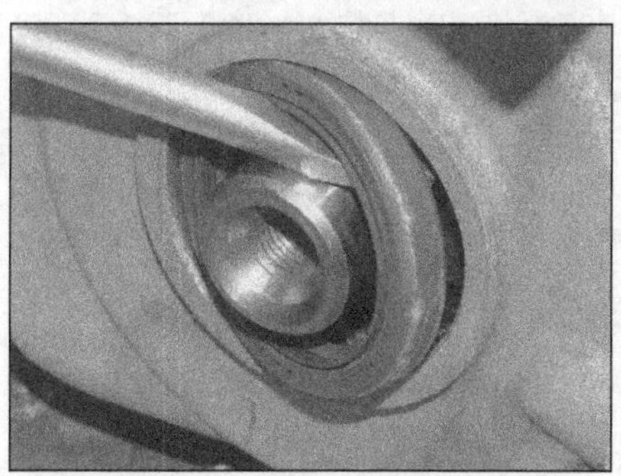

7.4 Carefully prise the oil seal out with a screwdriver

5 Clean the bore in the cover and coat the outer edge of the new seal with engine oil or multipurpose grease. Apply a little grease to the seal lip.
6 Using a socket with an outside diameter slightly smaller than the outside diameter of the seal, carefully drive the new seal into place. Make sure it's installed squarely and driven in so the outer edge of the seal is flush with the timing cover **(see illustration)**. If a socket isn't available, a short section of large diameter pipe will also work.

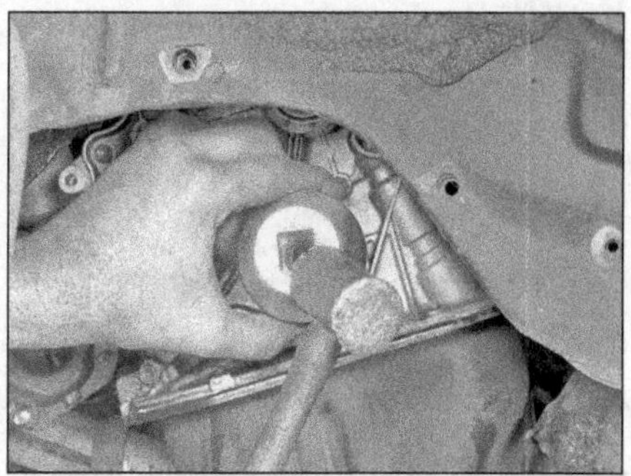

7.6 Gently drive the new seal into place with the spring side fitted towards the engine

7 Refit the crankshaft pulley and tighten the retaining bolt to the specified torque. Prevent the crankshaft from rotating using the same method employed during removal.
8 Refit the auxiliary drivebelt as described in Chapter 1A.

8 Camshafts and followers – removal, inspection and refitting

Removal

1 Remove the timing chain as described in

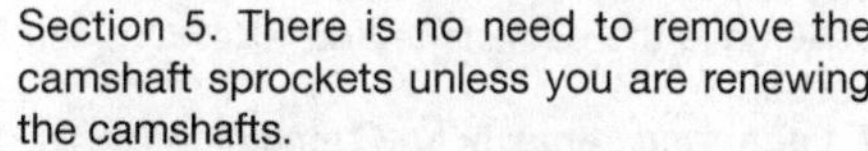

Section 5. There is no need to remove the camshaft sprockets unless you are renewing the camshafts.
2 Rotate the crankshaft 90° anti-clockwise to eliminate any possibility of accidental valve-to-piston contact during the camshaft removal procedure.
3 Working from both ends of the camshafts, gradually and evenly slacken and remove the bearing caps from the inlet and exhaust camshafts. Lift off the bearing caps.
Caution: As the centre bearing cap bolts are being loosened, make sure the camshafts are moving up evenly. If one end or the other stops moving and the camshaft gets jammed, start over by refitting the bearing caps. DO NOT try to lever or force the camshafts out.
4 Lift the camshaft straight up and out of the cylinder head.

8.5 Lift the followers from position

5 Clean the oil off the camshaft followers, mark them with a felt-tip marker and remove them **(see illustration)**. Store the camshaft bearing caps and followers so they can be reinstalled without mixing them up. These need to be installed in the same position as removal, so as to prevent engine wear.

Inspection

6 Inspect each follower for scuffing and score marks **(see illustration)**.
7 Visually examine the cam lobes and bearing journals for score marks, pitting, galling and evidence of overheating (blue, discoloured areas). Look for flaking away of the hardened surface layer of each lobe.
8 If in any doubt as to the condition of the components, have them examined and measured by an automotive engineering workshop.

8.6 Wipe off the oil and inspect each follower for wear and scuffing

8.11 The camshaft bearing caps are marked (arrowed) E for exhaust and I for inlet

Refitting

9 Apply a little clean engine oil to the exhaust camshaft followers, then install them in their original locations. Repeat this procedure for the inlet camshaft.

10 Apply a little clean engine oil to the exhaust camshaft lobes and bearing journals. Repeat this procedure for the inlet camshaft.

11 Position the exhaust and inlet camshaft with the lobes for No 1 cylinder pointing upwards, away from the followers **(see illustration)**.

12 Refit the camshaft bearing caps to their original positions. Note that the exhaust bearing caps are marked E and the inlet caps are marked I, as well as being numbered 2 to 5 from the timing chain end. No 1 bearing cap is the 'double' cap fitted adjacent to the timing chain. Apply a little clean engine oil to the threads and underside of the heads, then install the retaining bolts and tighten them gradually and evenly from the middle of the camshafts outwards **(see illustration)**.

13 Align the camshaft sprocket timing marks **(see illustration 3.7)**, then rotate the crankshaft 90° clockwise, back to TDC position (with the crankshaft key upright in the 12 o'clock position).

14 Refit the timing chain as described in Section 5.

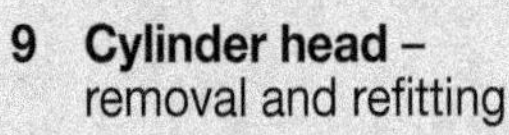

9 Cylinder head – removal and refitting

Note: *The engine must be completely cool before beginning this procedure.*

8.12 Position the No 1 cylinder camshaft lobes away from the followers

Note: *Measure the valve clearances before removing the camshafts (Chapter 1A) to save repeating work later.*

Removal

1 Drain the coolant from the engine block and radiator (see Chapter 1A).

2 Drain the engine oil and remove the oil filter (see Chapter 1A).

3 Remove the throttle body, fuel injectors, fuel rail, inlet and exhaust manifolds (see Chapter 4A).

4 Remove the timing chain as described in Section 5.

5 Undo the bolt and withdraw the VVT-i oil control valve from the cylinder head **(see illustration 6.3)**.

6 Remove the camshafts and followers (see Section 8).

7 Label and remove any remaining items, such as coolant fittings, tubes, cables, hoses or wires.

8 Using an M12 bi-hexagon bit, loosen the cylinder head bolts in 1/4-turn increments until they can be removed by hand. Loosen the cylinder head bolts in the **reverse** of the recommended tightening sequence **(see illustration 9.21)** to avoid warping or cracking the cylinder head. Recover the washers.

9 Lift the cylinder head off the engine block. If it's stuck, very carefully pry up at the transmission end, beyond the gasket surface **(see illustration)**.

10 Remove all external components from the cylinder head to allow for thorough cleaning and inspection. See Chapter 2C for cylinder head servicing procedures.

Refitting

11 The mating surfaces of the cylinder head and block must be perfectly clean when the cylinder head is installed.

12 Use a gasket scraper to carefully remove all traces of carbon and old gasket material **(see illustration)**, and then clean the mating surfaces with brake cleaner. If there's oil on the mating surfaces when the cylinder head is installed, the gasket may not seal correctly and leaks could develop. When working on the block, stuff the cylinders with clean rags to keep out debris. Use a vacuum cleaner to remove material that falls into the cylinders.

13 Check the block and cylinder head mating surfaces for nicks, deep scratches and other damage. If damage is slight, it can be removed with a file; if it's excessive, machining may be the only alternative.

14 Use a tap of the correct size to chase the threads in the cylinder head bolt holes, then clean the holes with compressed air – make sure that nothing remains in the holes.

Warning: Wear eye protection when using compressed air.

15 Mount each bolt in a vice and run a die down the threads to remove corrosion and restore the threads. Dirt, corrosion, sealant and damaged threads will affect torque readings.

16 Measure the overall length of the cylinder head bolts. If any of the bolts lengths exceeds that given in the Specifications (indicating excessive stretching), renew all the cylinder head bolts **(see illustration)**.

17 Install any components that were removed from the cylinder head.

18 Position the new gasket over the dowels in the cylinder block, the 'Lot number' must be facing upwards **(see illustration)**.

19 Carefully set the cylinder head on the block without disturbing the gasket.

20 Before installing the cylinder head bolts, apply a small amount of clean engine oil to the threads and under the bolt heads.

21 Install the cylinder head bolts and washers, and then tighten them in sequence to the Stage 1 torque setting **(see illustration)**.

22 Angle tighten the bolts a further 90° in sequence.

9.9 Lever only at the overhang, not between the mating surfaces

9.12 Remove all traces of old gasket material

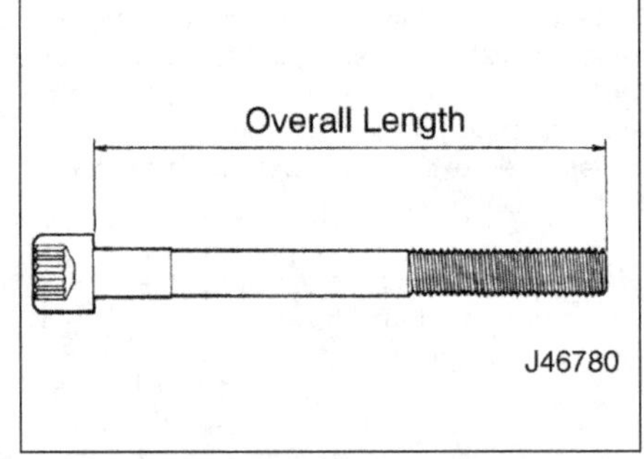

9.16 Check the overall length of the cylinder head bolts

9.18 The 'Lot number' (arrowed) must face upwards

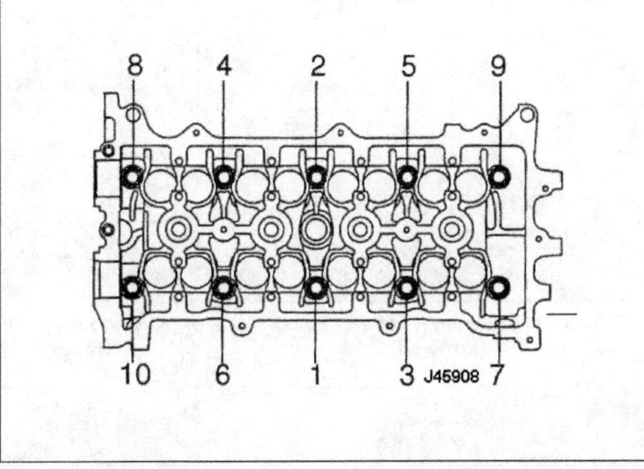

9.21 Cylinder head bolts tightening sequence

23 Check and adjust the valve clearances as necessary (see Chapter 1A).

24 The remainder of refitting is a reversal of removal, noting the following points:

a) Refill the cooling system, install a new oil filter and add oil to the engine (see Chapter 1A).

b) Run the engine and check for leaks.

c) Road test the vehicle.

10 Oil sump – removal and refitting

Removal

1 Set the parking brake and block the rear wheels.

2 Raise the front of the vehicle and support it securely on axle stands (see *Jacking and vehicle support*).

3 Remove the splash shields from under the engine.

4 Drain the engine oil and remove the oil filter (see Chapter 1A). Remove the oil dipstick.

5 Pull down the plastic cover slotted into the left-hand end of the engine block to access the left-hand sump bolts **(see illustration)**.

6 Remove the bolts and detach the oil sump. If it's stuck, pry it loose very carefully with a putty knife. Don't damage the mating surfaces of the sump and block or oil leaks could develop.

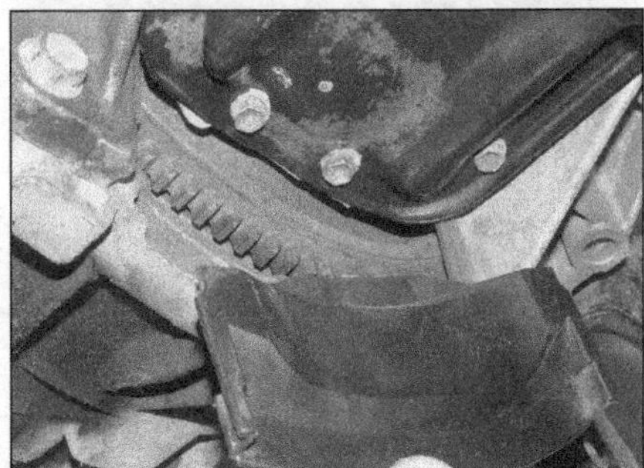

10.5 Pull down the plastic cover slotted into the engine block

7 Unbolt the pick-up tube/oil strainer assembly and remove it for cleaning. Discard the pick-up pipe gasket; a new one must be fitted.

Refitting

8 Use a scraper to remove all traces of old gasket material and sealant from the block and oil sump. Take great care not to gouge the mating surfaces. Clean the mating surfaces with brake cleaner.

9 Make sure the threaded bolt holes in the block are clean.

10 Check the oil sump flange for distortion, particularly around the bolt holes. On steel sumps, if necessary, place the oil sump on a wood block and use a hammer to flatten and restore the gasket surface.

11 Inspect the oil pump pick-up tube assembly for cracks and a blocked strainer. If the pick-up was removed, clean it thoroughly and install it now, using a new gasket. Tighten the nuts/bolts to the torque listed in this Chapter's Specifications.

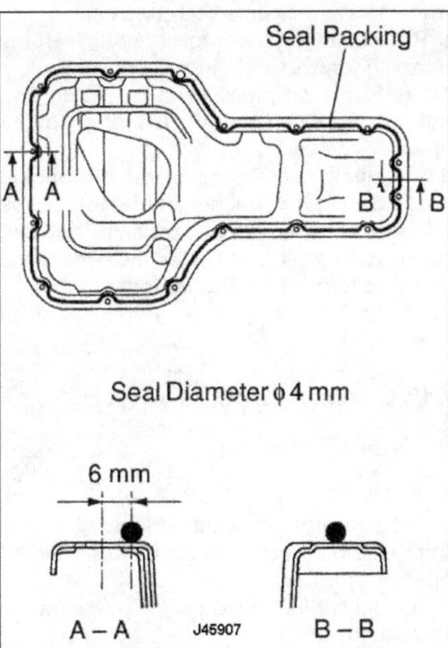

10.12 Sealant application details

12 Apply a 5 mm (approximately) wide bead of RTV sealant (steel sumps) or Toyota sealant No 08826-00080 (aluminium sumps) to the sump flange **(see illustration)**. **Note:** *Refitting must be completed within 5 minutes once the sealer has been applied.*

13 Carefully position the oil sump on the engine block and install the bolts. Working from the centre out. Tighten the bolts to the torque listed in this Chapter's Specifications.

14 The remainder of refitting is the reverse of removal. Be sure to add oil and fit a new oil filter.

15 Run the engine and check for oil pressure and leaks.

11 Oil pump – removal, inspection and refitting

Removal

1 Remove the timing chain as described in Section 5.

2 Undo the five bolts and remove the oil pump from the engine block **(see illustration)**.

11.2 Oil pump bolts (arrowed)

11.3 Oil pressure relief valve plug (arrowed)

11.4 Undo the three screws (arrowed) and remove the pump cover

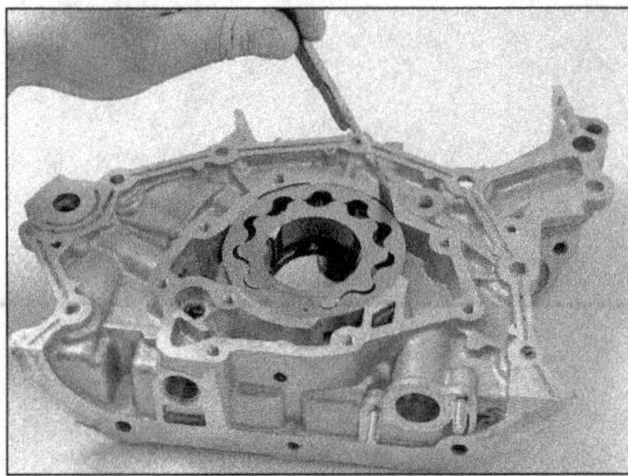

11.7a Measure the driven rotor-to-body clearance with a feeler gauge

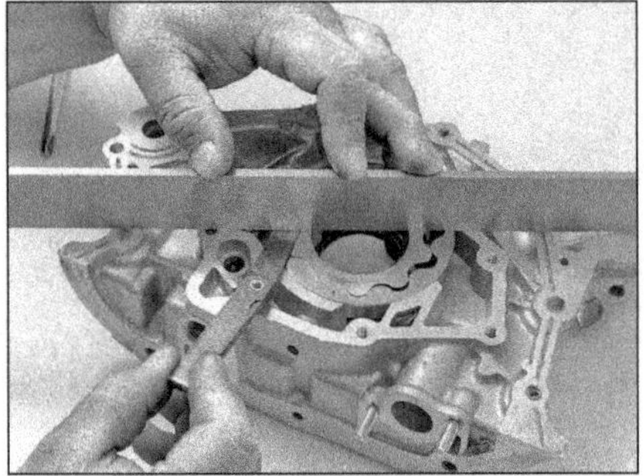

11.7b Use a straight-edge and feeler gauges to measure the rotor-to-cover clearance

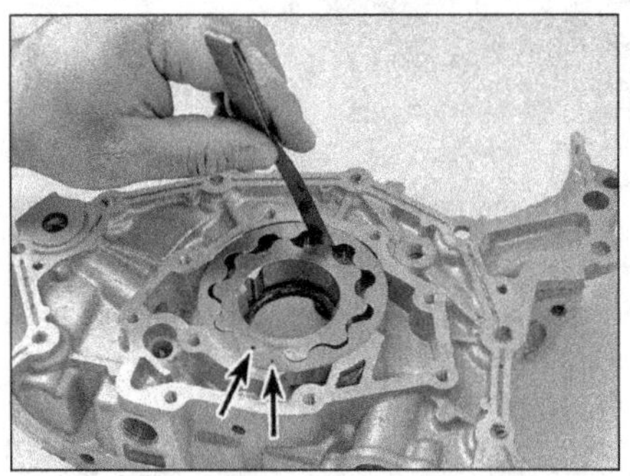

11.7c Measure the rotor tip clearance with a feeler gauge – rotor marks (arrowed)

11.11 Align the flats on the crankshaft with the flats on the pump rotor

3 Undo the plug and remove the pressure relief spring and piston **(see illustration)**.

4 Undo the 3 screws remove the pump cover. Lift out the pump rotors **(see illustration)**.

Inspection

5 Clean all components with solvent and inspect them for wear and damage. Use compressed air to blow through the oilways in the pump body.

Warning: Wear eye protection when using compressed air.

6 Check the oil pressure relief valve piston-sliding surface and valve spring. If either the spring or the piston is damaged, they must be renewed as a set. The piston must free to slide up and down the bore in the pump body without binding at any point.

7 Check the driven rotor-to-body clearance, rotor-to-cover clearance and drive rotor tip clearance with a feeler gauge **(see illustrations)** and compare the results to this Chapter's Specifications. If any clearance is excessive, renew the rotors as a set. If necessary, renew the oil pump body.

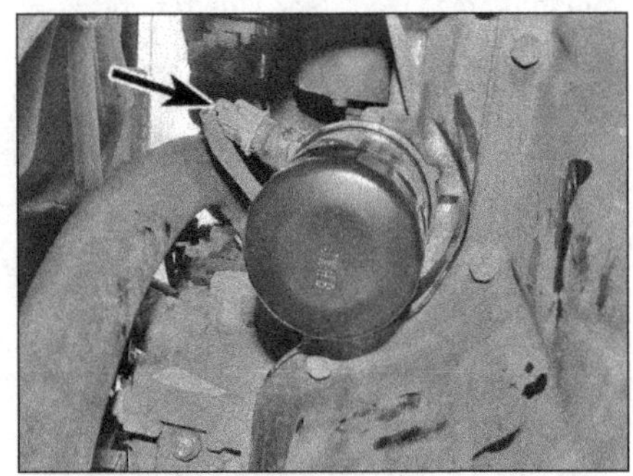

12.2 The oil pressure switch is above the oil filter

Refitting

8 Lubricate the pump rotors with clean engine oil, and place them in the pump body with the marks facing the pump body cover side.

9 Refit the pump body cover and tighten the retaining screws to the specified torque.

10 Refit the oil pressure relief piston and spring, and then tighten the plug to the specified torque.

11 Position a new gasket on the engine block, then refit the oil pump. Ensure the flats on the drive rotor align with the flats machined on the crankshaft, and tighten the bolts to the specified torque **(see illustration)**.

12 Refit the timing chain as described in Section 5.

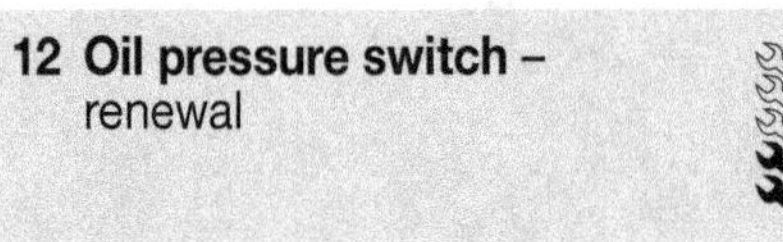

12 Oil pressure switch – renewal

1 The oil pressure switch is located on the front face of the engine block, above the oil filter.

2 Disconnect the wiring plug from the switch **(see illustration)**.

3 Unscrew the switch from the engine block. Be prepared for oil spillage.

4 Prior to refitting apply a small quantity of Loctite 242, Three Bond 1344 (or similar) to the threads of the switch.

5 Refit the switch and tighten it to the specified torque.

6 Reconnect the wiring plug.

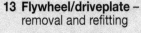

13 Flywheel/driveplate – removal and refitting

Removal

1 Remove the transmission as described in Chapter 7A or 7B.

2 Remove the pressure plate and clutch disc on manual transmission vehicles (Chapter 6).

3 Use a centre punch or paint to make alignment marks on the flywheel/driveplate and crankshaft to ensure correct alignment during refitting **(see illustration)**.

13.3 Mark the flywheel/driveplate and the crankshaft so they can be reassembled in the same relative positions

4 Remove the bolts that secure the flywheel/driveplate to the crankshaft. If the crankshaft turns, wedge a screwdriver in the ring gear teeth to jam the flywheel, or use a tool to lock the flywheel in position **(see illustration)**.

5 Remove the flywheel/driveplate from the crankshaft. Since the flywheel is fairly heavy, be sure to support it while removing the last bolt. Some automatic transmission equipped vehicles have spacers on both sides of the driveplate **(see illustration)**. Keep them with the driveplate, fitting them in the correct order.

Warning: The ring gear teeth may be sharp, wear gloves to protect your hands.

13.4 Lock the flywheel in place using a tool bolted to the engine block

13.5 On vehicles equipped with a spacer plate, note the position of the locating pin (arrowed)

Refitting

6 Clean the flywheel to remove grease and oil. Inspect the surface for cracks, rivet grooves, burned areas and score marks. Light scoring can be removed with emery cloth. Check for cracked and broken ring gear teeth. Lay the flywheel on a flat surface and use a straight-edge to check for warpage.

7 Clean and inspect the mating surfaces of the flywheel/driveplate and the crankshaft. If the crankshaft seal is leaking, renew it before reinstalling the flywheel/driveplate (see Section 14).

8 Position the flywheel/driveplate against the crankshaft. Be sure to align the marks made during removal. Note that some engines have an alignment dowel or staggered bolt holes to ensure correct refitting. Before installing the bolts, apply thread-locking compound to the threads.

9 Wedge a screwdriver in the ring gear teeth to keep the flywheel/driveplate from turning and tighten the bolts to the torque listed in this Chapter's Specifications. Follow a criss-cross pattern and work up to the final torque in three or four steps.

10 The remainder of refitting is the reverse of the removal procedure.

14 Crankshaft left-hand oil seal – renewal

1 Remove the flywheel/driveplate (Section 13).

2 The seal can be renewed without removing the oil sump or seal housing. Carefully prise out the old seal with a screwdriver **(see illustration)**. Take great care not to damage the seal bore or the surface of the crankshaft.

3 Apply multipurpose grease to the crankshaft seal journal and the lip of the new seal and carefully push the new seal into place. The lip is stiff so carefully work it onto the seal journal of the crankshaft with a smooth object like the end of an extension, then tap into place using a block of wood **(see illustrations)**. Don't rush it or you may damage the seal.

4 The remainder of refitting is the reverse of removal.

15 Engine/transmission mountings – check and renewal

1 Engine/transmission mountings seldom require attention, but broken or deteriorated mountings should be renewed immediately or the added strain placed on the driveline components may cause damage or wear.

Check

2 During the check, the engine must be raised slightly to remove the weight from the mountings.

3 Raise the vehicle and support it securely on axle stands (see *Jacking and vehicle support*), and then position a jack under the engine oil sump. Place a large wood block between the jack head and the oil sump, then carefully raise the engine just enough to take the weight off the mountings. Do not position the wood block under the drain plug.

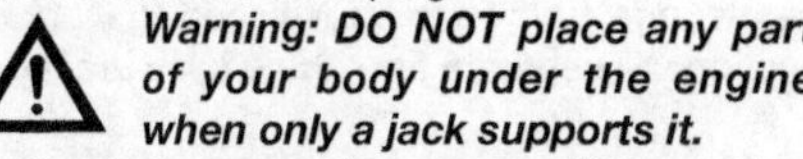

Warning: DO NOT place any part of your body under the engine when only a jack supports it.

4 Check the mountings to see if the rubber is cracked, hardened or separated from the metal plates. Sometimes the rubber will split right down the centre.

5 Check for relative movement between the mounting plates and the engine or body (use a large screwdriver or pry bar to attempt to move the mountings). If movement is noted, lower the engine and tighten the mounting fasteners.

6 Rubber preservative should be applied to the mountings to slow deterioration.

Renewal

7 Raise the vehicle and support it securely on axle stands (if not already done). Support the engine as described in paragraph 3.

14.2 Carefully prise out the old seal – take great care not to damage the crankshaft

14.3a Tap the oil seal into place using a block of wood . . .

14.3b . . . until the outer edge of the seal is flush with the engine block

15.8 Right-hand engine mounting

15.10 Left-hand transmission mounting

15.13 Front engine mounting lower retaining bolts

8 To remove the right engine mounting **(see illustration)**, remove the two nuts from underneath, one bolt from above, and the upper section will separate from the engine bracket.

9 Remove the mounting-to-chassis nuts and detach the mounting.

10 To remove the left-hand transmission mounting **(see illustration)**, remove the centre bolt and nut from through the mounting, the upper mounting bolts, and the upper section will separate from the lower mounting bracket.

11 Remove the mounting-to-transmission bolts and detach the mounting.

12 To remove the rear engine mounting, pull the rubber plugs (where fitted) from the longitudinal chassis brace to access the two nuts.

13 To remove the front engine mounting, remove the two bolts retaining the insulator to the longitudinal chassis brace **(see illustration)**, then the three nuts retaining the insulator to the chassis.

14 Refitting is the reverse of removal. Use thread locking-compound on the mounting bolts/nuts and be sure to tighten them securely.

Chapter 2 Part B:
Diesel engine in-car repair procedures

Contents

Degrees of difficulty

Easy, suitable for novice with little experience 

Fairly easy, suitable for beginner with some experience

Fairly difficult, suitable for competent DIY mechanic

Difficult, suitable for experienced DIY mechanic

Very difficult, suitable for expert DIY or professional

Specifications

General

Engine code	1CD-TV
Capacity	1995 cc
Bore and stroke	82.2 x 94.0 mm
Compression ratio	18.6 : 1
Cylinder numbers	1-2-3-4 (timing belt end-to-transmission end)
Firing order	1-3-4-2

Oil pump

Driven rotor-to-case clearance:	
Standard	0.10 to 0.17 mm
Service limit	0.20 mm
Rotor tip clearance:	
Standard	0.08 to 0.16 mm
Service limit	0.20 mm
Oil pressure:	
At idle speed	0.29 bar min
At 3000 rpm	2.45 to 5.88 bar

Cylinder head bolts limit

Thread outside diameter (approximately 25mm from bottom of threads)	10.75 to 11.00 mm
Minimum outside diameter	10.40 mm

Manifolds

Warpage limits:	
Inlet	0.1 mm
Exhaust	0.4 mm

Camshafts

Endfloat	0.035 to 0.110 mm
Journal oil clearance:	
Standard	0.025 to 0.062 mm
Maximum	0.08 mm
Journal diameter	26.969 to 26.985 mm
Runout (max)	0.06 mm
Lobe height:	
Standard:	
Inlet	46.57 to 46.67 mm
Exhaust	47.52 to 47.62 mm
Minimum:	
Inlet	46.10 mm
Exhaust	47.05 mm

Torque wrench settings

	Nm	lbf ft
Alternator bracket	37	27
Auxiliary drivebelt tensioner pulley (for alternator)	40	30
Auxiliary heater	12	9
Camshaft bearing caps	20	15
Camshaft oil seal housing	9	7
Camshaft sprocket	88	65
Common rail bolts	43	32
Connecting rod (big-end) bolts:		
Stage 1	22	16
Stage 2	Angle tighten a further 90°	
Coolant outlet elbow	21	15
Crankshaft oil seal housing	7	5
Crankshaft position sensor	9	7
Crankshaft pulley centre bolt	176	130
Cylinder head bolts:		
Stage 1	45	33
Stage 2	Angle-tighten a further 90°	
Stage 3	Angle-tighten a further 90°	
Stage 4	Angle-tighten a further 90°	
EGR valve to cylinder head	18	13
Engine mounting bracket to block	37	27
Engine mounting bracket to water pump	64	47
Exhaust manifold	47	35
Flywheel	88	65
Glow plug	12	9
High-pressure fuel pump sprocket	103	76
Idler pulley to cylinder head	34	25
Injector leak-off pipe to cylinder head	21	15
Inlet manifold	21	15
Oil dipstick tube	18	13
Oil filter bracket/adapter	34	25
Oil level sensor	6	4
Oil pick-up tube/strainer to upper housing:		
Bolt	21	15
Nut	13	10
Oil pressure switch	15	11
Oil pump	31	23
Oil pump sprocket	37	27
Relief valve plug to oil pump	49	36
Strainer to oil pump	13	10
Sump drain plug	34	26
Sump to upper housing	12	9
Sump upper housing:		
10 mm (head size) nut/bolt	11	8
12 mm (head size) bolt	21	15
Throttle body to inlet manifold	21	15
Timing belt cover	7	5
Timing belt plate to oil seal housing	9	7
Timing belt tensioner to water pump	21	15
Vacuum pump to cylinder head	27	20
Valve cover	13	10

1 General information

This Part of Chapter 2 is devoted to in-vehicle repair procedures for the 2.0 litre diesel in-line four-cylinder engine. This engine utilises a cast-iron engine block with an aluminium cylinder head. The aluminium cylinder head is equipped with pressed-in valve guides, hardened valve seats and houses the double overhead camshafts, which are driven from the crankshaft by a timing belt. Standard, adjustable followers with shims are used to actuate the valves. The oil pump is mounted at the timing belt end of the engine and is driven by the timing belt.

All information concerning engine removal and refitting and engine block and cylinder head overhaul can be found in Part C of this Chapter.

The following repair procedures are based on the assumption that the engine is fitted in the vehicle. If the engine has been removed from the vehicle and mounted on a stand, many of the steps outlined in this Part of Chapter 2 will not apply.

The Specifications included in this Part of Chapter 2 apply only to the procedures contained in this Part. Part C of Chapter 2 contains the Specifications necessary for cylinder head and engine block overhauling.

2 Repair operations possible with the engine in the vehicle

Many major repair operations can be accomplished without removing the engine from the vehicle.

Clean the engine compartment and the exterior of the engine with some type of degreaser before any work is done. It will make the job easier and help keep dirt out of the internal areas of the engine.

Depending on the components involved, it may be helpful to remove the bonnet to improve access to the engine as repairs are

3.6a The TDC mark on the exhaust camshaft must be aligned with the upper surface of the cylinder head

3.6b TDC marks on the crankshaft sprocket and oil pump housing

performed (refer to Chapter 11 if necessary). Cover the wings to prevent damage to the paint. Special pads are available, but an old bedspread or blanket will also work.

If inlet, exhaust, oil or coolant leaks develop, indicating a need for gasket or seal renewal, the repairs can generally be made with the engine in the vehicle. The inlet and exhaust manifold gaskets, sump gasket, crankshaft oil seals and cylinder head gasket are all accessible with the engine in place.

Exterior engine components, such as the inlet and exhaust manifolds, the sump, the oil pump, the water pump, the starter motor, the alternator and the fuel system components can be removed for repair with the engine in place.

Since the cylinder head can be removed without removing the engine, camshaft and valve component servicing can also be accomplished with the engine in the vehicle. Renewal of the timing belt and sprockets is also possible with the engine in the vehicle.

In extreme cases caused by a lack of necessary equipment, repair or renewal of piston rings, pistons, connecting rods and big-end bearings is possible with the engine in the vehicle. However, this practice is not recommended because of the cleaning and preparation work that must be done to the components involved.

3 Top Dead Centre (TDC) for number one piston – locating

1 Top Dead Centre (TDC) is the highest point in the cylinder that each piston reaches as it travels up-and-down when the crankshaft turns. Each piston reaches TDC on the compression stroke and again on the exhaust stroke, but TDC generally refers to piston position on the compression stroke. The timing marks on the flywheel are referenced to the number one piston at TDC.

2 Positioning the piston(s) at TDC is an essential part of procedures such as timing belt and sprocket renewal.

Warning: Before beginning this procedure, be sure to place the transmission in Neutral, apply the handbrake and remove the ignition key.

3 In order to bring any piston to TDC, the crankshaft must be turned with a large socket and bar attached to the large bolt threaded into the centre of the crankshaft pulley. When looking at the timing belt end of the engine, normal crankshaft rotation is clockwise.

4 Disable the fuel injection system by disconnecting the wiring to the fuel injectors on the top of the engine.

5 Remove the timing belt upper cover and the glow plugs (see Chapter 5A) and fit a compression gauge in the number one cylinder glow plug hole. **Note:** *Be sure to use a diesel compression gauge that can handle at least 35 bar. Turn the crankshaft clockwise with a socket and bar as described above.*

6 When the piston approaches TDC, compression will be noted on the compression gauge. Continue turning the crankshaft until the timing mark on the exhaust camshaft sprocket is at the 3 o'clock position and aligned with the upper surface of the cylinder head. At this point, the number one cylinder is at TDC on the compression stroke. To make a further check that the crankshaft is accurately positioned, it will be necessary to remove the crankshaft pulley and lower timing belt cover in order to check that the TDC mark on the crankshaft sprocket is aligned with the corresponding mark on the oil pump. At the same time, the TDC mark on the fuel pump sprocket will be in alignment with the mark on the water pump housing **(see illustrations)**. **Note:** *If a diesel compression gauge is not available, you can simply place your finger over the glow plug hole and feel for compression as the engine is rotated. Once compression at the No 1 glow plug hole is noted the remainder of the procedure is the same.*

7 After the number one piston has been positioned at TDC on the compression stroke, TDC for any of the remaining cylinders can be located by turning the crankshaft 180 degrees and following the firing order (refer to the Specifications). Rotating the engine 180 degrees past TDC for No 1 will put the engine at TDC compression for cylinder No 3.

3.6c TDC marks on the fuel pump sprocket and water pump housing

4 Valve cover – removal and refitting

Removal

1 Undo the retaining nuts and remove the engine upper cover **(see illustration)**.

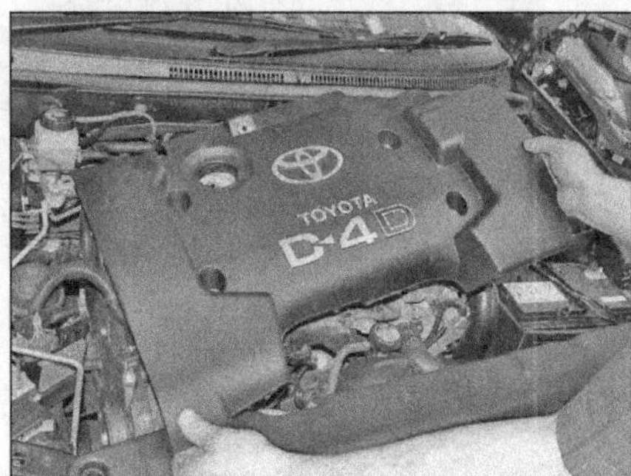

4.1 Remove the engine upper cover

4.2a Undo the retaining bolts . . .

4.2b . . . and remove the timing belt upper cover

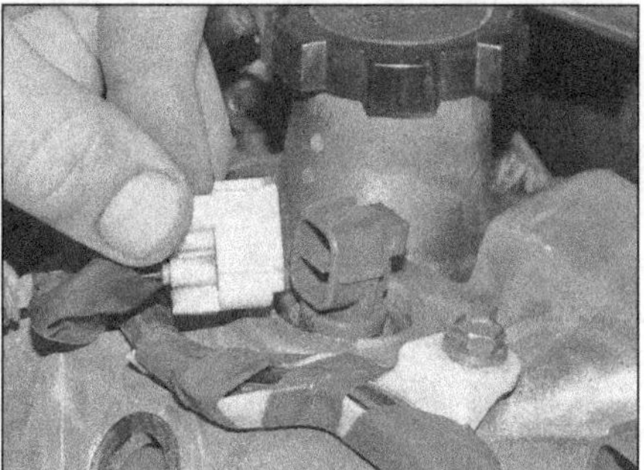

4.4a Disconnect the wiring connectors from the injectors . . .

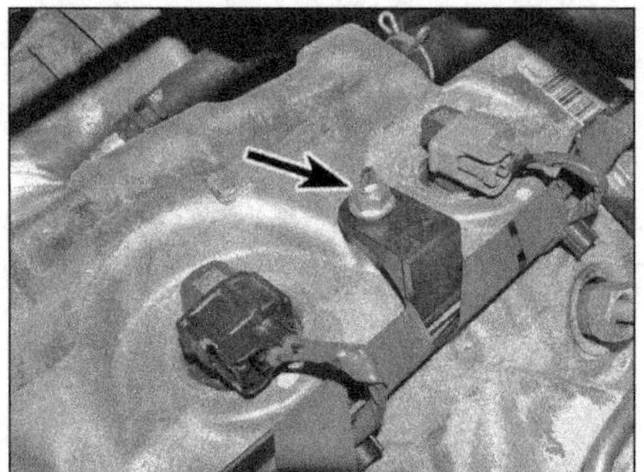

4.4b . . . and undo the wiring loom retaining nuts (arrowed)

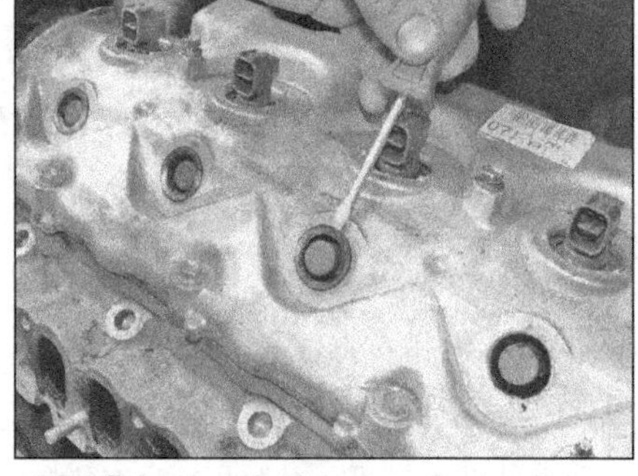

4.6a Prise out the injector pipe seals . . .

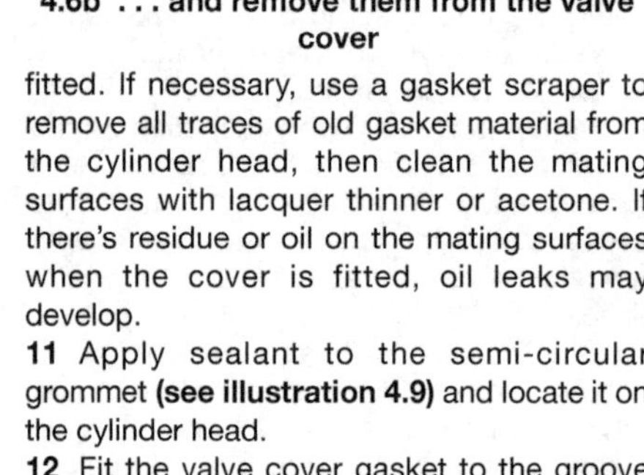

4.6b . . . and remove them from the valve cover

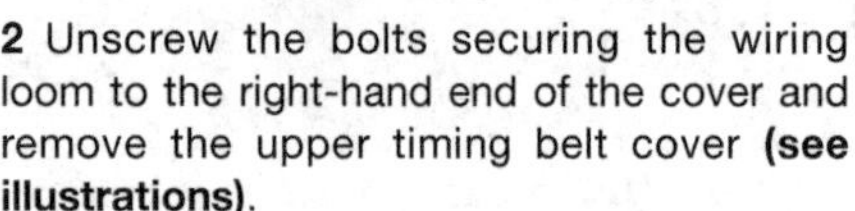

2 Unscrew the bolts securing the wiring loom to the right-hand end of the cover and remove the upper timing belt cover **(see illustrations)**.

3 Refer to Chapter 4B and remove the high-pressure injector pipes from the injectors and common rail. Tape over the open fuel apertures to prevent entry of dust and dirt.

4 Disconnect the wiring from the injectors and undo the retaining nuts to move the wiring loom to one side **(see illustrations)**.

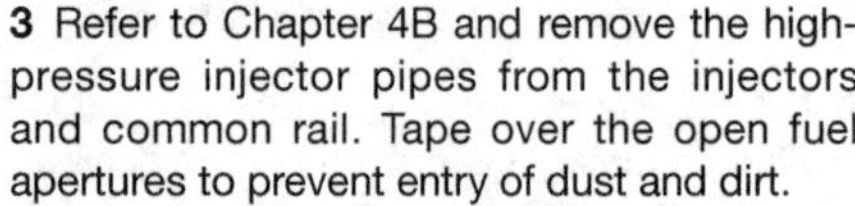

5 Disconnect the crankcase ventilation hose from the left-hand side of the valve cover. Also undo the retaining bolts/nuts and move the air inlet pipe from the left-hand side of the valve cover.

6 Prise the seals out from the valve cover, where the injector pipes connect to the injectors **(see illustrations)**.

7 Progressively unscrew the bolts and detach the valve cover from the cylinder head **(see illustration)**. Remove the gasket and renew if necessary.

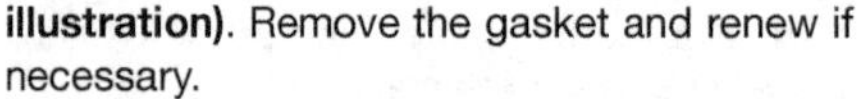

8 If the cover is stuck to the head, tap the end with a block of wood and a hammer to jar it loose. If that doesn't work, try to slip a flexible putty knife between the head and cover to break the seal. Be careful not to damage the gasket.

Caution: Don't prise at the cover-to-head joint or damage to the sealing surfaces may occur, leading to oil leaks after the cover is reinstalled.

9 Remove the semi-circular rubber grommet from the cylinder head and clean away any traces of sealant **(see illustration)**. If necessary, also remove the injector seals from the valve cover.

Refitting

10 The mating surfaces of the cylinder head and cover must be clean when the cover is fitted. If necessary, use a gasket scraper to remove all traces of old gasket material from the cylinder head, then clean the mating surfaces with lacquer thinner or acetone. If there's residue or oil on the mating surfaces when the cover is fitted, oil leaks may develop.

11 Apply sealant to the semi-circular grommet **(see illustration 4.9)** and locate it on the cylinder head.

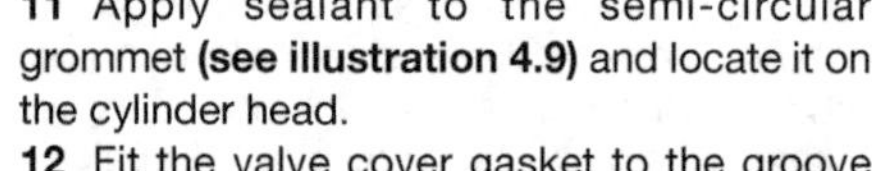

12 Fit the valve cover gasket to the groove in the valve cover **(see illustration)**. Ensure that the gasket is correctly seated, and take care to avoid displacing it as the valve cover is lowered into position.

13 Apply sealant to the joints where the camshaft end housings contact the cylinder head on the right-hand side, then lower the valve cover into position.

14 Insert the bolts and tighten them progressively to the specified torque.

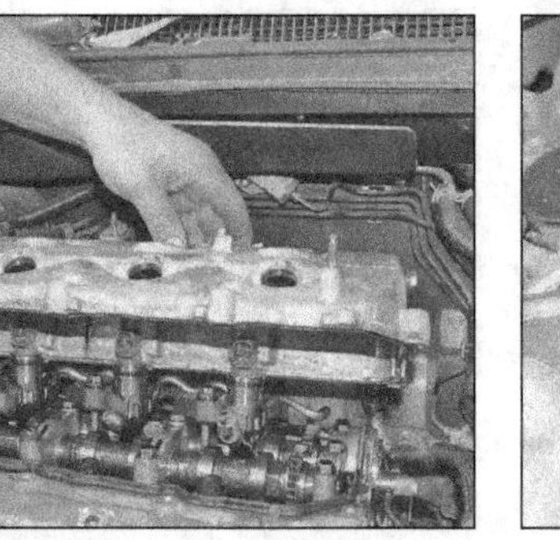

4.7 Removing the valve cover

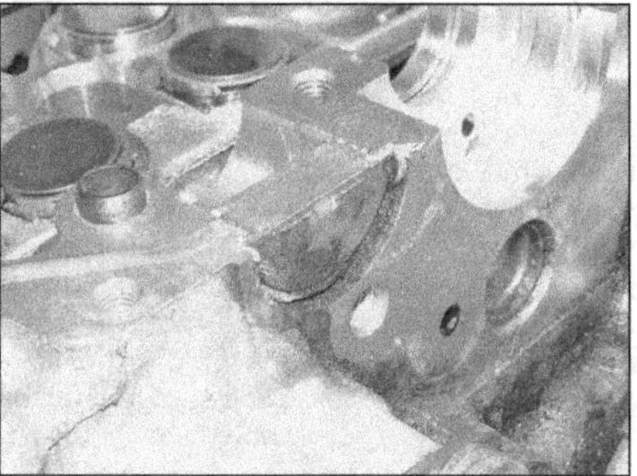

4.9 Semi-circular rubber grommet located in the cylinder head

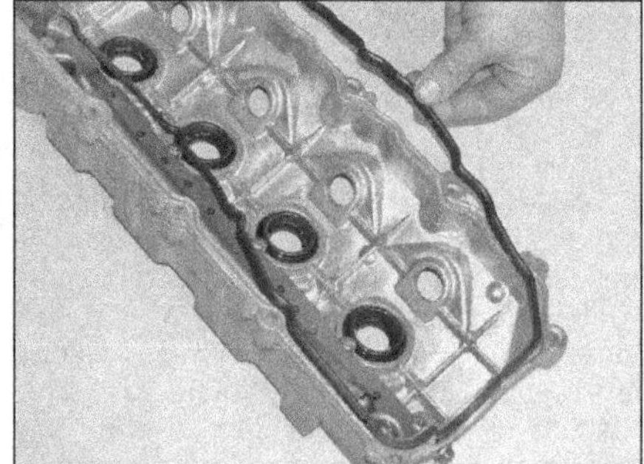

4.12 Fit the new gasket to the groove in the valve cover

15 Refit the seals to the injector pipe recess in the valve cover **(see illustration)**.
16 Fit the high-pressure pipes to the injectors and common rail with reference to Chapter 4B.
17 Refit the crankcase ventilation hose to the left-hand side of the valve cover. Also refit the retaining bolts/nuts and secure the air inlet pipe to the left-hand side of the valve cover.
18 Reconnect the wiring connector to the injectors and secure the wiring loom.
19 Refit the upper timing belt cover, wiring loom brackets and engine upper cover.

4.15 Refit the injector pipe recess seals

5.5 Remove the air inlet duct together with throttle body and gasket

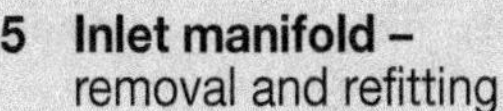

5 Inlet manifold – removal and refitting

Removal

1 The inlet manifold is located on the front of the cylinder head. First, remove the engine upper cover.
2 Refer to Chapter 4B and remove the high-pressure injector pipes from the injectors, common rail and high-pressure pump. Tape over the open fuel apertures to prevent entry of dust and dirt. **Note:** *Toyota recommends renewal of the injector pipes whenever the injectors and/or the common rail are removed. They also recommend renewal of the fuel inlet pipe whenever the common rail or supply pump are removed.*
3 Unbolt the cover from over the high-pressure fuel pump, and remove the insulator.
4 Unscrew the nuts/bolts and remove the inlet air duct from the transmission end of the cylinder head.
5 Undo the retaining bolts and remove throttle body together with the gasket **(see illustration)**.
6 Loosen the common rail mounting bolts. This is necessary to allow room for the inlet manifold to be removed.
7 Unscrew the bolts and nuts, and remove the inlet manifold together with the gasket **(see illustrations)**.

Refitting

8 Use a scraper to remove all traces of old gasket material and sealant from the manifold and cylinder head, then clean the mating surfaces with lacquer thinner or acetone. Keep in mind that the inlet manifold and the cylinder head are made of aluminium, so aggressive scraping is not suggested. If the gasket was leaking, have the manifold checked for warpage and resurfaced if necessary.
9 Refit the inlet manifold together with a new gasket and tighten the bolts and nuts to the specified torque.
10 Fully tighten the common rail bolts to the specified torque.
11 Refit the throttle body together with a new gasket, and tighten the bolts to the specified torque.
12 Refit the insulator and cover over the high-pressure pump, and tighten the bolts.
13 Refit the high-pressure injector pipes with reference to Chapter 4B.
14 Refit the inlet air duct to the transmission end of the cylinder head and check all wiring connectors are secure, and then refit the engine upper cover.

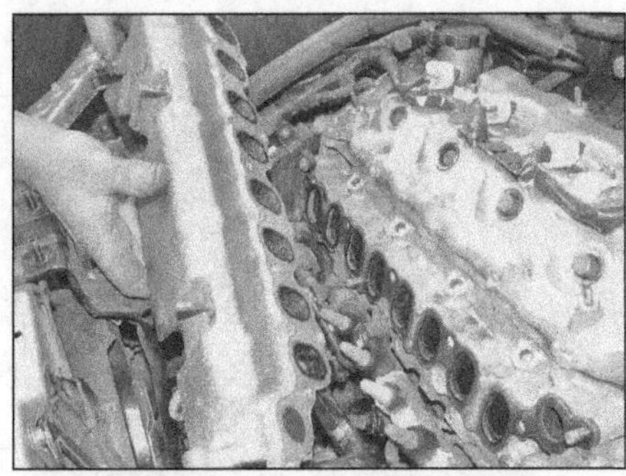
5.7a Removing the inlet manifold . . .

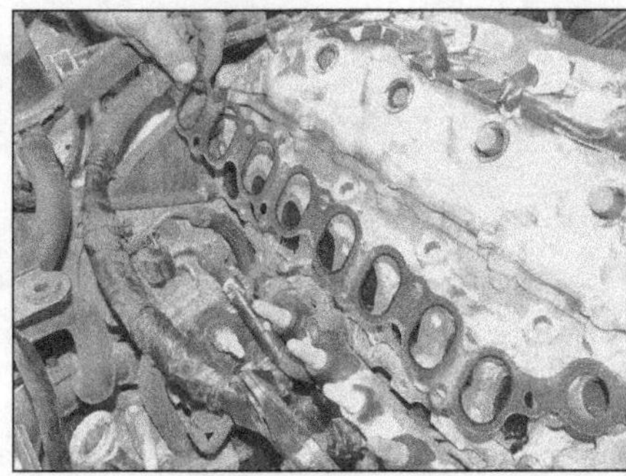
5.7b . . . and gasket

6 Exhaust manifold – removal and refitting

Warning: Wait until the engine is completely cool before beginning this procedure.

Removal

1 The exhaust manifold is located on the rear of the cylinder head. First, remove the turbocharger as described in Chapter 4B.
2 Unbolt the EGR cooler tube from the exhaust manifold and cylinder head, and recover the gaskets **(see illustrations)**.
3 Apply penetrating oil to the exhaust manifold mounting nuts, then unscrew them and remove the exhaust manifold from the cylinder head. Recover the collars, noting their fitted position and gasket **(see illustrations)**.

6.2a Unbolt and remove the EGR tube . . .

6.2b . . . and remove the gaskets from the exhaust manifold . . .

6.2c . . . and cylinder head

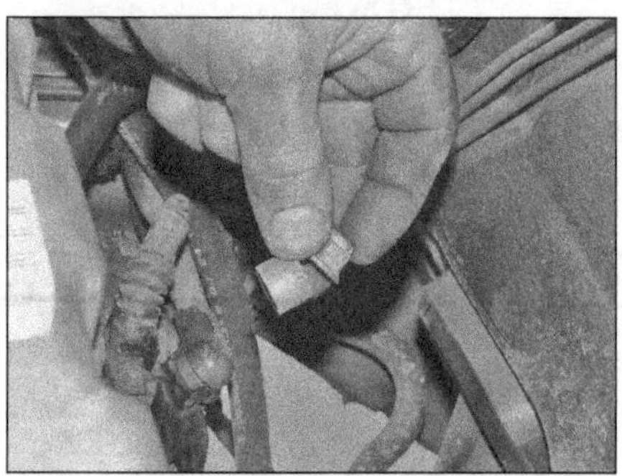

6.3a Unscrew the nuts and recover the collars . . .

6.5b . . . then refit the exhaust manifold . . .

Refitting

4 Use a scraper to remove all traces of old gasket material and carbon deposits from the manifold and cylinder head mating surfaces. If the gasket was leaking, have the manifold checked for warpage.

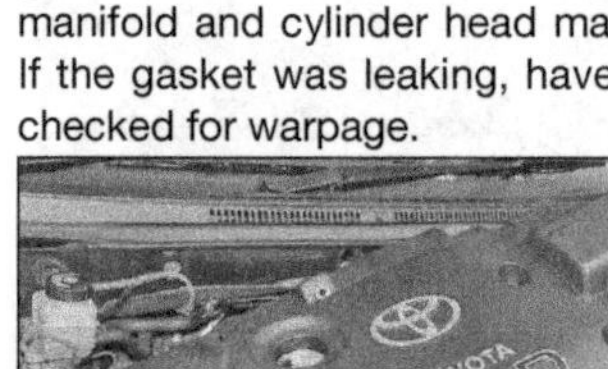

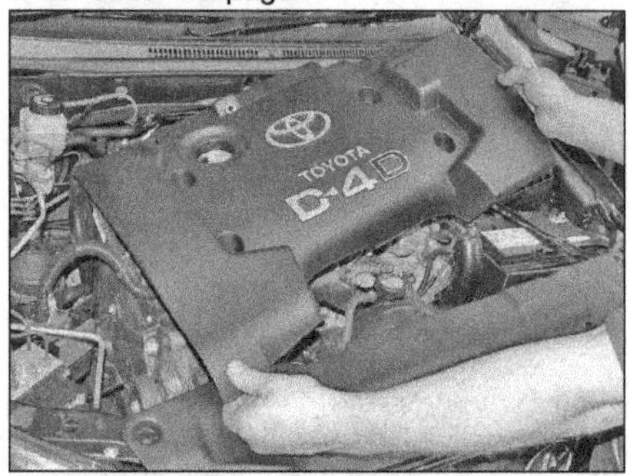

7.3 Remove the engine upper cover

6.3b . . . then remove the exhaust manifold

6.5c . . . making sure that the collars are located beneath the nuts

5 Locate the new gasket on the cylinder head studs, then refit the exhaust manifold followed by the collars and nuts **(see illustrations)**. Progressively tighten the nuts to the specified torque.

6 Refit the EGR cooler tube together with new gaskets, and tighten the mounting nuts/bolts.

7.6a Hold the crankshaft pulley stationary with a suitable tool while loosening the bolt

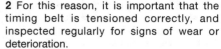

6.5a Locate a new gasket on the cylinder head studs . . .

7 Refit the turbocharger as described in Chapter 4B.

8 Run the engine and check for exhaust leaks.

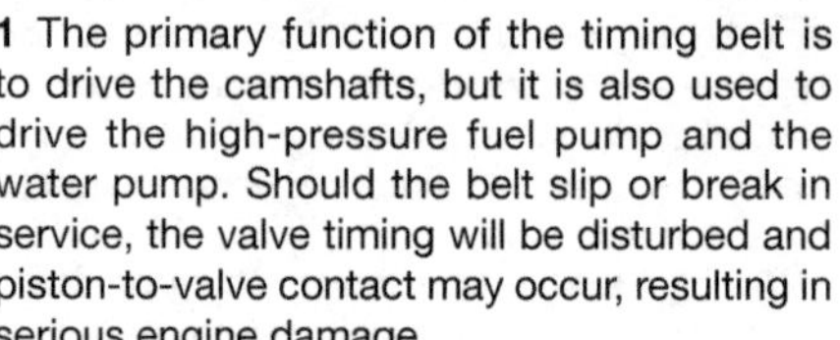

7 Timing belt and sprockets – removal, inspection and refitting

1 The primary function of the timing belt is to drive the camshafts, but it is also used to drive the high-pressure fuel pump and the water pump. Should the belt slip or break in service, the valve timing will be disturbed and piston-to-valve contact may occur, resulting in serious engine damage.

2 For this reason, it is important that the timing belt is tensioned correctly, and inspected regularly for signs of wear or deterioration.

Removal

3 Undo the retaining nuts and remove the engine upper cover **(see illustration)**.

4 Remove the glow plugs as described in Chapter 5A, in order to facilitate turning the engine later.

5 Apply the handbrake, then jack up the front of the vehicle and support on axle stands. Remove the right-hand front wheel. Remove the auxiliary drivebelt(s) as described in Chapter 1B.

6 Working under the wheel arch, remove the crankshaft pulley **(see illustrations)**.

7.6b . . . then use a puller to release the pulley from the nose of the crankshaft . . .

7.6c . . . remove the pulley bolt . . .

7.6d . . . and withdraw the crankshaft pulley

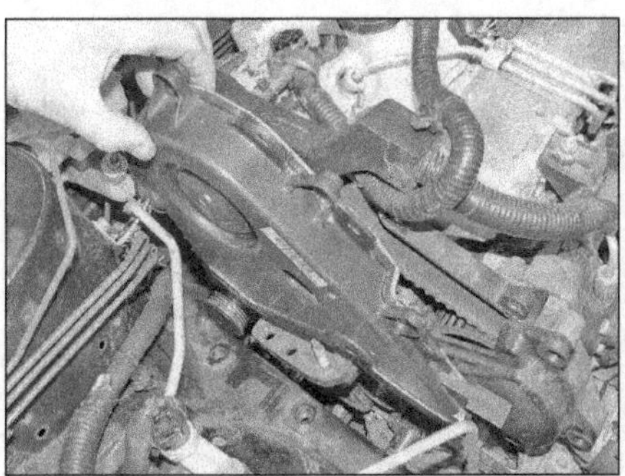

7.7 Removing the upper timing belt cover

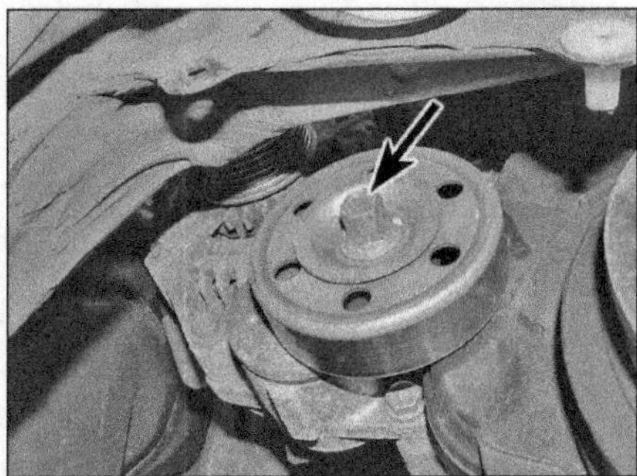

7.8a Undo the retaining bolt . . .

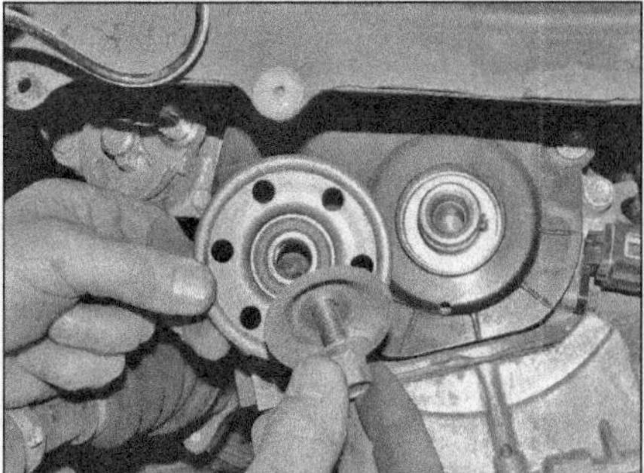

7.8b . . . and remove the alternator drivebelt tensioner pulley . . .

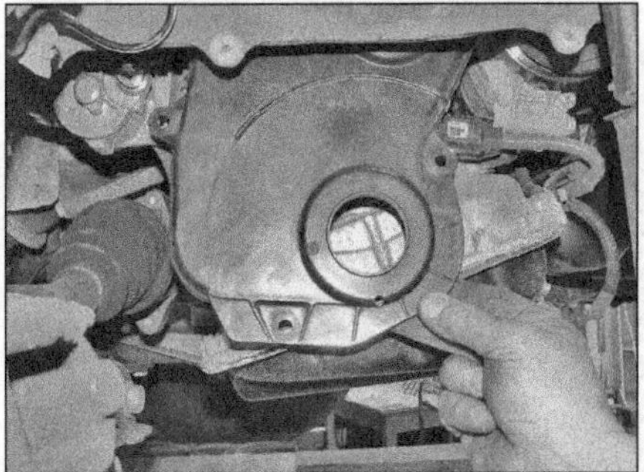

7.8c . . . then unbolt the lower timing belt cover from the cylinder block

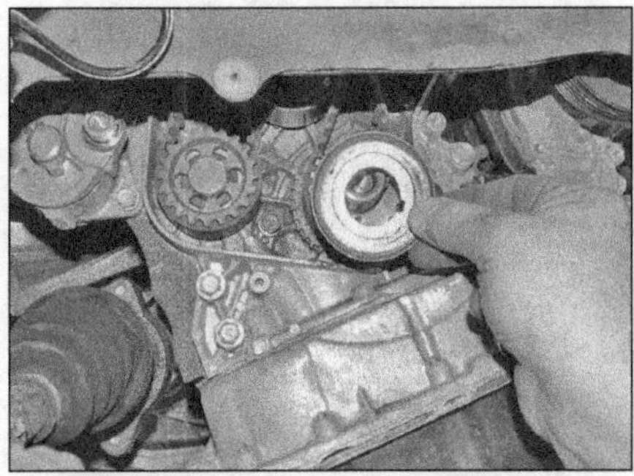

7.9 Removing the timing belt guide/ washer from the end of the crankshaft

7.10 Remove the right-hand engine mounting

7 Unscrew the bolts and remove the upper timing belt cover from the cylinder head/valve cover **(see illustration)**.

8 Unbolt and remove the alternator drivebelt tensioner pulley, then unscrew the bolts and remove the lower timing belt cover from the cylinder block **(see illustrations)**.

9 Remove the timing belt guide/washer from the end of the crankshaft **(see illustration)**.

10 Support the engine with a hydraulic jack and block of wood, then remove the right-hand side engine mounting **(see illustration)**.

11 Undo the mounting bolts and remove the auxiliary belt idler and adjuster pulleys, then remove the engine mounting bracket from the engine **(see illustrations)**.

12 Set the engine to TDC on No 1 cylinder as described in Section 3.

13 If the timing belt is to be re-used, mark its normal direction of rotation to ensure it is refitted correctly. **Note:** *It is always recommended to fit a new belt once it has been removed.*

14 Where fitted, unscrew the bolt and remove the timing belt spacer/guide located beneath the camshaft sprocket **(see illustration)**.

15 Progressively unscrew the two bolts and remove the tensioner **(see illustrations)**. Also if necessary, unbolt the tensioner roller and arm.

16 Release the timing belt from the camshaft,

7.11a Unbolt the idler pulley bracket . . .

7.11b . . . and then remove the right-hand lower engine mounting from the engine

7.14 Removing the timing belt spacer/ guide from beneath the camshaft sprocket

7.15a Unscrew the two mounting bolts . . .

7.15b . . . and remove the tensioner

7.16 Removing the timing belt

7.17a Undo the camshaft sprocket bolt . . .

7.17b . . . remove the camshaft sprocket . . .

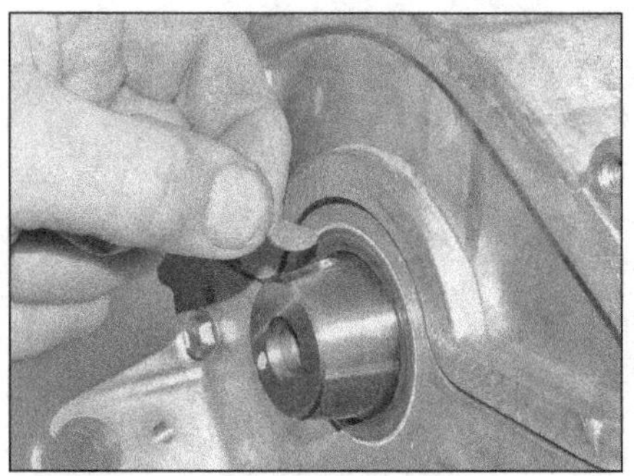
7.17c . . . and recover the Woodruff key

7.18a Remove the crankshaft sprocket . . .

7.18b . . . and recover the Woodruff keys from the nose of the crankshaft

high-pressure pump, water pump, crankshaft and oil pump sprockets, and withdraw from the engine **(see illustration)**.

17 To remove the camshaft sprocket, hold it stationary with a suitable lever inserted in the holes, then unscrew and remove the centre bolt. Using a puller, draw the sprocket from the end of the exhaust camshaft, and recover the Woodruff key **(see illustrations)**. Due to the minimal clearance between the sprocket and inner body, it may not be possible to use a puller with the engine *in place*; however, careful use of two levers may be sufficient to release it.

18 To remove the crankshaft sprocket, slide it from the end of the crankshaft. If it is tight, use a suitable puller attached to the bolt holes provided. Remove the Woodruff keys **(see illustrations)**.

19 Removal of the high-pressure supply pump sprocket is covered in Chapter 4B. It is removed by holding it stationary and unscrewing the nut, then withdrawing using a suitable puller.

20 Unscrew the bolt and remove the tensioner idler pulley from the cylinder block. If necessary, also unbolt and remove the front idler.

Inspection

Caution: Do not bend, twist or turn the timing belt inside out. Do not allow it to come in contact with oil, coolant or fuel. Do not turn the crankshaft or camshaft more than a few degrees (if necessary for tooth alignment) while the timing belt is removed.

21 Check the sprockets and idlers for excessive wear and renew them if necessary. Check the tensioner as follows. First check the integrity of the internal oil seal – if there is more that the faintest trace of oil on the seal, renew the tensioner. With the tensioner pushrod on the side of the workbench, press on the body to check that the pushrod does not move. Measure the protrusion of the pushrod – if it is more than 10.6 mm, renew the tensioner **(see illustration)**.

22 Examine the belt for evidence of contamination by coolant or lubricant. If this is the case, find the source of the contamination before progressing any further. Check the belt for signs of wear or damage, particularly around the leading edges of the belt teeth **(see illustration)**.

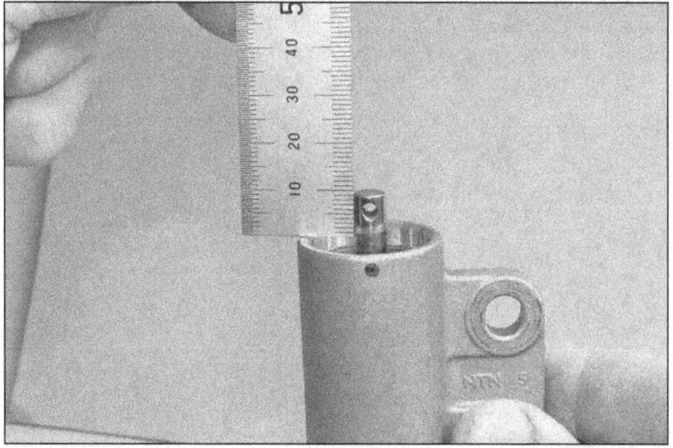
7.21 Measuring the protrusion of the timing belt tensioner pushrod

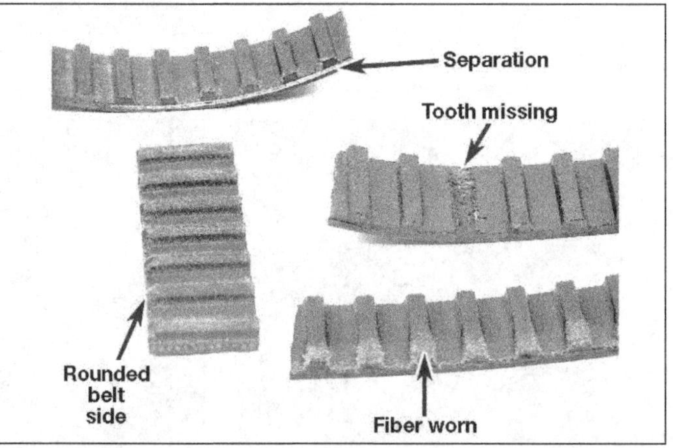

7.22 Check the timing belt for cracked and missing teeth – wear on one side of the belt indicates sprocket misalignment problems

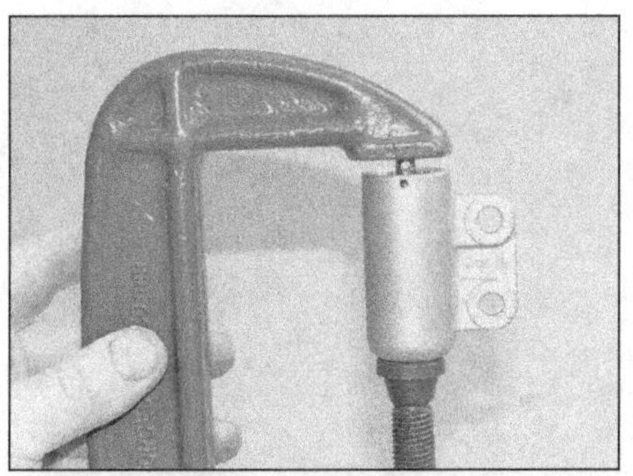
7.29a Using a G-clamp to compress the tensioner pushrod

7.29b Using an Allen key to set the tensioner

7.30a Refit the tensioner roller and arm . . .

7.30b . . . then refit the tensioner . . .

7.30c . . . and insert and tighten the mounting bolts

Caution: If the belt appears to be in good condition and can be re-used, it is essential that it is reinstalled the same way around, otherwise accelerated wear will result, leading to premature failure.

23 Renew the belt if its condition is in doubt; the cost of belt renewal is negligible compared with potential cost of the engine repairs, should the belt fail in service. Similarly, if the belt is known to have covered more than 36 000 miles, it is prudent to renew it regardless of condition, as a precautionary measure.

Refitting

24 Ensure that the crankshaft is still set to TDC on No 1 cylinder, as described in Section 3.

25 Refit the idler pulley and idlers, and tighten the bolts to the specified torque.

26 If removed, refit the high-pressure pump sprocket with reference to Chapter 4B.

27 Fit the Woodruff key, then refit the crankshaft sprocket, using a metal tube if necessary to drive it into position.

28 Fit the Woodruff key, then refit the camshaft sprocket on the camshaft. Hold the sprocket stationary, then refit the centre bolt and tighten to the specified torque.

29 Before refitting the tensioner, it must be set as follows. Using a press or suitable alternative, press the pushrod into the tensioner body until the holes are aligned, then insert a 1.3 mm diameter pin or alternative through the holes and release the press **(see illustrations)**.

30 Where removed, refit the tensioner roller and arm and tighten the bolt, then refit the tensioner to the cylinder block and tighten the bolts to the specified torque **(see illustrations)**.

31 Check that the crankshaft and camshaft are both still set to TDC on No 1 cylinder, then fit the timing belt onto the camshaft sprocket, high-pressure pump sprocket, water pump sprocket, crankshaft sprocket, rear idler pulley, water pump and tensioner pulley, in that order **(see illustration)**.

Caution: If refitting a used belt, observe the direction of rotation markings on the belt.

32 Check the position of the timing belt, then pull out the pin to release the pushrod against the tensioner pulley and tension the belt **(see illustration)**.

33 Temporarily refit the crankshaft pulley bolt, then turn the engine through two complete revolutions and set it to TDC again. **Do not** turn the engine anti-clockwise during this procedure. Check that the timing marks on the crankshaft and camshaft sprockets align correctly, and then remove the crankshaft pulley bolt.

34 Refit the timing belt spacer/guide (where

7.31 Refitting the timing belt

7.32 Pull out the pin to set the tensioner

7.35a Refit the right-hand side engine mounting bracket to the engine . . .

7.35b . . . and the idler pulley bracket

7.36 Refit the engine mounting

7.37 Refit the timing belt guide/washer to the end of the crankshaft

7.39 Refitting the lower timing belt cover . . .

7.41 . . . and upper timing belt cover

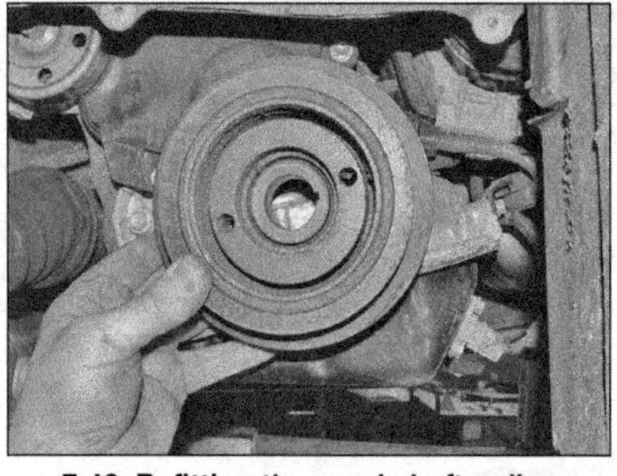
7.42 Refitting the crankshaft pulley

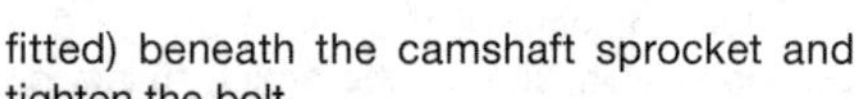

fitted) beneath the camshaft sprocket and tighten the bolt.

35 Refit the right-hand side engine mounting bracket and the auxiliary belt idler/adjuster pulley mounting bracket and tighten the mounting bolts **(see illustrations)**.

36 Refit the mounting to the inner body and tighten the bolts to the specified torque **(see illustration)**. Remove the hydraulic jack.

37 Refit the timing belt guide/washer to the end of the crankshaft **(see illustration)**.

38 Clean the mating surfaces of the lower timing belt cover, and check the condition of the gasket. If it requires renewal, remove the old gasket then remove the backing paper and fit the new gasket to the cover, making sure it is fully in the groove. If there is a gap between the ends of the gasket, apply sealant with the same profile as the gasket.

39 Fit the oil pump insulator (where fitted) then refit the lower timing belt cover and tighten the bolts **(see illustration)**.

40 Clean the mating surfaces of the upper timing belt cover, and check the condition of the gasket. If necessary, renew the gasket as described in paragraph 38.

41 Refit the upper timing belt cover and tighten the bolts **(see illustration)**.

42 Refit the crankshaft pulley **(see illustration)**.

43 Refit the auxiliary drivebelt(s) as described in Chapter 1B.

44 Refit the glow plugs as described in Chapter 5A.

45 Refit the right-hand front wheel and tighten the bolts to the specified torque setting. Refit the engine upper cover.

8 Crankshaft right-hand oil seal – renewal

1 Remove the timing belt and crankshaft sprocket (see Section 7).

2 Note how far the seal is recessed in the bore, then carefully lever it out of the oil pump housing with a screwdriver or seal removal tool. The seal may be easier to remove if the old seal lip is cut with a sharp utility knife first **(see illustrations)**. Don't scratch the housing bore or damage the crankshaft in the process (if the crankshaft is damaged, the new seal will end up leaking).

3 Clean the bore in the housing and coat the outer edge of the new seal with engine oil or multipurpose grease. Apply multipurpose grease to the seal lip.

4 Put the new seal over the crankshaft and then use the crankshaft sprocket and centre bolt to press the seal into place. Make sure it's fitted squarely and driven in to the same depth as the original using a block of wood **(see illustrations)**. Check the seal after refitting to

8.2a If necessary, cut away the oil seal lip before . . .

8.2b . . . using a screwdriver to lever out the old seal

8.4a Locate the new oil seal over the crankshaft . . .

8.4b . . . and use the crankshaft sprocket and centre bolt to press the seal into position . . .

8.4c . . . using a block of wood to ensure it is flush with the surface of the oil pump

make sure it has not been damaged and the spring is still in place.

5 Refit the crankshaft sprocket and timing belt (see Section 7).

6 Run the engine and check for oil leaks at the seal.

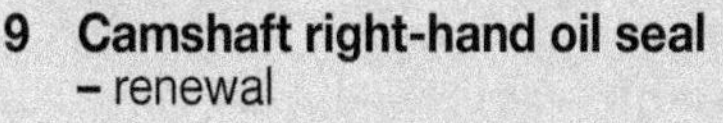

9 Camshaft right-hand oil seal – renewal

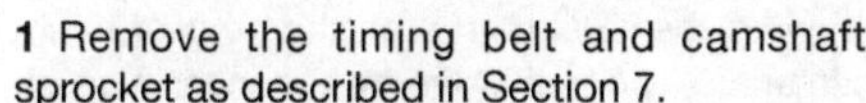

1 Remove the timing belt and camshaft sprocket as described in Section 7.

2 Note how far the seal is recessed in the bore, and then carefully prise it out of the housing with a screwdriver or seal removal tool. Don't scratch the housing bore or damage the camshaft in the process otherwise the seal will leak. **Note:** *The seal may be easier to remove if the old seal lip is cut with a sharp utility knife first (see illustrations in Section 8 of this Chapter).*

3 Clean the bore in the housing and coat the outer edge of the new seal with engine oil or multipurpose grease. Apply multipurpose grease to the seal lip.

4 Using a socket with an outside diameter slightly smaller than the outside diameter of the seal, carefully drive the new seal into place with a hammer. Make sure it's fitted squarely and driven in to the same depth as the original. If a socket isn't available, a short section of large diameter pipe will also work. Check the seal after refitting to make sure it has not been damaged and the spring is still in place.

5 Refit the timing belt and camshaft sprocket as described in Section 7.

6 Run the engine and check for leaks at the front seal.

10 Camshafts and followers – removal and refitting

Removal

1 Drain the engine coolant (see Chapter 1B).

2 Remove the valve cover as described in Section 4.

3 Remove the timing belt and camshaft sprocket as described in Section 7.

4 Unscrew the bolt and remove the camshaft position sensor from the rear of the cylinder head **(see illustration)**.

5 Unscrew the two mounting bolts and remove the brake vacuum pump from the cylinder head. Recover the two O-ring seals **(see illustrations)**.

6 Unbolt and remove the injector leak-off pipe.

7 Unscrew the bolts and lever the camshaft oil seal housing away from the front of the cylinder head **(see illustration)**. Prise out the oil seal as a new one must be fitted on reassembly.

8 Identify the position of each of the camshaft bearing caps on the cylinder head.

9 Progressively loosen the camshaft bearing cap bolts using the sequence shown, and then remove the bearing caps followed by the camshafts and camshaft carrier **(see illustrations)**.

Caution: Failure to unscrew the bolts in sequence may result in damage to the cylinder head.

10.4 Removing the camshaft position sensor

10.5a Remove the brake vacuum pump from the rear of the cylinder head . . .

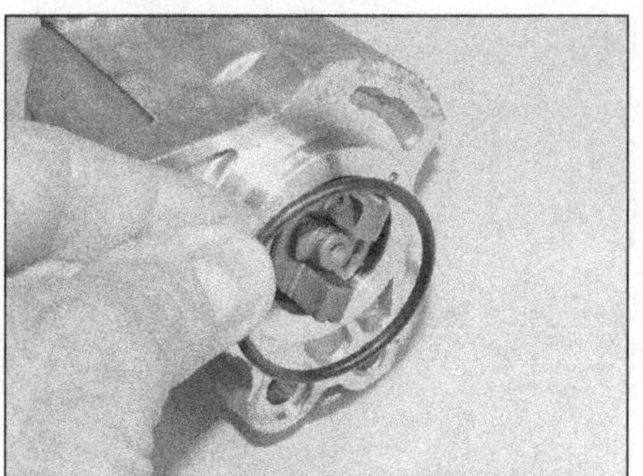

10.5b . . . and recover the large O-ring seal . . .

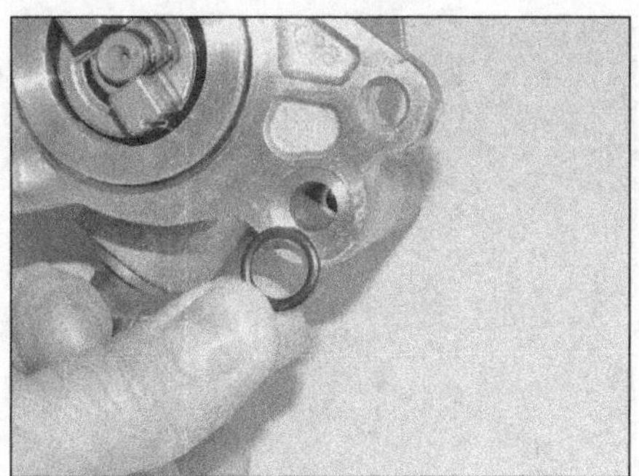

10.5c . . . and small O-ring seal

10.7 Removing the camshaft oil seal housing from the cylinder head

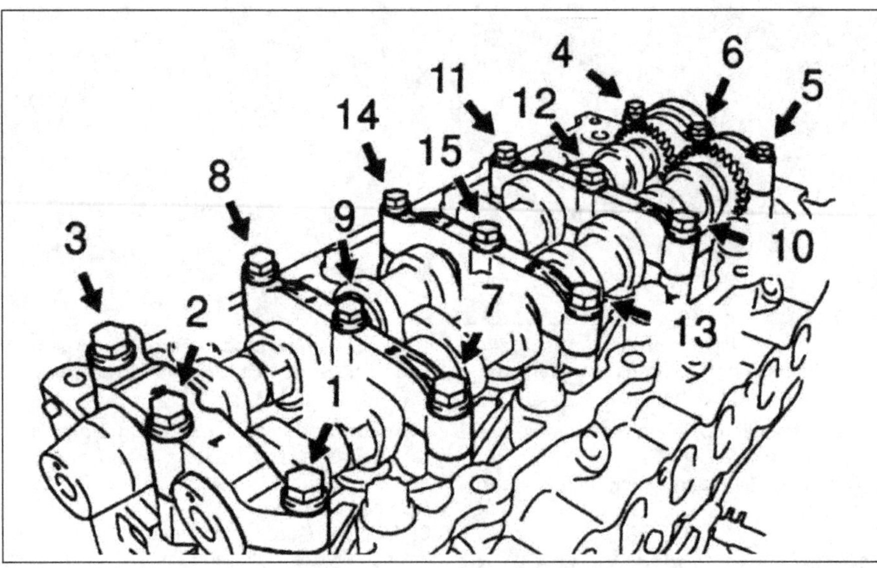

10.9a Camshaft bearing cap bolt loosening sequence

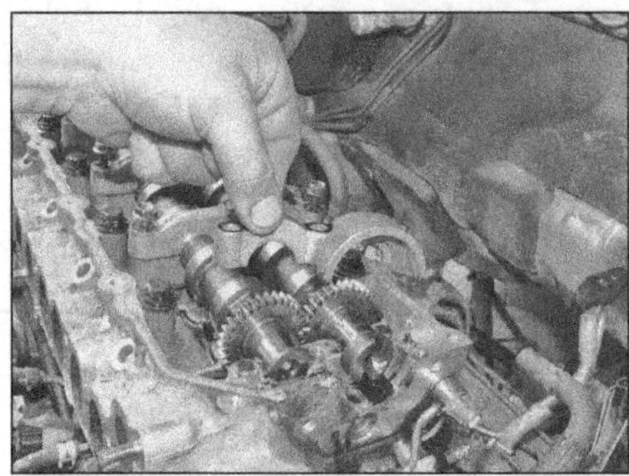
10.9b Remove the camshaft bearing caps . . .

10 Using a magnet or suction pad, withdraw the camshaft followers and shims from their bores, keeping them identified for position to ensure correct refitting **(see illustration)**.

11 Inspect the camshaft and followers as described in Chapter 2A.

Refitting

12 Insert the camshaft followers and shims to their correct bores, having lightly oiled the bores; check that the followers can be rotated smoothly in the bores by hand **(see illustration)**.

13 Locate the camshaft carrier on the cylinder head **(see illustration)**.

14 Oil the bearing surfaces of the carrier and inlet camshaft, then lower the inlet camshaft onto the cylinder head, in its position nearest the front of the head **(see illustrations)**. Position the camshaft so that the lobes of cylinders 3 and 4 are facing downwards.

15 Oil the bearing surfaces of the carrier and exhaust camshaft, then lower the exhaust camshaft onto the cylinder head, in its position at the rear of the head, at the same time aligning the TDC marks on the gear of each camshaft. The marks are on the inner face of each gear **(see illustration)**.

10.9c . . . followed by the camshafts . . .

10.9d . . . and camshaft carrier

10.10 Removing the camshaft followers

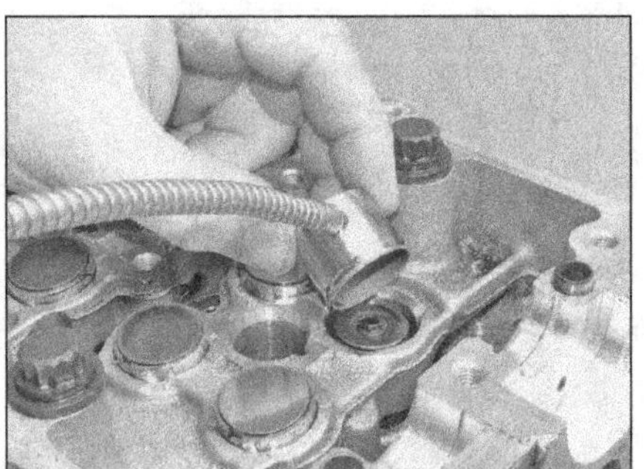
10.12 Insert the camshaft followers and shims to their correct bores

10.13 Locate the camshaft carrier on the cylinder head

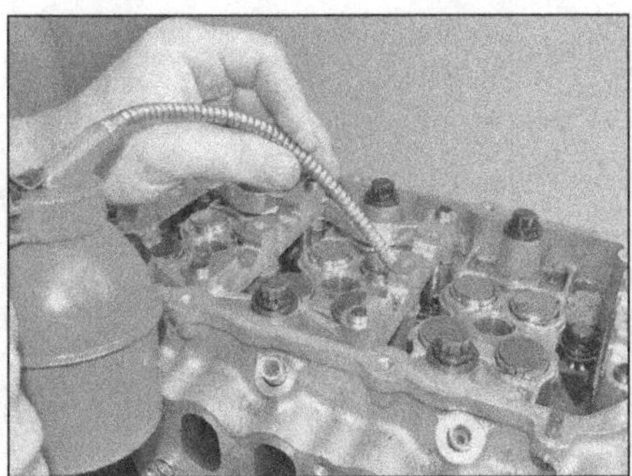
10.14a Oil the bearing surfaces . . .

10.14b . . . then lower the inlet camshaft onto the cylinder head

10.15 Align the TDC marks on the camshaft gears before fitting the bearing caps

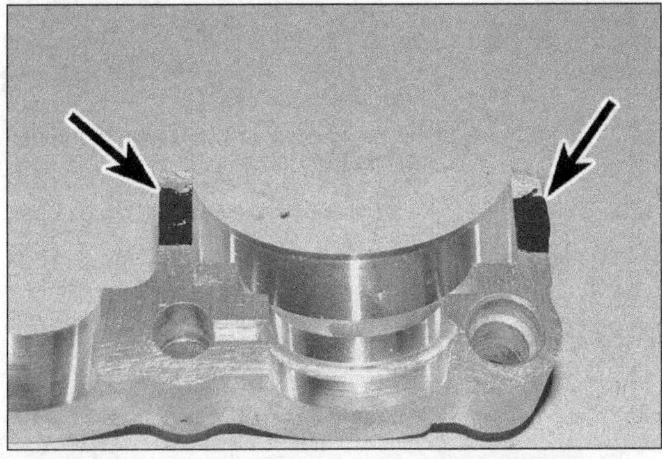
10.16 Apply sealant to the camshaft bearing cap 5 as shown

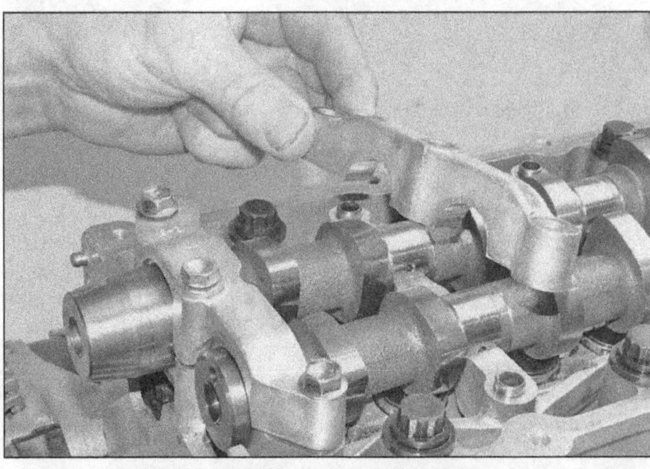
10.17a Refitting the camshaft bearing caps

16 Clean the mating surface of camshaft bearing cap 5 and apply sealant as shown **(see illustration)**.

17 Refit all the camshaft bearing caps in their correct position, then progressively tighten them to the specified torque in sequence **(see illustrations)**

18 Check and adjust the valve clearances as described in Chapter 1B.

19 Clean the mating surface of the camshaft oil seal housing, and apply a 2 to 4 mm wide bead of sealant as shown **(see illustration)**. Refit the housing and tighten the bolts to the specified torque.

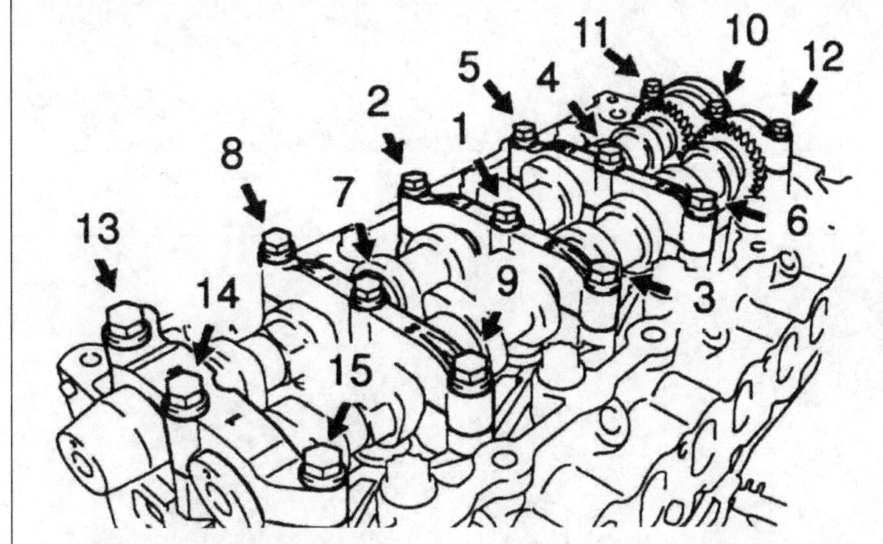

10.17b Camshaft bearing cap bolt tightening sequence

20 Fit a new oil seal to the housing as follows. Locate the new oil seal over the end of the camshaft, and then use a metal tube to drive it in the housing until flush with the outer edge.

21 Clean the semi-circular grommet and apply sealant to its grooves, then locate it on the end of the cylinder head.

22 Refit the injector leak-off pipe and tighten the union bolts to the specified torque.

23 Fit new O-ring seals to the vacuum pump, then align the drive lugs with the slot in the camshaft and refit the pump. Insert the bolts and tighten to the specified torque.

24 Refit the timing belt and camshaft sprocket as described in Section 7.

25 Refit the valve cover as described in Section 4.

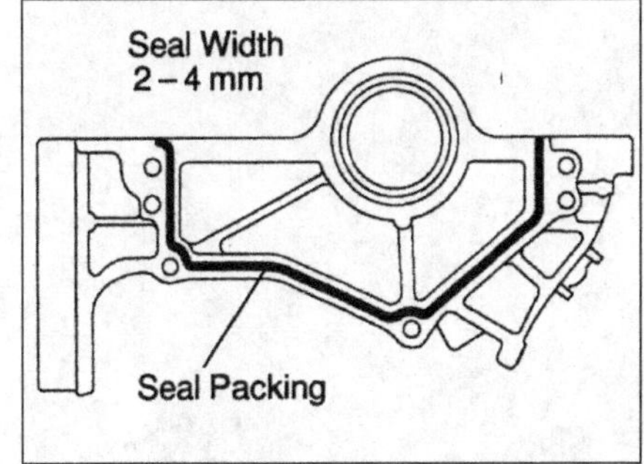

10.19 Apply sealant to the camshaft oil seal housing as shown

11.3 Removing the timing belt triangular inner cover

11.8a Unscrew the bolts . . .

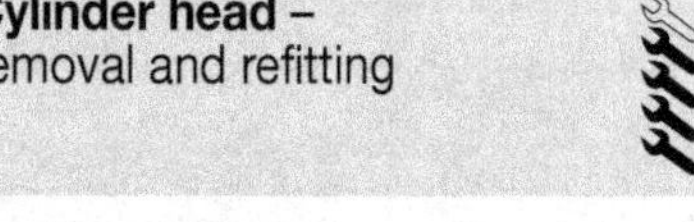

11 Cylinder head – removal and refitting

Warning: Wait until engine is completely cool before beginning this procedure.

Removal

1 Drain the engine coolant (see Chapter 1B).

2 Remove upper engine plastic cover.

3 Refer to Section 7 and remove the timing belt and the camshaft sprocket. Also unbolt and remove the timing belt triangular inner cover **(see illustration)**.

4 Remove the turbocharger as described in Chapter 4B.

5 Unscrew the nuts and remove the exhaust manifold from the cylinder head. Recover the collars and gasket.

6 Unscrew the bolt and remove the camshaft position sensor from the rear of the cylinder head.

7 Where fitted, unbolt the cover from over the high-pressure fuel pump, and remove the insulator.

8 Disconnect the wiring and vacuum hose, then unscrew the bolts and remove the inlet air duct and throttle body together with the gasket **(see illustrations)**.

9 Loosen the common rail mounting bolts. This is necessary to allow room for the inlet manifold to be removed.

10 Unscrew the bolts and nuts, and remove the inlet manifold together with the gasket **(see illustration)**.

11 Unbolt the timing belt cover bracket.

12 Remove the crankcase ventilation hose.

13 Unbolt the water outlet elbow and recover the gasket **(see illustrations)**.

14 Remove the bolts and withdraw the common rail **(see illustration)**.

15 If necessary, unscrew and remove the water temperature sensor.

16 Unscrew the single bolt and two nuts and remove the EGR valve and gasket **(see illustration)**.

11.8b . . . and remove the air inlet duct together with throttle body and gasket

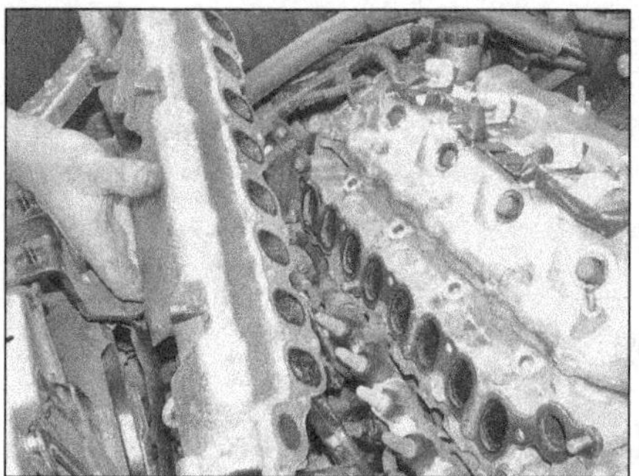
11.10a Removing the inlet manifold . . .

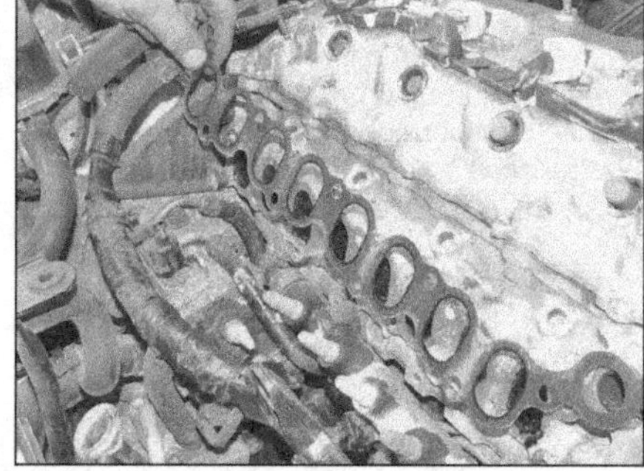
11.10b . . . and gasket

11.13a Unbolt the water outlet elbow . . .

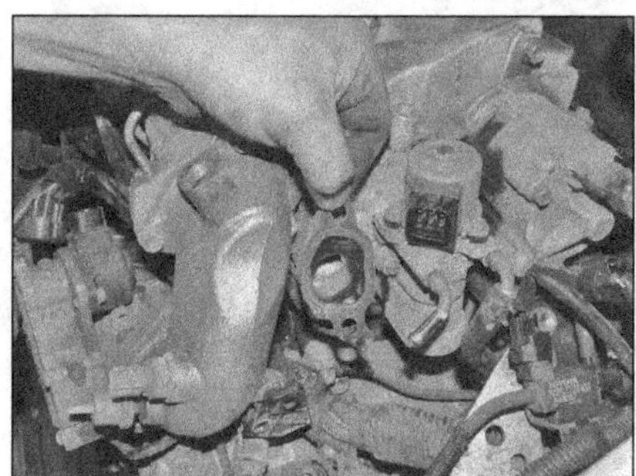
11.13b . . . and recover the gasket

11.14 Removing the common rail

11.16a EGR valve location

11.16b Removing the EGR valve

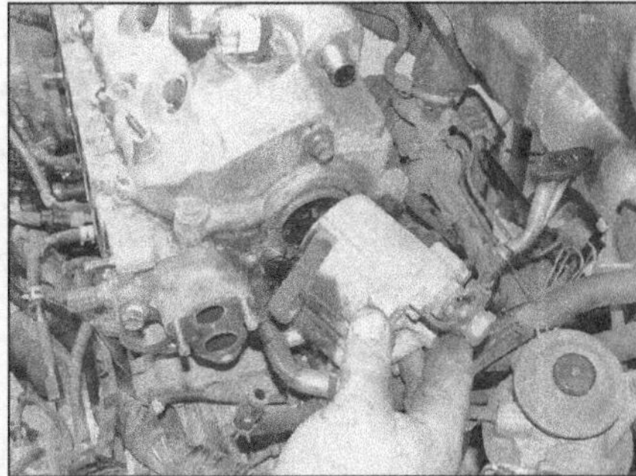

11.17 Removing the vacuum pump

11.21a Unscrew the union bolts . . .

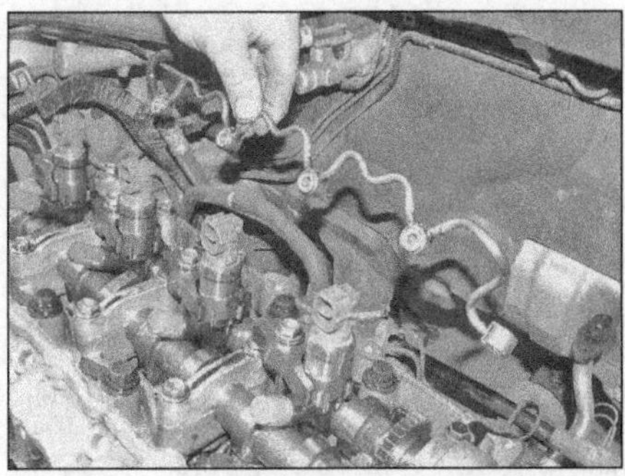

11.21b . . . and remove the injector leak-off pipe

11.23 Removing the camshaft oil seal housing

17 Unscrew the two mounting bolts and remove the vacuum pump from the end of the cylinder head **(see illustration)**. Recover the two O-ring seals.

18 Where fitted on the end of the cylinder head, remove the caps and unscrew the three nuts from the auxiliary heater plug supply terminals. Unscrew and remove the heater plugs. **Note:** *An auxiliary heater is only fitted to models in cold climates.*

19 Loosen the clips and disconnect the fuel hose and oil cooler hose.

20 Unscrew and remove the injector leak-off valve, pipe and gasket.

21 Unbolt and remove the injector leak-off pipe **(see illustrations)**

22 Remove the injectors as described in Chapter 4B. This procedure includes removal of the valve cover.

23 Unscrew the bolts and lever the camshaft oil seal housing away from the cylinder head **(see illustration)**. Prise out the oil seal, as a new one must be fitted on reassembly.

24 Identify the position of each of the camshaft bearing caps on the cylinder head.

25 Progressively loosen the camshaft bearing cap bolts using the sequence shown **(see illustration 10.9a)**, and then remove the bearing caps followed by the camshafts and camshaft carrier.

Caution: Failure to unscrew the bolts in sequence may result in damage to the cylinder head.

26 Progressively loosen the cylinder head bolts using the sequence shown **(see illustration)** then remove the bolts together with their washers. Note the different lengths of bolts; the inner bolts are shorter than the outer bolts.

Caution: Failure to unscrew the bolts in sequence may result in cylinder head warpage or cracking.

27 Check that all wiring has been disconnected, then carefully lift the cylinder head from the dowels on the cylinder block, and place it on the workbench.

28 Remove the gasket from the top of the block. Do not discard the gasket – it will be needed for identification purposes.

Refitting

29 The mating faces of the cylinder head and cylinder block must be perfectly clean before refitting the head. Use a hard plastic or wood scraper to remove all traces of gasket and carbon; also clean the piston crowns. Take particular care during the cleaning operations,

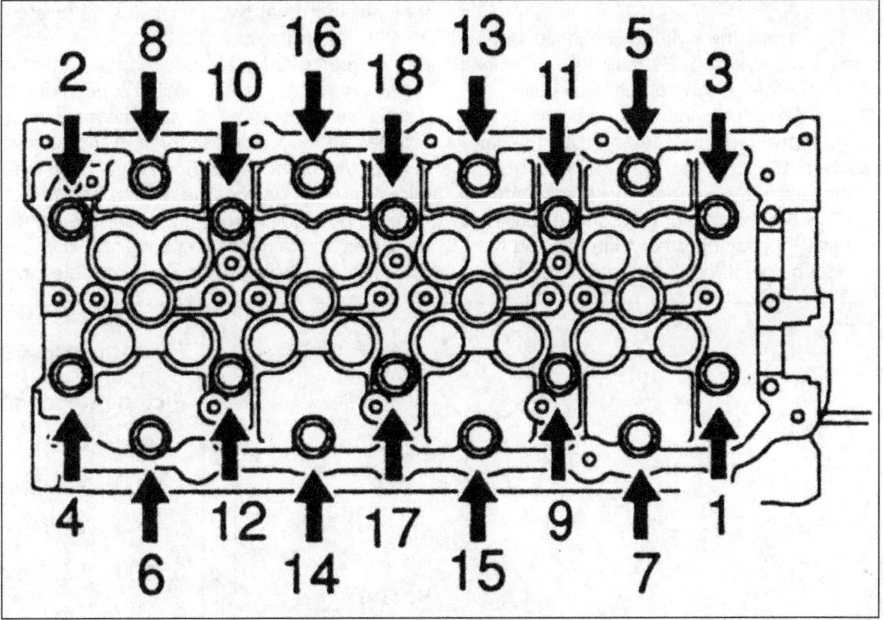

11.26 Cylinder head bolt loosening sequence

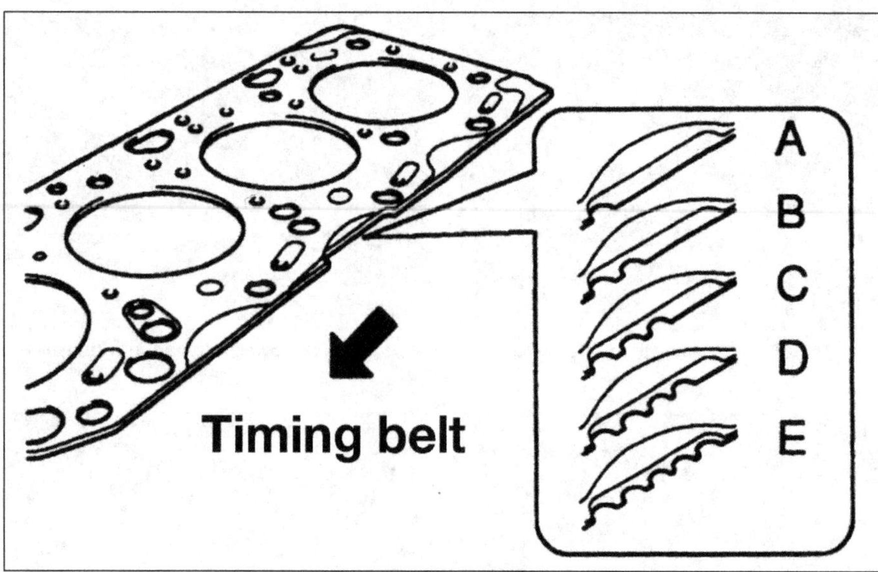

11.34 Cylinder head gasket identification cut-outs

as aluminium alloy is easily damaged. Also, make sure that the carbon is not allowed to enter the oil and water passages – this is particularly important for the lubrication system, as carbon could block the oil supply to the engine's components. Using adhesive tape and paper, seal the water, oil and bolt holes in the cylinder block.

30 Check the mating surfaces of the cylinder block and the cylinder head for nicks, deep scratches and other damage. If slight, they may be removed carefully with abrasive paper.

31 If warpage of the cylinder head gasket surface is suspected, use a straight-edge to check it for distortion (see Specifications), but note that head machining may not be possible.

32 Clean out the cylinder head bolt holes using a suitable tap. Be sure they are clean and dry before refitting of the head bolts.

33 On diesel engines it is possible for the piston crowns to strike and damage the valve heads if the camshaft is rotated with the timing belt removed and the crankshaft set to TDC. For this reason, the crankshaft must be set to a position other than TDC on No 1 cylinder before the cylinder head is reinstalled. Use a spanner and socket on the crankshaft pulley centre bolt to turn the crankshaft anti-clockwise until all four pistons are positioned halfway down their bores (approximately 90 degrees before TDC).

34 Examine the old cylinder head gasket for manufacturer's identification markings. These will be in the form of punched cut-outs on the front edge of the gasket **(see illustration)**. Unless new pistons have been fitted, the new cylinder head gasket must be the same type as the old one.

35 If new pistons have been fitted as part of an engine overhaul, before purchasing the new cylinder head gasket, measure the piston projection as follows to determine the thickness of head gasket to be used. Rotate the engine so that the No 1 piston is located at TDC. Using a dial indicator or a depth micrometer measure the distance that the piston protrudes past the gasket surface of the block **(see illustration)**. Repeat the measuring process on the remaining three cylinders and record the highest reading. Five different-thickness head gaskets are available for diesel engines depending on the amount the piston protrudes above the gasket surface. Compare the highest reading to the gasket selection chart below to select the proper head gasket thickness. Purchase a new gasket according to the results of the measurement (see table below).

36 Cut off the heads from two of the old cylinder head bolts to use as alignment dowels during cylinder head refitting. Also cut a slot in the end of the each bolt, big enough for a screwdriver blade so that the alignment dowels can be removed after the cylinder head is fitted. A simple hand-held hacksaw can be used to fabricate the alignment dowels.

37 Refit the alignment dowels in the outer rear holes of the cylinder block and position the new head gasket on the cylinder block, engaging it with the locating dowels. Ensure that the manufacturer's TOP and part number markings face up.

38 With the help of an assistant, place the cylinder head centrally on the cylinder block, ensuring that the locating dowels engage with the recesses in the cylinder head. Check that the head gasket is correctly seated before allowing the full weight of the cylinder head to rest upon it.

39 Oil the threads and the underside of the bolt heads and washers, then carefully guide each bolt into its relevant hole and screw them in hand tight. Be sure to use NEW cylinder head bolts, as the old bolts are stretch-type that will not obtain the correct torque readings if re-used. Note that the bolts for the outer rows are longer than those for the inner rows.

40 Unscrew the homemade alignment dowels using a flat-bladed screwdriver and refit the remaining two bolts hand-tight.

41 Working progressively and in sequence **(see illustration)**, tighten the cylinder head bolts to the Stage 1 torque wrench setting.

42 Angle-tighten the bolts in the same sequence by the Stage 2 angle. **Note:** *It is recommended that an angle-measuring gauge be used to ensure accuracy. If a gauge is not available, use white paint to make alignment marks between the bolt head and cylinder head prior to tightening; the marks can then be used to check the bolt has been rotated through the correct angle during tightening.*

43 Angle-tighten the bolts in the same sequence by the Stage 3 angle.

44 Angle-tighten the bolts in the same sequence by the Stage 4 angle.

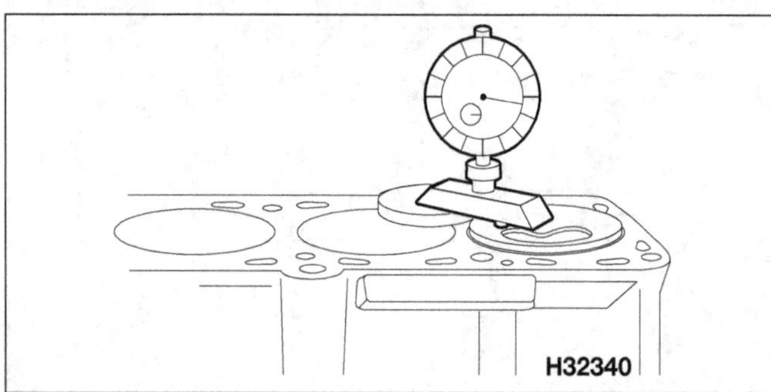

11.35 Measuring the piston projection with a dial indicator (DTI)

Piston projection table

Piston projection	Gasket cut-outs	Gasket thickness
0.165 to 0.220 mm	1 (A)	0.85 to 0.95 mm
0.220 to 0.270 mm	2 (B)	0.90 to 1.00 mm
0.270 to 0.320 mm	3 (C)	0.95 to 1.05 mm
0.320 to 0.370 mm	4 (D)	1.00 to 1.10 mm
0.370 to 0.425 mm	5 (E)	1.05 to 1.15 mm

45 Locate the camshaft carrier on the cylinder head.

46 Oil the bearing surfaces of the carrier and inlet camshaft, then lower the inlet camshaft onto the cylinder head, in its position nearest the front of the head. Position the camshaft so that the lobes of cylinders 3 and 4 are facing downwards.

47 Oil the bearing surfaces of the carrier and exhaust camshaft, then lower the exhaust camshaft onto the cylinder head, in its position at the rear of the head, at the same time aligning the marks on the gear of each camshaft. The marks are on the inner face of each gear.

48 Clean the mating surface of camshaft bearing cap 5 and apply sealant as shown **(see illustration)**.

49 Refit all the camshaft bearing caps in their correct position, then progressively tighten them to the specified torque in sequence **(see illustration 10.17b)**.

50 Check and adjust the valve clearances as described in Chapter 1B.

51 Clean the mating surface of the camshaft oil seal housing, and apply a 2 to 4 mm wide bead of sealant as shown **(see illustration)**. Refit the housing and tighten the bolts to the specified torque.

52 Fit a new oil seal to the housing as follows. Locate the new oil seal over the end of the camshaft, and then use a metal tube to drive it in the housing until flush with the outer edge.

53 Clean the semi-circular grommet and apply sealant to its grooves, then locate it on the end of the cylinder head.

54 Refit the injectors as described in Chapter 4B.

55 Refit the injector leak-off pipe and tighten the union bolts to the specified torque.

56 Refit the injector leak-off valve, pipe and gasket.

57 Refit the fuel hose and oil cooler hose.

58 Where fitted, refit the auxiliary heater plugs and caps.

59 Fit new O-ring seals to the vacuum pump, then align the drive lugs with the slot in the camshaft and refit the pump. Insert the bolts and tighten to the specified torque.

60 Refit the EGR valve together with a new gasket, and tighten the bolts to the specified torque.

61 Refit the water temperature sensor.

62 Refit the common rail but do not tighten the bolts at this stage.

63 Refit the coolant outlet elbow together with a new gasket, and tighten the bolts to the specified torque.

64 Refit the crankcase ventilation hose.

65 Refit the timing belt cover bracket and tighten the bolts to the specified torque.

66 Refit the inlet manifold together with a new gasket and tighten the bolts and nuts to the specified torque

67 Fully tighten the common rail bolts to the specified torque.

68 Refit the inlet air duct and throttle body together with a new gasket, and tighten the

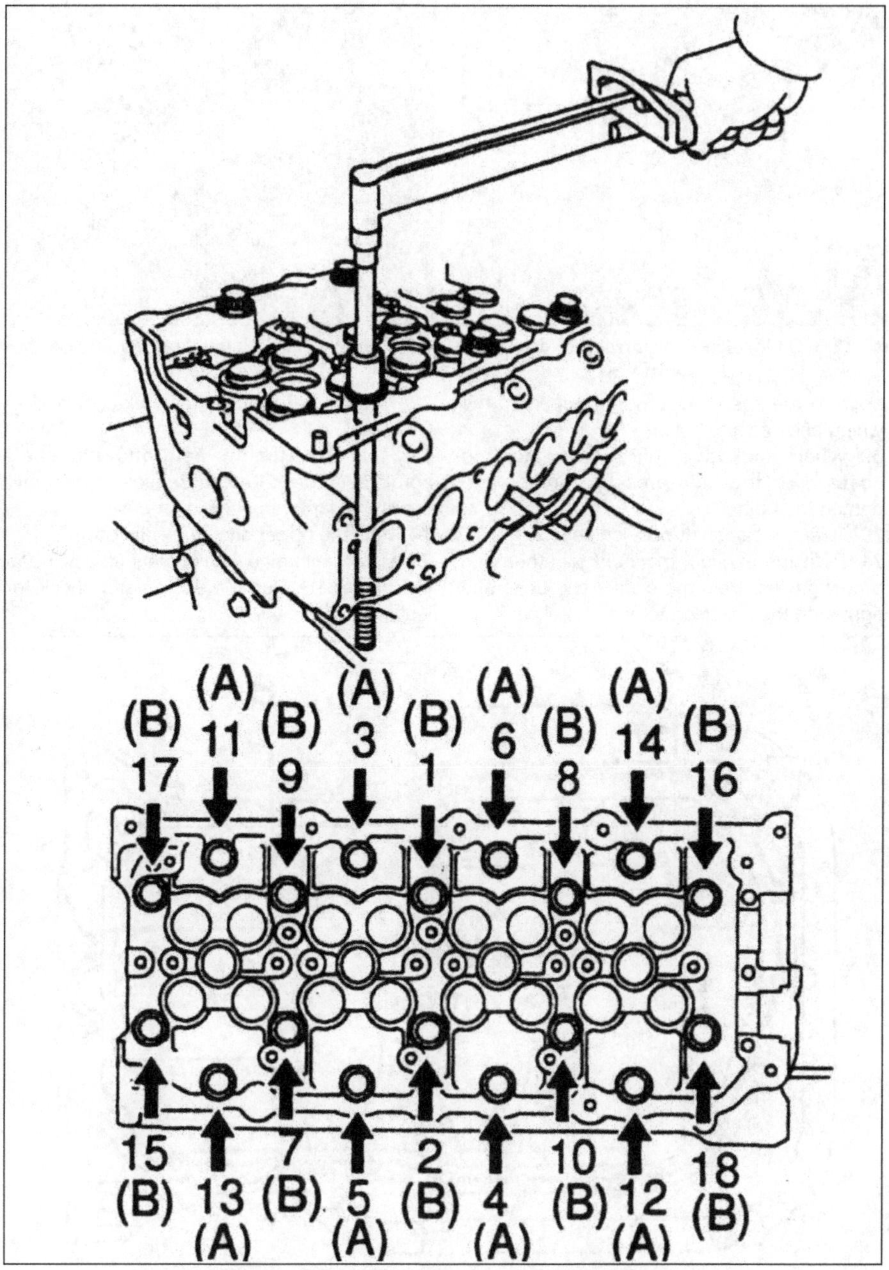

11.41 Cylinder head bolt tightening sequence

A = 160 mm *B = 104 mm*

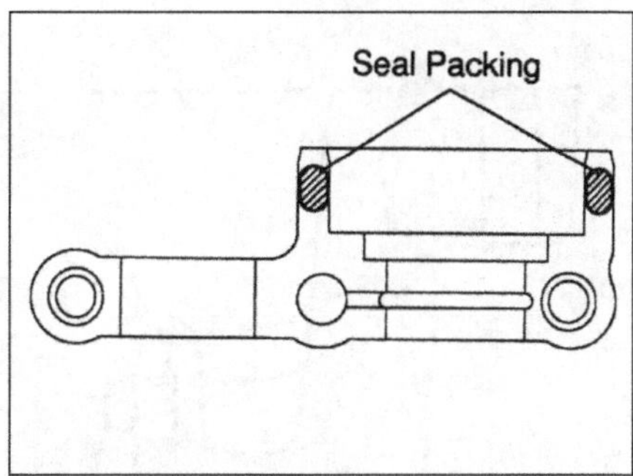

11.48 Apply sealant to the shaded area of bearing cap 5

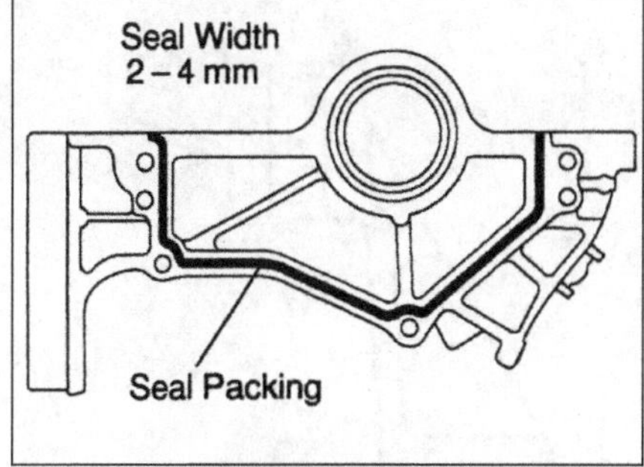

11.51 Apply sealant to the camshaft oil seal housing as shown

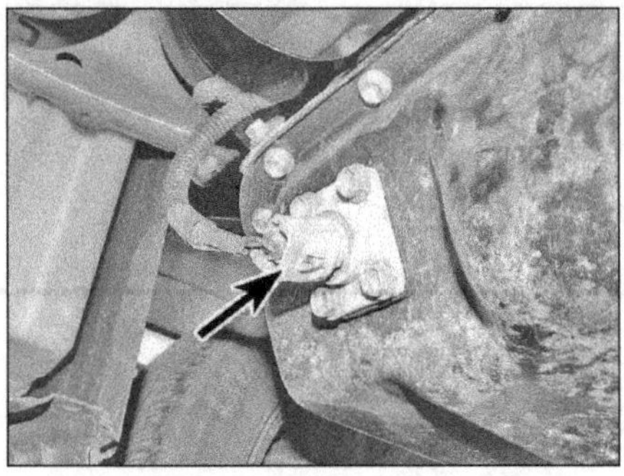
12.3 Oil level sensor (arrowed) on the sump

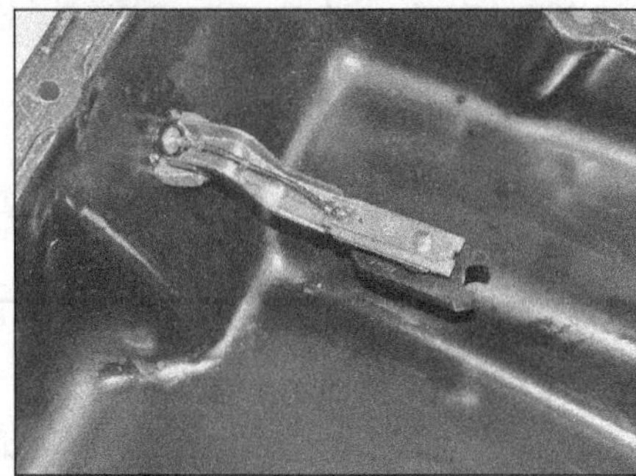
12.5 View of the oil level sensor inside the sump

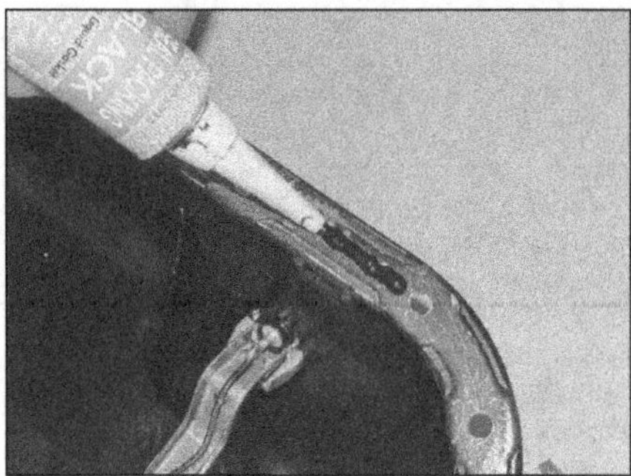
12.8a Apply sealant to the sump . . .

bolts to the specified torque. Reconnect the wiring and vacuum hose.

69 Where applicable, refit the insulator and cover over the high-pressure pump, and tighten the bolts.

70 Refit the camshaft position sensor.

71 Refit the exhaust manifold together with a new gasket. Refit the collars and bolts and tighten to the specified torque.

72 Refit the turbocharger as described in Chapter 4B.

73 Refit the timing belt and camshaft sprocket as described in Section 7. Also refit the triangular timing belt inner cover.

74 Refit the upper engine plastic cover.

75 Refill the engine with coolant as described in Chapter 1B. Run the engine and check for leaks.

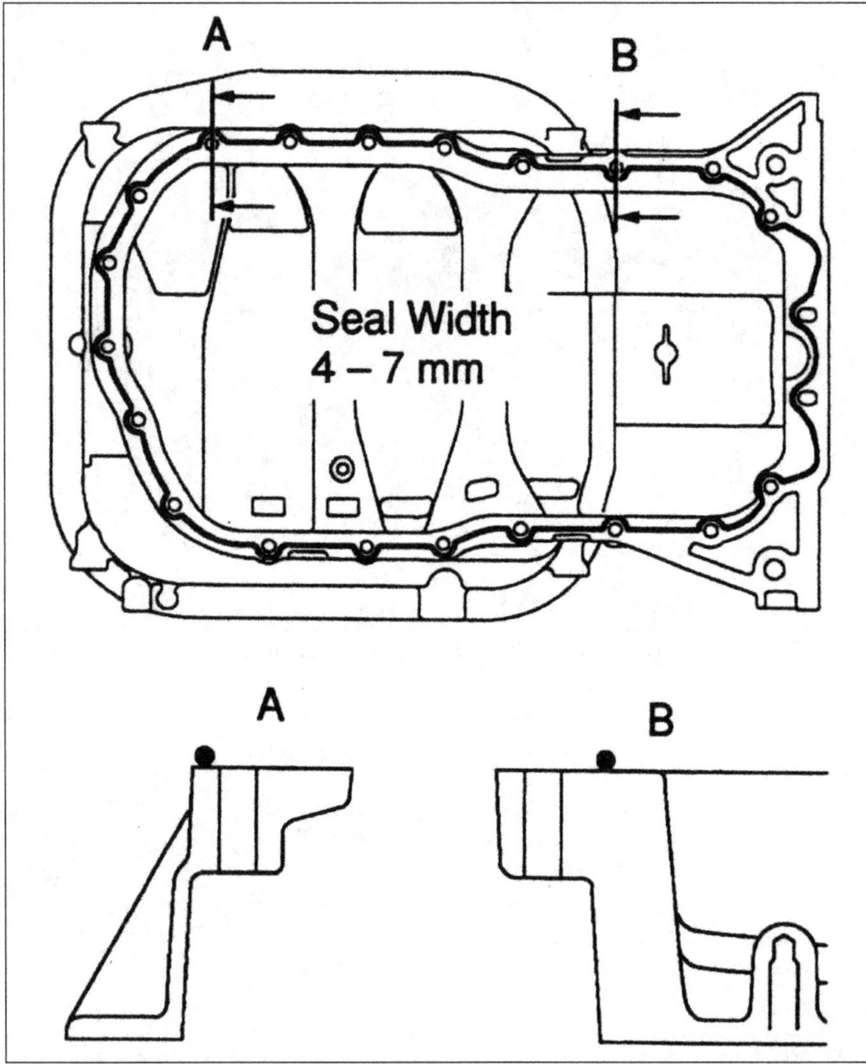

12.8b . . . as shown in the diagram

12 Sump – removal and refitting

Removal

1 Apply the handbrake, then jack up the front of the vehicle and support on axle stands. Remove the undertray.

2 Drain the engine oil and remove the oil filter (see Chapter 1B). Remove the oil dipstick.

3 Disconnect the wiring from the oil level sensor **(see illustration)**.

4 Unscrew the bolts and remove the sump. If it's stuck, prise it loose very carefully with a screwdriver or putty knife. Don't damage the mating surfaces of the sump and housing or oil leaks could develop.

5 If required, unbolt the oil level sensor from the sump and recover the gasket **(see illustration)**.

Refitting

6 Clean all sealant from the sump and block mating surfaces.

7 If removed, refit the oil level sensor together with a new gasket and tighten the bolts.

8 Apply a 4 to 7 mm wide bead of sealant on the sump flange; making sure that it is around the inner side of the bolt holes **(see illustrations)**.

9 Carefully position the sump on the engine block and insert the bolts. Progressively tighten them to the specified torque wrench setting.

10 The remainder of refitting is a reversal of removal. Add oil and a new filter, then run the engine and check for leaks.

13 Oil pump and sump upper housing – removal, inspection and refitting

Removal

1 Remove the sump as described in Section 12.

2 Remove the timing belt as described in Section 7. Also remove the crankshaft sprocket and front idler **(see illustration)**.

3 Unbolt and remove the auxiliary drivebelt

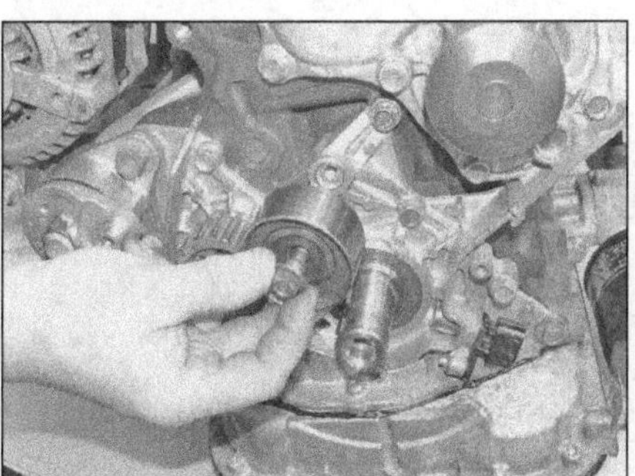

13.2 Removing the timing belt front idler

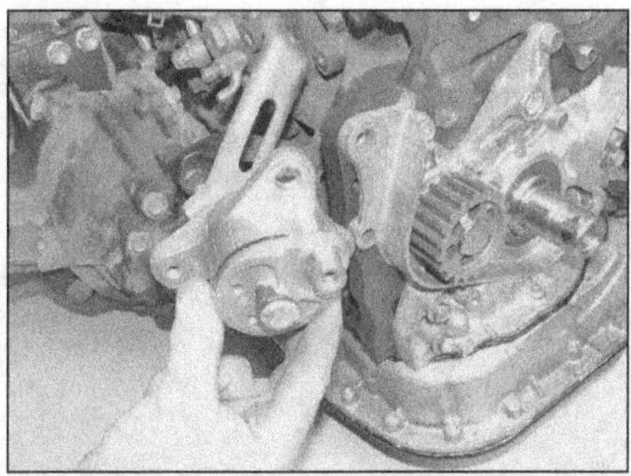

13.3 Removing the auxiliary drivebelt tensioner bracket from below the alternator

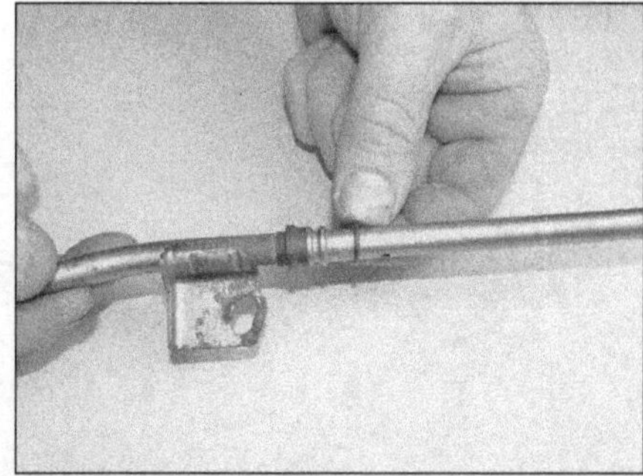

13.4 Removing the O-ring from the dipstick tube

13.5 Removing the oil pressure relief valve from the the upper housing

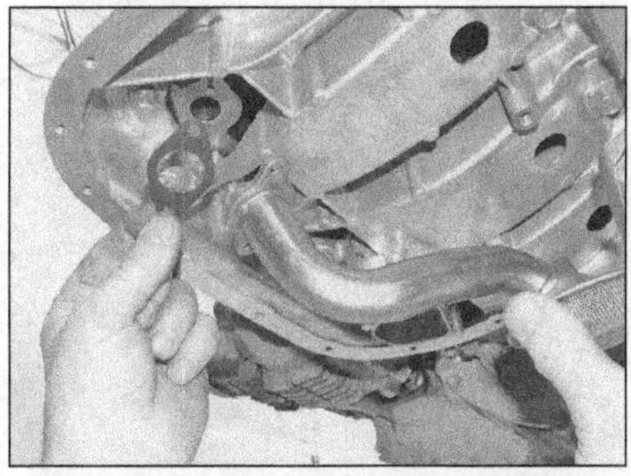

13.6 Removing the oil pick-up tube and gasket

13.7 Removing the sump insulator

tensioner bracket from below the alternator **(see illustration)**.

4 Unscrew the support bolt, then remove the dipstick tube from the sump upper housing. Remove the O-ring from the tube **(see illustration)**.

5 If required, unbolt and remove the oil level sensor. Also, if required, the oil pressure relief valve may be unbolted from the sump upper housing **(see illustration)**.

6 Unscrew the flange and support nuts and bolts, and remove the oil pick-up tube and gasket **(see illustration)**.

7 Unscrew the bolt and remove the sump insulator **(see illustration)**.

8 Unscrew the bolts and withdraw the sump upper housing from the bottom of the engine block, then recover the two O-ring seals. If it's stuck, prise it loose very carefully with a screwdriver or putty knife. Don't damage the mating surfaces of the sump and block or oil leaks could develop. If necessary, the oil filter housing may be removed from the upper housing and the O-ring seal recovered **(see illustrations)**.

9 Unscrew the bolt and remove the crankshaft position sensor from the oil pump housing **(see illustration)**.

10 Unscrew the bolts and remove the oil pump over the front of the crankshaft and from the cylinder block. If it's stuck, carefully lever it away by inserting a screwdriver from below. Remove the O-ring seal **(see illustration)**.

Inspection

11 Refer to Part A of this Chapter. Fit a new crankshaft oil seal to the oil pump housing with reference to Section 8 **(see illustrations)**.

Refitting

12 If fitting a new oil pump, remove the stud from the old one and transfer to the new one.

13 Clean the mating surfaces of the oil pump and cylinder block, then apply a 2 to 4 mm wide bead of sealant to the oil pump housing

13.8a Remove the oil filter housing . . .

13.8b . . . and recover the O-ring seal

13.9 Crankshaft position sensor on the oil pump housing

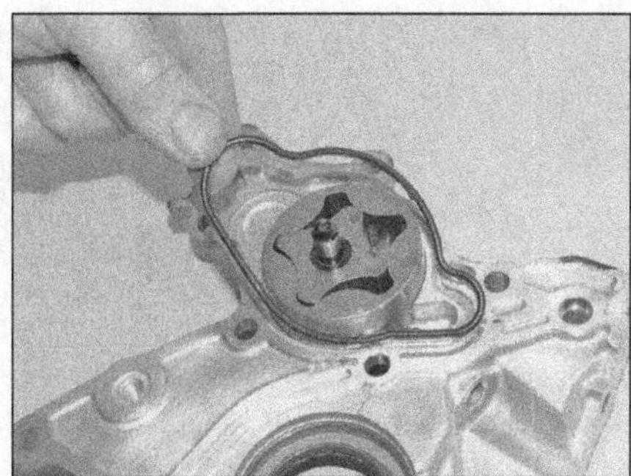

13.10 Removing the oil pump O-ring seal

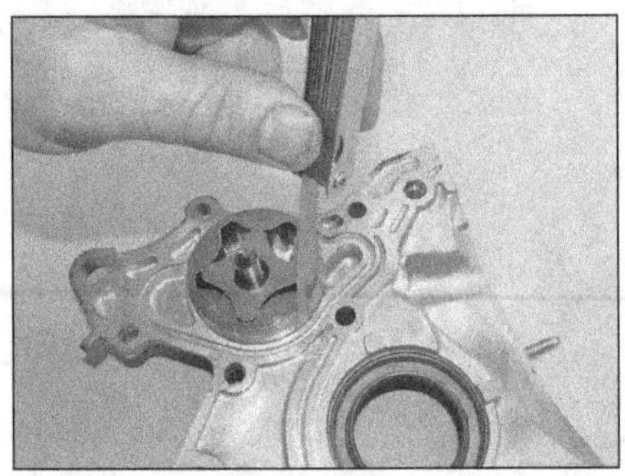
13.11a Checking the driven rotor-to-case clearance . . .

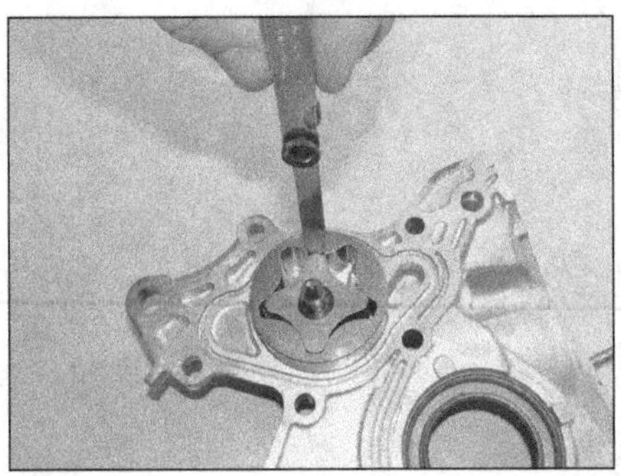
13.11b . . . and the rotor tip clearance with a feeler gauge

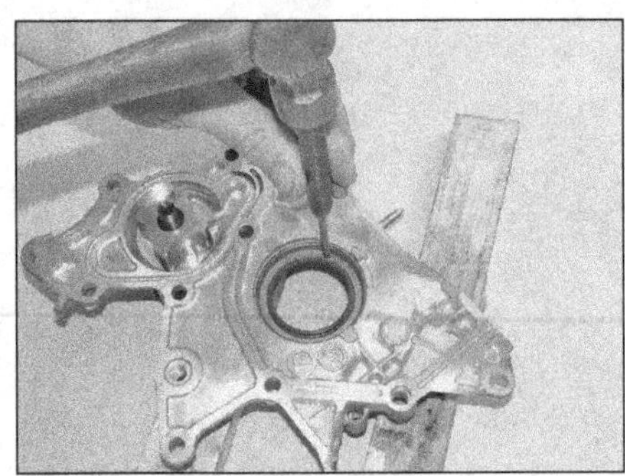
13.11c Drive out the old oil seal from the inside of the housing . . .

13.11d . . . then use a drift to drive in the new oil seal until flush with the outside surface of the housing

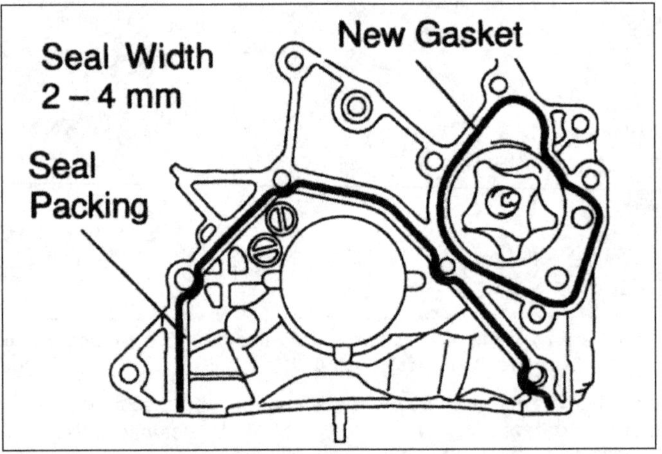

13.13a Apply sealant to the oil pump as shown

13.13b Cut the sealant tube to provide a 2 to 4 mm wide bead of sealant

13.14a Inject oil into the oil pump cavity . . .

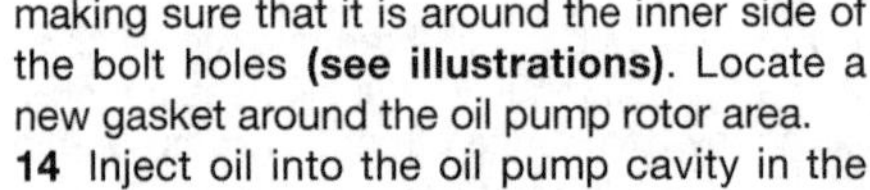
making sure that it is around the inner side of the bolt holes **(see illustrations)**. Locate a new gasket around the oil pump rotor area.

14 Inject oil into the oil pump cavity in the block, then refit the oil pump onto the location dowels and tighten the bolts to the specified torque **(see illustrations)**. Check that the pump sprocket turns freely.

15 Refit the crankshaft position sensor and tighten the bolts to the specified torque.

16 Clean the mating surfaces of the sump upper housing and block, then apply a 4 to 7 mm wide bead of sealant to the housing as shown **(see illustrations 12.8a and 12.8b)**. Note how the bead runs on the inner and outer sides of the bolt holes **(see illustration)**.

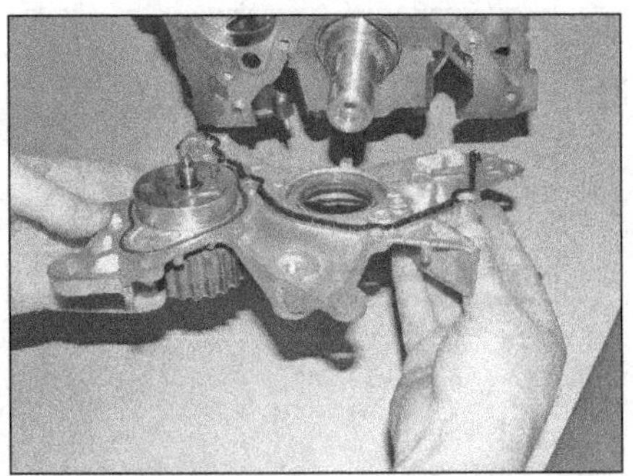
13.14b . . . then refit the oil pump . . .

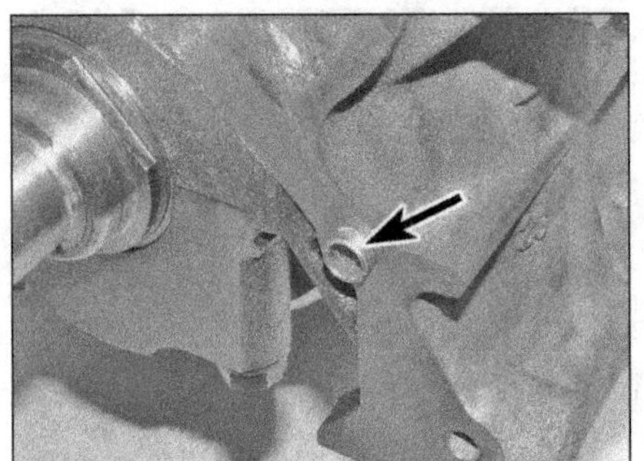
13.14c . . . onto the location dowels

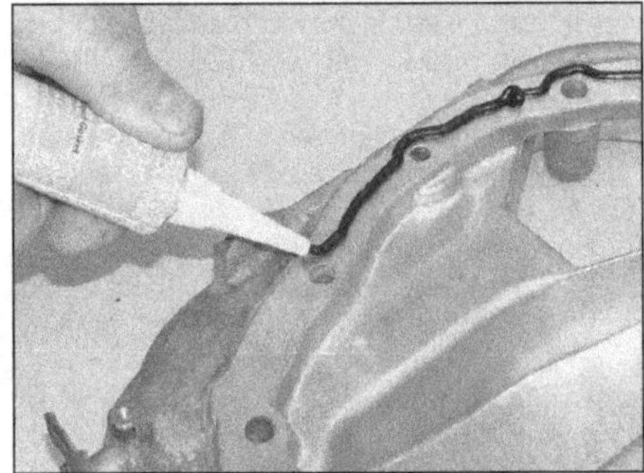
13.16 Apply a 4 to 7 mm wide bead of sealant to the upper sump housing

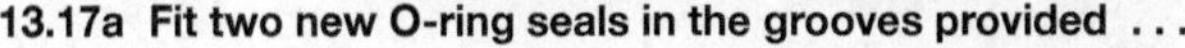

13.17a Fit two new O-ring seals in the grooves provided . . .

13.17b . . . then refit the upper housing

17 Fit two new O-ring seals, then refit the upper housing and progressively tighten the bolts to the specified torque **(see illustrations)**.

18 If removed, refit the oil filter housing together with a new O-ring seal, and tighten the mounting nuts/bolt.

19 Refit the sump insulator and tighten the bolt to the specified torque.

20 Refit the oil pick-up tube together with a new gasket, and tighten the nuts and bolts to the specified torque.

21 Refit the oil level sensor and tighten to the specified torque.

22 Refit the dipstick tube together with a new O-ring and tighten the support bolt.

23 Refit the auxiliary drivebelt adjustment bracket and tighten the bolts to the specified torque.

24 Refit the timing belt, crankshaft sprocket and front idler as described in Section 7.

25 Refit the sump as described in Section 12.

14 Flywheel – removal and refitting

Removal

1 The flywheel removal and refitting procedure is identical to that described in Chapter 2A, however, use the torque settings given in the Specifications at the beginning of this Chapter.

2 If necessary, for example to renew the crankshaft oil seal, unbolt and remove the engine endplate.

Refitting

3 Refitting is a reversal of removal.

15 Crankshaft left-hand oil seal – renewal

1 The transmission, flywheel and engine endplate must be removed from the vehicle for this procedure (see Chapter 7A and Section 14 of this Chapter).

2 The seal can be renewed without removing the sump, sump upper housing or the seal housing. However, this method is not recommended because the lip of the seal is quite stiff and it's possible to cock the seal in the housing bore or damage it during fitting. If you want to take the chance, prise out the old seal with a screwdriver. Apply multipurpose grease to the crankshaft seal journal and the lip of the new seal and carefully push the new seal into place. The lip is stiff so carefully work it onto the journal of the crankshaft with a smooth object like the end of an extension as you tap the seal into place. Don't rush it or you may damage the seal.

3 The following method is recommended but requires removal of the sump, sump upper housing and the seal housing. Refer to Sections 12 and 13 for the removal of the sump and upper housing, but do not remove the oil pump.

4 Unscrew the bolts and remove the seal housing, then clean away all traces of sealant from the housing and block.

5 Position the seal and housing assembly between two wood blocks on a workbench and drive the old seal out from the back side with a screwdriver.

6 Drive the new seal into the housing with a block of wood or a section of pipe slightly smaller in diameter than the outside diameter of the seal.

7 Apply a 2 mm to 3 mm wide bead of sealant to the flange of the housing, so that it is on the inner sides of the bolt holes.

8 Lubricate the crankshaft seal journal and the lip of the new seal with multipurpose grease.

9 Slowly and carefully push the seal and housing onto the crankshaft. The seal lip is stiff, so work it onto the crankshaft with a smooth object such as the end of an extension as you push the housing against the block.

10 Insert and tighten the housing bolts to the specified torque.

11 Refit the sump upper housing and the sump as described in Sections 12 and 13.

12 Refit the engine endplate, flywheel and transmission.

16 Engine mountings – removal and refitting

Refer to Chapter 2A.

Chapter 2 Part C: Engine removal and overhaul procedures

Contents

Degrees of difficulty

Easy, suitable for novice with little experience	**Fairly easy,** suitable for beginner with some experience	**Fairly difficult,** suitable for competent DIY mechanic	**Difficult,** suitable for experienced DIY mechanic	**Very difficult,** suitable for expert DIY or professional

Specifications

General

Engine codes:	
Petrol:	
1.4 litre (1398 cc)	4ZZ-FE
1.6 litre (1598 cc)	3ZZ-FE
Diesel (1995 cc)	1CD-FTV

Cylinder head

Warpage limits:	
Petrol engines:	
Block surface	0.05 mm
Manifold surfaces	0.10 mm
Diesel engine:	
Block surface	0.08 mm
Manifold surfaces	0.20 mm

Engine block

Petrol engines:	
Block warpage limit	0.05 mm
Cylinder bore diameter (nominal)	79.00 to 79.013 mm
Stroke:	
1.4 litre	71.3 mm
1.6 litre	81.5 mm
Diesel engine:	
Block warpage limit	0.05 mm
Cylinder bore diameter (nominal)	82.200 to 82.213 mm
Stroke	94.0 mm

Valves and related components

Petrol engines:	
Valve stem diameter:	
Inlet	5.470 to 5.485 mm
Exhaust	5.465 to 5.480 mm
Valve spring free length	43.40 mm
Diesel engine:	
Valve stem diameter:	
Inlet	5.970 to 5.985 mm
Exhaust	5.960 to 5.975 mm
Valve spring free length	40.45 mm

Crankshaft

Petrol engines:		
Crankshaft endfloat:		
Standard	0.04 to 0.24 mm	
Service limit	0.30 mm	
Thrustwasher thickness	2.430 to 2.480 mm	
Diesel engine:		
Crankshaft endfloat:		
Standard	0.04 to 0.24 mm	
Service limit	0.30 mm	
Thrustwasher thickness	2.680 to 2.730 mm	

Pistons and rings

Petrol engines:		
Piston diameter:		
1.4 litre engine	78.917 to 78.927 mm	
1.6 litre engine	78.955 to 78.965 mm	
Piston ring end gap:	**Standard**	**Service limit**
No 1 (top) compression ring	0.25 to 0.35 mm	1.05 mm
No 2 (middle) compression ring	0.35 to 0.50 mm	1.20 mm
Oil control ring	0.15 to 0.40 mm	1.05 mm
Diesel engine:		
Piston diameter	82.148 to 82.182 mm	
Piston ring end gap:	**Standard**	**Service limit**
No 1 (top) compression ring	0.27 to 0.43 mm	0.82 mm
No 2 (middle) compression ring	0.39 to 0.58 mm	1.00 mm
Oil control ring	0.20 to 0.44 mm	0.90 mm

Torque wrench settings

Refer to Chapter 2A or 2B as applicable for torque specifications.

1 General information

Included in this portion of Chapter 2 are the general overhaul procedures for the cylinder head and internal engine components.

The information ranges from advice concerning preparation for an overhaul and the purchase of new parts to detailed, step-by-step procedures covering removal and installation of internal engine components and the inspection of parts.

The following Sections have been written based on the assumption that the engine has been removed from the vehicle. For information concerning in-vehicle engine repair, as well as removal and installation of the external components necessary for the overhaul, see Chapter 2A or 2B and Section 6 of this Chapter.

The Specifications included in this Part are only those necessary for the inspection and overhaul procedures, which follow. Refer to Chapter 2A or 2B for additional Specifications.

2 Engine overhaul – general information

1 It is not always easy to determine when, or if, an engine should be completely overhauled, as a number of factors must be considered.

2 High mileage is not necessarily an indication that an overhaul is needed, while low mileage does not preclude the need for an overhaul. Frequency of servicing is probably the most important consideration. An engine, which has had regular and frequent oil and filter changes, as well as other required maintenance, should give many thousands of miles of reliable service. Conversely, a neglected engine may require an overhaul very early in its life.

3 Excessive oil consumption is an indication that piston rings, valve seals and/or valve guides are in need of attention. Make sure that oil leaks are not responsible before deciding that the rings and/or guides are worn. Perform a compression test, as described in Chapter 2A, to determine the likely cause of the problem, but note that introducing oil into the cylinder isn't a effective test for diesel engines.

4 Check the oil pressure with a gauge fitted in place of the oil pressure switch, and compare it with that specified. If it is extremely low, the main and big-end bearings, and/or the oil pump, are probably worn out.

5 Loss of power, rough running, knocking or metallic engine noises, excessive valve gear noise, and high fuel consumption may also point to the need for an overhaul, especially if they are all present at the same time. If a complete service does not remedy the situation, major mechanical work is the only solution.

6 A full engine overhaul involves restoring all internal parts to the specification of a new engine. During a complete overhaul, the pistons and the piston rings are renewed, and the cylinder bores are reconditioned. New main and big-end bearings are generally fitted; if necessary, the crankshaft may be reground, to compensate for wear in the journals. The valves are also serviced as well, since they are usually in less-than-perfect condition at this point. Always pay careful attention to the condition of the oil pump when overhauling the engine, and renew it if there is any doubt as to its serviceability. The end result should be an as-new engine that will give many trouble-free miles.

7 Critical cooling system components such as the hoses, thermostat and water pump should be renewed when an engine is overhauled. The radiator should be checked carefully, to ensure that it is not clogged or leaking. Also, it is a good idea to renew the oil pump whenever the engine is overhauled.

8 Before beginning the engine overhaul, read through the entire procedure, to familiarise yourself with the scope and requirements of the job. Overhauling an engine is not difficult if you follow carefully all of the instructions, have the necessary tools and equipment, and pay close attention to all specifications. It can, however, be time-consuming. Plan on the car being off the road for a minimum of two weeks, especially if parts must be taken to an engineering works for repair or reconditioning. Check on the availability of parts and make sure that any necessary special tools and equipment are obtained in advance. Most work can be done with typical hand tools, although a number of precision measuring tools are required for inspecting parts to determine if they must be renewed. Often the engineering works will handle the inspection of parts and offer advice concerning reconditioning and renewal.

9 Always wait until the engine has been completely dismantled, and until all components (especially the cylinder block/ crankcase and the crankshaft) have been inspected, before deciding what service and repair operations must be performed by an engineering works. The condition of these components will be the major factor to consider when determining whether to overhaul the original engine, or to buy a reconditioned unit. Do not, therefore, purchase parts or have overhaul work done on other components until they have been thoroughly inspected. As a general rule, time is the primary cost of an overhaul, so it does not pay to fit worn or sub-standard parts.

10 As a final note, to ensure maximum life and minimum trouble from a reconditioned engine, everything must be assembled with care, in a spotlessly-clean environment.

3 Engine removal – methods and precautions

1 If you have decided that the engine must be removed for overhaul or major repair work, several preliminary steps should be taken.

2 Locating a suitable place to work is extremely important. Adequate workspace, along with storage space for the car, will be needed. If a workshop or garage is not available, at the very least, a flat, level, clean work surface is required.

3 Cleaning the engine compartment and engine/transmission before beginning the removal procedure will help keep tools clean and organised.

4 An engine hoist or A-frame will also be necessary. Make sure the equipment is rated in excess of the weight of the engine. Safety is of primary importance, considering the potential hazards involved in lifting the engine/ transmission out of the car.

5 If this is the first time you have removed an engine, an assistant should ideally be available. Advice and aid from someone more experienced would also be helpful. There are many instances when one person cannot simultaneously perform all of the operations required when lifting the engine out of the vehicle.

6 Plan the operation ahead of time. Before starting work, arrange for the hire of or obtain all of the tools and equipment you will need. Some of the equipment necessary to perform engine/transmission removal and installation safely and with relative ease (in addition to an engine hoist) is as follows: a heavy duty trolley jack, complete sets of spanners and sockets (see *Tools and working facilities*), wooden blocks, and plenty of rags and cleaning solvent for mopping-up spilled oil, coolant and fuel. If the hoist must be hired, make sure that you arrange for it in advance, and perform all of the operations possible without it beforehand. This will save you money and time.

7 Plan for the car to be out of use for quite a while. An engineering works will be required to perform some of the work, which the do-it-yourselfer cannot accomplish without special equipment. These places often have a busy schedule, so it would be a good idea to consult them before removing the engine, in order to accurately estimate the amount of time required to rebuild or repair components that may need work.

8 Always be extremely careful when removing and refitting the engine/transmission. Serious injury can result from careless actions. Plan ahead and take your time, and a job of this nature, although major, can be accomplished successfully.

Note: *Such is the complexity of the power unit arrangement on these vehicles, and the variations that may be encountered according to model and optional equipment fitted, that the following should be regarded as a guide to the work involved, rather than a step-by-step procedure. Where differences are encountered, or additional component disconnection or removal is necessary, make notes of the work involved as an aid to refitting.*

4 Engine – removal and refitting

Note: *Read through the entire Section before beginning this procedure. The factory recommends removing the engine and transmission from the top as a unit, then separating the engine from the transmission on the workshop floor. If the transmission is not being serviced, it is possible to leave the transmission in the vehicle and remove the engine from the top by itself, by removing the crankshaft pulley and tilting up the timing belt/ chain end of the engine for clearance.*

Warning: These models are equipped with airbags. The airbag is armed and can deploy (inflate) anytime the battery is connected. To prevent accidental deployment (and possible injury), turn the ignition key to LOCK and disconnect the negative battery cable whenever working near airbag components. After the battery is disconnected, wait at least two minutes before beginning work (the system has a back-up capacitor that must fully discharge). For more information see Chapter 12.

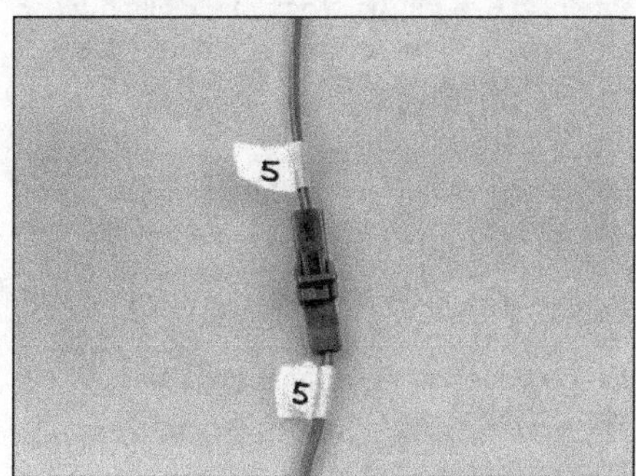

4.6 Label both ends of each wire and hose before disconnecting it

Removal

1 Relieve the fuel system pressure (see Chapter 4A). On diesel models, cover any connections with cloth and undo them.

2 Remove the battery as described in Chapter 5A, then lift out the plastic battery tray.

3 Remove the bonnet as described in Chapter 11.

4 Remove the air cleaner assembly (see Chapter 4A or 4B).

5 Raise the vehicle and support it securely on axle stands. Drain the cooling system and engine oil and remove the drivebelts (see Chapter 1A or 1B).

6 Clearly label, and then disconnect, all vacuum lines, coolant and emissions hoses, wiring harness connectors, earth straps and fuel lines. Masking tape and/or a touch up paint applicator work well for marking items **(see illustration)**. Take photos or sketch the locations of components and brackets.

7 Remove the windscreen washer tank and coolant reservoir tank.

8 Remove the cooling fan(s) and radiator (see Chapter 3).

9 Disconnect the heater hoses.

10 Release the residual fuel pressure in the tank by removing the fuel tank cap, then detach the fuel lines connecting the engine to the chassis. Plug or cap all open fittings.

11 Disconnect the accelerator cable, transmission Throttle Valve (TV) linkage and speed control cable, if equipped, from the engine.

12 Refer Chapter 4A or 2B and remove the inlet and exhaust manifolds.

13 On air conditioned models, unbolt the compressor and set it aside. Do not disconnect the refrigerant hoses. **Note:** *Don't let the compressor hang on the hoses.*

14 Attach a lifting sling to the engine.

15 Position a hoist and connect the sling to it. Take up the slack until there is slight tension on the hoist.

16 Refer to Chapter 8 and remove the driveshafts.

17 Remove the auxiliary drivebelt(s), coolant pump pulley and crankshaft pulley.

18 On automatic transmission-equipped models, pry out the plastic torque converter dust shield from the lower bellhousing. Remove the torque converter-to-driveplate fasteners (see Chapter 7B) and push the converter back slightly into the bellhousing.

19 Remove the engine-to-transmission bolts and separate the engine from the transmission (see Chapter 7A or 7B). The torque converter should remain in the transmission. **Note:** *If the transmission is to be removed at the same time, the left-side engine mounting should be removed, along with any wires, cables or hoses connected to the transmission. The engine-to-transmission bolts should remain in place at this time.*

20 Recheck to be sure nothing except the mountings are still connecting the engine to the vehicle or to the transmission. Disconnect and label anything still remaining.

21 Support the transmission with a trolley jack. Place a block of wood on the jack head to prevent damage to the transmission. Remove the bolts from the engine mountings, leaving those attached to the transmission in place.

Warning: Do not place any part of your body under the engine/transmission when its supported only by a hoist or other lifting device.

22 Slowly lift the engine (or engine/transmission) out of the vehicle **(see illustration)**. It may be necessary to lever the mountings away from the frame brackets. **Note:** *When removing the engine from a manual transmission-equipped vehicle and the transmission is to remain in the vehicle, you may have to use the jack supporting the transmission to tilt the transmission enough to allow the engine to be angled out of the vehicle.*

23 Move the engine away from the vehicle and carefully lower the hoist until the engine can be set on the floor; or remove the flywheel/driveplate and mount the engine on an engine stand. **Note:** *On automatic transmission-equipped models, mark the front and rear spacer plates (where fitted) and keep them with the driveplate.*

Refitting

24 Check the engine/transmission mountings. If they're worn or damaged, renew them.

25 On manual transmission-equipped models, inspect the clutch components (see Chapter 6) and on automatic models inspect the converter seal and bushing.

26 On automatic transmission-equipped models, apply a dab of grease to the nose of the converter.

27 Carefully guide the transmission into place, following the procedure outlined in Chapter 7A or 7B.

4.22 Lift the engine out of the vehicle

Caution: Do not use the bolts to force the engine and transmission into alignment. They may crack or damage major components.

28 Install the engine-to-transmission bolts and tighten them to the torque listed in the Chapter 7A or 7B Specifications.

29 Attach the hoist to the engine and carefully lower the engine/transmission assembly into the engine compartment. **Note:** *If the engine was removed with the transmission remaining in the car, lower the engine into the car until an assistant can help you line up the dowel pins on the block with the transmission. Some twisting and angling of the engine and/or the transmission will be necessary to secure proper alignment of the two.*

30 Install the mounting bolts and tighten them securely.

31 Reinstall the remaining components and fasteners in the reverse order of removal.

32 Add coolant, oil and transmission fluids as needed (see Chapter 1A or 1B).

33 Run the engine and check for proper operation and leaks. Shut off the engine and recheck the fluid levels.

5 Engine rebuilding alternatives

The do-it-yourselfer is faced with a number of options when performing an engine overhaul. The decision to renew the engine block, piston/connecting rod assemblies and crankshaft depends on a number of factors, with the number one consideration being the condition of the block. Other considerations are cost, access to machine shop facilities, parts availability, time required to complete the project and the extent of prior mechanical experience on the part of the do-it-yourselfer.

Some of the rebuilding alternatives include:

Individual parts

If the inspection procedures reveal that the engine block and most engine components are in re-usable condition, purchasing individual parts may be the most economical alternative. The block, crankshaft and piston/connecting rod assemblies should all be inspected carefully. Even if the block shows little wear, the cylinder bores should be surface honed.

Short engine

A short engine consists of an engine block with a crankshaft and piston/connecting rod assemblies already installed. All new bearings are incorporated and all clearances will be correct. The existing camshafts, valve train components, cylinder head and external parts can be bolted to the short engine with little or no machine shop work necessary.

Reconditioned engine

A reconditioned engine usually consists of a short engine plus an oil pump, oil sump, cylinder head, valve cover, camshaft and valve train components, timing sprockets and timing belt/chain covers. All components are installed with new bearings, seals and gaskets incorporated throughout. The installation of manifolds and external parts is all that's necessary.

Give careful thought to which alternative is best for you and discuss the situation with local automotive machine shops, auto parts dealers and experienced rebuilders before ordering or purchasing new parts.

6 Engine overhaul – disassembly sequence

1 It's much easier to disassemble and work on the engine if it's mounted on a portable engine stand. A stand can often be rented quite cheaply from an equipment rental yard. Before the engine is mounted on a stand, the flywheel/driveplate and oil seal housing should be removed from the engine.

2 If a stand isn't available, it's possible to disassemble the engine with it blocked up on the floor. Be extra careful not to tip or drop the engine when working without a stand.

3 If you're going to obtain a reconditioned engine, all external components must come off first, to be transferred to the new engine, just as they will if you're doing a complete engine overhaul yourself. These include:

Alternator and brackets.
Emissions control components.
Thermostat and housing cover.
Coolant pump and remaining cooling system components.
EFI components (sensors, etc).
Glowplug/preheating system components (diesel models).
Ignition coils (petrol models).
Inlet/exhaust manifolds.
Engine mountings.
Clutch and flywheel/driveplate.
Engine endplate.

Note: *When removing the external components from the engine, pay close attention to details that may be helpful or important during installation. Note the installed position of gaskets, seals, spacers, pins, brackets, washers, bolts and other small items.*

4 If you're obtaining a short engine, which consists of the engine block, crankshaft, pistons and connecting rods all assembled, then the cylinder head, oil sump and oil pump will have to be removed as well from your engine. See *Engine rebuilding alternatives* for additional information regarding the different possibilities to be considered.

5 If you're planning a complete overhaul, the engine must be disassembled and the internal components removed in the following order.

Inlet and exhaust manifolds.
Cylinder head cover.
Timing belt/chain covers.
Timing belt/chain and sprockets.

7.2 A small plastic bag, with an appropriate label, can be used to store the valve components

7.3 Compress the spring until the collets can be removed with a small magnetic screwdriver or thin-nosed pliers

Cylinder head.
Oil sump.
Oil pump.
Piston/connecting rod assemblies.
Crankshaft oil seal housing.
Crankshaft and main bearings.

7 Cylinder head – disassembly

Note: *New and reconditioned cylinder heads can be obtained from the manufacturer and engine overhaul specialists. Be aware that some specialist tools are required for the dismantling and inspection procedures, and new components may not be readily available. It may therefore be more practical and economical for the home mechanic to purchase a reconditioned head, rather than dismantle, inspect and recondition the original head.*

1 Cylinder head disassembly involves removal of the inlet and exhaust valves and related components. It's assumed that the followers and camshafts have already been removed (see Chapter 2A or 2B as needed).

2 Before the valves are removed, arrange to label and store them, along with their related components, so they can be kept separate and reinstalled in the same valve guides they are removed from **(see illustration)**.

3 Compress the springs on the first valve with a spring compressor and remove the collets **(see illustration)**.

4 Carefully release the valve spring compressor and remove the retainer, the spring and the spring seat (where fitted) **(see illustrations)**.

Caution: Be very careful not to nick or otherwise damage the follower bores when compressing the valve springs.

5 Pull the valve out of the head, then remove the oil seal from the guide **(see illustrations)**. If the valve binds in the guide (won't pull through), push it back into the head and deburr the area around the keeper groove (where collets locate) with a fine file or whetstone.

6 Repeat the procedure for the remaining valves. Remember to keep all the parts for each valve together so they can be reinstalled in the same locations.

7 Once the valves and related components have been removed and stored in an organised manner, the head should be thoroughly cleaned and inspected. If a complete engine overhaul is being done, finish the engine disassembly procedures before beginning the cylinder head cleaning and inspection process.

7.4a Remove the spring retaining washer . . .

7.4b . . . spring . . .

7.4c . . . and the spring seating washer

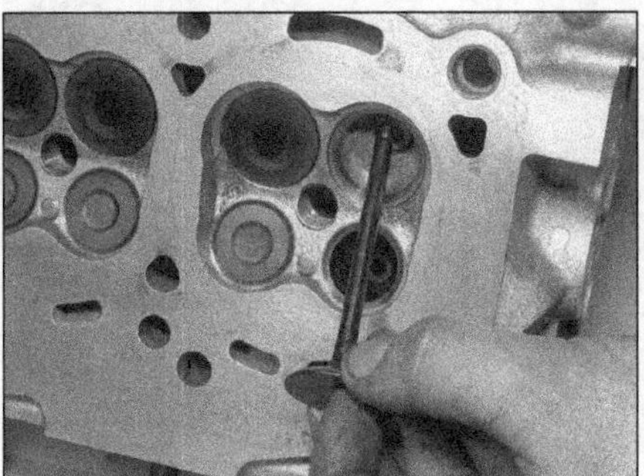

7.5a Remove the valve . . .

7.5b . . . and then the valve stem oil seal

8 Cylinder head - cleaning and inspection

1 Thorough cleaning of the cylinder head and related valve train components, followed by a detailed inspection, will enable you to decide how much valve service work must be done during the engine overhaul. **Note:** *If the engine was severely overheated, it is best to assume that the cylinder head is warped - check carefully for signs of this (see paragraph 12).*

Cleaning

2 Scrape all traces of old gasket material and sealing compound off the head gasket, inlet manifold and exhaust manifold sealing surfaces. Be very careful not to gouge the cylinder head. Special gasket removal solvents that soften gaskets and make removal much easier are available at automotive accessory/ parts retailers.

3 Remove all built-up scale from the coolant passages.

4 Run a stiff wire brush through the various holes to remove deposits that may have formed in them. If there are heavy rust deposits in the water passages, the bare head should be professionally cleaned.

5 Run an appropriate-size tap into each of the threaded holes to remove corrosion and thread sealant that may be present. If compressed air is available, use it to clear the holes of debris produced by this operation.

Warning: Wear eye protection when using compressed air.

6 Clean the exhaust and inlet manifold stud threads with a wire brush.

7 Clean the cylinder head with solvent and dry it thoroughly. Compressed air will speed the drying process and ensure that all holes and recessed areas are clean. **Note:** *Decarbonising chemicals are available and may prove very useful when cleaning cylinder heads and valve train components. They are very caustic and should be used with caution. Be sure to follow the instructions on the container.*

8 Clean the followers with solvent and dry them thoroughly. Compressed air will speed the drying process and can be used to clean

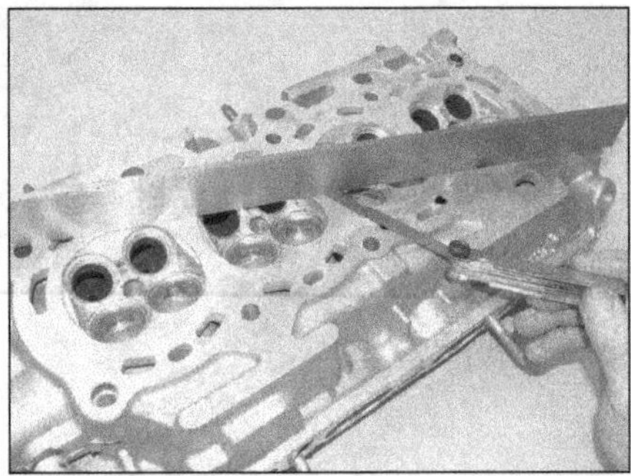

8.12 Check the cylinder head gasket surface for warpage by trying to slip a feeler gauge under the straight-edge

out the oil passages. Don't mix them up during the cleaning process; keep them in a box with numbered compartments.

9 Clean all the valve springs, spring seats, collets and retainers with solvent and dry them thoroughly. Work on the components from one valve at a time to avoid mixing up the parts.

10 Scrape off any heavy deposits that may have formed on the valves, then use a motorised wire brush to remove deposits from the valve heads and stems. Again, make sure the valves don't get mixed up.

Inspection

Note: *Be sure to perform all of the following inspection procedures before concluding that machine shop work is required. Make a list of the items that need attention. The inspection procedures for the followers and camshafts can be found in Chapter 2A or 2B.*

Cylinder head

11 Inspect the head very carefully for cracks, evidence of coolant leakage and other damage. If cracks are found, check with an automotive machine workshop concerning repair. If repair isn't possible, a new cylinder head should be obtained.

12 Using a straight-edge and feeler gauge, check the head gasket mating surface for warpage **(see illustration)**. If the warpage exceeds the limit found in this Chapter's Specifications, it can be resurfaced at an automotive machining workshop.

13 Examine the valve seats in each of the combustion chambers. If they're pitted, cracked or burned, the head will require valve service that's beyond the scope of the home mechanic.

14 If in any doubt as to the condition of the cylinder head, have it inspected by an automotive engine overhaul specialist.

Valves

15 Carefully inspect each valve face for uneven wear, deformation, cracks, pits and burned areas. Check the valve stem for scuffing and galling and the neck for cracks. Rotate the valve and check for any obvious indication that it's bent. Look for pits and excessive wear on the end of the stem. The presence of any of these conditions indicates the need for valve service by an automotive machine shop.

16 If in any doubt as to the condition of the valves, have them inspected by an automotive engine overhaul specialist.

Valve components

17 Check each valve spring for wear (on the ends) and pits. Measure the free length and compare it to this Chapter's Specifications **(see illustration)**. Any springs that are shorter than specified have sagged and should not be re-used.

18 Stand each spring on a flat surface and check it for squareness **(see illustration)**. If any of the springs are distorted or sagged, renew all of them.

19 Check the spring seats and collets for obvious wear and cracks. Any questionable parts should be renewed, as extensive damage will occur if they fail during engine operation.

20 Any damaged or excessively worn parts must be renewed.

21 If the inspection process indicates that the valve components are in generally poor condition and worn beyond the limits specified, which is usually the case in an engine that's being overhauled, reassemble the valves in the cylinder head and refer to Section 9 for valve servicing recommendations.

9 Valves - servicing

1 Because of the complex nature of the job and the special tools and equipment needed, servicing of the valves, the valve seats and the valve guides, should be done by a professional.

2 The home mechanic can remove and disassemble the head, do the initial cleaning and inspection, then reassemble and deliver them to an automotive engine overhaul specialist for the actual service work. Doing the inspection will enable you to see what condition the head and valve train components are in and will ensure that you know what work and new parts are required when dealing with the overhaul specialist.

3 The engine overhaul specialist will remove the valves and springs, recondition or renew

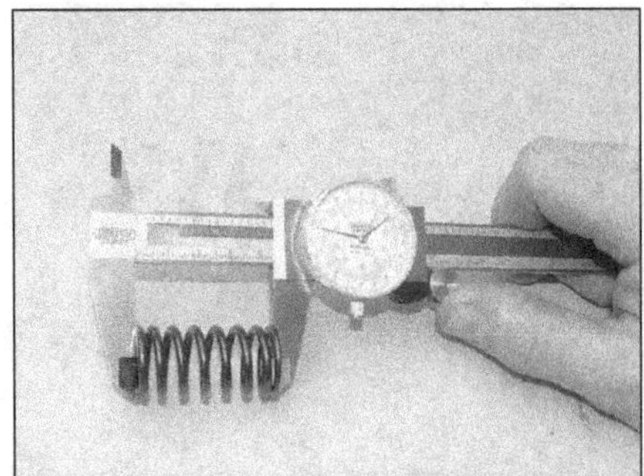

8.17 Measure the free length of each valve spring

8.18 Check each valve spring for squareness

the valves and valve seats, recondition the valve guides, check and renew the valve springs, spring retainers and collets (as necessary), renew the valve seals, reassemble the valve components and make sure the installed spring height is correct. The cylinder head gasket surface will also be resurfaced if it's warped.

4 After a professional has performed this work, the head will be in like new condition. When the head is returned, be sure to clean it again before installation on the engine to remove any metal particles and abrasive grit that may still be present from the valve service or head resurfacing operations. Use compressed air, if available, to blow out all the oil holes and passages.

Warning: Wear eye protection when using compressed air.

10 Cylinder head – reassembly

1 Regardless of whether or not the head was sent for reconditioning, make sure it's clean before beginning reassembly.

2 If the head was sent out for valve servicing, the valves and related components will already be in place.

3 Install new seals on each of the valve guides. On early engines, the inlet seal *body* is grey and the exhaust seal *body* is black. On later engines, it may be possible to see identification marks on the top of the seal face (you will probably need a magnifying glass to see this). With careful observation it will be seen that the exhaust valve stem seals are marked EX, and the inlet seals are marked IN **(see illustration) Note:** *Inlet and exhaust valves require different seals – DO NOT mix them up.*

4 Gently tap each inlet valve seal into place until it's seated on the guide **(see illustration)**.

Caution: Don't hammer on the valve seals once they're seated or you may damage them. Don't twist or cock the seals during installation or they won't seat properly on the valve stems.

5 Beginning at one end of the head, lubricate and install the first valve **(see illustration)**. Apply clean engine oil to the valve stem.

6 Drop the spring seat or shim(s) over the valve guide and set the valve spring and retainer in place.

7 Compress the springs with a valve spring compressor and carefully install the collets in the upper groove, then slowly release the compressor and make sure the collets seat properly. Apply a small dab of grease to each collet to hold it in place if necessary **(see illustration)**.

8 Repeat the procedure for the remaining valves. Be sure to return the components to their original locations – don't mix them up.

10.3 The exhaust valve stem seals are marked EX and the inlet seals are marked IN

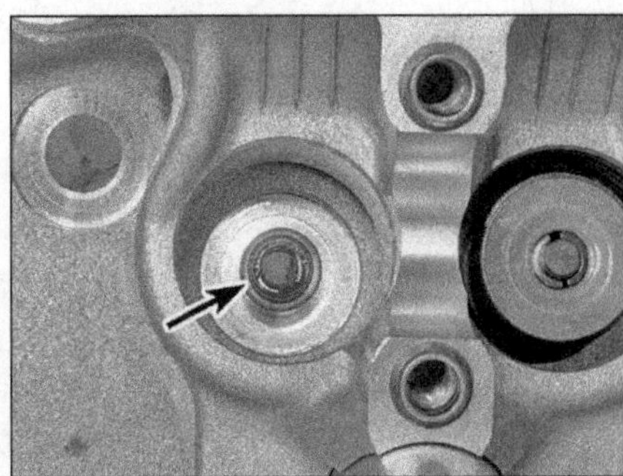

10.4 Tap the valve stem seals (arrowed) into place with a deep socket and hammer

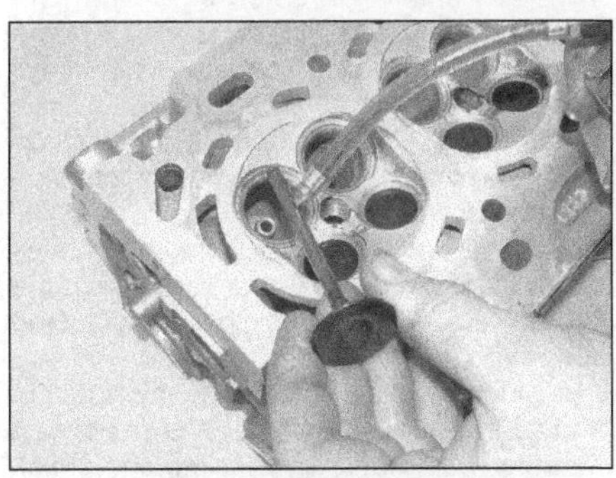

10.5 Lubricate the stems of the valves before inserting them into their guides

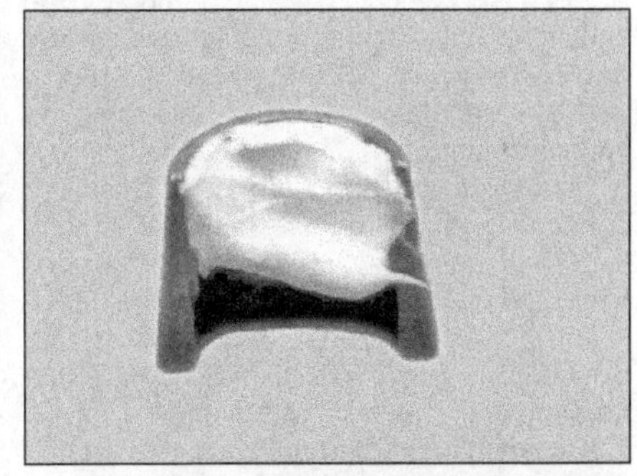

10.7 The small valve stem collets are easier to position when coated with grease

11 Pistons/connecting rods – removal

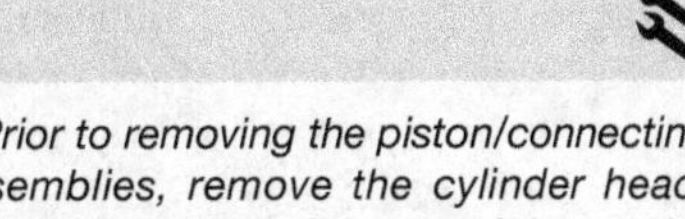

Note: *Prior to removing the piston/connecting rod assemblies, remove the cylinder head, the oil sump and the oil pump pick-up tube by referring to the appropriate Sections in Chapter 2A or 2B.*

1 Use your fingernail to feel if a ridge has formed at the upper limit of ring travel (about 8 mm down from the top of each cylinder). If carbon deposits or cylinder wear have produced ridges, they must be completely removed with a special tool **(see illustration)**. Follow the manufacturer's instructions provided with the tool. Failure to remove the ridges before attempting to remove the piston/connecting rod assemblies may result in piston damage.

2 After the cylinder ridges have been removed, turn the engine upside-down so the crankshaft is facing up.

3 Check the connecting rods and caps for identification marks. If they aren't plainly marked, use a small centre punch to make the appropriate number of indentations on each rod and cap (1, 2, 3, etc, depending on the cylinder they're associated with) **(see illustration)**.

4 Loosen each of the connecting rod cap nuts/bolts ½ turn at a time until they can be removed by hand. Remove the number one connecting rod cap and bearing shell. Don't drop the bearing shell out of the cap.

11.1 A ridge reamer is required to remove the ridge from the top of each cylinder

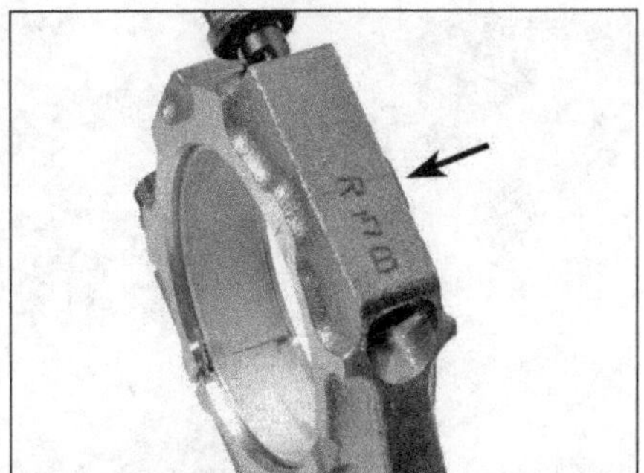

11.3 Do not confuse these markings as rod numbers; they are bearing size identifications

11.5 Slip sections of hose over the rod bolts before removing the pistons

5 Slip a short length of plastic or rubber hose over each connecting rod cap bolt (where applicable) to protect the crankshaft journal and cylinder wall as the piston is removed **(see illustration)**.

6 Remove the bearing shell and push the connecting rod/piston assembly out through the top of the engine. Use a wooden hammer handle to push on the upper bearing surface in the connecting rod. If resistance is felt, double-check to make sure that the entire ridge was removed from the cylinder.

7 Repeat the procedure for the remaining cylinders. **Note:** *Turn the crankshaft as needed to put the rod to be removed close to parallel with the cylinder bore, ie, don't try to drive it out while at a large angle to the bore.*

8 After removal, reassemble the connecting rod caps and bearing shells in their respective connecting rods and install the cap nuts/bolts finger tight. Leaving the old bearing shells in place until reassembly will help prevent the connecting rod bearing surfaces from being accidentally nicked or gouged.

9 Don't separate the pistons from the connecting rods (see Section 15 for additional information).

12 Crankshaft – removal

Note: *The crankshaft can be removed only after the engine has been removed from the vehicle. It's assumed that the flywheel or driveplate, crankshaft sprocket, timing belt/chain, oil sump, oil pick-up tube, oil pump and piston/connecting rod assemblies have already been removed. The left-hand oil seal and housing (where applicable) must be removed from the block before proceeding with crankshaft removal.*

1 Before the crankshaft is removed, check the endfloat. Mount a dial indicator with the stem in line with the crankshaft throws **(see illustration)**.

2 Push the crankshaft fully one way and zero the dial indicator. Next, lever the crankshaft the other way as far as possible and check the reading on the dial indicator. The distance that it moves is the endfloat. If it's greater than specified, check the crankshaft thrust surfaces for wear. If no wear is evident, new thrustwashers should correct the endfloat.

3 If a dial indicator isn't available, feeler gauges can be used. Gently pry or push the crankshaft fully one way. Slip feeler gauges between the crankshaft and the face of the number 3 (thrust) main bearing to determine the clearance **(see illustration)**.

4 Working is the **reverse** of the tightening sequence **(see illustration 20.10)**, gradually and evenly slacken and remove the bolts securing the main bearing ladder/sump upper housing to the engine block.

5 Use a flat-bladed screwdriver to gently prise the main bearing ladder/sump upper housing from the engine block at the cast-in leverage points. Ensure the lower bearing shells stay in their original positions in the bearing ladder/sump upper housing.

6 Carefully lift the crankshaft out of the engine. It may be a good idea to have an assistant available, since the crankshaft is quite heavy. With the bearing shells in place in the engine block and main bearing cap assembly, return the ladder/sump upper housing to the engine block and tighten the bolts finger tight.

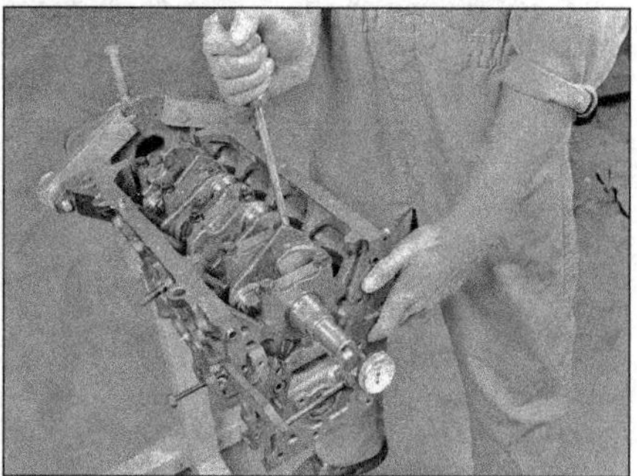

12.1 Check the crankshaft endfloat with a dial indicator . . .

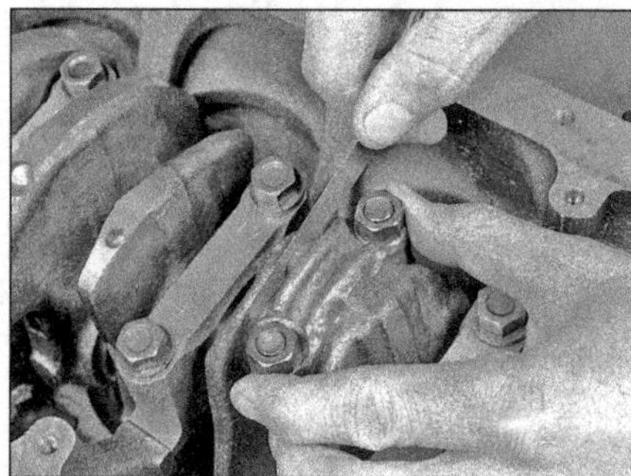

12.3 . . . or a feeler gauge

13.1a Use a hammer and punch to knock the core plugs sideways in their bores

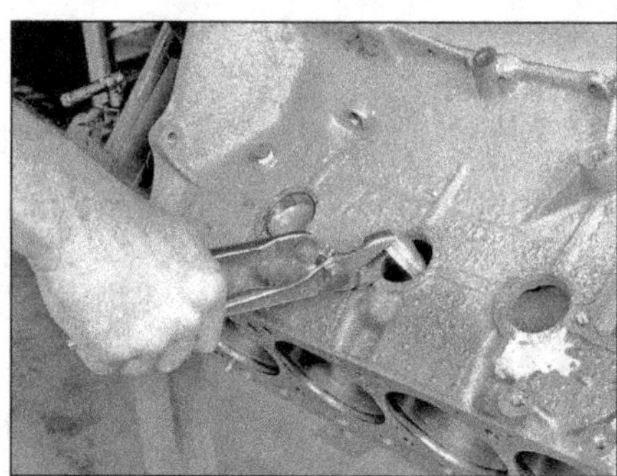

13.1b Pull the core plugs from the block with pliers

13 Engine block – cleaning

Caution: The core plugs may be difficult or impossible to retrieve if they're driven completely into the block coolant passages.

1 Using the blunt end of a punch, tap in on the outer edge of the core plug to turn the plug sideways in the bore. Then using pliers, pull the core plug from the engine block **(see illustrations)**.

2 Using a gasket scraper, remove all traces of gasket material from the engine block. Be very careful not to nick or gouge the gasket sealing surfaces.

3 Remove the main bearing cap assembly and separate the bearing shells from the caps and the engine block. Tag the bearings, indicating which cylinder they were removed from and whether they were in the cap or the block, then set them aside.

4 Remove all of the threaded oil gallery plugs from the block. The plugs are usually very tight – they may have to be drilled out and the holes retapped. Use new plugs when the engine is reassembled.

5 If the engine is extremely dirty, it should be steam cleaned.

6 After the block is returned, clean all oil holes and oil galleries one more time. Brushes specifically designed for this purpose are available at most automotive accessory retailers. Flush the passages with warm water until the water runs clear, dry the block thoroughly and wipe all machined surfaces with a light, rust preventive oil. If you have access to compressed air, use it to speed the drying process and to blow out all the oil holes and galleries.

Warning: Wear eye protection when using compressed air.

7 If the block isn't extremely dirty or sludged

up, you can do an adequate cleaning job with hot soapy water and a stiff brush. Take plenty of time and do a thorough job. Regardless of the cleaning method used, be sure to clean all oil holes and galleries very thoroughly, dry the block completely and coat all machined surfaces with light oil.

8 The threaded holes in the block must be clean to ensure accurate torque readings during reassembly. Run the proper size tap into each of the holes to remove rust, corrosion, thread sealant or sludge and restore damaged threads **(see illustration)**. If possible, use compressed air to clear the holes of debris produced by this operation. Now is a good time to clean the threads on the head bolts and the main bearing cap bolts as well.

9 Reinstall the main bearing caps and tighten the bolts finger tight.

10 After coating the sealing surfaces of the new core plugs with sealant, install them in the engine block **(see illustration)**. Make sure they're driven in straight and seated properly or leakage could result. Special tools are available for this purpose, but a large socket, with an outside diameter that will just slip into the core plug; a ½ inch drive extension and a hammer will work just as well.

11 Apply non-hardening sealant to the new oil gallery plugs and thread them into the holes in the block. Make sure they're tightened securely.

12 If the engine isn't going to be reassembled right away, cover it with a large plastic bag to keep it clean.

14 Engine block – inspection

1 Before the block is inspected, it should be cleaned as described in Section 13.

2 Visually check the block for cracks, rust and corrosion. Look for stripped threads in the threaded holes. It's also a good idea to have the block checked for hidden cracks by an engine overhaul specialist that has the equipment to do this type of work, especially if the vehicle had a history of overheating or using coolant. If defects are found, have the block repaired, if possible, or renewed.

13.8 All bolt holes in the block should be cleaned and restored with a tap

13.10 A large socket can be used to drive the new core plugs into the bores

3 If in any doubt as to the condition of the cylinder block, have it inspected and measured by an engine reconditioning specialist. If the bores are worn or damaged, they will be able to carry out any necessary reboring, and supply appropriate oversized pistons, etc.

15 Pistons/connecting rods – inspection

1 Before the inspection process can be carried out, the piston/connecting rod assemblies must be cleaned and the original piston rings removed from the pistons. **Note:** *Always use new piston rings when the engine is reassembled.*

2 Carefully expand the old rings over the top of the pistons. The use of two or three old feeler blades will be helpful in preventing the rings dropping into empty grooves **(see illustration)**. Be careful not to scratch the piston with the ends of the ring. The rings are brittle, and will snap if they are spread too far. They are also very sharp – protect your hands and fingers.

3 Scrape all traces of carbon from the top of the piston. A hand-held wire brush or a piece of fine emery cloth can be used once the majority of the deposits have been scraped away. Do not, under any circumstances, use a wire brush mounted in a drill motor to remove deposits from the pistons. The piston material is soft and may be eroded away by the wire brush.

4 Use a piston ring groove-cleaning tool to remove carbon deposits from the ring grooves. If a tool isn't available, a piece broken off the old ring will do the job. Be very careful to remove only the carbon deposits – don't remove any metal and do not nick or scratch the sides of the ring grooves **(see illustrations)**.

5 Once the deposits have been removed, clean the piston/rod assemblies with solvent and dry them with compressed air (if available). Make sure the oil return holes in the back sides of the ring grooves and the oil hole in the lower end of each rod are clear.

6 If the pistons and cylinder walls aren't damaged or worn excessively, and if the engine block is not rebored, new pistons won't be necessary. Normal piston wear appears as even vertical wear on the piston thrust surfaces and slight looseness of the top ring in its groove. New piston rings, however, should always be used when an engine is rebuilt.

7 Carefully inspect each piston for cracks around the skirt, at the pin bosses and at the ring lands.

8 Look for scoring and scuffing on the thrust faces of the skirt, holes in the piston crown and burned areas at the edge of the crown. If the skirt is scored or scuffed, the engine may have been suffering from overheating and/or abnormal combustion, which caused excessively high operating temperatures. The cooling and lubrication systems should be checked thoroughly. A hole in the piston crown is an indication that abnormal combustion (pre-ignition) was occurring. Burned areas at the edge of the piston crown are usually

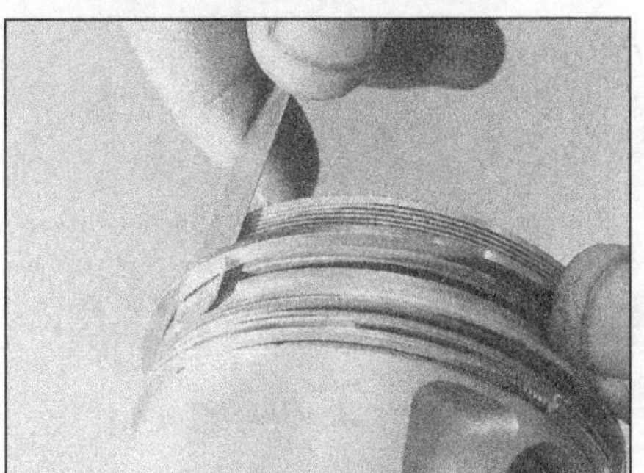

15.2 Use old feeler gauge blades to carefully expand the piston rings

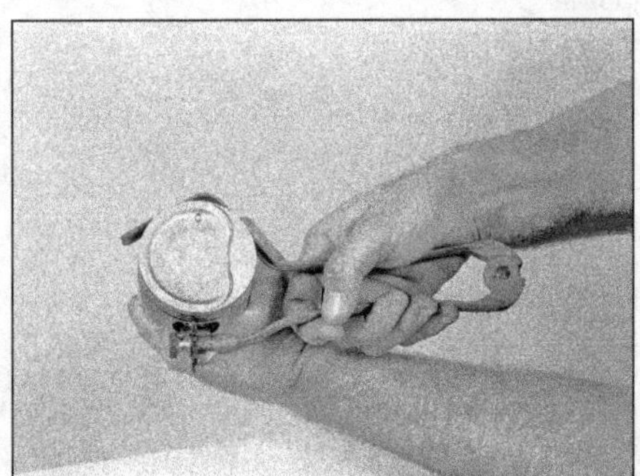

15.4a The ring grooves can be cleaned with a special tool, as shown here . . .

15.4b . . . or a section of broken ring

evidence of spark knock (detonation). If any of the above problems exist, the causes must be corrected or the damage will occur again. The causes may include inlet air leaks, incorrect air/fuel mixture, incorrect ignition timing and EGR system malfunctions.

9 Corrosion of the piston, in the form of small pits, indicates that coolant is leaking into the combustion chamber and/or the crankcase. Again, the cause must be corrected or the problem may persist in the rebuilt engine.

10 If in any doubt as to the condition of the pistons and connecting rods, have them inspected and measured by an engine reconditioning specialist. If new parts are required, they will be able to supply appropriate-sized pistons/rings, and rebore the cylinder block (where necessary).

16 Crankshaft - inspection

1 Clean the crankshaft using paraffin or a suitable solvent, and dry it, preferably with compressed air if available. Be sure to clean the oil holes with a pipe cleaner or similar probe, to ensure that they are not obstructed.

Warning: Wear eye protection when using compressed air.

2 Check the main and big-end bearing journals for uneven wear, scoring, pitting and cracking.

3 Big-end bearing wear is accompanied by distinct metallic knocking when the engine is running (particularly noticeable when the engine is pulling from low speed) and some loss of oil pressure.

4 Main bearing wear is accompanied by severe engine vibration and rumble – getting progressively worse as engine speed increases – and again by loss of oil pressure.

5 Check the bearing journal for roughness by running a finger lightly over the bearing surface. Any roughness (which will be accompanied by obvious bearing wear) indicates that the crankshaft requires regrinding (where possible) or renewal.

6 If the crankshaft has been reground, check for burrs around the crankshaft oil holes (the holes are usually chamfered, so burrs should not be a problem unless regrinding has been carried out carelessly). Remove any burrs with a fine file or scraper, and thoroughly clean the oil holes as described previously.

7 Have the crankshaft journals measured by an automotive engineering workshop. If the crankshaft is worn or damaged, they may be able to regrind the journals and supply suitable undersize bearing shells. If no undersize shells are available and the crankshaft has worn beyond the specified limits, it will have to be renewed. Consult your Toyota dealer or engine specialist for further information on parts availability.

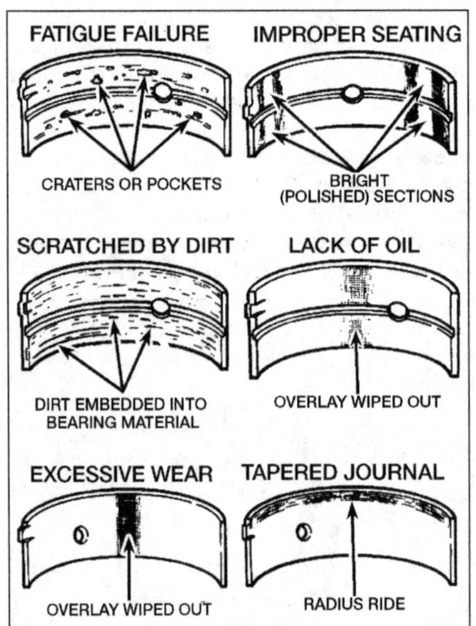

17.1 Typical bearing failures

17 Main and connecting rod bearings - inspection

1 Even though the main and connecting rod bearings should be renewed during the engine overhaul, the old bearings should be retained for close examination, as they may reveal valuable information about the condition of the engine **(see illustration)**.

2 Bearing failure occurs because of lack of lubrication, the presence of dirt or other foreign particles, overloading the engine and corrosion. Regardless of the cause of bearing failure, it must be corrected before the engine is reassembled to prevent it from happening again.

3 When examining the bearings, remove them from the engine block, the main bearing caps, the connecting rods and the rod caps and lay them out on a clean surface in the same general position as their location in the engine. This will enable you to match any bearing problems with the corresponding crankshaft journal.

4 Dirt and other foreign particles get into the engine in a variety of ways. It may be left in the engine during assembly, or it may pass through filters or the PCV system. It may get into the oil, and from there into the bearings. Metal chips from machining operations and normal engine wear are often present. Abrasives are sometimes left in engine components after reconditioning, especially when parts are not thoroughly cleaned using the proper cleaning methods. Whatever the source, these foreign objects often end up embedded in the soft bearing material and are easily recognised. Large particles will not embed in the bearing and will score or gouge the bearing and journal. The best prevention for this cause of bearing failure is to clean all parts thoroughly and keep everything spotlessly clean during engine assembly. Frequent and regular engine oil and filter changes are also recommended.

5 Lack of lubrication (or lubrication breakdown) has a number of interrelated causes. Excessive heat (which thins the oil), overloading (which squeezes the oil from the bearing face) and oil leakage or throw off (from excessive bearing clearances, worn oil pump or high engine speeds) all contribute to lubrication breakdown. Blocked oil passages, which usually are the result of misaligned oil holes in a bearing shell, will also oil starve a bearing and destroy it. When lack of lubrication is the cause of bearing failure, the bearing material is wiped or extruded from the steel backing of the bearing. Temperatures may increase to the point where the steel backing turns blue from overheating.

6 Driving habits can have a definite effect on bearing life. Low speed operation in too high a gear (lugging the engine) puts very high loads on bearings, which tends to squeeze out the oil film. These loads cause the bearings to flex, which produces fine cracks in the bearing face (fatigue failure). Eventually the bearing material will loosen in pieces and tear away from the steel backing. Short trip driving leads to corrosion of bearings because insufficient engine heat is produced to drive off the condensed water and corrosive gases. These products collect in the engine oil, forming acid and sludge. As the oil is carried to the engine bearings, the acid attacks and corrodes the bearing material.

7 Incorrect bearing installation during engine assembly will lead to bearing failure as well. Tight-fitting bearings leave insufficient bearing oil clearance and will result in oil starvation. Dirt or foreign particles trapped behind a bearing insert results in high spots on the bearing, which lead to failure.

8 *Do not* touch any shell's bearing surface with your fingers during reassembly; there is a risk of scratching the delicate surface, or of depositing particles of dirt on it.

9 As mentioned at the beginning of this Section, the bearing shells should be renewed as a matter of course during engine overhaul; to do otherwise is false economy.

18 Engine overhaul - reassembly sequence

1 Before beginning engine reassembly, make sure you have all the necessary new parts, gaskets and seals as well as the following items on hand:

Common hand tools.
A ½ inch drive torque wrench.
Piston ring installation tool.
Piston ring compressor.
Short lengths of rubber or plastic hose to fit over connecting rod bolts.

Feeler gauges.
A fine-tooth file.
New engine oil.
Engine assembly lube or moly-base grease.
Gasket sealant.
Thread-locking compound.

2 In order to save time and avoid problems, engine reassembly must be done in the following general order:

Piston rings (Section 19).
Crankshaft and main bearings (Section 20).
Piston/connecting rod assemblies (Section 21).
Crankshaft oil seal (Chapter 2A or 2B).
Cylinder head and followers (Chapter 2A or 2B).
Camshafts (Chapter 2A or 2B).
Oil pump (Chapter 2A or 2B).
Timing belt/chain and sprockets (Chapter 2A or 2B).
Timing covers (Chapter 2A or 2B).
Oil pick-up (Chapter 2A or 2B).
Oil sump (Chapter 2A or 2B).
Inlet and exhaust manifolds (Chapter 4A or 2B).
Cylinder head cover (Chapter 2A or 2B).
Flywheel/driveplate (Chapter 2A or 2B).

19 Piston rings – refitting

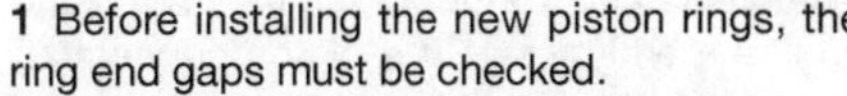

1 Before installing the new piston rings, the ring end gaps must be checked.

2 Lay out the piston/connecting rod assemblies and the new ring sets so the ring sets will be matched with the same piston and cylinder during the end gap measurement and engine assembly.

3 Insert the top (number one) ring into the first cylinder and square it up with the cylinder walls by pushing it in with the top of the piston **(see illustration)**. The ring should be near the bottom of the cylinder, at the lower limit of ring travel.

4 To measure the end gap, slip feeler gauges between the ends of the ring until a gauge equal to the gap width is found **(see illustration)**. The feeler gauge should slide between the ring ends with a slight amount of drag. Compare the measurement to that found in this Chapter's Specifications. If the gap is larger or smaller than specified, double-check to make sure you have the correct rings before proceeding.

5 If the gap is too small (unlikely if genuine Toyota parts are used), it must be enlarged, or the ring ends may contact each other during engine operation, causing serious damage. Ideally, new piston rings providing the correct end gap should be fitted. As a last resort, the end gap can be increased by filing the ring ends very carefully with a fine file. Mount the file in a vice equipped with soft jaws, slip the ring over the file with the ends contacting the file face, and slowly move the ring to remove material from the ends. Take care, as piston rings are sharp, and are easily broken.

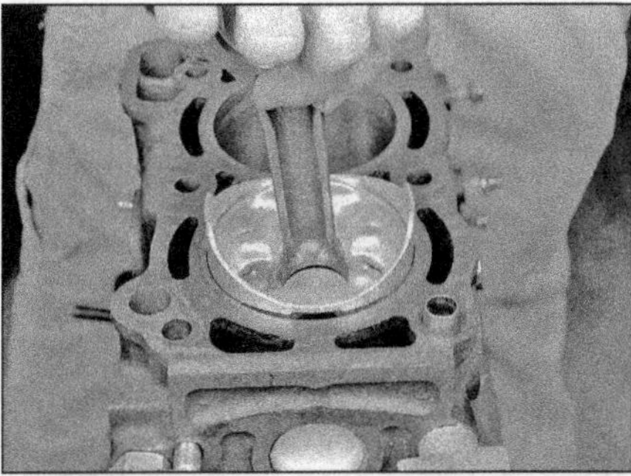

19.3 The ring must be square in the bore when checking the piston ring end gap

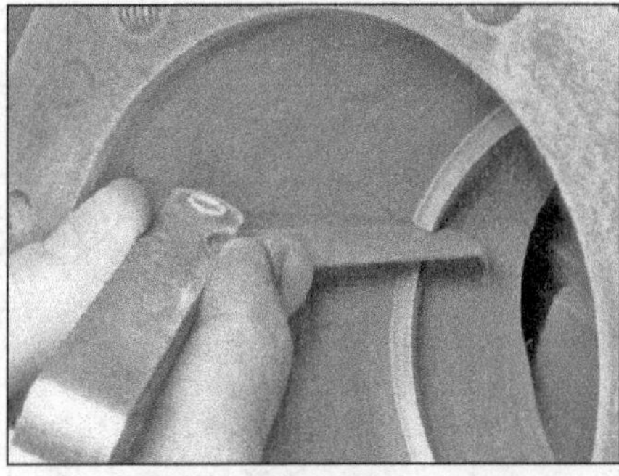

19.4 With the ring square in the bore, measure the end gap with a feeler gauge

6 Excess end gap isn't critical unless it's greater than the service limit listed in this Chapter's Specifications. Again, double-check to make sure you have the correct rings for your engine.

7 Repeat the procedure for each ring that will be installed in the first cylinder and for each ring in the remaining cylinders. Remember to keep rings, pistons and cylinders matched up.

8 Once the ring end gaps have been checked/corrected, the rings can be installed on the pistons.

9 Fit the piston rings using the same technique as for removal. Fit the bottom (oil control) ring first, and work up. When fitting a three-piece oil control ring, first insert the expander, and then fit the lower rail with its gap positioned 120° from the expander gap, and then fit the upper rail with its gap positioned 120° from the lower rail. When fitting a two-piece oil control ring, first insert the expander, then fit the control ring with its gap positioned 180° from the expander gap. Ensure that the second compression ring is fitted the correct way up, with its identification mark (either a dot of paint or the word TOP stamped on the ring surface) at the top, and the stepped surface at the bottom **(see illustrations)**. Arrange the gaps of the top and second compression rings 120° either side of the oil control ring gap, but make sure that none of the rings gaps are positioned over the gudgeon pin hole. **Note:** *Always follow any instructions supplied with the new piston ring sets – different manufacturers may specify different procedures. Do not mix up the top and second compression rings, as they have different cross-sections.*

19.9a Fit the spacer/expander in the oil control ring groove

19.9b Do not use a piston ring installation tool when installing the oil ring side rails

20 Crankshaft – refitting

1 Crankshaft installation is the first major step in engine reassembly. It's assumed at this point that the engine block and crankshaft have been cleaned, inspected and repaired or reconditioned.

2 Position the engine with the bottom facing up.

3 Remove the main bearing cap assembly bolts and lift out the ladder/sump upper housing.

4 If they're still in place, remove the old bearing shells from the block and the main bearing cap assembly. Wipe the main bearing surfaces of the block and cap assembly with a clean, lint-free cloth. They must be kept spotlessly clean.

5 Clean the back sides of the new main bearing inserts and lay the bearing half with the oil groove in each main bearing saddle in the block. Lay the other bearing half from each bearing set in the main bearing cap assembly. Make sure the tab on each bearing insert fits into the recess in the block or cap assembly. Also, the oil holes in the block must line up with the oil holes in the bearing insert.

6 Clean the bearing faces in the block, then apply a thin, uniform layer of clean moly-based grease or engine assembly lube to each of the

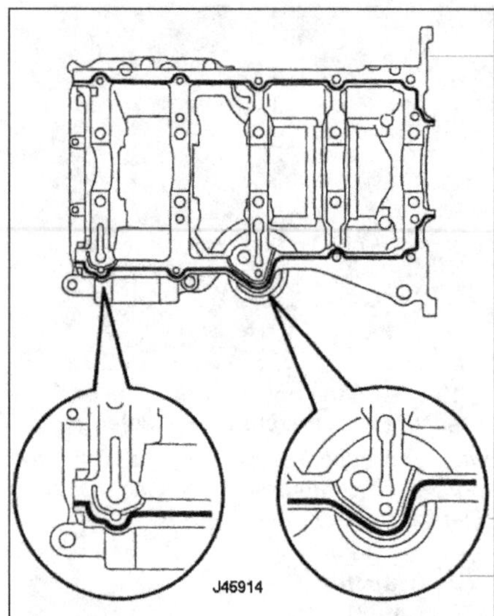

20.9 Apply a 2 mm wide bead of sealant to the main bearing ladder – petrol engine shown

bearing surfaces. Coat the thrustwashers as well and position them either side of the No 3 bearing position with the oil grooves facing outwards.

7 Lubricate the crankshaft surfaces that contact the oil seals with moly-based grease, engine assembly lube or clean engine oil.

8 Make sure the crankshaft journals are clean, and then lay the crankshaft back in place in the block. Clean the faces of the bearings in the main bearing ladder/sump upper housing, then apply lubricant to them.

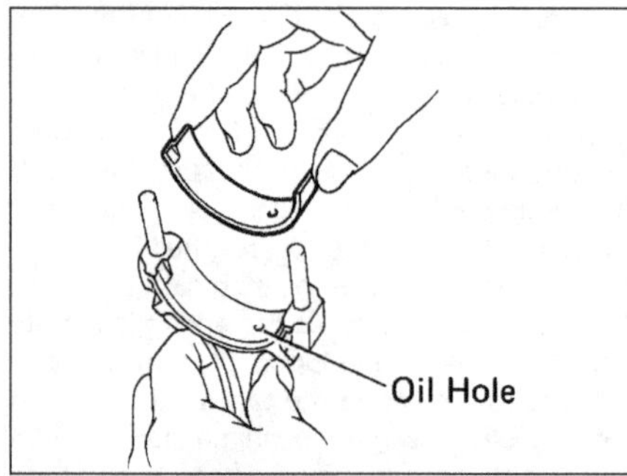

21.3 Align the hole in the bearing with the oil hole in the rod

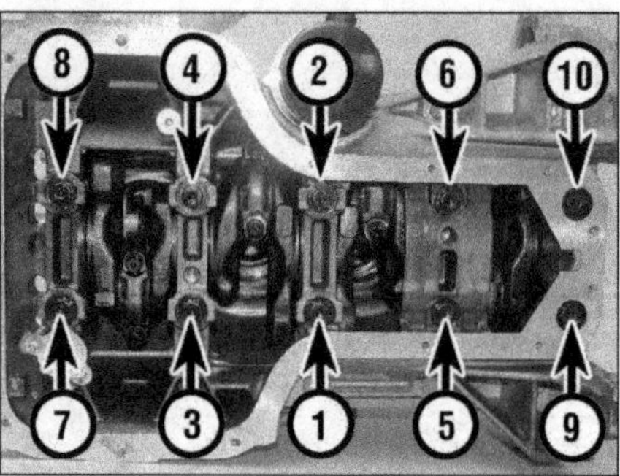

20.10 Main bearing ladder bolt tightening sequence – petrol engine shown

9 Apply a 2 mm wide bead of sealant (Toyota No 08826-00080) to the main bearing ladder/sump upper housing **(see illustration)**. Install the main bearing cap assembly within 3 minutes or the sealant will harden.

10 Refit the main bearing cap assembly bolts, and tighten the inner row of 10 bolts in sequence to the Stage 1 torque setting, followed by the Stage 2 angle-tightening setting **(see illustration)**. Tighten the remaining main bearing bolts to the specified torque.

11 Rotate the crankshaft a number of times by hand to check for any obvious binding.

12 Check the crankshaft endfloat with a feeler gauge or a dial indicator as described in Section 12. The endfloat should be correct if the crankshaft thrust faces aren't worn or damaged and new thrustwashers have been installed.

13 Install a new oil seal, then bolt the housing to the block (where applicable) – see Chapter 2A or 2B.

21 Pistons/connecting rods – refitting

1 Before installing the piston/connecting rod assemblies, the cylinder walls must be perfectly clean, the top edge of each cylinder must be chamfered, and the crankshaft must be in place.

2 Remove the cap from the end of the number one connecting rod (refer to the marks made during removal). Remove the original bearing shells and wipe the bearing surfaces of the connecting rod and cap with a clean, lint-free cloth. They must be kept spotlessly clean.

3 Clean the back side of the new upper bearing shell, then lay it in place in the connecting rod. Make sure the tab on the bearing fits into the recess in the rod so the oil holes line up **(see illustration)**. Don't hammer the bearing insert into place and be very careful not to nick or gouge the bearing face.

4 Clean the back side of the other bearing shell and install it in the rod cap. Again, make sure the tab on the bearing fits into the recess in the cap, and don't apply any lubricant. It's critically important that the mating surfaces of the bearing and connecting rod are perfectly clean and oil-free when they're assembled.

5 Position the piston ring gaps at staggered intervals around the piston **(see illustration).**

6 Slip a section of plastic or rubber hose over each connecting rod cap bolt to protect the cylinder bore.

7 Lubricate the piston and rings with clean engine oil and attach a piston ring compressor to the piston. Leave the skirt protruding about 8.0 mm to guide the piston into the cylinder. The rings must be compressed until they're flush with the piston.

8 Rotate the crankshaft until the number one connecting rod journal is at BDC (bottom dead centre) and apply a coat of engine oil to the cylinder wall.

9 With the dimple or arrow on top of the piston **(see illustration)** facing the front of the engine, gently insert the piston/connecting rod assembly into the number one cylinder bore and rest the bottom edge of the ring compressor on the engine block.

10 Tap the top edge of the ring compressor to make sure it's contacting the block around its entire circumference.

11 Gently tap on the top of the piston with the end of a wooden hammer handle **(see illustration)** while guiding the end of the connecting rod into place on the crankshaft journal. The piston rings may try to pop out of the ring compressor just before entering the cylinder bore, so keep some downward pressure on the ring compressor. Work slowly,

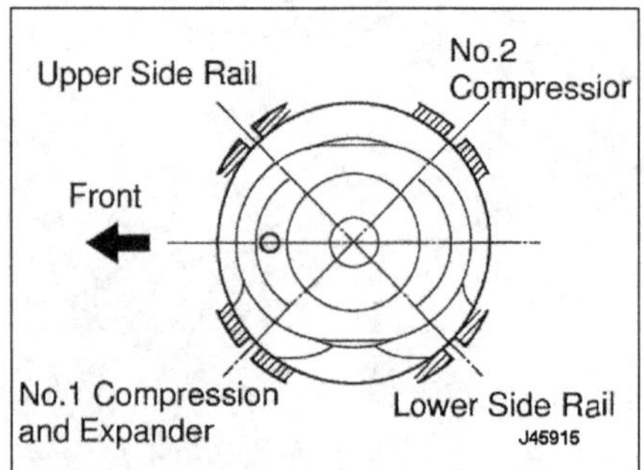

21.5a Piston ring end gap positions for petrol engines

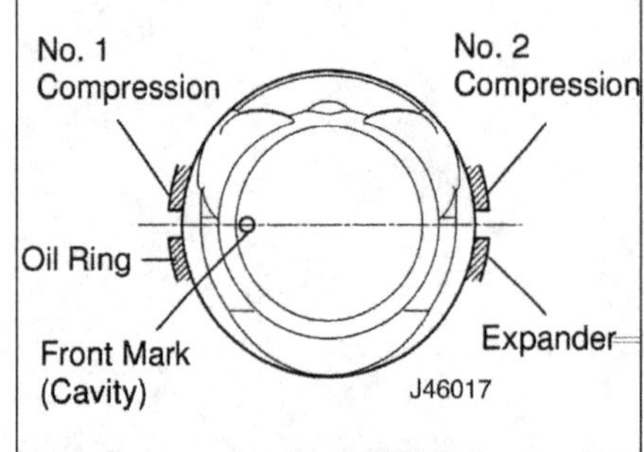

21.5b Piston ring end gap positions for diesel engines

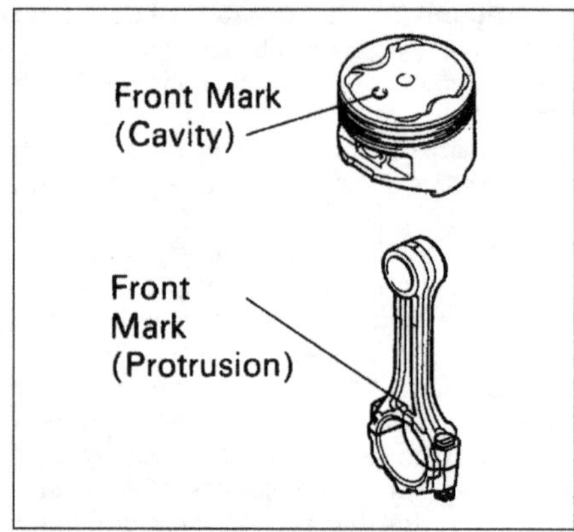

21.9 Check to be sure both the mark on the piston and the mark on the connection rod are aligned

and if any resistance is felt as the piston enters the cylinder, stop immediately. Find out what's binding and fix it before proceeding.

Caution: Do not, for any reason, force the piston into the cylinder – you might break a ring and/or the piston.

12 Make sure the bearing faces are perfectly clean, and then apply a uniform layer of clean moly-based grease or engine assembly lube to both of them. You'll have to push the piston higher into the cylinder to expose the face of the bearing shell in the connecting rod, be sure to slip the protective hoses over the rod bolts first.

13 Slide the connecting rod back into place on the journal, remove the protective hoses from the rod cap bolts, install the rod cap and tighten the nuts to the correct torque.

14 Repeat the entire procedure for the remaining pistons/connecting rods.

15 The important points to remember are:

- *a) Keep the back sides of the bearing shells and the insides of the connecting rods and caps perfectly clean when assembling them.*
- *b) Make sure you have the correct piston/ rod assembly for each cylinder.*
- *c) The dimple or arrow on the piston must face the front of the engine.*
- *d) Lubricate the cylinder walls with clean oil.*
- *e) Lubricate the bearing faces.*

16 After all the piston/connecting rod assemblies have been properly installed, rotate the crankshaft a number of times by hand to check for any obvious binding.

21.11 The piston can be (gently) driven into the cylinder bore with the end of a hammer handle

22 Initial start-up after overhaul

Warning: Have a fire extinguisher handy when starting the engine for the first time.

1 Once the engine has been installed in the vehicle, double-check the engine oil and coolant levels.

2 Remove the spark plugs (petrol engines) or glow plugs (diesel engines) from the engine.

3 On petrol engines, disable the fuel and ignition systems by disconnecting the wiring from the ignition coil pack/modules. On diesel engines, disconnect the wiring from the injectors.

4 Crank the engine until oil pressure registers on the gauge or the oil light goes out.

5 Install the spark plugs (petrol engines) and glow plugs (diesel engines) and reconnect any wiring.

6 Start the engine. It may take a few moments for the fuel system to build-up pressure, but the engine should start without a great deal of effort.

7 After the engine starts, it should be allowed to warm-up to normal operating temperature. While the engine is warming-up, make a thorough check for fuel, oil and coolant leaks.

8 Shut the engine off and recheck the engine oil and coolant levels.

9 Drive the vehicle to an area with minimum traffic, accelerate from 30 to 50 mph, and then allow the vehicle to slow to 30 mph with the throttle closed. Repeat the procedure 10 or 12 times. This will load the piston rings and cause them to seat properly against the cylinder walls. Check again for oil and coolant leaks.

10 Drive the vehicle gently for the first 500 miles (no sustained high speeds) and keep a constant check on the oil level. It is not unusual for an engine to use oil during the run-in period.

11 At approximately 500 to 600 miles, change the oil and filter.

12 For the next few hundred miles, drive the vehicle normally. Do not pamper it or abuse it.

13 After 2000 miles, change the oil and filter again and consider the engine run-in.

Notes

Chapter 3
Cooling, heating and air conditioning systems

Contents

Degrees of difficulty

Easy, suitable for novice with little experience 	**Fairly easy,** suitable for beginner with some experience	**Fairly difficult,** suitable for competent DIY mechanic	**Difficult,** suitable for experienced DIY mechanic	**Very difficult,** suitable for expert DIY or professional 

Specifications

General

Radiator cap pressure rating:	
Petrol	0.75 to 1.05 bar
Diesel	0.95 to 1.25 bar
Thermostat:	
Petrol:	
Opening temperature	74 to 78°C
Valve lift (at 95°C)	10.0 mm
Diesel:	
Opening temperature	80 to 84°C
Valve lift (at 95°C)	8.5 mm
Cooling fan:	
Petrol:	
Standard amperage (at 20°C)	8 to 12 amps
Resistance (at 20°C)	1.17 to 1.43 ohms
Diesel:	
Standard amperage (at 20°C)	Approximately 13.2 amps
Resistance (at 20°C)	1.17 to 1.43 ohms
Air conditioning system refrigerant:	
Type	R-134a
Charge volume	490 ± 30g
Thermostatic switch:	
Open at	93°C
Closed at	83°C
Air conditioning oil type	ND-Oil 8

Torque wrench settings	Nm	lbf ft
Coolant elbow to cylinder head	10	7
Compressor mounting bolts:		
12 mm head bolts	25	18
14 mm head bolts	54	40
Coolant pump-to-block bolts:		
Petrol:		
2 x 30mm length	9	7
4 x 35mm length	11	8
Diesel	31	23
Coolant pump to injection pump (diesel)	21	15
Thermostat cover bolts	9	7

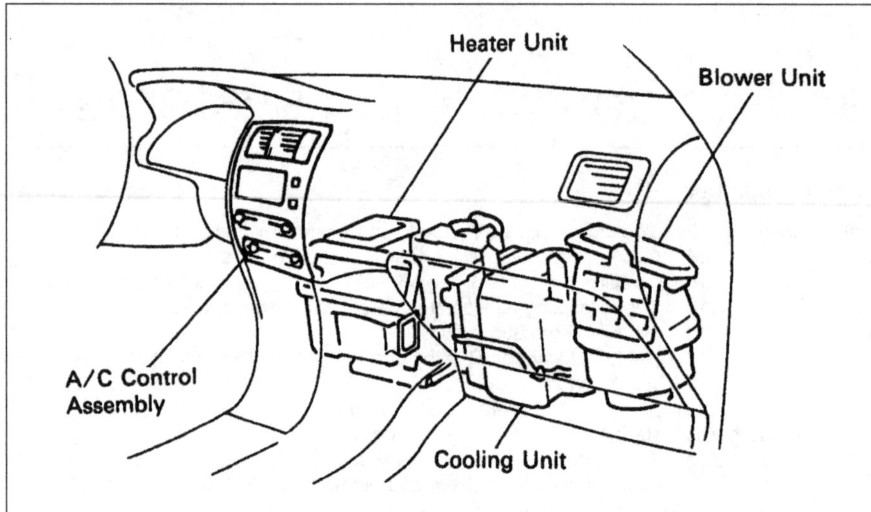

1.6 Underfacia arrangement of the blower unit, evaporator, and heater unit (LHD model shown, RHD is a mirror image)

1 General information

Engine cooling system

All vehicles covered by this manual employ a pressurised engine cooling system with thermostatically-controlled coolant circulation. An impeller type coolant pump mounted on the front of the block pumps coolant through the engine. The coolant flows around each cylinder and toward the rear of the engine. Cast-in coolant passages direct coolant around the inlet and exhaust ports, near the spark plug areas and in proximity to the exhaust valve guides.

A wax-type thermostat is located in the thermostat housing on the front face of the engine block. During warm-up, the closed thermostat prevents coolant from circulating through the radiator. When the engine reaches normal operating temperature, the thermostat opens and allows hot coolant to travel through the radiator, where it is cooled before returning to the engine.

The cooling system is sealed by a pressure-type radiator cap. This raises the boiling point of the coolant, and the higher boiling point of the coolant increases the cooling efficiency of the radiator. If the system pressure exceeds the cap pressure-relief value, the excess pressure in the system forces the spring-loaded valve inside the cap off its seat and allows the coolant to escape through the overflow tube into a coolant reservoir. When the system cools, the excess coolant is automatically drawn from the reservoir back into the radiator.

This type of cooling system is known as a closed design because coolant that escapes past the pressure cap is saved and re-used.

The coolant reservoir does double duty as both the point at which fresh coolant is added to the cooling system to maintain the proper fluid level and as a holding tank for hot coolant.

Heating system

The heating system consists of a blower fan and heater matrix located within the heater box under the facia, the inlet and outlet hoses connecting the heater matrix to the engine cooling system and the heater/air conditioning control panel on the facia **(see illustration)**. Engine coolant is circulated through the heater matrix. When the heater mode is activated, a flap door opens to expose the heater box to the passenger compartment. A fan switch on the control head activates the blower motor, which forces air through the matrix, heating the air.

Air conditioning system

The air conditioning system consists of a condenser mounted in front of the radiator, an evaporator mounted adjacent to the heater matrix, a compressor mounted on the engine, a receiver/drier which contains a high pressure relief valve and the plumbing connecting all of the above.

A blower fan forces the warmer air of the passenger compartment through the evaporator matrix (sort of a radiator-in-reverse), transferring the heat from the air to the refrigerant. The liquid refrigerant boils off into low-pressure vapour, taking the heat with it when it leaves the evaporator. The compressor keeps refrigerant circulating through the system, pumping the warmed refrigerant through the condenser where it is cooled and then circulated back to the evaporator.

2.4 Use a hydrometer to test the strength of the antifreeze mixture

2 Antifreeze/coolant – general information

Warning: Do not allow antifreeze to come in contact with your skin or painted surfaces of the vehicle. Rinse off spills immediately with plenty of water. Antifreeze is highly toxic if ingested. Never leave antifreeze lying around in an open container or in puddles on the floor; children and pets are attracted by its sweet smell and may drink it. Check with local authorities about disposing of used antifreeze. Many communities have collection centres, which will see that antifreeze is disposed of safely. Never dump used antifreeze on the ground or into drains.

The cooling system should be filled with Toyota coolant or a water/ethylene glycol-based antifreeze solution, which will prevent freezing down to at least -30° C, or lower if local climate requires it. It also provides protection against corrosion and increases the coolant boiling point.

The cooling system should be drained, flushed and refilled regularly (see Chapter 1A or 1B). The use of antifreeze solutions for extended periods is likely to cause damage and encourage the formation of rust and scale in the system. If your tap water is 'hard', ie, contains a lot of dissolved minerals, use distilled water with the antifreeze.

Before adding antifreeze to the system, check all hose connections, because antifreeze tends to search out and leak through very minute openings. Engines do not normally consume coolant. Therefore, if the level goes down, find the cause and correct it.

The exact mixture of antifreeze-to-water you should use depends on the relative weather conditions. The mixture should contain at least 50 percent antifreeze, but should never contain more than 70 percent antifreeze. Consult the mixture ratio chart on the antifreeze container before adding coolant. Hydrometers are available at most motor parts/accessory stores to test the ratio of antifreeze to water **(see illustration)**. Use antifreeze, which meets the vehicle manufacturer's specifications. **Note:** *The antifreeze available from a Toyota dealer is ready-mixed and doesn't require further dilution.*

3.8 Undo the thermostat cover nuts

3.9a Remove the hoses . . .

3.9b . . . and undo the thermostat housing bolts

3 Thermostat – testing and renewal

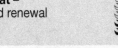

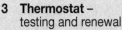

Warning: Do not attempt to remove the radiator cap, coolant or thermostat until the engine has cooled completely.

Testing

1 Before assuming the thermostat is responsible for a cooling system problem, check the coolant level (*Weekly checks*), drivebelt tension (Chapter 1A or 1B) and temperature gauge (or light) operation.

2 If the engine takes a long time to warm-up (as indicated by the temperature gauge or heater operation), the thermostat is probably stuck open. Renew the thermostat.

3 If the engine runs hot, use your hand to check the temperature of the radiator top hose. If the hose is not hot, but the engine is, the thermostat is probably stuck in the closed position, preventing the coolant inside the engine from travelling through the radiator. Renew the thermostat.

Caution: Do not drive the vehicle without a thermostat. The engine management ECM may stay in open loop and emissions and fuel economy will suffer.

4 If the radiator top hose is hot, it means that the coolant is flowing and the thermostat is open. Consult the *Fault finding* Section at the rear of this manual for further diagnosis.

Renewal

5 Drain the coolant from the radiator (see Chapter 1A or 1B).

6 Disconnect the earth/negative cable from the battery.

7 On petrol models, to make access easier, remove the alternator as described in Chapter 5A.

8 On petrol models, undo the two retaining nuts and remove the thermostat cover **(see illustration)**. Be prepared for some coolant to spill as the gasket seal is broken. The radiator hose can be left attached to the cover, unless the cover itself is to be renewed.

9 On diesel models, undo the retaining clips and remove the hoses from the coolant pipe

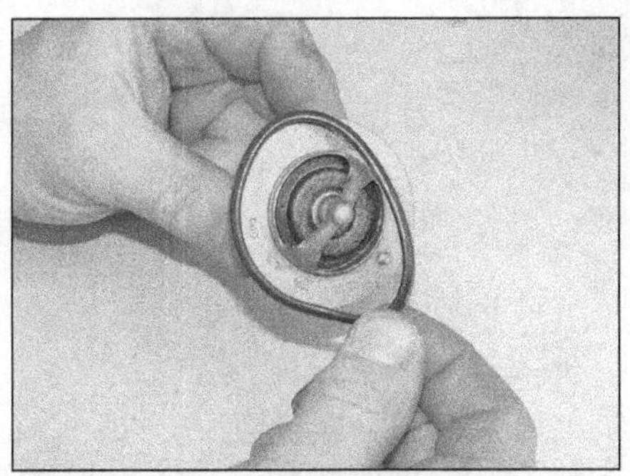

3.10 Discard the thermostat old seal and fit a new one

(see illustrations). Then undo the retaining nuts and remove the coolant elbow from the cylinder block. Be prepared for some coolant to spill as the gasket seal is broken.

10 Remove the thermostat; noting its fitted position. Discard the seal; a new one must be fitted **(see illustration)**.

11 Fit a new seal to the thermostat, and fit it into position on the engine block with the jiggle pin at the 12 o'clock position **(see illustration)**.

12 Refit the thermostat cover/coolant elbow and tighten the nuts to the specified torque.

13 If removed, reconnect the coolant hoses to the thermostat cover/coolant elbow.

14 On petrol modes, refit the alternator as described in Chapter 5A. Reconnect the earth/negative cable to the battery.

15 Refill the cooling system (see Chapter 1A or 1B), run the engine and check for leaks and proper operation.

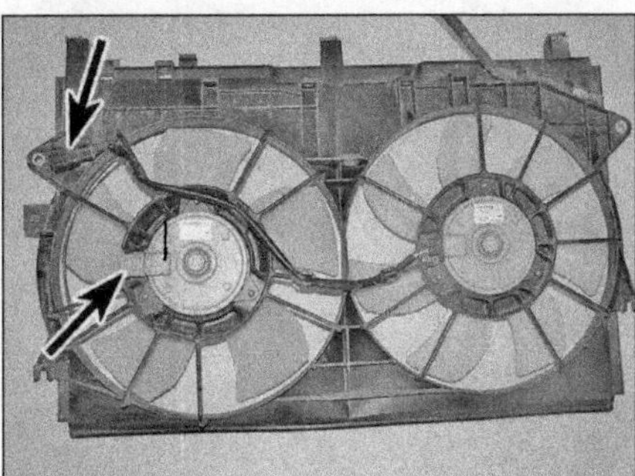

4.1 Wiring connectors (arrowed) for twin fans

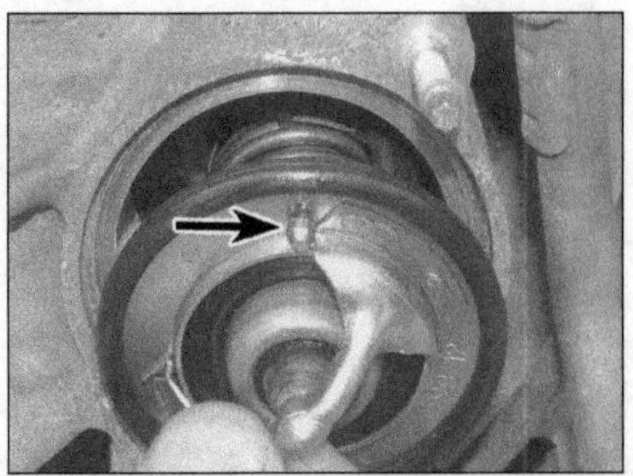

3.11 Fit the thermostat with the jiggle pin at the 12 o'clock position

4 Engine cooling fans and relay – checking and renewal

Warning: To avoid possible injury, keep clear of the fan blades, as they may start turning at any time.

Checking

Note 1: *The coolant temperature is monitored by the engine management ECM via the coolant temperature sensor, and the fans are operated by energising the cooling fan relay(s).*

Note 2: *The coolant reservoir on petrol models is part of the radiator fan shroud.*

1 To test an inoperative fan motor (one that doesn't come on when the engine gets hot or when the air conditioner is on) first check the fuses and/or fusible links (see Chapter 12). Then disconnect the electrical connector at the m otor and use fused jumper wires to connect the fan directly to the battery **(see illustration)**. If the fan still does not work, renew the fan motor.

Warning: Do not allow the test clips to contact each other or any metallic part of the vehicle.

2 If the motor tested OK in the previous test but is still inoperative, then the fault lies in the relays, fuse or wiring.

3 On diesel models, there are three fan relays, which are located in the relay box at the front

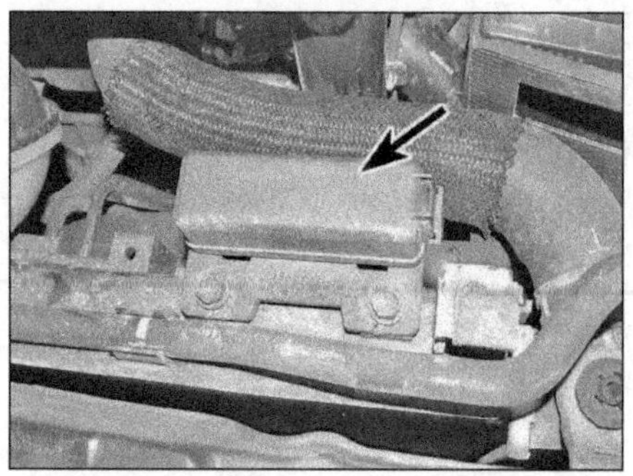
4.3a Fan relay box – diesel models

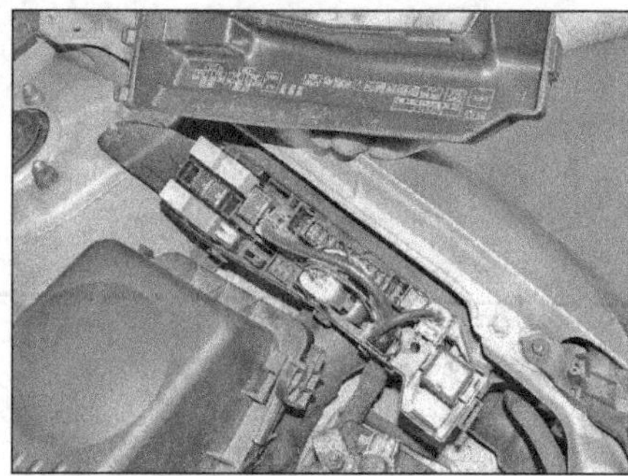
4.3b Fan relays in main fusebox – petrol models

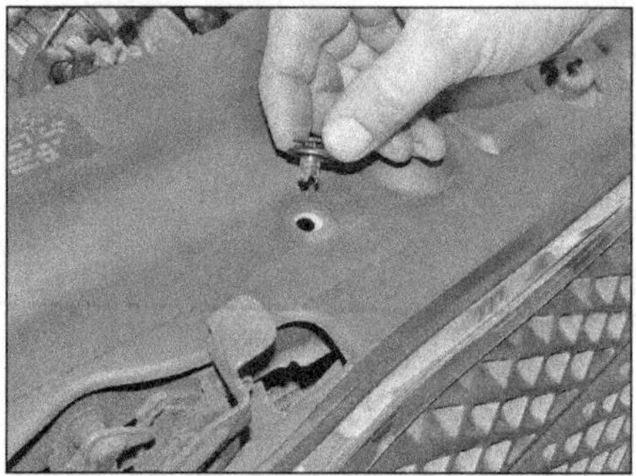
4.5a Remove the retaining clips . . .

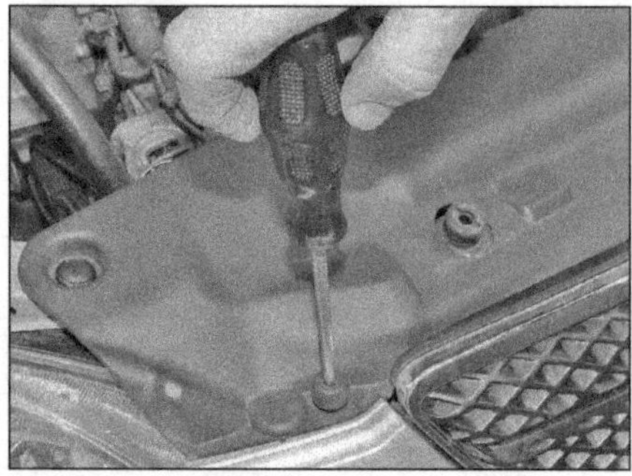
4.5b . . . undo the retaining screws . . .

4.5c . . . and remove the upper trim cover

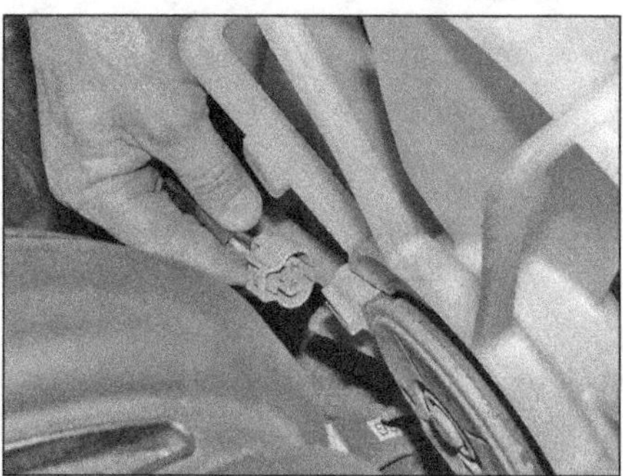
4.6 Disconnect the wiring connector from the fan

of the engine compartment **(see illustration)**. On petrol models, there are two fan relays, which are located in the fuse/relay box at the left-hand side of the engine compartment **(see illustration)**.

Cooling fan renewal

4 Disconnect the negative battery cable (see Chapter 5A).

5 Release the securing clips, undo the retaining screws and remove the plastic trim panel from across the front of the engine compartment **(see illustrations)**.

Petrol models

6 Disconnect the wiring connectors at the fan motor **(see illustration)**.

7 Disconnect the coolant resrvoir hose from the right-hand side top of the radiator **(see illustration)**. Note there may be some spillage from the pipe as it is removed.

8 Release the retaining clips, one at each side of the fan shroud and lift the fan/shroud assembly from the vehicle **(see illustrations)**.

Diesel models

9 Undo the retaining bolts and remove the relay box from the top of the fan cowling **(see illustration)**.

10 Drain enough coolant to disconnect the upper radiator hose at the radiator **(see illustration)**.

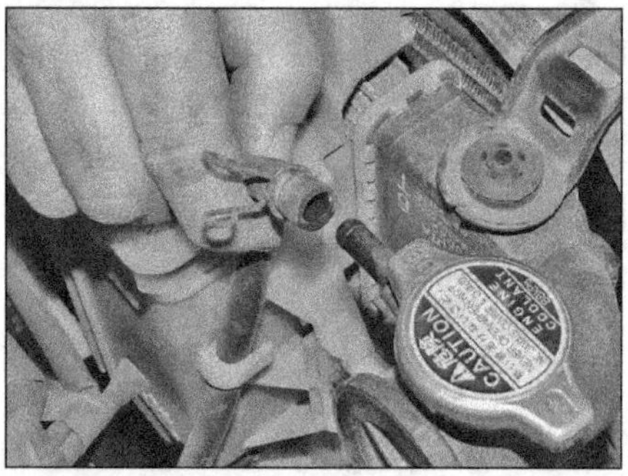

4.7 Disconnect the pipe from the radiator

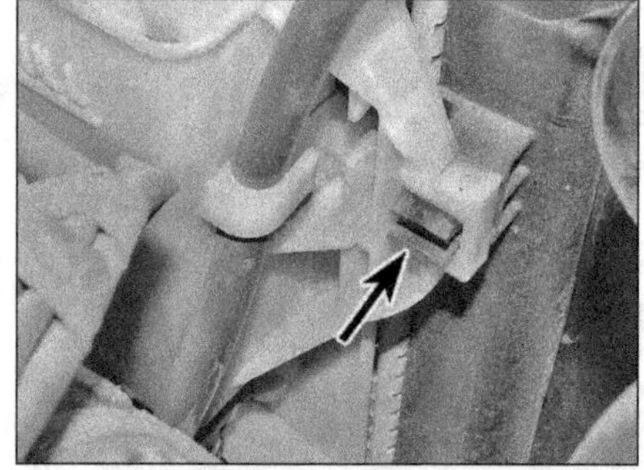
4.8a Release the securing clips (arrowed) . . .

4.8b . . . and withdraw the fan assembly

4.9 Remove the relay box

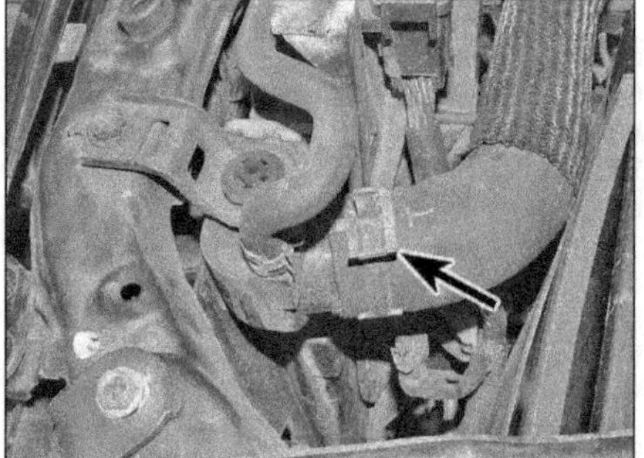
4.10 Remove the upper hose retaining clip (arrowed)

4.11a Disconnect the hoses . . .

4.11b . . . undo the bolts and remove the coolant reservoir

4.12 Disconnect the two wiring connectors

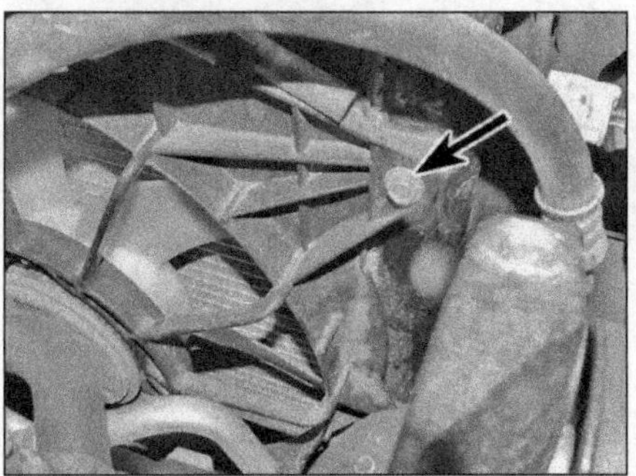

4.13a Undo the retaining bolts (arrowed) . . .

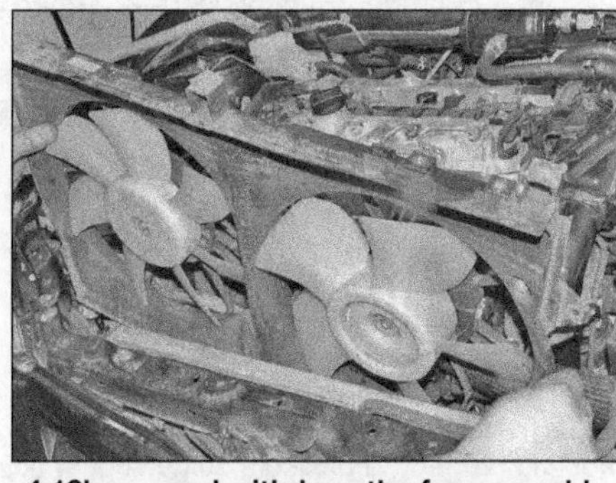

4.13b . . . and withdraw the fan assembly

4.14 Undo the fan blade retaining nut

11 Disconnect the hoses from the coolant reservoir and unbolt it from the top of the radiator fan cowling **(see illustrations)**

12 Disconnect the two wiring connectors from the fan motors **(see illustration)**.

13 Undo the retaining bolts, one at each side of the fan shroud, and lift the fan/shroud assembly from the vehicle **(see illustrations)**.

All models

14 If required, hold the fan blades and remove the fan retaining nut (and spacer, where fitted) **(see illustration)**.

15 Unbolt the fan motor from the shroud **(see illustration)**.

16 Refitting is the reverse of removal.

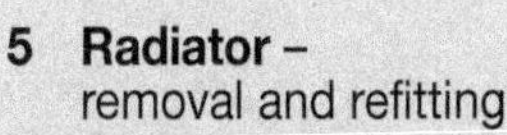

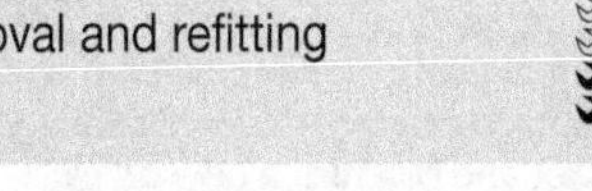

5 Radiator – removal and refitting

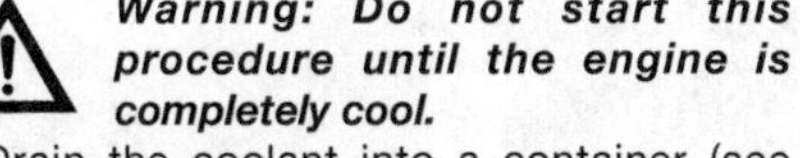

Warning: Do not start this procedure until the engine is completely cool.

1 Drain the coolant into a container (see Chapter 1A or 1B).

2 Remove the cooling fan assembly (see Section 4).

3 Remove both the upper and lower radiator hoses **(see illustration)**.

4 If equipped with an automatic transmission, disconnect the fluid cooler pipes from the radiator. Place a drip pan to catch the fluid and cap the fittings.

5 Remove the two upper radiator mounting brackets **(see illustrations)**. **Note:** *The bottom of the radiator is retained by two grommets located in the lower front crossmember.*

6 On diesel models, disconnect the wiring connector from the temperature sensor in the side of the radiator **(see illustration)**.

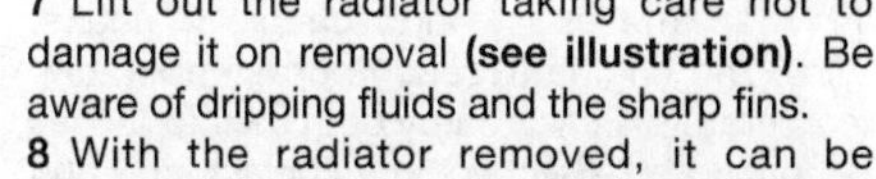

7 Lift out the radiator taking care not to damage it on removal **(see illustration)**. Be aware of dripping fluids and the sharp fins.

8 With the radiator removed, it can be inspected for leaks, damage and internal

4.15 Unbolt the fan motor from the shroud

5.3 Remove the radiator hoses

5.5a Remove the upper mounting brackets

5.5b Lower mounting bushes

5.6 Disconnect temperature sensor wiring connector – diesel model

blockage. If in need of repairs, have a professional radiator workshop or dealer service department perform the work, as special techniques are required.

9 Insects and dirt can be cleaned from the radiator with compressed air and a soft brush. Don't bend the cooling fins as this is done.

Warning: Wear eye protection when using compressed air.

10 Refitting is the reverse of the removal procedure. Be sure the rubber mounts are in place on the bottom of the radiator.

11 After refitting, fill the cooling system with the proper mixture of antifreeze and water. Refer to Chapter 1A or 1B, if necessary.

12 Start the engine and check for leaks. Allow the engine to reach normal operating temperature, indicated by both radiator hoses becoming hot. Recheck the coolant level and add more if required.

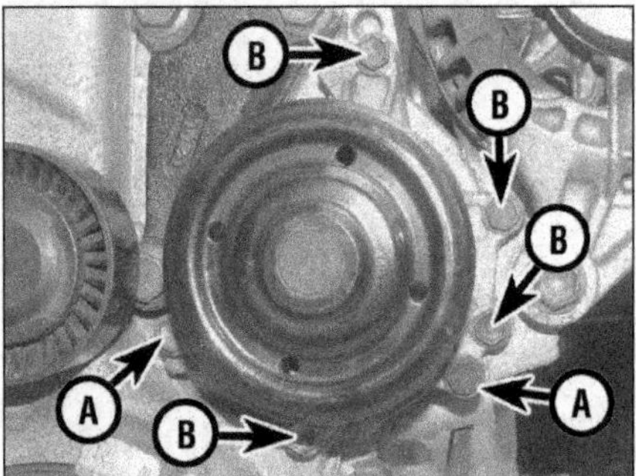

7.3 The bolts marked A are 30 mm long whilst the ones marked B are 35 mm long

7.9b . . . and recover the gasket

5.7 Carefully lift out the radiator

13 On automatic transmission-equipped models, check and add fluid as needed.

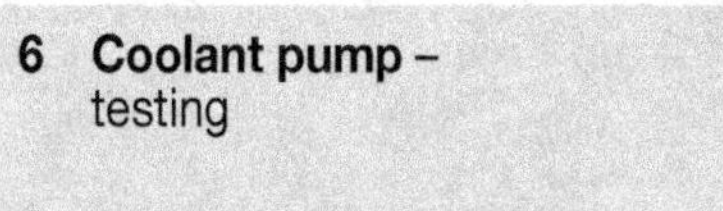

6 Coolant pump – testing

1 A failure in the coolant pump can cause serious engine damage due to overheating.

2 With the engine running and warmed to normal operating temperature, squeeze the upper radiator hose. If the coolant pump is working properly, a pressure surge should be felt as the hose is released.

Warning: Keep hands away from fan blades.

3 Coolant pumps are normally equipped with weep or vent holes. If a failure occurs in the pump seal, coolant will leak from this hole.

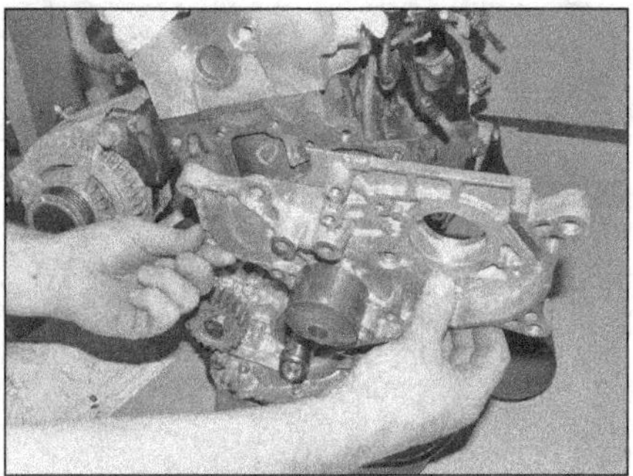

7.9a Remove the coolant pump and housing . . .

7.10 Renew the coolant pump O-ring – petrol model

In most cases it will be necessary to use a flashlight to find the hole on the coolant pump by looking through the space behind the pulley just below the coolant pump shaft.

4 If the coolant pump shaft bearings fail there may be a howling sound at the front of the engine while it is running. Bearing wear can be felt if the coolant pump pulley is rocked up-and-down. Do not mistake drivebelt slippage, which causes a squealing sound, for coolant pump failure.

7 Coolant pump – removal and refitting

Warning: Do not start this procedure until the engine is completely cool.

Removal

1 Drain the engine coolant as described in Chapter 1A or 1B.

Petrol engines

2 Remove the auxiliary drivebelt as described in Chapter 1A or 1B.

3 Undo the 6 bolts (there are two different lengths of bolts, note their fitted position), and remove the coolant pump **(see illustration)**. Discard the O-ring seal; a new one must be fitted.

Diesel engine

Note: *Toyota recommend renewal of the fuel inlet pipe whenever a new coolant pump is fitted.*

4 Remove the timing belt, crankshaft sprocket, idler pulley and high-pressure fuel pump pulley as described in Chapter 2B.

5 Unbolt the cover from over the high-pressure fuel pump, and remove the insulation.

6 Remove the fuel inlet pipe and injector pipes (see Chapter 4B).

7 Remove the inlet manifold as described in Chapter 2B.

8 Unscrew the mounting nuts securing the high-pressure fuel pump to the coolant pump housing studs.

9 Progressively unscrew the coolant pump mounting bolts and remove the pump from the cylinder block **(see illustrations)**. Remove the gasket and discard, a new one will be required for refitting.

Refitting

10 On petrol models, ensure the mating faces of the coolant pump and timing chain cover are clean, and then refit the pump using a new O-ring seal **(see illustration)**.

11 On diesel models, ensure the mating faces of the coolant pump and cylinder block are clean, and then refit the pump using a new gasket.

12 Refit the retaining bolts and tighten them to the specified torque.

13 On diesel models, refit the crankshaft sprocket, inlet manifold, timing belt and high-

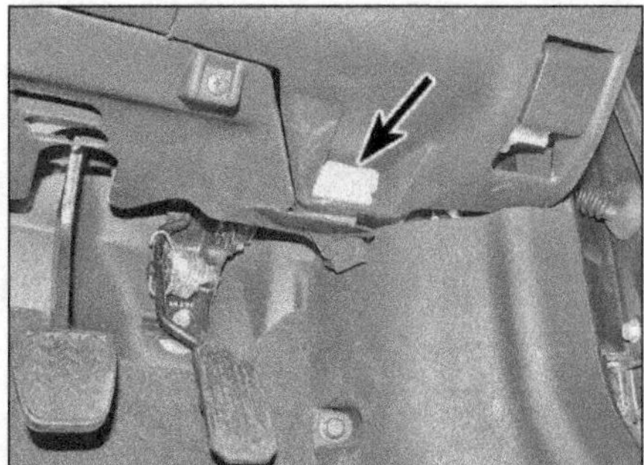
8.1 Vehicle diagnostic connector

8.7a Temperature sensor – diesel model

8.7b Temperature sensor – petrol model

pressure fuel pump pulley as described in Chapter 2B.

14 Refit the auxiliary drivebelt as described in Chapter 1A or 1B.

15 Refill the coolant system (Chapter 1A or 1B), and then run the engine and check for leaks.

8 Coolant temperature gauge sender unit – testing and renewal

Warning: Do not start this procedure until the engine is completely cool.

Testing

Note: *The following procedures only apply to the diesel engine. On petrol engines, have the engine management ECM self-diagnosis system interrogated by a suitably-equipped repair workshop. The vehicle's diagnostic connector is located under the right-hand side of the facia **(see illustration)**.*

1 If the coolant temperature gauge is inoperative, check the fuses first (see Chapter 12).

2 If the temperature gauge indicates excessive temperature after running a while, see the *Fault finding* Section in the rear of the manual.

3 If the temperature gauge indicates hot as soon as the engine is started from cold, disconnect the wire at the coolant temperature sender. The sender is located on the right-hand side of the radiator. If the gauge reading drops, renew the sender unit. If the reading remains high, the wire to the gauge may be shorted to earth or the gauge may be faulty.

4 If the coolant temperature gauge fails to show any indication after the engine has been warmed-up (approximately 10 minutes) and the fuses checked out OK, shut off the engine. Disconnect the wires at the sender unit and, using a jumper wire, connect the two wires together. Briefly turn on the ignition without starting the engine. If the gauge now indicates Hot, renew the sender unit.

5 If the gauge fails to respond, the circuit may be open or the gauge may be faulty – see Chapter 12 for additional information.

Renewal

6 Drain the coolant, until the level is lower than the sensor.

7 Disconnect the wiring connector from the sender unit **(see illustrations)**.

8 Using a deep socket or a spanner, remove the sender unit.

9 Fit the new unit and tighten it securely. Do not use thread sealer as it may electrically insulate the sender unit.

10 Reconnect the wiring connector, refill the cooling system and check for coolant leakage and proper gauge function.

9 Blower motor and resistor – removal and refitting

1 The blower unit is located in the passenger compartment above the left-hand front footwell. If the blower doesn't work, check the fuse and all connections in the circuit for looseness and corrosion. Make sure the battery is fully-charged.

2 On manual A/C models a resistor is fitted in the blower motor housing, on automatic A/C models, this is replaced with a control module.

3 Remove the glovebox (see Chapter 11).

Removal

4 Unclip the trim panel from below the facia **(see illustration)**.

5 Undo the retaining screws and unclip the ECM from below the blower motor **(see illustration)**.

6 Disconnect the electrical connector from the blower motor resistor/control module. Remove the screws and withdraw the resistor/module from the housing **(see illustrations)**.

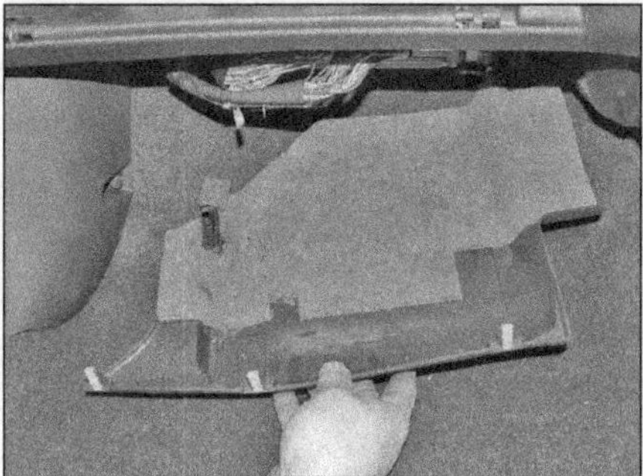
9.4 Remove the facia trim panel

9.5 Withdraw the electronic control module

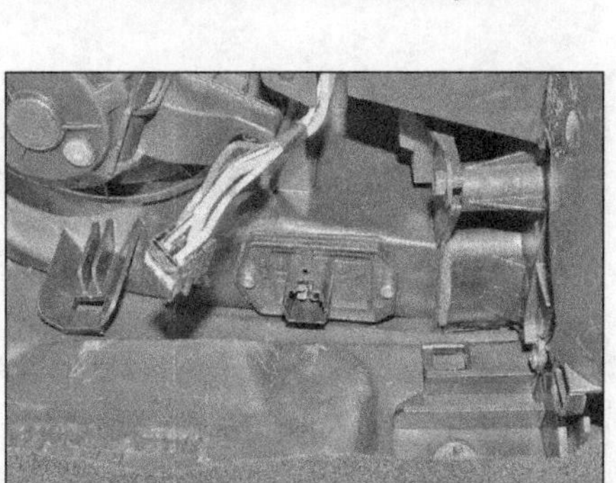
9.6a Disconnect the wiring connector . . .

9.6b . . . and remove the heater blower resistor

9.7a Disconnect the wiring connector . . .

9.7b . . . and remove the heater blower

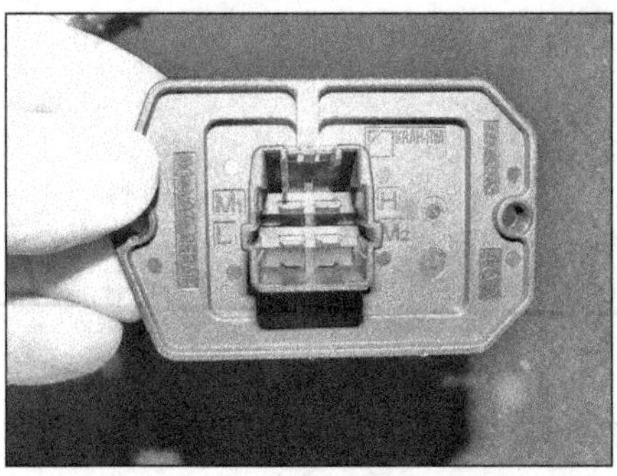

9.8 Note the terminal markings on the cover

7 Disconnect the wiring plug, then remove the three mounting screws and lower the blower assembly from the housing **(see illustrations)**. If required, the fan can be removed from the motor.

Testing

8 Using a continuity tester on the blower motor resistor, there should be continuity between all terminals **(see illustration)**. If not, renew the resistor. **Note:** *This is only on manual A/C models that have a resistor fitted, models with automatic A/C there is a control module which will need to be checked by your local Toyota dealer.*

Terminals

H to M1	*1.398 to 1.605 ohms*
H to M2	*0.465 to 0.535 ohms*
H to L	*3.069 to 3.531 ohms*

9 To check the blower motor, disconnect the wiring connector and run a positive (+) and negative (-) wire directly to the motor. If blower motor does not operate a new motor will be required.

Refitting

10 Refitting is the reverse of removal. Check for operation of heater blower when completed.

10 Heater matrix – removal and refitting

Warning: These models are equipped with airbags. The airbag is armed and can deploy (inflate) anytime the battery is connected. To prevent accidental deployment (and possible injury), turn the ignition key to LOCK and disconnect the negative battery cable whenever working near airbag components. After the battery is disconnected, wait at least two minutes before beginning work (the system has a back-up capacitor that must fully discharge). For more information see Chapter 12.

Removal

1 Remove the air conditioning evaporator as described in Section 16.

2 Undo the retaining screw and remove heater matrix pipe clamp from the housing **(see illustration)**.

3 Remove the plastic cover from the heater matrix pipes, and then withdraw the heater matrix complete with pipes, out from the housing **(see illustrations)**.

Refitting

4 Refitting is the reverse order of removal, noting that new air conditioning pipe O-rings must be fitted. Refer to Section 16 for the refitting of the air conditioning evaporator.

5 Refill the cooling system, reconnect the battery and run the engine. Check for leaks and proper system operation.

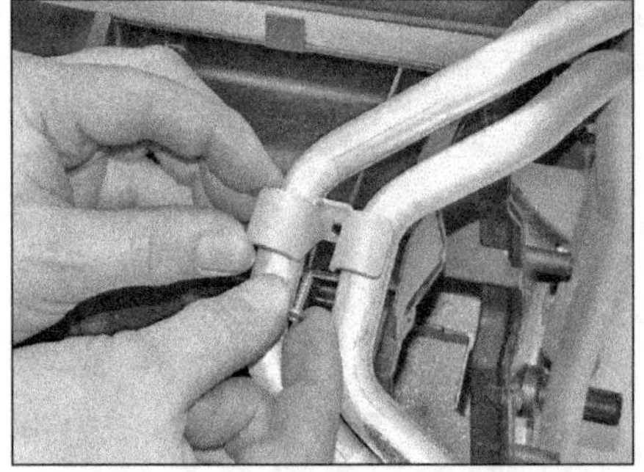
10.2 Remove the pipe clamp

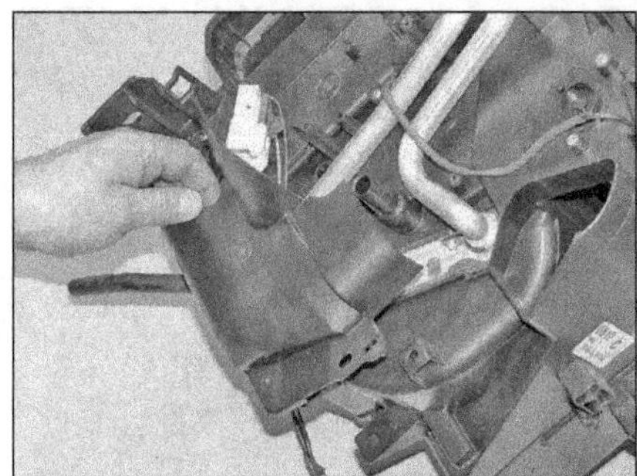
10.3a Remove the plastic cover . . .

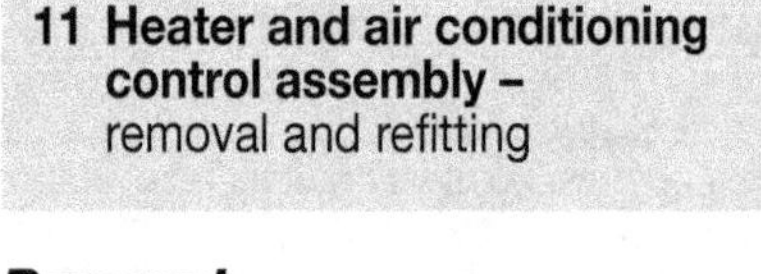

11 Heater and air conditioning control assembly – removal and refitting

Removal

1 Remove the rear section of the centre console (see Chapter 11).

2 On models with manual air conditioning, pull off the centre fan speed control knob, and undo the retaining screw **(see illustrations)**.

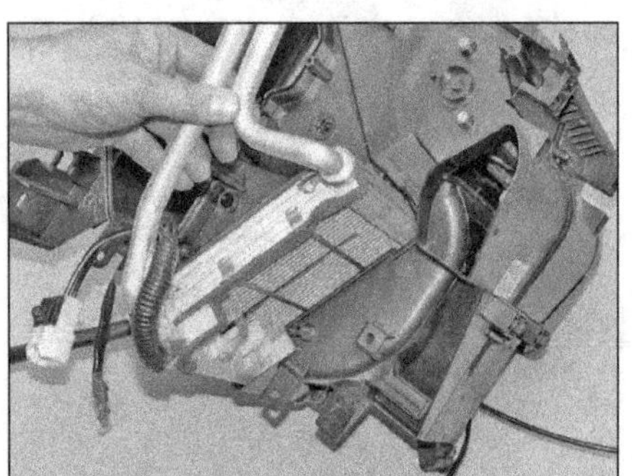
10.3b . . . and withdraw the heater matrix

11.2a Remove the centre control knob . . .

11.2b . . . and undo the retaining screw

3 Carefully unclip the centre cluster finish panel from the facia. Disconnect the wiring plugs as the panel is removed **(see illustrations)**.

4 Release the securing clips at each side of the heater control unit and pull it out from the facia **(see illustration)**.

5 On models with manual air conditioning, release the locking clips and disconnect the heater control cables from the rear of the control panel **(see illustrations)**. Note the fitted position of the cables, blue for the direction control knob and black for the temperature control knob.

6 Disconnect the wiring block connectors from the rear of the control panel **(see illustration)**.

7 On models with manual air conditioning, to remove the cables, remove the trim panel from the right-hand side of the heater housing, to the left of the clutch pedal. Release the retaining clips and disconnect the cables from the control levers **(see illustrations)**.

Refitting

8 Refitting is the reverse of the removal procedure.

9 Run the engine and check for proper functioning of the heater (and air conditioning, if equipped).

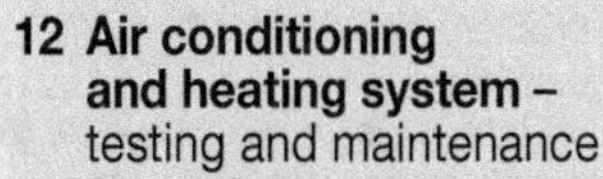

12 Air conditioning and heating system – testing and maintenance

Air conditioning system

Warning: The air conditioning system is under high pressure. Do not loosen any hose fittings or remove any components until the system has been discharged. Air conditioning refrigerant may only be discharged by a dealer service department or an automotive air conditioning specialist. Always wear eye protection when disconnecting air conditioning system fittings even after the system has been discharged.

1 The following maintenance checks should be performed on a regular basis to ensure that the air conditioner continues to operate at peak efficiency:

a) Inspect the condition of the compressor drivebelt. If it is worn or deteriorated, renew it (see Chapter 1A or 1B).

b) Check the drivebelt tension and, if necessary, adjust it (see Chapter 1A or 1B).

c) Inspect the system hoses. Look for cracks, bubbles, hardening and deterioration. Inspect the hoses and all fittings for oil bubbles or seepage. If there is any evidence of wear, damage or leakage, renew the hose(s).

d) Inspect the condenser fins for leaves, insects and any other foreign material that may have embedded itself in the fins. Use a 'fin comb' or compressed air to remove debris from the condenser.

11.3a Unclip the centre trim panel . . .

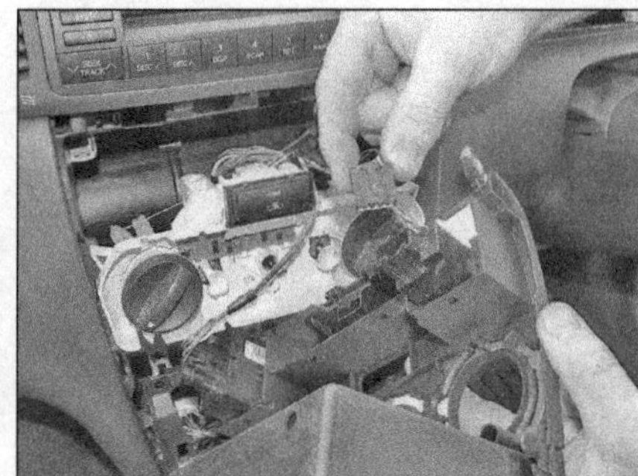

11.3b . . . and disconnect the wiring connectors

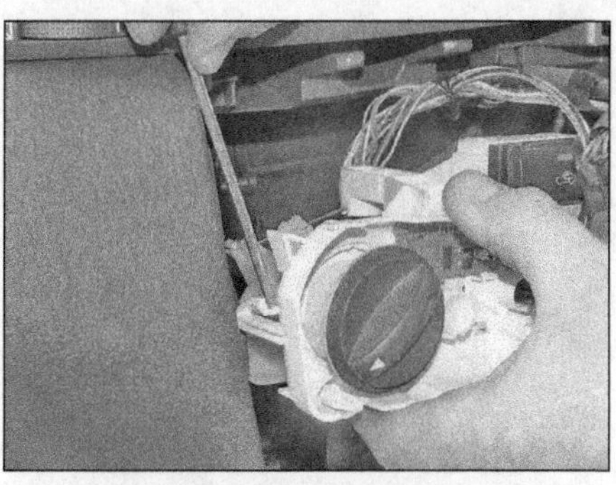

11.4 Releasing the securing clips

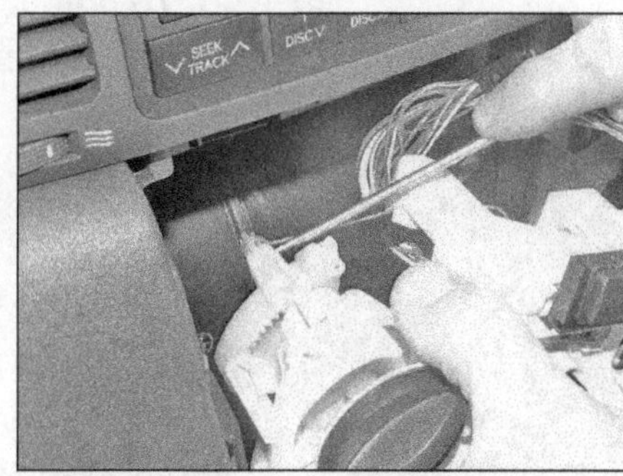

11.5a Release the inner cable . . .

2 It's a good idea to operate the system for about ten minutes at least once a month. This is particularly important during the winter months because long-term non-use can cause hardening, and subsequent failure, of the seals.

3 Leaks in the air conditioning system are best spotted when the system is brought up to operating temperature and pressure, by running the engine with the air conditioning on for five minutes. Shut the engine off

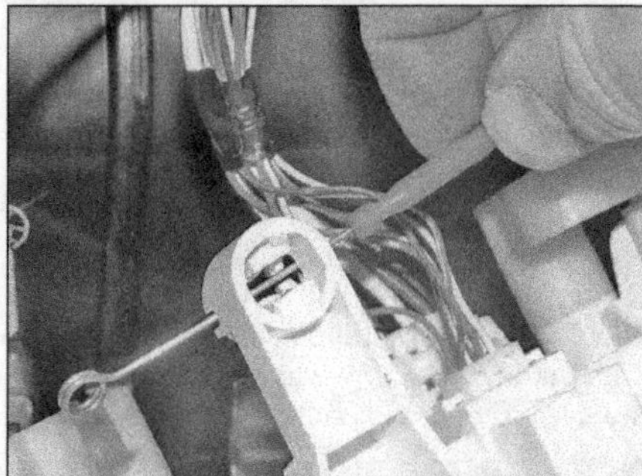

11.5b . . . and the outer cable

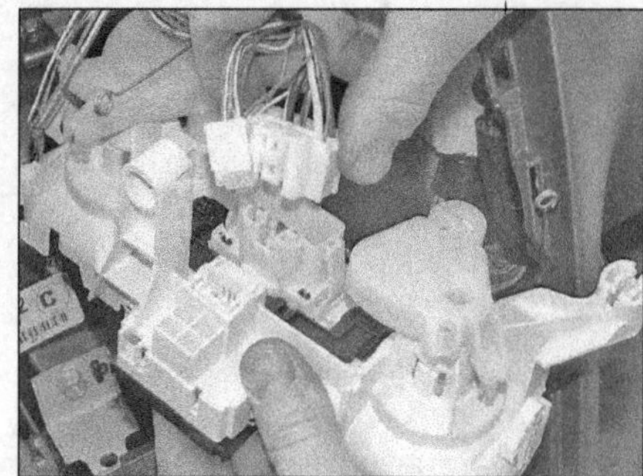

11.6 Disconnect the wiring connectors

11.7a Heater direction control cable (blue)

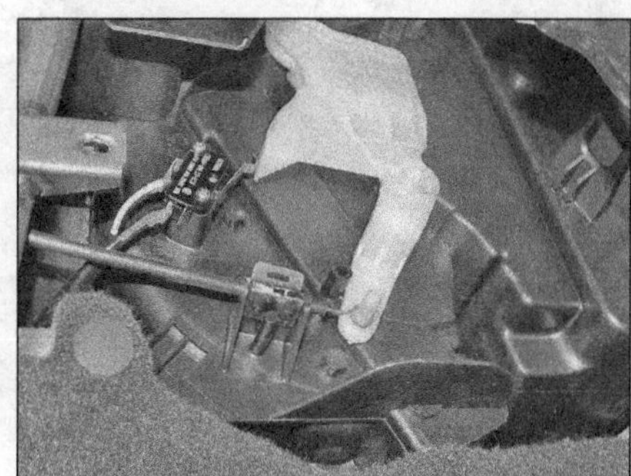

11.7b Heater temperature control cable (black)

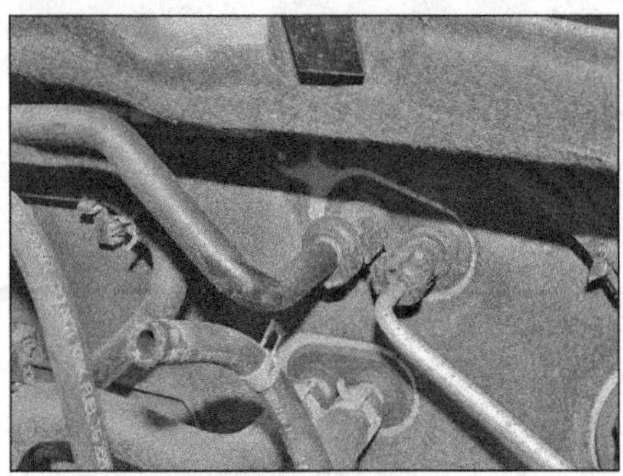
12.8 Air conditioning pipes going through the bulkhead

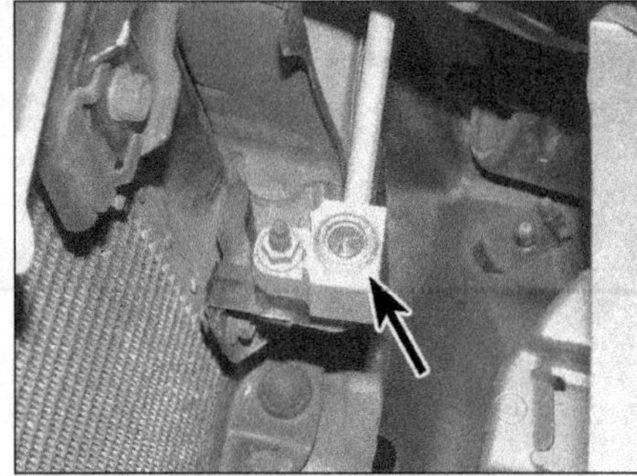
12.10 Air conditioning refrigerant sight glass (arrowed)

12.12a High-pressure service port (arrowed) – diesel model

12.12b High-pressure service port (arrowed) – petrol model

and inspect the air conditioning hoses and connections. Traces of oil usually indicate refrigerant leaks.

4 If the air conditioning system doesn't operate at all, check the fuse panel and the air conditioning relay, located in the fuse/relay box in the engine compartment.

5 The most common cause of poor cooling is simply a low system refrigerant charge. If a noticeable drop in cool air output occurs, the following quick check will help you determine if the refrigerant level is low.

Checking refrigerant charge

6 Warm the engine up to normal operating temperature.

7 Place the air conditioning temperature selector at the coldest setting and put the blower at the highest setting. Open the doors (to make sure the air conditioning system doesn't cycle off as soon as it cools the passenger compartment).

8 With the compressor engaged – the clutch will make an audible click and the centre of the clutch will rotate. After the system reaches operating temperature, feel the two pipes connected to the evaporator at the bulkhead **(see illustration)**.

9 The pipe leading from the condenser outlet to the evaporator (small tubing) should be cold, and the evaporator outlet line (the larger tubing that leads back to the compressor) should be slightly colder. If the evaporator outlet is considerably warmer than the inlet, the system needs a charge. If the air isn't as cold as it used to be, the system probably needs a charge. Further inspection or testing of the system is beyond the scope of the home mechanic and should be left to a professional.

10 Where fitted, inspect the sight glass, in the pipe union alloy block **(see illustration)**. If the refrigerant looks foamy when running, it's low. When ambient temperatures are very hot, bubbles may show in the sight glass even with the proper amount of refrigerant. With the proper amount of refrigerant, when the air conditioning is turned off, the sight glass should show refrigerant that foams, and then clears.

11 If the previous checks indicate that the refrigerant charge is low, take the vehicle to a Toyota dealer or automotive air conditioning repair facility to have the system recharged.

Air conditioning service ports

12 The high-pressure service port is located in front of the condenser, or on the inner wing panel, depending on model **(see illustrations)**.

13 The low-pressure service port is located at the rear of the engine compartment, next to the bulkhead **(see illustrations)**.

Heating systems

14 If the air coming out of the heater vents isn't hot, the problem could stem from any of the following causes:

a) *The thermostat is stuck open, preventing the engine coolant from warming-up enough to carry heat to the heater matrix. Renew the thermostat (see Section 3).*

b) *A heater hose is blocked, preventing the flow of coolant through the heater matrix. Feel both heater hoses at the bulkhead. They should be hot. If one of them is cold, there is an obstruction in one of the hoses or in the heater matrix, or the heater control valve is shut. Detach the hoses and back flush the heater matrix with a garden hose. If the heater matrix is clear but circulation is impeded, remove the two hoses and flush them out with a garden hose.*

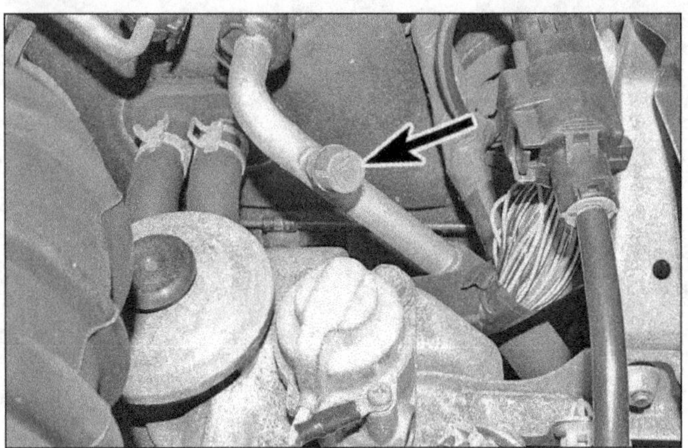
12.13a Low-pressure service port – diesel model

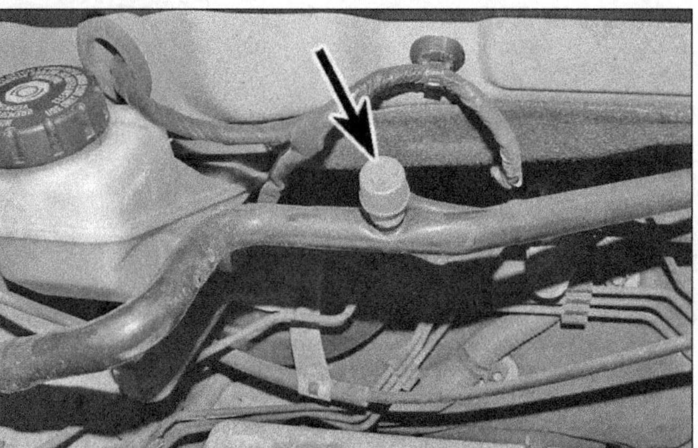
12.13b Low-pressure service port – petrol model

c) If flushing fails to remove the blockage from the heater matrix, the matrix must be renewed (see Section 10).

15 If the blower motor speed does not correspond to the setting selected on the blower switch, the problem could be a bad fuse, circuit, switch, blower motor resistor or motor.

16 If there isn't any air coming out of the vents:

a) Turn the ignition on and activate the fan control. Place your ear at the heating/ air conditioning register (vent) and listen. Most motors are audible. Can you hear the motor running?

b) If you can't (and have already verified that the blower switch and the blower motor resistor are good), the blower motor itself is probably defective (see Section 9).

17 If the carpet under the heater matrix is damp, or if antifreeze vapour or steam is coming through the vents, the heater matrix is leaking. Remove it (see Section 10) and install a new unit (most radiator workshops will not repair a leaking heater matrix).

18 Inspect the drain hose from the heater/air conditioning assembly at the left-hand side bottom of the heater housing **(see illustration)** and make sure it is not clogged.

13 Air conditioning receiver/drier – removal and refitting

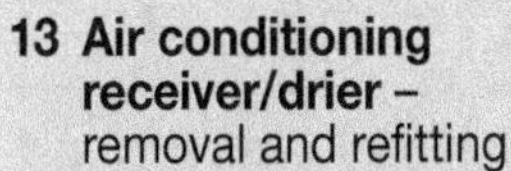

Warning: The air conditioning system is under high pressure. Do not loosen any hose fittings or remove any components until the system has been discharged. Air conditioning refrigerant may only be discharged by a dealer service department or an automotive air conditioning specialist. Always wear eye protection when disconnecting air conditioning system fittings even after the system has been discharged.

Note: *The receiver/drier is integral with the condenser.*

Removal

1 Have the refrigerant discharged and recovered by a Toyota dealer or automotive air conditioning specialist.

2 Remove the condenser as described in Section 15.

3 Turn the condenser upside down and remove the cap from the end of the condenser. Discard the O-ring seal(s); new ones must be fitted.

4 Using a pair of long-nose pliers, withdraw the cooler drier out from the side of the condenser.

Refitting

5 Refitting is the reverse of removal.

6 Apply compressor oil to the O-ring seal(s) and cap before refitting to the condenser.

7 Have the system evacuated, charged and leak-tested by the workshop that discharged it.

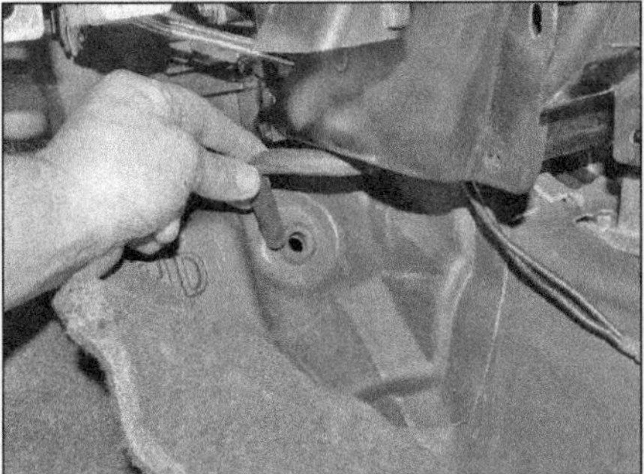

12.18 Check the heater drain hose

14 Air conditioning compressor – removal and refitting

Warning: The air conditioning system is under high pressure. Do not loosen any hose fittings or remove any components until the system has been discharged. Air conditioning refrigerant may only be discharged by a dealer service department or an automotive air conditioning specialist. Always wear eye protection when disconnecting air conditioning system fittings even after the system has been discharged.

Removal

1 Have the refrigerant discharged and recovered by a Toyota dealer or automotive air conditioning specialist.

2 Remove the drivebelt from the compressor (see Chapter 1A or 1B).

3 Detach the wiring connector and disconnect the refrigerant pipes, then cap the open fittings to prevent entry of moisture **(see illustration)**. Discard the pipe O-ring seals, new ones must be fitted.

4 Unbolt the compressor and lift it from the vehicle. Petrol engines have three mounting bolts and the diesel have four mounting bolts.

5 If a new or rebuilt compressor is being installed, follow the directions supplied with the compressor regarding the proper level of oil prior to refitting.

14.3 Air conditioning compressor wiring connector

Refitting

6 Refitting is the reverse of removal. Renew any O-rings with new ones specifically made for the type of refrigerant in your system and lubricate them with refrigerant oil, also designed specifically for your system.

7 Have the system evacuated, recharged and leak-tested by the workshop that discharged it.

15 Air conditioning condenser – removal and refitting

Warning: The air conditioning system is under high pressure. Do not loosen any hose fittings or remove any components until the system has been discharged. Air conditioning refrigerant may only be discharged by a dealer service department or an automotive air conditioning specialist. Always wear eye protection when disconnecting air conditioning system fittings even after the system has been discharged.

Removal

1 Have the refrigerant discharged and recovered by a Toyota dealer or automotive air conditioning repair facility.

2 Remove the radiator as described in Section 5.

3 Disconnect the condenser inlet and outlet fittings **(see illustrations)**. Cap the open fittings immediately to keep moisture and contamination out of the system. Discard the O-ring seals; new ones must be fitted.

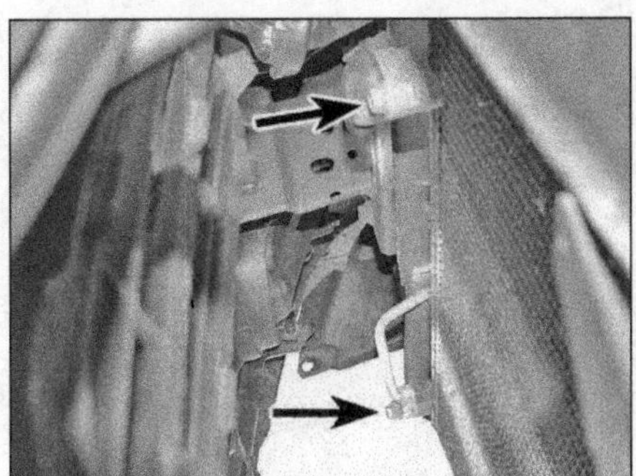

15.3a Condenser inlet and outlet pipes – diesel model

15.3b Condenser inlet . . .

15.3c . . . and outlet pipes – petrol model

15.5 Condenser upper mounting bracket

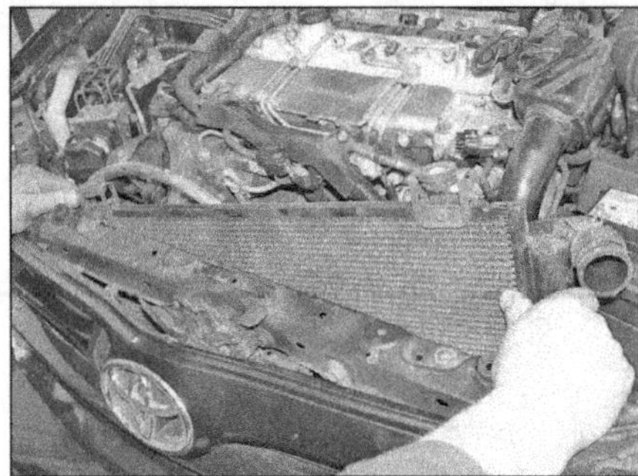
15.6 Carefully withdraw the condenser

4 Trace the pipes back and undo any support bracket retaining bolts.

5 Undo the bolts for the upper condenser supports brackets on both sides **(see illustration)**.

6 Push the condenser back towards the engine, and then lift the condenser upwards from the engine compartment **(see illustration)**.

7 if required, remove the cooler drier as described in Section 13.

Refitting

8 Fit the condenser, brackets and bolts, making sure the rubber cushions fit on the mounting points properly.

9 Reconnect the refrigerant pipes, using new O-rings. Apply compressor oil to the O-ring seal(s), before refitting.

10 Refit the remaining parts in the reverse order of removal.

11 Have the system evacuated, charged and leak-tested by the workshop that discharged it. If a new condenser has been installed, add approximately 40 cc of new refrigerant oil of the correct type.

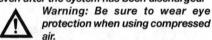

16 Air conditioning evaporator – removal and refitting

Warning: The air conditioning system is under high pressure. Do not loosen any hose fittings or remove any components until the system has been discharged. Air conditioning refrigerant may only be discharged by a dealer service department or an automotive air conditioning specialist. Always wear eye protection when disconnecting air conditioning system fittings even after the system has been discharged.

Warning: Be sure to wear eye protection when using compressed air.

Removal

1 Have the air conditioning refrigerant discharged (where applicable) by an automotive air conditioning specialist.

2 Disconnect the negative cable from the battery (see Chapter 5A).

3 Drain the cooling system (see Chapter 1A or 1B), unless you have access to hose clamps (see next paragraph).

4 Working in the engine compartment, release the clips and disconnect the heater hoses at the bulkhead. If you have access to hose clamps, use them on the heater hoses – then there's no need to drain the coolant **(see illustrations)**. Recover the rubber grommet from the bulkhead.

5 On air conditioned vehicles, disconnect the refrigerant pipes at the engine compartment bulkhead **(see illustrations)**. Discard the O-ring seals, as new ones must be fitted. Plug or cover the ends of the

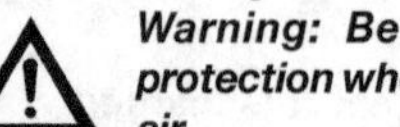

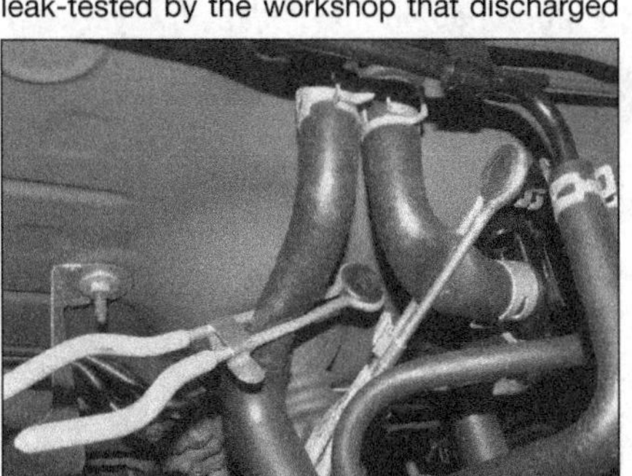
16.4a If available, use clamps on the heater hoses . . .

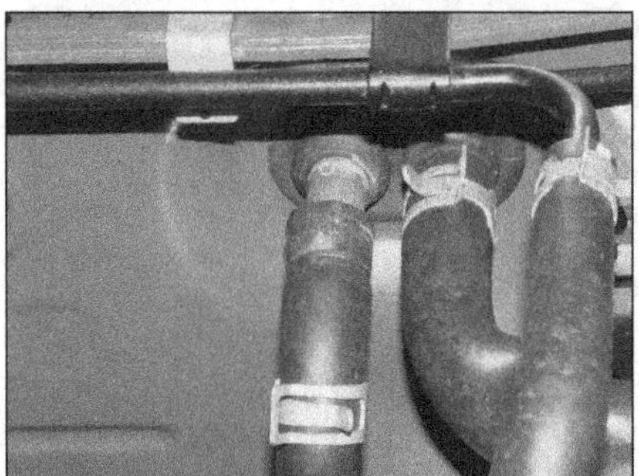
16.4b . . . then release the clips and disconnect the hose from the bulkhead . . .

16.4c Recover the grommet from the pipes

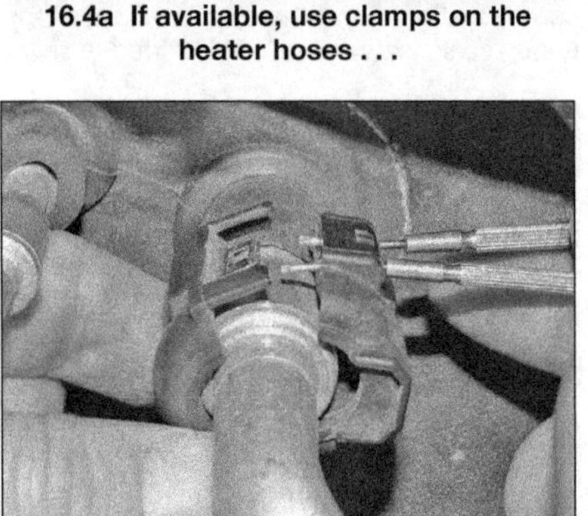
16.5a Release the securing clips . . .

16.5b . . . remove the retaining clamp . . .

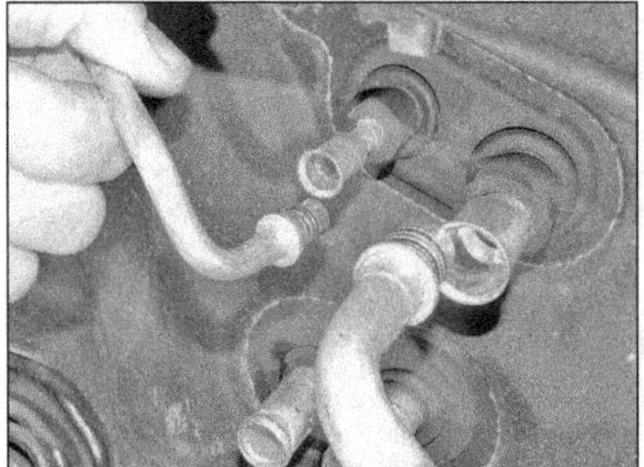
16.5c . . . and disconnect the pipes

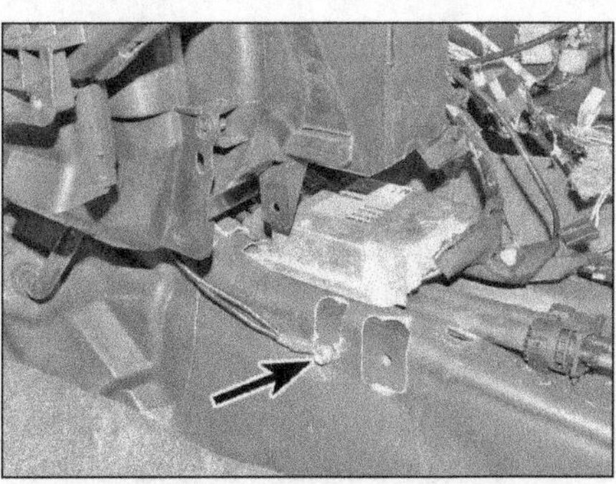
16.8 Disconnect earth cable – arrowed

16.9a Undo the centre nuts (arrowed) . . .

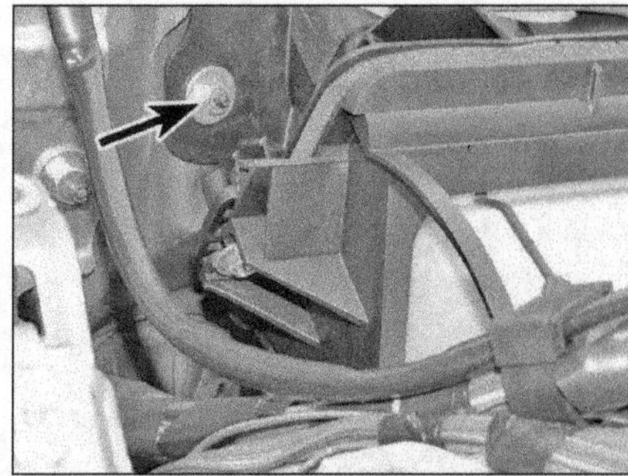
16.9b . . . upper nut (arrowed) . . .

pipes, and recover the grommet from the bulkhead.

6 Remove the entire facia and support crossbrace as described in Chapter 11.

7 Working your way around the heater and blower motor housing, make a note of their fitted positions, and then disconnect any wiring plugs and cables from the heater unit.

8 Disconnect the earth cable from below the centre of the heater unit **(see illustration)**

9 Undo the nuts, around the heater blower motor/evaporator housing to bulkhead noting there fitted position **(see illustrations)**. With all the nuts/bolts removed the complete unit can now be removed from the vehicle.

10 Undo the nuts/bolts securing the blower unit, and split it from the heater housing unit **(see illustrations)**. Unclip the wiring connectors and note their fitted position as the two parts are split.

11 Undo the retaining screws and remove the plastic cover from the evaporator pipes **(see illustrations)**.

12 Undo the retaining screws and withdraw the evaporator from the housing **(see illustrations)**.

13 If required remove the thermistor sensor probe from the evaporator matrix as described in Section 17.

14 The evaporator matrix can be cleaned with a 'fin comb' and blown off with compressed air.

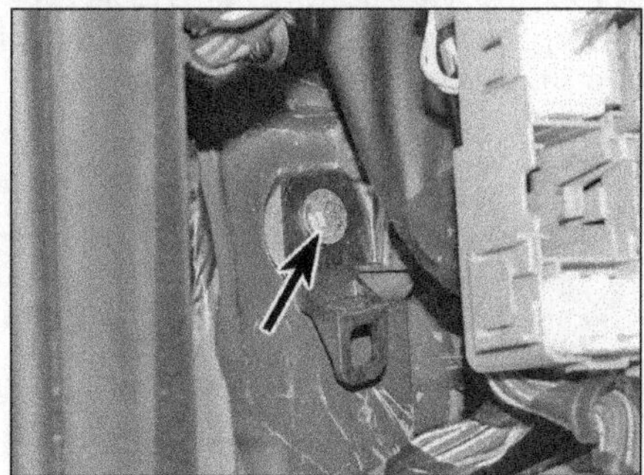
16.9c . . . left-hand end retaining bolt . . .

16.9d . . . and lower housing nut (arrowed)

16.10a Undo the bolts securing the blower to the evaporator housing

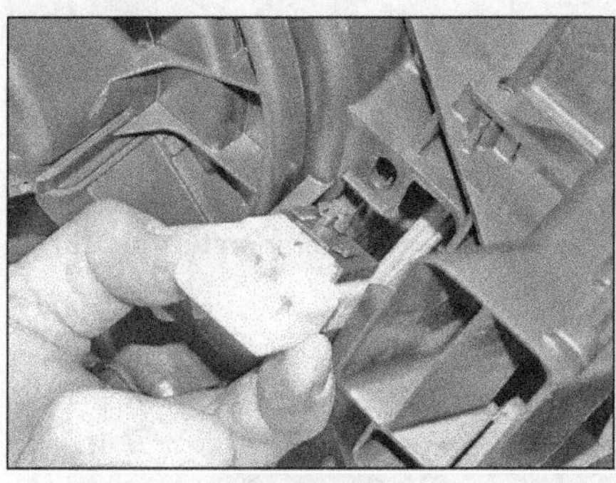
16.10b Release the wiring loom and connectors

16.10c Split the blower from the evaporator housing

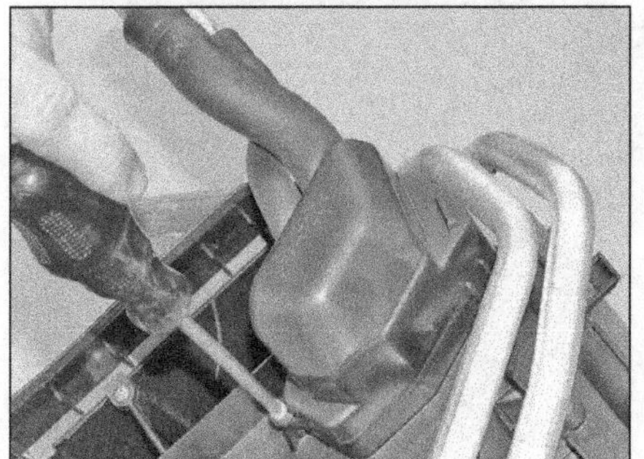
16.11a Undo the retaining screws . . .

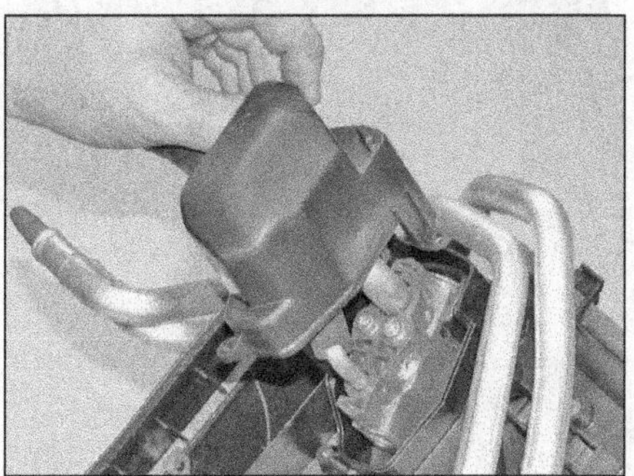
16.11b . . . and remove the plastic cover

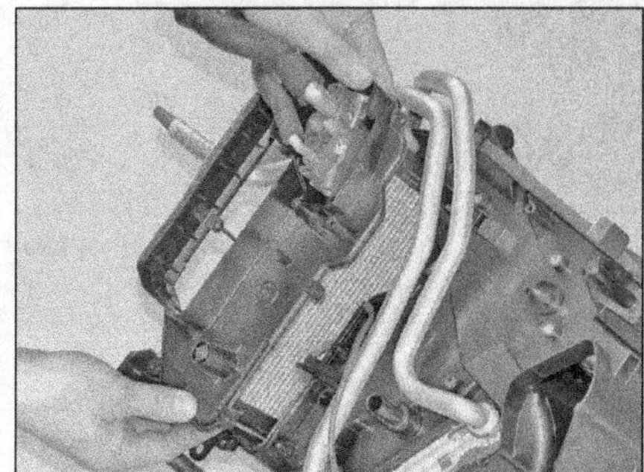
16.12a Undo the retaining screws . . .

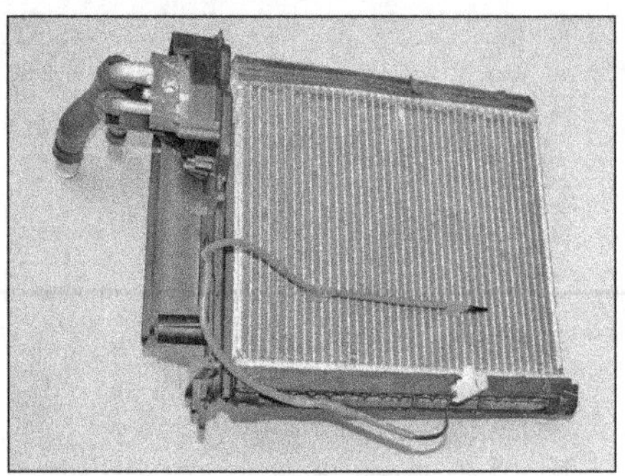

16.12b . . . and remove the evaporator from the housing

16.16 Make sure the drain hose is located correctly

Refitting

15 Refitting is the reverse order of removal, noting that new air conditioning pipe O-rings must be fitted. Apply compressor oil to the O-ring seal(s) before refitting.

16 When refitting the evaporator housing, ensure the drain hose is correctly located at the bulkhead **(see illustration)**.

17 Refill the cooling system, reconnect the battery and run the engine. Check for leaks and proper system operation.

18 Have the air conditioning system evacuated, charged and leak-tested by the workshop that discharged it. If the evaporator matrix is renewed, add 40 cc of new refrigerant oil of the correct type to the system during the recharge.

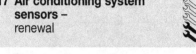

17 Air conditioning system sensors – renewal

Ambient temperature sensor

1 Remove the upper trim panel from across the top of the radiator **(see illustration)**.

2 Disconnect the wiring plug, release the connector clamp, then carefully prise the sensor from position **(see illustration)**.

3 To test the sensor, connect the leads from an ohmmeter to the sensor terminals, and measure the resistance. At 25°C the resistance should be 1.6 to 1.8 kΩ, and at 40°C the resistance should be 0.5 to 0.7 kΩ.

4 Refitting is a reversal of removal.

Evaporator temperature sensor

5 To test the sensor in place, remove the glovebox (Chapter 11, Section 27), connect the leads from an ohmmeter to the sensor terminals, and measure the resistance. At 25°C the resistance should be 1.5 kΩ **(see illustration)**.

6 To renew the sensor, remove the evaporator as described in Section 16.

7 Pull the thermistor sensor probe from the evaporator matrix, and if required, unbolt the expansion valve and the two short refrigerant pipes **(see illustrations)**. Discard the O-ring seals, as new ones must be fitted.

8 Refitting is a reversal of removal.

17.1 Remove the radiator upper trim cover

17.2 Ambient air temperature sensor

17.5 Disconnect the wiring connector – arrowed

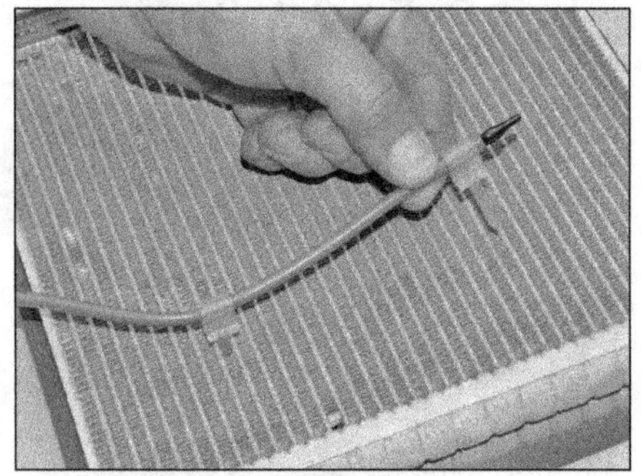

17.7a Carefully unclip the sensor from the evaporator

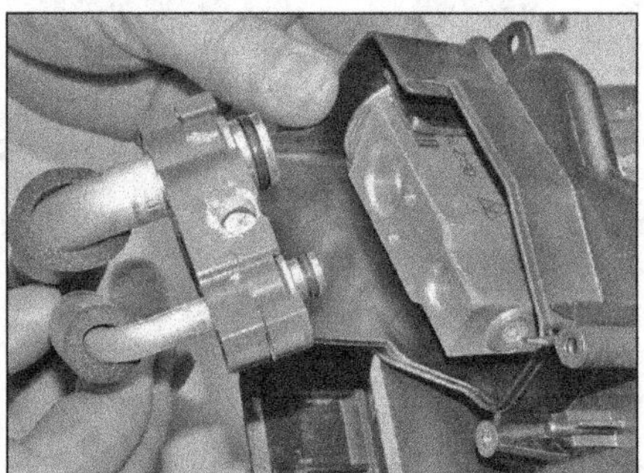

17.7b Remove the pipes . . .

17.7c . . . and the housing

Chapter 4 Part A: Fuel and exhaust systems – petrol engines

Contents

Degrees of difficulty

Easy, suitable for novice with little experience 	**Fairly easy,** suitable for beginner with some experience	**Fairly difficult,** suitable for competent DIY mechanic	**Difficult,** suitable for experienced DIY mechanic	**Very difficult,** suitable for expert DIY or professional

Specifications

General

Engine codes:	
1.4 litre (1398 cc) engine	4ZZ-FE
1.6 litre (1598 cc) engine	3ZZ-FE

Fuel system

Fuel system hold pressure	3.01 to 3.47 bar
Fuel pump resistance (at 20°C)	0.2 to 3.0 ohms
Fuel injector resistance (at 20°C)	13.4 to 14.2 ohms
Fuel injector volume (15 seconds)	39.3 to 52.4 cc

Inlet airflow meter

Resistance at connections 1 (E2) and 2 (THA):	
-20°C	13.6 to 18.4 k ohms
20°C	2.21 to 2.69 k ohms
60°C	0.49 to 0.67 k ohms

Crankshaft position sensor

Resistance:	
Cold (up to 50°C)	1630 to 2740 ohms
Hot (from 50°C)	2065 to 3225 ohms

Camshaft position sensor

Resistance:	
Cold (up to 50°C)	835 to 1400 ohms
Hot (from 50°C)	1060 to 1645 ohms
Camshaft timing oil control valve (at 20°C)	6.9 to 7.9 ohms

Idle speed

Automatic transmission	650 to 750 rpm
Manual transmission	600 to 700 rpm

Torque wrench settings	Nm	lbf ft
Camshaft oil control valve	7	5
Camshaft position sensor	9	7
Crankshaft position sensor	9	7
Exhaust manifold	37	27
Fuel rail mounting bolts	18	13
Inlet manifold	30	23
Throttle body	30	22

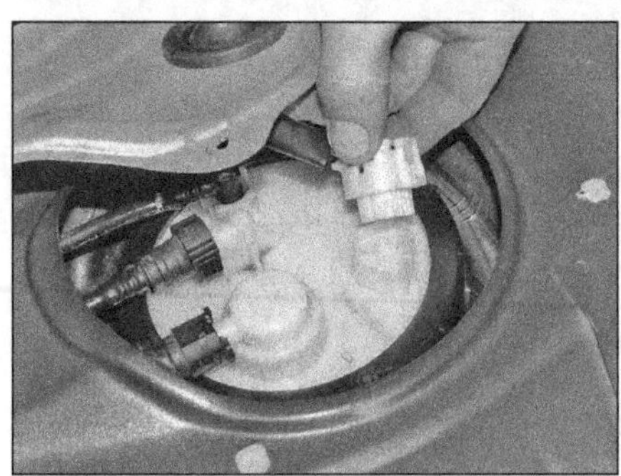

2.4 Disconnecting the fuel pump

1 General information

The fuel system consists of a fuel tank, an electric fuel pump (located in the fuel tank), an EFI/fuel pump relay, fuel injectors, a fuel pressure regulator, an air cleaner assembly and a throttle body unit. All models covered by this manual are equipped with the Multi Point Fuel Injection (MPFI) system.

Multi Point Fuel Injection

Multi Point Fuel Injection (MPFI) uses timed impulses to sequentially inject the fuel directly into the inlet port of each cylinder. The injectors are controlled by the Electronic Control Module (ECM). The ECM monitors various engine parameters and delivers the exact amount of fuel, in the correct sequence, into the inlet ports. The throttle body serves only to control the amount of air passing into the system. Because each cylinder is equipped with an injector mounted immediately adjacent to the inlet valve, much better control of the fuel/air mixture ratio is possible.

The engine management ECM also varies the timing of the inlet camshaft. The camshaft timing is varied according to engine speed and load. Retarding the timing (opening the valves later) at low and high engine speeds improves low speed driveability and maximum power respectively, whilst advancing the timing at medium engine speeds increases mid-range torque and reduces exhaust emissions.

Fuel pump and pipes

The fuel sender/pump unit incorporates a pressure regulator. Fuel is pumped along a single pipe to the front of the vehicle – any excess pressure created by the pump is released directly back into the tank via the regulator.

Fuel vapour is routed into a carbon canister where it is stored, until it's then fed back into the inlet manifold and burnt during the normal combustion process.

The fuel pump will operate as long as the engine is cranking or running and the ECM is receiving ignition reference pulses from the electronic ignition system (see Chapter 5B). If there are no reference pulses, the fuel pump will shut off after 2 or 3 seconds.

Exhaust system

The exhaust system includes a manifold fitted with an exhaust oxygen sensor, a catalytic converter, an exhaust pipe, and a silencer. An additional oxygen sensor is fitted after the catalytic converter to further fine-tune the engine and monitor the performance of the converter.

The catalytic converter is an emission control device added to the exhaust system to reduce pollutants. A single-bed converter is used in combination with a three-way (reduction) catalyst. Refer to Chapter 4C for more information regarding the catalytic converter.

Warning: Petrol is extremely flammable, so take extra precautions when you work on any part of the fuel system. Don't smoke or allow open flames or bare light bulbs near the work area, and don't work in a garage where a natural gas-type appliance (such as a water heater or a clothes dryer) with a pilot light is present. Since petrol is carcinogenic, wear latex gloves when there's a possibility of being exposed to fuel, and, if you spill any fuel on your skin; rinse it off immediately with soap and water. Mop-up any spills immediately and do not store fuel-soaked rags where they could ignite. The fuel system is under constant pressure, so, if any fuel pipes are to be disconnected, the fuel pressure in the system must be relieved first. When you perform any kind of work on the fuel system, wear safety glasses and have a Class B type fire extinguisher on hand.

2 Fuel injection system – depressurisation

1 Before servicing any fuel system component, you must relieve the fuel pressure to minimise the risk of fire or personal injury.

2 Remove the fuel filler cap – this will relieve any pressure built-up in the tank.

3 Remove the rear seat from the passenger cabin, then prise up the fuel pump/sender unit access cover.

4 Remove the fuel pump connector **(see illustration)**.

5 Start the engine and wait for the engine to stall, and then turn the ignition off.

6 The fuel system is now depressurised. **Note:** *Place a rag around the fuel line before removing any hose clamp or fitting to prevent any residual fuel from spilling onto the engine.*

7 Before working on the fuel system, disconnect the cable from the negative terminal of the battery (see Chapter 5A).

8 Refit the connector when the job is completed.

3 Fuel pump – removal and refitting

Warning: Petrol is extremely flammable, so take extra precautions when you work on any part of the fuel system. Don't smoke or allow open flames or bare light bulbs near the work area, and don't work in a garage where a natural gas-type appliance (such as a water heater or a clothes dryer) with a pilot light is present. Since petrol is carcinogenic, wear latex gloves when there's a possibility of being exposed to fuel, and, if you spill any fuel on your skin, rinse it off immediately with soap and water. Mop-up any spills immediately and do not store fuel-soaked rags where they could ignite. The fuel system is under constant pressure, so, if any fuel pipes are to be disconnected, the fuel pressure in the system must be relieved first. When you perform any kind of work on the fuel system, wear safety glasses and have a Class B type fire extinguisher on hand.

TMC (Toyota Motor Co) pump

1 Remove the fuel tank cap.

2 Disconnect the cable from the negative terminal of the battery (see Chapter 5A).

3 Remove the rear seat cushion, and lift the carpet underneath it (see Chapter 11).

4 Using a flat-bladed tool, carefully prise up the fuel pump/sender unit access cover **(see illustration)**.

5 Disconnect the electrical connector, and disconnect the fuel pipe(s) **(see illustrations)**.

3.4 Prise up the access cover over the fuel pump

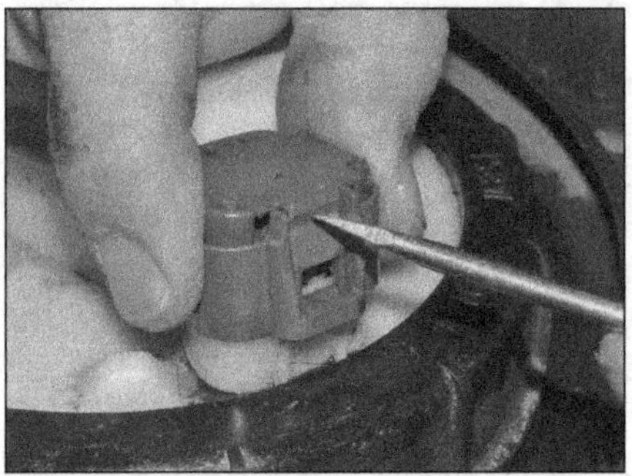

3.5a Depress the clips and disconnect the pump/sender wiring plug

6 Remove the fuel pump/sender unit retaining bolts **(see illustration)**.
7 Carefully withdraw the fuel pump/fuel level sender unit assembly from the fuel tank **(see illustration)**.
8 Before further dismantling, check with your local dealer for availability of parts.
9 Refitting is the reverse of removal. Make sure a new sealing ring is fitted.

Denso pump

10 Remove the fuel tank cap.
11 Disconnect the cable from the negative terminal of the battery (see Chapter 5A).
12 Remove the rear seat cushion, and lift the carpet underneath it (see Chapter 11).
13 Undo the retaining bolts and carefully prise up the fuel pump/sender unit access cover **(see illustration)**.
14 Disconnect the electrical connector, and disconnect the fuel pipe(s) **(see illustrations)**.
15 Unscrew the sender unit plastic retaining collar using a pair of large, crossed-screwdrivers, or improvise a tool **(see illustrations)**. Make sure the alignment marks between the collar and the tank are noted before removal.
16 Carefully lift the sender/pump assembly from position.
17 Before further dismantling, check with your local dealer for availability of parts.
18 Refitting is the reverse of removal. On vehicles where the pump/sender assembly is retained by a locking collar, the collar must be tightened up to the same point as before disassembly. Make sure a new sealing ring is fitted **(see illustration)**.

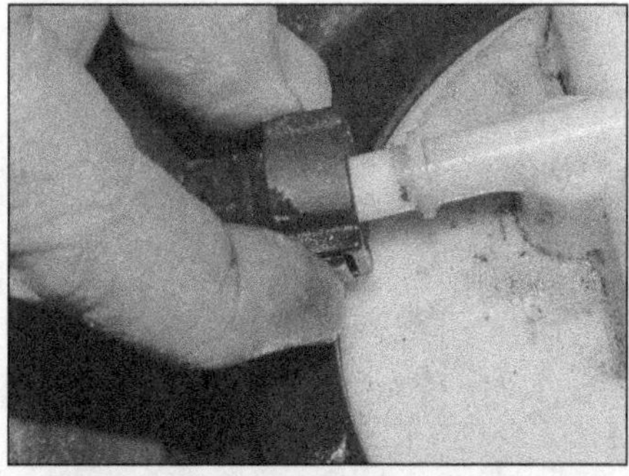
3.5b Squeeze in the release buttons and pull the fuel pipe from the pump cover

3.5c On some models, there are two fuel connections to the pump cover - one for feed and one for return

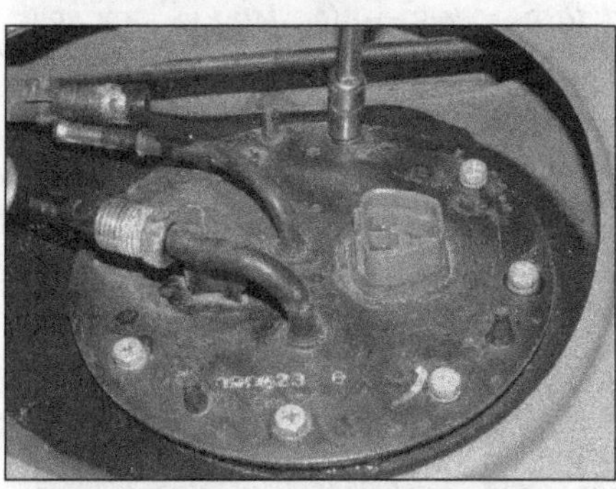
3.6 Undo the pump/sender unit cover retaining bolts

3.7 Carefully lift the pump/sender unit from the tank

Bosch pump

19 Remove the fuel tank cap.
20 Disconnect the cable from the negative terminal of the battery (see Chapter 5A).
21 Remove the rear seat cushion, and lift the carpet underneath it (see Chapter 11).
22 Undo the retaining bolts and carefully prise up the fuel pump/sender unit access cover **(see illustration 3.13)**.

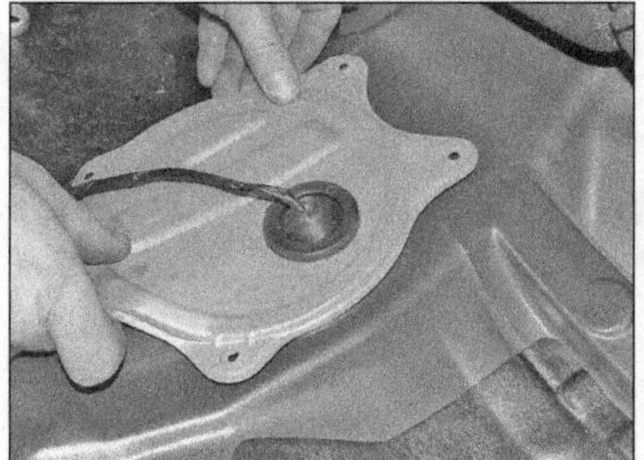
3.13 Remove the access cover

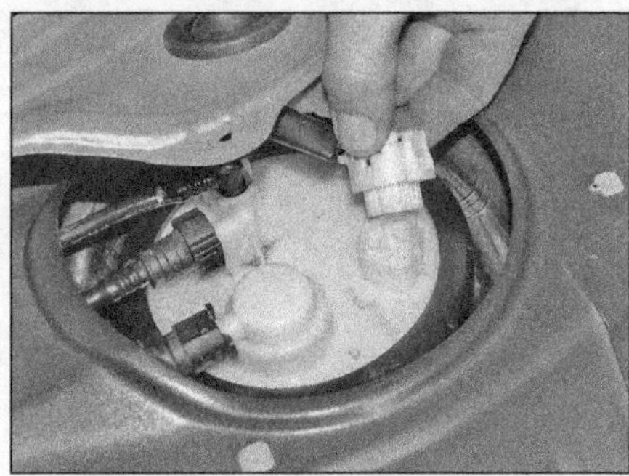
3.14a Disconnect the wiring connector . . .

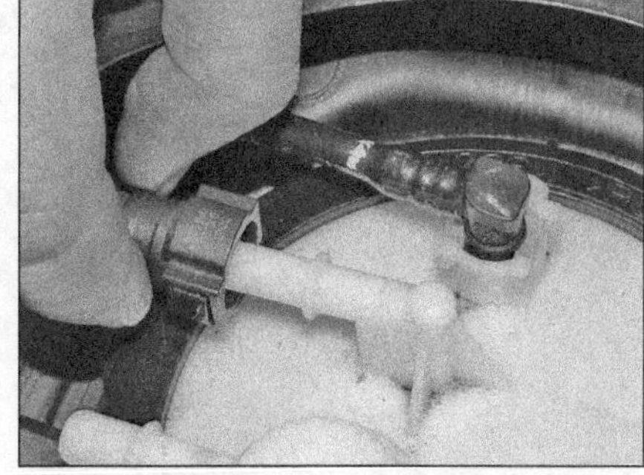
3.14b . . . and disconnect the fuel pipes

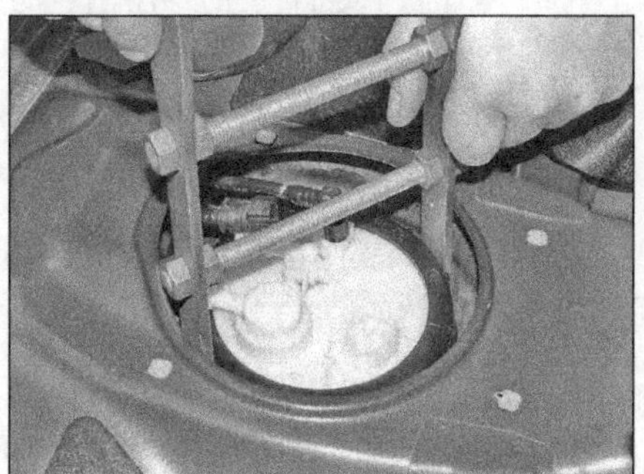
3.15a Improvise a tool to unscrew the plastic collar . . .

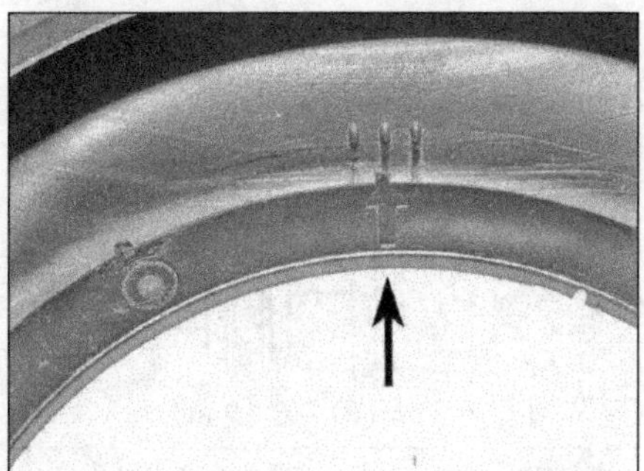
3.15b . . . make a note of the alignment marks (arrowed)

3.18 Use new sealing ring when refitting

23 Disconnect the electrical connector, and disconnect the fuel pipe(s) **(see illustrations 3.14a and 3.14b)**.

24 Unscrew the sender unit plastic retaining collar using a pair of large, crossed-screwdrivers, or improvise a tool **(see illustrations 3.15a and 3.15b)**. Make alignment marks between the collar and the tank to aid reassembly.

25 Carefully lift the sender/pump assembly from position **(see illustration)**.

26 Before further dismantling, check with your local dealer for availability of parts.

27 Refitting is the reverse of removal. On vehicles where the pump/sender assembly is retained by a locking collar, the collar must be tightened upto the same point as before disassembly. Make sure a new sealing ring is fitted.

4 Fuel level sender unit – testing and renewal

Warning: Petrol is extremely flammable, so take extra precautions when you work on any part of the fuel system. Don't smoke or allow open flames or bare light bulbs near the work area, and don't work in a garage where a natural gas-type appliance (such as a water heater or a clothes dryer) with a pilot light is present. Since petrol is carcinogenic, wear latex gloves when there's a possibility of being exposed to fuel, and, if you spill any fuel on your skin; rinse it off immediately with soap and water. Mop-up any spills immediately and do not store fuel-soaked rags where they could ignite. The fuel system is under constant pressure, so, if any fuel pipes are to be disconnected, the fuel pressure in the system must be relieved first. When you perform any kind of work on the fuel system, wear safety glasses and have a Class B type fire extinguisher on hand.

4.1 Remove the access cover

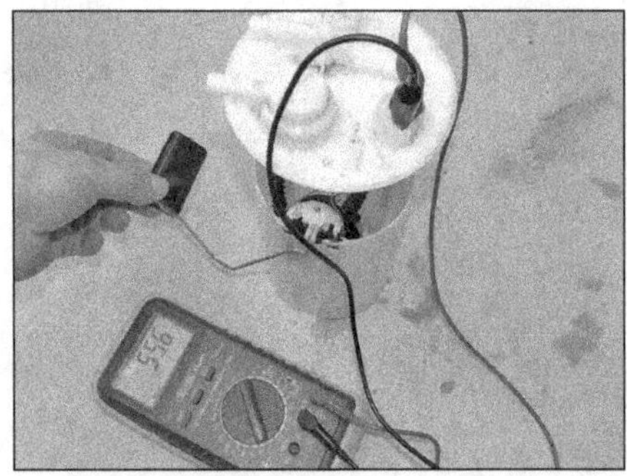

4.4 Connect an ohmmeter to the sender unit terminals

3.25 Removing the fuel pump/sender assembly

Testing

1 Before performing any tests on the fuel level sender unit, remove the rear seat and the fuel pump/sending unit access cover **(see illustration)**.

2 Disconnect the fuel level sender unit electrical connector located on top of the fuel tank.

3 Position the ohmmeter probes on the electrical connector terminals (terminals 1 and 2) check for resistance, it should be between 0.2 and 3.0 ohms (at 20°C).

4 If the readings are incorrect, renew the sender unit. **Note:** *The test can also be performed with the fuel level sending unit removed from the fuel tank. Using an ohmmeter, check the resistance of the sending unit with the float arm completely down (tank empty) and with the arm up (tank full)* ***(see illustration)****. The resistance should change steadily from 62 ohms to approximately 2.0 ohms.*

Renewal

5 Remove the fuel pump/fuel level sending unit assembly from the fuel tank (see Section 3).

6 Carefully angle the sending unit out of the opening without damaging the fuel level float located at the bottom of the assembly **(see illustration 3.7)**. **Note:** *On Bosch units, the sender unclips from the container inside the tank.*

7 Disconnect the electrical connectors from the sending unit.

8 Remove the screw from the side of the sending unit bracket and separate the sending unit from the assembly.

9 Refitting is the reverse of removal.

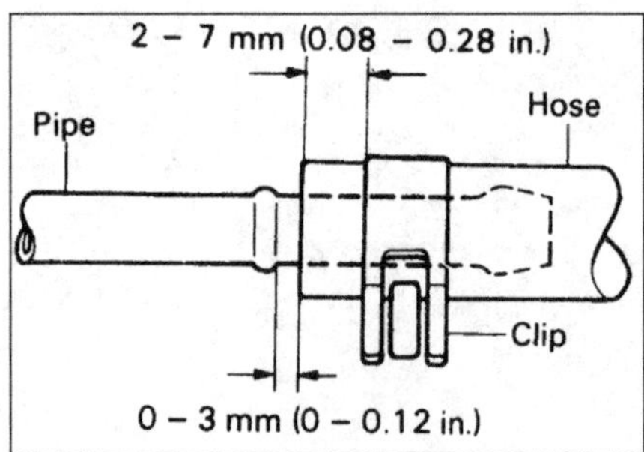

5.6 When attaching a section of rubber hose to a metal fuel line, be sure to overlap the hose as shown

5 Fuel pipes and fittings – inspection and renewal

Warning: Petrol is extremely flammable, so take extra precautions when you work on any part of the fuel system. Don't smoke or allow open flames or bare light bulbs near the work area, and don't work in a garage where a natural gas-type appliance (such as a water heater or a clothes dryer) with a pilot light is present. Since petrol is carcinogenic, wear latex gloves when there's a possibility of being exposed to fuel, and, if you spill any fuel on your skin, rinse it off immediately with soap and water. Mop-up any spills immediately and do not store fuel-soaked rags where they could ignite. The fuel system is under constant pressure, so, if any fuel pipes are to be disconnected, the fuel pressure in the system must be relieved first. When you perform any kind of work on the fuel system, wear safety glasses and have a Class B type fire extinguisher on hand.

Inspection

1 Once in a while, you will have to raise the vehicle to service or renew some component (an exhaust pipe mounting, for example). Whenever you work under the vehicle, always inspect fuel pipes and all fittings and connections for damage or deterioration.

2 Check all hoses and pipes for cracks, kinks, deformation or obstructions.

3 Make sure all hoses and pipe clips attach their associated hoses or pipes securely to the underside of the vehicle.

4 Verify all hose clamps attaching rubber hoses to metal fuel pipes or pipes are snug enough to ensure a tight fit between the hoses and pipes.

Renewal

5 If you must renew any damaged sections, use original equipment hoses or pipes constructed from exactly the same material as the section you are renewing. Do not install substitutes constructed from inferior or inappropriate material or you could cause a fuel leak or a fire.

6 Always, before detaching or disassembling any part of the fuel line system, note the routing of all hoses and pipes and the orientation of all clamps and clips to ensure that new sections are installed in exactly the same manner.

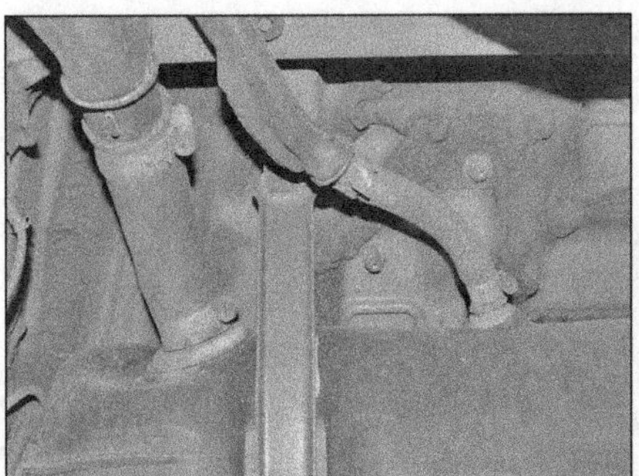

6.6 Slacken the clamps and disconnect the fuel tank hoses

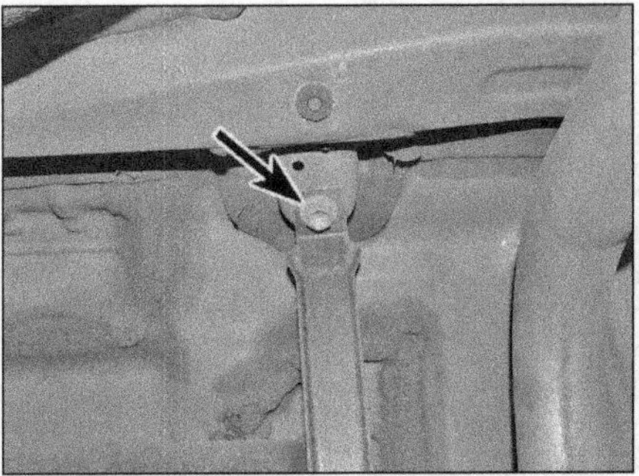

6.7a Remove the fuel retaining strap rear bolts . . .

6.7b . . . and the front bolts

When attaching hoses to metal pipes, overlap them as shown **(see illustration)**.

7 Before detaching any part of the fuel system, be sure to relieve the fuel line and tank pressure by removing the fuel tank cap and disconnecting the battery (see Chapter 5A). Cover the fitting being disconnected with a rag to absorb any fuel that may spray out.

6 Fuel tank – removal and refitting

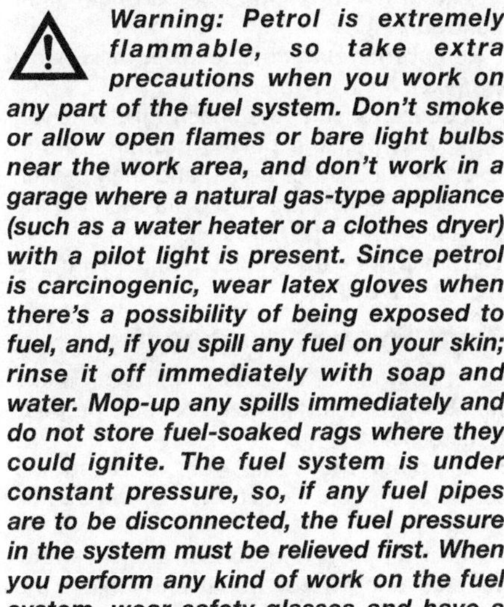

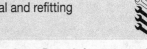

Warning: Petrol is extremely flammable, so take extra precautions when you work on any part of the fuel system. Don't smoke or allow open flames or bare light bulbs near the work area, and don't work in a garage where a natural gas-type appliance (such as a water heater or a clothes dryer) with a pilot light is present. Since petrol is carcinogenic, wear latex gloves when there's a possibility of being exposed to fuel, and, if you spill any fuel on your skin; rinse it off immediately with soap and water. Mop-up any spills immediately and do not store fuel-soaked rags where they could ignite. The fuel system is under constant pressure, so, if any fuel pipes are to be disconnected, the fuel pressure in the system must be relieved first. When you perform any kind of work on the fuel system, wear safety glasses and have a Class B type fire extinguisher on hand.

Removal

1 This procedure is much easier to perform if the fuel tank is empty. Some models may have a drain plug for this purpose. If for some reason the drain plug can't be removed, postpone the job until the tank is empty or syphon the fuel into an approved container using a syphoning kit (available at most automotive parts/accessory stores).

Warning: Do not start the syphoning action by mouth.

2 Remove the fuel pump/fuel level sending unit assembly from the fuel tank (see Section 3).

3 Raise the vehicle and place it securely on axle stands (see *Jacking and vehicle support*).

4 Remove the centre exhaust pipe and the heat insulator from the vehicle (see Section 15).

5 Support the fuel tank with a trolley jack. Place a sturdy plank between the jack head and the fuel tank to protect the tank.

6 Disconnect the fuel pipe(s), and the fuel filler hose **(see illustration)**. **Note:** *Be sure to plug the hoses to prevent leakage and contamination of the fuel system.*

7 Remove the bolts from the fuel tank retaining straps **(see illustrations)**.

8 Lower the tank enough to disconnect the electrical connector and earth strap from the fuel pump/fuel gauge sender unit, if you have not already done so.

9 Remove the tank from the vehicle.

Refitting

10 Refitting is the reverse of removal.

7 Fuel tank cleaning and repair – general information

1 Any repairs to the fuel tank or filler neck should be carried out by a professional who has experience in this critical and potentially dangerous work. Even after cleaning and flushing of the fuel system, explosive fumes can remain and ignite during repair of the tank.

2 If the fuel tank is removed from the vehicle, it should not be placed in an area where sparks or open flames could ignite the fumes coming out of the tank. Be especially careful inside garages where a natural gas-type appliance is located, because the pilot light could cause an explosion.

8.2a Slacken the retaining clip . . .

8 Air cleaner assembly – removal and refitting

Removal

1 Disconnect the wiring connector from the mass airflow sensor (MAF) **(see illustration)**.

2 Slacken the retaining clips and disconnect the air inlet hose from the air cleaner housing **(see illustrations)**. Note the alignment markings and slot for refitting.

3 Release the retaining clips, and remove the air filter cover and the filter element **(see illustrations)**.

8.1 Disconnect the wiring connector

8.2b . . . noting the alignment marks

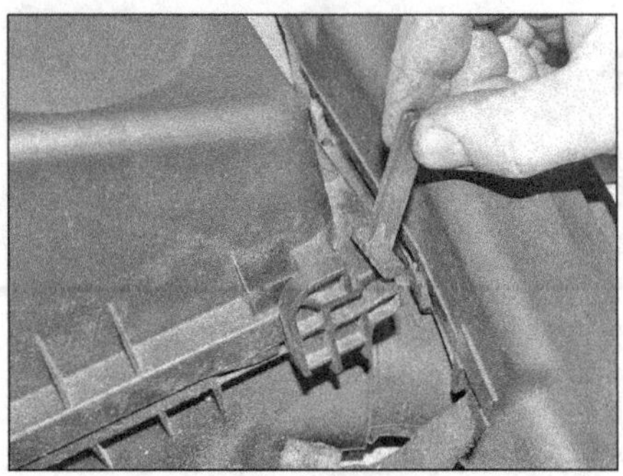
8.3a Release the air cleaner cover clips . . .

8.3b . . . lift of the upper cover . . .

8.3c . . . and withdraw the filter element

8.4a Undo the retaining bolts . . .

8.4b . . . and remove the filter lower housing

4 Remove the three bolts and remove the air cleaner assembly from the engine compartment, disconnecting the inlet hose as the assembly is withdrawn **(see illustrations)**.

Refitting

5 Refitting is the reverse of removal.

9.1 Slacken the locknut on the accelerator cable

9.2 Remove the cable end fitting from the slot in the lever

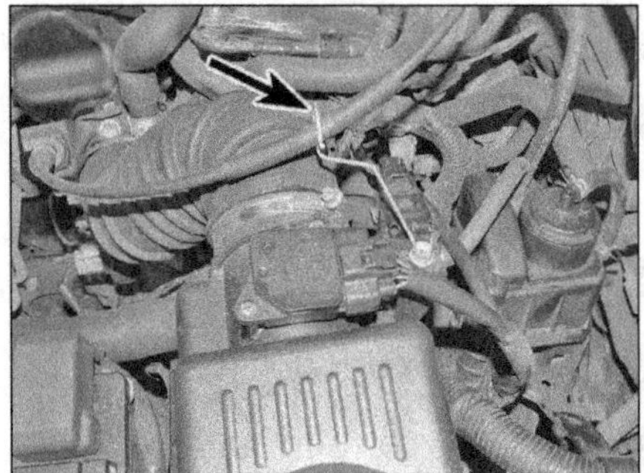
9.3a Release the cable . . .

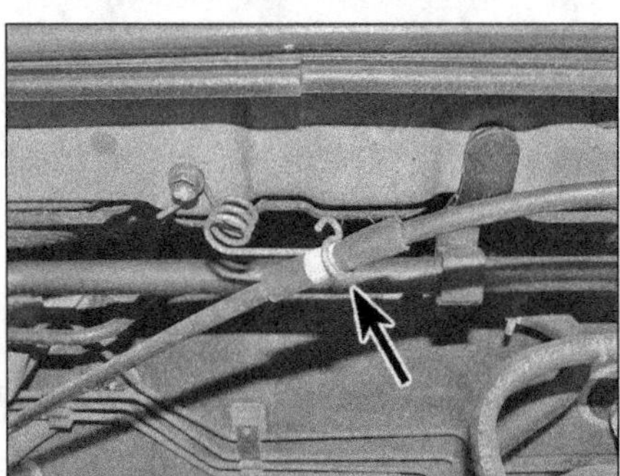
9.3b . . . from the retaining brackets

9 Accelerator cable – removal, refitting and adjustment

Removal

1 Loosen the locknut on the threaded portion of the throttle cable at the throttle body **(see illustration)**.

2 Rotate the throttle lever and slip the cable end out of the slot in the lever **(see illustration)**.

3 Release the cable from the retaining clips/brackets in the engine compartment **(see illustrations)**.

4 Remove the driver's side lower facia panel as described in Chapter 11.

5 Squeeze together the ends of the retaining clips, and pull the plastic grommet/fitting from the accelerator pedal, and then detach the cable. Remove the two bolts securing the cable retainer to the bulkhead.

6 From inside the vehicle, pull the cable through the bulkhead.

Refitting and adjustment

7 Refitting is the reverse of removal. Make sure the cable casing grommet seats properly in the bulkhead.

8 To adjust the cable, fully depress the accelerator pedal and check that the throttle is fully opened.

9 If not fully opened, loosen the locknuts, depress accelerator pedal and adjust the cable until the throttle is fully open.

10 Tighten the locknuts and recheck the adjustment. Make sure the throttle closes fully when the pedal is released.

10 Fuel injection system – general information

These models are equipped with an Electronic Fuel Injection (EFI) system. The EFI system is composed of three basic subsystems: fuel system, air induction system and electronic control system.

Fuel system

An electric fuel pump located inside

the fuel tank supplies fuel under constant pressure to the fuel rail, which distributes fuel evenly to all injectors. From the fuel rail, fuel is injected into the inlet ports, just above the inlet valves, by fuel injectors. The amount of fuel supplied by the injectors is precisely controlled by an Electronic Control Module (ECM).

Air induction system

The air induction system consists of an air filter housing, the throttle body and the duct connecting the two. An airflow meter is located in the air filter outlet ducting, which also measures the air temperature. This information helps the ECM determine the amount of fuel to be injected by the injectors.

The throttle plate inside the throttle body is controlled by the driver. As the throttle plate opens, the speed of the incoming air increases, which lowers the temperature of the air, and the manifold vacuum decreases. The sensors send this information to the ECM, which then signals the injectors to increase the amount of fuel delivered to the inlet ports.

Electronic control system

The Computer Control System controls the EFI and other systems by means of an Electronic Control Module (ECM), which employs a microcomputer. The ECM receives signals from a number of information sensors which monitor such variables as inlet air temperature, throttle angle, coolant temperature, engine rpm, vehicle speed and exhaust oxygen content. These signals help the ECM determine the injection duration necessary for the optimum air/fuel ratio. Some of these sensors and their corresponding ECM-controlled relays are not contained within EFI components, but are located throughout the engine compartment.

11 Fuel injection system – testing and adjustment

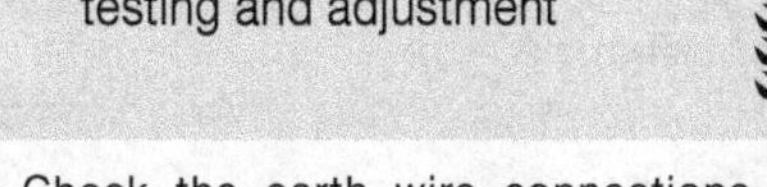

1 Check the earth wire connections for tightness. Check all wiring and electrical connectors that are related to the system. Loose electrical connectors and poor earths can cause many problems that resemble more serious malfunctions.

2 Check to see that the battery is fully-charged, as the control unit and sensors depend on an accurate supply voltage in order to properly meter the fuel.

3 Check the air filter element – a dirty or partially blocked filter will severely impede performance and economy (see Chapter 1A).

4 If a blown fuse is found, renew it and see if it blows again. If it does, search for an earthed wire in the harness related to the system.

5 Check the air inlet duct from the air cleaner housing to the inlet manifold for leaks, which will result in an excessively lean mixture. Also check the condition of the vacuum hoses connected to the inlet manifold.

11.6 Remove the air inlet hose

6 Remove the air inlet duct from the throttle body and check for carbon and residue build-up. If it's dirty, clean it with aerosol carburettor cleaner (make sure the can says it's safe for use with oxygen sensors and catalytic converters) and a toothbrush **(see illustration)**.

7 With the engine running, place a stethoscope against each injector, one at a time, and listen for a clicking sound, indicating operation. If you don't have an automotive stethoscope you can use a long screwdriver; just place the tip of the screwdriver against the injector body and press your ear against the handle.

8 With the engine off and the fuel injector electrical connectors disconnected, measure the resistance of each injector. Each injector should measure about 13.4 to 14.2 ohms. If not, the injector is probably faulty.

9 The remainder of the system checks should be left to a dealer service department or other suitably-equipped repairer, as there is a chance that the control unit may be damaged if not performed properly.

10 All models are equipped with a sophisticated self-diagnosis system, whereby any faults are stored as codes within the engine management ECM. By connecting suitable hand-held diagnostic equipment to the relevant connector **(see illustration)**, the stored code can be retrieved, and the fault identified. See your dealer or repair specialist.

12.4 Throttle position sensor (TPS) wiring connector

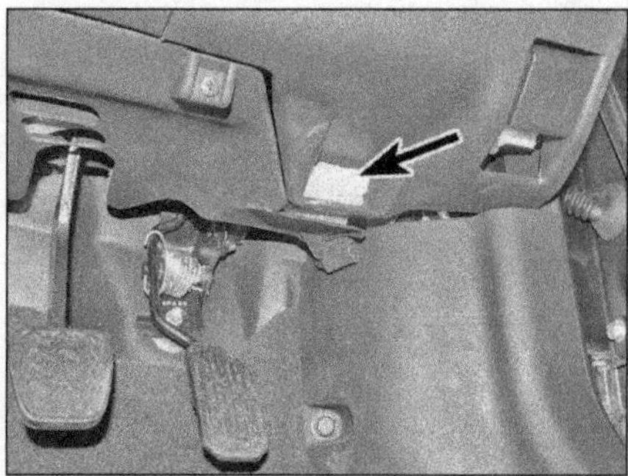

11.10 Diagnostic connector inside vehicle

12 Fuel injection system – component testing and renewal

Warning: Petrol is extremely flammable, so take extra precautions when you work on any part of the fuel system. Don't smoke or allow open flames or bare light bulbs near the work area, and don't work in a garage where a natural gas-type appliance (such as a water heater or a clothes dryer) with a pilot light is present. Since petrol is carcinogenic, wear latex gloves when there's a possibility of being exposed to fuel, and, if you spill any fuel on your skin; rinse it off immediately with soap and water. Mop up any spills immediately and do not store fuel-soaked rags where they could ignite. The fuel system is under constant pressure, so, if any fuel pipes are to be disconnected, the fuel pressure in the system must be relieved first. When you perform any kind of work on the fuel system, wear safety glasses and have a Class B type fire extinguisher on hand.

Throttle body

Testing

1 Verify that the throttle linkage operates smoothly.

2 Start the engine, detach each vacuum hose and, using a vacuum gauge, check there is no vacuum at idle, but that there is vacuum at all other times.

Renewal

Warning: Wait until the engine is completely cool before beginning this procedure.

3 Loosen the hose clamps and remove the air inlet duct from the throttle body.

4 Disconnect the electrical connector from the throttle position sensor (TPS) **(see illustration)**

Caution: Do not clean the throttle position sensor with anything. Just wipe it off carefully with a clean, soft cloth.

5 Disconnect the wiring connector from the idle speed control valve (ISCV) on the underside of the throttle body **(see illustration)**

12.5 Idle speed control valve (ISCV)

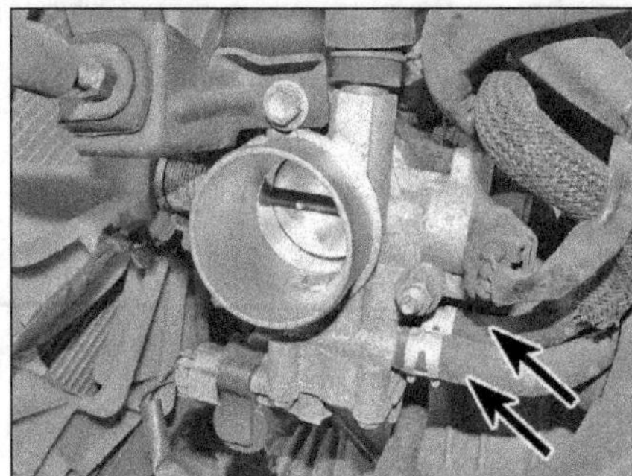
12.7 Disconnect the coolant hoses – arrowed

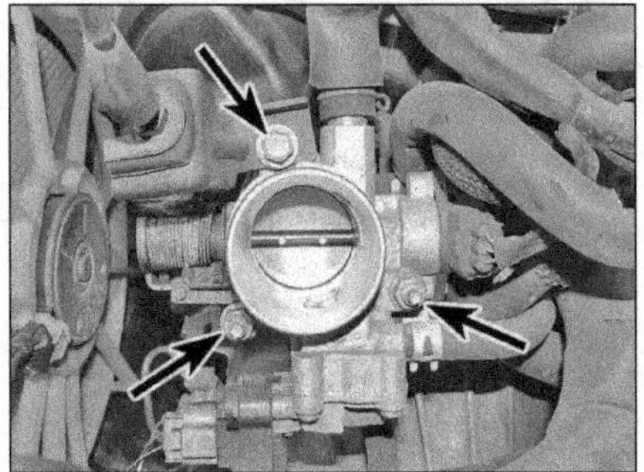
12.9 Throttle body mounting nuts – arrowed

12.10 Fit a new throttle body gasket/seal

6 Detach the accelerator cable from the throttle lever (see Section 9).

7 Drain the cooling system (see Chapter 1A) and disconnect the hoses from the throttle housing **(see illustration)**.

8 Release the retaining clip and disconnect the breather hose from the top of the throttle body.

9 Remove the throttle body mounting bolts/nuts **(see illustration)**. Note the upper mounting bolt also secures the accelerator cable mounting bracket.

10 Detach the throttle body and rubber gasket **(see illustration)** from the inlet manifold. Discard the gasket/seal; a new one must be fitted.

11 Using a soft brush and carburettor cleaner, thoroughly clean the throttle body casting, then blow out all passages with compressed air.

Warning: Wear eye protection when using compressed air.

12 Refitting of the throttle body is the reverse of removal, remembering to use a new gasket.

13 Be sure to tighten the throttle body mounting bolts to the torque listed in this Chapter's Specifications. Refill the cooling system (see Chapter 1A).

Throttle position sensor (TPS)

Testing

14 Disconnect the electrical connector from the throttle position sensor (TPS).

15 Using an ohmmeter, measure the resistance between the indicated terminal pairs. The resistances should be as follows **(see illustration)**:

Throttle valve position	Between terminals	Resistance value
Fully open	*VTA and E2*	*0.2 to 5.7 k ohms*
Fully closed	*VTA and E2*	*2.0 to 10.2 k ohms*
Any position	*VC and E2*	*2.5 to 6.0 k ohms*

16 If the resistance values are not as specified, renew the sensor.

Renewal

17 Undo the screws and remove the sensor **(see illustration)**.

18 Refitting is a reversal of removal.

Fuel pressure regulator

19 The fuel pressure regulator is incorporated into the fuel pump/level sender unit fitted into the fuel tank. Refer to Section 3 for details.

Fuel rail and fuel injectors

Testing

20 Refer to the fuel injection system checking procedure (see Section 11).

Renewal

21 Relieve the fuel pressure (Section 2).

22 Remove the cover from the top of the engine **(see illustration),** and then disconnect the PCV hose from the front of the cylinder head cover.

23 Disconnect the wiring plugs from the top of the injectors **(see illustration)**.

24 Undo the bolt securing the fuel pipe to the cylinder head.

25 Disconnect the fuel supply pipe from the fuel rail by sliding the clamp from the pipe using a piece of stiff plastic to release the internal clips inside the connection **(see illustrations)**.

26 Undo the two mounting bolts and remove the fuel rail complete with injectors **(see illustration)**.

27 Remove the two spacers and 4 grommets, and then pull the injectors from the fuel rail **(see illustrations)**.

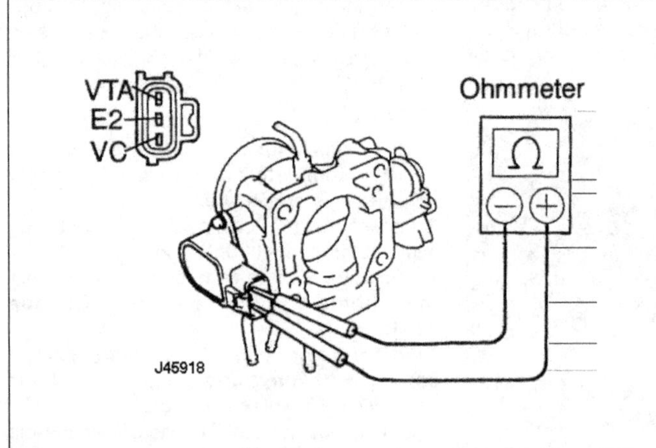

12.15 Throttle body connector terminal identification (see text)

12.17 Throttle position sensor screws (arrowed)

12.22 Remove the engine upper cover

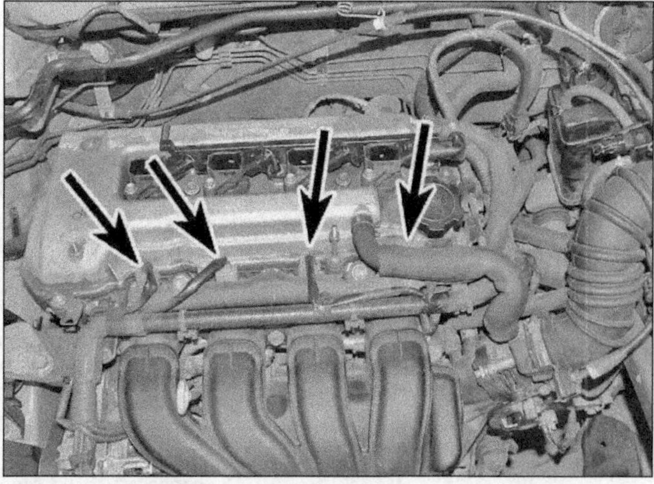

12.23 Fuel injector wiring connectors (arrowed)

28 If you intend to re-use the same injectors, renew the grommets and O-rings **(see illustration)**.

29 Refitting of the fuel injectors is the reverse of removal.

30 Tighten the fuel rail mounting bolts to the torque listed in this Chapter's Specifications.

Airflow meter/ temperature sensor

Testing

31 Connect the leads of an ohmmeter to the terminals E2 and THA of the sensor **(see illustration)**.

12.25a Slide the clamp from the fuel hose connection . . .

12.25b . . . then using a stiff piece of plastic . . .

12.25c . . . release the internal catches and disconnect the fuel hose

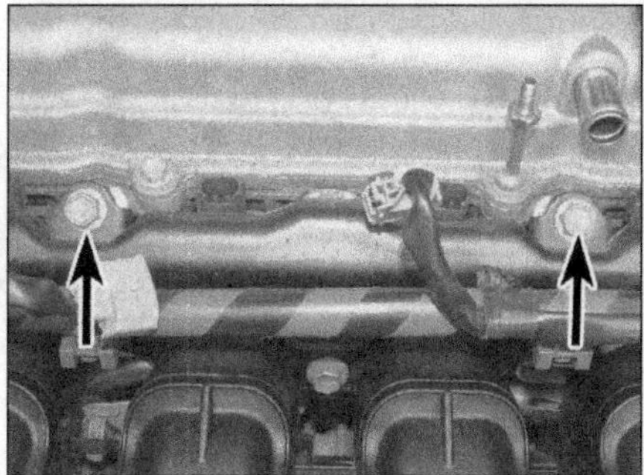

12.26 Undo the two fuel rail mounting bolts (arrowed)

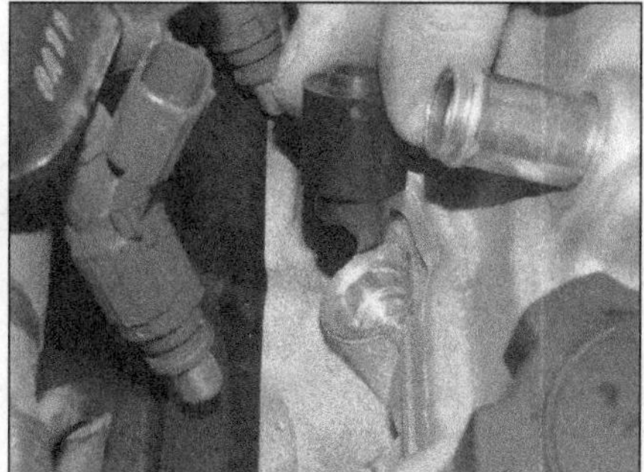

12.27a Recover the spacers from the cylinder head . . .

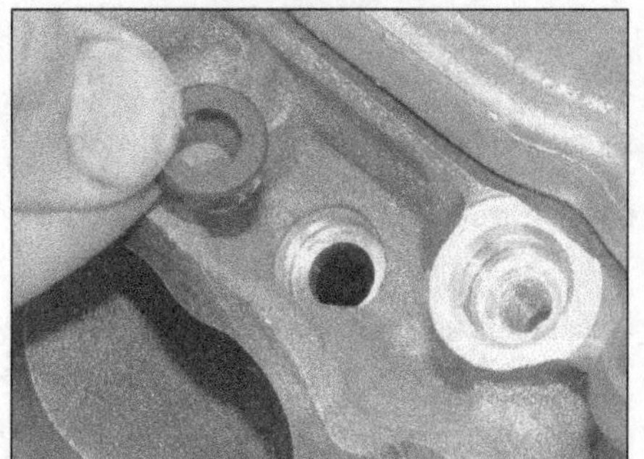

12.27b . . . and pull the grommets from the injector bores

12.28 Renew the injector O-rings and grommets (arrowed)

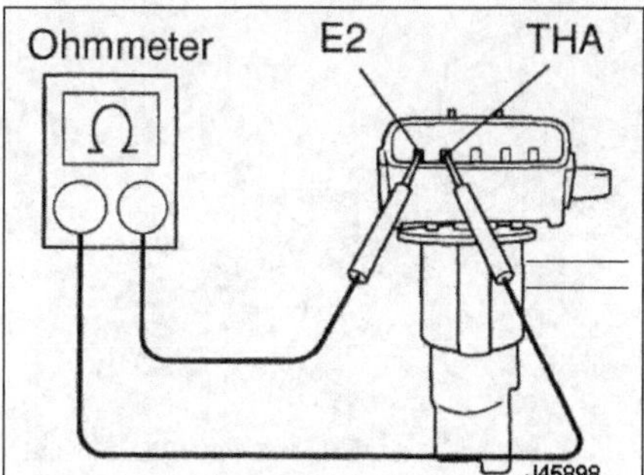

12.31 Connect an ohmmeter to the airflow meter terminals as shown

12.33 Disconnecting the airflow meter wiring

32 At -20°C the resistance across the terminals should be 13.6 to 18.4 k ohms, at 20° it should be 2.21 to 2.69 k ohms, and at 60°C 0.49 to 0.67 k ohms.

Renewal

33 The airflow meter is located in the air filter outlet ducting. Disconnect the sensor wiring plug **(see illustration)**.
34 Undo the two screws, and pull the sensor from the ducting. Discard the O-ring; a new one must be fitted.
35 Fit the sensor to the ducting, using a new O-ring seal, and tighten the screws securely.

Engine management ECM

Testing

36 Have the engine management ECM self-diagnosis system interrogated for any stored fault codes relating to the ECM (see Section 11).

Removal

37 Disconnect the battery negative lead (see Chapter 5A). **Note:** *Disconnecting the battery will erase any fault codes stored in the ECM. It is recommended that the fault code memory of the module is interrogated using special test equipment prior to battery disconnection. Entrust this task to a Toyota dealer or suitably-equipped specialist.*
38 Remove the trim panel from under the passenger side facia panel.
39 Undo the retaining bolts and remove the ECM.
40 Release the locking clips and disconnect the ECM wiring plugs **(see illustration)**.

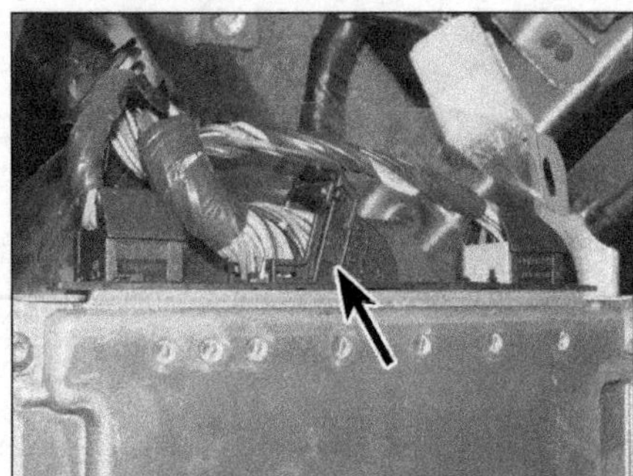
12.40 Release the locking catch (arrowed) and disconnect the ECM wiring plugs

Refitting

41 Refitting is a reversal of removal. **Note:** *If a new module has been fitted, it may be necessary to be recode it using special test equipment. Entrust this task to a Toyota dealer or suitably-equipped specialist. After reconnecting the battery, the vehicle must be driven for several miles so that the ECM can learn its basic settings. If the engine still runs erratically, the basic settings may be reinstated by a Toyota dealer or specialist using special diagnostic equipment.*

Camshaft position sensor

Testing

Note: *The following procedure only applies to those sensors manufactured by Denso. No information concerning Bosch sensors was available.*
42 The sensor is located at the front, left-hand end of the cylinder head. Disconnect the sensor wiring plug, and connect the leads of an ohmmeter to the sensor terminals.
43 On a cold engine, then resistance should be 835 to 1400 ohms. On a hot engine, the resistance should be 1060 to 1645 ohms.

Renewal

44 Disconnect the sensor wiring plug.
45 Undo the retaining bolt, and pull the sensor from position **(see illustration)**. Discard the O-ring seal; a new one must be fitted.
46 Insert the sensor into the cylinder head, with a new O-ring seal.
47 Tighten the retaining bolt to the specified torque, and reconnect the wiring plug.

12.49 The crankshaft position sensor is located adjacent to the crankshaft pulley (arrowed)

12.53 Undo the bolt and pull the sensor from the timing chain cover. Renew the O-ring (arrowed)

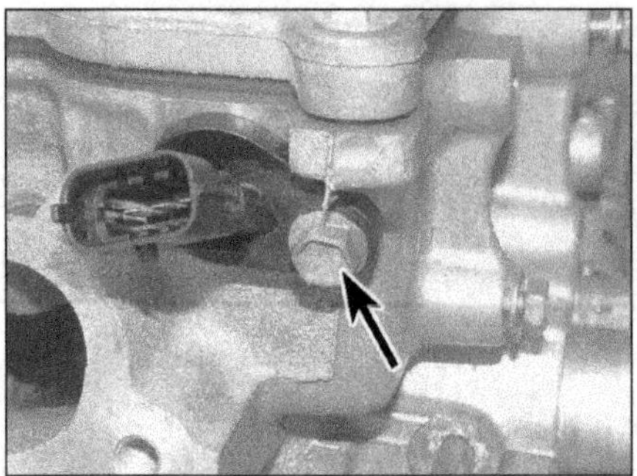
12.45 Camshaft position sensor retaining bolt (arrowed)

Crankshaft position/ speed sensor

Testing

48 Remove the alternator as described in Chapter 5A.
49 The sensor is located adjacent to the crankshaft pulley at the front of the engine. Trace the wiring back from the sensor and disconnect the wiring plug **(see illustration)**.
50 Connect the leads of an ohmmeter to the sensor terminals, and measure the resistance of the sensor. Compare the readings obtained with those given in the Specifications at the start of this Chapter.

Renewal

51 Proceed as described in paragraphs 48 and 49.
52 Undo the bolt securing the sensor wiring loom retaining bracket to the engine block.
53 Undo the retaining bolt and withdraw the sensor from position **(see illustration)**. Discard the sensor O-ring seal; a new one must be fitted.
54 Insert the sensor into position, with a new O-ring seal.
55 Tighten the retaining bolt to the specified torque, and reconnect the wiring plug.

13 Inlet manifold – removal and refitting

Removal

1 Remove the throttle body as described in Section 12.
2 Release the clips securing the engine wiring loom to the 2 brackets on the top of the manifold, then disconnect the camshaft position sensor plug and move the loom to one side.
3 Undo the two bolts and release the hose bracket from the manifold **(see illustration)**.
4 Disconnect the brake servo vacuum pipe and the PCV (positive crankcase ventilation) hose from the manifold **(see illustration)**.
5 Undo the three bolts and two nuts, remove the 2 brackets, and then remove the inlet manifold **(see illustration)**. Recover the inlet

13.3 Undo the two bolts (arrowed) and remove the hose bracket

manifold O-ring seals. Release the wiring loom clip as the manifold is removed.

Refitting

6 Clean the mating surfaces of the inlet manifold and the cylinder head mounting surface with brake cleaner or a suitable solvent. If the gasket shows signs of leaking, have the manifold checked for warpage at an automotive machine workshop and resurfaced if necessary.

7 Fit a new gasket/O-ring seals, then position the manifold on the cylinder head and refit the nuts/bolts.

8 Tighten the nuts/bolts in three or four equal steps to the torque listed in this Chapter's Specifications. Work from the centre out towards the ends to avoid warping the manifold.

9 Refit the remaining parts in the reverse order of removal.

10 Before starting the engine, check the throttle linkage for smooth operation.

11 Run the engine and check for coolant and vacuum leaks.

12 Road test the vehicle and check for proper operation of all accessories.

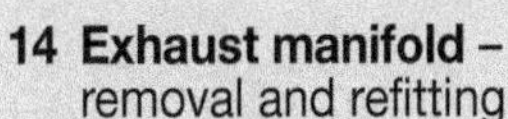

14 Exhaust manifold – removal and refitting

Warning: The engine must be completely cool before beginning this procedure.

Removal

1 Remove the upper heat shield from the manifold **(see illustration)**. **Note:** *There may also be a lower heat shield, but this is attached to the manifold from underneath and does not need to be removed.*

2 Apply penetrating oil to the exhaust manifold mounting nuts/bolts, and the nuts/bolts retaining the exhaust pipe to the manifold. After the nuts/bolts have soaked, remove the nuts/bolts retaining the exhaust pipe to the manifold **(see illustration)**

3 Where fitted, unbolt the exhaust manifold brace.

4 Where the manifold has an oxygen sensor fitted, trace the wiring from the sensor back to the connector and unplug it.

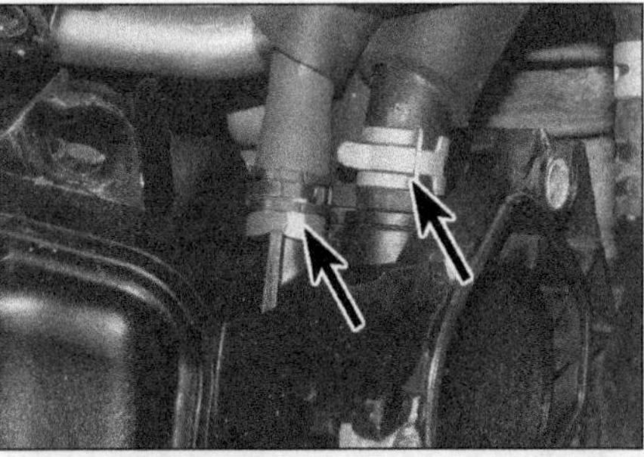

13.4 Release the clamps and disconnect the servo vacuum hose (right arrow) and the PCV hose (left arrow)

5 Remove the nuts/bolts and detach the manifold and gasket.

Refitting

6 Use a scraper to remove all traces of old gasket material and carbon deposits from the manifold and cylinder head mating surfaces. If the gasket was leaking, have the manifold checked for warpage at an automotive machine workshop and resurfaced if necessary.

7 Position a new gasket over the cylinder head studs. **Note:** *The marks on the gasket should face out (away from the cylinder head) and the arrow should point toward the transmission end of the engine.*

8 Refit the manifold and thread the mounting nuts/bolts into place.

9 Working from the centre out, tighten the nuts/bolts to the torque listed in this Chapter's Specifications in three or four equal steps.

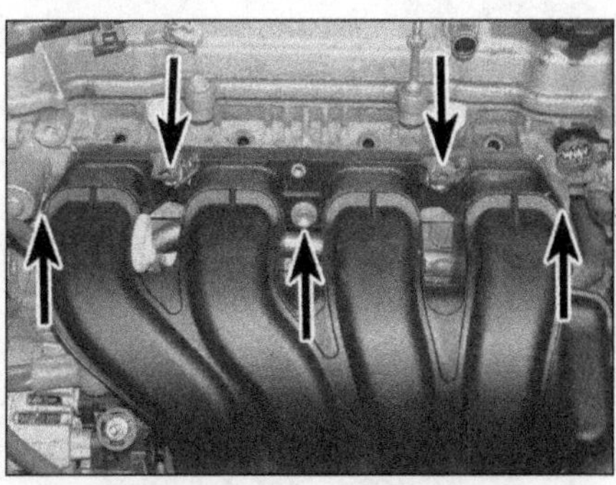

13.5 Undo the nuts and bolts (arrowed) and remove the inlet manifold

10 Refit the remaining parts in the reverse order of removal.

11 Run the engine and check for any leaks.

15 Exhaust system – removal and refitting

Warning: Inspection and repair of exhaust system components should be done only after the system components have cooled completely.

1 The exhaust system consists of the exhaust manifold, catalytic converter, the silencer, the tailpipe and all connecting pipes, brackets, rubber-mountings and clamps. The exhaust system is attached to the body with mounting brackets and rubber hangers **(see illustrations)**. If any of these parts are

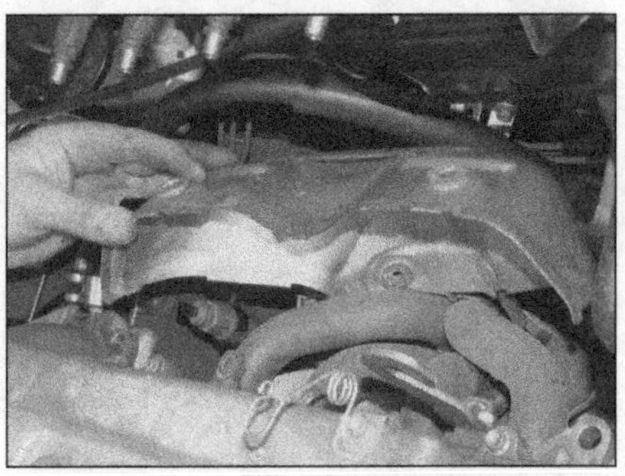

14.1 Remove the upper heat shield from the manifold

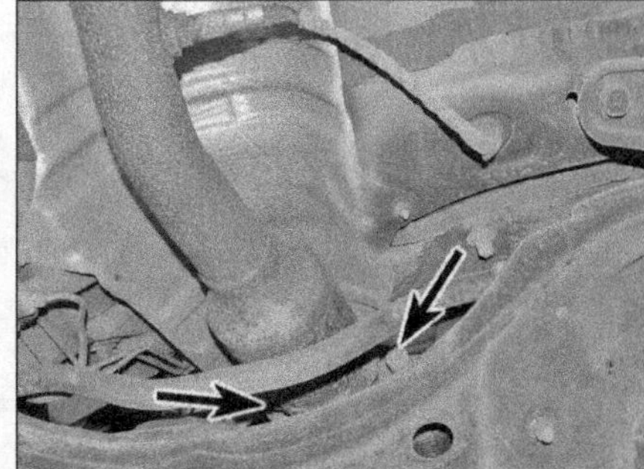

14.2 Front pipe retaining bolts (arrowed)

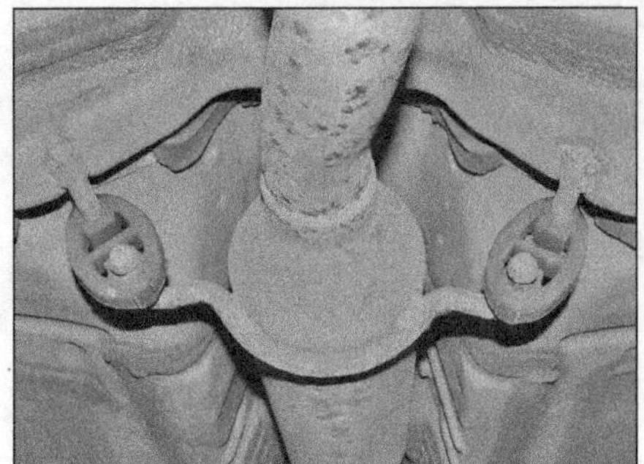

15.1a Check the exhaust rubber mountings . . .

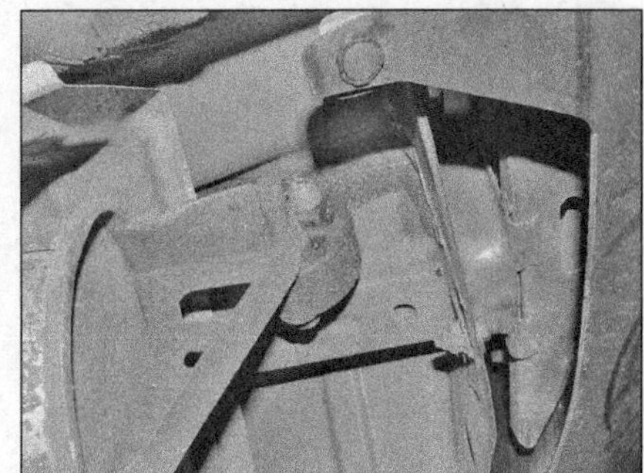

15.1b . . . and mounting brackets

15.4 Check condition and security of heat shields

damaged or deteriorated, excessive noise and vibration will be transmitted to the body.

2 Conducting regular inspections of the exhaust system will keep it safe and quiet. Look for any damaged or bent parts, open seams, holes, loose connections, excessive corrosion or other defects, which could allow exhaust fumes to enter the vehicle. Deteriorated exhaust system components should not be repaired – they should be renewed.

3 If the exhaust system components are extremely corroded or rusted together, they will probably have to be cut from the exhaust system. The convenient way to accomplish this is to have an exhaust specialist remove the corroded sections with a cutting torch. If, however, you want to save money by doing it yourself and you don't have an oxy-acetylene welding outfit with a cutting torch, simply cut off the old components with a hacksaw. If you have compressed air, special pneumatic cutting chisels can also be used. If you do decide to tackle the job at home, be sure to wear eye protection to protect your eyes from metal chips and work gloves to protect your hands.

4 Here are some simple guidelines to apply when repairing the exhaust system:

a) Work from the back to the front when removing exhaust system components.

b) Apply penetrating oil to the exhaust system component fasteners to make them easier to remove.

c) Use new gaskets, rubber-mountings and clamps when installing exhaust system components.

d) Apply anti-seize compound to the threads of all exhaust system fasteners during reassembly.

*e) Check that the heat shields between the underbody and the exhaust system are secure **(see illustration)**.*

f) Be sure to allow sufficient clearance between newly fitted parts and all points on the underbody to avoid overheating the floorpan and possibly damaging the interior carpet and insulation. Pay particularly close attention to the catalytic converter and its heat shield.

Warning: The catalytic converter operates at very high temperatures and takes a long time to cool. Wait until it's completely cool before attempting to remove the converter. Failure to do so could result in serious burns.

Chapter 4 Part B:
Fuel and exhaust systems – diesel engines

Contents

Degrees of difficulty

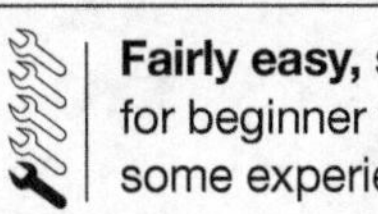
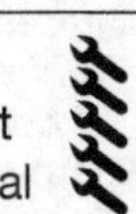

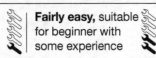

Easy, suitable for novice with little experience	**Fairly easy,** suitable for beginner with some experience	**Fairly difficult,** suitable for competent DIY mechanic	**Difficult,** suitable for experienced DIY mechanic	**Very difficult,** suitable for expert DIY or professional

Specifications

Fuel injection system

Type	Turbocharged direct injection common rail

High-pressure fuel pump

Resistance between terminals at 20°C	1.5 to 1.7 ohms

Fuel temperature sensor

Resistance:	
At approximately 20°C	2.21 to 2.69 ohms
At approximately 80°C	0.287 to 0.349 ohms

Fuel injectors

Resistance between terminals 3 and 4 at 20°C	2.6 to 2.8 ohms

Common rail

Resistance between terminals:	
Between terminals 2 and 3	3.0 k ohms or less
Between terminals 1 and 2	16.4 k ohms or less

Camshaft and crankshaft position sensor

Resistance:	
Cold (up to 50°C)	1630 to 2740 ohms
Hot (from 50°C)	2065 to 3225 ohms

Inlet airflow meter

Resistance at connections 1 (E2) and 2 (THA):	
-20°C	12.5 to 16.9 k ohms
20°C	2.19 to 2.67 k ohms
60°C	0.50 to 0.68 k ohms

Inlet air temperature sensor

Resistance:	
20°C	2.0 to 3.0 k ohms
60°C	400 to 700 ohms

Throttle control motor (inlet shutter)

Resistance at 20°C:	
Between terminals 2 and 1 or 2 and 3	18 to 22 k ohms
Between terminals 5 and 4 or 5 and 6	18 to 22 k ohms

Coolant temperature sensor

Resistance:	
At approximately 20°C	2320 to 2590 ohms
At approximately 80°C	310 to 326 ohms

Turbo inlet air temperature sensor

Resistance at 20°C	2210 to 2650 ohms

Turbo pressure sensor

Connections 1 (E2) and 3 (VC) – wiring harness side	4.5 to 5.5 volts (with ignition on)

Torque wrench settings

	Nm	lbf ft
Air temperature sensor	34	25
Camshaft position sensor	9	7
Common rail bolts	43	32
Crankshaft position sensor	9	7
Exhaust manifold nuts and bolts	46	34
Fuel injectors	27	20
High-pressure fuel pump:		
Mounting nuts	21	15
Support bracket bolts	21	15
Drive sprocket	103	76
High-pressure injector pipe union nuts:		
To injectors	34	25
To common rail	41	30
High-pressure pump fuel inlet pipe:		
To common rail	37	27
To pump	31	23
Support bolt	8	6
Inlet manifold nuts and bolts	21	15
Leak-off check valve	21	15
Leak-off check valve plug	10	7
Leak-off pipe hollow bolts	18	13
Leak-off pipe union bolt	22	16
Oil dipstick tube support	18	13
Throttle body/module inlet elbow to inlet manifold	21	15
Throttle body/module to inlet elbow	21	15
Turbocharger:		
To exhaust manifold	53	39
To catalytic converter	25	18
Turbocharger EGR cooler tube	25	18

1 General information

Warning 1: Diesel fuel isn't as volatile as petrol, but it is flammable, so take extra precautions when you work on any part of the fuel system. Don't smoke or allow naked flames or bare light bulbs near the work area. Don't work in a garage or other enclosed space where there is a gas-type appliance (such as a water heater or clothes dryer). Avoid direct skin contact with diesel fuel – wear protective clothing, safety glasses and gloves when handling fuel system components and have a fire extinguisher on hand. Ensure that the work area is well-ventilated.

Warning 2: Fuel injectors operate at extremely high pressures and the jet of fuel produced at the nozzle is capable of piercing skin, with potentially fatal results. When working with pressurised injectors, take great to avoid exposing any part of the body to the fuel spray. It is recommended that any pressure testing of the fuel system components should be carried out by a diesel fuel systems specialist.

Caution: Under no circumstances should diesel fuel be allowed to come into contact with coolant hoses, wiring or rubber components – wipe off accidental spillage immediately. Hoses that have been contaminated with fuel for an extended period should be renewed. Diesel fuel systems are particularly sensitive to contamination from dirt, air and water. Pay particular attention to cleanliness when working on any part of the fuel system, to prevent the entry of dirt. Thoroughly clean the area around fuel unions before disconnecting them. Store dismantled components in sealed containers to prevent contamination and the formation of condensation. Only use lint-free cloths and clean fuel for component cleaning. Avoid using compressed air when cleaning components in place.

Diesel models covered by this manual are equipped with a Turbocharged Direct Injection Common Rail fuel injection system. The fuel lift pump is immersed in the fuel inside the tank, and delivers a constant supply of fuel to the fuel filter in the engine compartment. Fuel from the fuel filter is delivered to the high-pressure fuel pump, then by the common rail and pipes to the electronic fuel injectors, where it is sequentially injected directly into the combustion chamber of each cylinder. A fuel pressure regulator on the common rail maintains a constant fuel pressure to the fuel injectors, and returns excess fuel to the tank through the return line. This constant flow system also helps to reduce fuel temperature.

The electronic fuel injectors are located beneath the engine valve cover in the cylinder head, directly above the combustion chambers, and are controlled by the Engine Control Module (ECM). The ECM monitors various engine parameters and delivers the exact amount of fuel, in the correct sequence, to each cylinder. This Chapter's information pertains to the air and fuel delivery components of the system only.

The exhaust system consists of an exhaust

manifold and catalytic converter, turbocharger, front exhaust pipe and catalytic converter, centre pipe and silencer, and tailpipe and silencer. Each of these components is renewable.

All diesel models are equipped with a variable-nozzle-vane turbocharger and intercooler. The turbocharger increases power by using an exhaust gas-driven turbine to pressurise the inlet charge before it enters the combustion chambers. The amount of inlet manifold pressure (boost) is regulated by an exhaust by-pass valve (wastegate). The wastegate regulator valve is controlled by the ECM. The heated compressed air is routed through an air-to-air radiator (intercooler). The intercooler removes excess heat from the compressed air, increasing its density and allowing for more boost pressure.

2 Fuel lines and fittings – general information

1 The main fuel supply line extends from the fuel tank to the fuel filter on the left-hand side of the engine compartment, and is secured to the underbody with clips. This line should be inspected occasionally for leaks, kinks and dents.

2 Fuel enters the fuel filter through a flexible hose, and is taken from the filter to the high-pressure fuel pump also by flexible hose **(see illustration)**. To remove a hose, loosen the clips at each end and disconnect it. Make sure the clips are fully tightened when refitting.

3 From the high-pressure fuel pump, the fuel is taken to the common rail by a single high-pressure fuel inlet pipe, then by individual high-pressure pipes to the four electronic injectors. These high-pressure pipes must be renewed if the components at either end of them are renewed, however, they may be re-used if the components are the original components. To remove them, unscrew the union nuts and release the pipes from any support clips. Refitting is a reversal of removal, but tighten the union nuts to the specified torque.

4 A leak-off pipe returns excess fuel from the injectors to the fuel tank. Access to the leak-off pipe and injectors is by removal of the valve cover, and details are given in Section 11 for the removal of the injectors. Also in Section 11 are details of pressure-checking the leak-off pipe.

2.2 Diesel fuel filter assembly

3 Fuel level sender unit – removal and refitting

The procedure is similar to that for removing the fuel level sender unit on petrol engine models. Refer to Chapter 4A, Section 4.

4 Fuel tank – removal and refitting

The procedure is similar to that for removing the fuel tank on petrol engine models. Refer to Chapter 4A, Section 6.

5 Fuel tank cleaning and repair

Refer to Section 7 in Chapter 4A.

6 Air cleaner and inlet system – removal and refitting

Removal

1 The air cleaner and housing assembly is located on the left-hand side of the engine compartment. Loosen the securing clip and disconnect the air inlet hose from the top cover **(see illustration)**.

2 Disconnect the wiring from the airflow meter, which is fitted to the air cleaner top cover, and unclip it from the support **(see illustration)**.

3 Release the spring clips and remove the top cover from the air cleaner body **(see illustrations)**.

4 Remove the filter element, noting its fitted position, with UP marked on the upper side **(see illustration)**.

5 Unscrew the mounting bolt securing the air cleaner body to the inner wing panel, and then release the inlet elbow from the housing on removal **(see illustrations)**.

6.1 Remove the air inlet hose

6.2 Disconnect the wiring from the airflow meter

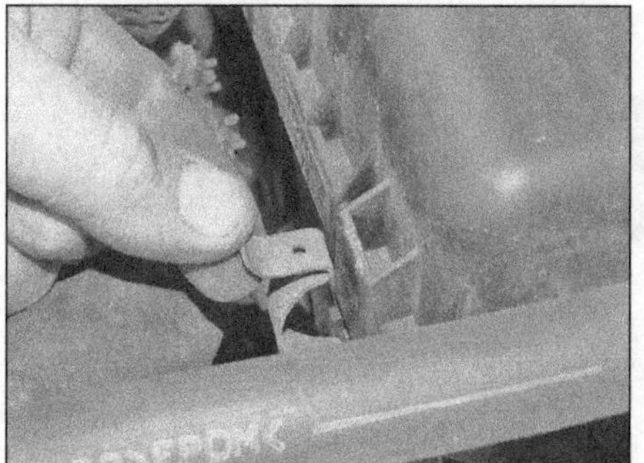

6.3a Release the retaining clips . . .

6.3b . . . and remove the air filter upper cover

6.4 Note the fitted position of the filter element

6.5a Unscrew the mounting bolts (arrowed) . . .

6.5b . . . and remove the air cleaner lower housing while releasing it from the air inlet elbow

Refitting

6 Clean the air cleaner body and top cover of dust and dirt and any leaves, then locate the body in position making sure that the inlet elbow is engaged securely with the housing. Insert the mounting bolts and tighten.

7 Fit the filter element in the position noted on removal, and refit the top cover, securing it with the spring clips.

8 Reconnect the air outlet hose to the top cover and secure by tightening the clip.

9 Reconnect the wiring to the airflow meter.

7 Fuel filter – removal, renewal and refitting

Refer to Chapter 1B.

8 High-pressure fuel pump – checking, removal and refitting

Checking

1 The only check that can be made by the home mechanic is the resistance across the terminals in the two wiring sockets. First, disconnect the wiring plugs.

2 Connect an ohmmeter across the terminals in each of the wiring sockets, and check that the resistance is within the limits given in the Specifications.

3 If either of the checks gives an incorrect result, renew the high-pressure fuel pump.

Removal

4 Remove the auxiliary drivebelt as described in Chapter 1B.

5 Clean the area around the high-pressure fuel pump, in particular the fuel pipes and union nuts, to prevent entry of dust and dirt into the fuel system.

6 Remove the timing belt as described in Chapter 2B.

7 Unscrew the union nuts and remove the injector pipes from the injectors and common rail. Tape over or plug the open apertures of the pipes, injectors and common rail. **Note:** *Toyota recommends renewal of the injector pipes whenever the injectors and/or the common rail are renewed.*

8 Unscrew the bolt securing the fuel inlet pipe to the inlet manifold, then unscrew the union nuts and remove the pipe from the high-pressure fuel pump and common rail. **Note:** *Toyota recommends renewal of the fuel inlet pipe whenever the common rail or supply pump are renewed.*

9 Unbolt the cover from the high-pressure fuel pump. Also remove the insulator.

10 Loosen the common rail mounting bolts. Also disconnect the wiring from the fuel pressure sensor fly-lead.

11 Disconnect the wiring from the throttle body/module, then unscrew the bolts securing the air inlet elbow to the inlet manifold, and withdraw the elbow together with the throttle body/module.

12 Unscrew the nuts and bolts and remove the inlet manifold and common rail. Recover the gasket.

13 Disconnect the two wiring plugs from the rear of the high-pressure pump. Also disconnect the fuel temperature sensor wiring from the top of the pump.

14 Remove the high-pressure fuel pump drive sprocket as follows. Hold the sprocket stationary with a suitable lever engaged in the holes, and then unscrew the retaining nut. Using a suitable puller, draw the sprocket from the pump driveshaft **(see illustrations)**.

15 Unbolt the engine oil dipstick tube from the high-pressure pump bracket, then pull the tube from the sump upper housing and recover the O-ring seal **(see illustration)**.

16 Unscrew the bolts and remove the pump support bracket **(see illustration)**.

17 Release the clips and disconnect the two fuel hoses from the pump. Tape over the apertures to prevent entry of dust and dirt.

8.14a Hold the sprocket stationary and unscrew the sprocket retaining nut . . .

8.14b . . . then use a puller to release the sprocket from the fuel pump driveshaft . . .

8.14c . . . and withdraw the sprocket

8.15 Removing the engine oil dipstick tube from the sump upper housing

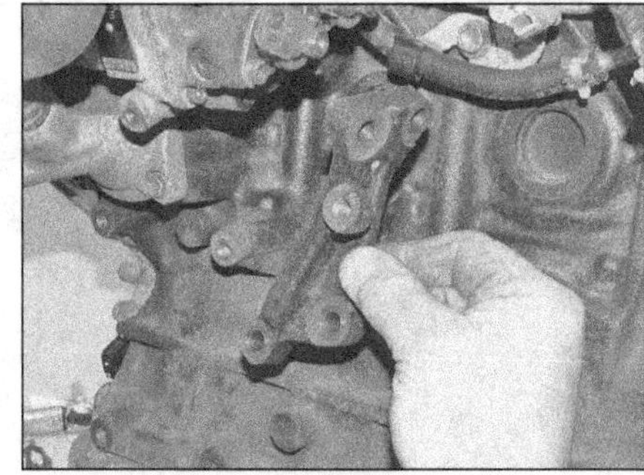

8.16 Removing the high-pressure fuel pump support bracket

8.18 Removing the high-pressure fuel pump from the mounting studs

18 Unscrew the mounting nuts and remove the high-pressure fuel pump from the studs **(see illustration)**. **Note:** *The pump may be difficult to release from the water pump housing due to corrosion.*

Refitting

19 Locate the high-pressure fuel pump on the mounting studs, and then fit the nuts and tighten them to the specified torque.

20 Reconnect the fuel hoses and secure with the clips.

21 Refit the pump support bracket and initially hand-tighten all the bolts. Now fully-tighten the bolts on the cylinder block to the specified torque, followed by the bolts on the pump.

22 Refit the oil dipstick tube together with a new O-ring seal and tighten the support bolts to the specified torque.

23 Align the high-pressure fuel pump drive sprocket with the groove in the driveshaft, and fully press on. Screw on the retaining nut, then hold the sprocket with a suitable lever while the nut is tightened to the specified torque.

24 Reconnect the two wiring plugs to the rear of the high-pressure pump, and the wiring plug to the fuel temperature sensor on the top of the pump.

25 Refit the inlet manifold and common rail together with a new gasket, then progressively tighten the inlet manifold mounting nuts and bolts to the specified torque.

26 Tighten the common rail mounting bolts to the specified torque.

27 Reconnect the wiring to the fuel pressure sensor fly-lead.

28 Refit the throttle body/module and inlet elbow to the inlet manifold together with a new gasket, and tighten the bolts to the specified torque. Reconnect the wiring.

29 Refit the insulator over the high-pressure pump, making sure it is correctly aligned with the inlet manifold. The insulator must not touch the union bolt of the pump **(see illustration)**.

30 Refit the pump cover and tighten the bolts.

31 Refit the fuel inlet pipe to the high-pressure pump and common rail and tighten the union nuts to the specified torque. Fit the support bolt and tighten to the specified torque.

32 Refit the injector pipes to the injectors and common rail, and tighten the union nuts to the specified torque.

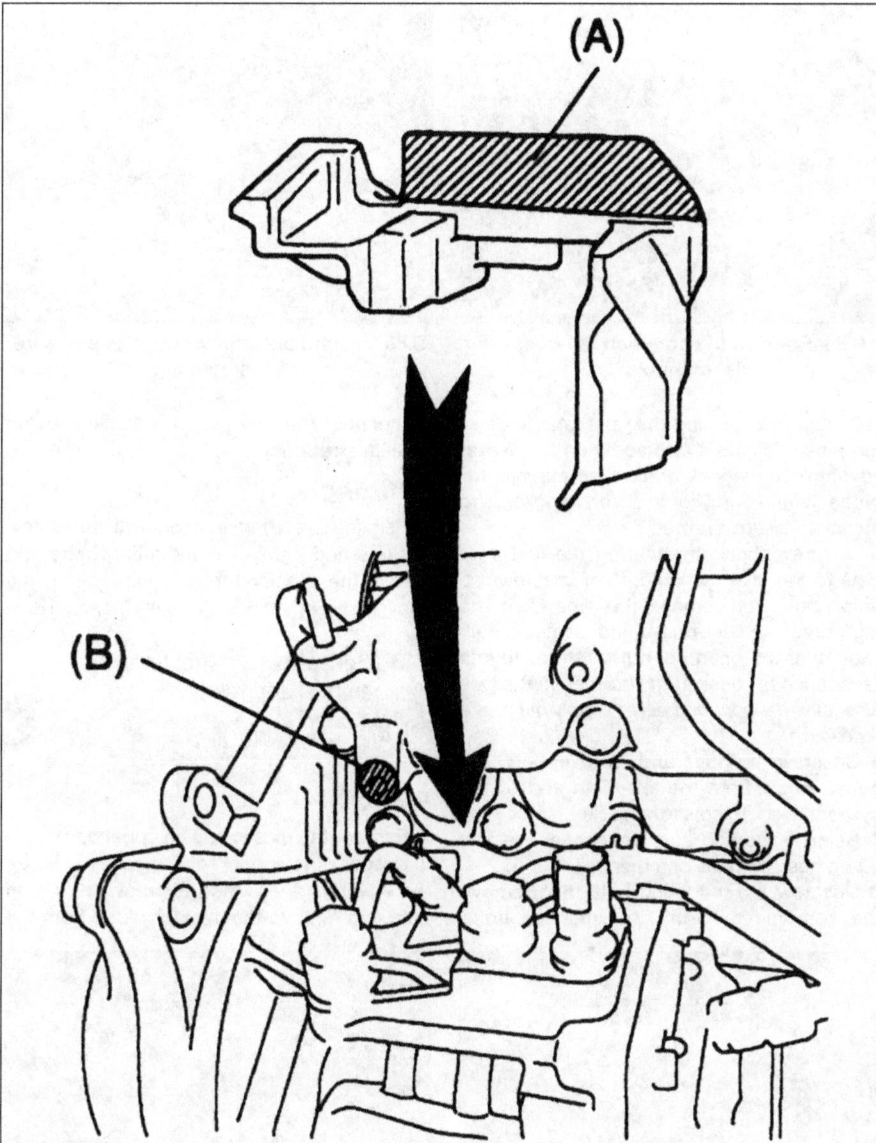

8.29 Align the shaded areas of the insulator (A) and inlet manifold (B) with each other

33 Refit the injector pipes as described in Section 10.

34 Refit the timing belt and crankshaft pulley as described in Chapter 2B.

9.3 Remove the engine upper cover

35 Refit the auxiliary belt as described in Chapter 1B.

36 Start the engine and check for fuel leaks.

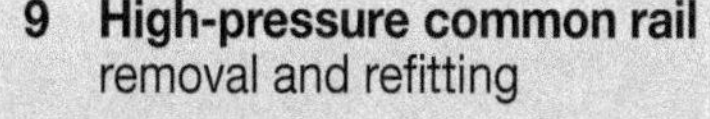

9 High-pressure common rail – removal and refitting

Removal

1 Clean the area around the high-pressure fuel pipes and union nuts, to prevent entry of dust and dirt into the fuel system.

2 Drain the cooling system as described in Chapter 1B.

3 Remove the plastic engine upper cover **(see illustration)**.

4 Unscrew the union nuts and remove the injector pipes from the injectors and common

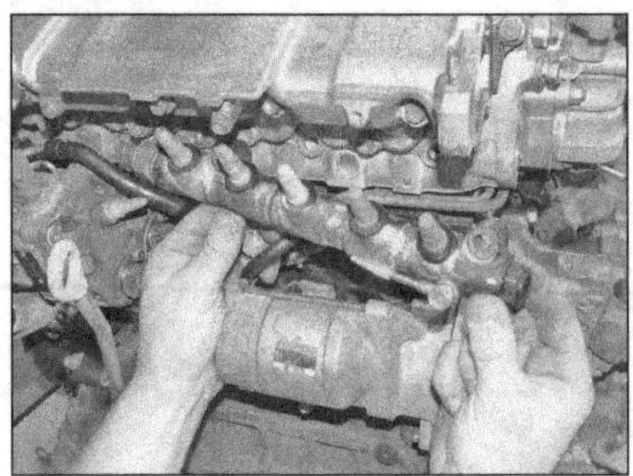

9.8a Remove the common rail from the inlet manifold . . .

rail. Tape over or plug the open apertures of the pipes, injectors and common rail. **Note:** *Toyota recommends renewal of the injector pipes whenever the injectors and/or the common rail are renewed.*

5 Unscrew the bolt securing the fuel inlet pipe to the inlet manifold, then unscrew the union nuts and remove the pipe from the high-pressure fuel pump and common rail. Tape over the open apertures. **Note:** *Toyota recommends renewal of the fuel inlet pipes whenever the common rail or supply pump are renewed.*

6 Unscrew the bolts and remove the water outlet elbow from the left-hand end of the cylinder head. Recover the gasket.

7 Release the clip and disconnect the fuel return hose from the common rail.

8 Unscrew the mounting bolts and remove the common rail from the inlet manifold.

9.8b . . . and disconnect the fuel pressure sensor wiring

Disconnect the fuel pressure sensor wiring **(see illustrations)**.

Refitting

9 Refitting is a reversal of removal, but fit new gaskets and tighten all mounting bolts and nuts to the specified torque. Finally, refill the cooling system as described in Chapter 1B.

10 High-pressure fuel lines – removal and refitting

Removal

1 Remove the plastic engine upper cover.

2 Unscrew the support clamp nuts to release the injector pipes, then unscrew the union nuts and remove the injector pipes from the injectors and common rail. Tape over or plug the open apertures of the pipes, injectors and common rail **(see illustrations)**. **Note:** *Toyota recommends renewal of the injector pipes whenever the injectors and/or the common rail are renewed.*

3 Unscrew the bolt securing the fuel inlet pipe to the inlet manifold, then unscrew the union nuts and remove the pipe from the high-pressure fuel pump and common rail **(see illustration)**. Tape over the open apertures. **Note:** *Toyota recommends renewal of the fuel inlet pipes whenever the common rail or supply pump are renewed.*

Refitting

4 Refitting is a reversal of removal, but tighten the union nuts to the specified torque. As a socket cannot be used, a 'crow's foot' adapter will be required **(see illustration)**.

11 Injectors – testing, removal and refitting

Testing

1 The resistance of the injectors may be checked before removing them from the engine. First, remove the engine upper cover.

2 Disconnect the wiring from the injectors **(see illustration)**.

3 Connect an ohmmeter between the terminals of each of the injectors in turn, and check that the resistance is within the limits given in the Specifications.

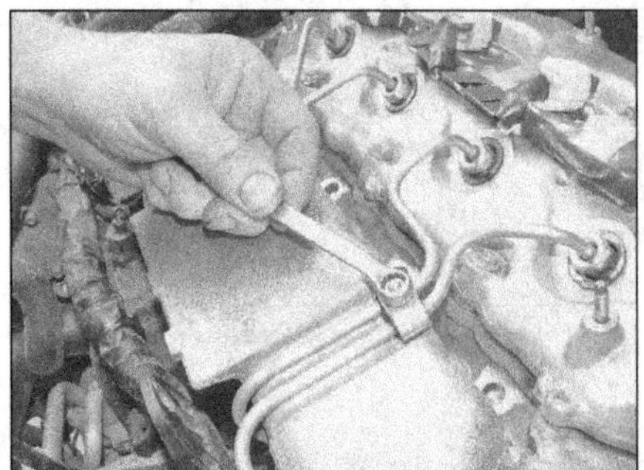

10.2a Unscrew the support clamp nuts . . .

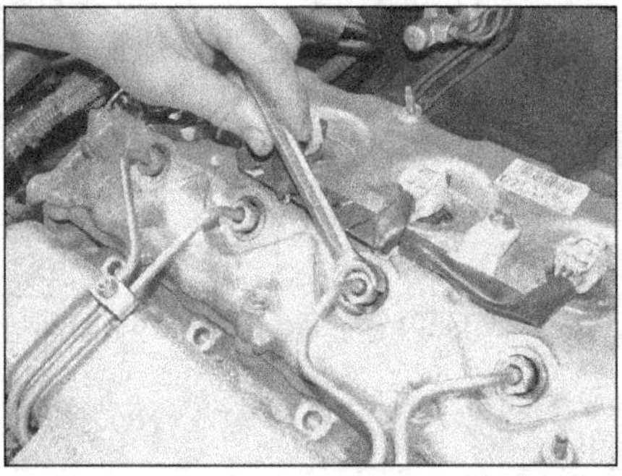

10.2b . . . then unscrew the union nuts . . .

10.2c . . . and remove the injector pipes

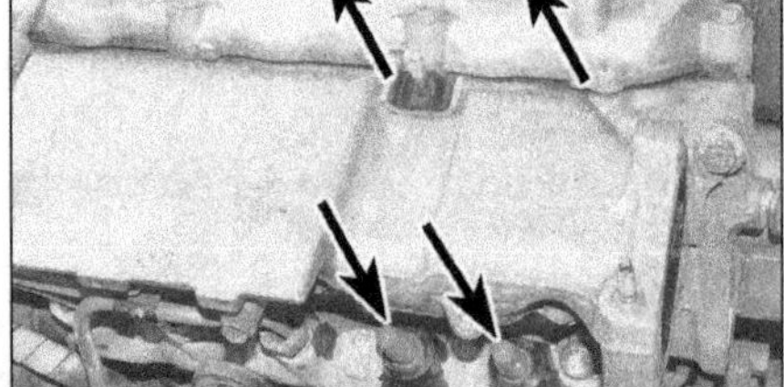

10.2d Cover the open apertures to prevent entry of dust and dirt

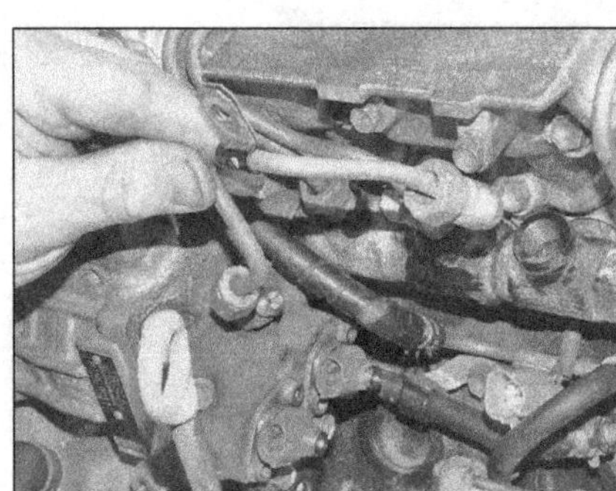

10.3 Removing the fuel inlet pipe from the high-pressure fuel pump and common rail

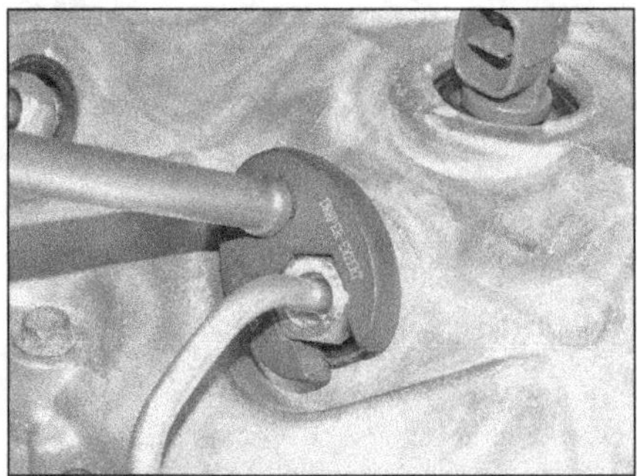

10.4 Using a crow's foot adapter to tighten the union nuts to the correct torque

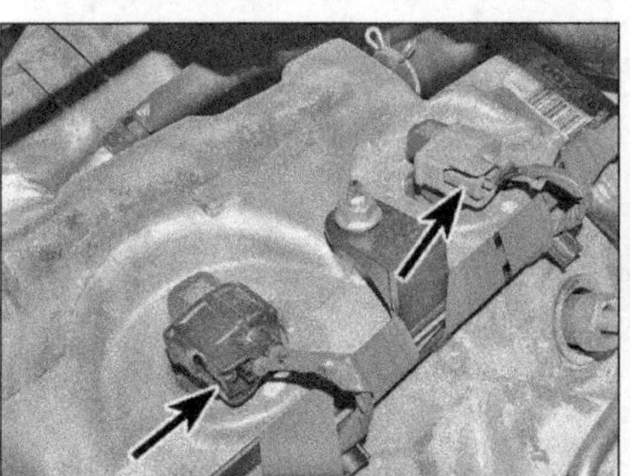
11.2 Injector wiring connectors (two shown)

11.12a Unscrew the four hollow bolts . . .

11.12b . . . remove the leak-off pipe, and recover the double sealing washers

4 Now use the ohmmeter to check that there is no continuity between the terminals and earth.

5 If the resistance is not correct, renew the injectors.

Removal

6 Release the engine wiring harness from its location near the common rail.

7 Remove the high-pressure fuel lines as described in the previous Section. Tape over the open apertures to prevent entry of dust and dirt. **Note:** *Toyota recommend renewal of the injector pipes whenever the injectors and/or the common rail are renewed. Toyota recommend renewal of the fuel inlet pipe whenever the common rail or supply pump are renewed.*

8 Remove the lower injection pipe support clamps from the inlet manifold.

9 Remove the valve cover as described in Chapter 2B.

10 Place cloth rags beneath the fuel leak-off pipe, to collect spilt fuel.

11 At the timing belt end of the fuel leak-off pipe, unscrew and remove the union bolt and recover the double sealing washer.

12 Unscrew the four hollow bolts securing the leak-off pipe to the cylinder head, remove the leak-off pipe, and recover the double sealing washers **(see illustrations)**.

13 Identify the fuel injectors for position to ensure correct refitting, as the engine control module (ECM) uses this information when injecting fuel.

14 Unscrew and remove the injector mounting bolts and recover the washers and clamps. Note the convex side of the washer abuts the top of the clamp **(see illustrations)**.

15 Using a lever or screwdriver, withdraw the injectors from the cylinder head, keeping them identified for position. It is a good idea to place each injector in a plastic bag **(see illustrations)**.

16 Remove the O-ring and back-up ring seals from the injectors.

17 Remove the nozzle seats from the cylinder head.

Refitting

18 Before refitting the injectors, thoroughly clean the cylinder head, injectors, leak-off pipe, and fuel lines.

19 Locate four new nozzle seats in the cylinder head. To ensure they locate correctly, use a narrow screwdriver to guide them into position **(see illustration)**.

20 Position the spring on each injector so

11.14a Unscrew the mounting bolt, and remove it together with the clamp

11.14b The convex side of the washer abuts the top of the clamp

11.15a Use a lever to release the injector . . .

11.15b . . . and remove from the cylinder head

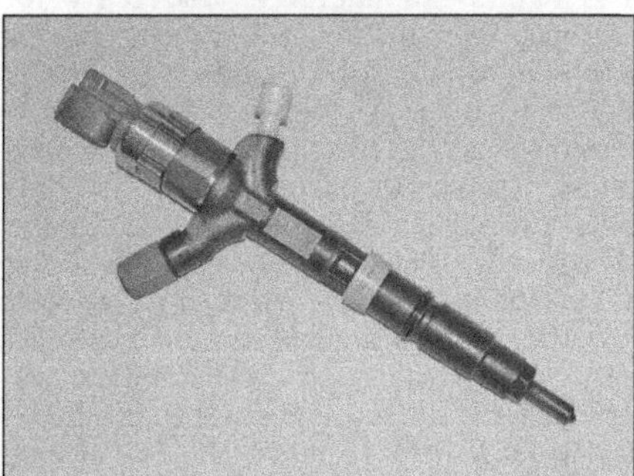
11.15c Injector removed from the cylinder head

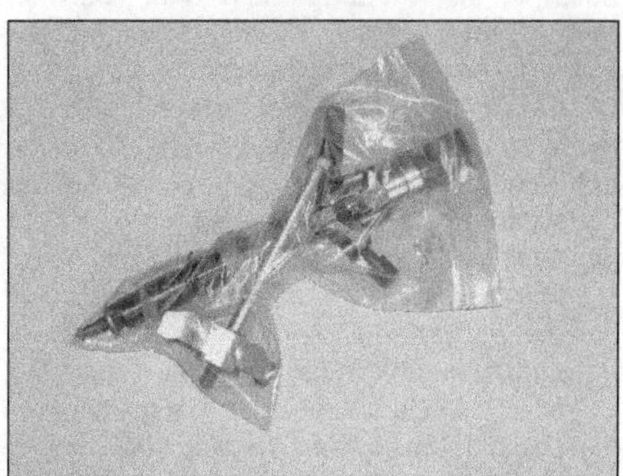
11.15d Keep the injectors in separate plastic bags

11.19 Use a narrow screwdriver to guide the new nozzle seats into the cylinder head

11.21 Insert the injector in the cylinder head so that the tag locates in the slot. Note also that the spring opening is aligned with the tag

that it's opening is over the injector locating tag. Fit new O-ring and back up ring seals to the injectors, and smear some fresh engine oil on the O-rings.

21 Align the injector tag with the slot in the cylinder head, and press the injector into position **(see illustration)**. If the injector moves up due to the reaction of the O-ring seal, remove it completely and insert again.

Caution: Make sure the injector is located in the correct cylinder as noted previously.

22 Insert the remaining injectors in the same manner, and then lightly oil under the heads of the clamp bolts and fit them together with the clamps and washers. The washers must be located on the clamps with the tapered side facing downwards.

23 Hand-tighten the bolts initially, then fully tighten them to the specified torque.

24 Refit the fuel leak-off pipe together with new double sealing washers, making sure that the washer ties are facing forward. Oil under the heads of the four hollow bolts, then insert them and tighten to the specified torque. **Note:** *If the bolts are overtightened, the leak-off pipe must be renewed.*

25 Refit the timing belt end of the leak-off pipe to the cylinder head together with a new double sealing washer. Oil under the head of the union bolt, then insert it and tighten to the specified torque. **Note:** *If the bolt is overtightened, the leak-off pipe must be renewed.*

26 At this stage, Toyota recommend making a pressure check of the leak-off pipe, however, if the following check is made, it will be necessary to obtain a new check valve.

a) First, disconnect the flexible leak-off hose from the fuel outlet check valve pipe on the timing belt end of the cylinder head, then use an Allen key to unscrew the plug from the check valve. Remove the spring and ball, and tighten the plug back into the check valve, then connect a pump and gauge to the check valve pipe, and apply 1.0 bar for 10 minutes.

b) Use soapy water to check for any air bubbles from the leak-off pipe connections. If evident, remove the leak-off pipe and renew the double washers, then refit it and make the check again.

c) After confirming the connections are good, unscrew the check valve and remove the union pipe, then fit a new check valve with new double washers to the pipe, and tighten to the specified torque. Reconnect the hose to the check valve pipe.

27 Refit the valve cover as described in Chapter 2B.

28 Refit the lower injection pipe support clamps to the inlet manifold.

29 Refit the high-pressure fuel lines as described in the previous Section.

30 Refit the engine wiring harness, and connect the wiring to the injectors.

31 Start the engine and check for fuel leaks.

12 On-Board Diagnostic (OBD) system and fault codes

Diagnostic tool information

1 A digital multimeter is necessary for checking fuel injection and emission related components. A digital volt-ohmmeter is preferred over the older style analogue multimeter for several reasons. The analogue multimeter cannot display the volts-ohms or amps measurement in hundredths and thousandths increments. When working with electronic circuits, which are often very low voltage, this accurate reading is most important. Another good reason for the digital multimeter is the high impedance circuit. The digital multimeter is equipped with a high resistance internal circuitry (10 million ohms). Because a voltmeter is hooked up in parallel with the circuit when testing, it is vital that none of the voltage being measured should be allowed to travel the parallel path set up by the meter itself. This dilemma does not show itself when measuring larger amounts of voltage (9 to 12 volt circuits) but if you are measuring a low voltage circuit such as sensor signal voltage, a fraction of a volt may be a significant amount when diagnosing a problem. However, there are several exceptions when using an analogue voltmeter may be necessary to test certain sensors.

2 Hand-held scanners are the most powerful and versatile tools for analysing engine management systems used on later model vehicles. Each brand scan tool must be examined carefully to match the year, make and model of the vehicle you are working on. Often interchangeable cartridges are available to access the particular manufacturer (Toyota, Ford, Vauxhall, etc). Some manufacturers will specify by continent (Asia, Europe, USA, etc).

3 The On-Board Diagnostic (OBD) facility built into the vehicle's electronic systems can only be accessed by a dedicated scan tool **(see illustration)**. Although hand-held scan tools are now becoming generally available, your local dealer or specialist will have the necessary equipment to interrogate the OBD system.

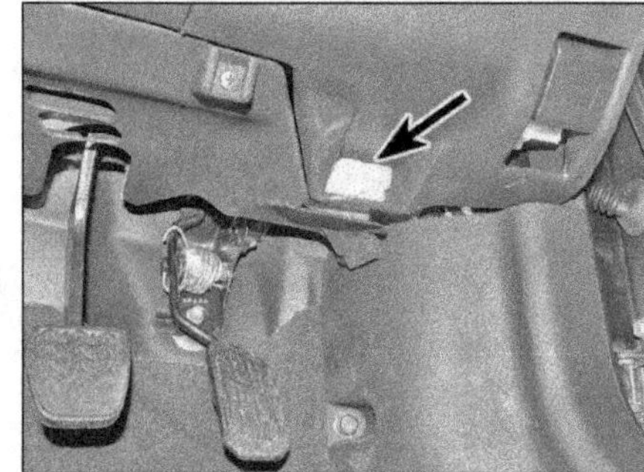
12.3 Diagnostic connector inside vehicle

On-Board Diagnostic system

4 All models described in this manual are equipped with the second generation On-Board Diagnostic system. The system consists of an on-board computer, known as the Engine Control Module (ECM), information sensors and output actuators.

5 The information sensors monitor various functions of the engine and send data to the ECM. Based on the data and the information programmed into the computer's memory, the ECM generates output signals to control various engine functions via control relays, solenoids and other output actuators. The ECM is specifically calibrated to optimise the emissions, fuel economy and driveability of the vehicle. It isn't a good idea to attempt diagnosis or renewal of the ECM at home while the vehicle is under warranty. Take the vehicle to a dealer service department if the ECM or a system component malfunctions.

Information sensors

Airflow meter

The airflow meter measures the amount of air passing through the sensor body and ultimately entering the engine. The ECM uses this information to control fuel injection quantity and turbocharger boost pressure.

Coolant temperature sensor

The engine coolant temperature sensor monitors engine coolant temperature. The ECM uses this information to control fuel injection quantity and timing.

Fuel temperature sensor

The fuel temperature sensor monitors the temperature of the fuel being delivered to the fuel injectors. The ECM uses this information to control fuel injection quantity and timing.

Inlet air temperature sensor

The inlet air temperature sensor monitors the temperature of the air entering the inlet manifold. The ECM uses this information to control fuel injection quantity and timing.

Fuel pressure sensor

The fuel pressure sensor monitors the fuel pressure in the common rail. The ECM uses this information to control fuel injection quantity and timing.

Turbo pressure sensor

The turbo pressure sensor monitors the air pressure in the inlet manifold. The ECM uses this information to control the turbocharger wastegate. The ECM calculates the engine torque needed depending on driver demand and engine operating conditions, and then adjusts the boost pressure to meet the demands.

Camshaft position sensor

The camshaft position sensor produces a signal which the ECM uses to identify number 1 cylinder and to time the sequential fuel injection.

Crankshaft position sensor

The crankshaft position sensor monitors crankshaft position (TDC) and speed during each engine revolution. The ECM uses this information to control fuel injection quantity and timing.

Accelerator pedal and position sensor

The throttle position sensor forms part of the accelerator pedal module, and senses throttle movement and position. The ECM uses this information to control fuel delivery and engine speed according to driver demand.

Vehicle speed sensor

The vehicle speed sensor provides information to the ECM to indicate vehicle speed.

Miscellaneous ECM inputs

In addition to the various sensors, the ECM monitors various switches and circuits to determine vehicle operating conditions. The switches and circuits include:

a) Air conditioning system.
b) Antilock brake system.
c) Barometric pressure sensor (inside ECM).
d) Battery voltage.
e) Brake switch.
f) Clutch pedal switch.
g) Cruise control system.
h) Park/neutral position switch.
i) Power steering pressure switch.

Output actuators

Check Engine light

The ECM will illuminate the CHECK ENGINE light if a malfunction in the electronic engine control system occurs.

Glow plugs

The ECM controls the operation of the glow plug system. The glow plugs allow the engine to start easily in cold conditions.

Wastegate regulator valve

The ECM monitors inlet manifold pressure and controls the turbocharger wastegate with the wastegate regulator valve. The engine control system calculates the engine torque needed depending on driver demand and engine operating conditions; the ECM will then adjust the boost pressure to meet the demands.

Obtaining fault codes

Note: *The diagnostic fault codes on all models can only be extracted from the Engine Control Module (ECM) using a specialised diagnostic tool. Have the vehicle diagnosed by a dealer service department or other qualified repair facility if the proper tool is not available.*

6 The ECM will illuminate the CHECK ENGINE light on the dash if it recognises a fault in the system. The light will remain illuminated until the problem is repaired and the code is cleared or the ECM does not detect any malfunction for several consecutive drive cycles.

7 The diagnostic codes for the On-Board Diagnostic (OBD) system can only be extracted from the ECM using a diagnostic tool. The tool is programmed to interface with the OBD system by plugging into the diagnostic connector **(see illustration 12.3)**. When used, the diagnostic tool has the ability to diagnose in-depth driveability problems. If the tool is not available and intermittent driveability problems exist, have the vehicle checked at a dealer service department or other qualified garage.

Clearing fault codes

8 After the system has been repaired, the codes must be cleared from the ECM memory using a scan tool. Do not attempt to clear the codes by disconnecting battery power. If battery power is disconnected from the ECM, the ECM will lose the current engine operating parameters and driveability will suffer until the ECM is programmed with a scan tool.

9 Always clear the codes from the ECM before starting the engine after a new electronic emission control component is fitted onto the engine. The ECM stores the operating parameters of each sensor. The ECM may set a fault code if a new sensor is allowed to operate before the parameters from the old sensor have been erased.

13 Injection system electrical components – testing, removal and refitting

Throttle body/module

Testing

1 The throttle body is located on an air inlet elbow on the left-hand end of the inlet manifold. The internal windings may be checked for resistance without removing the unit. First, disconnect the wiring plug.

2 Using an ohmmeter, check that the resistance between terminals 1 or 3 and 2, and 4 or 6 and 5 are as given in the Specifications. If not, renew the throttle body.

Renewal

3 Undo the retaining bolts and move the air inlet pipe/ducting away from the air inlet elbow and throttle body **(see illustration)**. **Note:** *It may be necessary to disconnect the*

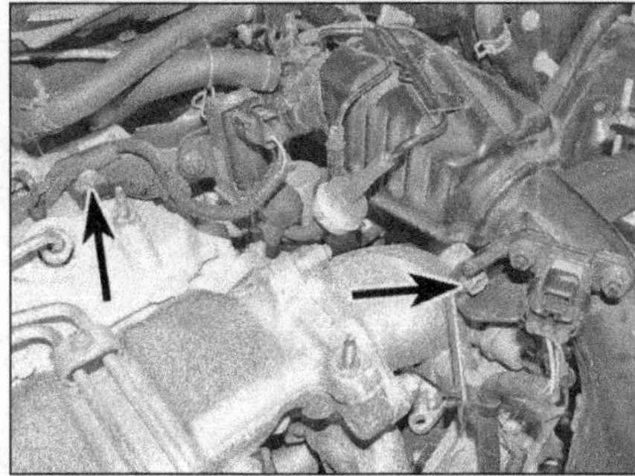

13.3 Undo the air inlet pipe mounting bolts (arrowed)

13.4 Disconnecting the wiring

13.5a Unscrew the mounting bolts and remove the throttle body and air inlet elbow from the inlet manifold . . .

13.5b . . . then recover the gasket

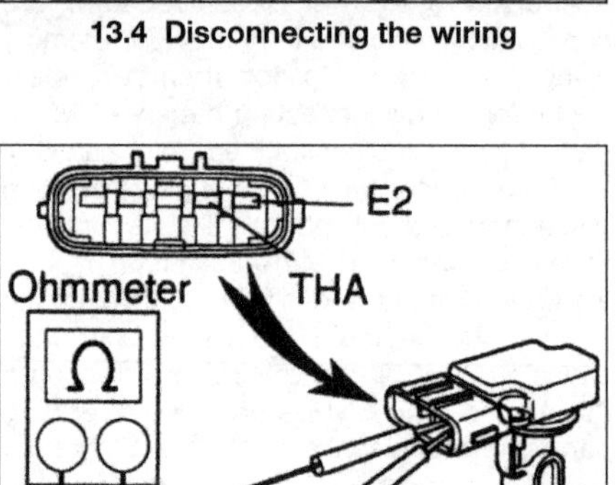

13.8 Checking the resistance of the airflow meter

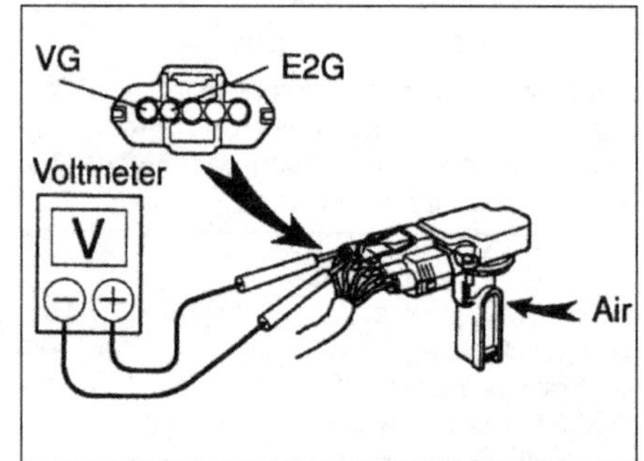

13.9 Using a voltmeter to check the operation of the airflow meter

wiring connectors and hose from the air inlet pipe/ducting, to allow it to be moved away.

4 Disconnect the wiring and the vacuum hose **(see illustration)**.

5 Unscrew the mounting bolts and remove the throttle body complete with air inlet elbow from the inlet manifold. Recover the gasket **(see illustrations)**.

6 Unscrew the mounting nuts and remove the throttle body from the air inlet elbow. Recover the gasket.

7 Refitting is a reversal of removal, but fit new gaskets and tighten the mounting nuts to the specified torque.

Airflow meter

Testing

8 Using an ohmmeter as shown **(see illustration)**, check that the resistance of the airflow meter is as given in the Specifications.

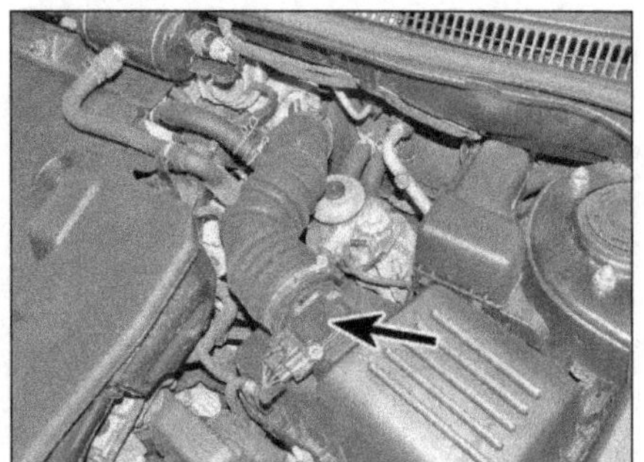
13.11 Location of airflow meter

9 Now reconnect the wiring and use a voltmeter to back-probe the terminals as shown **(see illustration)**. With the ignition switched on, blow air through the airflow meter and check that the voltage fluctuates.

10 If the airflow meter is faulty, renew it.

Renewal

11 The airflow meter is located in the outlet of the air cleaner top cover. First, disconnect the wiring **(see illustration)**.

12 Undo the screws and remove the airflow meter.

13 Refitting is a reversal of removal.

Coolant temperature sensor

14 The coolant temperature sensor is located in the cylinder head, beneath the left-hand end of the inlet manifold. The sensor is a thermistor (a resistor which varies the value of its resistance in accordance with temperature changes). The change in the resistance values will directly affect the voltage signal from the sensor to the ECM. As the sensor temperature INCREASES, the resistance values will DECREASE. As the sensor temperature DECREASES, the resistance values will INCREASE.

Testing

15 Check the terminals in the connector and the wires leading to the sensor for looseness and breaks. Repair as required.

16 With the ignition switch off, disconnect the wiring plug from the inlet air temperature sensor. Using an ohmmeter, measure the resistance between the terminals. With the engine cool (20°C), the resistance should be 2320 to 2590 ohms. Reconnect the wiring plug to the sensor, start the engine and warm it up until it reaches operating temperature. Disconnect the connector and check the resistance again. At 60°C the resistance should be 310 to 326 ohms. If the sensor resistance test results are incorrect, renew the engine coolant temperature sensor.

Renewal

Warning: Wait until the engine is completely cool before beginning this procedure.

17 Partially drain the cooling system (see Chapter 1B).

18 Disconnect the wiring plug from the sensor and use a 19 mm socket to unscrew the sensor from the cylinder head. Recover the seal.

19 Refitting is a reversal of removal, and refill the cooling system (see Chapter 1B).

Fuel temperature sensor

20 The fuel temperature sensor is a thermistor (a resistor which varies the value of its resistance in accordance with temperature changes). The change in the resistance values will directly affect the voltage signal from the sensor to the ECM. As the sensor temperature INCREASES, the resistance values will DECREASE. As the sensor temperature DECREASES, the resistance values will INCREASE.

Testing

21 The fuel temperature sensor is located in the high-pressure fuel pump body. It cannot be renewed separately. Check the terminals in the connector and the wires leading to the high-pressure pump for looseness and breaks. Repair as required.

22 With the ignition off, disconnect the wiring from the sensor.

23 Connect an ohmmeter between the terminals, and check that the resistance as specified at the beginning of this Chapter.

Renewal

24 If the resistance is not as specified, the complete high-pressure fuel pump must be renewed as described in Section 8. Note also that the fuel inlet pipe must also be renewed at the same time.

Inlet air temperature sensor

25 The inlet air temperature sensor is located in the air inlet elbow on the left-hand end of the inlet manifold **(see illustration)**. The sensor is a thermistor (a resistor which varies the value of its resistance in accordance with temperature changes). The change in the resistance values will directly affect the voltage signal from the sensor to the ECM. As the sensor temperature INCREASES, the resistance values will DECREASE. As the sensor temperature DECREASES, the resistance values will INCREASE.

Testing

26 Check the terminals in the connector and the wires leading to the sensor for looseness and breaks. Repair as required.

27 With the ignition switch off, disconnect the wiring plug from the inlet air temperature sensor. Using an ohmmeter, measure the resistance between the terminals. With the engine cool (20°C), the resistance should be 2.0 to 3.0 k ohms. Reconnect the wiring plug to the sensor, start the engine and warm it up until it reaches operating temperature. Disconnect the connector and check the resistance again. At 60°C the resistance should be 400 to 700 ohms. If the sensor resistance test results are incorrect, renew the temperature sensor.

Renewal

28 Disconnect the wiring plug from the sensor and use a 22 mm socket to unscrew the sensor from the air inlet elbow.

29 Refitting is a reversal of removal, but tighten the sensor to the specified torque.

Fuel pressure sensor

Testing

30 The fuel pressure sensor is located on the right-hand end of the common rail. It cannot be renewed separately, and if faulty, the complete common rail must be renewed.

31 Thorough testing of the fuel pressure sensor is best left to a Toyota dealer who will have the equipment necessary to make the check, however, the following check will determine if the sensor is receiving the correct supply voltage.

32 Disconnect the wiring plug from the sensor – it is located on a support mid-way along the common rail.

33 Switch on the ignition, then connect a voltmeter to the terminals in the socket, and check that the supply voltage is between 4.5 and 5.5 volts. If not, check the wiring.

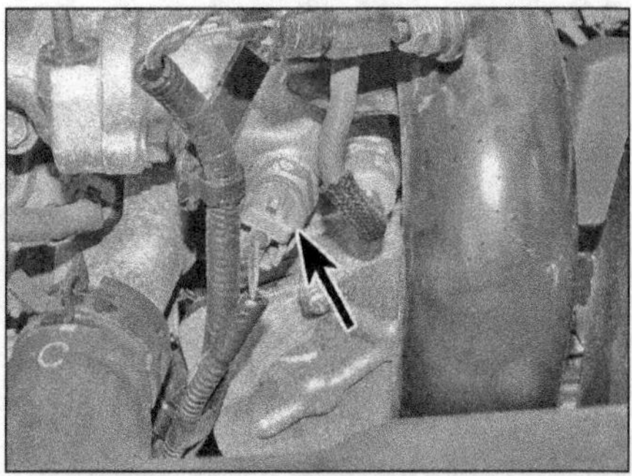

13.25 Location of inlet air temperature sensor

34 Reconnect the wiring plug.

Turbo pressure sensor

Testing

35 The turbo pressure sensor is located on a bracket at the left-hand end of the inlet manifold. Thorough testing of the turbo pressure sensor is best left to a Toyota dealer who will have the equipment necessary to make the check, however, the following check will determine if the sensor is receiving the correct supply voltage.

36 Disconnect the wiring plug from the sensor.

37 Switch on the ignition, then connect a voltmeter to the terminals in the socket, and check that the supply voltage is between 4.5 and 5.5 volts. If not, check the wiring.

38 Reconnect the wiring plug.

Camshaft position sensor

Testing

39 The camshaft position sensor is located on a support bracket at the right-hand rear of the cylinder head.

40 Disconnect the wiring plug from the sensor, then connect an ohmmeter between the terminals on the sensor and check that the resistance is as given in the Specifications. If not, renew the sensor.

Renewal

41 With the wiring plug disconnected, unscrew the mounting bolt and remove the sensor from the support bracket **(see illustration)**.

13.43 Crankshaft position sensor

13.41 Removing the camshaft sensor

42 Apply a little engine oil to the O-ring seal, then refit the sensor and tighten the mounting bolt to the specified torque. Reconnect the wiring.

Crankshaft position sensor

Testing

43 The crankshaft position sensor is located on the oil pump housing at the right-hand front of the engine **(see illustration)**. Access is limited and is best gained by raising the front of the vehicle and supporting on axle stands.

44 Disconnect the wiring plug from the sensor, then connect an ohmmeter between the terminals on the sensor and check that the resistance is as given in the Specifications. If not, renew the sensor.

Renewal

45 With the wiring plug disconnected, unscrew the mounting bolt and remove the sensor from the oil pump housing.

46 Apply a little engine oil to the O-ring seal, then refit the sensor and tighten the mounting bolt to the specified torque. Reconnect the wiring.

Accelerator pedal and position sensor

Testing

47 The accelerator pedal and position sensor are integral as a single module. The sensor detects the opening angle of the accelerator pedal, and outputs a corresponding voltage to the engine ECM.

48 For reasons of safety, testing of the sensor is best left to a Toyota dealer.

Renewal

49 Pull back the carpet as necessary for access, and then disconnect the two wiring plugs.

50 Unscrew the mounting bolts and remove the accelerator pedal assembly from inside the vehicle.

51 Refitting is a reversal of removal, but tighten the mounting bolts securely.

14.4 Remove the air inlet hose

14.6 Removing the intercooler hose

14.7a Remove the upper . . .

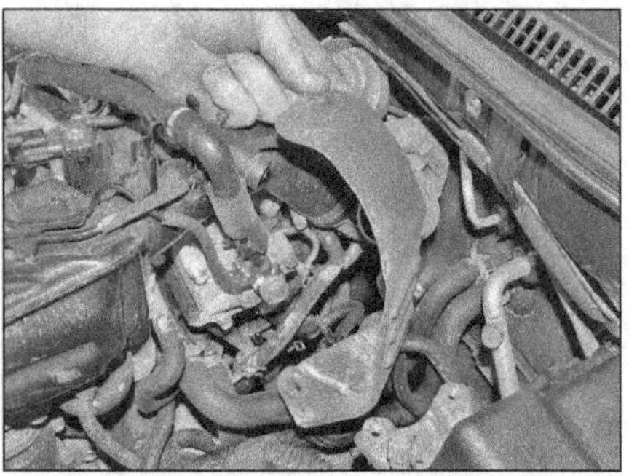
14.7b . . . and side heat shields

14.8 Turbocharger heat shields

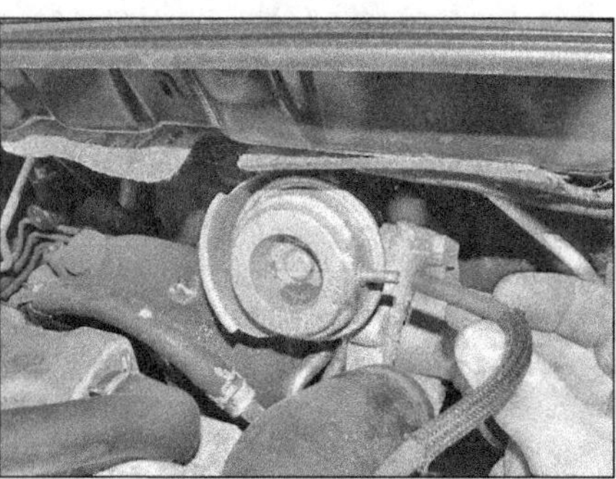
14.9 Disconnect the vacuum hose from the turbocharger wastegate

14 Turbocharger – testing, removal and refitting

Testing

1 The turbocharger is a precision component, which can be severely damaged by a lack of lubrication or from foreign material entering the air inlet duct. Turbocharger failure may be indicated by poor engine performance, blue/grey exhaust smoke or unusual noises from the turbocharger. If a turbocharger failure is suspected, check the following areas:

a) Check the inlet air duct for looseness or damage. Make sure there are no restrictions in the air inlet system, dirty air filter element or damaged intercooler.

b) Check the system vacuum hoses for restrictions or damage.

c) Check the system wiring for damage and electrical connectors for looseness or corrosion.

d) Make sure the wastegate actuator linkage is not binding.

e) Check the exhaust system for damage or restrictions.

f) Check the lubricating oil supply and return pipes for damage or restrictions.

g) If the turbocharger requires renewal due to failure, be sure to change the engine oil and filter (see Chapter 1B).

2 Complete diagnosis of the turbocharger and control system requires special techniques and equipment. If the previous checks fail to identify the problem, take the vehicle to a dealership service department or other properly-equipped repair facility for diagnosis.

Removal

Warning: Wait until the engine is completely cool before beginning this procedure.

3 Drain the cooling system as described in Chapter 1B.

4 Loosen the clips and disconnect the air filter inlet hose from the turbocharger **(see illustration)**.

5 Unscrew the mounting nuts and remove the plastic cover from the top of the engine.

6 Loosen the clips and disconnect the intercooler hose from the turbocharger **(see illustration)**.

7 Unbolt and remove the upper heat shield from the turbocharger **(see illustrations)**.

8 Unbolt the lower heat shields from the rear of the exhaust manifold catalytic converter **(see illustration)**. Access to the lower bolts is best from below, due to the restricted access, the heat shield cannot be removed from behind the engine until after the turbocharger is removed.

9 Disconnect the vacuum hose from the turbocharger **(see illustration)**.

10 Undo the retaining bolts and remove the brake vacuum reservoir from the bulkhead and move it to one side.

11 Loosen the clips and disconnect the coolant hoses from the turbocharger **(see illustrations)**.

12 Undo the bolts and remove the manifold support bracket **(see illustration)**.

13 Unscrew the retaining bolts and separate the front pipe from the catalytic converter. Recover the gasket **(see illustration)**.

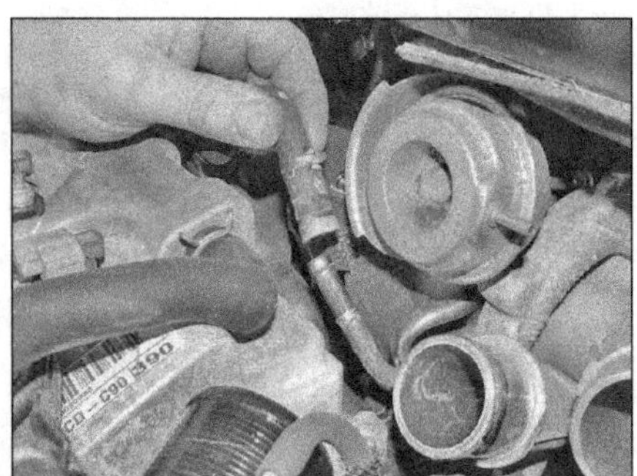
14.11a Release the retaining clips . . .

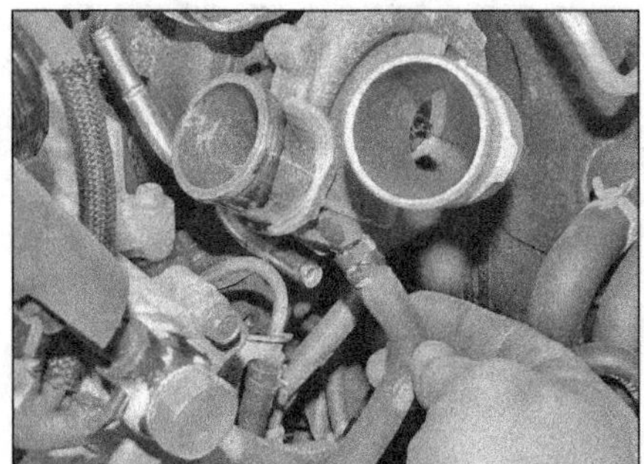
14.11b . . . and disconnect the coolant hoses

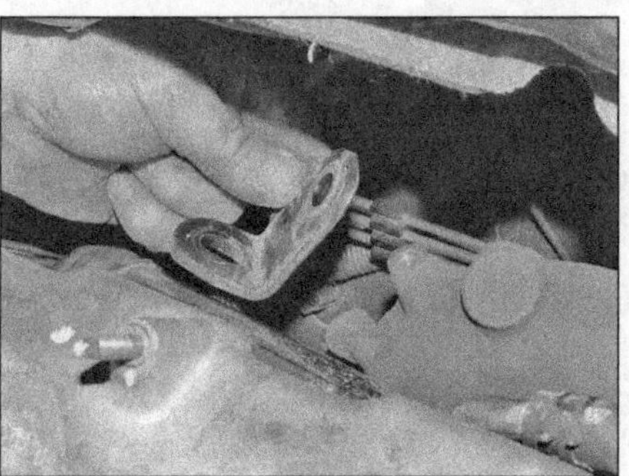
14.12 Remove the manifold support bracket

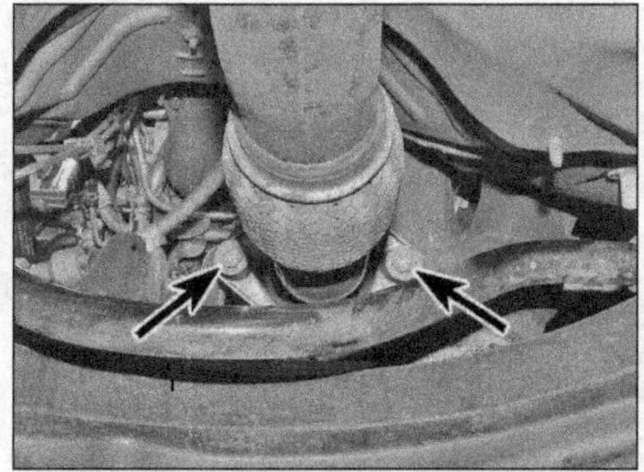
14.13 Exhaust front pipe retaining bolts (arrowed)

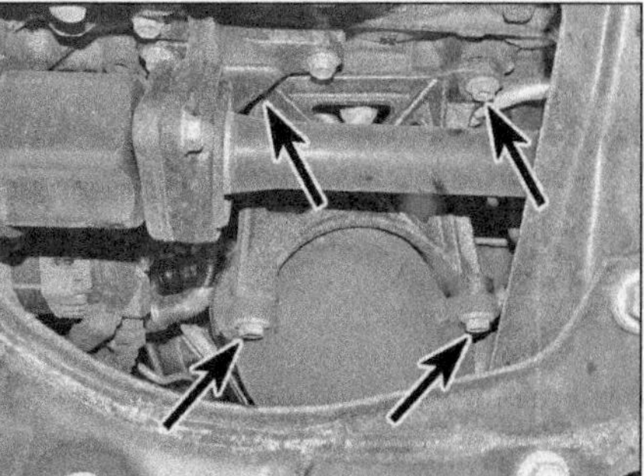
14.14a Undo the retaining bolts (arrowed) . . .

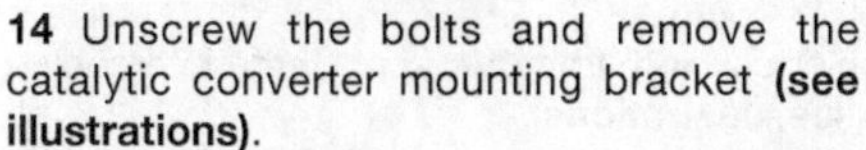
14.14b . . . and remove the lower mounting bracket

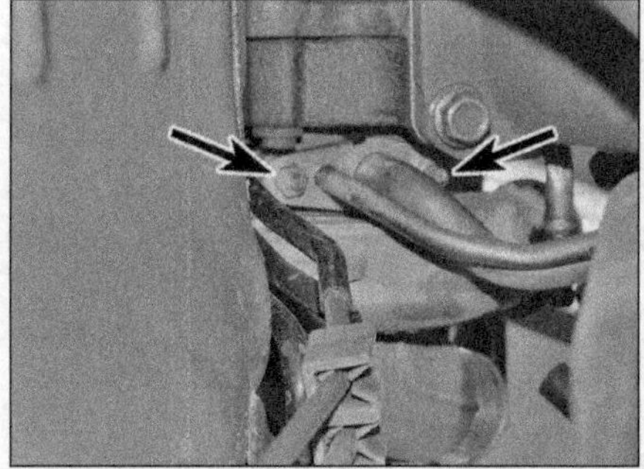
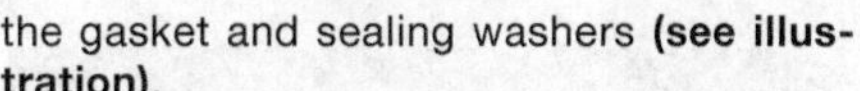
14.15 Oil return pipe retaining nuts (arrowed)

14.16 Remove the turbo mounting bracket

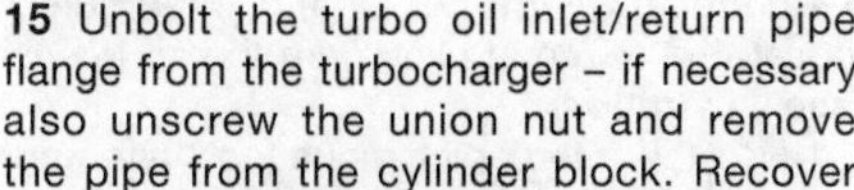
14 Unscrew the bolts and remove the catalytic converter mounting bracket **(see illustrations)**.

15 Unbolt the turbo oil inlet/return pipe flange from the turbocharger – if necessary also unscrew the union nut and remove the pipe from the cylinder block. Recover the gasket and sealing washers **(see illustration)**.

16 Unbolt the remaining stay, then unscrew the mounting nuts and remove the catalytic converter from the turbocharger **(see illustration).**

17 Undo the retaining nuts and disconnect the turbocharger from the exhaust manifold **(see illustrations)**. Recover the gasket. Take care not to damage the actuator pushrod.

18 If required, unbolt and remove the EGR cooler tube **(see illustration)**.

19 Recover the remaining heat shield from the rear of the engine **(see illustration)**.

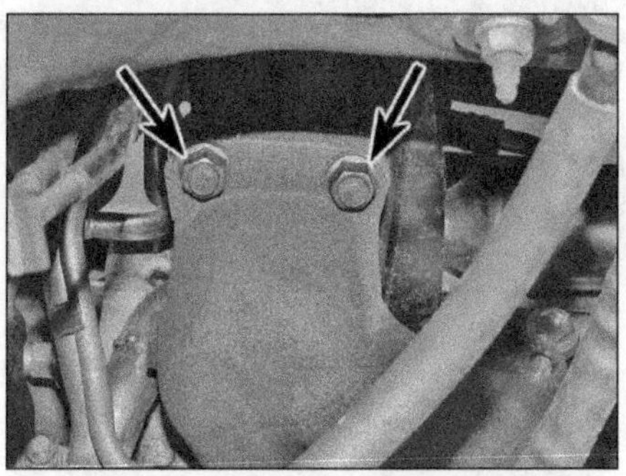
14.17a Undo the lower mounting nuts . . .

14.17b . . . upper mounting nut . . .

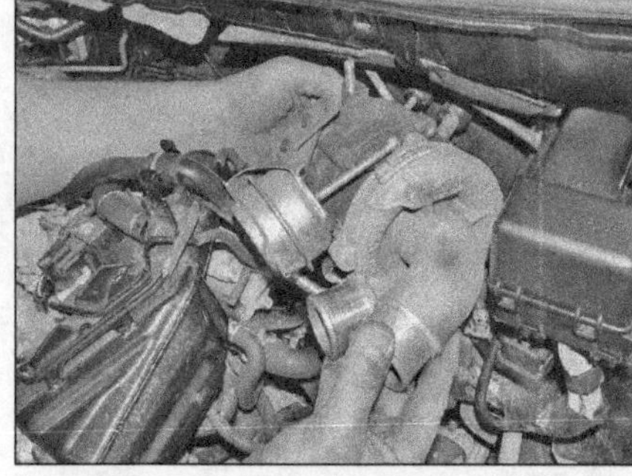
14.17c . . . and remove the turbocharger

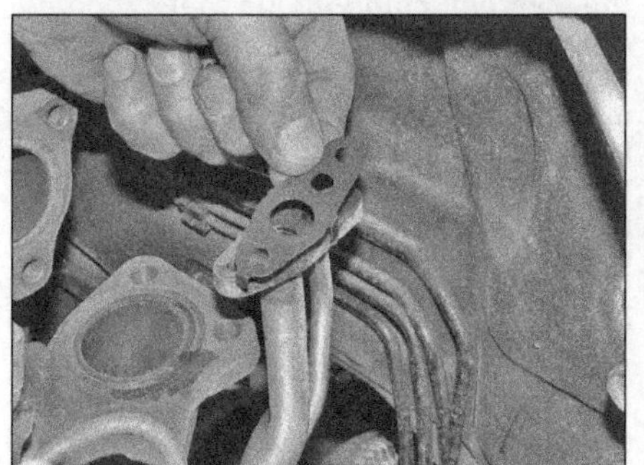
14.17d Recover the oil return pipe gasket

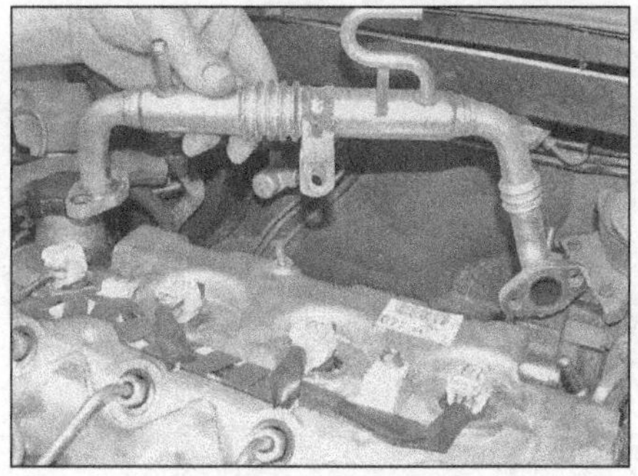
14.18 Removing the EGR tube

14.19 Recover the remaining heat shield

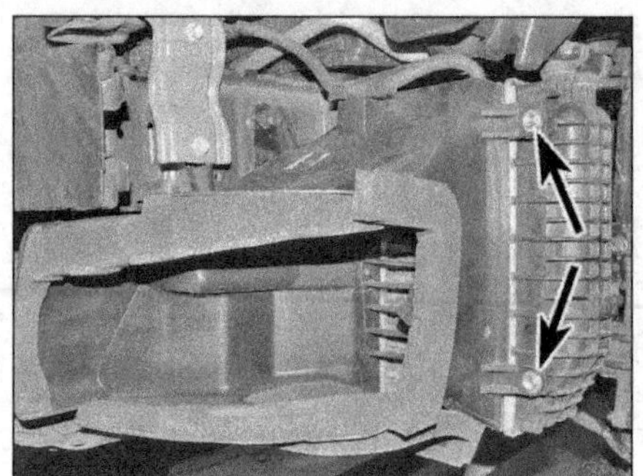
15.3a Undo the two retaining bolts (arrowed) . . .

15.3b . . . and remove the air inlet cowling

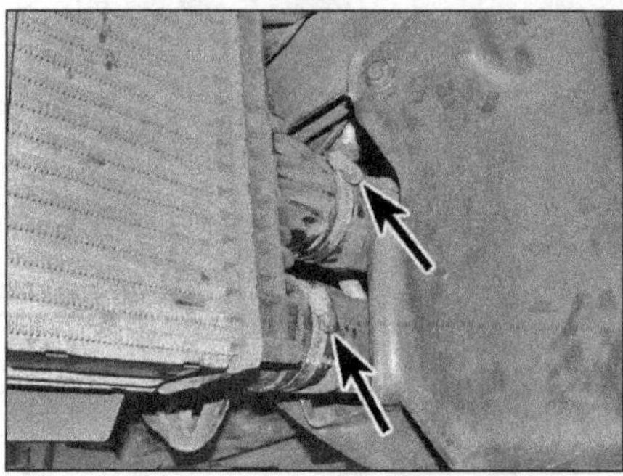
15.4 Slacken the air inlet hoses

15.5a Undo the rear mounting nut (arrowed) . . .

15.5b . . . the upper mounting bolts . . .

15.5c . . . and the front mounting bolts

15.6a Disconnect the hoses . . .

15.6b . . . and remove the intercooler

Refitting

20 Refitting is the reverse of removal with the following additions:

a) Renew all gaskets, seals, union bolt washers and self-locking nuts.

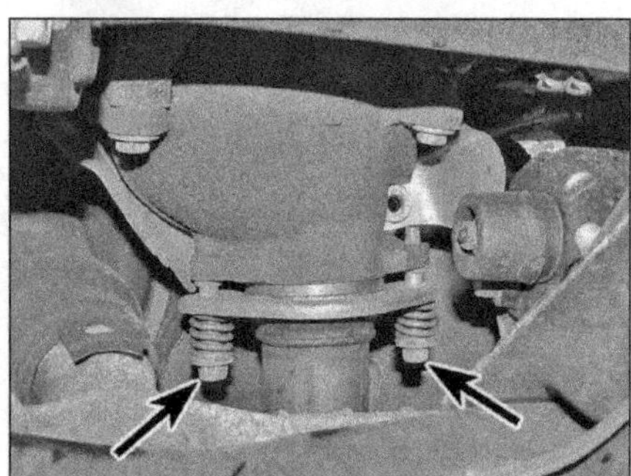
16.1a Front pipe retaining bolts and springs

b) Tighten the nuts and bolts to the torques listed in this Chapter's Specifications.

c) Change the engine oil and filter (see Chapter 1B).

d) Refill the cooling system (see Chapter 1B).

e) Before starting the engine, disconnect the injector feed wiring and crank the engine over until oil pressure builds.

15 Intercooler – removal and refitting

Removal

1 The intercooler is located behind the bumper at the left-hand side front of the vehicle.

2 Remove the front bumper as described in Chapter 11.

3 Undo the retaining bolts and remove the air inlet cowling, from the front of the intercooler **(see illustrations)**.

4 At the lower corner of the intercooler, loosen the securing clips from the air hoses **(see illustration)**.

5 Undo the intercooler mounting bolts and nuts **(see illustrations)**.

6 Withdraw the intercooler from the inlet hoses and disconnect the vacuum pump as it is being removed **(see illustrations)**.

Refitting

7 Refitting is a reversal of removal.

16 Exhaust system – general information

Warning: Inspection and repair of exhaust system components should be done only after the system components have cooled completely.

1 The exhaust system consists of the exhaust manifold and catalytic converter, turbocharger, front exhaust pipe and catalytic converter, centre pipe and silencer, and tailpipe and silencer. The front exhaust pipe is attached to the catalytic converter by spring-tensioned bolts and a circular exhaust gasket **(see illustrations)**.

2 The exhaust system is attached to the body with mounting brackets and rubber hangers. If any of these parts are damaged or deteriorated, excessive noise and vibration will be transmitted to the body **(see illustration)**.

16.1b Rear exhaust retaining bolts and springs

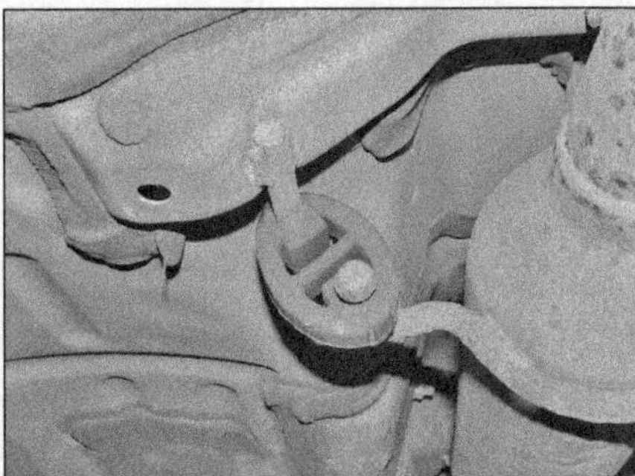
16.2 Check the exhaust mounting rubbers

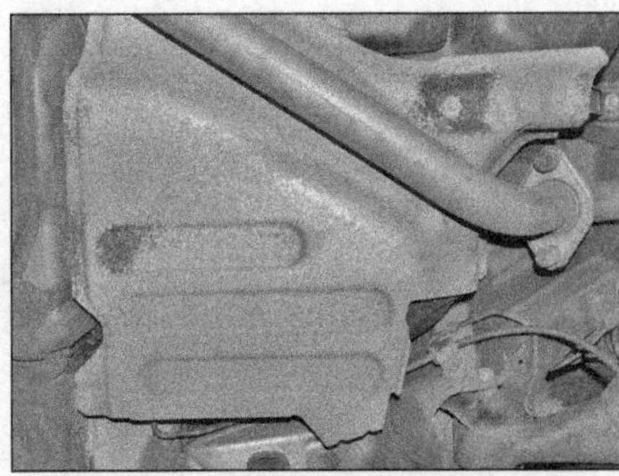
16.5 Check the condition and security of the heat shields

3 Conducting regular inspections of the exhaust system will keep it safe and quiet. Look for any damaged or bent parts, open seams, holes, loose connections, excessive corrosion or other defects, which could allow exhaust fumes to enter the vehicle. Deteriorated exhaust system components should not be repaired – they should be renewed.

4 If the exhaust system components are extremely corroded or rusted together, they will probably have to be cut from the exhaust system.

5 Here are some simple guidelines to apply when repairing the exhaust system:

a) Work from the back to the front when removing exhaust system components.

b) Apply penetrating oil to the exhaust system component fasteners to make them easier to remove.

c) Use new gaskets, hangers and clamps when installing exhaust system components.

d) Apply anti-seize compound to the threads of all exhaust system nuts and bolts during reassembly.

*e) Check that the heat shields between the underbody and the exhaust system are secure **(see illustration)**.*

f) Be sure to allow sufficient clearance between newly fitted parts and all points on the underbody to avoid overheating the floorpan and possibly damaging the interior carpet and insulation. Pay particularly close attention to the catalytic converters and heat shields.

Warning: The catalytic converters operate at very high temperatures and take a long time to cool. Wait until completely cool before attempting to remove the converters. Failure to do so could result in serious burns.

Chapter 4 Part C:
Emission control systems – petrol engines

Contents

Degrees of difficulty

Easy, suitable for novice with little experience 	**Fairly easy,** suitable for beginner with some experience	**Fairly difficult,** suitable for competent DIY mechanic	**Difficult,** suitable for experienced DIY mechanic	**Very difficult,** suitable for expert DIY or professional 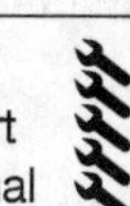

Specifications

Vacuum switching valve (VSV)

Resistance at 20°C	30.0 to 34.0 ohms

Oxygen sensor heater resistance

Connections 1 (+B) and 2 (HT) – resistance at 20°C	11.0 to 16.0 ohms

Torque wrench setting

	Nm	lbf ft
Oxygen sensor	44	32

1 General information

To minimise pollution of the atmosphere from incompletely burned and evaporating gases, and to maintain good driveability and fuel economy, a number of emission control systems are used on these vehicles, according to market territory. They include the:

Positive Crankcase Ventilation (PCV) system.
Evaporative Emission Control (EVAP) system.
Three-way catalytic converter (TWC) system.

The Sections in this Chapter include general descriptions, checking procedures within the scope of the home mechanic and component renewal procedures (when possible) for each of the systems listed above.

Before assuming an emissions control system is malfunctioning, check the fuel and ignition systems carefully (see Chapters 4A and 5A). The diagnosis of some emission control devices requires specialised tools, equipment and training. If checking and servicing become too difficult or if a procedure is beyond the scope of your skills, consult your dealer service department or other repair workshop.

This doesn't mean, however, that emission control systems are particularly difficult to maintain and repair. You can quickly and easily perform many checks and do most of the regular maintenance at home with common tune-up and hand tools. **Note:** *The most frequent cause of emissions problems is simply a loose or broken electrical connector or vacuum hose, so always check the electrical connectors and vacuum hoses first.*

Pay close attention to any special precautions outlined in this Chapter. It should be noted that the illustrations of the various systems may not exactly match the system installed on your vehicle because of changes made by the manufacturer during production or from year-to-year.

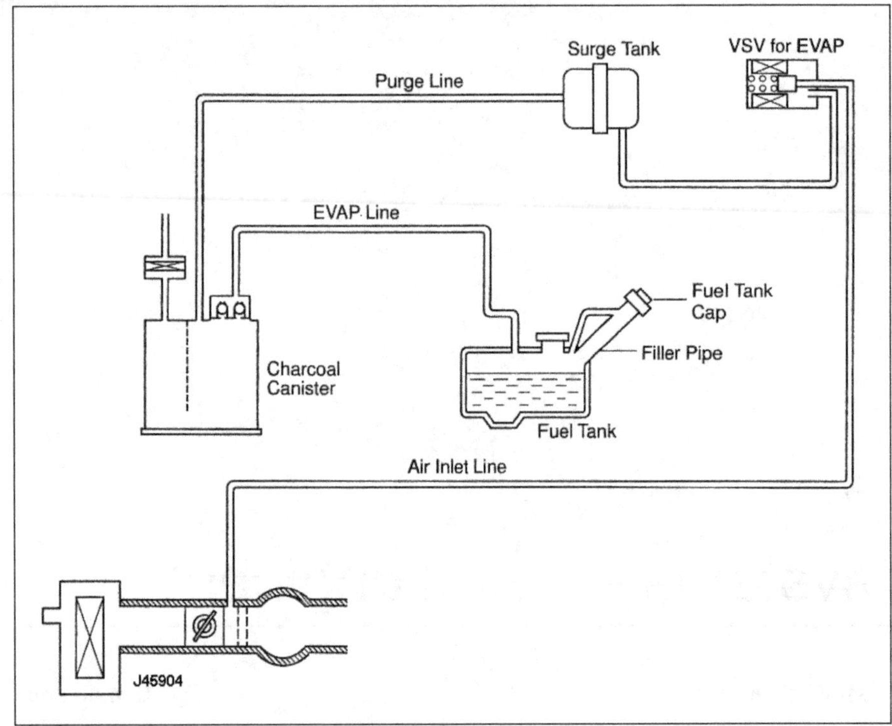

2.2 EVAP system

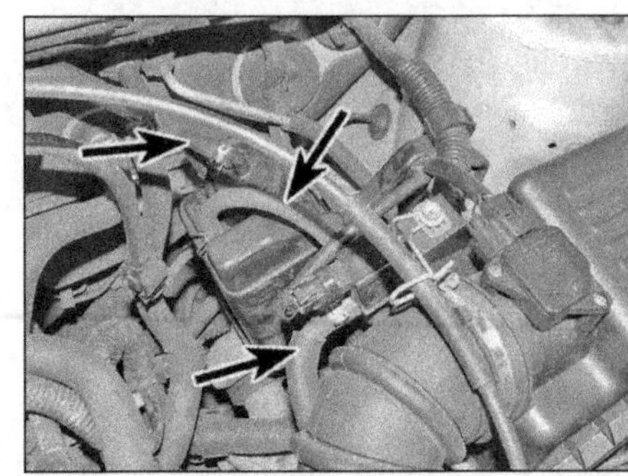

2.7 Charcoal canister hoses (arrowed)

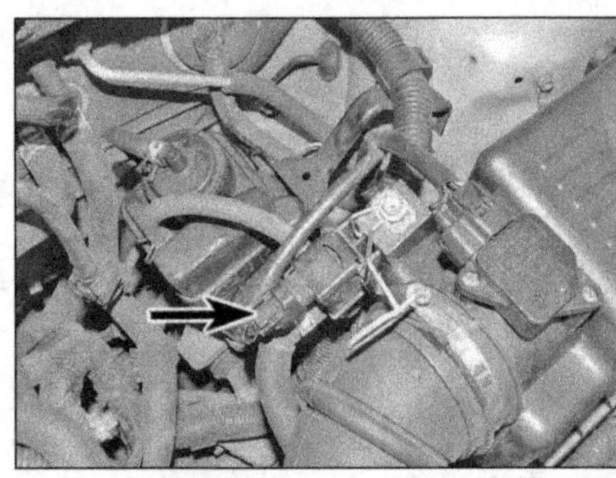

2.11 Location of purge valve (arrowed)

2 Evaporative Emission Control (EVAP) system

General description

1 This system is designed to trap and store fuel that evaporates from the fuel tank, throttle body and inlet manifold that would normally enter the atmosphere in the form of hydrocarbon (HC) emissions.

2 The Evaporative Emission Control (EVAP) system consists of a charcoal-filled canister, the pipes connecting the canister to the fuel tank, the Vacuum Switching Valve (VSV) and a surge tank **(see illustration)**.

3 Fuel vapours are transferred from the fuel tank and throttle body to a canister where they're stored when the engine isn't running. When the engine is running, the fuel vapours are purged from the canister by inlet airflow and consumed in the normal combustion process.

4 The charcoal canister is equipped with a check valve that incorporates three check balls. Depending upon the running conditions and the pressure in the fuel tank, the check balls open and close the passageways to the TVV/VSV (consequently the throttle body) and fuel tank.

Check

5 Poor idle, stalling and poor driveability can be caused by an inoperative check valve, a damaged canister, split or cracked hoses, or hoses connected to the wrong fittings. Check the fuel filler cap for a damaged or deformed gasket.

6 Evidence of fuel loss or fuel odour can be caused by liquid fuel leaking from fuel lines, a cracked or damaged canister, an inoperative check valve, or disconnected, misrouted, kinked, deteriorated or damaged vapour or control hoses.

7 Inspect each hose attached to the canister for kinks, leaks and cracks along its entire length **(see illustration)**. Repair or renew as necessary.

8 Look for fuel leaking from the bottom of the canister. If fuel is leaking, renew the canister and check the hoses and hose routing.

9 Inspect the canister. If it's cracked or damaged, renew it.

10 Check for a clogged filter or a stuck check valve. Using low-pressure compressed air, blow into the canister tank pipe. Air should flow freely from the other pipes. If a problem is found, renew the canister.

11 Disconnect the VSV (purge) valve wiring plug (located in front of the charcoal canister) **(see illustration)** and connect the leads of an ohmmeter to the valve terminals. The correct resistance should be 30 to 34 ohms at 20°C.

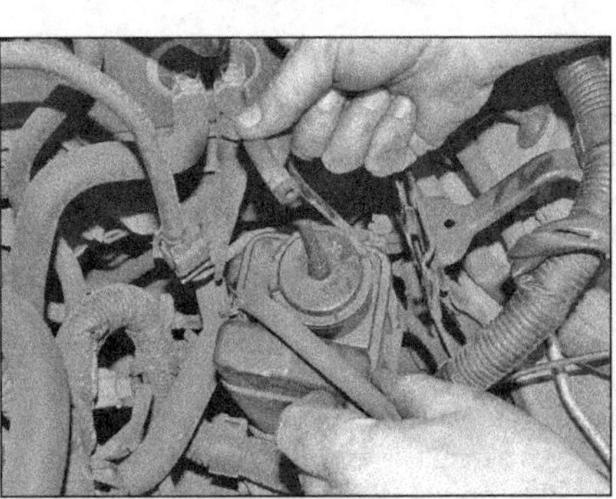

2.12 Disconnect the hoses . . .

2.13 . . . release the securing clip (arrowed) . . .

Charcoal canister renewal

12 Clearly label, and then detach the vacuum hoses from the canister **(see illustration)**.

13 Release the retaining clips and pull the canister upwards to remove it from its position in the mounting bracket **(see illustration)**.

14 To check the canister filter, unclip the cap and remove the filter from the top of the canister **(see illustration)**.

15 Installation is the reverse of removal.

2.14 . . . and withdraw the charcoal canister

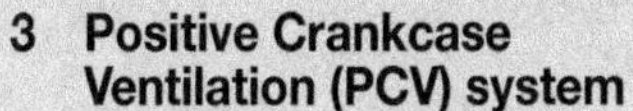

3 Positive Crankcase Ventilation (PCV) system

General description

1 The Positive Crankcase Ventilation (PCV) system reduces hydrocarbon emissions by scavenging crankcase vapours. It does this by circulating fresh air from the air cleaner through the crankcase, where it mixes with blow-by gases and is then rerouted through a PCV valve to the inlet manifold **(see illustration)**.

2 The main components of the PCV system are the PCV valve, a fresh air inlet and the vacuum hoses connecting these components to the engine.

3 To maintain idle quality, the PCV valve restricts the flow when the inlet manifold vacuum is high. If abnormal operating conditions (such as piston ring problems) arise, the system is designed to allow excessive amounts of blow-by gases to flow back through the crankcase vent tube into the air cleaner to be consumed by normal combustion.

4 This system directs the blow-by into the throttle body, which, over time, can cause an oily residue build-up in the area near the throttle plate. Consequently, it's a good idea to periodically clean this residue from the throttle body. Refer to Chapter 4A for this cleaning procedure.

3.8 Disconnect the hose and unscrew the PCV valve

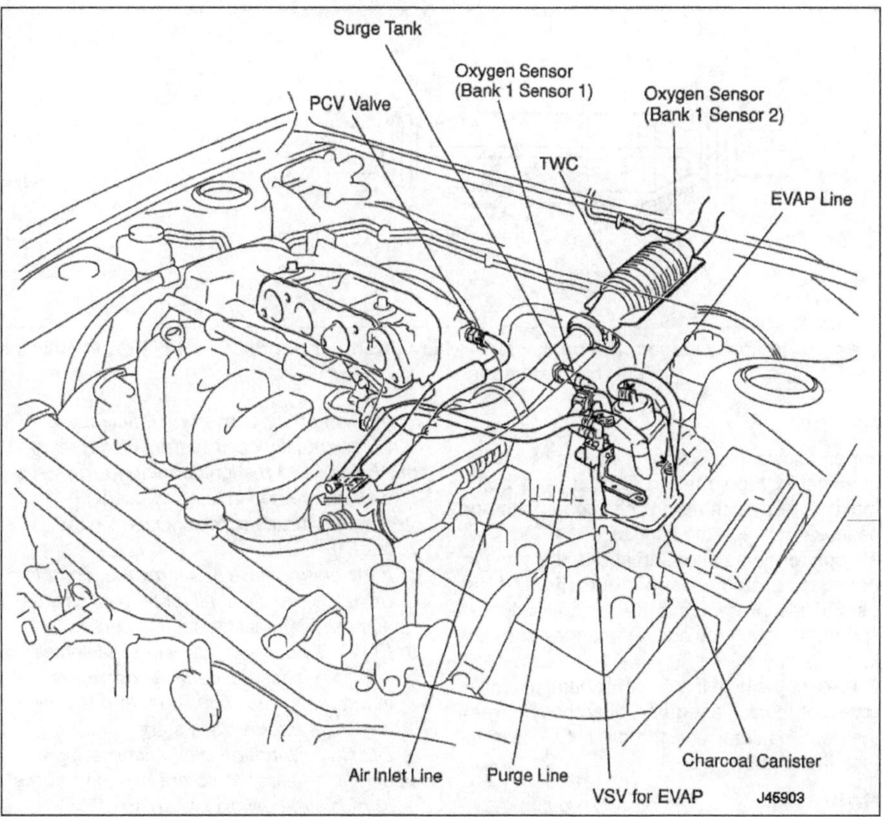

3.1 Emission systems pipework

Check

5 To check the valve, first unscrew it from the cover and shake the valve. It should rattle, indicating that it's not clogged with deposits. If the valve does not rattle, renew it.

6 Start the engine and allow it to idle, and then place your finger over the valve opening. If vacuum is felt, the PCV valve is working properly. If no vacuum is felt, the PCV valve may be defective or the hose may be blocked. Also check for vacuum leaks at the valve, filler cap and all the hoses.

Renewal

7 Undo the two nuts, prise out the plastic fasteners at the rear and remove the cover from the top of the engine.

8 Release the clamp, disconnect the hose, and unscrew the valve from the left-hand end of the cylinder head cover **(see illustration)**.

9 If the valve is clogged, the hose is also probably blocked. Remove the hose and clean it with solvent.

10 After cleaning the hose, inspect it for damage, wear and deterioration. Make sure it fits snugly on the fittings.

11 If necessary, install a new PCV valve.

12 Install the clean PCV hose. Make sure that the PCV valve and hose are secure.

4 Catalytic converter

General description

1 To reduce hydrocarbon, carbon monoxide and oxides of nitrogen emissions, all vehicles are equipped with a three-way catalyst system, which oxidises and reduces these chemicals, converting them into harmless nitrogen, carbon dioxide and water.

2 The catalytic converter is mounted in the exhaust system much like a silencer **(see illustration)**.

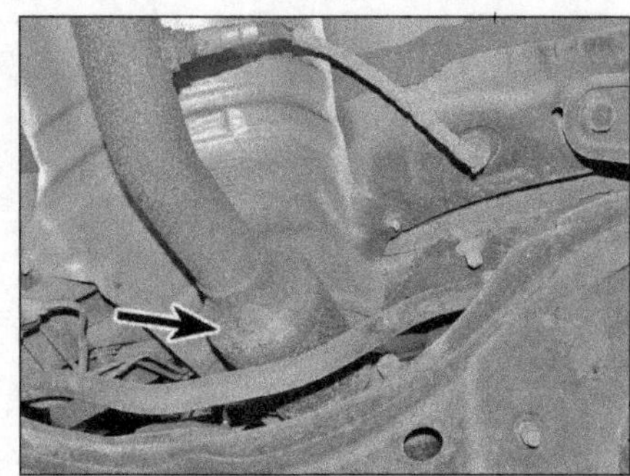

4.2 Catalytic converter (arrowed)

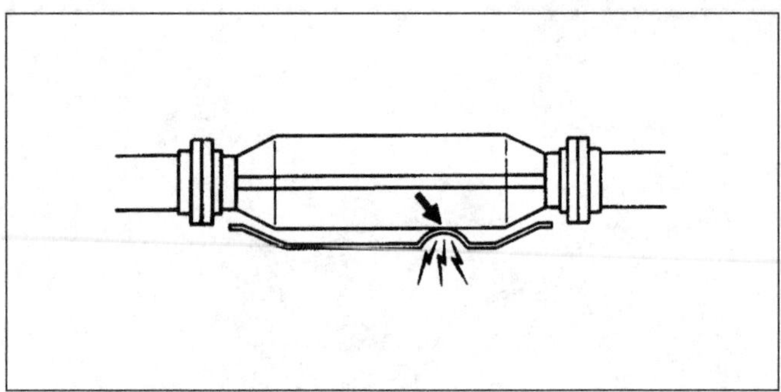
4.4 Periodically inspect the heat shield (where fitted) for dents and other damage

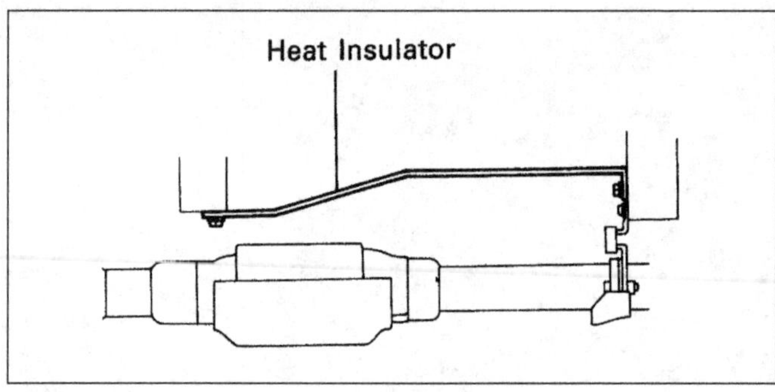

4.5 Periodically inspect the heat insulation panels to make sure there's adequate clearance

Check

3 Periodically inspect the catalytic converter-to-exhaust pipe mating flanges and bolts. Make sure that there are no loose bolts and no leaks between the flanges.

4 Look for dents in or damage to the catalytic converter protector **(see illustration)**. If any part of the protector is damaged or dented enough to touch the converter, repair or renew it.

5 Inspect the heat insulator for damage. Make sure that there is adequate clearance between the heat insulator and the catalytic converter **(see illustration)**.

Renewal

6 To renew the catalytic converter, refer to Chapter 4A.

Precautions

a) DO NOT use leaded petrol or LRP – the lead will coat the precious metals, reducing their converting efficiency, and will eventually destroy the converter.

b) Always keep the ignition and fuel systems well maintained in accordance with the manufacturer's schedule (see Chapter 1A).

c) If the engine develops a misfire, do not drive the vehicle at all (or at least as little as possible) until the fault is cured.

d) DO NOT push – or tow-start the vehicle – this will soak the catalytic converter in unburned fuel, causing it to overheat when the engine does start.

e) DO NOT switch off the ignition at high engine speeds, ie, do not blip the throttle immediately before switching off.

f) DO NOT use fuel or engine oil additives – these may contain substances harmful to the catalytic converter.

g) DO NOT continue to use the vehicle if the engine burns oil to the extent of leaving a visible trail of blue smoke.

h) Remember that the catalytic converter operates at very high temperatures. DO NOT, therefore, park the vehicle in dry undergrowth, over long grass or piles of dead leaves, after a long run.

i) Remember that the catalytic converter is FRAGILE. Do not strike it with tools during servicing work.

j) In some cases, a sulphurous smell (like that of rotten eggs) may be noticed from the exhaust. This is common to many catalytic converter-equipped vehicles. Once the vehicle has covered a few thousand miles, the problem should disappear – in the meantime, try changing the brand of petrol used.

k) The catalytic converter used on a well-maintained and well-driven vehicle should last for between 50 000 and 100 000 miles. If the converter is no longer effective, it must be renewed.

Chapter 4 Part D:
Emission control systems – diesel engines

Contents

Degrees of difficulty

Easy, suitable for novice with little experience 	**Fairly easy,** suitable for beginner with some experience	**Fairly difficult,** suitable for competent DIY mechanic	**Difficult,** suitable for experienced DIY mechanic	**Very difficult,** suitable for expert DIY or professional 

Specifications

Vacuum regulating valve

Resistance at 20ºC	11.0 to 13.0 ohms	

Torque wrench settings

	Nm	lbf ft
Air temperature sensor	34	25
Camshaft position sensor	9	7
Coolant temperature sensor	21	15
Crankshaft position sensor	9	7

1 General information

To prevent pollution of the atmosphere from incompletely burned fuel and to maintain good driveability and fuel economy, a number of emission control systems are incorporated. They include the:

Electronic engine control system.
Crankcase ventilation system.
Exhaust Gas Recirculation system.
Catalytic converters.

All of these systems are linked, directly or indirectly, to the emission control system.

The Sections in this Chapter include general descriptions, checking procedures within the scope of the home mechanic (when possible) and component renewal procedures for each of the systems listed above.

Before assuming that an emissions control system is malfunctioning, check the fuel system carefully. The diagnosis of some emission control devices requires specialised tools, equipment and training. If checking and servicing become too difficult or if a procedure is beyond your ability, consult a dealer service department or other properly-equipped repair facility. Remember, the most frequent cause of emissions problems is simply a loose or broken vacuum hose or lead, so always check the hose and wiring connections first.

This doesn't mean, however, that emission control systems are particularly difficult to maintain and repair. You can quickly and easily perform many checks and do most of the regular maintenance at home with common hand tools. Pay close attention to any special precautions outlined in this Chapter. It should be noted that the illustrations of the various systems might not exactly match the system fitted on the vehicle you're working on because of changes made by the manufacturer during production or from year-to-year.

2 Crankcase ventilation system – general information

1 When the engine is running, a certain amount of the gases produced during combustion escapes past the piston rings into the crankcase as blow-by gases. The crankcase ventilation system is designed to reduce the resulting hydrocarbon emissions (HC) by routing the gases and vapours from the crankcase into the inlet manifold and combustion chambers, where they are consumed during engine operation.

2 Crankcase vapours pass through a hose connected from the valve cover to the air inlet duct. The oil/air separator at the valve cover separates the oil suspended in the blow-by gases and allows the oil to drain back into the crankcase. The crankcase vapours are drawn from the oil/air separator through a hose connected to the air inlet duct where they mix with the incoming air and are burned during the normal combustion process.

3 A blocked breather, valve or hose will cause excessive crankcase pressures resulting in oil leaks and sludge build-up in the crankcase. Check the components for restrictions and clean or renew the components as necessary. Be sure to check the basic mechanical condition of the engine before condemning the crankcase ventilation system.

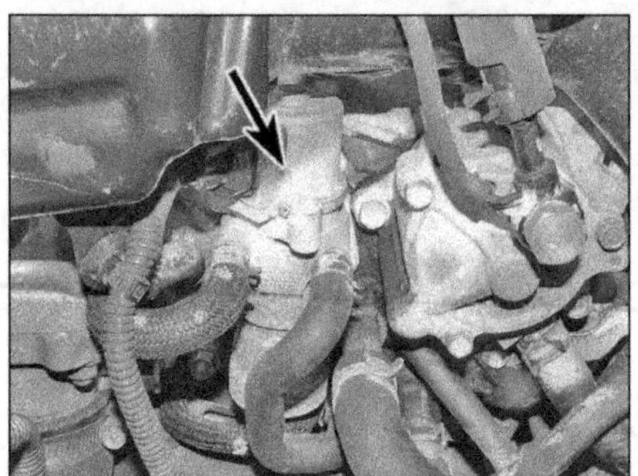
3.8 Location of exhaust gas recirculating valve

3.12 Location of vacuum regulating valve

3.16a Withdraw the EGR valve from the studs . . .

3.16b . . . and remove the gasket

3 Exhaust Gas Recirculation (EGR) system components – testing, removal and refitting

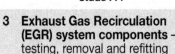

1 The Exhaust Gas Recirculation (EGR) system is used to lower NOx (oxides of nitrogen) emission levels caused by high combustion temperatures. The EGR valve recirculates a small amount of exhaust gases into the inlet manifold. The additional mixture lowers the temperature of combustion thereby reducing the formation of NOx compounds.

2 The EGR system consists of the EGR valve, EGR cooler tube (engine coolant-cooled), vacuum damper, electronic vacuum regulating valve, and the connecting vacuum hoses. The EGR valve is bolted to the left-hand end of the cylinder head. Vacuum for the system is supplied by the brake vacuum pump mounted on the left-hand end of the cylinder head.

3 The ECM controls the EGR flow rate by energising the EGR vacuum regulating valve. When the valve is energized, vacuum is applied to the EGR valve, opening the EGR passage. The vacuum is cut by the ECM, de-energising the EGR vacuum regulating valve.

Testing

Electronic vacuum regulating valve

4 The vacuum regulating valve may be checked *in situ*. First, disconnect the wiring plug.

5 Connect an ohmmeter between the two terminals on the valve, and check that the resistance is as given in the Specifications.

6 Using the ohmmeter, check that there is no continuity between either of the terminals and the valve body.

7 Apply 6 volts DC to the terminals, then apply vacuum to the outlet (outer) port, and check that there is no interruption of the supply voltage.

Exhaust gas recirculating (EGR) valve

8 Remove the EGR valve as described later in this Section **(see illustration)**.

9 Check the ports for heavy carbon deposits, which can cause the internal shaft to stick. Clean as necessary.

10 Apply a vacuum of 8.3 in-Hg to the diaphragm chamber, and check that the internal shaft rises to open the upper inlet port. Blow through the port and check that the passage is clear to the lower outlet port. Maintain the vacuum to check that the diaphragm holds the shaft open.

11 Refit the EGR valve as described later in this Section.

Removal

Electronic vacuum regulating valve

12 Unscrew the mounting nuts and remove the valve from the mounting bracket **(see illustration)**.

13 Disconnect the vacuum hoses and wiring plug as it is removed.

EGR valve

14 Remove the electronic vacuum regulating valve as described earlier.

15 Disconnect the vacuum hose from the diaphragm unit.

16 Unscrew the mounting bolt and nuts, and withdraw the EGR valve from the studs on the cylinder head. Remove the gasket and discard as a new one must be used on refitting **(see illustrations)**.

Refitting

17 Refitting is a reversal of removal. When refitting the EGR valve, renew the gasket and tighten the mounting nuts and bolt securely.

Chapter 5 Part A: Starting and charging systems

Contents

Degrees of difficulty

Easy, suitable for novice with little experience 	**Fairly easy,** suitable for beginner with some experience	**Fairly difficult,** suitable for competent DIY mechanic	**Difficult,** suitable for experienced DIY mechanic	**Very difficult,** suitable for expert DIY or professional

Specifications

General

Engine codes:	
1.4 litre (1398 cc) petrol engine	4ZZ-FE
1.6 litre (1598 cc) petrol engine	3ZZ-FE
2.0 litre (1995 cc) diesel engine	1CD-FTV

Charging system

Charging voltage	13.5 to 15.0 volts
Standard amperage:	
All lights and accessories turned off	Less than 10 amps
Headlights (high beam) and heater blower motor turned on	30 amps or more
Alternator brush exposed length:	
Denso alternator:	
Standard	9.5 to 11.5 mm
Minimum	1.5 mm
Bosch alternator:	
Standard	11.0 to 13.6 mm
Minimum	1.5 mm

Torque wrench settings

	Nm	lbf ft
Alternator mounting bolts:		
Petrol engine:		
12 mm head bolt	25	18
14 mm head bolt	54	40
Diesel engine:		
M8 bolt	21	15
M10 bolt	52	38
Glow plugs (diesel engines)	12	9
Starter motor mounting bolts	37	27

1 General information

General information

The engine electrical system consists mainly of the charging and starting systems. Because of their engine-related functions, these components are covered separately from the body electrical devices such as the lights, instruments, etc (which are covered in Chapter 12). Refer to Part B for information on the petrol engine ignition system.

The electrical system is of the 12 volt negative earth type.

The battery is of the low maintenance or 'maintenance-free' (sealed for life) type and is charged by the alternator, which is belt-driven from the crankshaft pulley.

The starter motor is of the pre-engaged type incorporating an integral solenoid. On starting, the solenoid moves the drive pinion into engagement with the flywheel ring gear before the starter motor is energised. Once the engine has started, a one-way clutch prevents the motor armature being driven by the engine until the pinion disengages from the flywheel.

Precautions

Further details of the various systems are given in the relevant Sections of this Chapter. While some repair procedures are given, the usual course of action is to renew the component concerned.

It is necessary to take extra care when working on the electrical system to avoid damage to semi-conductor devices (diodes and transistors), and to avoid the risk of personal injury. In addition to the precautions given in *Safety first!* at the beginning of this manual, observe the following when working on the system:

- Always remove rings, watches, etc, before working on the electrical system. Even with the battery disconnected, capacitive discharge could occur if a component's live terminal is earthed through a metal object. This could cause a shock or nasty burn.
- Do not reverse the battery connections. Components such as the alternator, electronic control units, or any other components having semi-conductor circuitry could be irreparably damaged.
- If the engine is being started using jump leads and a slave battery, connect the batteries positive-to-positive and negative-to-negative (see *Jump starting*). This also applies when connecting a battery charger.
- Never disconnect the battery terminals, the alternator, any electrical wiring or any test instruments when the engine is running.
- Do not allow the engine to turn the alternator when the alternator is not connected.
- Never 'test' for alternator output by 'flashing' the output lead to earth.
- Never use an ohmmeter of the type incorporating a hand-cranked generator for circuit or continuity testing.
- Always ensure that the battery negative lead is disconnected when working on the electrical system.
- Before using electric-arc welding equipment on the car, disconnect the battery, alternator and components such as the fuel injection/ignition electronic control unit to protect them from the risk of damage.
- When the battery is disconnected, any fault codes stored in the engine management ECM memory will be erased. If any faults are suspected, do not disconnect the battery until a Toyota dealer or specialist has read the fault codes.
- Several systems fitted to the vehicle require battery power to be available at all times, either to ensure their continued operation (such as the clock) or to maintain control unit memories of security codes which would be wiped if the battery were to be disconnected.

2 Battery – testing and charging

Testing

Standard and low maintenance battery

1 If the vehicle covers a small annual mileage, it is worthwhile checking the specific gravity of the electrolyte every three months to determine the state of charge of the battery. Use a hydrometer to make the check and compare the results with the following table. Note that the specific gravity readings assume an electrolyte temperature of 15°C; for every 10°C below 15°C subtract 0.007. For every 10°C above 15°C add 0.007.

	Above 25°C	Below 25°C
Fully-charged	*1.210 to 1.230*	*1.250 to 1.290*
70% charged	*1.170 to 1.190*	*1.230 to 1.250*
Discharged	*1.050 to 1.070*	*1.110 to 1.130*

2 If the battery condition is suspect, first check the specific gravity of electrolyte in each cell. A variation of 0.040 or more between any cells indicates loss of electrolyte or deterioration of the internal plates.

3 If the specific gravity variation is 0.040 or more, the battery should be renewed. If the cell variation is satisfactory but the battery is discharged, it should be charged as described later in this Section.

Maintenance-free battery

4 In cases where a 'sealed for life' maintenance-free battery is fitted, topping-up and testing of the electrolyte in each cell is not possible. The condition of the battery can therefore only be tested using a battery condition indicator or a voltmeter.

5 Certain models may be fitted with a particular type of maintenance-free battery, with a built-in charge condition indicator. The indicator is located in the top of the battery casing, and indicates the condition of the battery from its colour. If the indicator shows green, then the battery is in a good state of charge. If the indicator shows black, then the battery requires charging, as described later in this Section. If the indicator shows blue, then the electrolyte level in the battery is too low to allow further use, and the battery should be renewed.

Caution: Do not attempt to charge, load or jump start a battery when the indicator shows clear/yellow.

All battery types

6 If testing the battery using a voltmeter, connect the voltmeter across the battery and compare the result with those given in paragraph 7. The test is only accurate if the battery has not been subjected to any kind of charge for the previous six hours. If this is not the case, switch on the headlights for 30 seconds, then wait four to five minutes before testing the battery after switching off the headlights. All other electrical circuits must be switched off, so check that the doors, boot and/or tailgate are fully shut when making the test.

7 If the voltage reading is less than 12.2 volts, then the battery is discharged, whilst a reading of 12.2 to 12.4 volts indicates a partially discharged condition.

8 If the battery is to be charged, remove it from the vehicle (Section 3) and charge it as described later in this Section.

Charging

Note: *The following is intended as a guide only. Always refer to the manufacturer's recommendations (often printed on a label attached to the battery) before charging a battery.*

Standard and low maintenance battery

9 Charge the battery at a rate of 3.5 to 4 amps and continue to charge the battery at this rate until no further rise in specific gravity is noted over a four hour period.

10 Alternatively, a trickle charger charging at the rate of 1.5 amps can safely be used overnight.

11 Specially rapid 'boost' charges, which are claimed to restore the power of the battery in 1 to 2 hours, are not recommended, as they can cause serious damage to the battery plates through overheating.

12 While charging the battery, note that the temperature of the electrolyte should never exceed 38°C.

Maintenance-free battery

13 This battery type takes considerably longer to fully recharge than the standard type, the time taken being dependent on the extent of discharge, but it can take anything up to three days.

14 A constant voltage type charger is required to be set, when connected, to 13.9 to 14.9 volts with a charger current below 25 amps. Using

3.1a Slacken the nut and disconnect the lead from the battery negative terminal

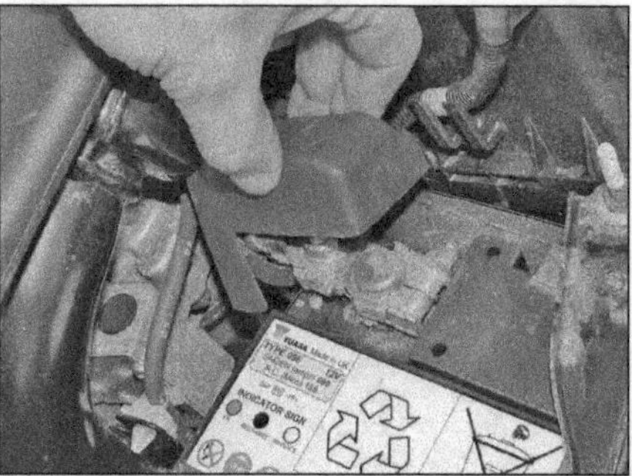

3.1b Undo the nut and disconnect the lead from the battery positive terminal

3.2 Battery hold-down clamp retaining bolt and nut (arrowed)

this method, the battery should be usable within three hours, giving a voltage reading of 12.5 volts, but this is for a partially-discharged battery and, as mentioned, full charging can take considerably longer.

15 If the battery is to be charged from a fully-discharged state (reading less than 12.2 volts), have it recharged by your Toyota dealer or local automotive electrician, as the charge rate is higher and constant supervision during charging is necessary.

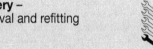

3 Battery – removal and refitting

Note: *When the battery is disconnected, any fault codes stored in the engine management ECM memory will be erased. If any faults are suspected, do not disconnect the battery until a Toyota dealer or specialist has read the fault codes.*

Removal

1 Starting with the negative battery cable **(see illustrations)**, disconnect both cables from the battery terminals.

Caution: If the stereo in your vehicle is equipped with an anti-theft system, make sure you have the correct activation code before disconnecting the battery.

2 Remove the battery hold-down clamp **(see illustration)**.

3 Lift out the battery. Be careful, it's heavy.

4 While the battery is out, lift out the plastic tray and inspect the bracket for corrosion.

5 If you are renewing the battery, make sure that you get one that's identical, with the same dimensions, amperage rating, cold cranking rating, etc, as the original.

Refitting

6 Refitting is the reverse of removal; always reconnect the positive lead first, and the negative lead last. Smear petroleum jelly on the terminals after reconnecting the leads, to combat corrosion

4 Charging system – general information and precautions

General information

The charging system includes the alternator, an internal voltage regulator, a charge indicator, the battery, a fusible link and the wiring between all the components. The charging system supplies electrical power for the ignition system, the lights, the radio, etc. The alternator is driven by a drivebelt at the right-hand side of the engine.

The purpose of the voltage regulator is to limit the alternator's voltage to a preset value. This prevents power surges, circuit overloads, etc, during peak voltage output.

There are two fuseboxes in the engine compartment on diesel engines and only one on petrol engines **(see illustrations)**. There is a fusebox inside the vehicle, behind the facia above the glove compartment on the passenger side.

The instrument cluster warning light should come on when the ignition key is turned to Start, and then should go off immediately. If it remains on, there is a malfunction in the charging system. Some vehicles are also equipped with a voltage gauge. If the voltage gauge indicates abnormally high or low voltage, check the charging system (see Section 5).

Precautions

Be very careful when making electrical circuit connections to a vehicle equipped with an alternator and note the following:

a) When reconnecting wires to the alternator from the battery, be sure to note the polarity.
b) Before using arc-welding equipment to repair any part of the vehicle, disconnect the wires from the alternator and the battery terminals.
c) Never start the engine with a battery charger connected.
d) Always disconnect both battery leads before using a battery charger.
e) The alternator is driven by an engine drivebelt, which could cause serious injury if your hand, hair or clothes become entangled in it with the engine running.
f) Because the alternator is connected directly to the battery, it could arc or cause a fire if overloaded or shorted out.
g) Wrap a plastic bag over the alternator and secure it with rubber bands before steam cleaning the engine.

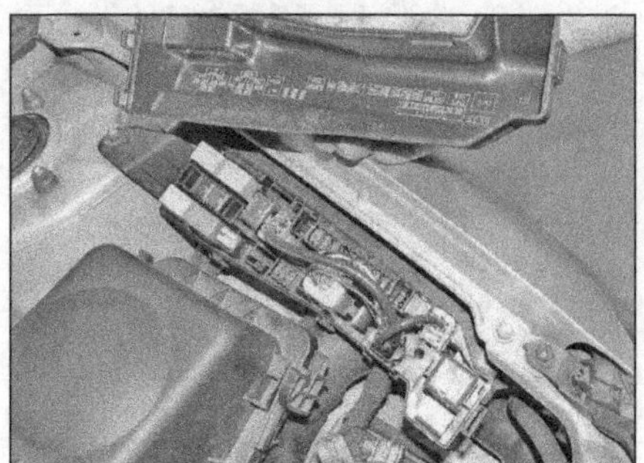

4.1a Underbonnet main fusebox

4.1b Underbonnet relay box – diesel models

4.1c Main fusebox inside passenger compartment behind glovebox

6.2 Alternator connections – petrol model shown

6.5 Alternator mounting bolts (arrowed) – petrol model shown

5 Charging system – testing

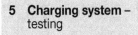

Note: *Refer to the warnings given in 'Safety first!' and in Section 1 of this Chapter before starting work.*

1 If the ignition warning light fails to illuminate when the ignition is switched on, first check the alternator wiring connections for security. If satisfactory, check that the warning light bulb has not blown, and that the bulb holder is secure in its location in the instrument panel. If the light still fails to illuminate, check the continuity of the warning light feed wire from the alternator to the bulb holder. If all is satisfactory, the alternator is at fault and should be renewed or taken to an auto-electrician for testing and repair.

2 If the ignition warning light illuminates when the engine is running, stop the engine and check that the drive belt is correctly tensioned (see Chapter 1A or 1B) and that the alternator connections are secure. If all is so far satisfactory, have the alternator checked by an auto-electrician for testing and repair.

3 If the alternator output is suspect even though the warning light functions correctly, the regulated voltage may be checked as follows.

4 Connect a voltmeter across the battery terminals and start the engine.

5 Increase the engine speed until the voltmeter reading remains steady; the reading should be approximately 12 to 13 volts, and no more than 14.2 volts.

6 Switch on as many electrical accessories as possible (eg, the headlights, heated rear window and heater blower), and check that the alternator maintains the regulated voltage at around 13 to 14 volts.

7 If the regulated voltage is not as stated, the fault may be due to worn alternator brushes, weak brush springs, a faulty voltage regulator, a faulty diode, a severed phase winding or worn or damaged slip-rings. The alternator should be renewed or taken to an auto-electrician for testing and repair.

7.2a Remove the three nuts from the rear cover (Denso alternator)

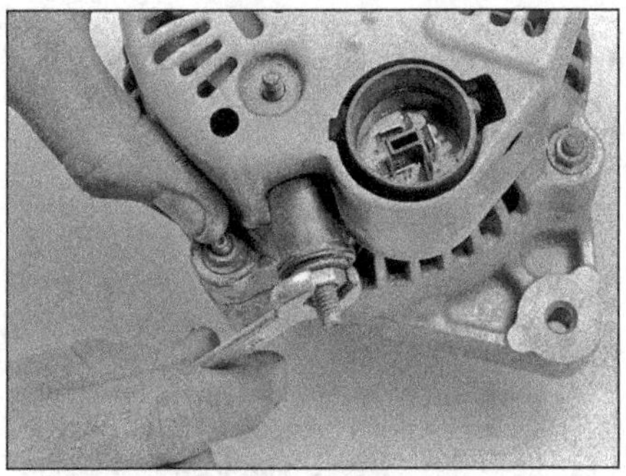
7.2b Take the nut, washer and insulator off terminal B and remove the rear cover (Denso alternator)

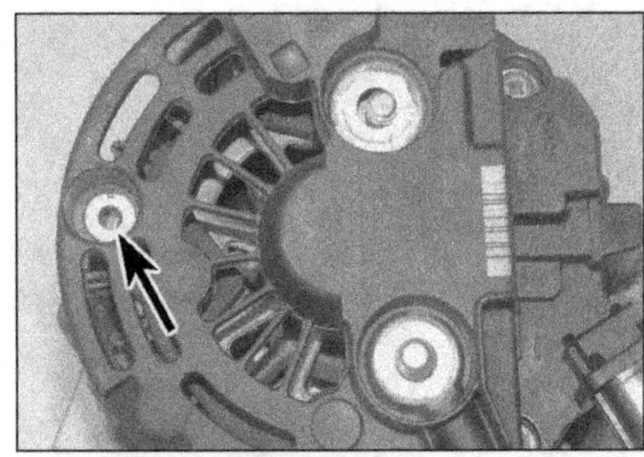
7.2c Undo the two nuts and undo the screw (arrowed), then lift off the rear cover (Bosch alternator)

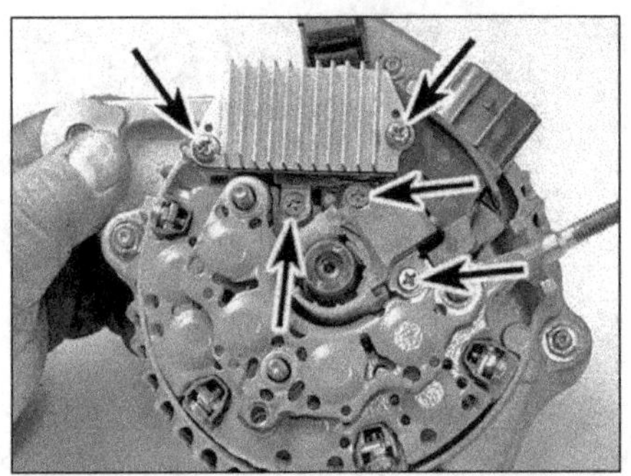
7.3a Undo the 5 screws (arrowed) . . .

6 Alternator – removal and refitting

Removal

1 Detach the cable from the negative terminal of the battery (see Section 3).

2 Detach the electrical connectors from the alternator **(see illustration)**.

3 Remove the drivebelt as described in Chapter 1A or 1B.

4 On diesel models, the alternator is down the back of the engine, to make access easier, remove the exhaust front pipe.

5 Undo the mounting bolts and remove the alternator **(see illustration)**.

6 If you are renewing the alternator, take the old alternator with you when purchasing a new unit. Make sure that the new/rebuilt unit is identical to the old alternator. Look at the terminals – they should be the same in number, size and locations as the terminals on the old alternator. Finally, look at the identification markings – they will be stamped in the housing or printed on a tag or plaque affixed to the housing. Make sure that these numbers are the same on both alternators.

7 Many new/rebuilt alternators do not have a pulley installed, so you may have to switch the pulley from the old unit to the new/rebuilt one. When buying an alternator, find out the workshop's policy regarding refitting of pulleys – some workshops will perform this service free of charge.

Refitting

8 Refitting is the reverse of removal, tightening the mounting bolts securely.

9 After the alternator is installed, adjust the drivebelt tension (see Chapter 1A and 1B).

10 Check the charging voltage to verify proper operation of the alternator (see Section 5).

7 Alternator regulator/ brush pack – renewal

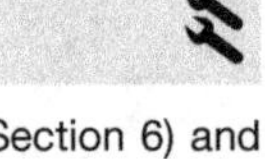

1 Remove the alternator (see Section 6) and place it on a clean workbench.

2 Remove the rear cover nuts, the screw and terminal insulator, and the rear cover **(see illustrations)**.

3 Undo the 5 screws (Denso alternator) or 3 screws (Bosch alternator) and remove the brush holder and the regulator from the rear end frame **(see illustrations)**.

7.3b . . . remove the brush holder . . .

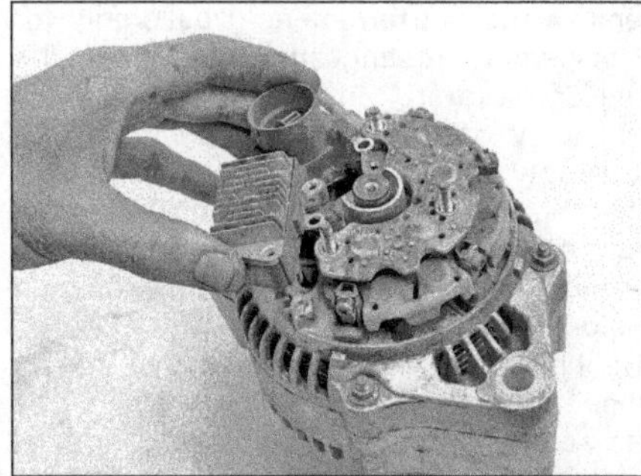

7.3c . . . and regulator (Denso alternator)

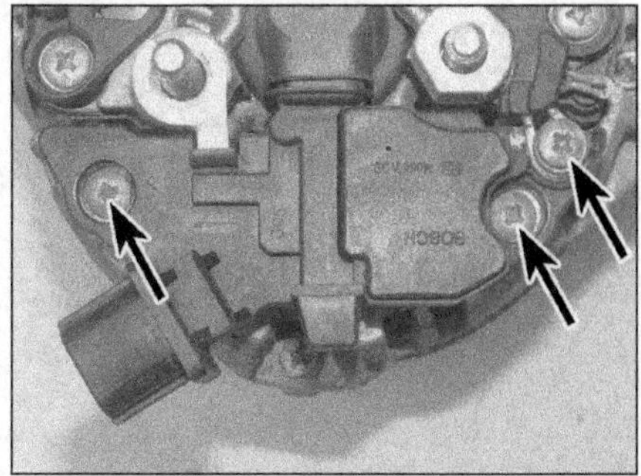

7.3d Undo the 3 screws (arrowed) and remove the brush holder (Bosch alternator)

4 Measure the exposed length of each brush **(see illustration)** and compare it to the minimum length listed in this Chapter's Specifications. If the length of either brush is less than the specified minimum, renew the brushes and brush holder assembly. **Note:** *On some models, it may be necessary to solder the new brushes in place.*

5 Make sure that each brush moves smoothly in the brush holder.

6 Install the components in the reverse order of removal, noting the following:

7 On Denso alternators, install the brush holder by depressing each brush with a small screwdriver to clear the shaft **(see illustration)**.

8 Install the voltage regulator and brush holder screws into the rear frame.

9 Install the rear cover and tighten the nuts/screw securely.

10 Install the terminal insulator and tighten it with the nut (where applicable).

11 Refit the alternator.

8 Alternator – testing and overhaul

If the alternator is thought to be suspect, it should be removed from the vehicle and taken to an auto-electrician for testing. Most auto-electricians will be able to supply and fit brushes at a reasonable cost. However, check on the cost of repairs before proceeding, as it may prove more economical to obtain a new or exchange alternator.

9 Starting system – general information and precautions

General information

The function of the starting system is to turn over the engine quickly enough to allow it to start.

The system consists of the battery, the starter motor, the starter solenoid and the electrical circuit connecting the components. The solenoid is mounted directly on the starter motor.

The solenoid/starter motor assembly is installed on the upper part of the engine, next to the transmission bellhousing.

When the ignition key is turned to the Start position, the starter solenoid is actuated through the starter control circuit. The starter solenoid then connects the battery to the starter. The battery supplies the electrical energy to the starter motor, which does the actual work of cranking the engine.

The starter motor on a vehicle equipped with a manual transmission can be operated only when the clutch pedal is depressed; the starter on a vehicle equipped with an automatic transmission can be operated only when the transmission selector lever is in Park or Neutral.

Precautions

Always observe the following precautions when working on the starting system:

a) *Excessive cranking of the starter motor can overheat it and cause serious damage. Never operate the starter motor for more than 15 seconds at a time without pausing to allow it to cool for at least two minutes.*

b) *The starter is connected directly to the battery and could arc or cause a fire if mishandled, overloaded or short-circuited.*

c) *Always detach the cable from the negative terminal of the battery before working on the starting system (see Section 3).*

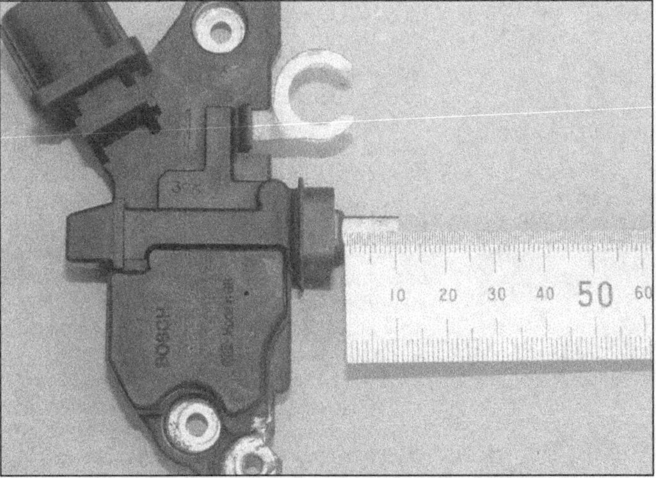

7.4 Measure the exposed length of each brush

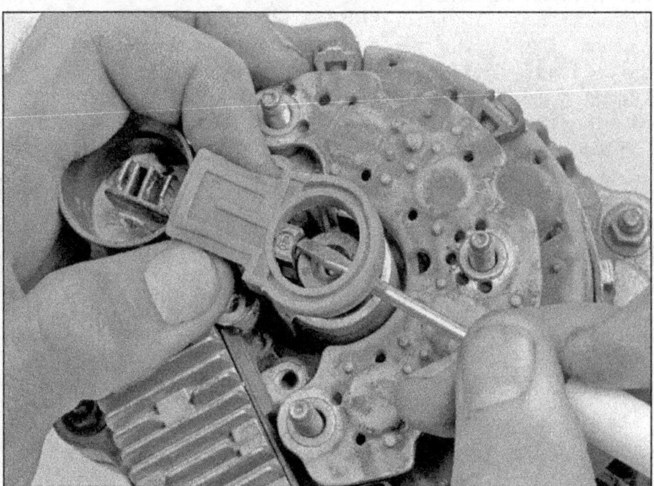

7.7 On Denso alternators, depress each brush with a small screwdriver to ease refitting

11.2 Disconnect the wiring from the starter motor/solenoid

10 Starter motor – testing in vehicle

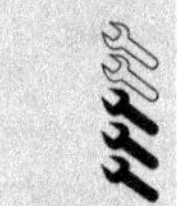

Note: *Before diagnosing starter problems, make sure the battery is fully-charged.*

1 If the starter motor does not turn at all when the switch is operated, make sure that the selector lever is in Neutral or Park (automatic transmission) or that the clutch pedal is depressed (manual transmission).

2 Make sure that the battery is charged and that all cables, both at the battery and starter solenoid terminals, are clean and secure.

3 If the starter motor spins but the engine is not cranking, the overrunning clutch in the starter motor is slipping and the starter motor must be renewed.

4 If, when the switch is actuated, the starter motor does not operate at all but the solenoid clicks, then the problem lies with either the battery, the main solenoid contacts or the starter motor itself (or the engine is seized).

5 If the solenoid plunger cannot be heard when the switch is actuated, the battery is faulty, the fusible link is burned (the circuit is open), the starter relay is defective or the starter solenoid itself is defective.

6 To check the solenoid, connect a jumper lead between the battery (+) and the ignition switch terminal (the small terminal) on the solenoid. If the starter motor now operates, the solenoid is OK and the problem is in the ignition switch, Neutral start switch or in the wiring.

7 If the starter motor still does not operate, remove the starter/solenoid assembly for disassembly, testing and repair. Take the starter motor to an auto-electrician for testing. Most auto-electricians will be able to supply and fit brushes at a reasonable cost. However, check on the cost of repairs before proceeding, as it may prove more economical to obtain a new or exchange motor.

8 If the starter motor cranks the engine at an abnormally slow speed, first make sure that the battery is charged and that all terminal connections are tight. If the engine is partially-seized, or has the wrong viscosity oil in it, it will crank slowly.

11 Starter motor – removal and refitting

Note: *The starter/solenoid assembly cannot be repaired using separate components. In the event of failure, exchange the starter/solenoid assembly for a complete new or reconditioned unit.*

Removal

1 Detach the cable from the negative terminal of the battery (see Section 3).

2 Detach the electrical connectors from the starter/solenoid assembly **(see illustration)**. Note the motor is located at the front of the engine block.

3 Remove the starter motor mounting bolts.

Refitting

4 Refitting is the reverse of removal.

12 Glow plug system (diesel models) – general information

To assist cold starting, diesel engine models are equipped with a preheating system, which comprises four glow plugs, a glow plug relay, a dash-mounted warning lamp, the Engine Control Module (ECM) and the associated electrical wiring.

The glow plugs are miniature electric heating elements, encapsulated in a metal case with a probe at one end and electrical connection at the other. Each combustion chamber has a glow plug threaded into it. When the glow plug is energised, the air in the combustion chamber is heated, allowing optimum combustion temperature to be achieved more readily before fuel is injected into the cylinder.

The duration of the preheating period is governed by the Engine Control Module, which monitors the temperature of the engine via the coolant temperature sensor and alters the preheating time to suit the conditions.

A dash-mounted warning lamp informs the driver that preheating is taking place. The lamp extinguishes when sufficient preheating has taken place to allow the engine to be started, but power will still be supplied to the glow plugs for a further period until the engine is started. If no attempt is made to start the engine, the power supply to the glow plugs is switched off to prevent battery drain and glow plug burnout.

After the engine has been started, the glow plugs continue to operate for a further period of time. This helps to improve fuel combustion while the engine is warming-up, resulting in quieter, smoother running and reduced exhaust emissions.

The Check Engine warning lamp will illuminate during normal driving if a preheating system malfunction occurs and a diagnostic trouble code will be stored in the ECM memory.

13 Glow plugs (diesel models) – testing and renewal

Testing

1 Remove the intercooler (Chapter 4B) followed by the engine top covers.

2 Disconnect the electrical connector from the engine coolant temperature sensor. **Note:** *This will allow the glow plugs to be energised, regardless of engine temperature.*

3 Remove the grommets from the tops of the glow plug terminals, then connect a 12 volt test light or voltmeter to one of the terminals and switch on the ignition. Battery voltage should be indicated on the meter for approximately 20 seconds. If no voltage is indicated, check the glow plug fuses and glow plug relay (see Chapter 12).

4 With the ignition switched off, remove the caps then unscrew the nuts and remove the electrical supply strip from the tops of the glow plugs. Position the strip to one side **(see illustrations)**.

5 Connect the clip of a 12 volt test light to the *positive* battery terminal. Touch the electrical terminal on each glow plug with the test light tip. If the glow plug is good, the test light will illuminate.

6 Also, to check the resistance of the glow plugs (with electrical supply strip removed,

13.4a Remove the caps and unscrew the nuts from the top of the glow plugs . . .

13.4b . . . then remove the electrical supply strip

see paragraph 4) use an ohmmeter to measure the resistance between the glow plug terminal and earth. The resistances should be approximately 0.7 ohms (at 20°C).

7 Renew any defective glow plugs. Refit the electrical supply strip and tighten the nuts, then reconnect the wiring to the coolant temperature sensor.

Renewal

8 If not already done, remove the engine upper plastic cover.

9 With the ignition switched off, remove the caps and unscrew the nuts from the glow plugs terminals, then remove the electrical supply strip and position to one side **(see illustrations 13.4a and 13.4b)**.

10 Using a deep socket, remove the glow plugs from the cylinder head **(see illustration)**.

11 Refitting is the reverse of removal. Tighten the glow plugs to the torque listed in this Chapter's Specifications **(see illustration)**.

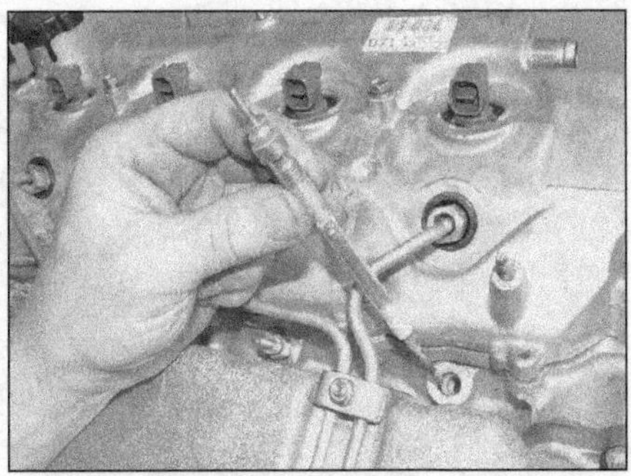

13.10 Unscrew and remove the glow plugs from the cylinder head

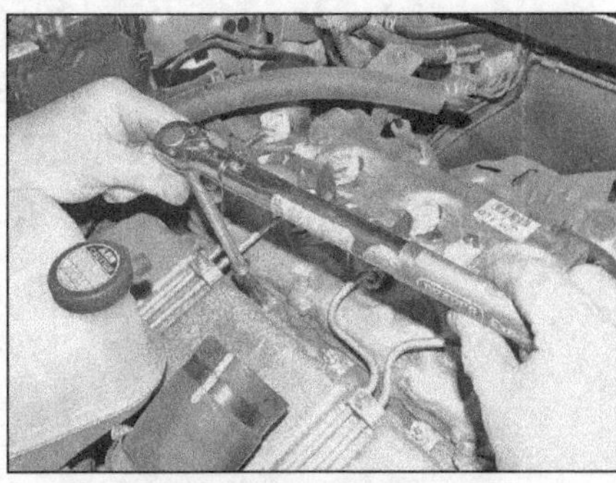

13.11 Use a torque wrench to tighten the glow plugs

Chapter 5 Part B:
Ignition systems – petrol engines

Contents

Degrees of difficulty

Easy, suitable for novice with little experience 	**Fairly easy,** suitable for beginner with some experience	**Fairly difficult,** suitable for competent DIY mechanic	**Difficult,** suitable for experienced DIY mechanic	**Very difficult,** suitable for expert DIY or professional 

Specifications

General

Engine codes:	
1.4 litre (1398 cc) engine	4ZZ-FE
1.6 litre (1598 cc) engine	3ZZ-FE

Firing order

All models	1 – 3 – 4 – 2

HT leads

Resistance	25 k ohms max

Torque wrench settings	**Nm**	**lbf ft**
Ignition coil to cylinder head	9	7
Knock sensor:		
Bosch:		
Stud	10	7
Nut	20	15
Denso	39	29

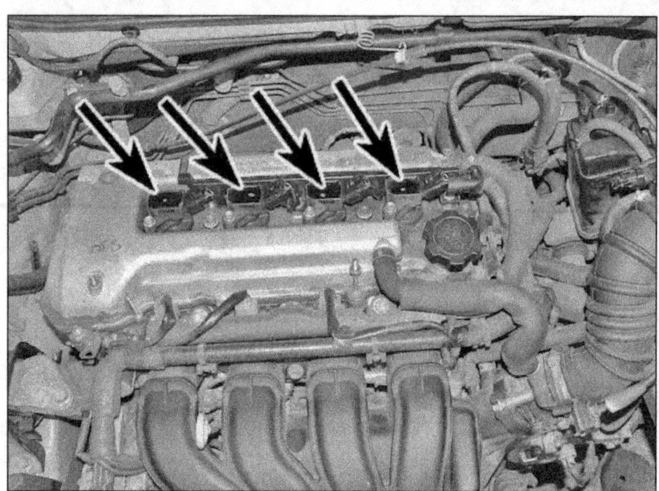

1.1 Location of ignition coils

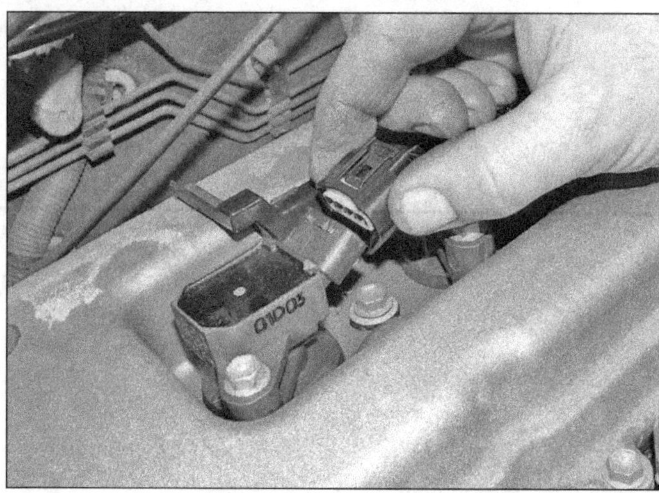

2.3 Disconnect the wiring connector

1 General information

The ignition system has one ignition coil per cylinder, fitted directly above each spark plug **(see illustration)**. The engine management ECM information from the crankshaft and camshaft position sensors to calculate the optimum to generate a spark at each cylinder sequentially. A knock sensor is also fitted, to monitor for any signs of pre-ignition. Should any be detected, the ECM will gradually retard the ignition timing until the symptoms disappear.

Precautions

When working on the ignition system, take the following precautions:

a) Do not keep the ignition switch on for more than 10 seconds if the engine will not start.

b) Always connect a tachometer in accordance with the manufacturer's instructions. Some tachometers may be incompatible with this ignition system.

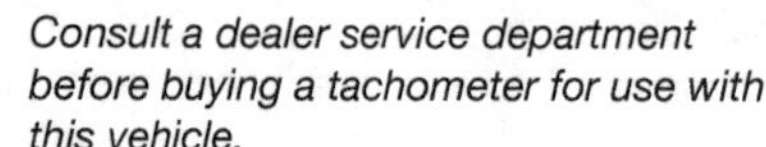

Consult a dealer service department before buying a tachometer for use with this vehicle.

c) Never allow the ignition coil terminals to touch earth. Earthing the coil could result in damage to the igniter and/or the ignition coil.

d) Do not disconnect the battery when the engine is running.

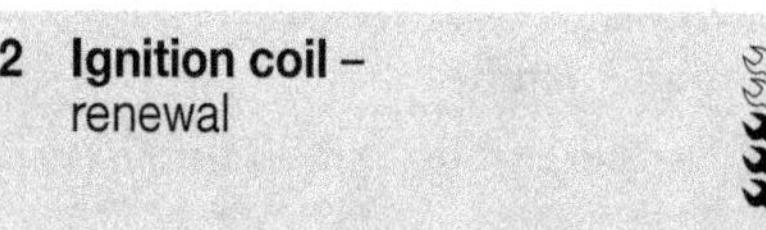

2 Ignition coil – renewal

1 Ensure the ignition is turned off.

2 Undo the two nuts, prise out the plastic fasteners at the rear, and remove the plastic cover from the top of the engine.

3 Disconnect the wiring plugs from the ignition coils **(see illustration)**.

4 Undo the bolts and pull the ignition coils from the top of the spark plugs **(see illustration)**. Recover the dust seal (where fitted).

5 Refitting is a reversal of removal.

3 Knock sensor – removal, testing and refitting

Removal

1 Remove the inlet manifold (see Chapter 4A).

2 Disconnect the sensor wiring plug, and then unscrew the sensor bolt (Denso) or undo the nut and pull the sensor (Bosch) from the engine block **(see illustration)**.

Testing

3 On Denso sensors, connect the leads of an ohmmeter across the sensor terminals. There should be a reading of 120 to 280 k ohms. If there is not, the sensor may be defective.

4 On Bosch sensors, connect the leads of an ohmmeter between terminals 1 and 2 of the sensor terminals. The resistance should be more than 1.0 M ohms **(see illustration)**. If the resistance is not as specified, the sensor may be defective.

Refitting

5 Refitting is a reversal of removal.

2.4 Undo the bolt and pull the coil from the cylinder head cover

3.2 Undo the nut and remove the knock sensor from the cylinder block (1.4 litre engine)

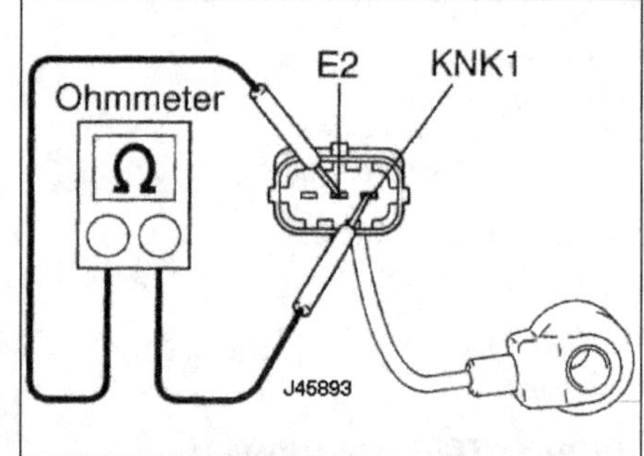

3.4 Connect the ohmmeter to terminals 1 and 2 of the knock sensor connector (1.4 litre engine)

Chapter 6
Clutch

Contents

Degrees of difficulty

Easy, suitable for novice with little experience 	**Fairly easy,** suitable for beginner with some experience	**Fairly difficult,** suitable for competent DIY mechanic	**Difficult,** suitable for experienced DIY mechanic	**Very difficult,** suitable for expert DIY or professional 

Specifications

Clutch

Fluid type	See *Lubricants and fluids* on page 0•16
Pedal height:	
Petrol models	142.0 to 152.0 mm
Diesel models	146.0 to 156.0mm
Pedal freeplay	5.0 to 15.0 mm
Pushrod play at top of pedal	1.0 to 5.0 mm

Torque wrench settings

	Nm	lbf ft
Clutch cover-to-flywheel bolts	19	14
Clutch master cylinder mounting nuts	12	9
Clutch release cylinder mounting bolts	12	9

1 General information

The clutch consists of a friction disc, a clutch cover assembly, a release bearing and release fork; all of these components are contained in the large cast-aluminium alloy bellhousing, sandwiched between the engine and the transmission. The release mechanism is hydraulic on all models **(see illustration)**.

The friction disc is fitted between the engine flywheel and the clutch cover, and is allowed to slide on the transmission input shaft splines.

The clutch cover assembly is bolted to the engine flywheel. When the engine is running, drive is transmitted from the crankshaft, via the flywheel, to the friction disc (these components being clamped securely together by the clutch cover assembly) and from the friction disc to the transmission input shaft.

To interrupt the drive, the spring pressure must be relaxed. This is done by means of the clutch release bearing, fitted concentrically around the transmission input shaft. The bearing is pushed onto the clutch cover assembly by means of the release fork actuated by clutch slave cylinder pushrod.

The clutch pedal is connected to the clutch master cylinder by a short pushrod. The master cylinder is mounted on the engine side of the bulkhead in front of the driver and receives its hydraulic fluid supply from the brake master cylinder reservoir. Depressing the clutch pedal moves the piston in the master cylinder forwards, so forcing hydraulic fluid through the clutch hydraulic pipe to the slave cylinder. The piston in the slave cylinder moves forward on the entry of the fluid and actuates the clutch release fork by means of a short pushrod. The release fork pivots on its mounting stud, and the other end of the fork then presses the release bearing against the clutch cover spring fingers. This causes the springs to deform and releases the clamping force on the clutch cover.

On all models the clutch operating mechanism is self-adjusting, and no manual adjustment is required.

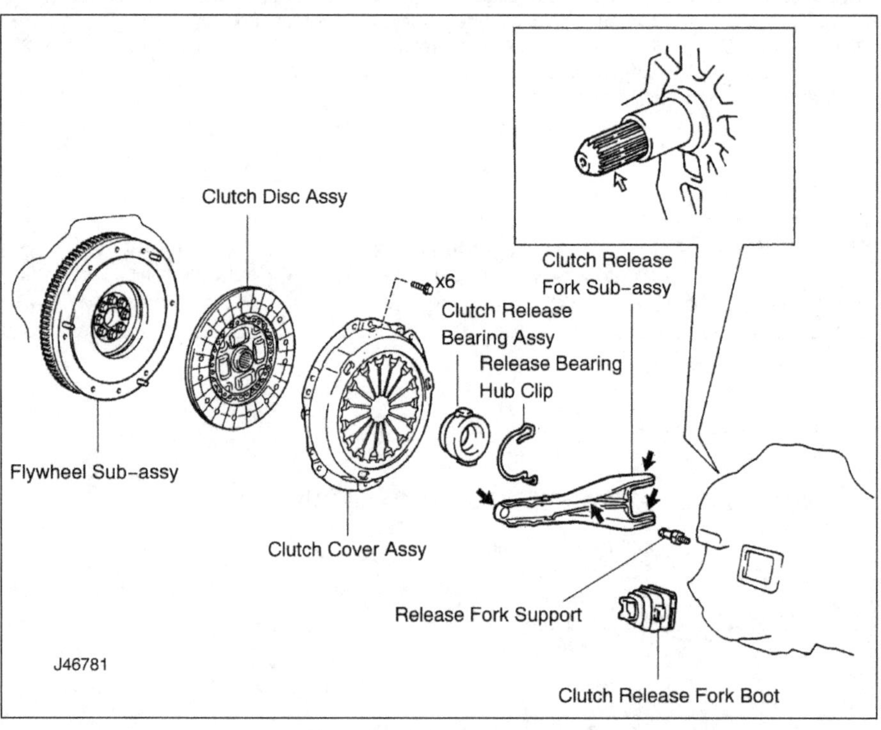

1.1 Typical clutch assembly details

2 Clutch hydraulic system – bleeding

Warning: Hydraulic fluid is poisonous; wash off immediately and thoroughly in the case of skin contact, and seek immediate medical advice if any fluid is swallowed or gets into the eyes. Certain types of hydraulic fluid are inflammable, and may ignite when allowed into contact with hot components; when servicing any hydraulic system, it is safest to assume that the fluid IS inflammable, and to take precautions against the risk of fire as though it is petrol that is being handled. Hydraulic fluid is also an effective paint stripper, and will attack plastics; if any is spilt, it should be washed off immediately, using copious quantities of clean water. When topping-up or renewing the fluid, always use the recommended type, and ensure that it comes from a freshly-opened sealed container.

1 The hydraulic system should be bled of all air whenever any part of the system has been removed or if the fluid level has been allowed to fall so low that air has been drawn into the master cylinder. The procedure is similar to bleeding a brake system.

2 Fill the master cylinder with fresh brake fluid of the specified type. Note the clutch master cylinder shares the fluid reservoir with the brake system.

Caution: Do not re-use any of the fluid coming from the system during the bleeding operation or use fluid, which has been inside an open container for an extended period of time.

3 Raise the vehicle and place it securely on axle stands to gain access to the release cylinder, which is located on the front side of the clutch housing.

4 Locate the bleed screw on the clutch release cylinder (adjacent to the fitting for the hydraulic fluid pipe) **(see illustration)**. Remove the dust cap, which fits over the bleed screw, and push a length of plastic hose over the valve. Place the other end of the hose into a clear container with sufficient fluid to submerge the end of the hose.

5 Have an assistant depress the clutch pedal and hold it. Open the bleed screw on the release cylinder, allowing fluid to flow through the hose. Close the bleed screw when fluid stops flowing from the hose. Once closed, have your assistant release the pedal.

6 Continue this process until all air is evacuated from the system, indicated by a full, solid stream of fluid being ejected from the bleed screw each time and no air bubbles in the hose or container. Keep a close watch on the fluid level inside the brake master cylinder reservoir, if the level drops too low, air will be sucked back into the system and the process will have to be started all over again.

7 Install the dust cap and lower the vehicle. Check carefully for proper operation before placing the vehicle in normal service.

3 Clutch components – removal, inspection and refitting

Warning: Dust produced by clutch wear and deposited on clutch components may contain

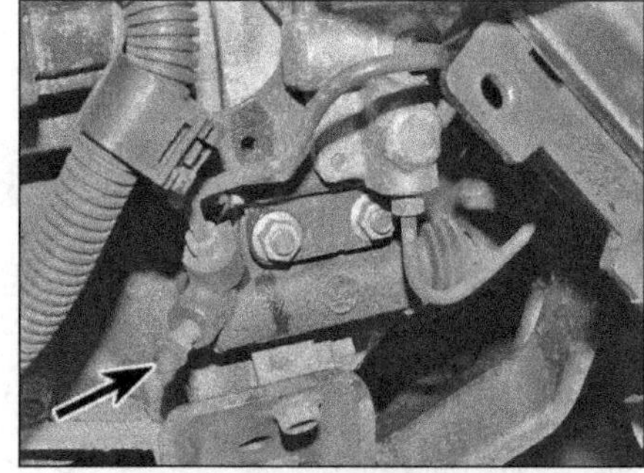

2.4 The clutch release cylinder bleed screw (arrowed)

asbestos, which is hazardous to your health. DO NOT blow it out with compressed air and DO NOT inhale it. DO NOT use petrol or petroleum-based solvents to remove the dust. Brake system cleaner should be used to flush the dust into a drain pan. After the clutch components are wiped clean with a rag, dispose of the contaminated rags and cleaner in a labeled, covered container.

Removal

1 Access to the clutch components is normally by removing the transmission, leaving the engine in the vehicle. If the engine is being removed for major overhaul, then the opportunity should be taken to check the clutch for wear and renew worn components as necessary. However, the relatively low cost of the clutch components compared to the time and labour involved in gaining access to them warrants their renewal any time the engine or transmission is removed, unless they are new or in near-perfect condition. The following procedures assume that the engine will stay in place.

2 Remove the release cylinder (see Section 6). Position it to one side out of the way – it isn't necessary to disconnect the hose.

3 Remove the transmission from the vehicle (see Chapter 7A). Support the engine while the transmission is out. Preferably, an engine hoist should be used to support it from above. **Note:** *If a jack is used underneath the engine, make sure a piece of wood is used between the jack and oil sump to spread the load.* ***Caution: The pick-up for the oil pump is very close to the bottom of the oil sump. If the sump is bent or distorted in any way, engine oil starvation could occur.***

4 The release fork and release bearing can remain attached to the transmission for the time being.

5 Carefully inspect the flywheel and clutch cover for alignment marks. The marks are usually an X an O or a white letter. If they cannot be found, scribe marks yourself so the clutch cover and the flywheel will be in the same alignment during refitting **(see illustration)**.

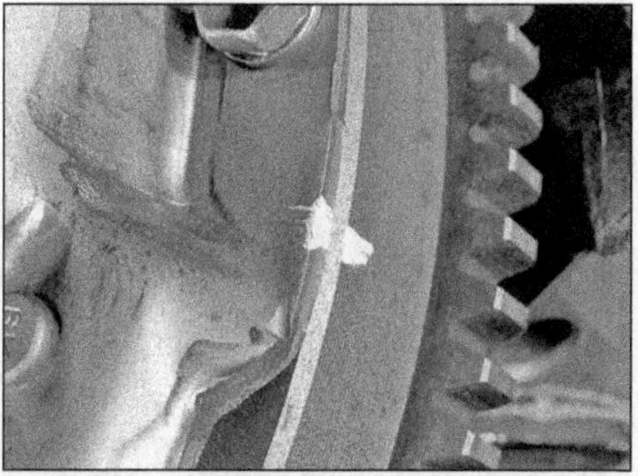

3.5 Mark the relationship of the clutch cover to the flywheel (in case you're going to re-use the same clutch cover)

6 Slowly loosen the clutch cover-to-flywheel bolts. Work in a diagonal pattern and loosen each bolt a little at a time until all spring pressure is relieved. Then hold the clutch cover securely and completely remove the bolts, followed by the clutch cover and clutch friction disc.

Inspection

7 Ordinarily, when a problem occurs in the clutch, it can be attributed to wear of the clutch driven plate assembly (clutch friction disc). However, all components should be inspected at this time.

8 Inspect the flywheel for cracks, score marks and other damage. If the imperfections are slight, a machine workshop can resurface it to make it flat and smooth. Refer to Chapter 2A or 2B for the flywheel removal procedure.

9 Inspect the lining on the friction disc. There should be at least 0.3 mm of lining above the rivet heads. Check for loose rivets, distortion, cracks, broken springs and other obvious damage **(see illustration)**. As mentioned above, ordinarily the friction disc is renewed as a matter of course, so if in doubt about the condition, renew it.

3.9 Examine the clutch friction disc

10 The release bearing should be renewed along with the friction disc (see Section 4).

11 Check the machined surface and the diaphragm spring fingers of the clutch cover **(see illustrations)**. If the surface is grooved or otherwise damaged, renew the clutch cover assembly. Also check for obvious damage, distortion, cracking, etc. Light glazing can be removed with emery cloth or sandpaper. If a new clutch cover is indicated, new or factory rebuilt units are available.

Refitting

12 Before refitting, carefully wipe the flywheel and clutch cover machined surfaces clean. It's important that no oil or grease is on these surfaces or the lining of the friction disc. Handle these parts with clean hands.

13 Position the friction disc and clutch cover, with the clutch held in place with an alignment tool **(see illustration)**. Make sure it's installed properly (most new friction discs will be marked 'flywheel side' or something similar – if not marked, install the friction disc with the damper springs or cushion toward the transmission).

14 Tighten the clutch cover-to-flywheel bolts only finger-tight, working around the clutch cover.

15 Centralise the friction disc by ensuring the alignment tool is through the splined hub and

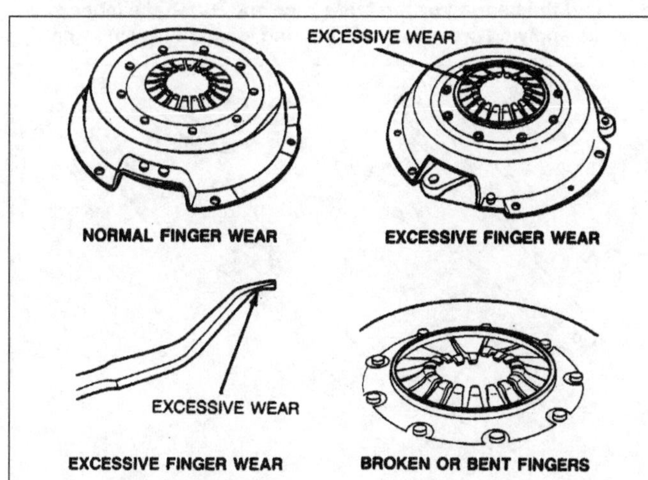

3.11a Renew the clutch cover is any of these conditions are noted

3.11b Examine the clutch cover friction surface for score marks, cracks and evidence of overheating (blue spots)

3.13 Centre the friction disc in the clutch cover with a clutch alignment tool

into the recess in the crankshaft. Wiggle the tool up, down or side-to-side as needed to bottom the tool. Tighten the clutch cover-to-flywheel bolts a little at a time, working in a crisscross pattern to prevent distortion of the cover. After all of the bolts are snug, tighten them to the torque listed in this Chapter's Specifications. Remove the alignment tool.

16 Using clutch assembly grease, lubricate the inner groove of the release bearing (see Section 4). Also place grease on the release lever contact areas and the transmission input shaft bearing retainer.

17 Fit the clutch release bearing (see Section 4).

18 Refit the transmission, release cylinder and all components removed previously, tightening all fasteners securely.

4 Clutch release bearing and lever – removal, inspection and refitting

Warning: Dust produced by clutch wear and deposited on clutch components may contain asbestos, which is hazardous to your health. DO NOT blow it out with compressed air and DO NOT inhale it. DO NOT use petrol or petroleum-based solvents to remove the dust. Brake system cleaner should be used to flush it into a drain pan. After the clutch components are wiped clean with a rag, dispose of the contaminated rags and cleaner in a labelled, covered container.

Removal

1 Remove the transmission (see Chapter 7A).

2 Remove the clutch release lever from the ball-stud, and then remove the bearing from the lever **(see illustration)**. Remove the release bearing hub clip **(see illustration 1.1)**.

Inspection

3 Hold the bearing by the outer race and rotate the inner race while applying pressure **(see illustration)**. If the bearing doesn't turn smoothly or if it's noisy, renew the bearing/hub assembly. Wipe the bearing with a clean rag and inspect it for damage, wear and cracks. Don't immerse the bearing in solvent – it's sealed for life and to do so would ruin it. Also check the release lever for cracks and bends.

Refitting

4 Apply a light coat of grease to the inner part of the release bearing with clutch assembly grease. Also apply a light coat of the same grease to the transmission input shaft splines and the bearing guide tube **(see illustration)**.

5 Lubricate the release lever ball socket, lever ends and release cylinder pushrod socket with clutch assembly grease **(see illustration)**.

6 Attach the release bearing to the release lever, making sure it is secured in place wit the retaining clip.

7 Slide the release bearing onto the transmission input shaft front bearing retainer while

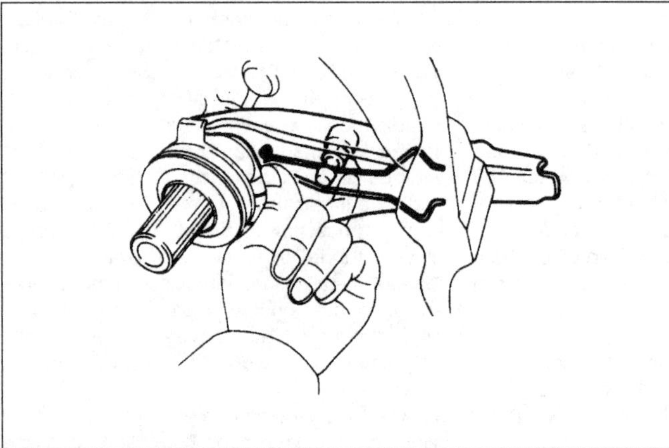

4.2 Disengage the lever from the ball-stud by pulling on the retention spring, then remove the lever and bearing

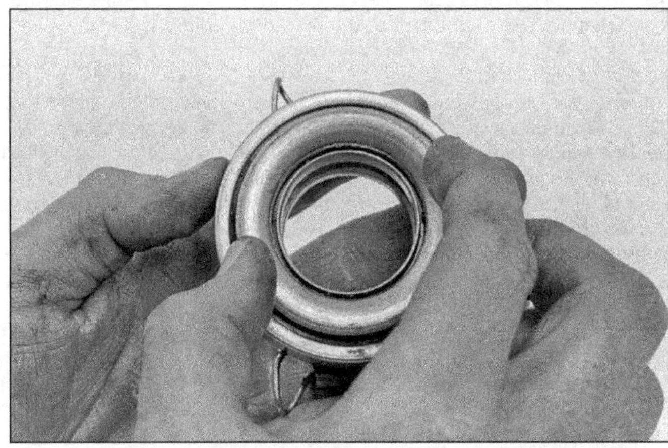

4.3 Hold the bearing by the outer race and rotate the inner race while applying pressure – the bearing should turn smoothly

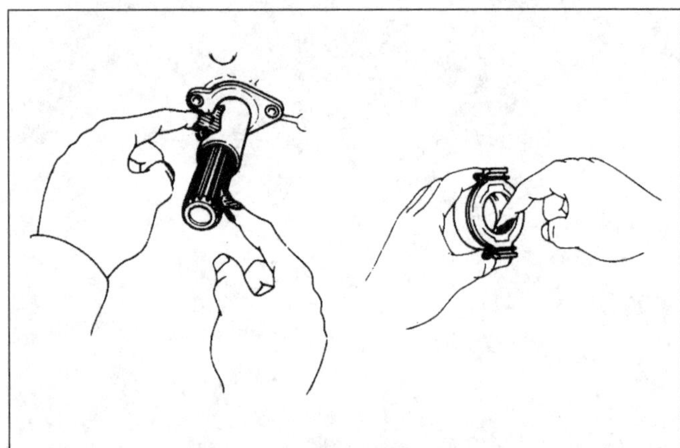

4.4 Apply a light coat of clutch assembly grease to the transmission bearing guide tube and also fill the release bearing groove

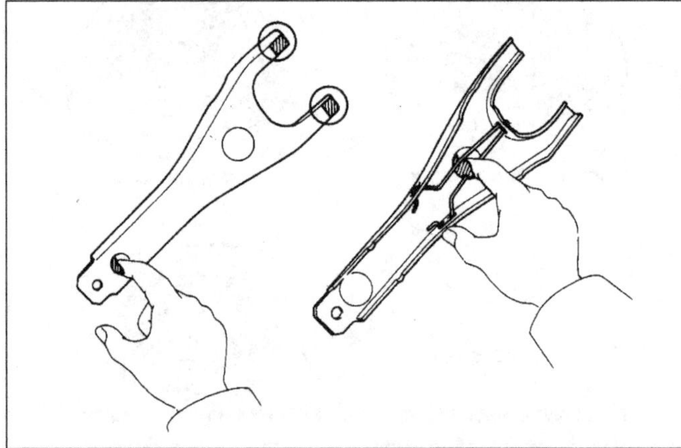

4.5 Apply clutch assembly grease to the release lever in the areas indicated

5.2a Unhook the clutch pedal return spring . . .

5.2b . . . and remove the clip and pull out the clevis pin

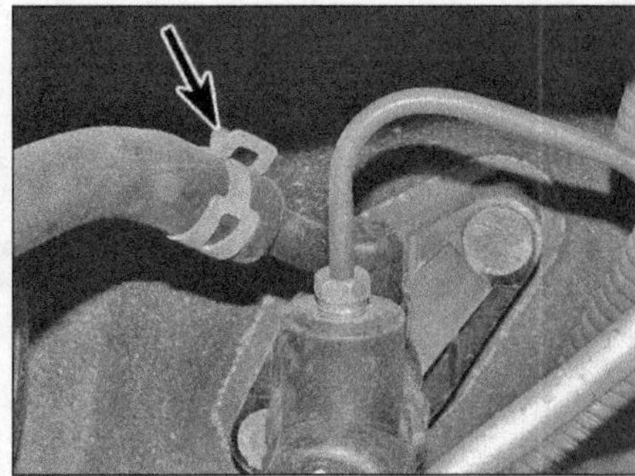

5.3 release the retaining clip (arrowed)

passing the end of the release lever through the opening in the clutch housing. Push the clutch release lever onto the ball-stud until it's firmly seated.

8 Apply a light coat of clutch assembly grease to the face of the release bearing where it contacts the clutch cover diaphragm fingers.

9 The remainder of refitting is the reverse of the removal procedure.

5 Clutch master cylinder – removal and refitting

Removal

1 Remove the driver's side lower facia panel as described in Chapter 11.

2 Working under the driver's side of the facia, unclip the return spring, and disconnect the pushrod from the top of the clutch pedal. It's held in place with a clevis pin. To remove the clevis pin, remove the clip **(see illustrations)**.

3 Open the bonnet, and working inside the engine compartment, release the retaining clip and disconnect the hose from the brake fluid reservoir **(see illustration)**. Clamp the pipe before removal or plug the end of the hose as it is removed. Have rags handy, as some fluid will be lost as the hose is removed.

4 Using a flare-nut spanner on the fitting, to protect the fitting from being rounded off, undo the hydraulic pipe at the clutch master cylinder **(see illustration)**. Have rags handy, as some fluid will be lost as the pipe is removed.

Caution: Don't allow clutch fluid to come into contact with the vehicle's paintwork, as it will damage it.

5 From inside the vehicle, remove the nuts which attach the master cylinder to the bulkhead **(see illustration)**.

6 Remove the master cylinder from the engine compartment, again being careful not to spill any of the fluid.

Refitting

7 Position the master cylinder on the bulkhead, refitting the mounting nuts finger-tight.

8 Connect the hydraulic pipe to the master cylinder, moving the cylinder slightly as necessary to thread the fitting properly into the bore. Don't cross-thread the fitting as it's installed.

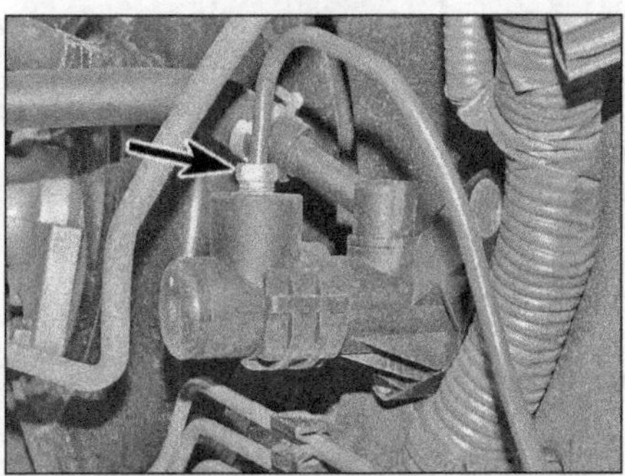

5.4 Undo the hydraulic fluid pipe (arrowed)

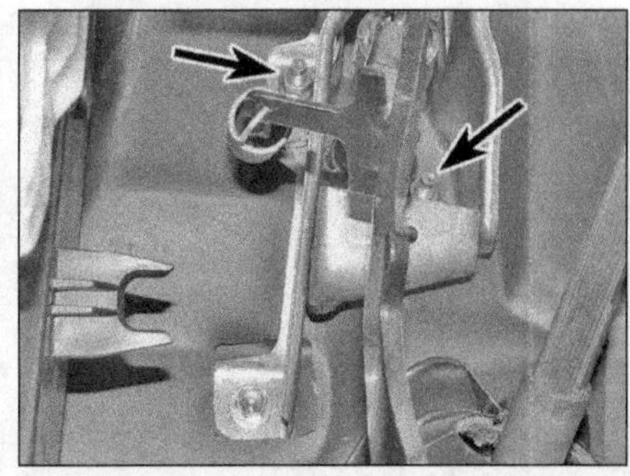

5.5 Master cylinder retaining nuts (arrowed)

9 Tighten the mounting nuts and the hydraulic pipe fitting securely.

10 Refit the reservoir hose to the master cylinder making sure the clip is secure.

11 Connect the pushrod to the clutch pedal and refit the return spring.

12 Top-up the brake fluid reservoir with fresh brake fluid of the specified type and then bleed the clutch system (see Section 2).

6 Clutch release cylinder – removal and refitting

Removal

1 Raise the vehicle and support it securely on axle stands (see *Jacking and vehicle support*). Undo the screws and remove the engine undertray (where fitted).

2 Disconnect the hydraulic pipe at the release cylinder. If available, use a flare-nut spanner on the fitting, which will prevent the fitting from being rounded off **(see illustration)**. Have a small can and rags handy, as some fluid will be spilled as the pipe is removed.

3 Slacken and remove the clutch release cylinder mounting bolts **(see illustration)**.

4 Remove the release cylinder.

Refitting

5 Refit the release cylinder on the clutch housing. Make sure the pushrod is seated in the release fork recess.

6 Connect the hydraulic pipe to the release cylinder. Tighten the connection.

7 Fill the brake fluid reservoir fresh brake fluid of the specified type and bleed the clutch system (see Section 2).

8 Refit the engine undertray (where fitted) and lower the vehicle.

6.2 Use a flare-nut spanner on the hydraulic pipe fitting (arrowed)

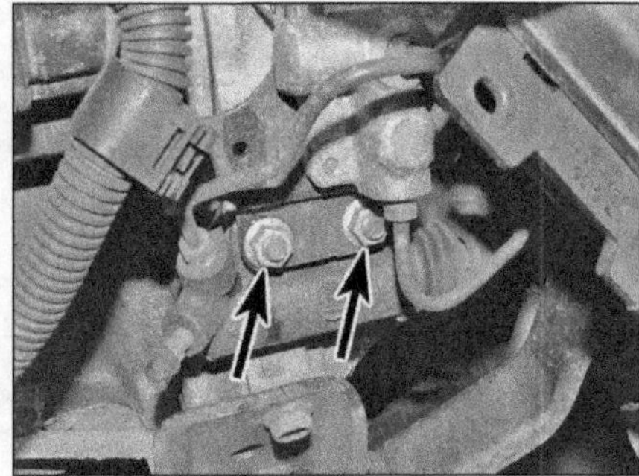

6.3 Clutch release cylinder mounting bolts (arrowed)

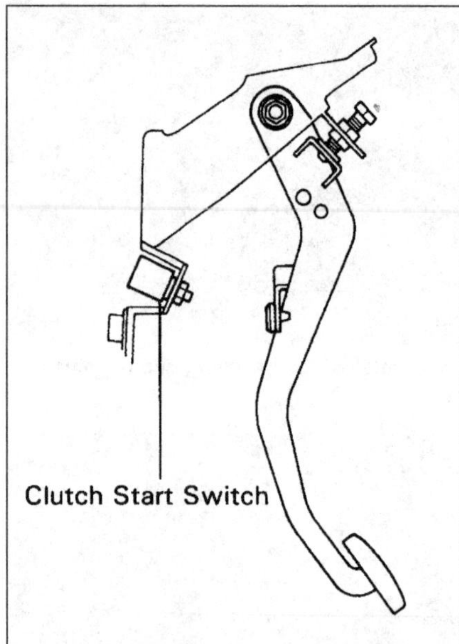

7.4 The clutch start switch is located under the facia on a bracket in front of the clutch pedal

7 Clutch pedal start switch - check and renewal

Note: *A clutch pedal start switch is not fitted to all models.*

Check

1 Check the clutch pedal height and free-play, and the pushrod freeplay (see Chapter 1A or 1B).

2 Verify that the engine will not start when the clutch pedal is released. Verify that the engine will start when the clutch pedal is depressed all the way.

3 If the clutch start switch doesn't perform as described, adjust and, if necessary, renew it.

4 Locate the switch **(see illustration)** and unplug the electrical connector.

5 Verify that there is continuity between the clutch start switch terminals when the switch is on (pedal depressed) **(see illustration)**.

6 Verify that no continuity exists between the switch terminals when the switch is off (pedal released).

7 If the switch fails either of the tests, renew it.

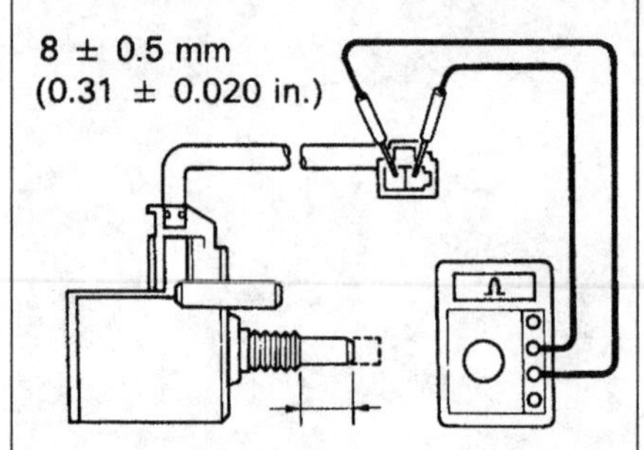

7.5 Using an ohmmeter, check the start switch

Renewal

8 Remove the nut nearest the plunger end of the switch and unscrew the switch. Unplug the electrical connector.

9 Refitting is the reverse of removal. The switch is self-adjusting, so there's no need for adjustment.

10 Verify again that the engine doesn't start when the clutch pedal is released, and does start when the pedal is depressed.

Chapter 7 Part A:
Manual transmission

Contents

Degrees of difficulty

Easy, suitable for novice with little experience 

Fairly easy, suitable for beginner with some experience

Fairly difficult, suitable for competent DIY mechanic

Difficult, suitable for experienced DIY mechanic

Very difficult, suitable for expert DIY or professional 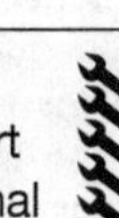

Specifications

Torque wrench settings	**Nm**	**lbf ft**
Lower transmission-to-engine bolts	23	17
Reversing light switch	40	30
Transmission earth cable	13	10
Transmission mounting front:		
To transmission	64	47
To subframe	52	38
Transmission mounting left-hand:		
To body	52	38
Through-bolt	80	59
To transmission	52	38
Transmission mounting rear:		
To transmission	64	47
Through-bolt	87	64
Upper transmission-to-engine bolts **(see illustration 5.26)**:		
Bolts A	64	47
Bolts B	47	35
Bolts C	23	17

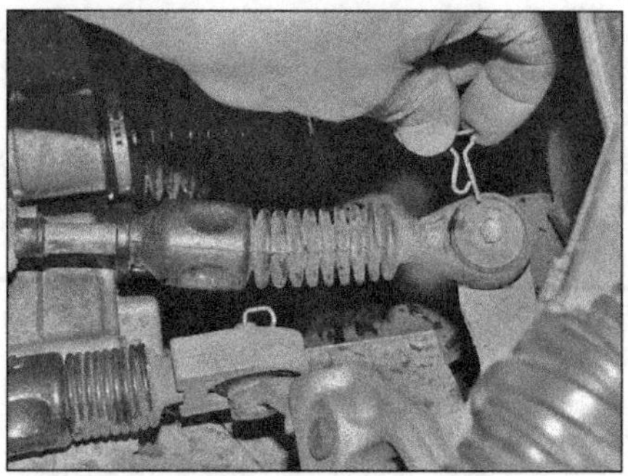
2.1 Prise out the clips and disconnect the gearchange cables from the levers

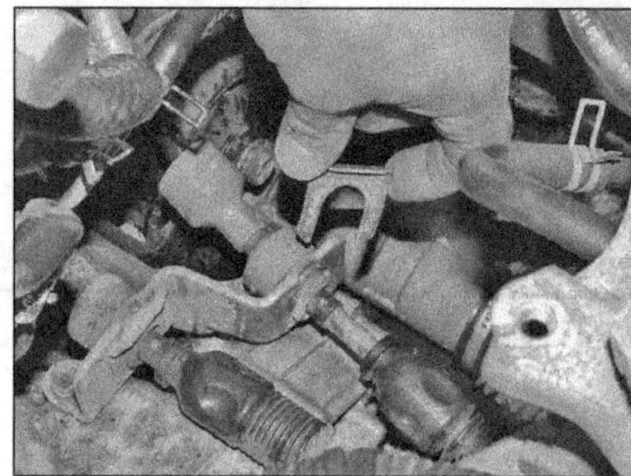
2.2a Slide up the cable retaining clips . . .

2.2b . . . and release the cables

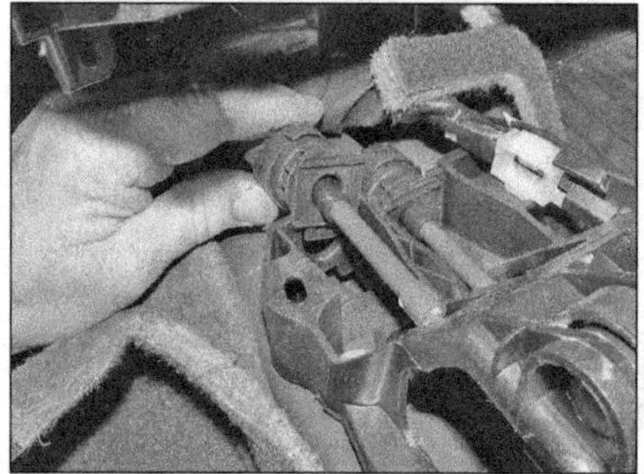
2.4 Slide the cables from the housing

1 General information

The vehicles covered by this manual are equipped with a 5-speed manual transmission or a 4-speed automatic transmission. Information on the manual transmission is included in this Part of Chapter 7. Service procedures for the automatic transmission are contained in Chapter 7B.

The transmission is contained in a cast-aluminium alloy casing bolted to the engine's left-hand end, and consists of the gearbox and final drive differential – often called a transaxle.

Drive is transmitted from the crankshaft via the clutch to the input shaft, which has a splined extension to accept the clutch friction disc, and rotates in sealed ball-bearings. From the input shaft, drive is transmitted to the output shaft, which rotates in a roller bearing at its right-hand end and a sealed ball-bearing at its left-hand end. From the output shaft, the drive is transmitted to the differential crownwheel, which rotates with the differential case and planetary gears, thus driving the sun gears and driveshafts. The rotation of the planetary gears on their shaft allows the inner roadwheel to rotate at a slower speed than the outer roadwheel when the car is cornering.

The input and output shafts are arranged side-by-side, parallel to the crankshaft and driveshafts, so that their gear pinion teeth are in constant mesh. In the neutral position, the output shaft gear pinions rotate freely, so that drive cannot be transmitted to the crownwheel.

Gear selection is via a floor-mounted lever and cable mechanism. The selector/gearchange cables causes the appropriate selector fork to move its respective synchro-sleeve along the shaft, to lock the gear pinion to the synchro-hub. Since the synchro-hubs are splined to the output shaft, this locks the pinion to the shaft, so that drive can be transmitted. To ensure that gearchanging can be made quickly and quietly, a synchromesh system is fitted to all forward gears, consisting of baulk rings and spring-loaded fingers, as well as the gear pinions and synchro-hubs. The synchromesh cones are formed on the mating faces of the baulk rings and gear pinions.

2 Gearchange cables – removal and refitting

Removal

1 In the engine compartment, remove the retaining clips and washers and disconnect the gearchange cables from the selecting bellcrank **(see illustration)**.

2 Remove the cable retaining clips from the cable bracket **(see illustrations)**.

3 Inside the vehicle, remove the centre console (see Chapter 11).

4 Remove the cable retainers from the gear-change lever base **(see illustration)**.

5 Remove the retaining clips and release the cable ends **(see illustration)** from the gearchange lever assembly.

6 Pull the outer cables upwards from the lever housing.

7 Trace the cable assembly to the bulk- head, undo the bolts and remove the weather-proofing grommet and retaining plate **(see illustration)**. Pull the cable assembly through the bulkhead.

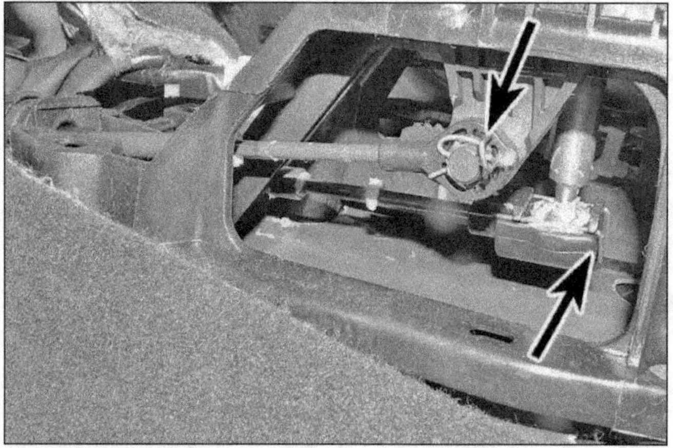
2.5 Remove the cable clips (arrowed) from the cable ends

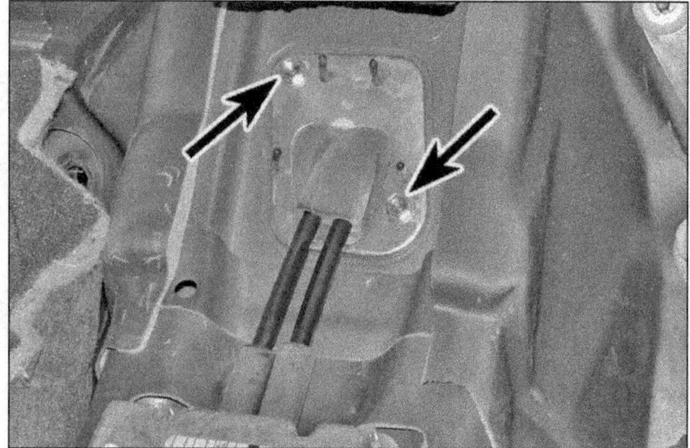
2.7 Undo the two bolts (arrowed) and remove the cable grommet/retaining plate assembly

3.3a Undo the 4 bolts (arrowed) . . .

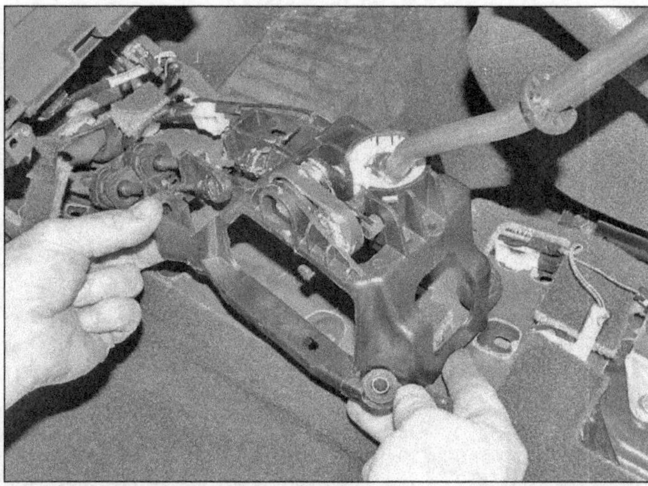
3.3b . . . and remove the gearchange lever base

Refitting

8 Refitting is the reverse of removal.

3 Gearchange lever – removal and refitting

Removal

1 Remove the centre console (see Chapter 11).

2 Remove the gearchange cable retainers and disconnect both cables from the gearchange lever (see Section 2).

3 Remove the retaining bolts from the gearchange lever base **(see illustrations)** and detach the gearchange lever from the vehicle.

Refitting

4 Refitting is the reverse of removal.

4 Reversing light switch – testing and renewal

Check

1 The reversing light switch is located on top of the transmission.

2 Turn the ignition key to the on position and move the gearchange lever to the Reverse position. The switch should close the reversing light circuit and turn on the reversing lights.

3 If it doesn't, check the reversing light fuse (see Chapter 12).

4 If the fuse is okay, verify that there's voltage available on the battery side of the switch (with the ignition turned on).

5 If there's no voltage on the battery side of the switch, check the wire between the fuse and the switch; if there is voltage, put the gearchange lever in reverse and see if there's voltage on the earth side of the switch.

6 If there's no voltage on the earth side of the switch, renew the switch (see below); if there is voltage, note whether one or both reversing lights are out.

7 If only one bulb is out, renew it, if they're both out, the bulbs could be the problem, but it's more likely that the wire between the switch and the bulbs has an open circuit somewhere.

Renewal

8 Remove the air filter housing as described in Chapter 4A or 4B.

9 Disconnect the electrical connector from the reversing light switch **(see illustration)**.

10 Unscrew and remove the old switch. Recover the sealing washer (where applicable)

11 To test the new switch before refitting, simply check continuity across the switch terminals: with the plunger depressed, there should be continuity; with the plunger free, there should be no continuity.

12 Check the condition of the sealing washer (where fitted) and renew where necessary. Screw in the new switch and tighten it to the specified torque.

13 Connect the electrical connector.

14 Put the ignition on and check the reversing lights, to ensure that the circuit is working properly.

15 Refit the air filter housing as described in Chapter 4A or 4B.

5 Manual transmission – removal and refitting

Removal

1 Disconnect the negative cable from the battery (see Chapter 5A). Remove the battery and battery tray from the engine compartment.

2 Remove the air cleaner assembly (see Chapter 4A or 4B).

3 Slacken the front roadwheel nuts, then jack up the front of the vehicle, and support it securely on axle stands (see *Jacking and vehicle support*). Remove the front roadwheels.

4 Undo the screws and remove the engine undertrays.

5 Remove the clutch release cylinder and the clutch hydraulic pipe (see Chapter 6).

6 Note their fitted locations, and then unplug the electrical connectors from the transmission. Trace the wiring loom along the transmission and disconnect any retaining clips, noting their fitted position for refitting.

7 Locate the earth cable to the transmission housing, remove the cable retaining bolt and detach the earth cable from the transmission.

8 Disconnect the gearchange cables from the transmission (see Section 2).

9 Remove the starter motor as described in Chapter 5A.

10 Remove the two upper and the single front transmission-to-engine mounting bolts. Note the location of any earth connectors or brackets, so that they may be refitted in their original location.

11 Support the engine. This can be done from above by using an engine hoist, or by placing a jack (with a wood block as an insulator) under the engine oil sump pan. The engine must be supported at all times while the transmission is out of the vehicle.

12 Remove the left-hand engine mounting from the top of the transmission **(see illustration)**.

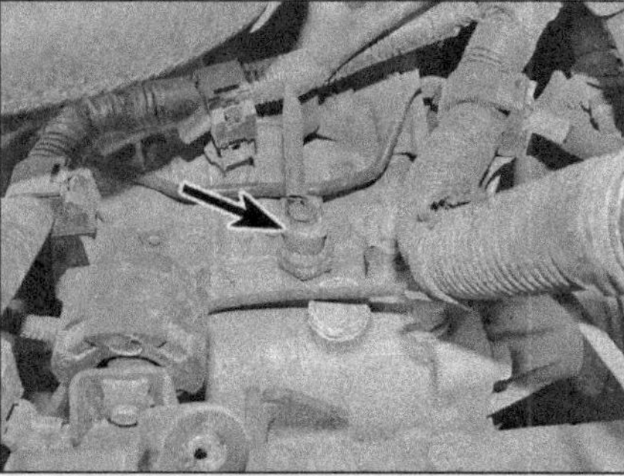
4.9 The reversing light switch (arrowed) is located on the top of the transmission housing

5.12 Remove the transmission mounting (arrowed)

5.16a Undo the lower mounting bolts . . .

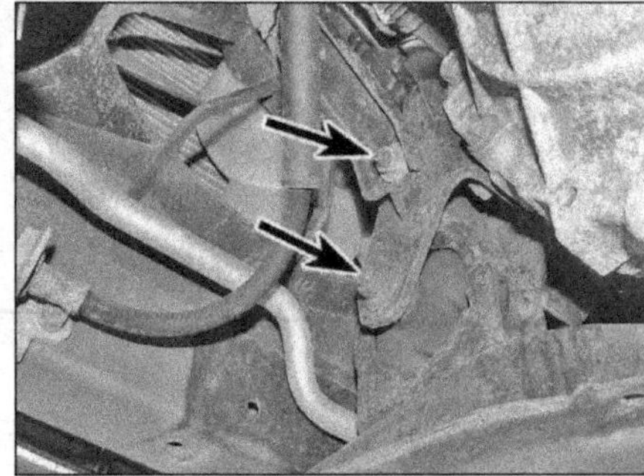

5.16b . . . the bracket mounting bolts . . .

5.16c . . . and the upper mounting bolts

13 Drain the transmission fluid (see Chapter 1A or 1B).

14 Remove the driveshafts (see Chapter 8), and unbolt the shield over the right-hand driveshaft inner joint (where fitted).

15 Remove the front exhaust pipe (see Chapter 4A or 4B).

16 Disconnect the front engine mounting **(see illustrations)**.

17 Remove the rear engine mounting **(see illustration)**.

18 Undo the front and rear mounting bolts and remove the centre support member **(see illustration)**.

19 Support the transmission with a jack (preferably a special jack made for this purpose). If you're using a floor jack, be sure to place a wood block between the lifting pad and the transmission to protect the cast aluminium housing. Safety chains will help steady the transmission on the jack.

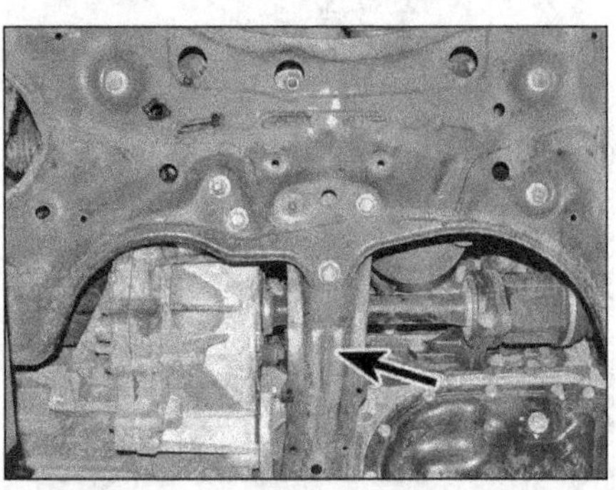

5.18 Remove the centre support member (arrowed)

5.17 Rear engine mounting – arrowed

20 Remove the rest of the bolts securing the transmission to the engine.

21 Make a final check that all wires and hoses have been disconnected from the transmission.

22 Lower the left-hand end of the engine, then roll the transmission and jack toward the side of the vehicle. Once the input shaft is clear of the splines in the clutch hub, lower the transmission and remove it from under the vehicle. Try to keep the transmission as level as possible.

Caution: Do not depress the clutch pedal while the transmission is removed from the vehicle.

23 The clutch components can now be inspected (see Chapter 6). In most cases, new clutch components should be routinely fitted whenever the transmission is removed.

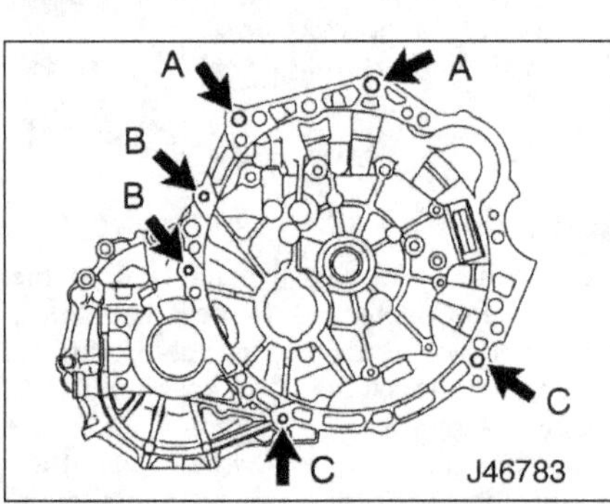

5.26 Tighten the bolts to the torque listed in the Specifications

Refitting

24 If removed, fit the clutch components (see Chapter 6).

25 With the transmission secured to the jack as on removal, raise it into position and then carefully slide it forward, engaging the input shaft with the splines in the clutch hub. Do not use excessive force to install the transmission – if the input shaft does not slide into place, readjust the angle of the transmission so it is level and/or turn the input shaft so the splines engage properly with the clutch.

26 Refit the transmission-to-engine bolts **(see illustration)**. Tighten the bolts to the torque listed in this Chapter's Specifications.

27 Refit the transmission mounting nuts and bolts. Tighten all nuts and bolts securely.

28 Refit any suspension components which were detached or removed. Tighten all nuts and bolts to the torque listed in the Chapter 10 Specifications.

29 Remove the jacks supporting the transmission and the engine.

30 Refit the various items removed previously. Refer to Chapter 4A or 4B for information regarding the exhaust pipe, Chapter 5A for the starter motor and Chapter 8 for the driveshafts.

31 Make sure that the wiring harness connectors for the reversing light switch and the speed sensor, and any other electrical devices, are plugged in. And make sure that all harness clamps are reattached to the engine and/or transmission.

32 If the transmission was drained, fill it with the specified lubricant to the proper level (see Chapter 1A or 1B).

33 Lower the vehicle.

34 Connect the gearchange cables (see Section 2).

35 Connect the negative battery cable (see Chapter 5A). Road test the vehicle to check for proper transmission operation, and check for leakage.

6 Manual transmission overhaul – general information

1 Overhauling a manual transmission is a difficult and involved job for the DIY home

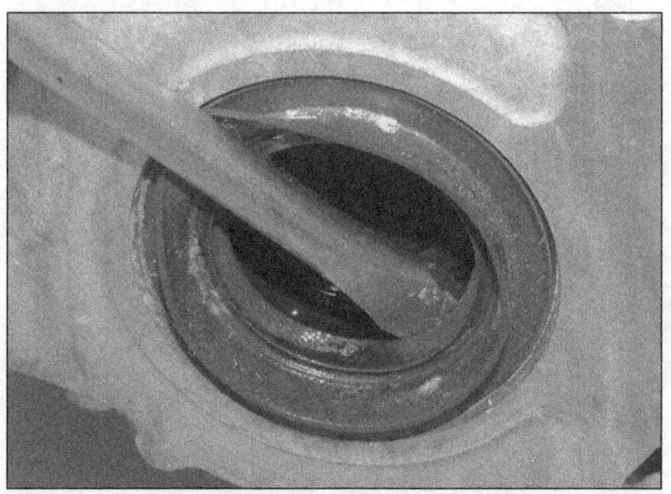

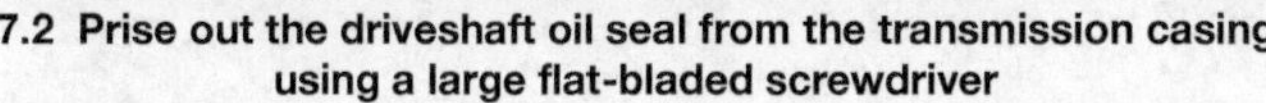
7.2 Prise out the driveshaft oil seal from the transmission casing using a large flat-bladed screwdriver

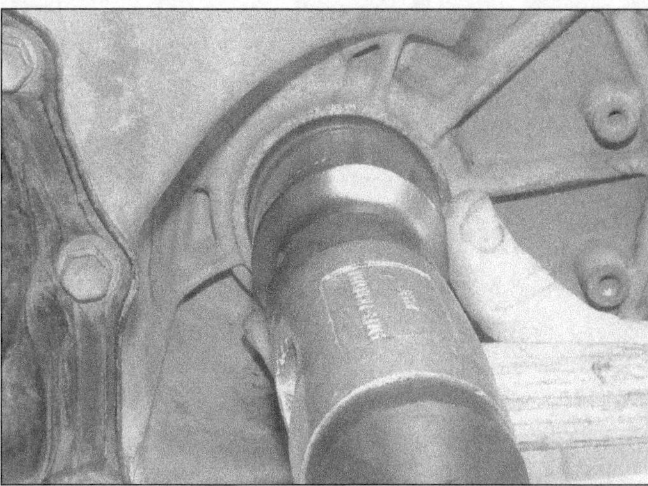
7.3 Use a suitable tubular drift or socket which bears only on the hard, outer edge of the new seal

mechanic. In addition to dismantling and reassembling many small parts, clearances must be precisely measured and, if necessary, changed by selecting shims and spacers. Internal transmission components are also often difficult to obtain, and in many instances, extremely expensive. Because of this, if the transmission develops a fault or becomes noisy, the best course of action is to have the unit overhauled by a specialist repairer, or to obtain an exchange reconditioned unit.

2 Nevertheless, it is not impossible for the more experienced mechanic to overhaul the transmission, provided the special tools are available, and the job is done in a deliberate step-by-step manner, so that nothing is overlooked.

3 The tools necessary for an overhaul include internal and external circlip pliers, bearing pullers, a slide hammer, a set of pin punches, a dial test indicator, and possibly a hydraulic press. In addition, a large, sturdy workbench and a vice will be required.

4 During dismantling of the transmission, make careful notes of how each component is fitted, to make reassembly easier and more accurate.

5 Before dismantling the transmission, it will help if you have some idea what area is malfunctioning. Certain problems can be closely related to specific areas in the transmission, which can make component examination and renewal easier. Refer to the *Fault finding* Section for more information.

7 Oil seals – renewal

Driveshaft oil seals

1 Remove the appropriate driveshaft as described in Chapter 8.

2 Carefully prise the oil seal out of the transmission, using a large flat-bladed screwdriver **(see illustration)**.

3 Remove all traces of dirt from the area around the oil seal aperture, then apply a smear of grease to the outer lip of the new oil seal. Fit the new seal into its aperture, and drive it squarely into position using a suitable tubular drift (such as a socket), which bears only on the hard outer edge of the seal, until it abuts its locating shoulder. If the seal was supplied with a plastic protector sleeve, leave this in position until the driveshaft has been refitted **(see illustration)**.

4 Apply a thin film of grease to the oil seal lip.

5 Refit the driveshaft as described in Chapter 8.

Input shaft oil seal

6 Remove the transmission as described in Section 5, and the clutch release mechanism as described in Chapter 6.

7 Undo the three bolts securing the clutch release bearing guide sleeve in position, and slide the guide off the input shaft. Recover any shims or thrustwashers, which have stuck to the rear of the guide sleeve, and refit them to the input shaft.

8 Carefully lever the oil seal out of the transmission casing using a suitable flat-bladed screwdriver.

9 Before fitting a new seal, check the input shaft's seal rubbing surface for signs of burrs, scratches or other damage, which may have caused the seal to fail in the first place. It may be possible to polish away minor faults of this sort using fine abrasive paper; however, more serious defects will require the renewal of the input shaft. Ensure that the input shaft is clean and greased, to protect the seal lips on refitting.

10 Dip the new seal in clean oil, and fit it to the casing.

11 Fit a new sealing ring or gasket (as applicable) to the rear of the guide sleeve, then carefully slide the sleeve into position over the input shaft. Refit the retaining bolts and tighten them securely.

12 Take the opportunity to inspect the clutch components if not already done (Chapter 6). Finally, refit the transmission as described in Section 5.

Notes

Chapter 7 Part B: Automatic transmission

Contents

Degrees of difficulty

Easy, suitable for novice with little experience 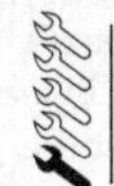	**Fairly easy,** suitable for beginner with some experience	**Fairly difficult,** suitable for competent DIY mechanic	**Difficult,** suitable for experienced DIY mechanic	**Very difficult,** suitable for expert DIY or professional

Specifications

Torque wrench settings	**Nm**	**lbf ft**
Manual valve	10	7
Neutral start switch	6	4
Speed sensor	6	4
Torque converter-to-driveplate bolts	28	21
Transmission drain plug	17	13
Transmission-to-engine bolts **(see illustration 7.26)**:		
Bolts A	64	47
Bolts B	46	34
Bolts C	23	17

1 General information

All vehicles covered in this manual are equipped with either a 5-speed manual transmission or a 4-speed automatic transmission. All information on the automatic transmission is included in this Part of Chapter 7. Information for the manual transmission can be found in Part A of this Chapter.

Because of the complexity of the automatic transmissions and the specialised equipment necessary to perform most service operations, this Chapter contains only those procedures related to general diagnosis, routine maintenance, adjustment, and removal and refitting.

If the transmission requires major repair work, it should be left to a dealer service department or an automotive or transmission repair workshop. You can, however, remove and install the transmission yourself and save the expense, even if the repair work is done by a transmission workshop.

2 Fault finding – general

Note: *Automatic transmission malfunctions may be caused by five general conditions: poor engine performance, improper adjustments, hydraulic malfunctions, mechanical malfunctions, or malfunctions in the computer or its signal network. Diagnosis of these problems should always begin with a check of the easily repaired items: fluid level and condition (see Chapter 1A), selector linkage adjustment and throttle linkage adjustment (where applicable). Next, perform a road test to determine if the problem has been corrected or if more diagnosis is necessary. If the problem persists after the preliminary tests and corrections are completed, additional diagnosis should be done by a dealer service department or transmission repair workshop. Refer to the 'Fault finding' section at the rear of this manual for information on symptoms of transmission problems.*

Preliminary checks

1 Drive the vehicle to warm the transmission to normal operating temperature.

2 Check the fluid level as described in Chapter 1A:

a) *If the fluid level is unusually low, add enough fluid to bring the level within the designated area of the dipstick, then check for external leaks (see below).*

b) *If the fluid level is abnormally high, drain off the excess, and then check the drained fluid for contamination by coolant. The presence of engine coolant in the automatic transmission fluid indicates that a failure has occurred in the internal radiator walls that separate the coolant from the transmission fluid (see Chapter 3).*

c) *If the fluid is foaming, drain it and refill the transmission, then check for coolant in the fluid, or a high fluid level.*

3 Check the engine idle speed. **Note:** *If the engine is malfunctioning, do not proceed with the preliminary checks until it has been repaired and runs normally.*

4 Check the accelerator cable for freedom of movement. Adjust it if necessary (see Chap-

3.4 Lever the driveshaft oil seal from the transmission casing

ter 4A). **Note:** *The cable may function properly when the engine is shut off and cold, but malfunction once the engine is hot. Check it when cold and at normal engine operating temperature.*

5 Inspect the selector cable (see Section 4). Make sure that it's properly adjusted and that the cable operates smoothly.

Fluid leak diagnosis

6 Most fluid leaks are easy to locate visually. Repair usually consists of renewing a seal or gasket. If a leak is difficult to find, the following procedure may help.

7 Identify the fluid. Make sure it's transmission fluid and not engine oil or brake fluid (automatic transmission fluid is a deep red colour).

8 Try to pinpoint the source of the leak. Drive the vehicle several miles, and then park it over a large sheet of cardboard. After a minute or two, you should be able to locate the leak by determining the source of the fluid dripping onto the cardboard.

9 Make a careful visual inspection of the suspected component and the area immediately around it. Pay particular attention to gasket mating surfaces. A mirror is often helpful for finding leaks in areas that are hard to see.

10 If the leak still cannot be found, clean the suspected area thoroughly with a degreaser or solvent, then dry it.

11 Drive the vehicle for several miles at normal operating temperature and varying speeds. After driving the vehicle, visually inspect the suspected component again.

12 Once the leak has been located, the cause must be determined before it can be properly repaired. If a gasket is renewed but the sealing flange is bent, the new gasket will not stop the leak. The bent flange must be straightened.

13 Before attempting to repair a leak, check to make sure that the following conditions are corrected or they may cause another leak. **Note:** *Some of the following conditions cannot be fixed without highly specialised tools and expertise. Such problems must be referred to a transmission workshop or a dealer service department.*

Gasket leaks

14 Check the pan periodically. Make sure the bolts are tight, no bolts are missing, the gasket is in good condition and the pan is flat (dents in the pan may indicate damage to the valve body inside).

15 If the pan gasket is leaking, the fluid level or the fluid pressure may be too high, the vent may be plugged, the pan bolts may be too tight, the pan sealing flange may be warped, the sealing surface of the transmission housing may be damaged, the gasket may be damaged or the transmission casting may be cracked or porous. If sealant instead of gasket material has been used to form a seal between the pan and the transmission housing, it may be the wrong sealant.

Seal leaks

16 If a transmission seal is leaking, the fluid level or pressure may be too high, the vent may be plugged, the seal bore may be damaged, the seal itself may be damaged or improperly installed, the surface of the shaft protruding through the seal may be damaged or a loose bearing may be causing excessive shaft movement.

17 Make sure the dipstick tube seal is in good condition and the tube is properly seated. Periodically check the area around the speedometer gear or sensor for leakage. If transmission fluid is evident, check the O-ring for damage.

Case leaks

18 If the case itself appears to be leaking, the casting is porous and will have to be repaired or renewed.

19 Make sure the oil cooler hose fittings are tight and in good condition.

Fluid from the vent pipe or fill tube

20 If this condition occurs, the transmission is overfilled, there is coolant in the fluid, the case is porous, the dipstick is incorrect, the vent is plugged or the drain-back holes are plugged.

3 Oil seal renewal

1 Oil leaks frequently occur due to wear of the driveshaft oil seals and/or the speedometer drive gear oil seal and O-rings. Renewal of these seals is relatively easy, since the repairs can usually be performed without removing the transmission from the vehicle.

Driveshaft oil seals

2 The driveshaft oil seals are located on the sides of the transmission, where the inner ends of the driveshafts are splined into the differential side gears. If you suspect that a driveshaft oil seal is leaking, raise the vehicle and support it securely on axle stands (see *Jacking and vehicle support*). If the seal is leaking, you'll see lubricant on the side of the transmission, below the seal.

3 Remove the driveshaft (see Chapter 8).

4 Using a screwdriver or pry bar, carefully lever the oil seal out of the transmission bore **(see illustration)**.

5 If the oil seal cannot be removed with a screwdriver or pry bar, a special oil seal removal tool (available at motor factors) will be required.

6 Using a seal installer, a large section of pipe or a large deep socket as a drift, install the new oil seal. Drive it into the bore squarely and make sure it's completely seated **(see illustration)**. A fully-seated left seal should be recessed about 5.3 mm, a right seal about 2.0 mm.

7 Lubricate the lip of the new seal with multipurpose grease, then refit the driveshaft (see Chapter 8). Be careful not to damage the lip of the new seal.

Speed sensor O-ring

8 The speed sensor is located on the transmission housing. Look for lubricant around the sensor housing to determine if the O-ring is leaking.

9 Unplug the electrical connector and unbolt

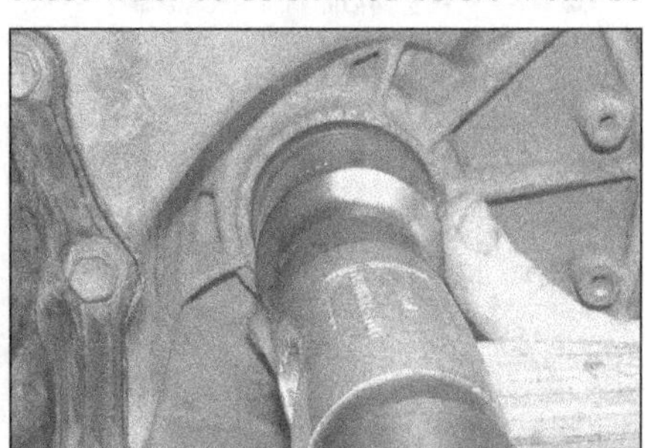

3.6 Drive the seal into place using a tubular drift or socket that bears only on the hard, outer edge of the seal

3.9 Unplug the speed sensor electrical connector (arrowed), remove the bolt (arrowed) and pull the speed sensor out

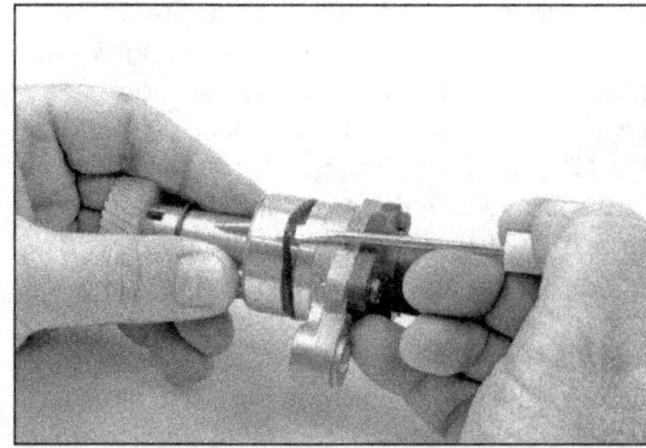

3.10 Remove the O-ring; make sure you don't scratch the surface of the sensor or gouge the O-ring groove

4.2a Undo the nut and disconnect the selector cable from the lever

4.2b Pull out the cable retaining clip

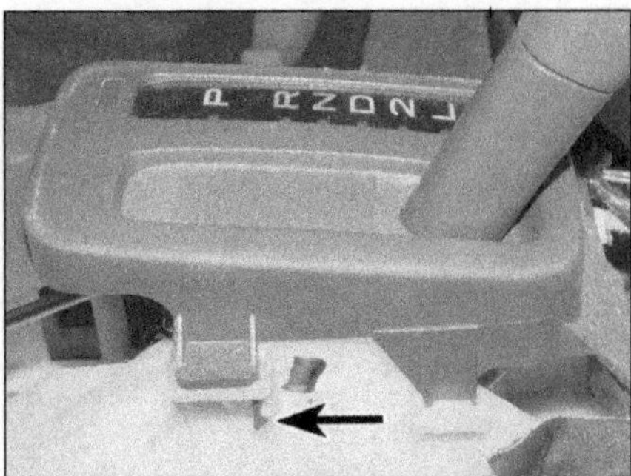
4.4a Release the indicator panel clips (arrowed)

4.4b Pull the light bulb and holder from the panel

4.5 Prise the end of the selector cable from the lever

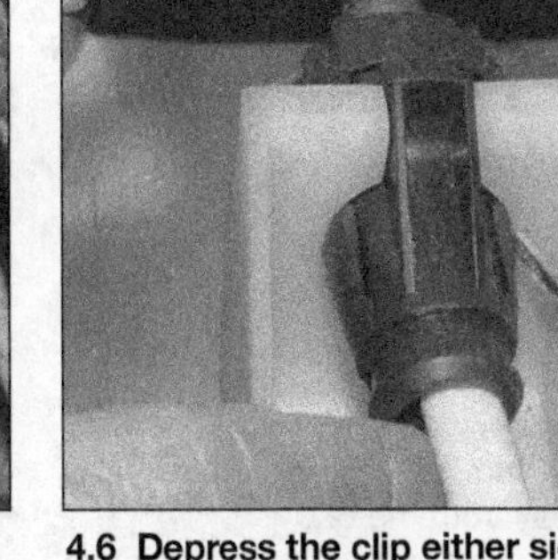
4.6 Depress the clip either side and pull the outer cable from the selector lever base

the vehicle speed sensor from the transmission **(see illustration)**.

10 Using a scribe or a small screwdriver, remove the O-ring from the sensor **(see illustration)** and install a new O-ring. Lubricate the new O-ring with automatic transmission fluid to protect it during refitting of the sensor.

11 Refitting is the reverse of removal.

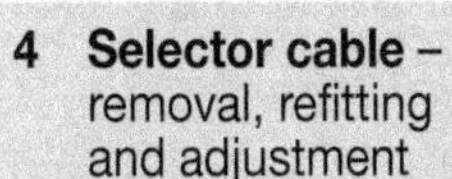

4 Selector cable – removal, refitting and adjustment

Removal and refitting

1 Apply the handbrake and block the rear wheels. Raise the front of the vehicle and place it securely on axle stands (see *Jacking and vehicle support*).

2 Disconnect the selector cable from the manual selector lever at the transmission and detach it from the bracket on the front of the transmission **(see illustrations)**.

3 Remove the centre console (see Chapter 11).

4 Release the clips, lift up the gear-position indicator panel and pull the light bulb from the panel **(see illustrations)**. Tie the gear-position indicator panel to the selector lever handle so that you have room to work.

5 Prise the end of the selector cable from the selector lever **(see illustration)**.

6 Depress the two retaining clips, and pull the selector lever outer cable from the front edge of the selector lever base **(see illustration)**.

7 Pull the cable through the grommet in the firewall.

8 Refitting is the reverse of removal.

9 When you're done, adjust the selector cable.

Adjustment

10 Loosen the nut on the manual selector lever at the transmission **(see illustration 4.2a)**.

11 Push the lever toward the right side of the vehicle until it stops, then return it two notches to the Neutral position.

12 Move the selector lever inside the vehicle to the Neutral position.

13 While holding the lever with a slight pressure toward the Reverse position, tighten the nut securely.

14 Check the operation of the transmission in each selector lever position (try to start the engine in each gear – the starter should operate in the Park and Neutral positions only).

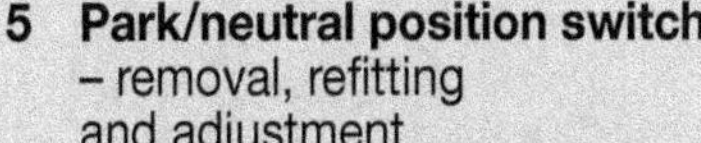

5 Park/neutral position switch – removal, refitting and adjustment

Removal

1 Move the transmission lever into the Neutral position.

2 Apply the handbrake and block the rear wheels. Raise the front of the vehicle and place it securely on axle stands (see *Jacking and vehicle support*).

3 Remove the nut and lift off the selector lever **(see illustration 4.2a)**.

4 Disconnect the wiring connector from the switch unit.

5 Using a screwdriver, prise back the tab on the lockwasher under the nut securing the switch to the valve shaft.

6 Unscrew the nut, and recover the lockwasher and shim(s).

7 Remove the retaining bolts and lift the switch off the shaft.

Refitting and adjustment

8 To install, line up the flats on the valve shaft with the flats in the switch and push the switch onto the shaft. Refit the shim(s), the lockwasher and securing nut. Tighten the securing nut, and bend over the lockwasher tab.

9 Rotate the switch until the neutral basic line aligns with the groove **(see illustration)**. Tighten the bolts securely and connect the electrical connector.

10 Install the selector lever to the switch, and verify the engine will not start with the

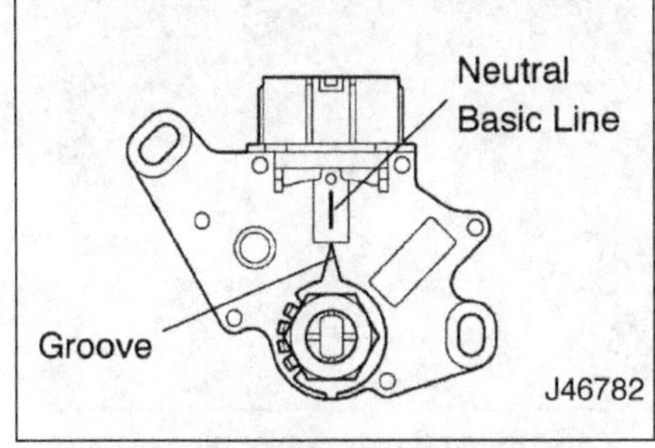

5.9 Rotate the switch until the neutral basic line aligns with the groove and tighten the bolts

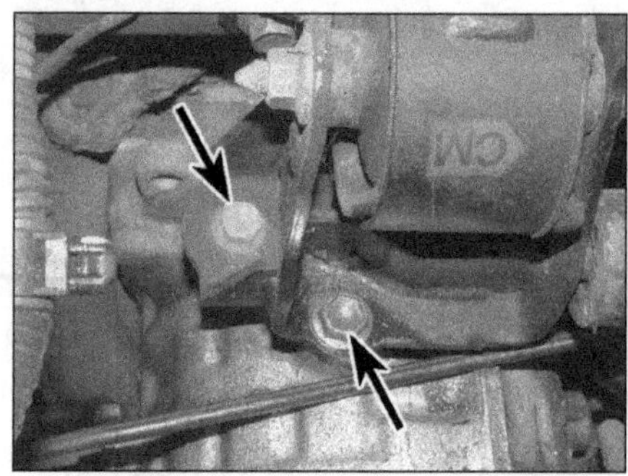

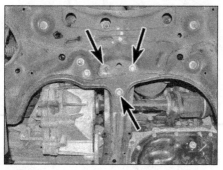

7.3 Undo the mounting-to-transmission casing bolts (rear ones arrowed)

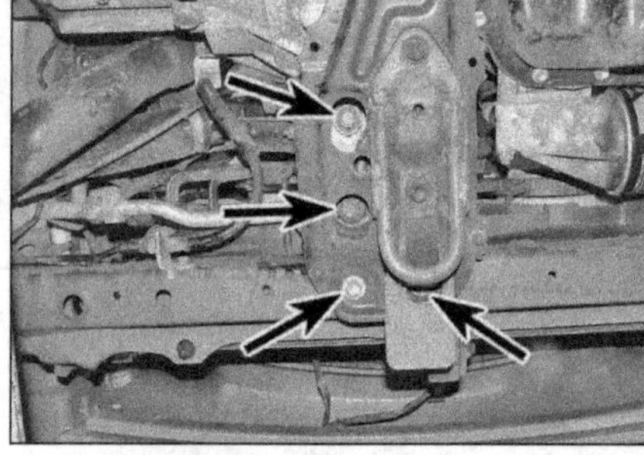

7.13a Undo the front mounting bolts (arrowed) . . .

7.13b . . . and the rear mounting bolts (arrowed)

selector lever in any position other than Park or Neutral, if necessary follow the adjustment procedure above.

6 Transmission mounting – check and renewal

Check

1 Insert a large screwdriver or pry bar between the transmission mounting and the body and try to lever it away from the body.

2 The transmission mounting should not move excessively. If it does, renew the mounting.

Renewal

3 To renew a mounting, support the transmission with a jack, remove the nuts and bolts and remove the mounting. It may be necessary to raise the transmission slightly to provide enough clearance to remove the mounting.

4 Refitting is the reverse of removal.

7 Automatic transmission – removal and refitting

Removal

1 Detach the cable from the negative battery terminal (see Chapter 5A).

2 Remove the air cleaner housing (see Chapter 4A).

3 Remove the bolts from the left-hand transmission mounting **(see illustration)**.

4 Note their fitted positions, then disconnect any all electrical connectors from the transmission, and detach any wiring harness clamps from the transmission and set the wiring harnesses aside.

5 Remove the upper transmission-to-engine bolts. Remove the transmission-to-starter motor bolt (see Chapter 5A).

6 Raise the vehicle and support it securely on axle stands (see *Jacking and vehicle support*).

7 Release the screws and remove the engine undertrays.

8 Disconnect the selector cable from the transmission (see Section 4).

9 Remove the exhaust pipe section between the exhaust manifold and the catalytic converter (see Chapter 4A).

10 Drain the transmission fluid (see Chapter 1A).

11 Remove the driveshafts (see Chapter 8). **Note:** *It's not absolutely necessary to completely remove the driveshafts; you can detach the inner CV joints and suspend them out of the way. However, you'll have more room to work if you remove the driveshafts. And this is a good time to inspect the CV joint boots for tears and deterioration and, if necessary, repack them with new CV joint grease (see Chapter 8).*

12 Support the engine using a hoist from above, or a jack and a wood block under the oil sump to spread the load.

13 Remove the bolts and nuts that attach the centre support brace and suspension member to the vehicle **(see illustrations)**.

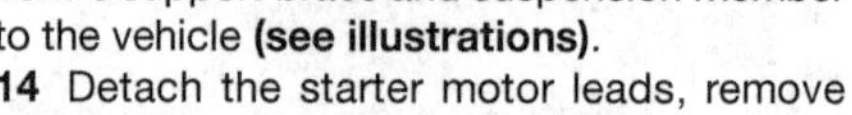

14 Detach the starter motor leads, remove the lower starter-to-transmission bolt and remove the starter (see Chapter 5A).

15 Detach the oil cooler pipe retaining clamps from the transmission, then disconnect the two pipe fittings from the transmission **(see illustration)**.

16 To detach the dipstick tube from the transmission, remove the single bracket bolt from the front of the bellhousing, and then pull straight up on the tube.

17 Support the transmission with a jack – preferably a special jack made for this purpose. Safety chains will help steady the transmission on the jack.

18 Remove the remaining bolts from the left-hand transmission mounting. Remove the bolts from the front and rear mountings **(see illustration)** so that the engine can be tilted slightly to the left to allow easier removal and refitting of the transmission.

19 Remove the torque converter inspection cover. Mark the relationship of the torque converter to the driveplate so they can be installed in the same position. Remove the six torque converter mounting bolts. Turn the crankshaft for access to each one in turn.

20 Working your way around the outside edge of the transmission, remove the engine-to-transmission bolts which are still fitted.

21 Move the transmission to the side to disengage it from the engine block dowel pins and make sure the torque converter is detached from the driveplate. Secure the torque converter to the transmission so that it will not fall out during removal. Lower the transmission from the vehicle.

Refitting

22 Make sure that the torque converter is located correctly in the transmission bellhousing and engaged with the output shaft, prior to refitting.

23 With the transmission secured to the jack, raise it into position. Be sure to keep it level so the torque converter does not slide forward. Connect the cooler lines.

24 Move the transmission carefully into place until the dowel pins are engaged and the torque converter is engaged.

25 Rotate the torque converter to align the

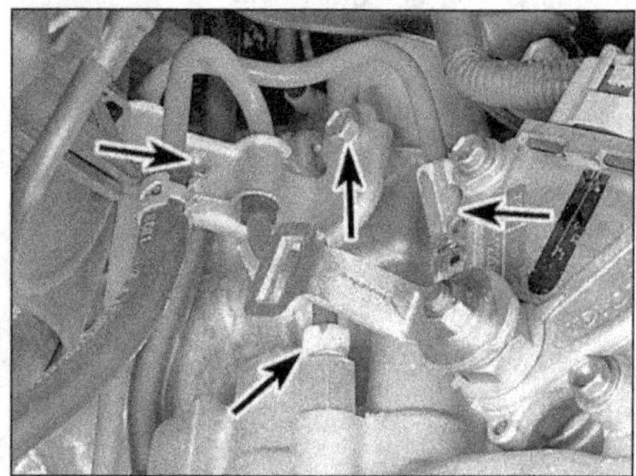

7.15 Unbolt the oil cooler pipe clamps (arrowed) from the transmission and unscrew the pipe fittings (arrowed)

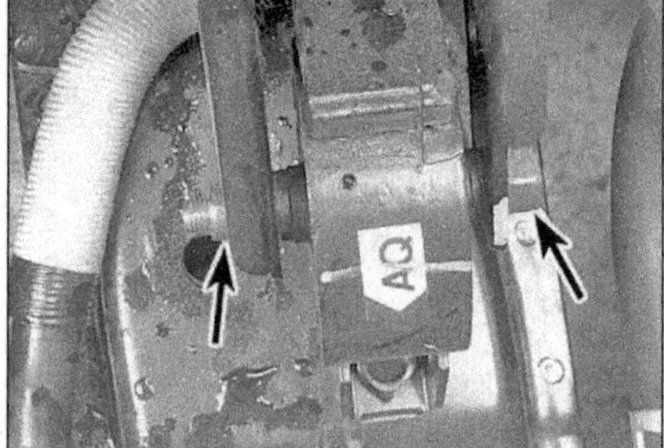

7.18 Remove the nut and through-bolt (arrowed) from the front and rear mountings (front mounting shown, rear mounting similar)

bolt holes with the holes in the driveplate. The match marks on the torque converter and driveplate, made during paragraph 19, must align.

26 Install the lower transmission-to-engine bolts and tighten them to the torque listed in this Chapter's Specifications **(see illustration)**.

27 Install the torque converter-to-driveplate bolts. Tighten them to the torque listed in this Chapter's Specifications. Install the torque converter cover.

28 Install the support brace and suspension member. Tighten the bolts and nuts securely.

29 Remove the jacks supporting the transmission and the engine.

30 Install the starter motor (see Chapter 5A). (It's easier to install the upper bolt after the vehicle has been lowered.)

31 Install the dipstick tube into the transmission and attach the dipstick bracket to the transmission.

32 Connect the oil cooler pipe fittings and the line retaining clamps to the transmission.

33 Install and/or connect the driveshafts to the transmission (see Chapter 8).

34 Install and adjust the park/neutral position switch (see Section 5).

35 Connect and adjust the selector cable (see Section 4) and the accelerator cable (see Chapter 4A).

36 Reconnect all electrical connectors. Make sure that the wiring harnesses are routed properly and clamped to the transmission housing.

37 Refit the exhaust pipe between the exhaust manifold and the catalytic converter (see Chapter 4A).

38 Remove the axle stands and lower the vehicle.

39 Refit the upper transmission bolts and tighten them to the torque listed in this Chapter's Specifications. Install the upper starter motor bolt, if you haven't already done so.

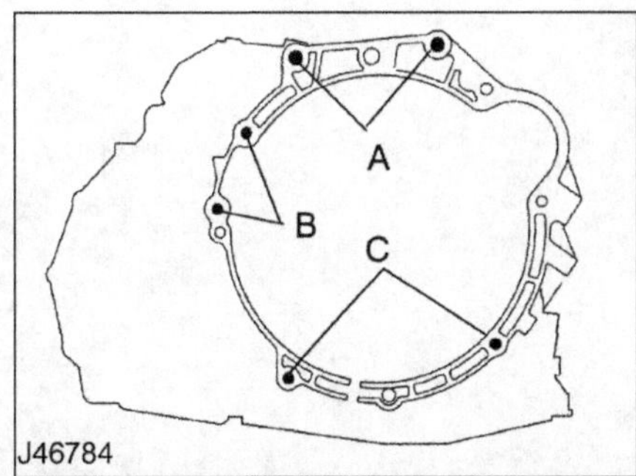

7.26 Tighten the bolts to the torque listed in the Specifications

40 Fill the transmission with the proper type and amount of fluid (see Chapter 1A). Run the vehicle and check for fluid leaks.

Notes

Chapter 8
Driveshafts

Contents

Degrees of difficulty

Easy, suitable for novice with little experience	**Fairly easy,** suitable for beginner with some experience	**Fairly difficult,** suitable for competent DIY mechanic	**Difficult,** suitable for experienced DIY mechanic	**Very difficult,** suitable for expert DIY or professional

Specifications

Driveshaft CV joints

Grease capacity:	
Petrol models:	
Inboard joint	126 to 136 g
Outboard joint	85 to 105 g
Diesel models:	
Inboard joint	170 to 190 g
Outboard joint	152 to 162 g

Driveshaft length

Petrol models:	
Left-hand driveshaft	570.8 ± 5.0 mm
Right-hand driveshaft	842.8 ± 5.0 mm
Diesel models:	
Left-hand driveshaft	532.8 ± 5.0 mm
Right-hand driveshaft	874.0 ± 5.0 mm

Driveshaft damper fitment

Petrol models:	
Hatchback:	
Left-hand driveshaft	213 ± 2.0 mm
Right-hand driveshaft	422 ± 2.0 mm
Estate and Saloon:	
Left-hand driveshaft	217 ± 2.0 mm
Right-hand driveshaft	440 ± 2.0 mm
Diesel models:	
Hatchback:	
Left-hand driveshaft	200 ± 2.0 mm
Right-hand driveshaft	Not available
Estate and Saloon:	
Left-hand driveshaft	204 ± 2.0 mm
Right-hand driveshaft	Not available

Torque wrench settings

	Nm	lbf ft
Driveshaft/hub nut	216	159
Wheel nuts	103	76

2.2 Release the locking tab

2.3 Use a large lever to immobilise the hub while slackening the driveshaft nut

1 General information

1 Power is transmitted from the transmission to the wheels through a pair of driveshafts. The inner end of each driveshaft is splined into the differential side gears. The outer ends of the driveshafts are splined to the axle hubs and locked in place by a large nut.

2 The inner ends of the driveshafts are equipped with sliding constant velocity joints, which are capable of both angular and axial motion. Each inner joint assembly consists of a tripod bearing and a joint housing (outer race) in which the joint is free to slide in and out as the driveshaft moves up and down with the wheel. The joints can be disassembled and cleaned in the event of a gaiter failure (see Section 3), but if any parts are damaged, the joints must be renewed as a unit.

3 The outer CV joints, which consist of ball-bearings running between an inner race and an outer cage, are capable of angular but not axial movement. The outer joints should be cleaned, inspected and repacked, but they cannot be disassembled. If an outer joint is damaged, it must be renewed along with the driveshaft (the outer joint and driveshaft are sold as a single component).

4 The gaiters should be inspected periodically for damage and leaking lubricant. Torn CV joint gaiters must be renewed immediately or the joints can be damaged. Gaiter renewal involves removal of the driveshaft (see Section 2). **Note:** *Some motor accessory/parts stores carry 'split' type renewal gaiters, which can be fitted without removing the driveshaft from the vehicle. This is a convenient alternative; however, the driveshaft should be removed and the CV joint disassembled and cleaned to ensure the joint is free from contaminants such as moisture and dirt which will accelerate CV joint wear.* The most common symptom of worn or damaged CV joints, besides lubricant leaks, is a clicking noise in turns, a clunk when accelerating after coasting, and vibration at highway speeds. To check for wear in the CV joints and driveshaft shafts, grasp each driveshaft (one at a time) and rotate it in both directions while holding the CV joint housings, feeling for play indicating worn splines or sloppy CV joints. Also check the driveshaft shafts for cracks, dents and distortion.

2 Driveshafts – removal and refitting

Removal

1 Loosen the front wheel nuts, raise the vehicle and support it securely on axle stands (see *Jacking and vehicle support*). Remove the wheel.

2 Using a small chisel, release the locking tab from the groove in the end of the driveshaft and remove the driveshaft hub nut **(see illustration)**.

3 To prevent the hub from turning, wedge a lever between two of the wheel studs and allow the lever to rest against the ground or the floor of the vehicle. Alternatively make up a special tool with a length of bar to fit on two of the wheel studs **(see illustration)**.

4 To loosen the driveshaft from the hub splines, tap the end of the driveshaft with a soft-faced hammer or a hammer and a brass punch. **Note:** *Don't attempt to push the end of the driveshaft through the hub yet. Applying force to the end of the driveshaft, beyond just breaking it loose from the hub, can damage the driveshaft or transmission.* If the driveshaft is stuck in the hub splines and won't move, it may be necessary to remove the brake disc (see Chapter 9) and push it from the hub with a two-jaw puller after the procedure in paragraph 6 is performed.

5 Release the screws and remove the engine undertrays. Place a drain pan underneath the transmission to catch the lubricant that will spill out when the driveshafts are removed.

6 Remove the nuts and bolt securing the balljoint to the control arm, then lever the control arm down to separate the components (see Chapter 10)

7 Pull out on the hub carrier and detach the driveshaft from the hub **(see illustration)**. Don't let the driveshaft hang by the inner CV joint after the outer end has been detached from the hub carrier, as the inner joint could become damaged. Support the outer end of the driveshaft with a piece of wire, if necessary.

8 On right-hand side driveshafts, undo the mounting bolts from the centre bearing assembly to the cylinder block **(see illustration)**.

9 Carefully lever the inner CV joint out of the transmission – you may need to give the lever bar a sharp rap with a soft hammer **(see illustration)**.

10 Refer to Chapter 7A or 7B for the driveshaft oil seal renewal procedure.

Refitting

11 Refitting is the reverse of the removal procedure, but with the following additional points:

a) *Push the driveshaft sharply in to seat the retaining ring on the inner CV joint in the groove in the differential side gear.*
b) *Tighten the driveshaft hub nut to*

2.7 Pull the hub carrier out and slide the end of the driveshaft out of the hub

2.8 Right-hand driveshaft centre bearing (arrowed)

2.9 To separate the end of the driveshaft from the transmission, lever on the CV joint housing

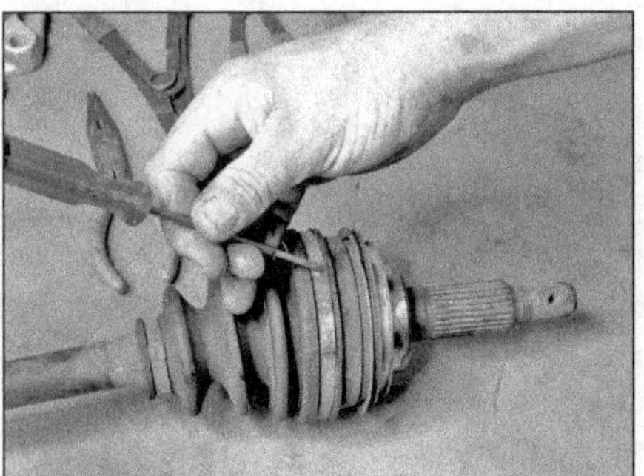

3.3 Lift the tabs on all the gaiter clamps with a screwdriver, then open the clamps

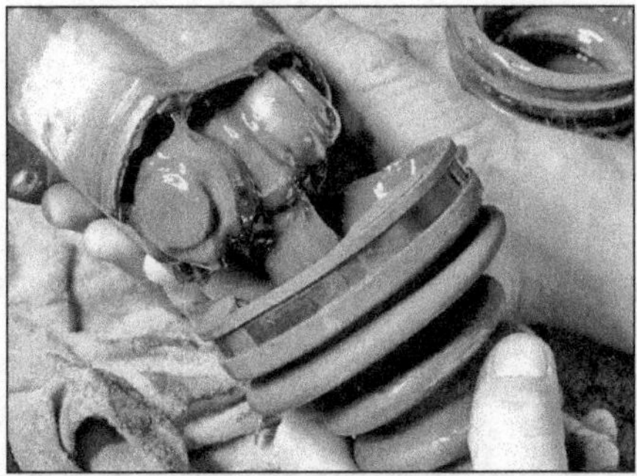

3.4 Remove the gaiter from the inner CV joint and slide the joint housing from the tripod

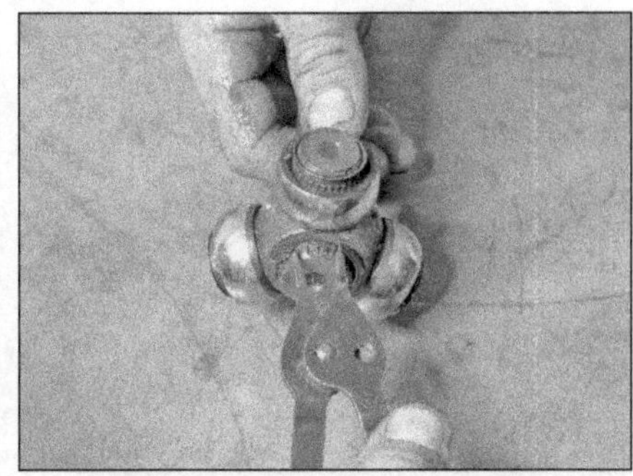

3.6 Remove the circlip with a pair of circlip pliers

the torque listed in this Chapter's Specifications, then install the locking cap and a new split pin.

c) Refit the wheel and nuts, lower the vehicle and tighten the nuts to the torque listed in the Specifications.

d) Check the transmission lubricant and add, if necessary, to bring it to the proper level (see Chapter 1A or 1B).

3 Driveshaft gaiter renewal and CV joint inspection

Note: *If the CV joints must be overhauled (usually due to torn gaiters), explore all options before beginning the job. Complete rebuilt driveshafts are available on an exchange basis, which eliminates much time and work. Whichever route you choose to take, check on the cost and availability of parts before disassembling the vehicle.*

1 Remove the driveshaft (see Section 2).

Disassembly

2 Mount the driveshaft in a vice with wood-lined jaws (to prevent damage to the driveshaft). Check the CV joint for excessive play in the radial direction, which indicates worn parts. Check for smooth operation throughout the full range of motion for each CV joint. If a gaiter is torn, disassemble the joint, clean the components and inspect for damage due to loss of lubrication and possible contamination by foreign matter.

3 Working on the inboard joint, using a small screwdriver, lever the retaining tabs on the clamps up to loosen them and slide them off **(see illustration)**.

4 Using a screwdriver, carefully lever up on the edge of the outer gaiter and push it away from the CV joint. Old and worn gaiters can be cut off. Pull the inner CV joint gaiter back from the housing and slide the housing from the tripod **(see illustration)**.

5 Mark the tripod and driveshaft to ensure that they are reassembled properly.

6 Remove the tripod joint circlip with a pair of circlip pliers **(see illustration)**.

7 Use a hammer and a brass punch to drive the tripod joint from the driveshaft; be careful not to damage the bearing surfaces or the splines on the shaft **(see illustration)**.

8 If you haven't already cut them off, remove both gaiters. Where fitted, cut off the clamp for the dynamic damper and slide the damper off, after first marking its position for reassembly.

9 Do not disassemble the outer joint.

Check

10 Thoroughly clean all components, including the outer CV joint assembly, with solvent until the old CV joint grease is completely removed. Inspect the bearing surfaces of the inner tripods and housings for cracks, pitting, scoring and other signs of wear. It's very difficult to inspect the bearing surfaces of the inner and outer races of the outer CV joint, but you can at least check the surfaces of the ball-bearings themselves. If they're in good shape, the races probably are too; if they're not, neither are the races. If the inner CV joint is worn, you can buy a new inner CV joint and install it on the old driveshaft; if the outer CV joint is worn, you'll have to purchase a new outer CV joint *and* driveshaft (they're sold preassembled).

Reassembly

11 Where fitted, be sure to install the dynamic damper and a new clamp onto the shaft, before installing the inner gaiter **(see illustration)**. See Specifications for the distance required for the fitment of the damper.

12 Wrap the splines on the end of the driveshaft with electrical tape to protect the gaiters from the sharp edges of the splines **(see illustrations)**. Slide the clamps and gaiter(s) onto the driveshaft, and then place the tripod on the shaft. Apply grease to the tripod assembly and inside the housing. Insert

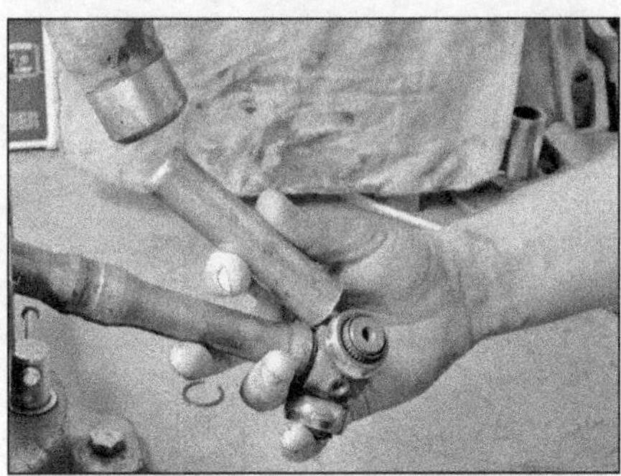

3.7 Drive the tripod joint from the driveshaft with a brass punch and hammer

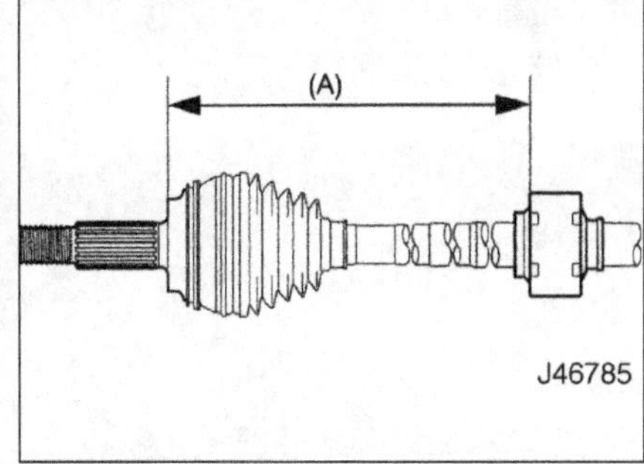

3.11 Measurement (A) distance for dynamic damper

3.12a Wrap the splined areas of the driveshaft with tape to prevent damage to the gaiters

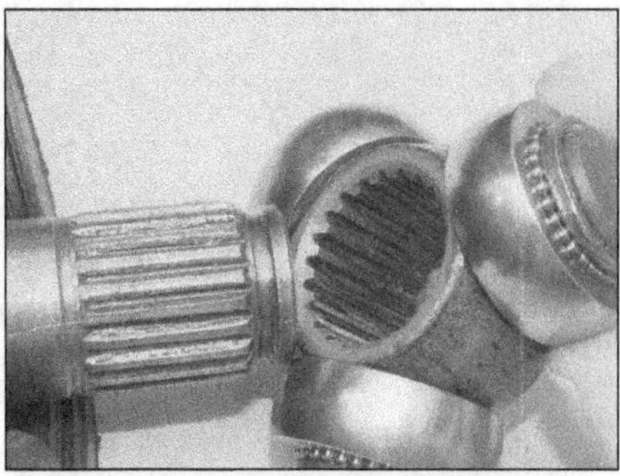

3.12b Fit the tripod with the chamfered section facing the driveshaft

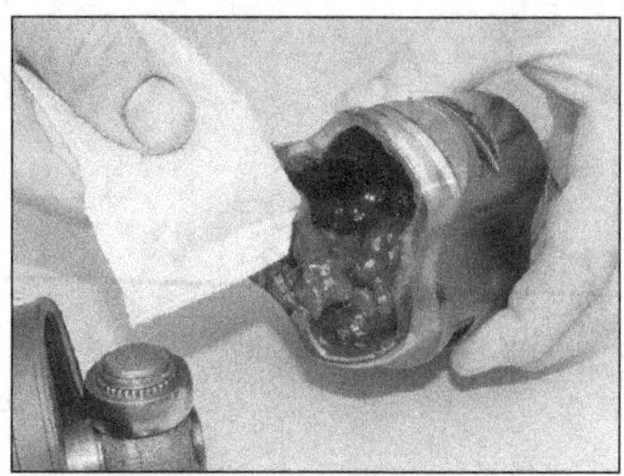
3.12c Apply the supplied grease to the joint housing

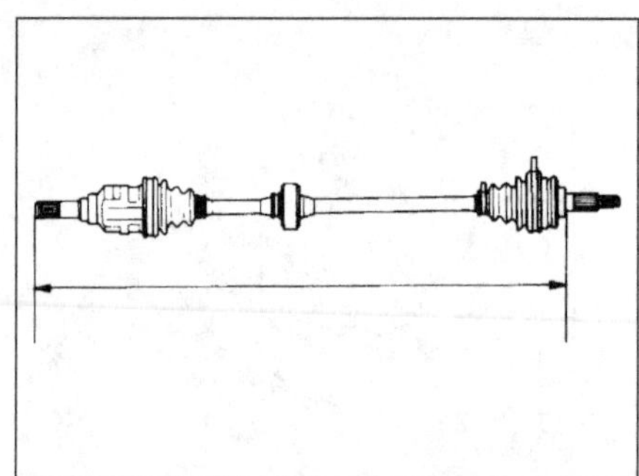
3.13 The driveshaft standard length should be set before the gaiter clamps are tightened

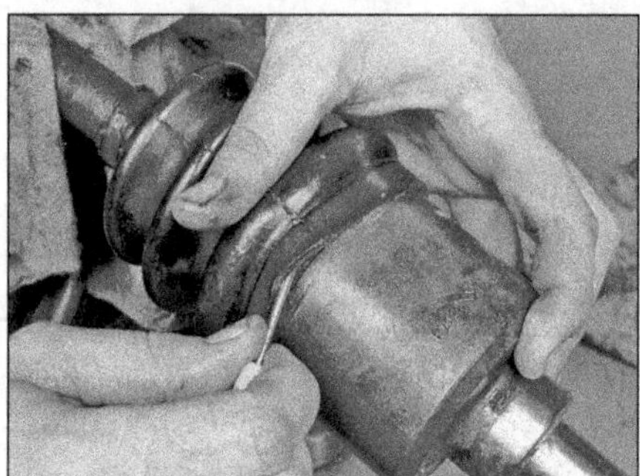
3.14a Equalise the pressure in the gaiter with a screwdriver between the gaiter and the housing

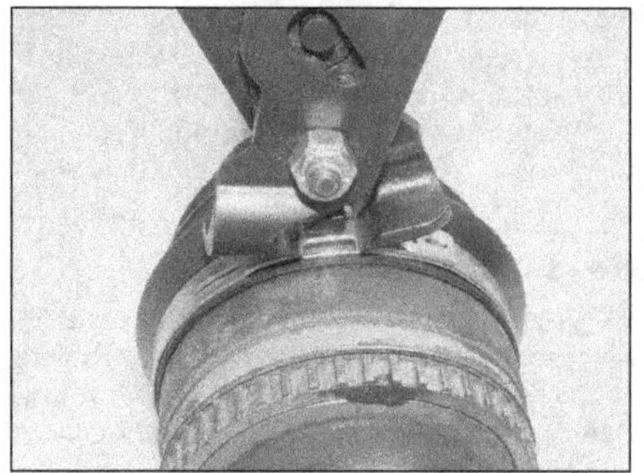
3.14b Use pincers . . .

3.14c . . . to tighten the gaiter clamps

the tripod into the housing and pack the remainder of the grease around the tripod.

13 Slide the gaiter into place, making sure both ends seat in their grooves. Adjust the length of the driveshaft to the dimension listed in this Chapter's Specifications **(see illustration)**.

14 Equalise the pressure in the gaiter, then tighten and secure the gaiter clamps **(see illustrations)**.

Chapter 9
Braking system

Contents

Degrees of difficulty

Easy, suitable for novice with little experience 	**Fairly easy,** suitable for beginner with some experience	**Fairly difficult,** suitable for competent DIY mechanic	**Difficult,** suitable for experienced DIY mechanic	**Very difficult,** suitable for expert DIY or professional 

Specifications

Front disc brakes

Type	Disc, with single-piston sliding caliper
Disc thickness:	
New	25.0 mm
Minimum	23.0 mm
Maximum disc run-out	0.05 mm
Brake pad friction material thickness:	
Petrol models:	
New	11.0 mm
Minimum	1.0 mm
Diesel models:	
New	11.5 mm
Minimum	1.0 mm

Rear disc brakes

Type	Disc, with single-piston sliding caliper
Disc thickness:	
New	9.0 mm
Minimum	8.0 mm
Maximum disc run-out	0.15 mm
Brake pad friction material thickness:	
New	10.0 mm
Minimum	1.0 mm

Handbrake

Inside disc diameter:	
New	173.0 mm
Maximum	174.0 mm
Handbrake shoe friction material thickness:	
New	3.5 mm
Minimum	1.0 mm

Brake pedal

Height from floor to centre of pedal pad:	
LHD	134.9 to 144.9 mm
RHD	131.6 to 141.6 mm

Torque wrench settings

	Nm	lbf ft
Front brake caliper:		
Guide pin bolts	34	25
Mounting bracket bolts	107	79
Handbrake lever nuts	15	11
Hydraulic hose/pipe union nuts	15	11
Master cylinder retaining nuts	25	18
Rear brake caliper:		
Guide pin bolts	27	20
Mounting bracket	47	35
Roadwheel nuts	103	76
Vacuum pump	27	20
Vacuum servo unit mounting nuts	13	10
Vacuum servo unit pushrod nut	25	18
Wheel speed sensor	8	6

1 General information

The braking system is of the servo-assisted, dual-circuit hydraulic type. The arrangement of the hydraulic system is such that each circuit operates one front and one rear brake from a tandem master cylinder. Under normal circumstances, both circuits operate in unison. However, in the event of hydraulic failure in one circuit, full braking force will still be available at two wheels.

All models are equipped with disc brakes at the front and the rear. ABS is fitted as standard (refer to Section 20 for further information on ABS operation). The disc brakes are actuated by single-piston sliding type calipers, which ensure that equal pressure is applied to each disc pad.

On all models, the handbrake provides an independent mechanical means of rear brake application. The handbrake operates the rear brake shoes by means of a floor-mounted lever and two cables. These cables operate separate handbrake shoes within the rear drum-in-disc arrangement.

Note: *When servicing any of the system, work carefully and methodically; also observe scrupulous cleanliness when overhauling any of the hydraulic system. Always renew components (in axle sets, where applicable) if in doubt about their condition, and use only genuine Toyota parts, or at least those of known good quality. Note the warnings given in 'Safety first!' and at relevant points in this Chapter concerning the dangers of asbestos dust and hydraulic fluid.*

2 Hydraulic system – bleeding

Warning: Hydraulic fluid is poisonous; wash off immediately and thoroughly in the case of skin contact, and seek immediate medical advice if any fluid is swallowed or gets into the eyes. Certain types of hydraulic fluid are inflammable, and may ignite when allowed into contact with hot components; when servicing any hydraulic system, it is safest to assume that the fluid is inflammable, and to take precautions against the risk of fire as though it is petrol that is being handled. Hydraulic fluid is also an effective paint stripper, and will attack plastics; if any is spilt, it should be washed off immediately, using copious quantities of fresh water. Finally, it is hygroscopic (it absorbs moisture from the air) – old fluid may be contaminated and unfit for further use. When topping-up or renewing the fluid, always use the recommended type, and ensure that it comes from a freshly-opened sealed container.

Caution: Ensure the ignition is switched off before starting the bleeding procedure to avoid any possibility of voltage being applied to the hydraulic modulator before the bleeding procedure is complete. Ideally, the battery should be disconnected. If voltage is applied to the modulator before the bleeding procedure is complete, this will effectively drain the hydraulic fluid in the modulator, rendering the unit unserviceable. Do not, therefore, attempt to 'run' the modulator in order to bleed the brakes.

General

1 The correct operation of any hydraulic system is only possible after removing all air from the components and circuit; this is achieved by bleeding the system.

2 During the bleeding procedure, add only clean, unused hydraulic fluid of the recommended type; never re-use fluid that has already been bled from the system. Ensure that sufficient fluid is available before starting work.

3 If there is any possibility of incorrect fluid being already in the system, the brake components and circuit must be flushed completely with uncontaminated, correct fluid, and new seals should be fitted to the various components.

4 If hydraulic fluid has been lost from the system, or air has entered because of a leak, ensure that the fault is cured before proceeding further.

5 Park the vehicle on level ground, switch off the engine and select first or reverse gear, then chock the wheels and release the handbrake.

6 Check that all pipes and hoses are secure, unions tight and bleed screws closed. Clean any dirt from around the bleed screws.

7 Unscrew the master cylinder reservoir cap, and top the master cylinder reservoir up to the MAX level line; refit the cap loosely, and remember to maintain the fluid level at least above the MIN level line throughout the procedure, or there is a risk of further air entering the system.

8 There is a number of one-man, do-it-yourself brake bleeding kits currently available from motor accessory shops. It is recommended that one of these kits is used whenever possible, as they greatly simplify the bleeding operation, and also reduce the risk of expelled air and fluid being drawn back into the system. If such a kit is not available, the basic (two-man) method must be used, which is described in detail below.

9 If a kit is to be used, prepare the vehicle as described previously, and follow the kit manufacturer's instructions, as the procedure may vary slightly according to the type being used; generally, they are as outlined below in the relevant sub-section.

10 Whichever method is used, the same sequence must be followed (paragraphs 11 and 12) to ensure that the removal of all air from the system.

Bleeding

Sequence

11 If the system has been only partially disconnected, and suitable precautions were taken to minimise fluid loss, it should be necessary only to bleed that of the system (ie, the primary or secondary circuit).

12 If the complete system is to be bled, then it should be done working in the following sequence:

a) Left-hand front brake.
b) Right-hand front brake.
c) Left-hand rear brake.
d) Right-hand rear brake.

Basic (two-man) method

13 Collect a clean glass jar, a suitable length of plastic or rubber tubing which is a tight fit over the bleed screw, and a ring spanner to fit the screw **(see illustration)**. The help of an assistant will also be required.

14 Remove the dust cap from the first screw in the sequence. Fit the spanner and tube to the screw, place the other end of the tube in the jar, and pour in sufficient fluid to cover the end of the tube.

15 Ensure that the master cylinder reservoir fluid level is maintained at least above the MIN level line throughout the procedure.

16 Have the assistant fully depress the brake pedal several times to build-up pressure, then maintain it on the final down stroke.

17 While pedal pressure is maintained, unscrew the bleed screw (approximately one turn) and allow the compressed fluid and air to flow into the jar. The assistant should maintain pedal pressure, following it down to the floor if necessary, and should not release it until instructed to do so. When the flow stops, tighten the bleed screw again, have the assistant release the pedal slowly, and recheck the reservoir fluid level.

18 Repeat the steps given in paragraphs 16 and 17 until the fluid emerging from the bleed screw is free from air bubbles. If the master cylinder has been drained and refilled, and air is being bled from the first screw in the sequence, allow approximately five seconds between cycles for the master cylinder passages to refill.

19 When no more air bubbles appear, tighten the bleed screw securely, remove the tube and spanner, and refit the dust cap. Do not overtighten the bleed screw.

20 Repeat the procedure on the remaining screws in the sequence, until all air is removed from the system and the brake pedal feels firm again.

Using a one-way valve kit

21 As their name implies, these kits consist of a length of tubing with a one-way valve fitted, to prevent expelled air and fluid being drawn back into the system; some kits include a translucent container, which can be positioned so that the air bubbles can be more easily seen flowing from the end of the tube.

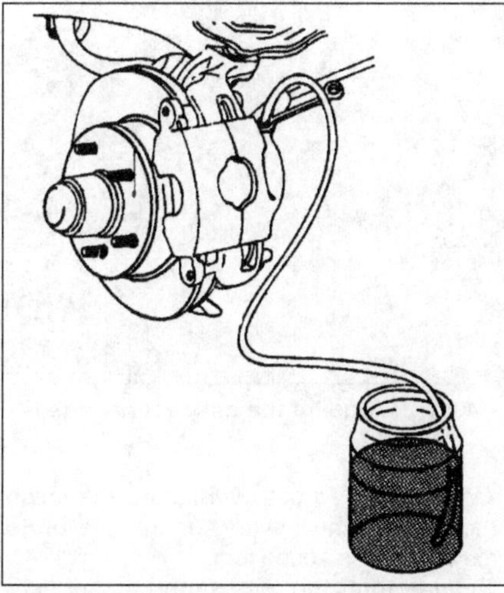

2.13 When bleeding the brakes, a hose is connected to the bleed screw at the caliper

22 The kit is connected to the bleed screw, which is then opened. The user returns to the driver's seat, depresses the brake pedal with a smooth, steady stroke, and slowly releases it; this is repeated until the expelled fluid is clear of air bubbles.

23 Note that these kits simplify work so much that it is easy to forget the master cylinder reservoir fluid level; ensure that this is maintained at least above the MIN level line at all times.

Using a pressure-bleeding kit

24 These kits are usually operated by the reservoir of pressurised air contained in the spare tyre. However, note that it will probably be necessary to reduce the pressure to a lower level than normal; refer to the instructions supplied with the kit.

25 By connecting a pressurised, fluid-filled container to the master cylinder reservoir, bleeding can be carried out simply by opening each screw in turn (in the specified sequence), and allowing the fluid to flow out until no more air bubbles can be seen in the expelled fluid.

26 This method has the advantage that the large reservoir of fluid provides an additional safeguard against air being drawn into the system during bleeding.

27 Pressure-bleeding is particularly effective when bleeding 'difficult' systems, or when bleeding the complete system at the time of routine fluid renewal.

All methods

28 When bleeding is complete, and firm pedal feel is restored, wash off any spilt fluid, tighten the bleed screws securely, and refit their dust caps.

29 Check the hydraulic fluid level in the master cylinder reservoir, and top-up if necessary (see *Weekly checks*).

30 Discard any hydraulic fluid that has been bled from the system; it will not be fit for re-use.

31 Check the feel of the brake pedal. If it feels at all spongy, air must still be present in the system, and further bleeding is required. Failure to bleed satisfactorily after a reasonable repetition of the bleeding procedure may be due to worn master cylinder seals.

3 Hydraulic pipes and hoses – renewal

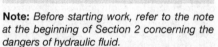

Note: *Before starting work, refer to the note at the beginning of Section 2 concerning the dangers of hydraulic fluid.*

1 If any pipe or hose is to be renewed, minimise fluid loss by first removing the master cylinder reservoir cap, then tightening it down onto a piece of polythene to obtain an airtight seal. Alternatively, flexible hoses can be sealed, if required, using a proprietary brake hose clamp **(see illustration)**; metal brake pipe unions can be plugged (if care is taken not to allow dirt into the system) or capped immediately they are disconnected. Place a wad of rag under any union that is to be disconnected to catch any spilt fluid.

2 If a flexible hose is to be disconnected, unscrew the brake pipe union nut before removing the spring clip which secures the hose to its mounting bracket **(see illustrations)**.

3 To unscrew the union nuts, it is preferable to obtain a brake pipe (flare-nut) spanner of the correct size; these are available from most large motor accessory shops. Failing this, a close-fitting open-ended spanner will be required, though if the nuts are tight or corroded, their flats may be rounded-off if the

3.1 Use a proprietary hose clamp to seal the rubber flexible hoses

3.2a Unscrew the brake pipe threaded fitting with a flare-nut spanner to protect the union corners from being rounded off

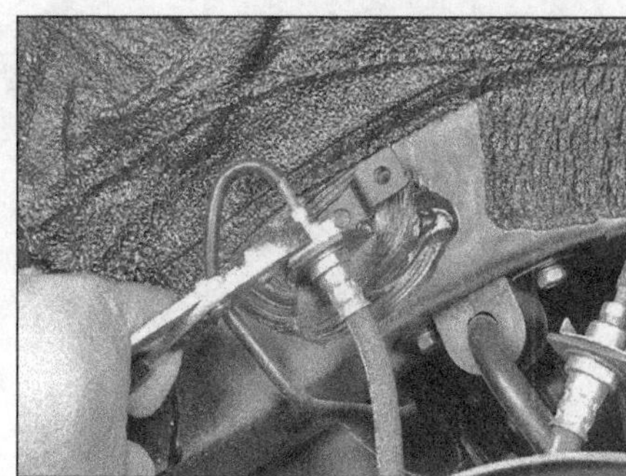

3.2b Pull of the union clip with a pair of pliers

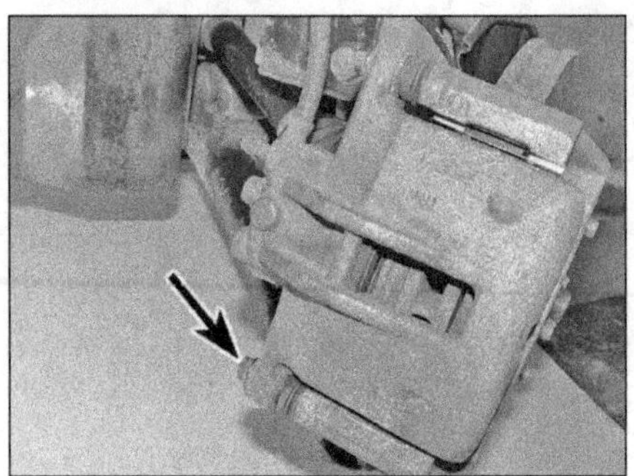

4.3a Remove the lower guide pin bolt (arrowed) . . .

4.3b . . . and lift the caliper upwards

4.4 Remove the anti-squeal disc from the piston

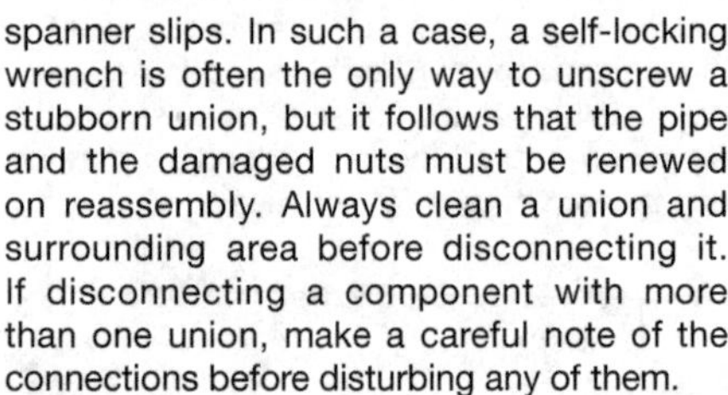

spanner slips. In such a case, a self-locking wrench is often the only way to unscrew a stubborn union, but it follows that the pipe and the damaged nuts must be renewed on reassembly. Always clean a union and surrounding area before disconnecting it. If disconnecting a component with more than one union, make a careful note of the connections before disturbing any of them.

4 If a brake pipe is to be renewed, it can be obtained, cut to length and with the union nuts and end flares in place, from Toyota dealers. All that is then necessary is to bend it to shape, following the line of the original, before fitting it to the car. Alternatively, most motor accessory shops can make up brake pipes from kits, but this requires very careful measurement of the original, to ensure that the new one is of the correct length. The safest answer is usually to take the original to the shop as a pattern.

5 On refitting, do not overtighten the union nuts. It is not necessary to exercise brute force to obtain a sound joint.

6 Ensure that the pipes and hoses are correctly routed, with no kinks, and that they are secured in the clips or brackets provided. After fitting, remove the polythene from the reservoir, and bleed the hydraulic system as described in Section 2. When all work is completed, wash off any spilt fluid, and check carefully for fluid leaks.

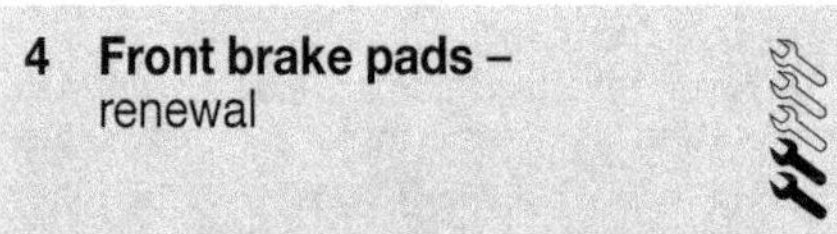

4 Front brake pads – renewal

Warning: Renew both sets of front brake pads at the same time – never renew the pads on only one wheel, as uneven braking may result. Note that the dust created by wear of the pads may contain asbestos, which is a health hazard. Never blow it out with compressed air, and don't inhale any of it. An approved filtering mask should be worn when working on the brakes. DO NOT use petrol or petroleum-based solvents to clean brake parts; use brake cleaner or methylated spirit only.

1 Apply the handbrake, slacken the front roadwheel nuts, then jack up the front of the vehicle and support it on axle stands (see *Jacking and vehicle support*). Remove the front roadwheels.

2 Push the piston into its bore by pulling the caliper outwards.

3 Undo the lower guide pin bolt and swivel the caliper upwards **(illustrations)**.

4 If required, unclip the anti-squeal disc from the caliper piston **(illustration)**.

5 Remove the inner and outer brake pad from the caliper mounting bracket **(illustrations)**.

6 Check the brake pad upper and lower support plates, if worn or distorted they will need to be renewed **(illustration)**.

7 If new brake pads are to be fitted, the caliper piston must be pushed back into the cylinder to make room for them. Either use a G-clamp or similar tool, or use suitable pieces of wood as levers **(illustration)**.

Caution: Pushing back the piston causes a reverse-flow of brake fluid, which has been known to 'flip' the master cylinder rubber seals, resulting in a total loss of braking. To avoid this, clamp the caliper flexible hose and open the bleed screw – as the piston is pushed back, the fluid can be directed into a suitable container using a hose attached to the bleed screw. Close the screw just before the piston is pushed fully back, to ensure no air enters the system.

8 Use a ruler to check the thickness of the friction material on the brake pads and compare it with the specifications at the beginning of this Chapter **(see illustration)**. If either pad is worn at any point to the specified minimum thickness or less, all four pads must be renewed. Also, the pads should be renewed if any are fouled with oil or grease; there is no satisfactory way of degreasing friction material, once

4.5a Remove the inner brake pad . . .

4.5b . . . and the outer brake pad

4.6 Check the upper and lower retaining plates

4.7 Using a special tool to push the piston back

contaminated. If any of the brake pads are worn unevenly, or fouled with oil or grease, trace and rectify the cause before reassembly.

9 If the brake pads are still serviceable, carefully clean them using a clean, fine wire brush or similar, paying particular attention to the sides and back of the metal backing. Clean out the grooves in the friction material, and pick out any large embedded particles of dirt or debris. Carefully clean the pad locations in the caliper body/mounting bracket.

10 Prior to fitting the pads, check that the guide pins are free to slide easily in the caliper body, and check that the rubber guide pin gaiters are undamaged. Brush the dust and dirt from the caliper and piston, but **do not** inhale it, as it is a health hazard. Inspect the dust seal around the piston for damage, and the piston for evidence of fluid leaks, corrosion or damage. If attention to any of these components is necessary, refer to Section 8.

11 Make sure the brake pad support plates are located in the mounting bracket correctly and apply a small amount of high-temperature grease.

12 Apply a small amount of high-temperature grease to the rear metal part of the brake pads and refit them to the caliper mounting bracket.

13 If removed refit the anti-squeal disc to the caliper piston **(illustration)**.

14 Swivel the caliper back into place over the brake pads and tighten the guide pin bolts to the specified torque setting.

15 Depress the brake pedal repeatedly, until the pads are pressed into firm contact with the brake disc, and normal (non-assisted) pedal pressure is restored.

16 Repeat the above procedure on the remaining front brake caliper.

17 Refit the roadwheels, then lower the vehicle to the ground and tighten the roadwheel nuts to the specified torque.

18 Check the hydraulic fluid level as described in *Weekly checks*.

Caution: New pads will not give full braking efficiency until they have bedded-in. Be prepared for this, and avoid hard braking as far as possible for the first hundred miles or so after pad renewal.

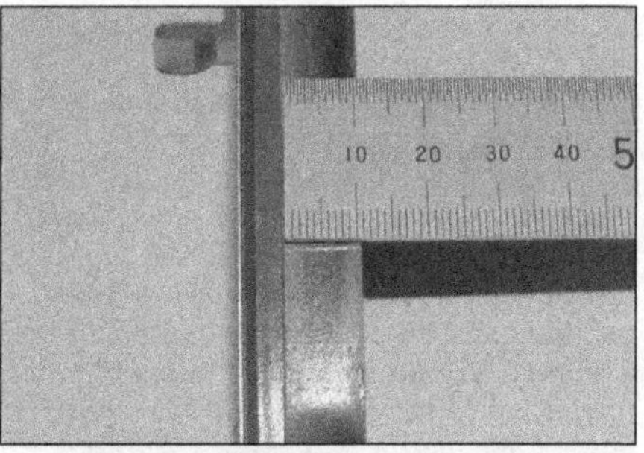

4.8 Measure the thickness of the pad's friction material; if it's less than specified, renew all four pads

4.13 Refit the anti-squeal disc

5 Rear brake pads – renewal

Warning: Renew both sets of rear brake pads at the same time – never renew the pads on only one wheel, as uneven braking may result. Note that the dust created by wear of the pads may contain asbestos, which is a health hazard. Never blow it out with compressed air, and don't inhale any of it. An approved filtering mask should be worn when working on the brakes. DO NOT use petrol or petroleum-based solvents to clean brake parts; use brake cleaner or methylated spirit only.

1 Chock the front wheels, slacken the rear roadwheel nuts, and then jack up the rear of the vehicle and support it on axle stands (see *Jacking and vehicle support*). Remove the rear roadwheels.

2 Slacken and remove the caliper guide pin bolts, and move the caliper, supporting it on the rear suspension arm **(illustrations)**. Do not let it hang on the brake hose.

3 Withdraw the inner and outer pads from the caliper bracket **(see illustration)**.

4 Recover the upper and lower pad support plates from the caliper mounting bracket **(see illustration)**.

5 First measure the thickness of the friction material of each brake pad **(see illustration 4.8)**. If either pad is worn at any point to the specified minimum thickness or less, all four pads must be renewed. Also, the pads should be renewed if any are fouled with oil or grease; there is no satisfactory way of degreasing friction material, once contaminated. If any of the brake pads are worn unevenly, or fouled with oil or grease, trace and rectify the cause before reassembly.

5.2a Undo the caliper guide pin bolts . . .

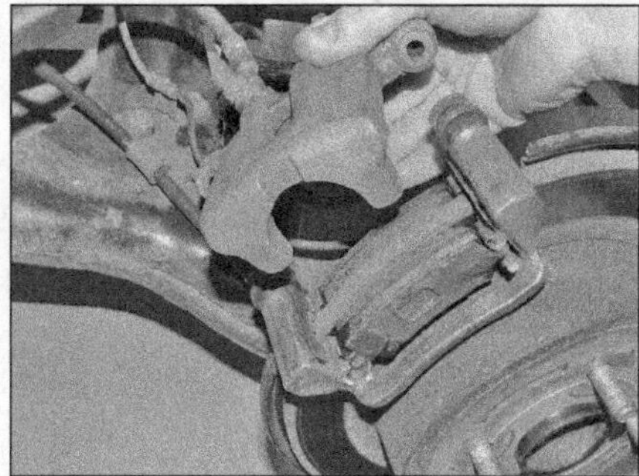

5.2b . . . remove the caliper . . .

5.2c . . . rest the caliper on the rear suspension arm

5.3 Remove the brake pads

5.4 Check the upper and lower retaining plates

5.8 Using a G-clamp to push back the piston

6 If the brake pads are still serviceable, carefully clean them using a clean, fine wire brush or similar, paying particular attention to the sides and back of the metal backing. Clean out the grooves in the friction material, and pick out any large embedded particles of dirt or debris. Carefully clean the pad locations in the caliper body/mounting bracket.

7 Prior to fitting the pads, check that the guide pins are free to slide easily in the caliper body, and check that the rubber guide pin gaiters are undamaged. Brush the dust and dirt from the caliper and piston, but **do not** inhale it, as it is a health hazard. Inspect the dust seal around the piston for damage, and the piston for evidence of fluid leaks, corrosion or damage. If attention to any of these components is necessary, refer to Section 9.

8 If new brake pads are to be fitted, the caliper piston must be pushed back into the cylinder to make room for them. Either use a G-clamp or similar tool, or use suitable pieces of wood as levers **(illustration)**.

Caution: Pushing back the piston causes a reverse-flow of brake fluid, which has been known to 'flip' the master cylinder rubber seals, resulting in a total loss of braking. To avoid this, clamp the caliper flexible hose and open the bleed screw – as the piston is pushed back, the fluid can be directed into a suitable container using a hose attached to the bleed screw. Close the screw just before the piston is pushed fully back, to ensure no air enters the system.

9 Make sure the brake pad support plates are located in the mounting bracket correctly and apply a small amount of high-temperature grease.

10 Slide the brake pads into position in the caliper mounting bracket, ensuring each pad's friction material is facing the brake disc. Apply a small amount of high-temperature grease to the rear metal part of the brake pads.

11 Refit the caliper over the brake pads and tighten the guide pin bolts to the specified torque setting.

12 Depress the brake pedal repeatedly until the pads are pressed into firm contact with the brake disc, and normal (non-assisted) pedal pressure is restored.

13 Repeat the above procedure on the remaining rear brake caliper.

14 Refit the roadwheels, then lower the vehicle to the ground and tighten the roadwheel nuts to the specified torque setting.

15 Check the hydraulic fluid level as described in *Weekly checks*.

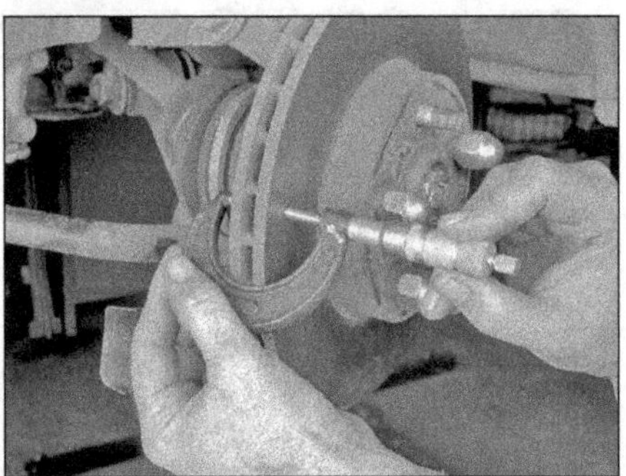

6.3 Use a micrometer to measure the disc thickness

6.4 To check disc run-out, mount a dial indicator as shown and rotate the disc

6.6a Undo the two caliper mounting bracket bolts (arrowed) . . .

6.6b . . . and remove the caliper mounting bracket

Caution: New pads will not give full braking efficiency until they have bedded-in. Be prepared for this, and avoid hard braking as far as possible for the first hundred miles or so after pad renewal.

6 Front brake disc – inspection, removal and refitting

Note: *Before starting work, refer to the note at the beginning of Section 4 concerning the dangers of asbestos dust.*

Inspection

Note: *If either disc requires renewal, BOTH should be renewed at the same time, to ensure even and consistent braking. New brake pads should also be fitted.*

1 Apply the handbrake, slacken the front roadwheel nuts, then jack up the front of the car and support it on axle stands (see *Jacking and vehicle support*). Remove the appropriate front roadwheel.

2 Slowly rotate the brake disc so that the full area of both sides can be checked; remove the brake pads if better access is required to the inboard surface. Light scoring is normal in the area swept by the brake pads, but if heavy scoring or cracks are found, the disc must be renewed.

3 It is normal to find a lip of rust and brake dust around the disc's perimeter; this can be scraped off if required. If, however, a lip has formed due to excessive wear of the brake pad swept area, then the disc's thickness must be measured using a micrometer. Take measurements at several places around the disc, at the inside and outside of the pad swept area; if the disc has worn at any point to the specified minimum thickness or less, the disc must be renewed **(see illustration)**.

4 If the disc is thought to be warped, it can be checked for run-out. Either use a dial gauge mounted on any convenient fixed point, while the disc is slowly rotated, or use feeler blades to measure (at several points all around the disc) the clearance between the disc and a fixed point, such as the caliper mounting bracket **(see illustration)**. If the measurements obtained are at the specified maximum or beyond, the disc is excessively warped and must be renewed; however, it is worth checking first that the hub bearing is in good condition (Chapter 1A or 1B). Also try the effect of removing the disc and turning it through 180°, to reposition it on the hub; if the run-out is still excessive, the disc must be renewed.

5 Check the disc for cracks, especially around the wheel bolt holes, and any other wear or damage, and renew if necessary.

Removal

6 With the caliper removed (see Section 8), slacken and remove the two bolts securing the brake caliper mounting bracket to the hub carrier, and remove it from the disc **(see illustrations)**.

7 Use chalk or paint to mark the relationship of the disc to the hub, and then remove the disc. If it is tight, lightly tap its rear face with a hide or plastic mallet **(see illustration)**.

Refitting

8 Refitting is the reverse of the removal procedure, noting the following points:

a) *Ensure that the mating surfaces of the disc and hub are clean and flat.*
b) *Align (if applicable) the marks made on removal.*
c) *If a new disc has been fitted, use a suitable solvent to wipe any preservative coating from the disc before refitting the caliper.*
d) *Refit the roadwheel then lower the vehicle to the ground and tighten the wheel bolts to the specified torque. Apply the footbrake several times to force the pads back into contact with the disc before driving the vehicle.*

6.7 Remove the brake disc

7.3a Undo the two caliper mounting bracket bolts (arrowed) . . .

7 Rear brake disc – inspection, removal and refitting

Note: *Before starting work, refer to the note at the beginning of Section 5 concerning the dangers of asbestos dust.*

Inspection

Note: *If either disc requires renewal, BOTH should be renewed at the same time, to ensure even and consistent braking. New brake pads should also be fitted.*

1 Firmly chock the front wheels, slacken the appropriate rear roadwheel nuts, and then jack up the rear of the car and support it on axle stands (see *Jacking and vehicle support*). Remove the relevant rear roadwheel.

2 Inspect the disc as described in Section 6.

Removal

3 With the caliper removed (see Section 9), slacken and remove the two bolts securing the brake caliper mounting bracket to the hub carrier, and remove it from the disc **(see illustrations)**.

4 Use chalk or paint to mark the relationship of the disc to the hub, and then remove the disc.

5 If the disc is tight, slacken the handbrake as described in Section 15, and then thread two bolts into the centre of the disc and tighten them evenly to push the disc off **(see illustration)**.

Refitting

6 Refitting is the reverse of the removal procedure, noting the following points:

a) *Ensure that the mating surfaces of the disc and hub are clean and flat.*
b) *Align (if applicable) the marks made on removal.*
c) *If a new disc has been fitted, use a suitable solvent to wipe any preservative coating from the disc before refitting the caliper.*
d) *Refit the roadwheel, then lower the vehicle to the ground and tighten the roadwheel nuts to the specified torque. Depress the brake pedal several times to force the pads back into contact with the disc.*

7.3b . . . and remove the caliper mounting bracket

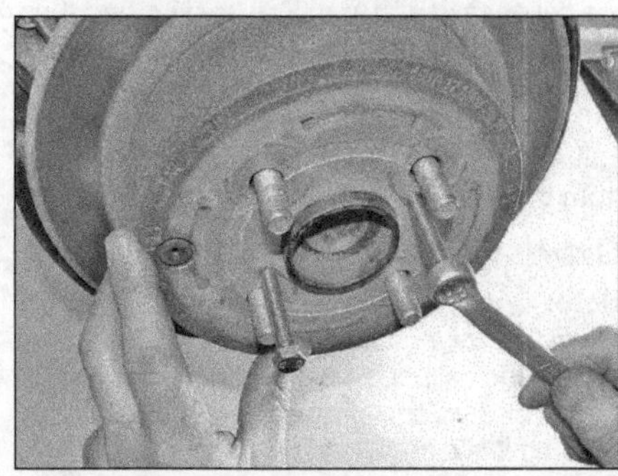
7.5 Using two bolts to push the disc off the hub

8 Front brake caliper – removal, overhaul and refitting

Caution: Ensure the ignition is switched off before disconnecting any braking system hydraulic union and do not switch it on until after the hydraulic system has been bled. Failure to do this could lead to air entering the modulator unit.

Note: *Before starting work, refer to the note at the beginning of Section 2 concerning the dangers of hydraulic fluid, and to the warning at the beginning of Section 4 concerning the dangers of asbestos dust.*

Removal

1 Apply the handbrake, slacken the relevant front roadwheel nuts, then jack up the front of the vehicle and support it on axle stands (see *Jacking and vehicle support*). Remove the appropriate roadwheel.

2 Minimise fluid loss by first removing the master cylinder reservoir cap, and then tightening it down onto a piece of polythene, to obtain an airtight seal. Alternatively, use a brake hose clamp, a G-clamp or a similar tool to clamp the flexible hose **(see illustration 3.1)**.

3 Clean the area around the caliper hose union, then loosen the union **(see illustration)**.

4 Slacken and remove the upper and lower caliper guide pin bolts **(see illustrations)**. Lift

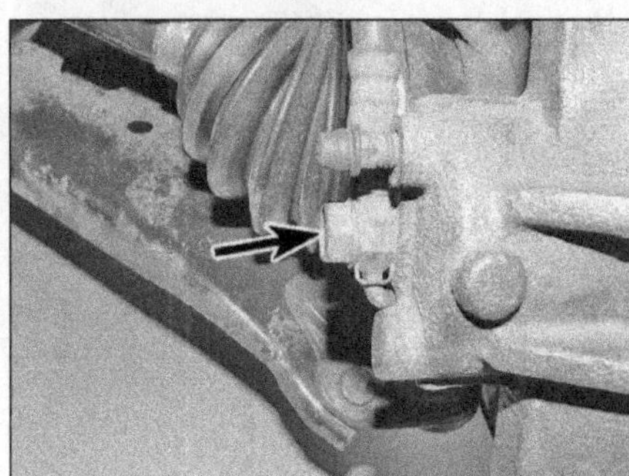
8.3 Slacken the brake pipe union

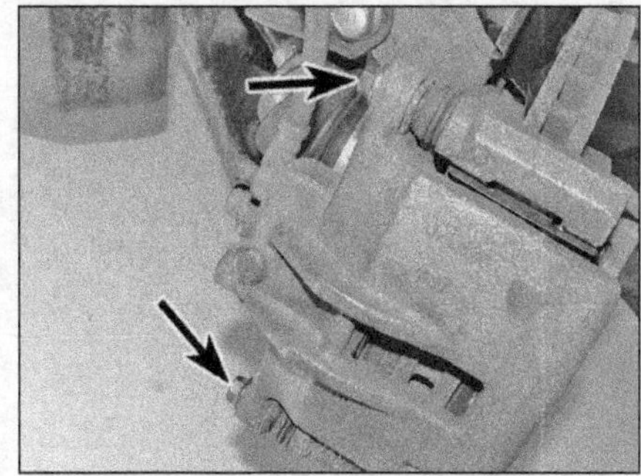
8.4a Undo the two brake caliper bolts . . .

8.4b . . . and remove the caliper

8.5a Remove the brake pads . . .

8.5b . . . and the mounting bracket

the caliper away from the brake disc, and then unscrew the caliper from the end of the brake hose.

5 If required, remove the pads and then the caliper mounting bracket can be unbolted from the hub carrier **(see illustrations)**.

Overhaul

Note: *Check the availability of repair kits for the caliper before dismantling.*

6 With the caliper on the bench, wipe away all traces of dust and dirt, but *avoid inhaling the dust, as it is a health hazard.*

7 Withdraw the partially-ejected piston from the caliper body, and remove the dust seal. The dust seal may be retained by a circlip **(see illustration)**

8 Using a small screwdriver, extract the piston hydraulic seal, taking great care not to damage the caliper bore.

9 Thoroughly clean all components, using only methylated spirit, isopropyl alcohol or clean hydraulic fluid as a cleaning medium. Never use mineral-based solvents such as petrol or paraffin, as they will attack the hydraulic system's rubber components. Dry the components immediately, using compressed air or a clean, lint-free cloth. Use compressed air to blow clear the fluid passages.

10 Check all components, and renew any that are worn or damaged. Check particularly the cylinder bore and piston; these should be renewed (note that this means the renewal of the complete body assembly) if they are scratched, worn or corroded in any way. Similarly check the condition of the guide pins and their gaiters; both pins should be undamaged and (when cleaned) a reasonably tight sliding fit in the caliper bracket. If there is any doubt about the condition of any component, renew it.

11 If the assembly is fit for further use, obtain the appropriate repair kit; the components should be available from Toyota dealers in various combinations. All rubber seals should be renewed as a matter of course; these should never be re-used.

12 On reassembly, ensure that all components are clean and dry.

13 Soak the piston and the new piston (fluid) seal in clean brake fluid. Smear clean fluid on the cylinder bore surface.

14 Fit the new piston (fluid) seal, using only your fingers (no tools) to manipulate it into the cylinder bore groove **(see illustration)**.

15 Fit the new dust seal to the rear of the piston and seat the outer lip of the seal in the caliper body groove. Carefully ease the piston squarely into the cylinder bore using a twisting motion **(see illustrations)**. Press the piston fully into position, and seat the inner lip of the dust seal in the piston groove. Fit the circlip, which retains the dust seal.

16 If the guide pins are being renewed, lubricate the pin shafts with the special grease supplied in the repair kit, and fit the gaiters to the pin grooves. Insert the pins into the caliper bracket and seat the gaiters correctly in the bracket grooves **(see illustrations)**. Note the guide pins are different and need to be fitted in the correct location.

Refitting

17 If previously removed, refit the caliper mounting bracket to the hub carrier, and tighten the new bolts to the specified torque.

18 Screw the caliper body fully onto the flexible hose union.

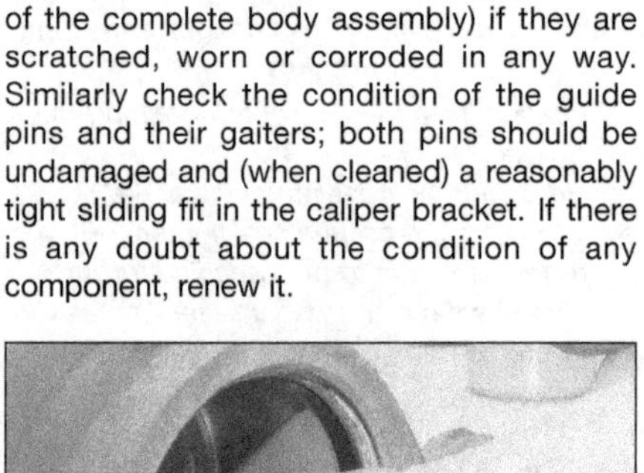

8.7 Remove the dust seal from the piston

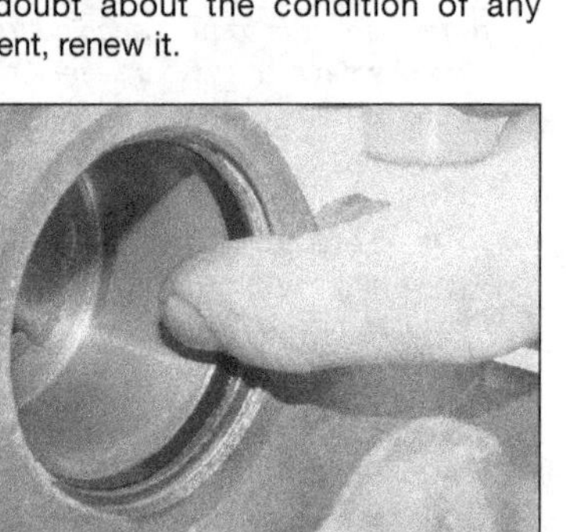

8.14 Fit the seal into the groove in the caliper bore

8.15a Fit the seal to the rear of the piston, and the outer lip to the caliper body groove . . .

8.15b . . . then push and twist the piston into the bore

8.16a New guide pin and seal kit

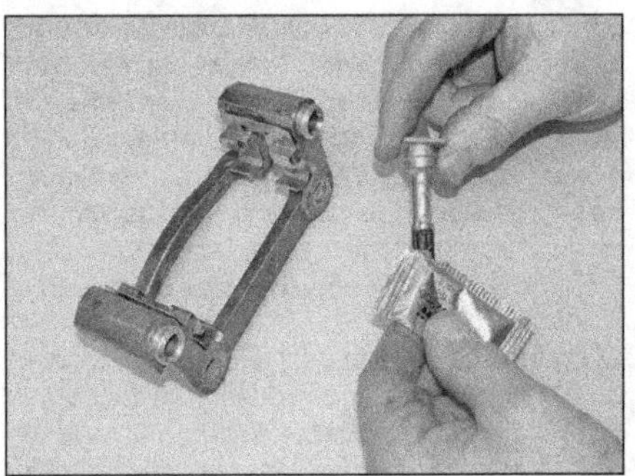

8.16b Apply grease to the guide pin and seal . . .

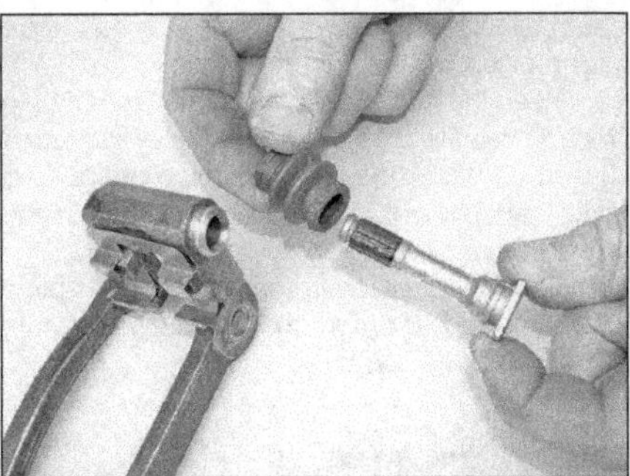

8.16c . . . fit the new dust cover . . .

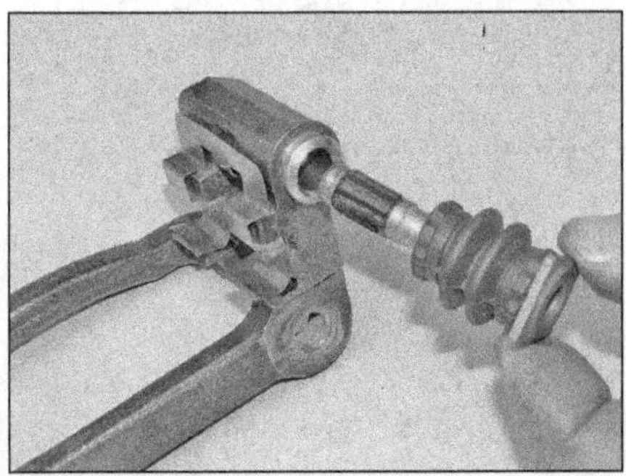

8.16d . . . and then insert it into the caliper mounting bracket

19 Ensure that the brake pads are correctly fitted in the caliper mounting bracket and refit the caliper (see Section 4).

20 Fit the lower guide pin bolt, then press the caliper into position and fit the upper guide pin bolt. Tighten both guide pin bolts to the specified torque.

21 Tighten the brake hose union nut to the specified torque, then remove the brake hose clamp or polythene (where fitted).

22 Bleed the hydraulic system as described in Section 2. Note that, providing the precautions described were taken to minimise brake fluid loss, it should only be necessary to bleed the relevant front brake.

23 Refit the roadwheel, then lower the vehicle to the ground and tighten the roadwheel nuts to the specified torque.

9 Rear brake caliper – removal, overhaul and refitting

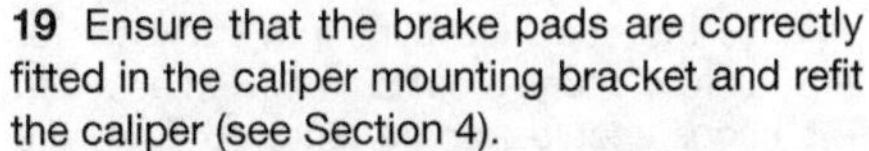

Caution: Ensure the ignition is switched off before disconnecting any braking system hydraulic union and do not switch it back on until after the hydraulic system has been bled. Failure to do this could lead to air entering the modulator unit requiring the unit to be bled (see Section 2).

Note: *Before starting work, refer to the note at the beginning of Section 2 concerning the dangers of hydraulic fluid, and to the warning at the beginning of Section 5 concerning the dangers of asbestos dust.*

Removal

1 Chock the front wheels, slacken the relevant rear roadwheel nuts, then jack up the rear of the vehicle and support on axle stands (see *Jacking and vehicle support*). Remove the relevant rear wheel.

2 Minimise fluid loss by first removing the master cylinder reservoir cap, and then tightening it down onto a piece of polythene, to obtain an airtight seal. Alternatively, use a brake hose clamp, a G-clamp or a similar tool to clamp the flexible hose at the nearest convenient point to the brake caliper.

3 Wipe away all traces of dirt around the brake hose union on the caliper. Unscrew the union bolt and disconnect the brake pipe from the caliper **(see illustration)**. Plug the pipe and caliper unions to minimise fluid loss and prevent dirt entry.

4 Slacken and remove the guide pin bolts. Remove the caliper from the vehicle **(see illustrations)**.

5 If required, remove the pads and then the caliper mounting bracket can be unbolted from the hub carrier **(see illustrations)**.

Overhaul

6 At the time of writing, no parts were available to recondition the rear caliper assembly, with the exception of the guide pin bolts, guide pins and guide pin gaiters. Check the condition of the guide pins and their gaiters; both pins should be undamaged and (when cleaned) a reasonably tight sliding fit in the caliper bracket. If there is any doubt about the condition of any component, renew it **(see illustrations 8.16a, 8.16b, 8.16c and 8.16d)**.

Refitting

7 If previously removed, refit the caliper mounting bracket to the hub carrier, and

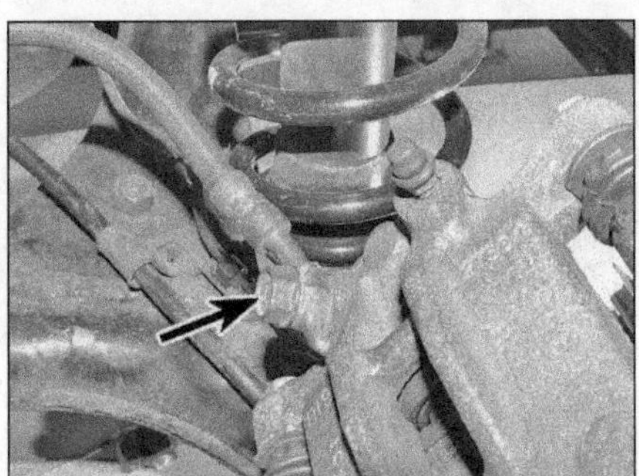

9.3 Slacken the brake pipe union

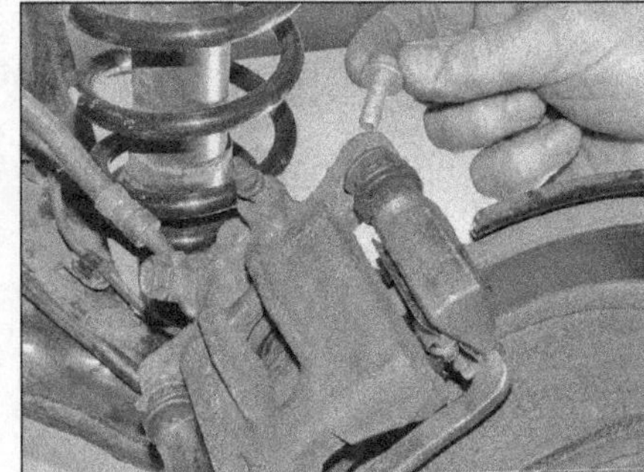

9.4a Undo the two brake caliper bolts . . .

9.4b . . . and remove the caliper

9.5a Remove the brake pads . . .

9.5b . . . and the mounting bracket

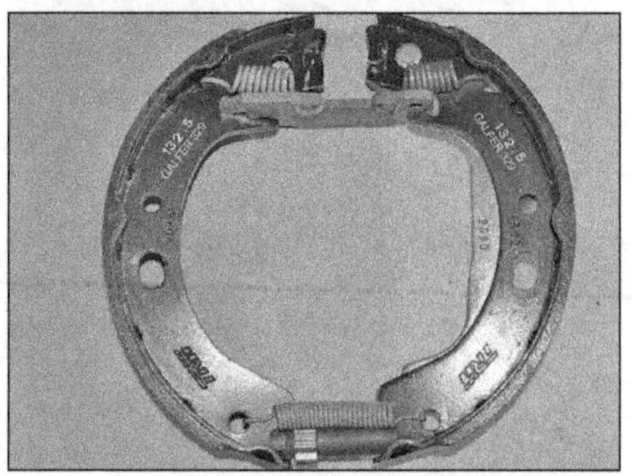
10.4 Layout of handbrake shoes

tighten the new bolts to the specified torque. Refit the brake pads, see Section 5.

8 Refit the caliper and tighten the guide pin bolts to the specified torque settings.

9 Reconnect the brake pipe to the caliper, and tighten the brake hose union nut to the specified torque. Remove the brake hose clamp or polythene (where fitted).

10 Bleed the hydraulic system as described in Section 2. Note that, providing the precautions described were taken to minimise brake fluid loss, it should only be necessary to bleed the relevant rear brake.

11 Refit the roadwheel, then lower the vehicle to the ground and tighten the roadwheel nuts to the specified torque.

10 Handbrake shoes – renewal

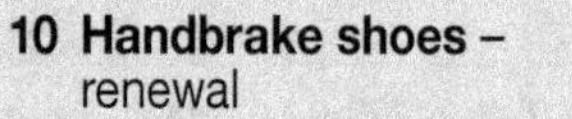

Warning: Renew both sets of brake shoes at the same time – never renew the shoes on only one wheel, as uneven braking may result. Note that the dust created by wear of the shoes may contain asbestos, which is a health hazard. Never blow it out with compressed air, and don't inhale any of it. An approved filtering mask should be worn when working on the brakes. DO NOT use petrol or petroleum-based solvents to clean brake parts; use brake cleaner or methylated spirit only.

1 Remove the rear brake disc as described in Section 7.

2 Taking precautions to avoid inhalation of dust, remove the brake dust from the brake disc, shoes and backplate. We recommend the use of aerosol brake cleaners, available from most automotive part/accessory retailers.

3 Measure the thickness of the friction material at several points; if either shoe is worn at any point to the specified minimum thickness or less, all four shoes must be renewed as a set. The shoes should also be renewed if any are contaminated with oil or grease, since there is no satisfactory way of degreasing the friction material.

4 Note the location and orientation of all components before disassembly as an aid to reassembly **(see illustration)**.

5 Follow the accompanying illustrations for the brake shoe removal procedure **(see illustrations)**. Be sure to stay in order and read the caption under each illustration.

6 Refitting is the reverse of the removal procedure, noting the following points:

a) Refit the rear brake disc as described in Section 7.

b) Repeat the operation on the remaining brake on the other side of the vehicle.

c) Check and adjust the handbrake as described in Section 15.

10.5a Remove the securing clip . . .

10.5b . . . and withdraw the locating pin from the backplate

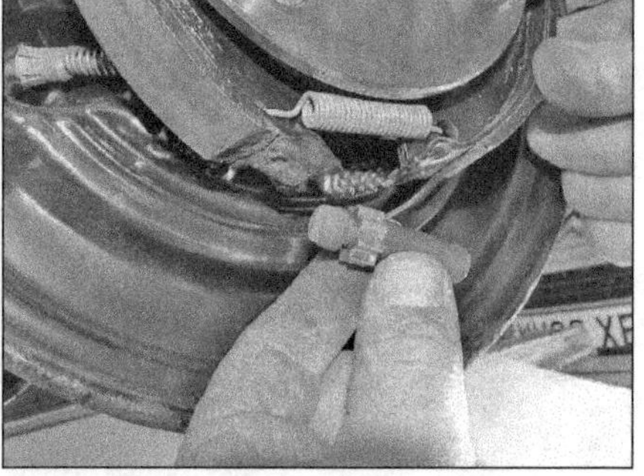
10.5c Remove the adjuster from between the bottom of the brake shoes . . .

10.5d . . . and then remove the spring, noting its fitted position

10.5e Pull the shoes outwards over the hub . . .

10.5f . . . and turn them over to access the handbrake cable

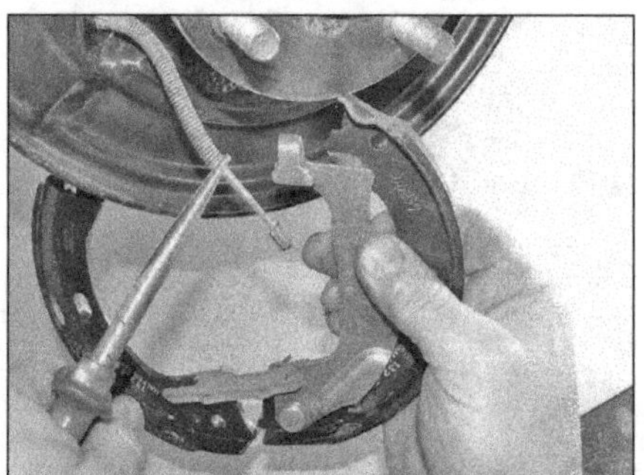
10.5g Use long-nose pliers to release the handbrake cable from the lever

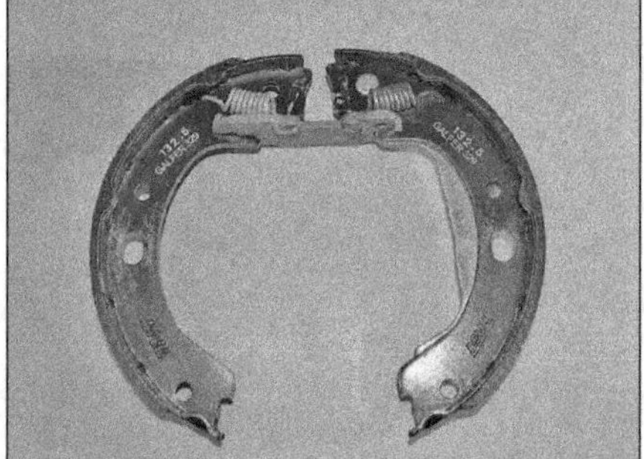
10.5h Check position of upper springs and locating plate before removal

11 Master cylinder – removal, overhaul and refitting

Caution: Ensure the ignition is switched off before disconnecting any braking system hydraulic union and do not switch it back on until after the hydraulic system has been bled. Failure to do this could lead to air entering the modulator unit requiring the unit to be bled (see Section 2).

Note: *Before starting work, refer to the warning at the beginning of Section 2 concerning the dangers of hydraulic fluid.*

Removal

1 Remove the master cylinder reservoir cap, and syphon the hydraulic fluid from the reservoir. **Note:** *Do not syphon the fluid by mouth, as it is poisonous; use a syringe or an old antifreeze tester.* Alternatively, open any convenient bleed screw in the system, and gently pump the brake pedal to expel the fluid through a plastic tube connected to the screw until the reservoir is emptied (see Section 2).

2 Note their fitted positions, and then undo the brake pipe unions from the master cylinder **(see illustration)**. Be prepared for fluid spillage. Plug or tape over the pipe ends and master cylinder orifices to minimise the loss of brake fluid, and to prevent the entry of dirt into the system. Wash off any spilt fluid immediately with cold water.

3 On manual transmission models, disconnect the clutch master cylinder supply hose from the brake fluid reservoir **(see illustration)**. Be prepared for fluid spillage. Plug the hose end and reservoir orifice to minimise the loss of brake fluid, and to prevent the entry of dirt into the system. Wash off any spilt fluid immediately with cold water.

4 Disconnect the fluid level sensor wiring plug, from the lower part of the reservoir **(see illustration)**.

5 Undo the nuts and pull the master cylinder from the brake servo unit **(see illustration)**. Recover the gasket fitted between the cylinder and brake servo. Where applicable, disconnect the wiring/cable bracket from the mounting stud.

6 If required, undo the screw, and pull the reservoir upwards from the master cylinder. Recover the two rubber grommets from the master cylinder ports **(see illustrations)**. If they are hard, cracked or damaged, or have been leaking, renew them.

Overhaul

7 The master cylinder may be overhauled after obtaining the relevant repair kit from a Toyota dealer. Ensure that the correct repair kit is obtained for the master cylinder being worked on. Note the locations of all components to ensure correct refitting, and lubricate the new seals using clean brake fluid. Follow the assembly instructions supplied with the repair kit.

Refitting

8 Remove all traces of dirt from the master cylinder and servo unit mating surfaces and check the condition of the gasket – renew if necessary.

9 Press the mounting seals fully into the master cylinder ports then carefully ease the fluid reservoir into position. Refit and tighten the retaining screw, or refit the retaining clip as applicable.

10 Fit the master cylinder to the servo unit. Refit the master cylinder mounting nuts, and tighten them to the specified torque.

11 Wipe clean the brake pipe unions and refit them to the master cylinder ports, tightening them to the specified torque.

12 Reconnect the level sensor wiring plug.

13 Reconnect the clutch master cylinder supply hose to the reservoir.

14 Refill the master cylinder reservoir with new fluid. Bleed the complete hydraulic system as described in Section 2.

12 Brake pedal – removal and refitting

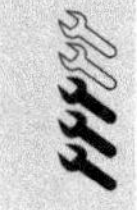

Removal

1 Remove the driver's side lower facia trim panel **(see illustration)** as described in Chapter 11.

2 Withdraw the retaining clip and withdraw the clevis pin securing the servo pushrod to the pedal **(see illustration)**.

3 Slacken and remove the pivot bolt and nut **(see illustration)**, and remove the brake pedal from the vehicle. Remove the pivot bolt and bushes, examine all components for

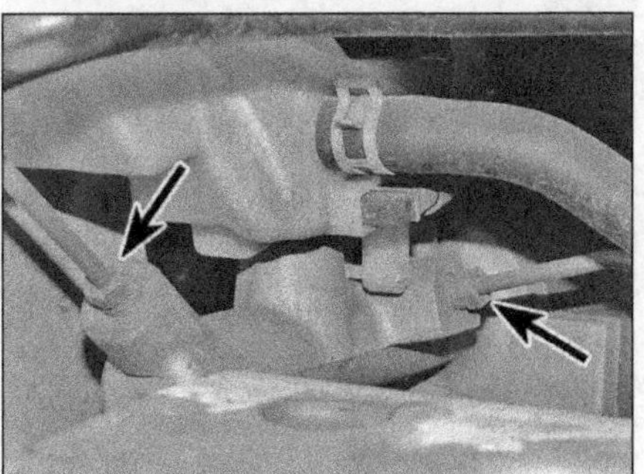

11.2 Disconnect the brake pipes from the master cylinder

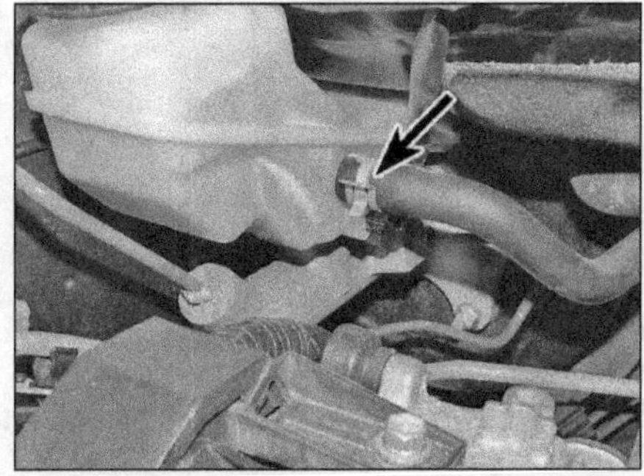

11.3 Clutch master cylinder supply hose

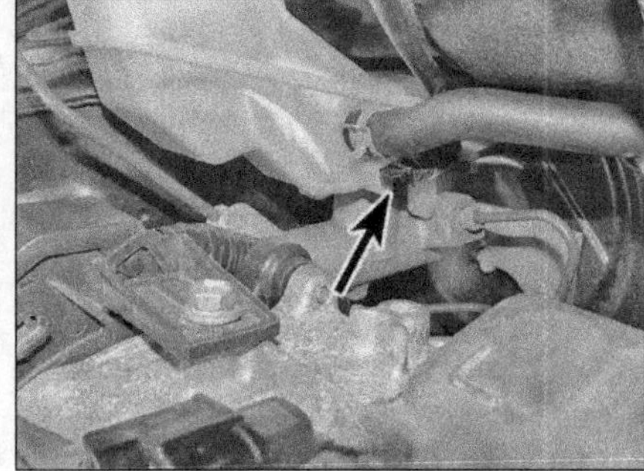

11.4 Disconnect the fluid level warning light switch

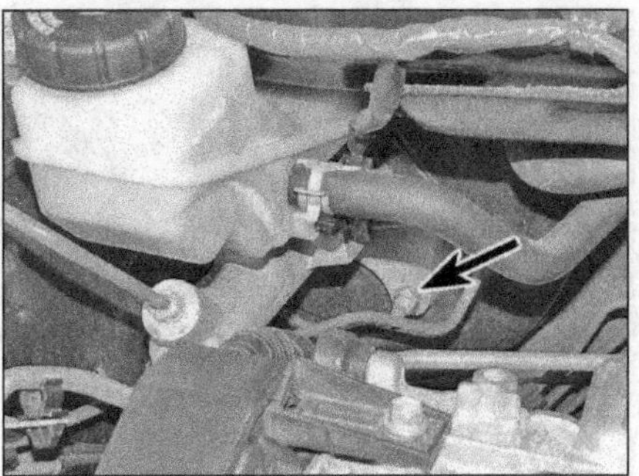

11.5 Undo the brake master cylinder mounting nuts (one shown)

11.6a Undo the retaining screw to remove the reservoir

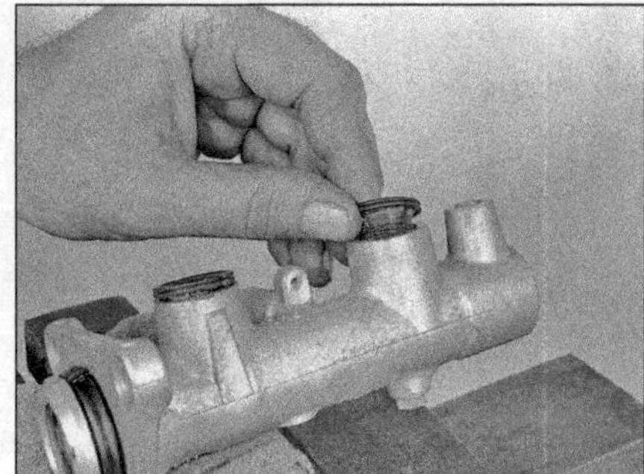

11.6b Pull the grommets from the master cylinder; renew if required

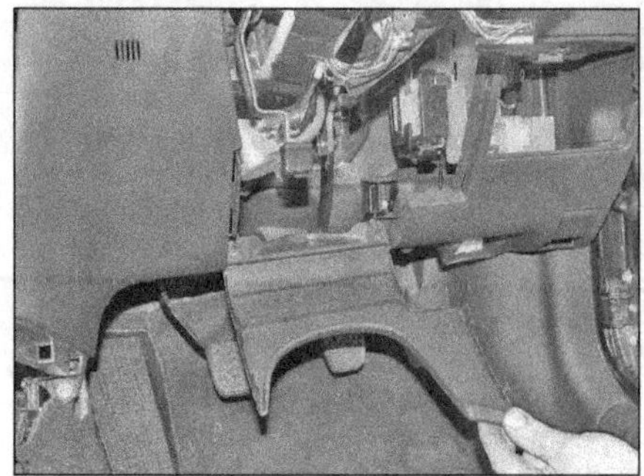

12.1 Unclip the lower trim panel

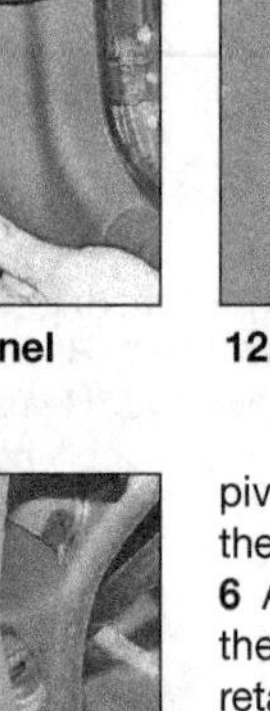

12.7a Locknut (arrowed) for adjustment

signs of wear or damage, renewing them as necessary.

Refitting

4 Apply a smear of lithium (soap-based) glycol grease to the bushes and to the pedal pivot bore.

5 Manoeuvre the pedal into position, making sure it is correctly engaged with the pushrod, and insert the pivot bolt. Refit the nut to the

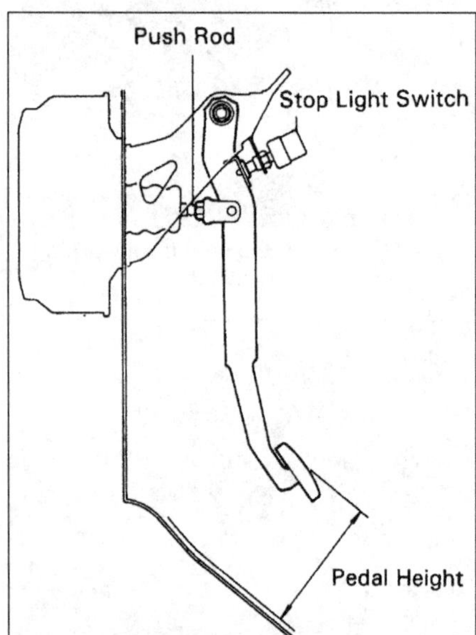

12.7b Brake pedal height is the distance between the pedal and the metal floor when the pedal is released

12.2 Withdraw the retaining clip and clevis pin

pivot bolt and tighten it securely, making sure the bushes are fitted correctly.

6 Align the pedal with the pushrod and insert the clevis pin, securing it in position with the retaining clip.

7 Pull back the carpet and measure the distance from the centre of the pedal pad to the metal floor. Compare the measurement obtained and compare it with that given in the Specifications. Slacken the servo pushrod locknut and adjust the length of the pushrod if necessary **(see illustrations)**. **Note:** *Before adjusting the pedal height, slacken the locknut and remove the brake light switch. Refit the switch after the pedal height has been adjusted.*

8 Refit the lower panel to the facia.

13 Vacuum servo unit – testing, removal and refitting

Testing

1 To test the operation of the servo unit, depress the footbrake several times to exhaust the vacuum, then start the engine whilst keeping the pedal firmly depressed. As the engine starts, there should be a noticeable 'give' in the brake pedal as the vacuum builds-up. Allow the engine to run for at least two minutes, and then switch it off. If the brake pedal is now depressed it should feel normal, but further applications should result in the pedal feeling firmer, with the pedal stroke decreasing with each application.

2 If the servo does not operate as described,

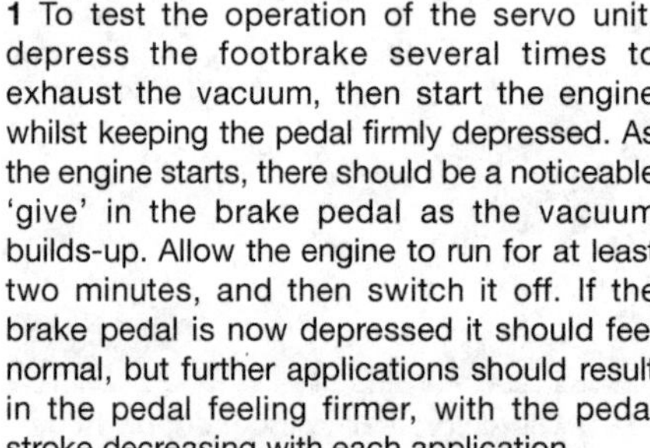

13.6 Unclip the lower trim panel

12.3 Remove pivot bolt (arrowed)

first inspect the servo unit check valve as described in Section 14.

3 If the servo unit still fails to operate satisfactorily, the fault lies within the unit itself. Repairs to the unit are not possible – if faulty, the servo unit must be renewed.

Removal

Warning: Before starting work on the removal of the servo unit, it must be noted that the engine will need to be supported and the engine mountings removed. This will allow the engine to come far enough forward to withdraw the servo unit from the bulkhead. Also depending on model, it will be necessary to remove the air intake housing, camshaft cover and timing belt/chain cover. See relevant Chapters to carry out these procedures.

4 Remove the master cylinder as described in Section 11.

5 Slacken or release the retaining clip (depending on type of securing clip), then disconnect the vacuum pipe from the servo unit check valve.

6 Remove the driver's side lower facia trim panel **(see illustration)** as described in Chapter 11.

7 Remove the clip and extract the servo pushrod clevis pin from the linkage **(see illustration 12.2)**.

8 On manual transmission models, remove the clutch master cylinder as described in Chapter 6.

9 Slacken and remove the four nuts securing the servo to the bulkhead **(see illustration)**.

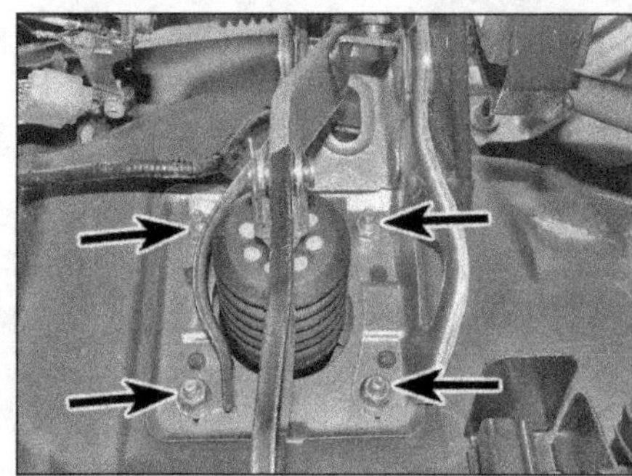

13.9 Remove the four nuts (arrowed) securing the servo to the bulkhead

10 Before the servo unit can be withdrawn, the engine will need to be tilted and moved forward to allow enough room. See *Warning* at the beginning of the removal procedure.

11 Manoeuvre the servo unit out of position, along with its gasket, which is fitted between the servo and bulkhead. Renew the gasket if it shows signs of damage.

Refitting

12 Refitting is the reverse of removal, noting the following points.

a) Lubricate all linkage pivot points with multipurpose grease.

b) Tighten the servo unit and mounting bracket nuts and bolts to their specified torque settings.

c) Refit the master cylinder as described in Section 11 and bleed the complete hydraulic system as described in Section 2.

14 Vacuum servo unit check valve – removal, testing and refitting

Removal

1 Slacken or release the retaining clip (depending on type of securing clip), then disconnect the vacuum hose from the servo unit check valve.

2 Withdraw the valve from its rubber sealing grommet, using a pulling and twisting motion **(see illustration)**. Remove the grommet from the servo.

Testing

3 Examine the check valve for signs of damage, and renew if necessary. The valve may be tested by blowing through it in both directions. Air should flow through the valve in one direction only – when blown through from the servo unit end of the valve. Renew the valve if this is not the case.

4 Examine the rubber sealing grommet and flexible vacuum hose for signs of damage or deterioration, and renew as necessary.

Refitting

5 Fit the sealing grommet into position in the servo unit.

6 Carefully ease the check valve into position, taking great care not to displace or damage the grommet. Reconnect the vacuum hose to the valve and, where necessary, securely tighten its retaining clip.

7 On completion, start the engine and check for air leaks from the check valve-to-servo unit connection.

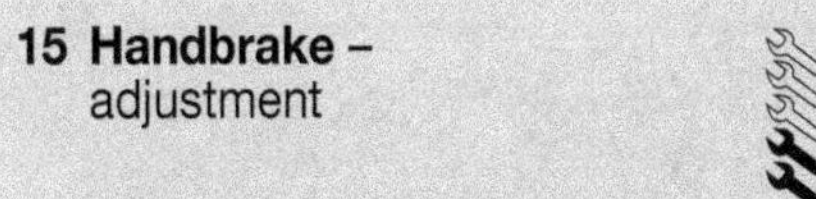

15 Handbrake – adjustment

1 Remove the rear section of the centre console as described in Chapter 11.

2 Slacken the locknut all the way off, and then undo the adjusting nut until the cable is slack **(see illustration).**

3 Chock the front wheels, slacken the rear roadwheel nuts, then jack up the rear of the vehicle and support on axle stands (see *Jacking and vehicle support*). Remove the rear wheels.

4 Remove the rubber grommet from the disc and, using a screwdriver inserted through the adjusting hole in the backing plate **(see illustrations)**, turn the adjuster star wheel until the brake shoes drag on the brake inside drum as the drum is rotated, then back off the star wheel until the shoes don't drag.

5 To check the handbrake adjustment, applying normal moderate pressure, pull the handbrake lever to the fully-applied position, counting the number of clicks emitted from the handbrake ratchet mechanism. If adjustment is correct, the handbrake should be fully applied after 6 to 9 clicks have been emitted. If this is not the case, adjust as follows.

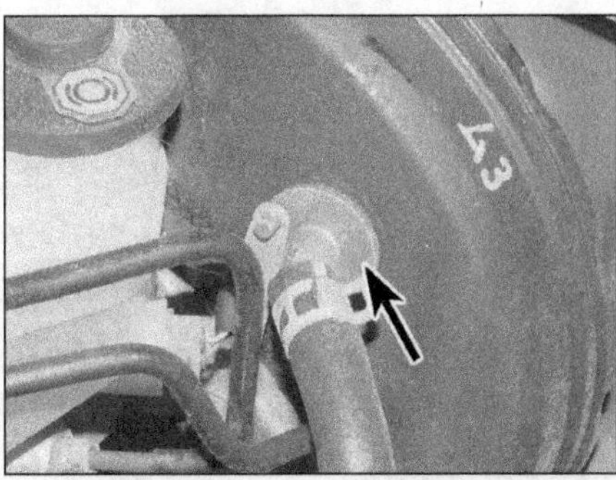

14.2 Servo check valve (arrowed)

6 Slacken the locknut (if not already done), and then rotate the adjusting nut until the correct setting (6 to 9 clicks) is achieved. Tighten the locknut **(see illustration).**

7 Refit the centre console, with reference to Chapter 11.

8 Refit the roadwheel, then lower the vehicle to the ground and tighten the roadwheel nuts to the specified torque.

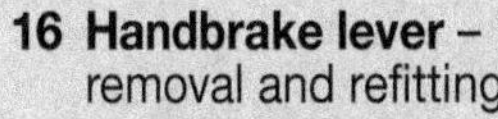

16 Handbrake lever – removal and refitting

Removal

1 Remove the centre console as described in Chapter 11.

2 Release the handbrake lever and back off the locknut and adjuster nut to detach the handbrake cable from the lever **(see illustration).**

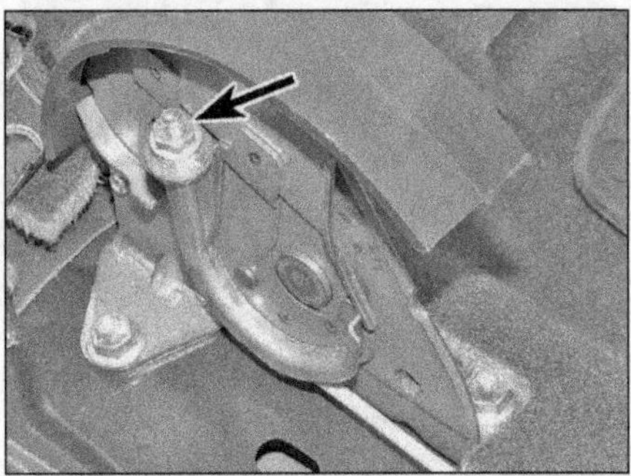

15.2 Slacken the upper locknut (arrowed)

15.4a Remove the rubber grommet . . .

15.4b . . . insert screwdriver and adjust

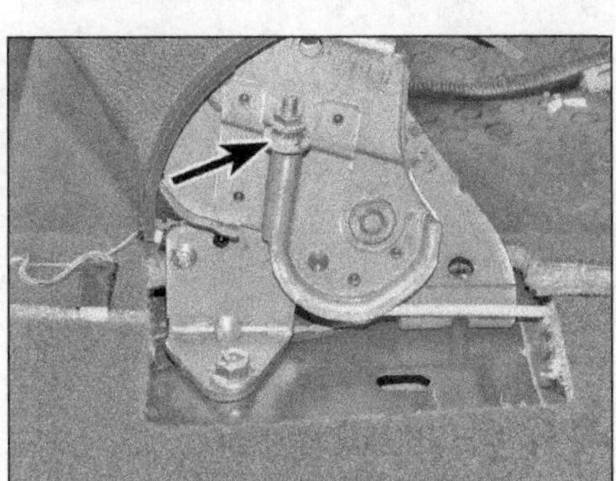

15.6 Lower adjusting nut (arrowed)

16.2 Disconnect the cable from the brake lever

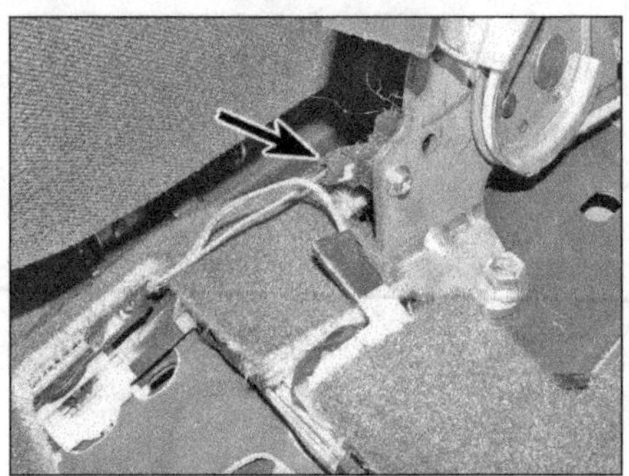
16.3 Disconnect the warning light switch connector (arrowed)

3 Disconnect the wiring connector from the handbrake warning light switch **(see illustration)**.

4 Slacken and remove the lever retaining bolts, and remove the lever from the vehicle **(see illustration)**.

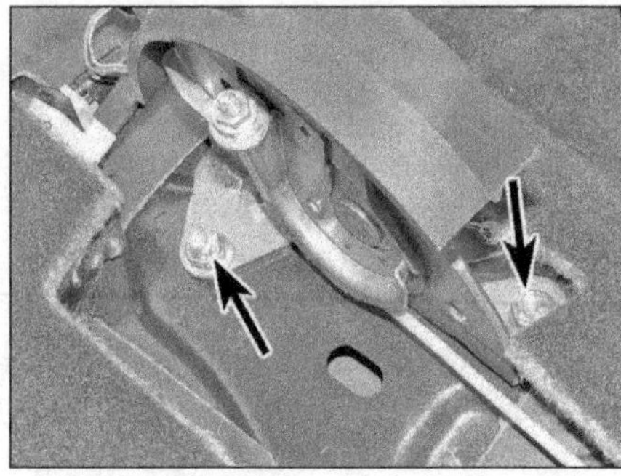
16.4 Handbrake lever mounting bolts (arrowed)

Refitting

5 Refitting is a reversal of removal. Tighten the lever retaining nuts to the specified torque, and adjust the handbrake (see Section 15).

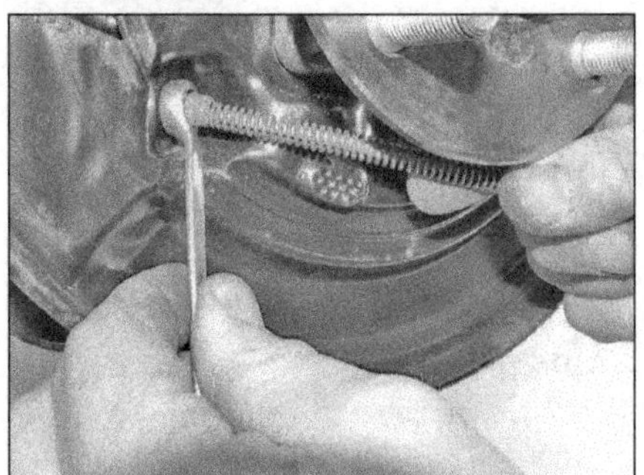
17.3a Using a ring spanner . . .

17 Handbrake cables – renewal

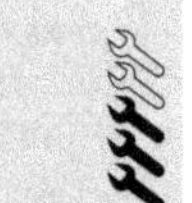

Equaliser-to-handbrake shoes

1 Firmly chock the front wheels, slacken the relevant rear roadwheel nuts, and then jack up the rear of the vehicle and support it on axle stands (see *Jacking and vehicle support*). Remove the rear wheel.

2 Ensure the handbrake is completely released, and then remove the relevant brake disc (see Section 7).

3 Remove the handbrake shoes and disconnect the cable from the lever on the shoe (see Section 10). Squeeze together the tangs of the retaining clip and pull the cable through the backing plate **(see illustrations)**.

4 Unbolt the cable clamp from the top of the rear suspension arm **(see illustration)**.

5 Unbolt the cable clamp from the floorpan, in front of the fuel tank above the exhaust system **(see illustration)**.

6 To make access easier, remove the exhaust pipe and heat shields (see Chapter 4A or 4B).

7 Unclamp the cable from the retaining bracket, and disconnect the cable from the equaliser **(see illustration)**.

8 Refitting is a reversal of the removal procedure, adjusting the handbrake as described in Section 15.

Equaliser-to-handbrake lever

9 Remove the centre console as described in Chapter 11.

10 Ensure the handbrake lever is fully released, then remove the locknut and adjusting nut (see Section 15), and detach the cable from the lever **(see illustration)**.

11 Firmly chock the front wheels, slacken the relevant rear roadwheel nuts, and then jack up the rear of the vehicle and support it on axle stands (see *Jacking and vehicle support*). Remove the rear wheel.

12 To make access easier, remove the exhaust pipe and heat shields (see Chapter 4A or 4B).

13 Rotate the cable end 90° and disconnect it from the equaliser **(see illustration)**.

14 Prise out the rubber grommet, and pull the cable up through the hole in the floorpan.

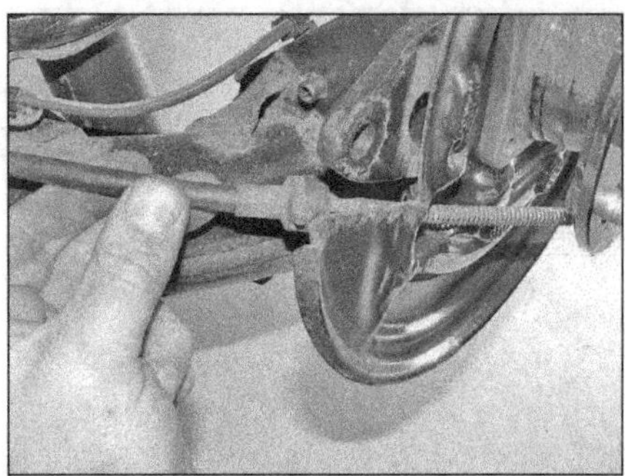
17.3b . . . to release the cable from the backplate

17.4 Disconnect the handbrake mounting bracket from the suspension arm

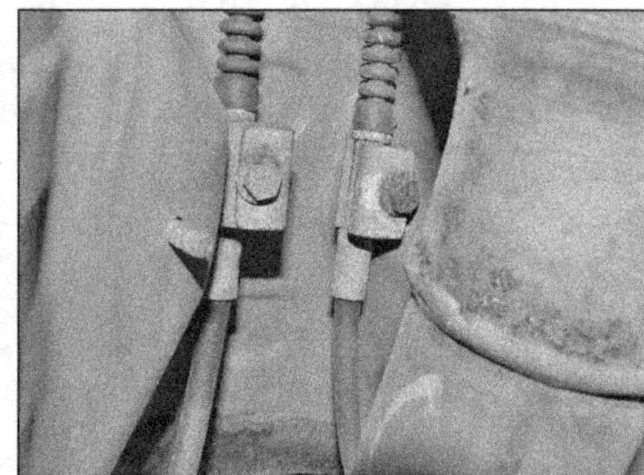
17.5 Handbrake cable clamps under the vehicle

17.7 Handbrake cable equaliser (arrowed)

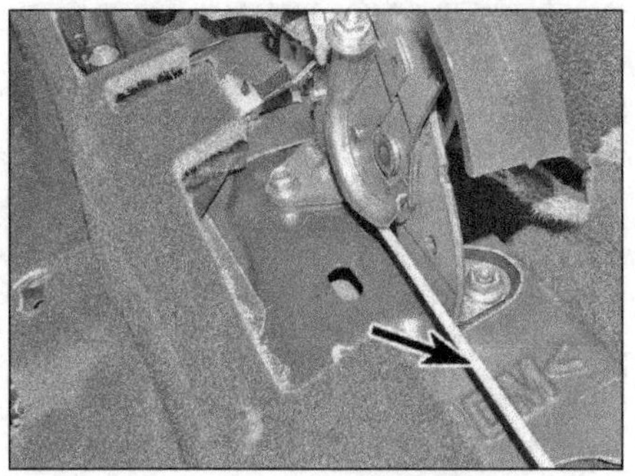
17.10 Handbrake front cable (arrowed)

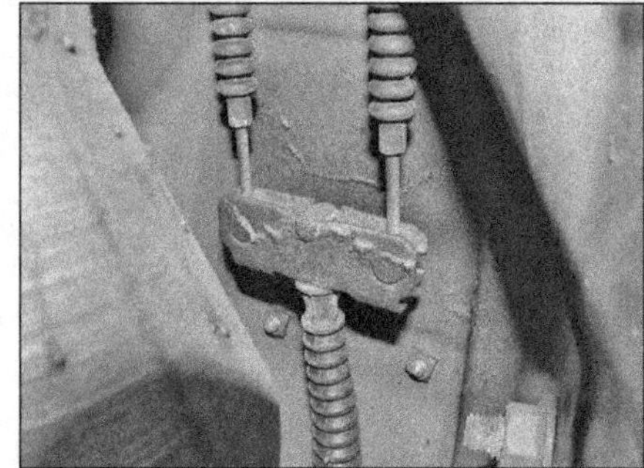
17.13 Disconnect the cables from the equaliser

15 Refitting is a reversal of removal. Apply a light coat of grease to the portion of the cable end the engages with the equaliser, and coat the sealing edge of the rubber grommet with silicone sealant to ensure that it remains watertight.

16 Adjust the handbrake as described in Section 15.

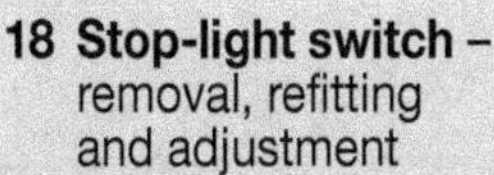

18 Stop-light switch – removal, refitting and adjustment

1 The stop-light switch is located on a bracket at the top of the brake pedal **(see illustration)**. The switch activates the brake lights at the rear of the vehicle when the brake pedal is depressed.

Removal

2 Remove the driver's side lower facia panel as described in Chapter 11.

3 Disconnect the wiring, then undo the locknut and unscrew the switch from the bracket **(see illustrations)**.

Refitting and adjustment

4 Screw the switch into the pedal bracket and loosely refit the locknut.

5 Continue to screw in the switch until the plunger makes light contact with the pedal, and then rotate the switch anti-clockwise one complete turn. Tighten the locknut.

6 Check the clearance between the switch and the pedal **(see illustration)**.

7 Reconnect the wiring connector, and check the operation of the stop-lights. Refit the facia panel.

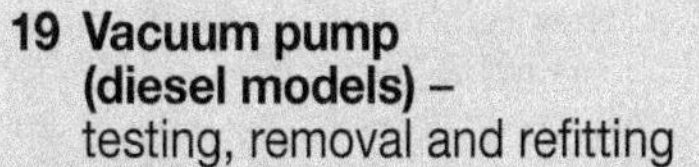

19 Vacuum pump (diesel models) – testing, removal and refitting

Testing

1 The most common symptom of a failed vacuum pump is a hard pedal. Check the operation of the brake servo as described in Section 13.

2 If the servo does not operate properly, remove the vacuum hose from the brake servo and connect a vacuum gauge to it.

3 Start the engine and watch the gauge. Vacuum should register on the gauge almost immediately.

4 If vacuum does not register on the gauge, renew the vacuum pump.

Removal

5 Loosen the retaining clip and disconnect the vacuum hoses from the pump **(see illustration)**.

6 Loosen the retaining clip and disconnect the oil return hose from the bottom of the pump **(see illustration)**.

7 Unscrew the mounting bolts and withdraw the vacuum pump from the transmission end of the cylinder head. Recover the two O-ring seals and discard them, as new ones will be needed for refitting. Be prepared for a small amount of engine oil to leak from the cylinder head.

18.1 Brake light warning switch (arrowed)

18.3b . . . and slacken the locknut (arrowed)

18.3a Disconnect the wiring connector . . .

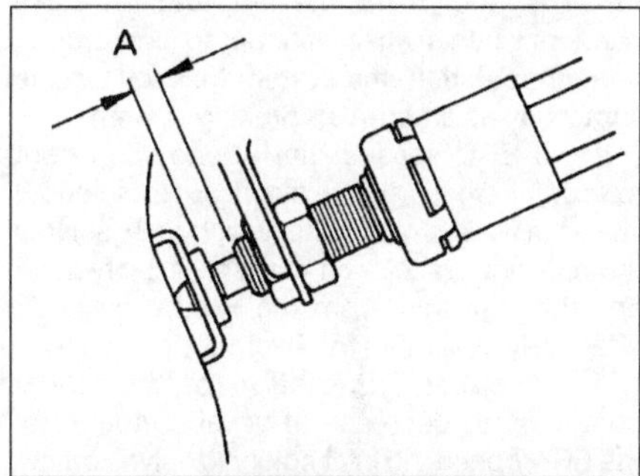

18.6 Clearance (A) between the end of the light switch body and the pedal should be 0.5 to 2.4 mm

Refitting

8 Wipe clean the mating surfaces of the vacuum pump and the cylinder head, then fit new O-ring seals to the vacuum pump, align the pump with the camshaft, and refit it. Insert the mounting bolts and tighten to the specified torque.

9 Reconnect the vacuum hoses, oil return hose and tighten the retaining clamps.

20 Anti-lock Braking System (ABS) – general information

ABS is fitted to all models as standard; the system comprises a hydraulic modulator unit and the four roadwheel sensors. The modulator unit contains the electronic control unit (ECU), the hydraulic solenoid valves and the electrically-driven return pump. The purpose of the system is to prevent the wheel(s) locking during heavy braking. This is achieved by automatic release of the brake on the relevant wheel, followed by re-application of the brake.

The solenoid valves are controlled by the ECU, which itself receives signals from the four wheel sensors (front sensors are fitted to the hubs, and the rear sensors are fitted to the stub axle assembly), which monitor the speed of rotation of each wheel. By comparing these signals, the ECU can determine the speed at which the vehicle is travelling. It can then use this speed to determine when a wheel is decelerating at an abnormal rate, compared

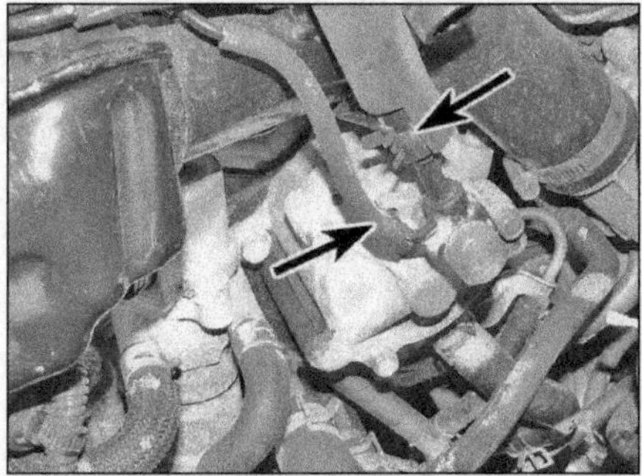

19.5 Disconnect the hoses (arrowed) from the vacuum pump

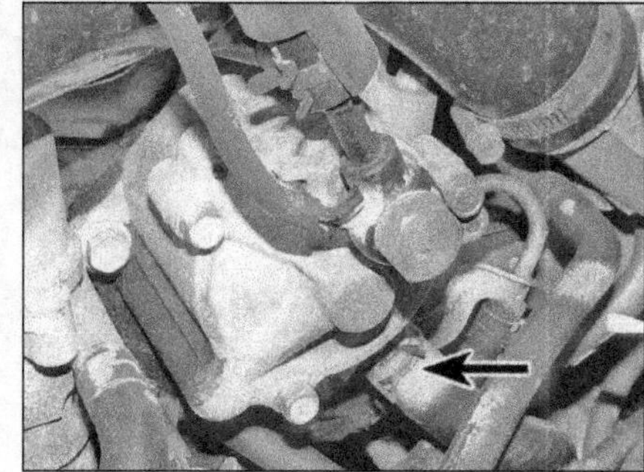

19.6 Disconnect the oil return hose (arrowed)

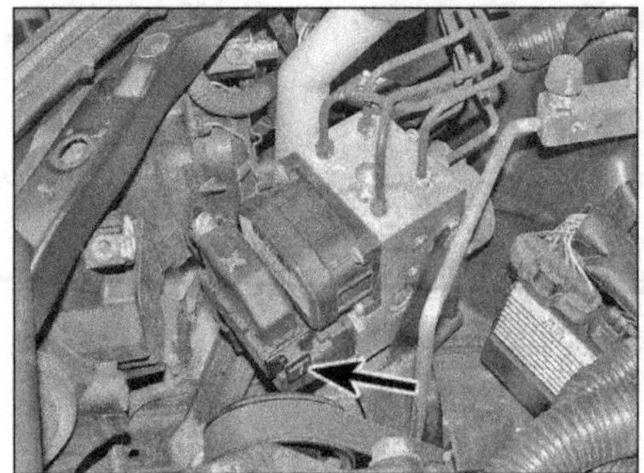
21.2 Pull the locking clip (arrowed) to disconnect the wiring connector

21.3 Note the location of the hydraulic pipes

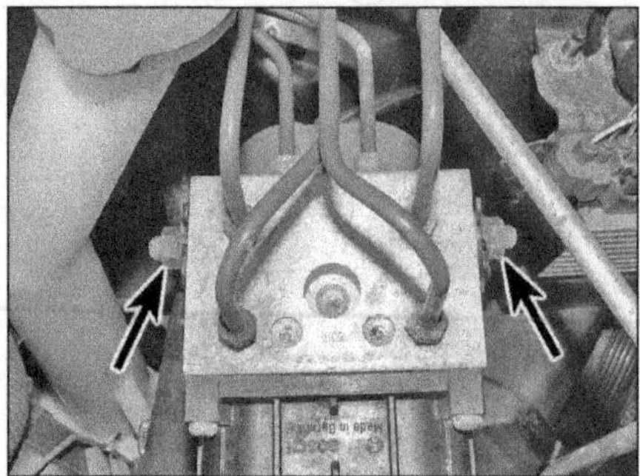
21.4 Brake modulator mounting nuts (arrowed)

to the speed of the vehicle, and therefore predicts when a wheel is about to lock. During normal operation, the system functions in the same way as a non-ABS braking system.

If the ECU senses that a wheel is about to lock, it closes the relevant outlet solenoid valves in the hydraulic unit, which then isolates the relevant brake(s) on the wheel(s) which is/are about to lock from the master cylinder, effectively sealing-in the hydraulic pressure.

If the speed of rotation of the wheel continues to decrease at an abnormal rate, the ECU opens the inlet solenoid valves on the relevant brake(s), and operates the electrically-driven return pump which pumps the hydraulic fluid back into the master cylinder, releasing the brake. Once the speed of rotation of the wheel returns to an acceptable rate, the pump stops; the solenoid valves switch again, allowing the hydraulic master cylinder pressure to return to the brake.

The action of the solenoid valves and return pump creates pulses in the hydraulic circuit. When the ABS system is functioning, these pulses can be felt through the brake pedal.

The operation of the ABS system is entirely dependent on electrical signals. To prevent the system responding to any inaccurate signals, a built-in safety circuit monitors all signals received by the ECU. If an inaccurate signal or low battery voltage is detected, the ABS system is automatically shut-down, and the warning light on the instrument panel is illuminated, to inform the driver that the ABS system is not operational. Normal braking should still be available, however.

If a fault does develop in the any of these systems, the vehicle must be taken to a Toyota dealer or suitably-equipped specialist for fault diagnosis and repair.

21 Anti-lock Braking System (ABS) components – removal and refitting

Modulator assembly

Caution: Disconnect the battery (see Chapter 5A) before disconnecting the modulator hydraulic unions, and do not reconnect the battery until after the hydraulic system has been bled. Also ensure that the unit is stored upright (in the same position as it is fitted to the vehicle) and is not tipped onto its side or upside down.

Note: *Before starting work, refer to the warning at the beginning of Section 2 concerning the dangers of hydraulic fluid.*

Removal

1 Disconnect the battery (see Chapter 5A).

2 Disconnect the modulator wiring plug connector **(see illustration)**.

3 Mark the locations of the hydraulic fluid pipes to ensure correct refitting, then unscrew the union nuts, and disconnect the pipes from the modulator assembly **(see illustration)**. Be prepared for fluid spillage, and plug the open ends of the pipes and the modulator, to prevent dirt ingress and further fluid loss.

4 Slacken and remove the modulator mounting nuts and remove the assembly from the engine compartment **(see illustration)**. If necessary, the mounting bracket can then be unbolted and removed from the vehicle. Renew the modulator mountings if they show signs of wear or damage.

Refitting

5 Manoeuvre the modulator into position and locate it in the mounting bracket. Refit the mounting nuts and tighten them securely.

6 Reconnect the hydraulic pipes to the correct unions on the modulator and tighten the union nuts to the specified torque.

7 Reconnect the wiring connector to the modulator.

8 Bleed the complete hydraulic system as described in Section 2. Once the system is correctly bled, check the operation of the brake system.

Electronic control unit (ECU)

9 The ECU is integral with the modulator assembly, and is not available separately.

Wheel speed sensors

Removal

10 Ensure the ignition is turned off.

11 Apply the handbrake, slacken the appropriate roadwheel nuts, then jack up the front/rear (as applicable) of the vehicle and support securely on axle stands (see *Jacking and vehicle support*). Remove the relevant roadwheel.

12 Trace the wiring back from the sensor, releasing it from all the relevant clips and ties whilst noting its correct routing, and disconnect the wiring connector **(see illustration)**.

13 On front wheel sensors, slacken and remove the retaining bolt and withdraw the sensor from the hub carrier assembly **(see illustrations)**.

14 On rear wheel sensors, a puller will be

21.12 Unclip the wiring from the strut

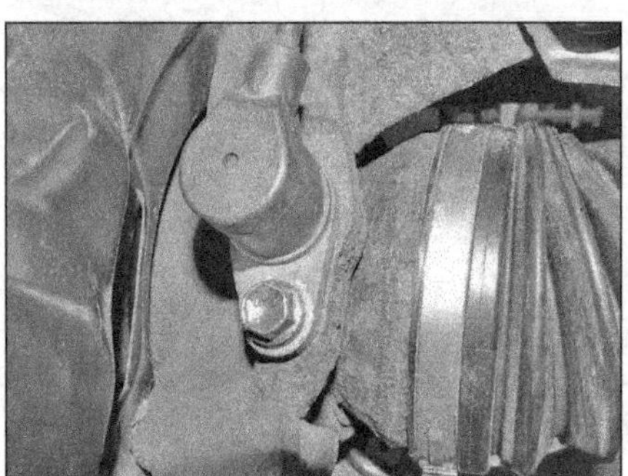
21.13a Undo the retaining nut . . .

21.13b . . . and withdraw the front sensor

required to remove the senor from the rear of the hub **(see illustration)**. If required, remove the rear hub bearing assembly as described in Chapter 10.

Refitting

15 Ensure that the mating faces of the sensor and the swivel hub are clean, and apply a little anti-seize grease to the hub carrier bore before refitting.

16 Make sure the sensor tip is clean and ease it into position in the hub carrier.

17 On front wheel sensors, refit the retaining bolt and tighten it to the specified torque.

18 On rear wheel sensors, refit the rear hub bearing assembly as described in Chapter 10.

19 Work along the sensor wiring, making sure it is correctly routed, and securing it in position with all the relevant clips and ties. Reconnect the wiring connector.

20 Refit the roadwheel, then lower the vehicle and tighten the wheel bolts to the specified torque.

21.14 Disconnect the rear sensor

Chapter 10
Suspension and steering systems

Contents

Degrees of difficulty

Easy, suitable for novice with little experience 	**Fairly easy,** suitable for beginner with some experience	**Fairly difficult,** suitable for competent DIY mechanic	**Difficult,** suitable for experienced DIY mechanic	**Very difficult,** suitable for expert DIY or professional 

Specifications

Front wheel alignment

Toe setting	0°06' ± 12' toe-in
Castor:	
1.4 litre (1398 cc) petrol engine	2°51' ± 45'
1.6 litre (1598 cc) petrol engine	2°53' ± 45'
2.0 litre (1995 cc) diesel engine	2°46' ± 45'
Camber:	
1.4 litre (1398 cc) petrol engine	-0°30' ± 45'
1.6 litre (1598 cc) petrol engine	-0°31' ± 45'
2.0 litre (1995 cc) diesel engine	-0°33' ± 45'
Steering axis inclination:	
1.4 litre (1398 cc) petrol engine	11°19'
1.6 litre (1598 cc) petrol engine	11°19'
2.0 litre (1995 cc) diesel engine	11°23'

Rear wheel alignment

Toe setting	0°13' ± 15' toe-in
Camber	-1°28' ± 30'

Torque wrench settings

	Nm	lbf ft
Front suspension		
Anti-roll bar:		
Drop link balljoints	44	32
Clamp bolts	19	14
Balljoints:		
Balljoint-to-control arm bolt/nuts	142	105
Balljoint-to-hub carrier nut	103	76
Control arm:		
Front pivot bolt	137	101
Rear pivot bolt	137	101
Roadwheel nuts	103	76
Subframe:		
Front upper mounting bolts	113	83
Rear mounting bolts	157	116
Support brace to front panel	39	29
Suspension struts:		
Strut-to-hub carrier bolts/nuts	153	113
Strut upper mounting nuts	39	29
Strut piston rod nut	47	35
Rear suspension		
Anti-roll bar	185	137
Axle mounting nuts/bolts	85	63
Hub and bearing assembly to axle	56	41
Roadwheel nuts	103	76
Suspension struts:		
Strut-to-axle	80	59
Strut upper mounting nuts	80	59
Strut piston rod nut	56	41
Steering		
Steering column:		
Mounting bolts	21	15
Protective shield bolt	18	13
Steering rack mounting bolts/nuts	49	36
Steering wheel nut	50	37
Track rod ends		
Track rod end-to-hub carrier nut	49	36
Track rod end locknut	74	55
Universal joint-to-pinion shaft pinch-bolt	35	26

1 General information

The front suspension is a MacPherson strut design. The upper end of each strut/coil spring assembly is attached to the vehicle's body. The lower end of the strut assembly is connected to the upper end of the hub carrier. The hub carrier is attached to a balljoint mounted on the outer end of the suspension control arm. An anti-roll bar reduces body roll.

The rear suspension also utilises strut/coil spring assemblies. The upper end of each strut is attached to the vehicle body. The lower end of each strut is attached to the rear beam axle. The rear anti-roll bar is located inside the box section of the rear beam axle.

The rack-and-pinion steering rack is located behind the engine/transmission assembly on the bulkhead and actuates the track rods, which are attached to the hub carriers. The inner ends of the track rods are protected by rubber gaiters, which should be inspected periodically for secure attachment, tears and leaking lubricant.

The steering power assist system is electric and consists of an electric motor attached to the steering column. The steering wheel operates the steering column, which actuates the steering rack through universal joints. Looseness in the steering can be caused by wear in the steering shaft universal joints, the steering rack, the track rod ends and loose retaining bolts.

Precautions

Frequently, when working on the suspension or steering system components, you may come across fasteners which seem impossible to loosen. These fasteners on the underside of the vehicle are continually subjected to water, road grime, mud, etc, and can become rusted or 'frozen', making them extremely difficult to remove. In order to unscrew these stubborn fasteners without damaging them (or other components), be sure to use lots of penetrating fluid and allow it to soak in for a while. Using a wire brush to clean exposed threads will also ease removal of the nut or bolt and prevent damage to the threads. Sometimes a sharp blow with a hammer and punch will break the bond between a nut and bolt threads, but care must be taken to prevent the punch from slipping off the fastener and ruining the threads. Heating the stuck fastener and surrounding area with a heat gun sometimes helps too, but isn't recommended because of the obvious dangers associated with fire. Sometimes tightening the nut or bolt first will help to break it loose. Fasteners that require drastic measures to remove should always be renewed.

Since most of the procedures dealt with in this Chapter involve jacking up the vehicle and working underneath it, a good pair of axle stands will be needed. A hydraulic trolley jack is the preferred type of jack to lift the vehicle, and it can also be used to support certain components during various operations.

Warning: Never, under any circumstances, rely on a jack to support the vehicle while working

2.2a Unclip the ABS wiring . . .

2.2b . . . undo the securing bolt . . .

2.2c . . . and remove the retaining bracket from the strut

on it. Whenever any of the suspension or steering fasteners are loosened or removed they must be inspected and, if necessary, renewed with ones of the same part number or of original equipment quality and design. Torque specifications must be followed for proper reassembly and component retention. Never attempt to heat or straighten any suspension or steering components. Instead, renew any bent or damaged part.

2 Suspension strut assembly (front) – removal, inspection and refitting

Removal

1 Loosen the wheel nuts, raise the vehicle and support it securely on axle stands (see *Jacking and vehicle support*). Remove the wheel.

2 Unbolt the brake hose bracket from the strut. Release the clip and detach the speed sensor wiring harness from the strut **(see illustrations)**.

3 Undo the retaining bolt and disconnect the anti-roll bar drop link from the strut **(see illustration)**.

4 Remove the strut-to-hub carrier nuts **(see illustration)** and tap the bolts out with a hammer and punch.

5 Separate the strut from the hub carrier. Be careful not to overextend the inner CV joint. Also, don't let the hub carrier fall outward and strain the brake hose.

6 Support the strut and spring assembly with one hand and remove the three strut-to-body nuts **(see illustration)**. Remove the assembly out from the wheel arch.

Inspection

7 Check the strut body for leaking fluid, dents, cracks and other obvious damage, which would warrant repair or renewal.

8 Check the coil spring for chips or cracks in the spring coating (this will cause premature spring failure due to corrosion). Inspect the spring seat for cuts, hardness and general deterioration.

9 If any undesirable conditions exist, proceed to the strut disassembly procedure (see Section 3).

Refitting

10 Guide the strut assembly up into the wheel arch and insert the upper mounting studs through the holes in the body. Once the studs protrude, install the nuts so the strut won't fall back through. This is most easily accomplished with the help of an assistant, as the strut is quite heavy and awkward.

11 Slide the hub carrier into the strut flange and insert the two bolts from the rear. Install the nuts and tighten them to the torque listed in this Chapter's Specifications.

12 Connect the brake hose bracket to the strut and tighten the bolt securely. Install the speed sensor wiring harness bracket.

13 Refit the anti-roll bar drop link to the strut and tighten the retaining nut to the correct torque setting.

14 Install the wheel and nuts, then lower the vehicle and tighten the nuts to the torque listed in the Specifications.

15 Tighten the upper mounting nuts to the torque listed in this Chapter's Specifications.

16 We recommend that the front wheel alignment be checked after fitting the suspension struts (see Section 21).

3 Strut/spring assembly – renewal

1 If the struts or coil springs exhibit the telltale signs of wear (leaking fluid, loss of damping capability, chipped, sagging or cracked coil springs) explore all options before beginning any work. The strut/shock absorber assemblies are not serviceable and must be renewed if a problem develops. However, strut assemblies complete with springs may be available on an exchange basis, which eliminates much time and work. Whichever route you choose to take, check on the cost and availability of parts before disassembling your vehicle.

Warning: Disassembling a strut is potentially dangerous and utmost attention must be directed to the job, or serious injury may result. Use only a high-quality spring compressor and carefully follow the manufacturer's instructions furnished with the tool. After removing the coil spring from the strut assembly, set it aside in a safe, isolated area.

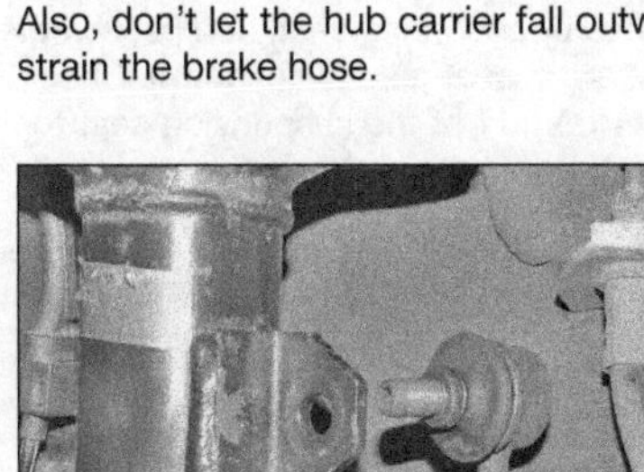

2.3 Disconnect the drop link

2.4 Undo the nuts and remove the strut-to-hub carrier bolts

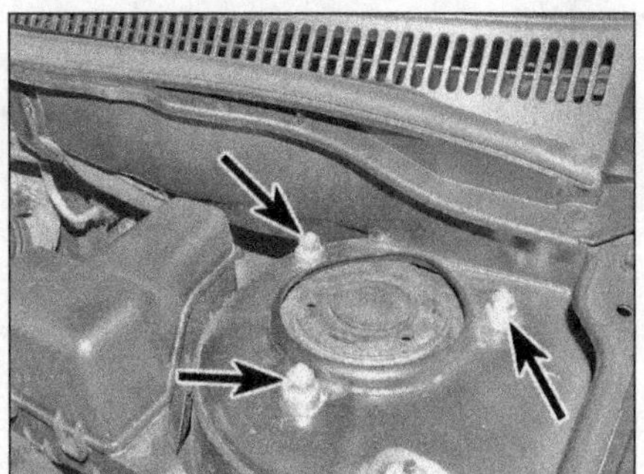

2.6 Undo the three strut-to-body nuts (arrowed)

3.3 Compress the spring until all pressure is relieved from the upper spring seat

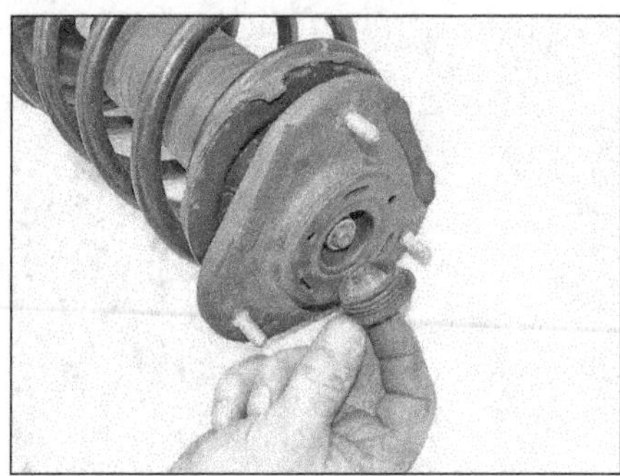

3.4a Remove the plastic centre cap . . .

3.4b . . . and remove the securing nut

3.5a Remove the upper mounting . . .

3.5b . . . and foam washer

Disassembly

2 Remove the strut assembly following the procedure described in the relevant Section. Mount the strut assembly in a vice. Line the vice jaws with wood or rags to prevent damage to the unit and don't tighten the vice excessively.

3 Following the tool manufacturer's instructions, install the spring compressor (which can be obtained at most automotive parts/accessory retailers or tool hire shops) on the spring and compress it sufficiently to relieve all pressure from the upper spring seat **(see illustration)**. This can be verified by wiggling the spring.

Front strut

4 With the spring compressed (see paragraph 3), remove the plastic cap and slacken the piston rod nut with a socket **(see illustrations)**.

5 Lift off the upper mounting, bearing and foam washer **(see illustrations)**. Inspect the bearing in the mounting for smooth operation. If it doesn't turn smoothly, renew the mounting.

6 Remove the upper spring seat, noting its fitted position **(see illustration)**. Check the rubber portion of the suspension seat for cracking and general deterioration. If there is any separation of the rubber, renew it.

7 Remove the bump stop and rubber gaiter from the strut piston rod **(see illustrations)**.

8 Carefully lift the compressed spring from the assembly, noting its fitted position in the lower seat **(see illustration)** and set it in a safe place.

9 Check the lower rubber insulator/seat for wear, cracking and hardness and renew it if necessary **(see illustration)**.

Rear strut

10 Mark the position of the spring to the upper seat. With the spring compressed (see paragraph 3), remove the piston rod nut with a socket. Recover the washer and rubber bush **(see illustrations)**.

11 Remove upper spring seat, complete with rubber insulator seat **(see illustration)**. Check the rubber portion of the suspension seat for

3.6 Remove the spring upper seat

3.7a Slide the bump stop from the piston rod . . .

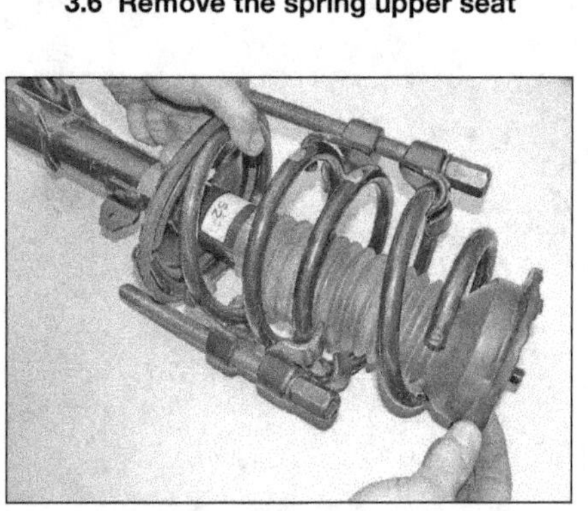

3.7b . . . and rubber gaiter

3.8 Lift the compressed spring from the strut

3.9 Check the rubber insulator for deterioration

3.10a Make alignment mark (arrowed) for the end of the spring

3.10b Remove the securing nut . . .

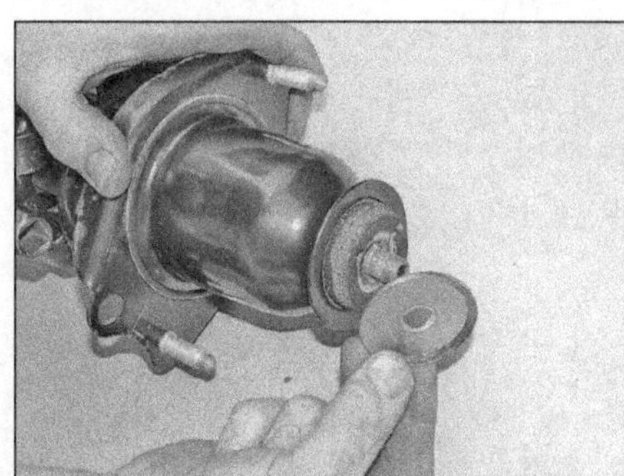
3.10c . . . washer . . .

cracking and general deterioration. If there is any separation of the rubber, renew it.

12 Slide the rubber bump stop and cover from the piston rod **(see illustrations)**.

13 Carefully lift the compressed spring from the assembly noting its fitted position in the lower seat, and then set it in a safe place **(see illustration)**.

14 Check the all components for leaking, wear, cracking and hardness and renew if necessary.

Reassembly

15 On front struts, if the lower insulator is being renewed, set it into position with the dropped portion seated in the lowest part of the seat.

16 Extend the piston rod to its full length and carefully place the coil spring onto the lower insulator, in the position noted on removal.

Front strut

17 Fit the rubber gaiter/spring seat to the top of the spring, aligning the end of the coil spring with the step in the rubber, and then install the rubber bump stop.

18 Fit the upper spring seat, ensuring the flats on its underside align with the flats machined on the piston rod, and the cut-away on its upper surface locates with the rubber gaiter **(see illustrations)**.

19 Fit the foam washer and upper mounting, and then tighten the piston rod nut to the specified torque. Fit plastic cap when nut has been tightened.

20 Install the strut assembly following the procedure as described in the relevant Section.

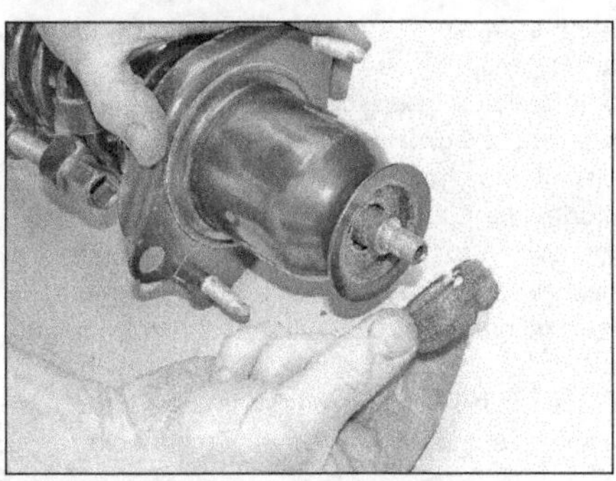
3.10d . . . and rubber bush

Rear strut

21 Slide the rubber bump stop and cover back into position on the piston rod.

22 Install the upper spring rubber and upper seat, making sure that the alignment marks made on removal are correct.

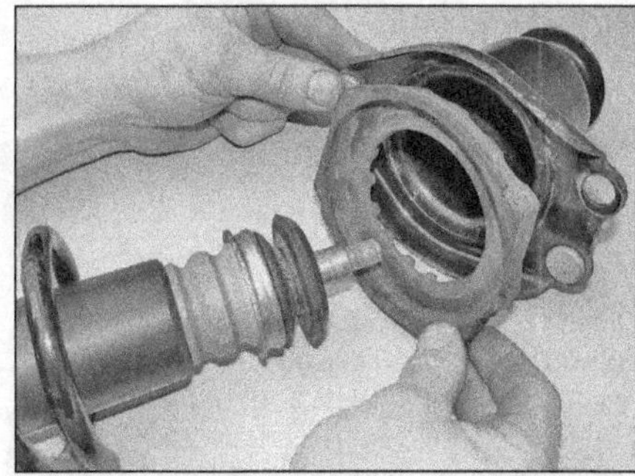
3.11 Remove the spring upper seat and insulator

23 Install the rubber bush, washer and nut and tighten it securely.

24 Install the strut assembly following the procedure as described in the relevant Section.

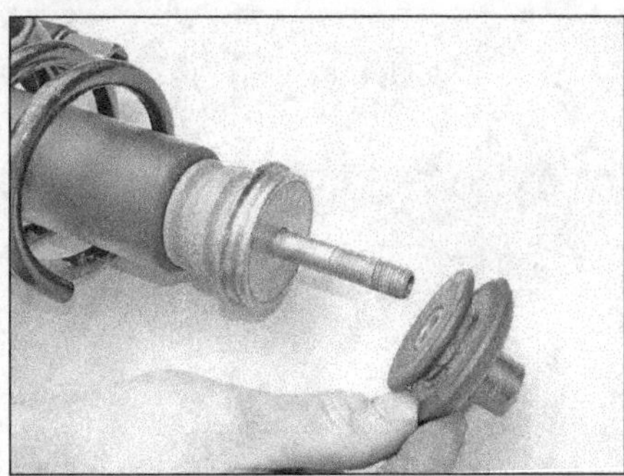
3.12a Remove the upper rubber bush . . .

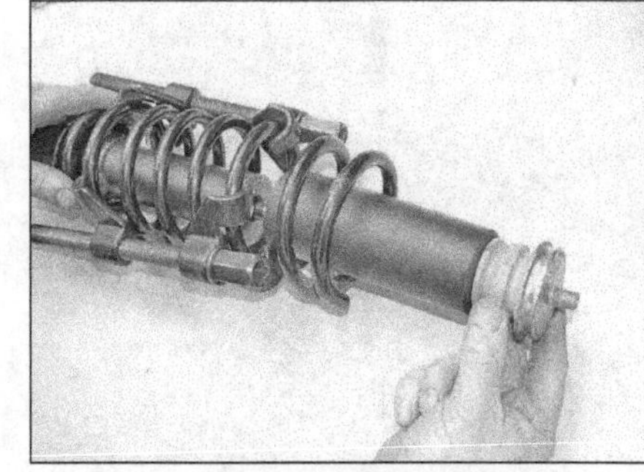
3.12b . . . and then slide the bump stop and cover from the piston rod

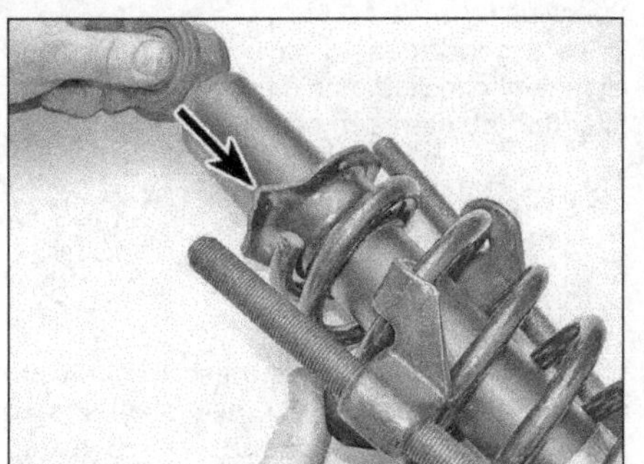
3.13 Note the fitted position (arrowed) for the end of the spring

3.18a Make sure the flats (arrowed) align with the upper seat . . .

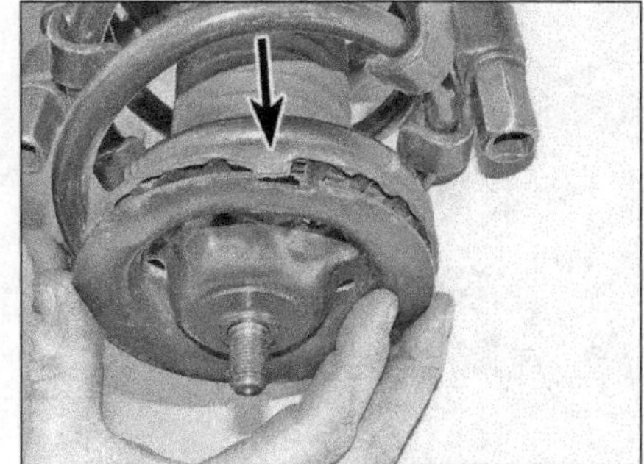
3.18b . . . and the rubber gaiter aligns (arrowed) with the upper seat

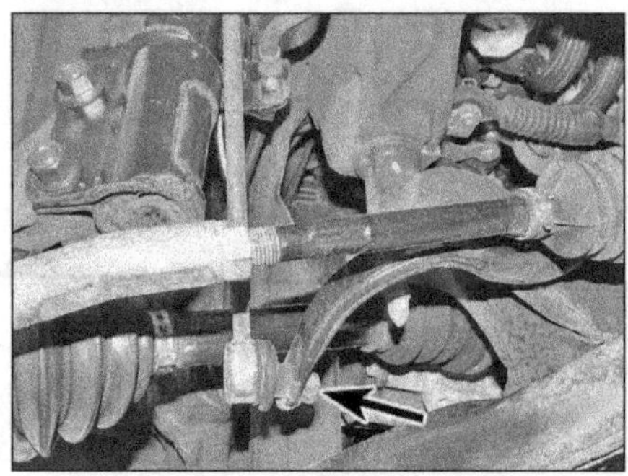

4.2 Undo the lower drop link balljoint nut (arrowed)

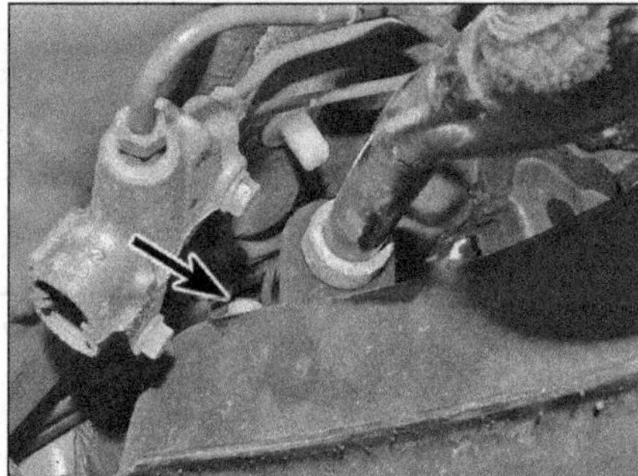

4.3 Anti-roll bar-to-subframe mounting bolts (one arrowed)

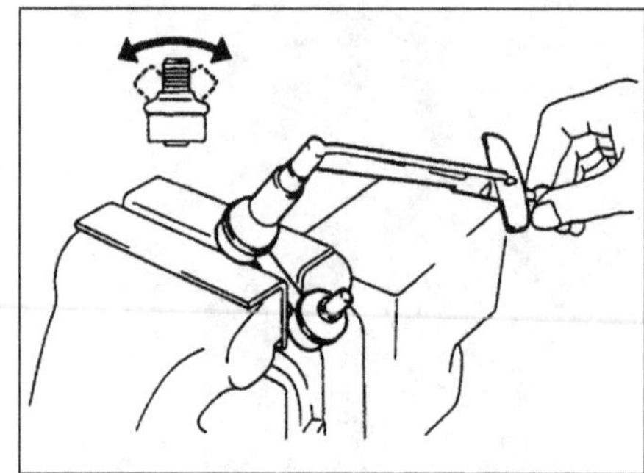

4.5 Check the balljoint in the anti-roll bar link as described in the text

4 Anti-roll bar and bushings (front) – removal and refitting

Removal

1 Loosen the front wheel nuts. Raise the front of the vehicle and support it securely on axle stands (see *Jacking and vehicle support*). Apply the handbrake and block the rear wheels to keep the vehicle from rolling off the stands. Remove the front wheels.

2 Remove the anti-roll bar drop link and lower balljoint nuts **(see illustration)**. If the balljoint shank turns with the nut, use an Allen key to hold the shank.

3 Unbolt the anti-roll bar bushing clamps from the top of the front subframe **(see illustration)**.

4 While the anti-roll bar is off the vehicle, slide off the rubber bushings and inspect them. If they're cracked, worn or deteriorated, renew them.

5 It is also a good idea to inspect the anti-roll bar drop links. To check them, flip the balljoint shank side-to-side five or six times **(see illustration)**, then install the nut. Using a torque wrench, turn the nut continuously one turn every two to four seconds and note the torque reading on the fifth turn. It should be about 0.05 to 1.0 Nm. If it isn't, renew the link assembly.

6 Clean the bushing area of the anti-roll bar with a stiff wire brush to remove any rust or dirt.

Refitting

7 Lubricate the inside and outside of the new bushing with vegetable oil (as used in cooking) to simplify reassembly.

Caution: Don't use petroleum or mineral-based lubricants, or brake fluid – they will lead to deterioration of the bushings.

8 Refitting is the reverse of removal.

5.2a Remove the nuts and bolt (arrowed) . . .

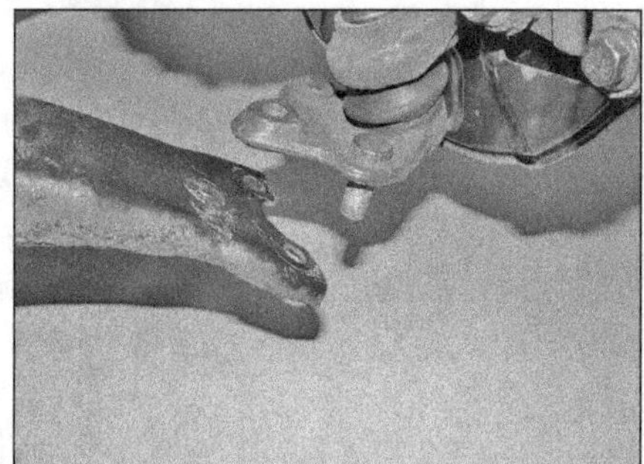

5.2b . . . and disconnect the lower balljoint

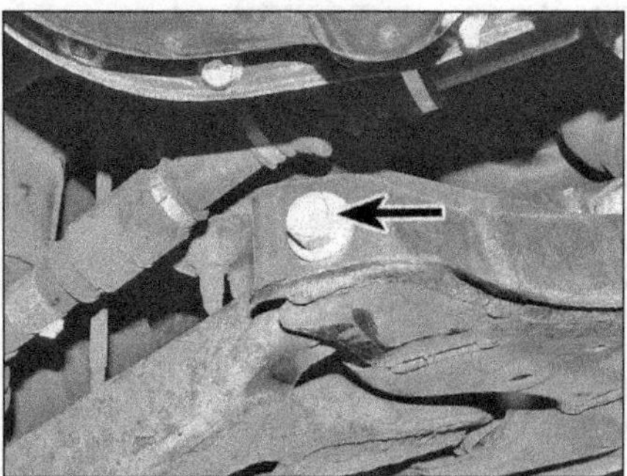

5.3 Remove the control arm front pivot bolt (arrowed)

5.4 Undo the control arm rear pivot bolt (arrowed)

5 Control arm – removal, inspection and refitting

Removal

1 Loosen the wheel nuts on the side to be dismantled, raise the front of the vehicle, support it securely on axle stands (see *Jacking and vehicle support*) and remove the wheel.

2 Remove the bolt and two nuts holding the control arm to the balljoint. Use a lever to disconnect the control arm from the balljoint **(see illustrations)**.

3 Remove the control arm front pivot bolt **(see illustration)**.

4 Remove the rear pivot bolt **(see illustration)**.

5 Remove the control arm.

Inspection

6 Check the control arm for distortion and the bushings for wear, renewing parts as necessary. Do not attempt to straighten a bent control arm.

Refitting

7 Refitting is the reverse of removal. Tighten all of the fasteners to the torque values listed in this Chapter's Specifications. **Note:** *Before tightening the pivot bolts, raise the outer end of the control arm with a floor jack to simulate normal ride height, or only tighten the bolts once the vehicle is lowered to the ground.*

8 Refit the wheel and nuts, lower the vehicle and tighten the nuts to the torque listed in the Specifications.

9 It's a good idea to have the front wheel alignment checked, and if necessary adjusted after this job has been performed.

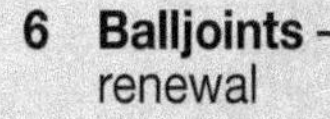

6 Balljoints – renewal

1 Loosen the wheel nuts, raise the vehicle and support it securely on axle stands (see *Jacking and vehicle support*). Remove the wheel.

2 Remove the bolt and nuts securing the balljoint to the control arm. Separate the balljoint from the control arm with a lever **(see illustration)**.

3 Slacken the driveshaft hub nut, and push the driveshaft through the hub to make access to the balljoint nut easier **(see illustration)**. If necessary undo the guide pin bolts and move the brake caliper to one side to prevent the hose being strained (see Chapter 9).

4 Remove the split pin (if equipped) from the balljoint shank and loosen the nut.

5 Separate the balljoint from the hub carrier with a balljoint separator **(see illustrations)**. Lubricate the rubber boot with grease and work carefully, so as not to tear the boot. Withdraw the balljoint from the stub axle.

6 To install the balljoint, insert the balljoint shank through the hole in the hub carrier and install the nut. Tighten the nut to the torque listed in this Chapter's Specifications and install a new split pin. If the split pin hole doesn't line up with the slots on the nut, tighten the nut additionally until it does line up – don't loosen the nut to insert the split pin.

7 Refit the driveshaft through the hub and tighten the retaining nut (Chapter 8). If removed, refit the brake caliper with reference to Chapter 9.

8 Attach the balljoint to the control arm and install the bolt and nuts, tightening them to the torque listed in this Chapter's Specifications.

9 Refit the wheel and nuts. Lower the vehicle and tighten the nuts to the torque listed in the Specifications.

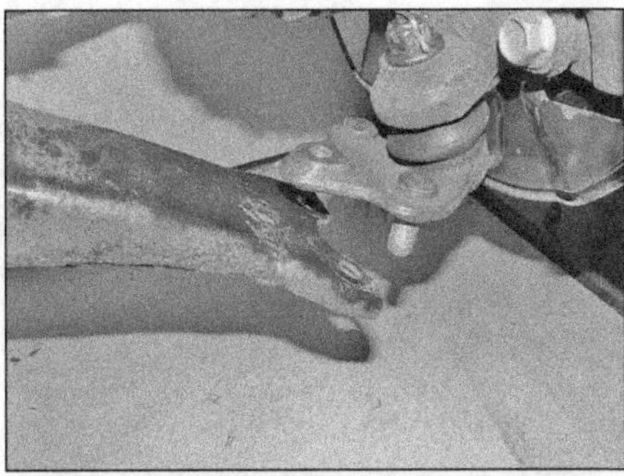

6.2 Disconnect the balljoint from the lower arm

6.3 Withdraw the hub from the driveshaft

6.5a Using a balljoint separator tool . . .

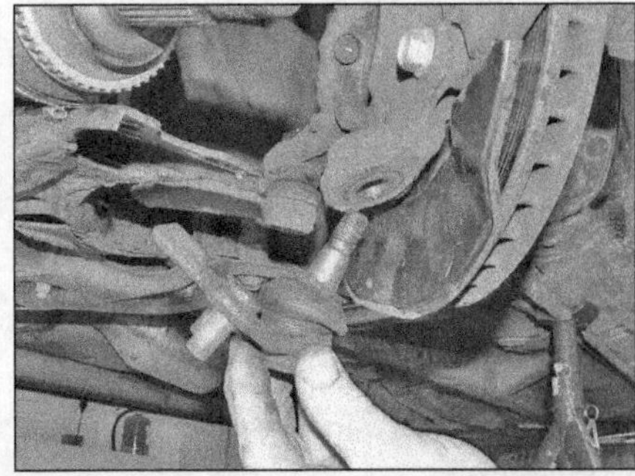

6.5b . . . to detach the balljoint shank from the hub carrier

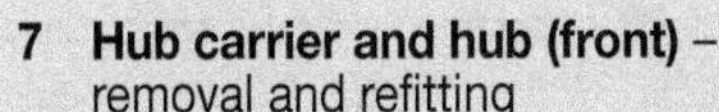

7 Hub carrier and hub (front) – removal and refitting

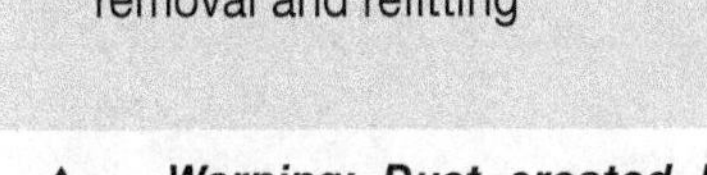

Warning: Dust created by the brake system may contain asbestos, which is harmful to your health. Never blow it out with compressed air and don't inhale any of it. Do not, under any circumstances, use petroleum-based solvents to clean brake parts. Use an aerosol brake cleaner.

Removal

1 Loosen the wheel nuts, raise the vehicle and support it securely on axle stands (see *Jacking and vehicle support*). Remove the wheel.

2 Release the locking tab and remove the driveshaft hub nut **(see illustrations)**. To prevent the hub from turning, wedge a lever between two of the wheel studs and allow the lever to rest against the ground or the floorpan of the vehicle.

3 Remove the brake caliper and the brake disc (see Chapter 9), and disconnect the brake hose from the strut.

4 Undo the retaining bolt and remove the wheel speed sensor (see Chapter 9).

5 Loosen, but don't remove the strut-to-hub carrier nuts and bolts **(see illustration)**.

6 Separate the track rod end from the hub carrier arm **(see illustration)**.

7 Remove the balljoint-to-lower arm as described in Section 6.

8 To loosen the driveshaft from the hub splines, tap the end of the driveshaft with a soft-faced hammer or a hammer and a brass punch.

9 The strut-to-hub carrier bolts can now be removed, and carefully separate the hub carrier from the strut **(see illustrations)**. As the hub carrier is removed, push the driveshaft from the hub and support the end of the driveshaft with a piece of wire.

7.2a Release the locking tab . . .

7.2b . . . and undo the driveshaft retaining nut

7.5 Slacken the strut-to-hub carrier nuts (arrowed)

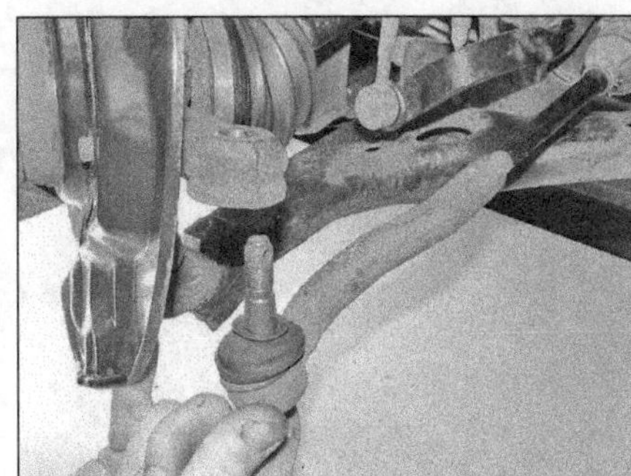

7.6 Disconnect the track rod end from the hub carrier

7.9a Remove the strut-to-hub carrier bolts (arrowed) . . .

7.9b . . . withdraw the driveshaft . . .

7.9c . . . and remove the hub assembly

Refitting

10 Guide the hub carrier and hub assembly into position, inserting the driveshaft into the hub.

11 Push the hub carrier into the strut flange and install the bolts and nuts, but don't tighten them yet.

12 If you removed the balljoint from the old hub carrier, and are planning to use it with the new hub carrier, connect the balljoint to the hub carrier and tighten the balljoint shank nut to the torque listed in this Chapter's Specifications.

13 Attach the balljoint to the control arm as describe in Section 6.

14 Attach the track rod to the hub carrier arm (see Section 16). Tighten the strut bolt nuts, the balljoint-to-control arm bolt and nuts and the track rod nut to the torque listed in this Chapter's Specifications.

15 Place the brake disc on the hub and install the caliper and wheel speed sensor as described in Chapter 9.

16 Install the driveshaft/hub nut, and then tighten it to the torque listed in the Chapter 8 Specifications. Using a drift, lock the tab on the nut to the groove in the driveshaft.

17 Install the wheel and nuts.

18 Lower the vehicle and tighten the nuts to the torque listed in the Specifications.

19 Drive the vehicle to a specialist workshop to have the front wheel alignment checked and, if necessary, adjusted.

8 Hub and bearing assembly (front) – removal and refitting

Removal

1 Remove the hub carrier and hub assembly as described in Section 7.

2 The hub must now be removed from the bearing inner races. It is preferable to use a press to do this, but it is possible to drive out the hub using a length of metal tube/socket of suitable diameter **(see illustration)**.

3 Part of the inner race may remain on the hub, and this should be removed using a puller or chisel **(see illustration)**.

4 Note that when renewing the hub, the wheel bearing will have to be renewed also, as it will be damaged on removal.

5 Using circlip pliers, extract the circlip securing the bearing in the hub carrier **(see illustration)**.

6 Press or drive out the bearing, using a length of metal tubing of diameter slightly less than the bearing outer race. Alternatively, refit the bearing inner race and press or drive against this – after all, as the bearing assembly is to be renewed, any damage to the bearing balls/races is of no importance **(see illustrations)**.

7 Clean the bearing seating faces in the hub carrier.

Refitting

8 Using a length of metal tube of diameter slightly less than the outer race, press or drive the new bearing into the hub carrier until it is fully located. Do not apply any pressure to the inner race.

9 Locate the circlip into the groove in the hub carrier.

10 Support the inner race on a length of metal tube, then press or drive the hub fully into the bearing.

11 Refit the hub carrier and hub assembly as described in Section 7.

8.2 Drive the hub from the bearing using a suitable tube or drift

8.3 If the bearing inner race remains on the hub, remove it using a puller or chisel

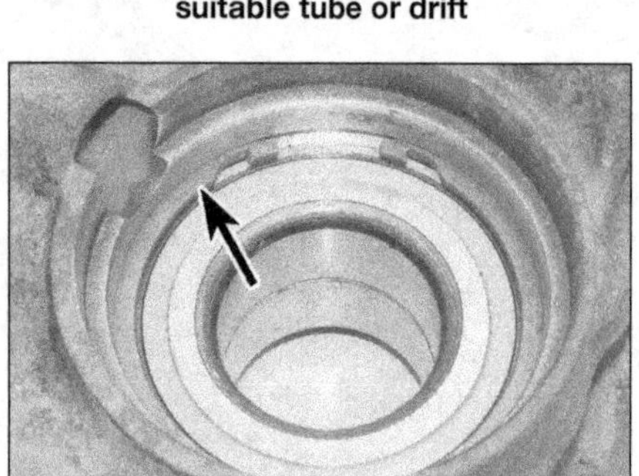
8.5 Extract the bearing circlip (arrowed) from the hub carrier

8.6a Refit the bearing inner race . . .

8.6b . . . and drive the bearing from the hub carrier

9 Anti-roll bar (rear) – removal and refitting

Removal

1 Raise the rear of the vehicle and place it securely on axle stands (see *Jacking and vehicle support*).

2 Remove the anti-roll bar retaining bolts from the rear beam axle **(see illustration)**.

3 The anti-roll bar can now be removed from the vehicle. Pull the anti-roll bar out from inside the box section of the rear beam axle.

4 Check the bushings at each end of the anti-roll bar for wear, hardness, distortion, cracking and other signs of deterioration, renewing them if necessary. Check with your local dealer for availability of parts.

Refitting

5 Refitting is the reverse of removal.

10 Suspension strut assembly (rear) – removal, inspection and refitting

Removal

1 Open the luggage compartment and remove the carpet from the floor area to access the suspension strut upper retaining nuts. On some models, it may be necessary to remove the rear seat back or fold the rear seats forward (see Chapter 11).

9.2 Anti-roll bar retaining bolt – one side shown

2 Loosen the rear wheel nuts, raise the rear of the vehicle and support it securely on axle stands (see *Jacking and vehicle support*). Remove the wheel.

3 Support the rear hub assembly with a trolley jack.

4 Remove the retaining nut and washer, and then disconnect the suspension strut from the hub carrier **(see illustrations)**.

5 Working inside the luggage compartment, remove the inner trim and undo the two strut upper retaining nuts **(see illustration)**.

6 Working under the wheel arch, support the strut and remove the upper strut-to-body mounting bolt **(see illustration)**.

7 Lower the suspension strut out from under the vehicle **(see illustration)**.

Inspection

8 Follow the inspection procedures described in Section 3. If you determine that the strut assembly must be disassembled for renewal of the strut or the coil spring, refer to Section 3.

9 When reassembling the strut, make sure the suspension upper support is aligned as noted on removal.

Refitting

10 Manoeuvre the assembly up into the wheel arch and insert the upper mounting bolt under the wheel arch, but do not tighten it yet.

11 Locate the lower part of the strut onto the stud on the hub carrier and install the nut and washer, tightening it to the torque listed in this Chapter's Specifications.

12 Working inside the luggage compartment fit the upper retaining nuts and tighten them to the specified torque setting. Also tighten the upper bolt under the wheel arch to the specified torque setting.

13 Install the wheel and nuts, lower the vehicle and tighten the nuts to the torque listed in the Specifications.

14 Where applicable, refit the luggage compartment carpet, seat and rear side seat backs (see Chapter 11).

11 Drop link – removal and refitting

Removal

1 The drop link is the linkage rod, with balljoints at each end, between the strut and the end of the anti-roll bar.

2 Loosen the wheel nuts, raise the vehicle

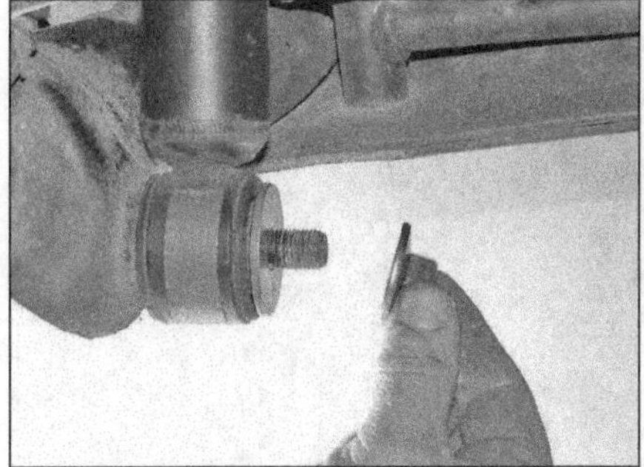

10.4a Remove the mounting nut . . .

10.4b . . . washer . . .

10.4c . . . and then disconnect the lower end of the strut

10.5 Undo the two upper mounting nuts (arrowed)

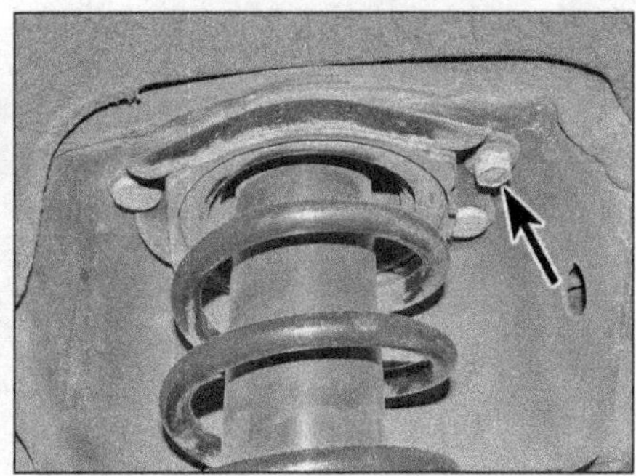

10.6 Undo the upper mounting bolt (arrowed)

10.7 Remove the strut from under the vehicle

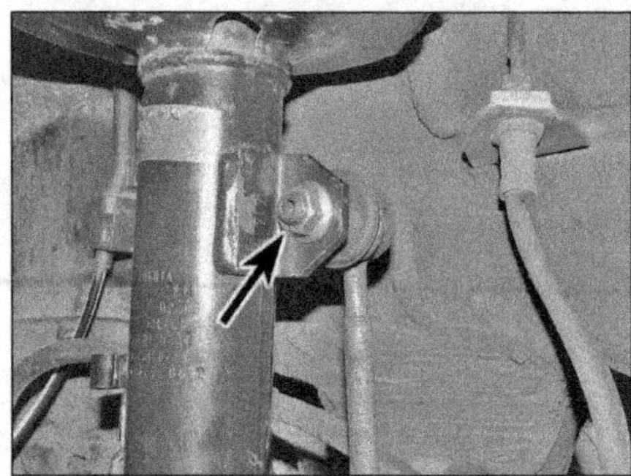

11.3a Remove the upper retaining nut (arrowed) . . .

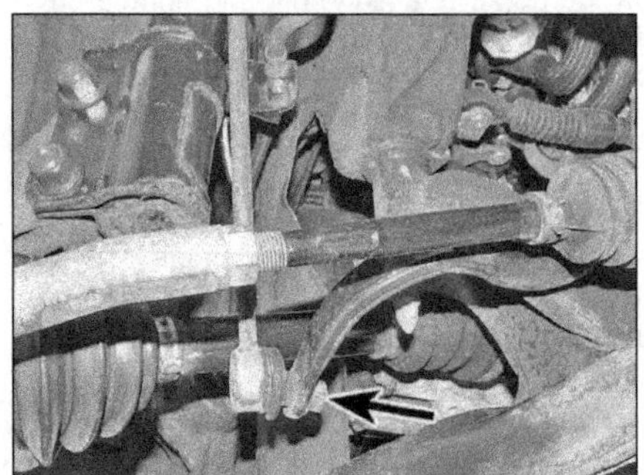

11.4 Remove the lower retaining nut (arrowed) and disconnect the drop link from the anti-roll bar

and support it securely on axle stands (see *Jacking and vehicle support*). Remove the wheel.

3 Undo the retaining nut and disconnect the upper part of the drop link from the suspension strut **(see illustrations)**.

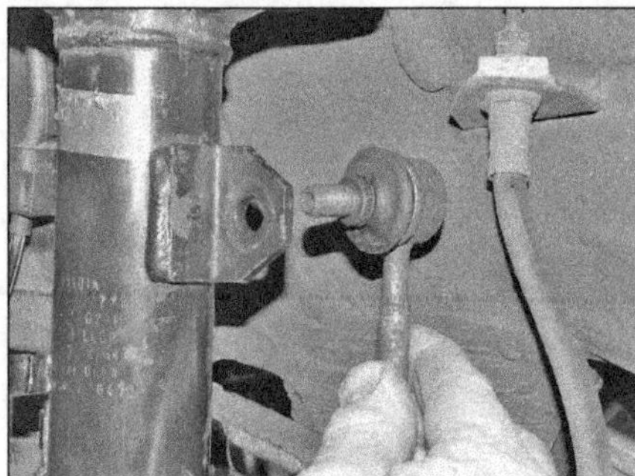

11.3b . . . and disconnect the drop link from the strut

4 Undo the retaining nut and disconnect the lower part of the drop link from the end of the anti-roll bar **(see illustration)**. The drop link can then be removed from the vehicle.

Refitting

5 Refitting is the reverse of the removal procedure. Be sure to tighten the bolts to the torque listed in this Chapter's Specifications. Tighten the wheel nuts to the torque listed in the Specifications.

12 Hub and bearing assembly (rear) – removal and refitting

Warning: Dust created by the brake system may contain asbestos, which is harmful to your health. Never blow it out with compressed air and don't inhale any of it. Do not use petroleum-based solvents. Use brake system cleaner only.

Removal

1 Loosen the rear wheel nuts, raise the rear of the vehicle and support it securely on axle stands (see *Jacking and vehicle support*). Remove the relevant rear wheel.

2 Remove the rear brake disc and caliper and handbrake shoes with reference to Chapter 9.

3 Disconnect the wiring connector from the rear wheel speed sensor at the rear of the hub **(see illustration)**.

4 Remove the four hub-to-hub carrier bolts, and remove the hub complete with brake backplate from the rear axle **(see illustrations)**.

5 The hub/bearing assembly is a tight fit in the brake backplate. Refit the four bolts by a couple of threads and tap the heads of them, while supporting the backplate, to remove the hub **(see illustration)**.

6 Remove the wheel speed sensor from the rear of the hub as described in Chapter 9, Section 21.

Refitting

7 Apply a light coat of copper grease to the rear of the hub/bearing assembly before refitting **(see illustration)**.

8 Clean the inner circumference of the brake backplate, before refitting the hub/bearing.

9 Refit the brake backplate to the rear axle and fit the handbrake shoes, with reference to Chapter 9. Use a nut and bolt to hold the

12.3 Disconnect the wiring connector from the speed sensor

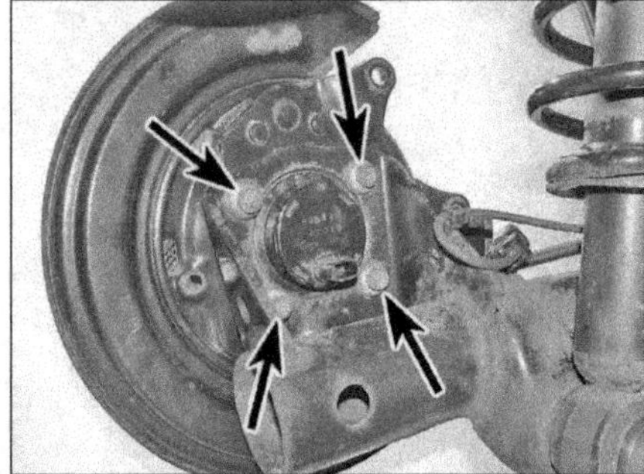

12.4a Undo the four hub bolts (arrowed) . . .

12.4b . . . and withdraw the hub from the rear axle

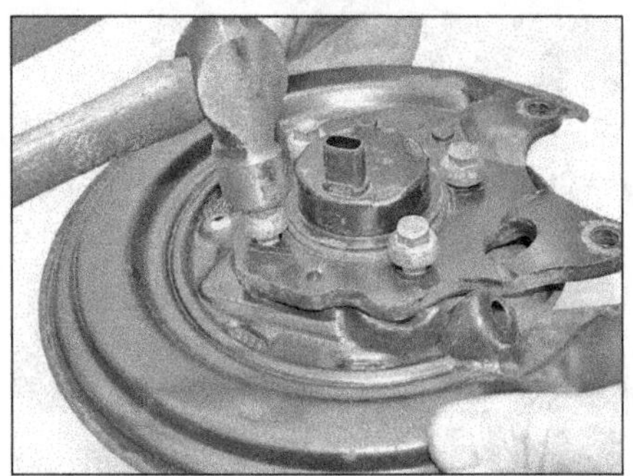

12.5a Support the backplate . . .

12.5b . . . and use a hammer to remove the hub

12.7 Apply copper grease around the hub flange before refitting

backplate in place while carrying out this procedure **(see illustration)**.

10 Remove the nut and bolt from the backplate and then position the hub/bearing assembly on the axle. Align the holes in the backing plate and install the four bolts **(see illustration)**. Tighten them to the torque listed in this Chapter's Specifications.

11 Refit the brake disc, caliper and wheel speed sensor (with reference to Chapter 9). Refit the roadwheel and lower the vehicle, tighten the nuts to the torque listed in the Specifications.

13 Rear beam axle – removal and refitting

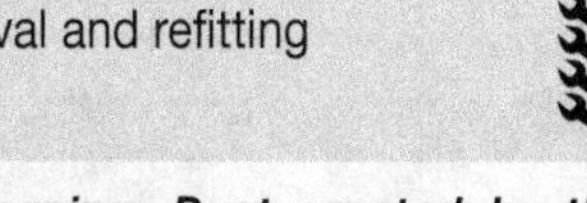

Warning: Dust created by the brake system may contain asbestos, which is harmful to your health. Never blow it out with compressed air and don't inhale any of it. Do not, under any circumstances, use petroleum-based solvents to clean brake parts. Use brake system cleaner only.

Note: *Due to the weight and size of the rear axle, it would be useful to have the aid of an assistant for this procedure.*

Removal

1 Loosen the wheel nuts, raise the vehicle and support it on axle stands (see *Jacking and vehicle support*). Block the front wheels and remove the rear wheels.

2 Remove the rear hub/bearing assembly as described in Section 12 of this Chapter. If a new axle is not being fitted, then the brake disc and hub assembly can remain fitted to the rear axle and the handbrake cable can be disconnected under the vehicle, see Chapter 9.

3 Undo the retaining bolts and disconnect the handbrake cable bracket and wheel speed sensor wiring bracket from each side of the rear axle **(see illustration)**.

4 Using a trolley jack to support the rear axle, undo the retaining nuts and disconnect the lower part of the rear shock absorbers from the axle **(see illustration)**.

5 Undo the rear axle-to-body mounting bolts **(see illustration)** and with the aid of an assistant, lower the rear axle from under the vehicle.

Refitting

6 Refitting is the reverse of the removal procedure. Be sure to tighten the bolts to the torque listed in this Chapter's Specifications.

14 Steering system – general information

All models are equipped with rack-and-pinion steering. The steering gear is bolted to the front suspension crossmember and operates the hub carriers via track rods. The inner ends of the track rods are protected by

12.9 Use a bolt (arrowed) to support the backplate

12.10 Fitting the rear hub into the backplate

rubber gaiters, which should be inspected periodically for secure attachment, tears and leaking lubricant.

All models are equipped with electric power-assisted steering. The power assist system consists of an electric motor, which is part of the steering column.

The steering wheel operates the steering column, which actuates the steering rack through universal joints. Looseness in the steering can be caused by wear in the steering column universal joints, the steering rack, the track rod ends and loose retaining bolts.

15 Steering wheel – removal and refitting

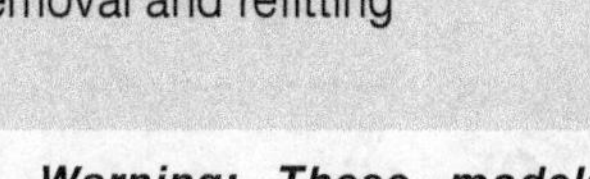

Warning: These models are equipped with airbags. The airbag is armed and can deploy (inflate) whenever the battery is connected. To prevent accidental deployment (and possible injury), turn the ignition key to LOCK and disconnect the negative battery cable whenever working near airbag components (see Chapter 5A). After the battery is disconnected, wait at least five minutes before beginning work (the system has a back-up capacitor that must fully discharge). For more information see Chapter 12.

Removal

1 Turn the ignition key to off, then disconnect the cable from the negative terminal of the battery (see Chapter 5A), then wait at least 5 minutes before proceeding.

2 From the straight-ahead position, turn the steering wheel a quarter of a turn anti-clockwise. Insert a screwdriver into the hole in the rear of the steering wheel on the right-hand side to release the locking clip **(see illustrations)**.

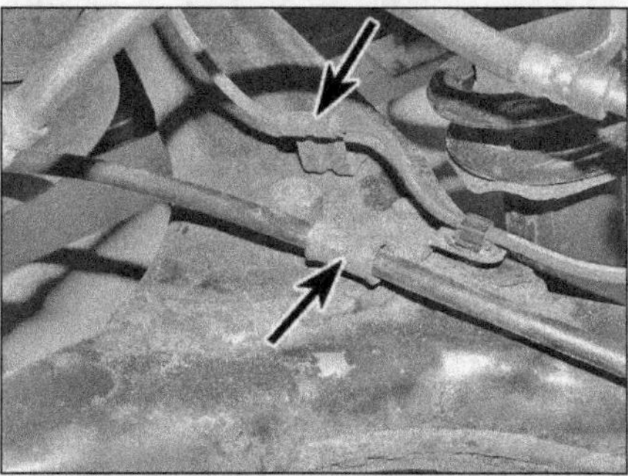

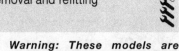

13.3 Disconnect the cable brackets (arrowed) from the axle

13.4 Disconnect the lower strut from the rear axle

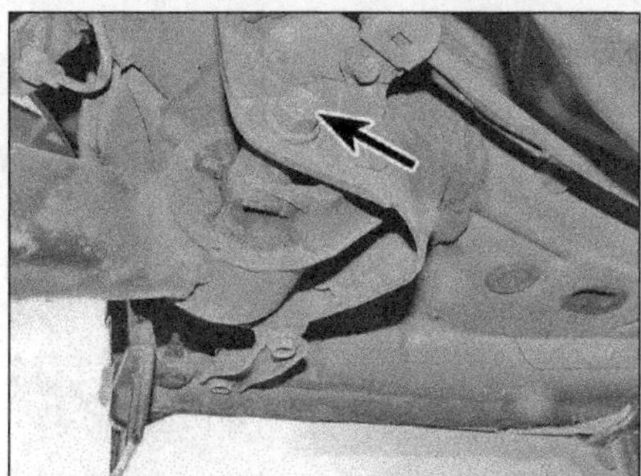

13.5 Rear axle mounting bolts – one side shown

15.2a Insert a screwdriver . . .

15.2b . . . and release the retaining spring clip arrowed

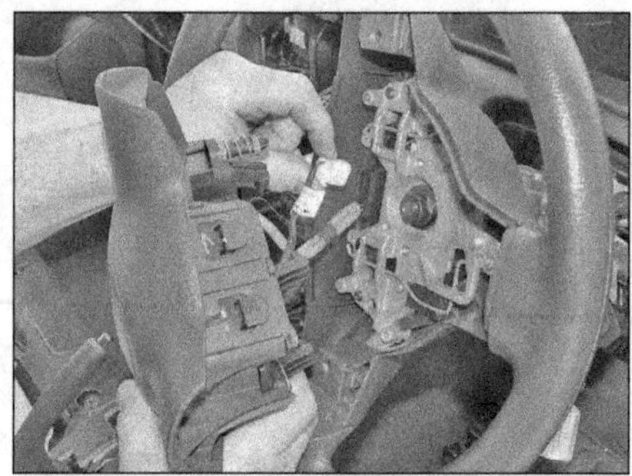
15.3 Disconnect the wiring connectors

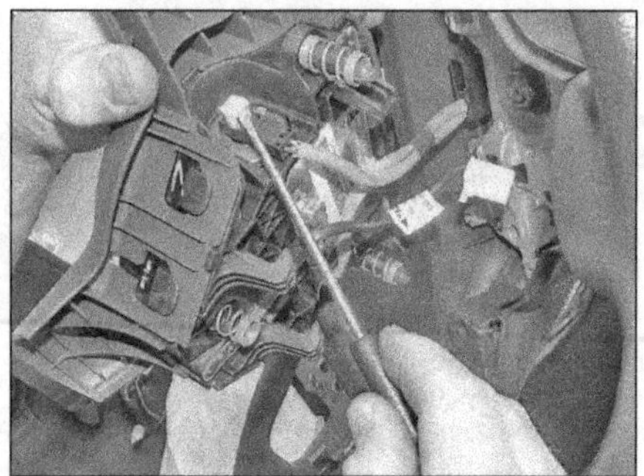
15.4a Release the locking clip . . .

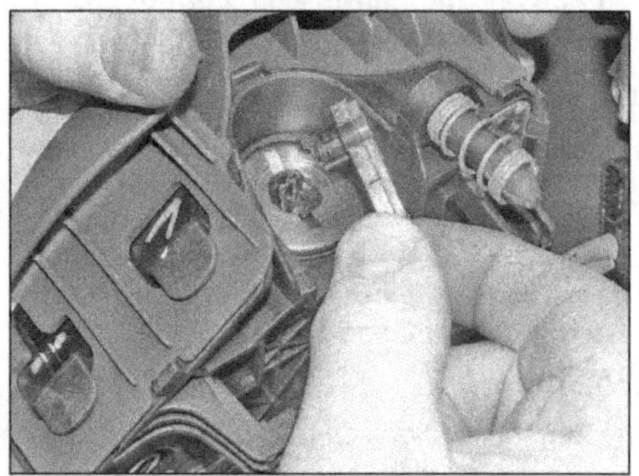
15.4b . . . and disconnect the connector from the airbag

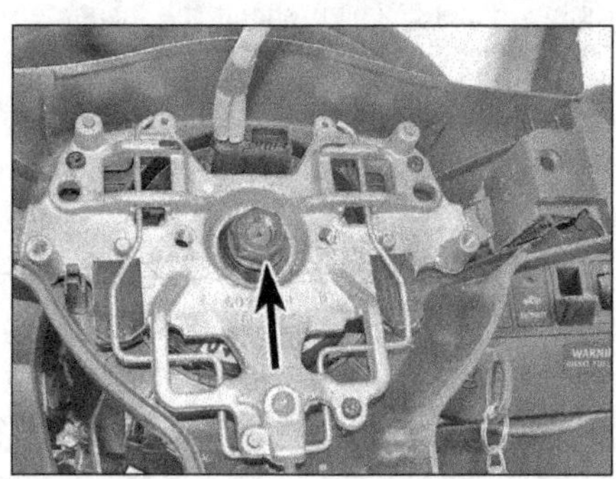
15.5 Steering wheel retaining nut

15.6a Using home-made puller . . .

3 With the clip released withdraw the airbag module from the steering wheel and unplug the electrical connector for the cruise control (if equipped) and horn contact **(see illustration)**.
4 Release the locking clips and disconnect the module electrical connectors **(see illustrations)**.

Warning: Set the airbag module down with the trim side facing up.

5 Slacken the steering wheel retaining nut, then mark the relationship of the steering column to the hub (if marks don't already exist or don't line up) to simplify installation and ensure steering wheel alignment **(see illustration)**.
6 Pull the wheel from the steering column using a rocking motion. If necessary, use a puller to disconnect the steering wheel from the column **(see illustrations)**. Feed the wiring out through the slot in the steering wheel as it is removed.

Refitting

7 To install the wheel, align the mark on the steering wheel hub with the mark on the shaft and slip the wheel onto the shaft. Install the nut and tighten it to the torque listed in this Chapter's Specifications.
8 Plug in the cruise control/horn contact connector.
9 Plug in the electrical connectors for the airbag module and fit the locking clips **(see illustration)**.
10 Make sure the airbag module electrical connector is positioned correctly and that the wires don't interfere with anything, then press the airbag module onto the steering wheel, making sure retaining clip secures the airbag.
11 Make sure that no one is inside the car, and then connect the negative battery cable (see Chapter 5A).

16 Track rod ends – removal and refitting

Removal

1 Loosen the wheel nuts. Raise the front of the vehicle, support it securely on axle stands (see *Jacking and vehicle support*), block the rear wheels and set the handbrake. Remove the front wheel.
2 Remove the split pin **(see illustration)** and loosen the nut on the track rod end balljoint shank.
3 Hold the track rod with a pair of locking

15.6b . . . to release the steering wheel from the splines . . .

15.6c . . . and remove it from the steering column

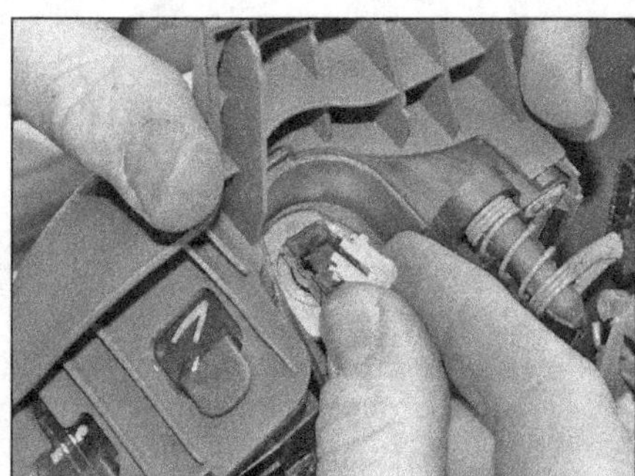
15.9 Make sure the locking clip is securely refitted

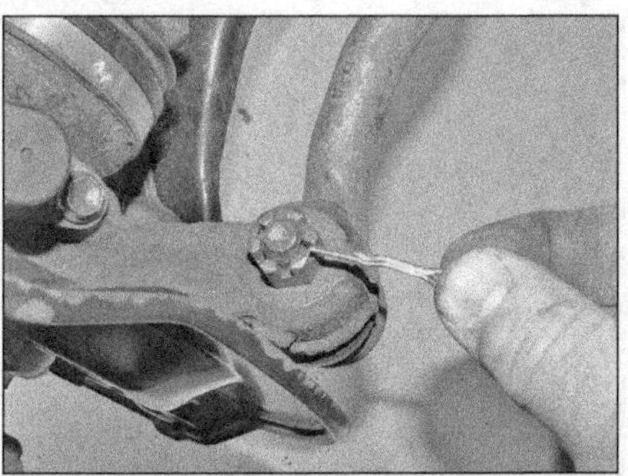

16.2 Remove the split pin from the track rod end retaining nut

16.3a Slacken the locknut (arrowed) . . .

16.3b . . . then mark the position of the track rod end in relation to the threads

pliers or spanner and loosen the locknut enough to mark the position of the track rod end in relation to the threads **(see illustrations)**.

4 Disconnect the track rod from the hub carrier arm using a universal balljoint separator. Remove the nut and detach the track rod **(see illustrations)**

5 The track rod end can then be unscrewed from the track rod, counting the number of turns, to aid refitting.

Refitting

6 Thread the track rod end on to the marked position (number of turns) and insert the track rod end balljoint shank into the hub carrier arm. Tighten the lock nut securely.

7 Refit the castellated nut on the balljoint shank and tighten it to the torque listed in this Chapter's Specifications. Install a new split pin. If the hole for the split pin doesn't line up with one of the slots in the nut, turn the nut an additional amount until it does.

8 Refit the wheel and nuts. Lower the vehicle and tighten the nuts to the torque listed in the Specifications.

9 It's advisable to have the wheel alignment checked by a dealer service department or an alignment workshop.

16.4a Using a balljoint separator tool . . .

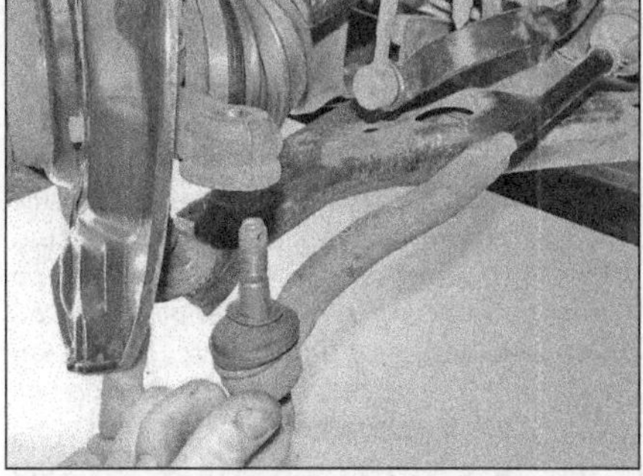

16.4b . . . to detach the balljoint shank from the hub carrier arm

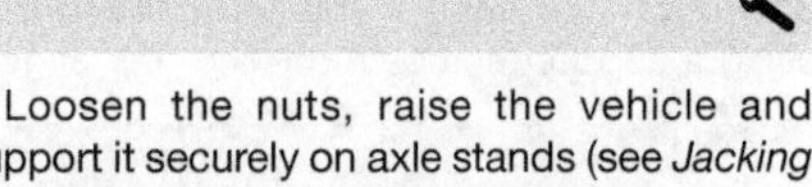

17 Steering rack gaiters – renewal

1 Loosen the nuts, raise the vehicle and support it securely on axle stands (see *Jacking and vehicle support*). Remove the wheel.

2 Remove the track rod end and locknut (see Section 16).

3 Remove the outer steering rack gaiter clamp with a pair of pliers. Release the inner gaiter clamp and slide off the gaiter **(see illustrations)**.

4 Before fitting the new gaiter, wrap the threads and serrations on the end of the steering rod with a layer of tape so the small end of the new gaiter isn't damaged.

5 Slide the new gaiter into position on the steering rack until it seats in the groove in the steering rod and install new clamps (where necessary).

6 Remove the tape and install the track rod end (see Section 16).

7 Refit the wheel and nuts. Lower the vehicle and tighten the nuts to the torque listed in the Specifications.

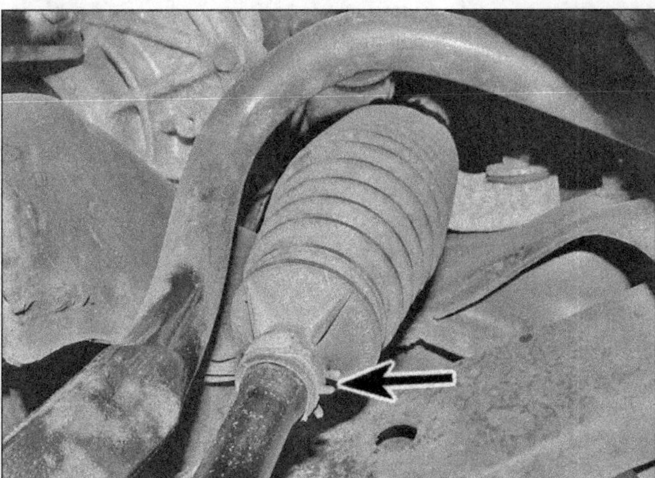

17.3a Release the band type clamp (arrowed) using a pair of pliers

17.3b The inner ends of the gaiters are retained by clamps that must be cut off and discarded

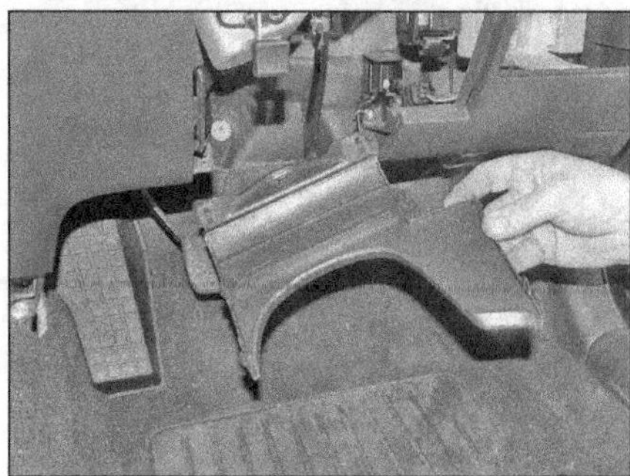
18.2 Unclip the lower facia trim panel

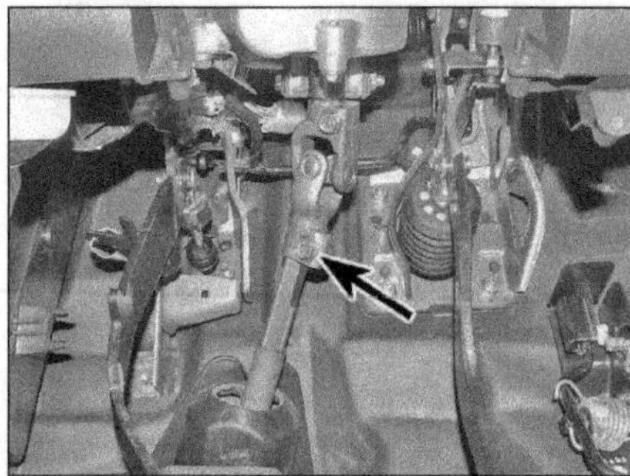
18.3 Undo the steering column joint bolt (arrowed)

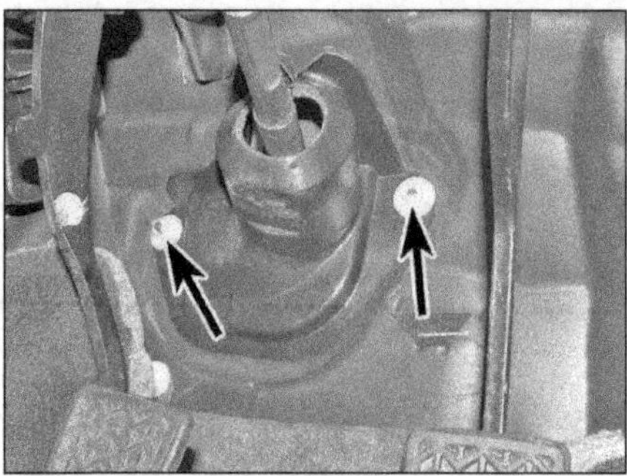
18.4 Undo the retaining nuts and remove cover

18 Steering rack – removal and refitting

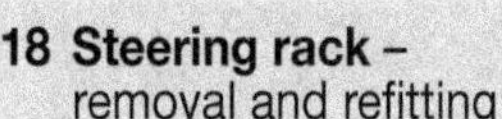

Warning: These models are equipped with airbags. Make sure the steering column is not turned while the steering rack is removed or you could damage the airbag system. To prevent the column from turning, turn the ignition key to the LOCK position before beginning work or run the seat belt through the steering wheel and clip the seat belt into place.

Removal

1 Loosen the front wheel nuts, raise the front of the vehicle and support it securely on axle stands (see *Jacking and vehicle support*). Apply the handbrake and remove the wheels. Remove the engine undertrays.

2 Working inside the driver's side footwell, undo the retaining screws and remove the lower facia trim panel **(see illustration)**.

3 Undo the securing bolt on the steering column universal joint and disconnect it from the steering rack shaft **(see illustration)**. Mark the position of the universal joint on the shafts, so that it can be refitted in the correct position.

4 Pull back the carpet and remove the lower cover from the bulkhead **(see illustration)**

5 Disconnect the track rod ends from the hub carrier as described in Section 16.

6 Undo the retaining nuts and disconnect the drop link upper balljoints from the front struts **(see illustration)**.

7 Disconnect the lower balljoints from the lower suspension control arm as described in Section 5.

8 Support the engine and transmission by using a support across the top of the engine compartment, secure the engine/transmission to the support.

9 With the engine/transmission supported, undo the retaining bolts and remove the centre brace from under the engine **(see illustration)**.

10 Undo the rear engine mounting to suspension crossmember retaining bolts.

11 Support the suspension crossmember using a trolley jack and remove the outer bracing plates from each side of the cross-member, and the rear crossmember mounting bolt **(see illustration)**. Mark around the outside of the crossmember, to aid with the alignment of the crossmember on refitting.

12 Undo the nuts/bolts and lower suspension crossmember out from under the vehicle, complete with steering rack and anti-roll bar attached across the top of the crossmember **(see illustration)**.

13 Undo the retaining bolts and remove the steering gear from the crossmember. Where applicable, check the steering rack mounting grommets for excessive wear or deterioration, renewing them if necessary.

18.6 Undo the retaining nut (arrowed) and disconnect the drop link

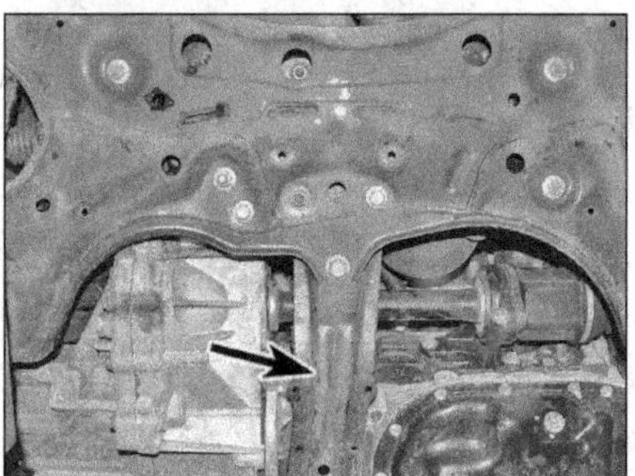
18.9 Remove the centre brace (arrowed)

Refitting

14 Refitting is the reverse of the removal procedure, noting the following points:

a) Align the crossmember, as noted on removal before tightening all the bolts.

b) Be sure to tighten the bolts to the torque listed in this Chapter's Specifications.

c) Position the steering rack and connect the universal joint, aligning the marks.

19 Steering column and motor – removal and refitting

Removal

1 Remove the steering wheel as described in Section 15.

2 Undo the securing bolt on the steering column universal joint and disconnect it from the steering rack shaft **(see illustration)**. Mark the position of the universal joint on the shafts, so that it can be refitted in the correct position.

3 Remove the indicator and lighting switches from the top of the steering column as described in Chapter 12.

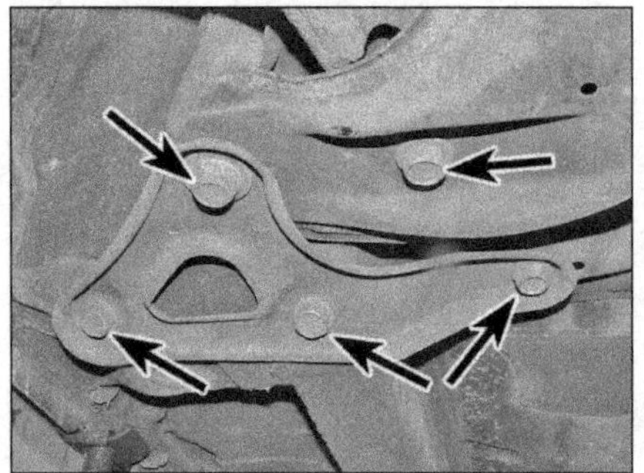
18.11 Undo the mounting bolts (arrowed)

18.12 Crossmember front mounting nuts – one side shown

19.2 Undo the steering column joint bolt (arrowed)

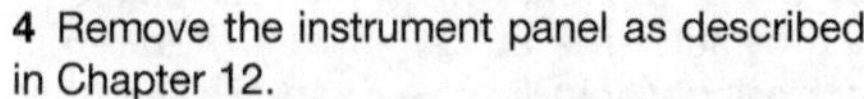

4 Remove the instrument panel as described in Chapter 12.

5 Trace the wiring from the power steering motor to the electronic control module and disconnect the wiring connector.

6 Disconnect the wiring connector from the ignition switch **(see illustration)**.

7 Unclip the wiring loom from the steering column, noting its fitted position **(see illustration)**.

8 Undo the retaining bolt and remove the protective shield from the lower part of the steering column **(see illustration)**.

9 With the protective shield removed, slacken and remove the lower steering column mounting bolt **(see illustration)**.

10 Slacken and remove the steering column upper mounting bolts and withdraw the steering column from inside the vehicle **(see illustration)**.

11 See your local Toyota dealer for further information and parts for the power steering motor **(see illustration)**.

Refitting

12 Refitting is the reverse of the removal procedure. Be sure to tighten all bolts to their specified torque setting where applicable. Refer to Chapter 12 for the refitting procedure of the instrument panel and switches as required.

19.6 Disconnect the wiring block connectors

19.8 Undo the shield retaining bolt (arrowed)

20 Wheels and tyres – general information

1 All vehicles covered by this manual are equipped with metric-sized fibreglass or steel belted radial tyres. Use of other size or type of tyres may affect the ride and handling of the vehicle. Don't mix different types of tyres, such as radials and bias belted on the same vehicle, as handling may be seriously affected. It's recommended that tyres be renewed in pairs on the same axle, but if only one tyre is being renewed, be sure it's the same size, structure and tread design as the other.

19.7 Release the wiring loom from the steering column

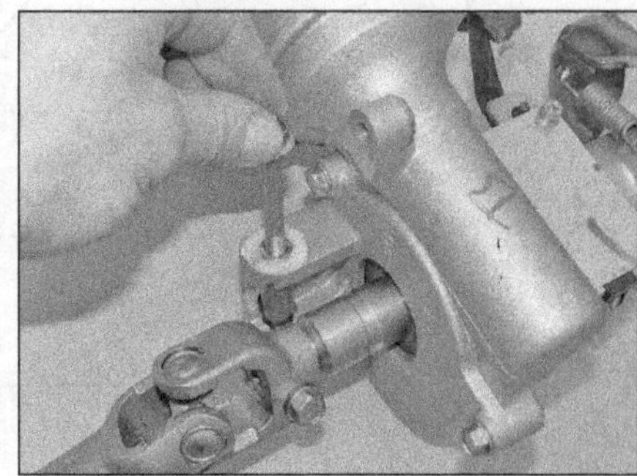

19.9 Remove the steering column lower mounting bolt (column removed for clarity)

2 Because tyre pressure has a substantial effect on handling and wear, the pressure on all tyres should be checked regularly and before any extended trips (see *Weekly checks*).

3 Wheels must be renewed if they are bent, dented, leak air, have elongated bolt holes, are heavily rusted, out of vertical symmetry or if the nuts won't stay tight. Wheel repairs that use welding or peening are not recommended.

4 Tyre and wheel balance is important in the overall handling, braking and performance of the vehicle. Unbalanced wheels can adversely affect handling and ride characteristics as well as tyre life. Whenever a tyre is installed on a wheel, the tyre and wheel should be balanced by a workshop with the proper equipment.

19.10 Remove the steering column upper mounting bolts (arrowed)

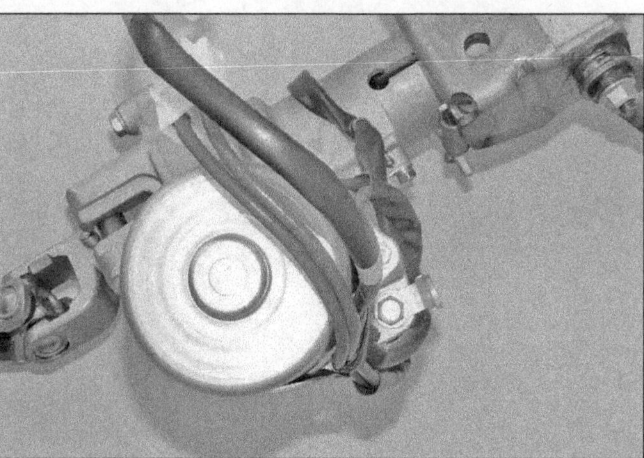

19.11 Steering motor part of steering column

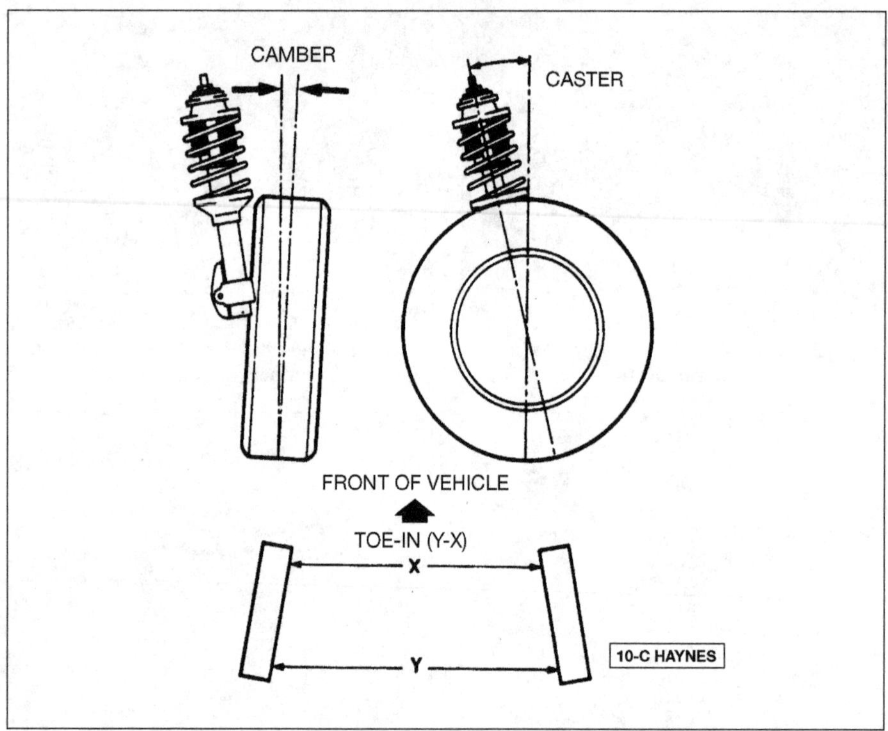

21.1 Camber, castor and toe-in angles

21 Wheel alignment – general information

A wheel alignment refers to the adjustments made to the wheels so they are in proper angular relationship to the suspension and the ground. Wheels that are out of proper alignment not only affect vehicle control, but also increase tyre wear. The front-end angles normally measured are camber, castor and toe-in **(see illustration)**; only toe-in is adjustable. The only adjustment possible on the rear is toe-in. The other angles should be measured to check for bent or worn suspension parts.

Getting the proper wheel alignment is a very exacting process, one in which complicated and expensive machines are necessary to perform the job properly. Because of this, you should have a technician with the proper equipment perform these tasks. We will, however, use this space to give you a basic idea of what is involved with a wheel alignment so you can better understand the process and deal intelligently with the workshop that does the work.

Toe-in is the turning in of the wheels. The purpose of a toe specification is to ensure parallel rolling of the wheels. In a vehicle with zero toe-in, the distance between the front edges of the wheels will be the same as the distance between the rear edges of the wheels. The actual amount of toe-in is normally only millimetre or so. On the front end, toe-in is controlled by the track rod end position on the track rod. Incorrect toe-in will cause the tyres to wear improperly by making them scrub against the road surface.

Camber is the tilting of the wheels from vertical when viewed from one end of the vehicle. When the wheels tilt out at the top, the camber is said to be positive (+). When the wheels tilt in at the top the camber is negative (-). The amount of tilt is measured in degrees from vertical and this measurement is called the camber angle. This angle affects the amount of tyre tread, which contacts the road and compensates for changes in the suspension geometry when the vehicle is cornering or travelling over an undulating surface.

Castor is the tilting of the front steering axis from the vertical. A tilt toward the rear is positive castor and a tilt toward the front is negative castor.

Chapter 11
Bodywork and fittings

Contents

Degrees of difficulty

Easy, suitable for novice with little experience 	**Fairly easy,** suitable for beginner with some experience	**Fairly difficult,** suitable for competent DIY mechanic	**Difficult,** suitable for experienced DIY mechanic	**Very difficult,** suitable for expert DIY or professional 

Specifications

Torque wrench settings	Nm	lbf ft
Seat belt mounting bolts	41	30
Seat belt tensioner stalk on seat	41	30
Seat mounting bolts	42	31

1 General information

The bodyshell is made of pressed-steel sections. Most components are welded together, but some use is made of structural adhesives.

The bonnet, door and some other vulnerable panels are made of zinc-coated metal, and are further protected by being coated with an anti-chip primer before being sprayed.

Extensive use is made of plastic materials, mainly in the interior, but also in exterior components. The front and rear bumpers and front grille are injection-moulded from a synthetic material that is very strong and yet light. Plastic components such as wheel arch liners are fitted to the underside of the vehicle, to improve the body's resistance to corrosion.

2 Maintenance – bodywork and underframe

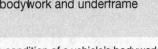

1 The condition of a vehicle's bodywork is the one thing that significantly affects its value. Maintenance is easy, but needs to be regular. Neglect, particularly after minor damage, can lead quickly to further deterioration and costly repair bills. It is important also to keep watch on those parts of the vehicle not immediately visible, for instance the underside, inside all the wheel arches, and the lower part of the engine compartment.

2 The basic maintenance routine for the bodywork is washing – preferably with a lot of water, from a hose. This will remove all the loose solids, which may have stuck to the vehicle. It is important to flush these off in such a way as to prevent grit from scratching the finish. The wheel arches and underframe need washing in the same way, to remove any accumulated mud, which will retain moisture and tend to encourage rust. Oddly enough, the best time to clean the underframe and wheel arches is in wet weather, when the mud is thoroughly wet and soft. In very wet weather, the underframe is usually cleaned of large accumulations automatically, and this is a good time for inspection.

3 Periodically, except on vehicles with a wax-based underbody protective coating, it is a good idea to have the whole of the underframe of the vehicle steam-cleaned, engine compartment included, so that a thorough inspection can be carried out to see what minor repairs and renovations are necessary. Steam cleaning is available at many garages, and is necessary for the removal of the accumulation of oily grime, which sometimes is allowed to become thick in certain areas. If steam-cleaning facilities are not available, there are some excellent grease solvents available which can be brush-applied; the dirt can then be simply hosed off. Note that these methods should not be used on vehicles with wax-based underbody protective coating, or the coating will be removed. Such vehicles should be inspected annually, preferably just before Winter, when the underbody should be washed down, and repair any damage to the wax coating. Ideally, a completely fresh coat should be applied. It would also be worth considering the use of such wax-based protection for injection into door panels, sills, box sections, etc, as an additional safeguard against rust damage, where such protection is not provided by the vehicle manufacturer.

4 After washing paintwork, wipe off with a chamois leather to give an unspotted clear finish. A coat of clear protective wax polish will give added protection against chemical pollutants in the air. If the paintwork sheen has dulled or oxidised, use a cleaner/polisher combination to restore the brilliance of the shine. This requires a little effort, but such dulling is usually caused because regular washing has been neglected. Care needs to be taken with metallic paintwork, as special non-abrasive cleaner/polisher is required to avoid damage to the finish. Always check that the door and ventilator opening drain holes and pipes are completely clear, so that water can be drained out. Brightwork should be treated in the same way as paintwork. Windscreens and windows can be kept clear of the smeary film that often appears, by proprietary glass cleaner. Never use any form of wax or other body or chromium polish on glass.

3 Maintenance – upholstery and carpets

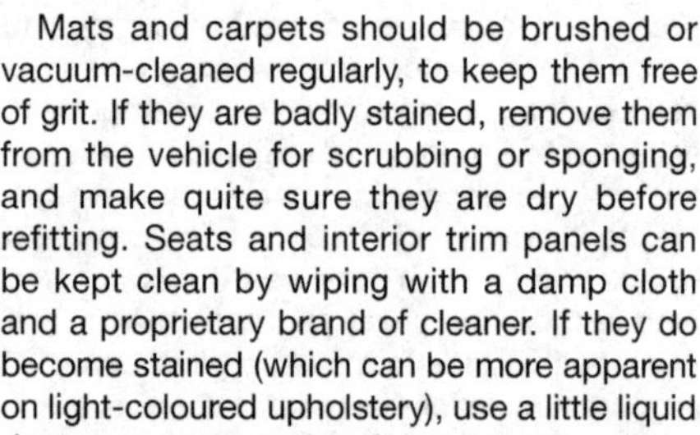

Mats and carpets should be brushed or vacuum-cleaned regularly, to keep them free of grit. If they are badly stained, remove them from the vehicle for scrubbing or sponging, and make quite sure they are dry before refitting. Seats and interior trim panels can be kept clean by wiping with a damp cloth and a proprietary brand of cleaner. If they do become stained (which can be more apparent on light-coloured upholstery), use a little liquid detergent and a soft nail brush to scour the grime out of the grain of the material. Do not forget to keep the headlining clean in the same way as the upholstery. When using liquid cleaners inside the vehicle, do not over-wet the surfaces being cleaned. Excessive damp could get into the seams and padded interior, causing stains, offensive odours or even rot. If the inside of the vehicle gets wet accidentally, it is worthwhile taking some trouble to dry it out properly, particularly where carpets are involved. Do not leave oil or electric heaters inside the vehicle for this purpose.

4 Minor body damage – repair

Minor scratches

1 If the scratch is very superficial, and does not penetrate to the metal of the bodywork, repair is very simple. Lightly rub the area of the scratch with a paintwork renovator or a very fine cutting paste to remove loose paint from the scratch, and to clear the surrounding bodywork of wax polish. Rinse the area with clean water.

2 Apply touch-up paint to the scratch using a fine paint brush; continue to apply fine layers of paint until the surface of the paint in the scratch is level with the surrounding paintwork. Allow the new paint at least two weeks to harden, and then blend it into the surrounding paintwork by rubbing the scratch area with a paintwork renovator or a very fine cutting paste. Finally, apply wax polish.

3 Where the scratch has penetrated right through to the metal of the bodywork, causing the metal to rust, a different repair technique is required. Remove any loose rust from the bottom of the scratch with a penknife, and then apply rust-inhibiting paint to prevent the formation of rust in the future. Using a rubber or nylon applicator, fill the scratch with body-stopper paste. If required, this paste can be mixed with cellulose thinners to provide a very thin paste, which is ideal for filling narrow scratches. Before the stopper-paste in the scratch hardens, wrap a piece of smooth cotton rag around the top of a finger. Dip the finger in cellulose thinners, and quickly sweep it across the surface of the stopper-paste in the scratch; this will ensure that the surface of the stopper-paste is slightly hollowed. The scratch can now be painted over as described earlier in this Section.

Dents

4 When deep denting of the vehicle's bodywork has taken place, the first task is to pull the dent out, until the affected bodywork almost attains its original shape. There is little point in trying to restore the original shape completely, as the metal in the damaged area will have stretched on impact, and cannot be reshaped fully to its original contour. It is better to bring the level of the dent up to a point that is about 3 mm below the level of the surrounding bodywork. In cases where the dent is very shallow anyway, it is not worth trying to pull it out at all. If the underside of the dent is accessible, it can be hammered out gently from behind, using a mallet with a wooden or plastic head. Whilst doing this, hold a suitable block of wood firmly against the outside of the panel, to absorb the impact from the hammer blows and thus prevent a large area of the bodywork from being 'belled-out'.

5 Should the dent be in a section of the bodywork, which has a double skin, or some other factor making it inaccessible from behind, a different technique is called for. Drill several small holes through the metal inside the area – particularly in the deeper section. Then screw long self-tapping screws into the holes, just sufficiently for them to gain a good purchase in the metal. Now the dent can be pulled out by pulling on the protruding heads of the screws with a pair of pliers.

6 The next stage of the repair is the removal of the paint from the damaged area, and from an inch or so of the surrounding 'sound' bodywork. This is accomplished most easily by using a wire brush or abrasive pad on a power drill, although it can be done just as effectively by hand, using sheets of abrasive paper. To complete the preparation for filling, score the surface of the bare metal with a screwdriver or the tang of a file, or alternatively, drill small holes in the affected area. This will provide a good 'key' for the filler paste.

7 To complete the repair, see the Section on filling and respraying.

Rust holes or gashes

8 Remove all paint from the affected area, and from an inch or so of the surrounding 'sound' bodywork, using an abrasive pad or a wire brush on a power drill. If these are not available, a few sheets of abrasive paper will do the job most effectively. With the paint removed, you will be able to judge the severity of the corrosion, and therefore decide whether to renew the whole panel (if this is possible) or to repair the affected area. New body panels are not as expensive as most people think, and it is often quicker and more satisfactory to fit a new panel than to attempt to repair large areas of corrosion.

9 Remove all fittings from the affected area, except those, which will act as a guide to the original shape of the damaged bodywork (eg, headlamp shells etc). Then, using tin snips or a hacksaw blade, remove all loose metal and any other metal badly affected by corrosion. Hammer the edges of the hole inwards, to create a slight depression for the filler paste.

10 Wire-brush the affected area to remove the powdery rust from the surface of the remaining metal. Paint the affected area with rust-inhibiting paint; if the back of the rusted area is accessible, treat this also.

11 Before filling can take place, it will be necessary to block the hole in some way. This can be achieved with aluminium or plastic mesh, or aluminium tape.

12 Aluminium or plastic mesh, or glass-fibre matting, is probably the best material to use for a large hole. Cut a piece to the approximate size and shape of the hole to be filled, then position it in the hole so that its edges are below the level of the surrounding bodywork. It can be retained in position by several blobs of filler paste around its periphery.

13 Aluminium tape should be used for small or very narrow holes. Pull a piece off the roll, trim it to the approximate size and shape required, then pull off the backing paper (if used) and stick the tape over the hole; it can be overlapped if the thickness of one piece is insufficient. Burnish down the edges of the tape with the handle of a screwdriver or similar, to ensure that the tape is securely attached to the metal underneath.

Filling and respraying

14 Before using this Section, see the Sections on dent, deep scratch, rust holes and gash repairs.

15 Many types of bodyfiller are available, but generally speaking, those proprietary kits which contain a tin of filler paste and a tube of resin hardener are best for this type of repair which can be used directly from the tube. A wide, flexible plastic or nylon applicator will be found invaluable for imparting a smooth and well-contoured finish to the surface of the filler.

16 Mix up a little filler on a clean piece of card or board – measure the hardener carefully (follow the maker's instructions on the pack), otherwise the filler will set too rapidly or too slowly. Using the applicator, apply the filler paste to the prepared area; draw the applicator across the surface of the filler to achieve the correct contour and to level the surface. When a contour that approximates to the correct one is achieved, stop working the paste – if you carry on too long, the paste will become sticky and begin to 'pick-up' on the applicator. Continue to add thin layers of filler paste at 20-minute intervals, until the level of the filler is just proud of the surrounding bodywork.

17 Once the filler has hardened, the excess can be removed using a metal plane or file. From then on, progressively finer grades of abrasive paper should be used, starting with a 40-grade production paper, and finishing with a 400-grade wet-and-dry paper. Always wrap the abrasive paper around a flat rubber, cork, or wooden block – otherwise the surface of the filler will not be completely flat. During the smoothing of the filler surface, the wet-and-dry paper should be periodically rinsed in water. This will ensure that a very smooth finish is imparted to the filler at the final stage.

18 At this stage, the 'dent' should be surrounded by a ring of bare metal, which in turn should be encircled by the finely 'feathered' edge of the good paintwork. Rinse the repair area with clean water, until all the dust produced by the rubbing-down operation has gone.

19 Spray the whole area with a light coat of primer – this will show up any imperfections in the surface of the filler. Repair these imperfections with fresh filler paste or bodystopper, and again smooth the surface with abrasive paper. If bodystopper is used, it can be mixed with cellulose thinners, to form a thin paste, which is ideal for filling small holes. Repeat this spray-and-repair procedure until you are satisfied that the surface of the filler, and the feathered edge of the paintwork, are perfect. Clean the repair area with clean water, and allow to dry fully.

20 The repair area is now ready for final spraying. Paint spraying must be carried out in a warm, dry, windless and dust-free atmosphere. This condition can be created artificially if you have access to a large indoor working area, but if you are forced to work in the open, you will have to pick your day very carefully. If you are working indoors, dousing the floor in the work area with water will help to settle the dust that would otherwise be in the atmosphere. If the repair area is confined to one body panel, mask off the surrounding panels; this will help to minimise the effects of a slight mis-match in paint colours. Bodywork fittings (eg chrome strips, door handles etc) will also need to be masked off. Use genuine masking tape, and several thickness of newspaper, for the masking operations.

21 Before starting to spray, agitate the aerosol can thoroughly, and then spray a test area (an old tin, or similar) until the technique is mastered. Cover the repair area with a thick coat of primer; the thickness should be built up using several thin layers of paint, rather than one thick one. Using 400-grade wet-and-dry paper, rub down the surface of the primer until it is smooth. While doing this, the work area should be thoroughly doused with water, and the wet-and-dry paper periodically rinsed in water. Allow to dry before spraying on more paint.

22 Spray on the top coat, again building up the thickness by using several thin layers of paint. Start spraying at the top of the repair area, and then, using a side-to-side motion, work downwards until the whole repair area and about 2 inches of the surrounding original paintwork is covered. Remove all masking material 10 to 15 minutes after spraying on the final coat of paint.

23 Allow the new paint at least two weeks to harden, then, using a paintwork renovator or a very fine cutting paste, blend the edges of the paint into the existing paintwork. Finally, apply wax polish.

Plastic components

24 With the use of more and more plastic body components by the vehicle manufacturers (e.g. bumpers. spoilers, and in some cases major body panels), rectification of more serious damage to such items has become a matter of either entrusting repair work to a specialist in this field, or renewing complete components. Repair of such damage by the DIY owner is not feasible, owing to the cost of the equipment and materials required for effecting such repairs. The basic technique involves making a groove along the line of the crack in the plastic, using a rotary burr in a power drill. The damaged part is then welded back together, using a hot air gun to heat up and fuse a plastic filler rod into the groove. Any excess plastic is then removed, and the area rubbed down to a smooth finish. It is important that a filler rod of the correct plastic is used, as body components can be made of different types (eg, polycarbonate, ABS, polypropylene).

25 Damage of a less serious nature (abrasions, minor cracks etc) can be repaired by the DIY owner using a two-part epoxy filler repair material, which can be used directly from the tube. Once mixed in equal proportions, this is used in similar fashion to the bodywork filler used on metal panels. The filler is usually cured in twenty to thirty minutes, ready for sanding and painting.

26 If the owner is renewing a complete component himself, or if he has repaired it with epoxy filler, he will be left with the problem of finding a suitable paint for finishing which is compatible with the type of plastic used. At one time, the use of a universal paint was not possible, owing to the complex range of plastics met with in body component applications. Standard paints, generally speaking, will not bond to plastic or rubber satisfactorily, but professional matched paints, to match any plastic or rubber finish, can be obtained from some dealers. However, it is now possible to obtain a plastic body parts finishing kit, which consists of a pre-primer treatment, a primer and coloured top coat. Full instructions are normally supplied with a kit, but basically the method of use is to first apply the pre-primer to the component concerned, and allow it to dry for up to 30 minutes. Then the primer is applied, and left to dry for about an hour before finally applying the special-coloured top coat. The result is a correctly coloured component, where the paint will flex with the plastic or rubber, a property that standard paint does not normally possess.

5 Major body damage – repair

Where serious damage has occurred, or large areas need renewal due to neglect, it means that complete new panels will need welding-in, and this is best left to professionals. If the damage is due to impact, it will also be necessary to check completely the alignment of the bodyshell, and this can only be carried out accurately by a Toyota dealer or specialist using special jigs. If the body is left misaligned, it is primarily dangerous, as the car will not handle properly, and secondly, uneven stresses will be imposed on the steering, suspension and possibly transmission, causing abnormal wear, or complete failure, particularly to such items as the tyres.

6 Front bumper – removal and refitting

Removal

1 Pull back the wheel arch liner (remove if required) and undo the retaining bolt at each side of the bumper, securing the rear edge to the wheel arch liner **(see illustration)**.

2 Working under the front edge of the bumper, remove the splash shield from across the front of the vehicle.

3 Open the bonnet, and undo the retaining screws from each end of the shield across the top of the grille **(see illustration)**.

4 Release the retaining clips and remove the shield from across the front of the engine compartment **(see illustrations)**.

5 Remove the retaining clips from the rear of the grille panel at the centre of the bumper **(see illustration)**.

6 Remove the retaining clips from each side of the grille **(see illustration)**.

7 Pull the rear edges of the bumper outwards to release them from the wing panel, and with the help of an assistant, pull the bumper forwards away from the vehicle, releasing it from the retaining clips under the headlamps **(see illustrations)**.

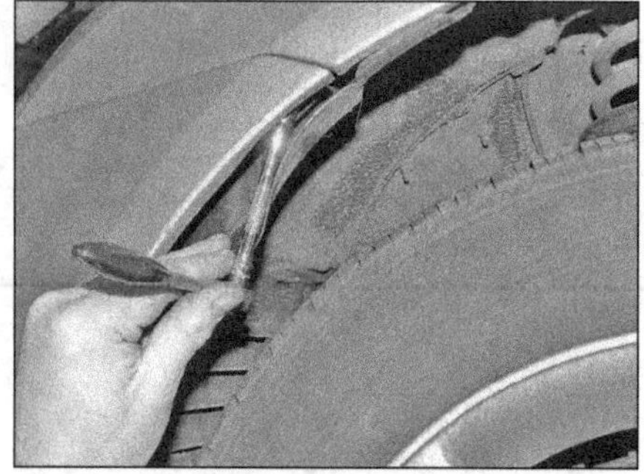

6.1 Undo the bolt each side securing the bumper to the wing

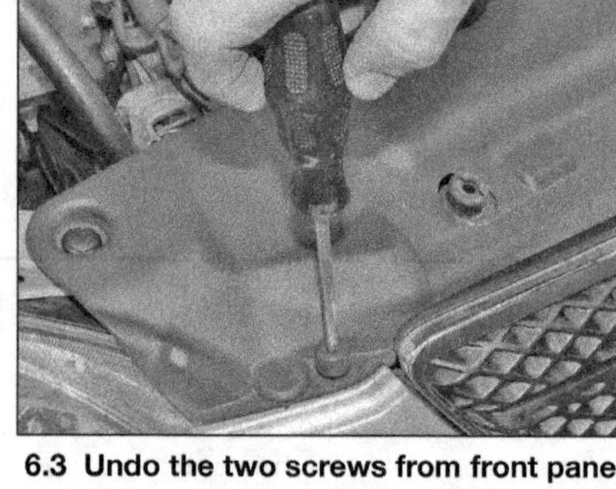

6.3 Undo the two screws from front panel

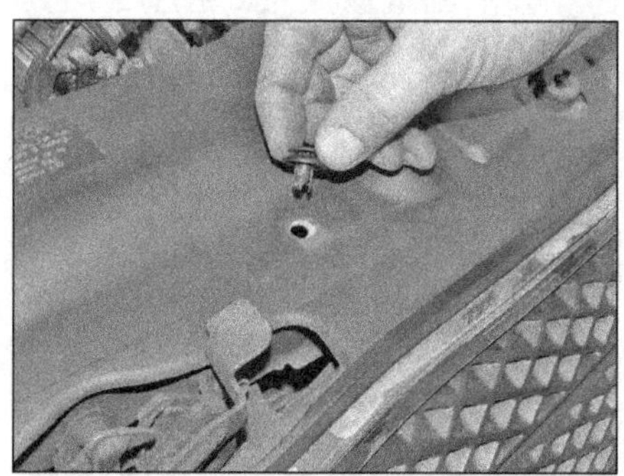

6.4a release the retaining clips . . .

6.4b . . . and remove the front trim panel

8 Where fitted, disconnect the wiring plugs from the front foglights as the bumper is withdrawn **(see illustration)**. Check for any other wiring as it is removed.

Refitting

9 Refitting is a reverse of the removal procedure, ensuring that the bumper mounting screws are securely tightened.

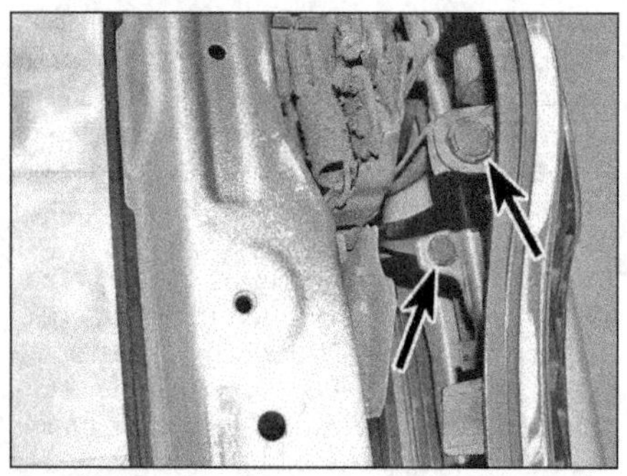

6.5 Remove the two clips (arrowed)

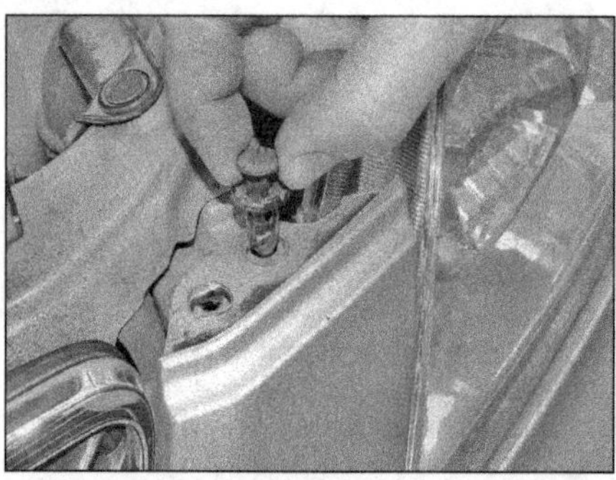

6.6 Remove the retaining clips from by the headlamps

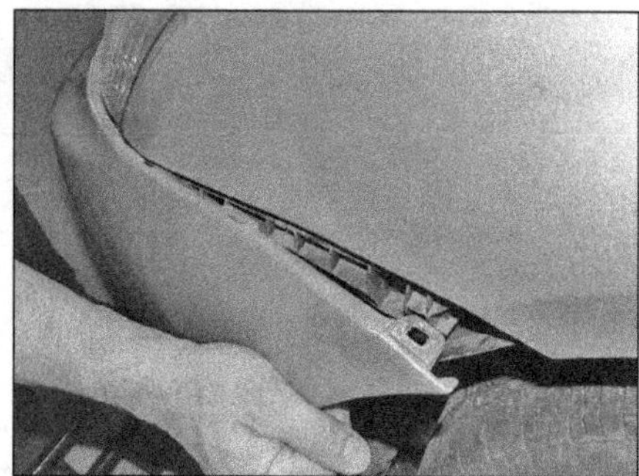

6.7a Release the bumper at each side . . .

6.7b . . and from the clips (arrowed) under the headlamps . . .

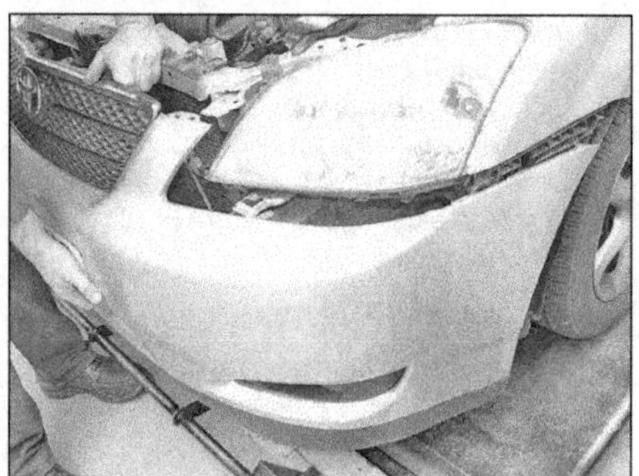

6.7c . . . and remove the bumper from the vehicle

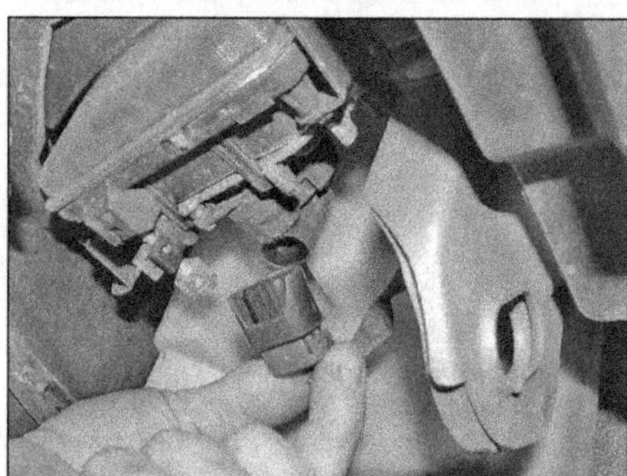

6.8 Disconnect the wiring connector from the foglights

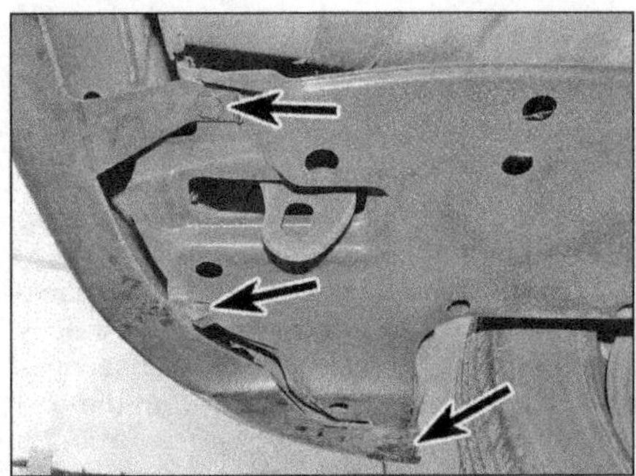
7.2a Release the securing clips . . .

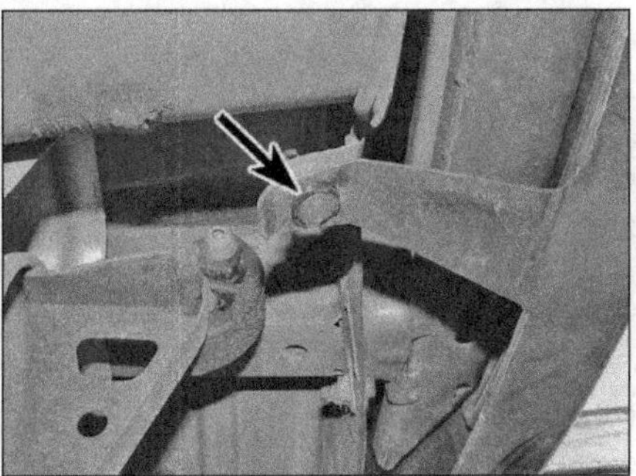
7.2b . . . from under the rear bumper

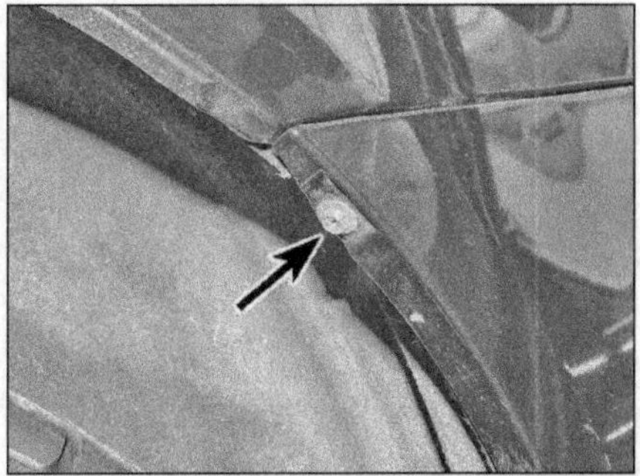
7.3 Undo the retaining screws (arrowed) at each side of the bumper

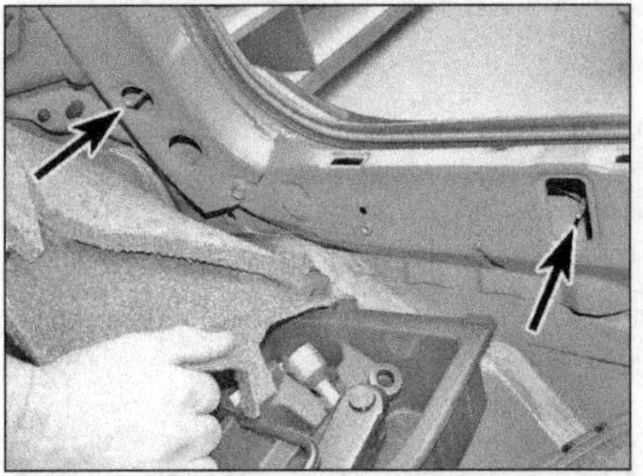
7.4a Pull back the carpet and undo the nuts (arrowed) . . .

7.4b . . . from inside the rear of the vehicle

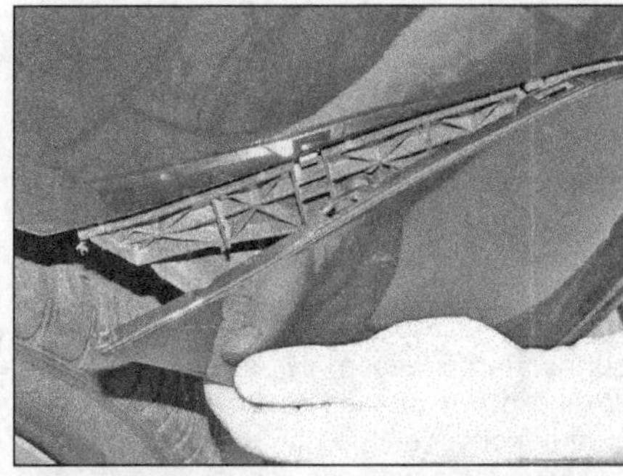
7.5a Release the bumper at each side . . .

7 Rear bumper – removal and refitting

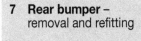

Note: *The following procedure is for the Hatchback model; Estate and Saloon models are similar.*

Removal

1 Open the tailgate, and remove the luggage compartment carpet.

2 Working under the rear of the vehicle, remove the retaining clips along the lower edge of the bumper **(see illustrations)**.

3 Where fitted, undo the screws and remove the mudflaps from both sides of the vehicle, then undo the screw and prise out the clip at the upper edge of the bumper at each side **(see illustration)**.

4 Pull back the carpet trim behind the rear lights forward, and then undo the four nuts securing the bumper to the rear panel **(see illustrations)**.

5 With the help of an assistant, unclip the sides of the bumper from the wing panel and then slide the bumper to the rear, unclipping it from under the rear light units **(see illustrations)**. On models with parking distance sensors, disconnect the wiring plugs as the bumper is withdrawn.

Refitting

6 Refitting is a reverse of the removal procedure, ensuring that the mounting bolts/nuts are tightened securely.

7.5b . . and from the clips under the rear lights . . .

8 Bonnet – removal, refitting and adjustment

Note: *The bonnet is heavy and somewhat awkward to remove and refit – at least two people should perform this procedure.*

Removal and refitting

1 Make marks around the hinge bracket on the bonnet to ensure proper alignment during refitting **(see illustration)**.

2 Use blankets or pads to cover the scuttle area of the body and wings. This will protect the body and paint as the bonnet is lifted off.

3 Disconnect any cables or wires that will interfere with removal.

4 Have an assistant support the bonnet. Remove the hinge-to-bonnet bolts.

5 Lift off the bonnet.

7.5c . . . and remove the bumper from the vehicle

6 Refitting is the reverse of removal.

Adjustment

7 Fore-and-aft and side-to-side adjustment of the bonnet is done by moving the hinge plate slot after loosening the bolts.

8.1 Bonnet hinge bracket retaining bolts

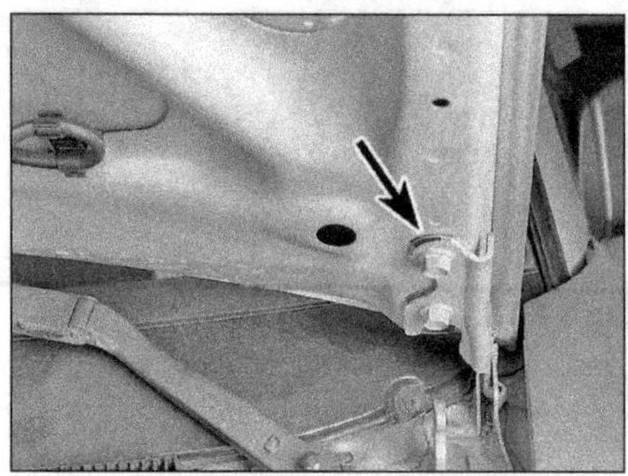

8.8 Before removing the bonnet, make marks around the hinge plate

8 Scribe a line around the entire hinge plate so you can judge the amount of movement **(see illustration)**

9 Loosen the bolts or nuts and move the bonnet into correct alignment. Move it only a little at a time. Tighten the hinge bolts and carefully lower the bonnet to check the position.

10 If necessary after refitting, the entire bonnet latch assembly can be adjusted up-and-down as well as from side-to-side on the radiator support so the bonnet closes securely, flush with the wings. To make the adjustment, scribe a line around the bonnet latch mounting bolts to provide a reference point, then loosen them and reposition the latch assembly, as necessary **(see illustration)**. Following adjustment, retighten the mounting bolts.

11 The bonnet latch assembly, as well as the hinges, should be periodically lubricated with white, lithium-base grease to prevent binding and wear.

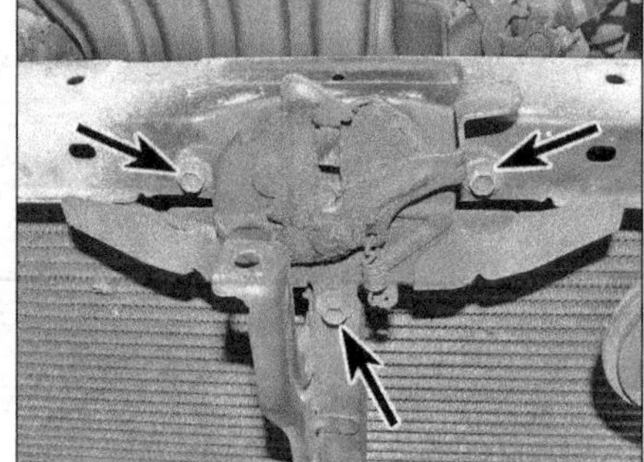

8.10 Bonnet catch securing bolts (arrowed)

9 Bonnet release cable – removal and refitting

Removal

1 The one-piece bonnet release cable connects the release handle under the driver's side of the facia, to the release mechanism in the centre of the bonnet slam panel.

2 Pull the release handle to open the bonnet, and then disengage the outer cable and cable end fitting from the handle **(see illustrations)**.

3 If required, to make access easier, remove the front bumper as described in Section 6.

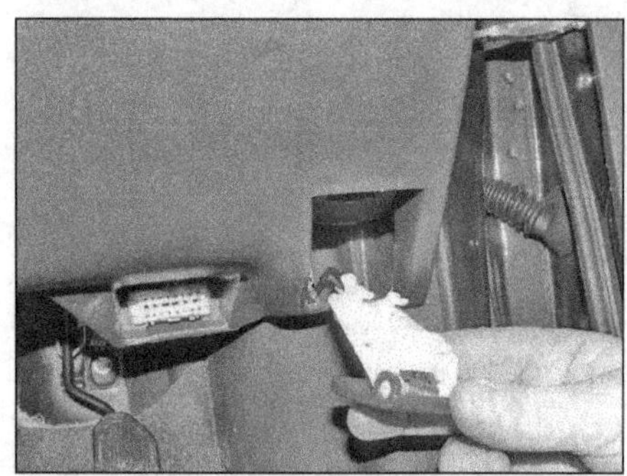

9.2a Unclip the bonnet release lever from the facia . . .

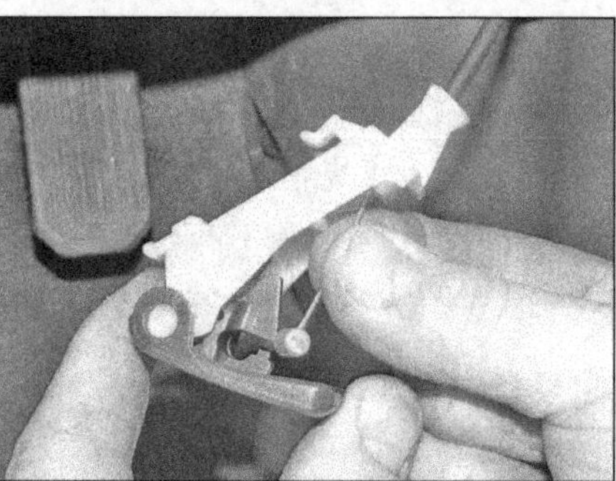

9.2b . . . and disconnect the release cable

9.5 Disconnect the bonnet release cable from the catch

11.2 Unclip the grille from the bumper

4 Make alignment marks around the bonnet lock to aid refitting, then undo the two retaining screws **(see illustration 8.10)**.

5 Disconnect the outer cable and end fitting from the bonnet lock **(see illustration)**.

6 Release the cable from any retaining clips along its length.

7 Tie a length of string to the end of the cable in the engine compartment, then carefully pull the cable through into the passenger compartment. Untie the string from the end of the cable, and leave it in position to aid refitting.

Refitting

8 Locate the cable in position in the passenger compartment.

9 Tie the end of the new cable to the string, and pull it through into the engine compartment. You may have to guide the cable through the grommet at the bulkhead.

10 Check that the cable is correctly routed, and then secure it in place with the retaining clips. Untie the string.

11 Reconnect the cable to the bonnet lock, then refit the lock using the previously-made alignment marks.

12 Where applicable refit the front bumper.

13 Reconnect the cable to the release lever. Check that the bonnet lock operates correctly before closing the bonnet.

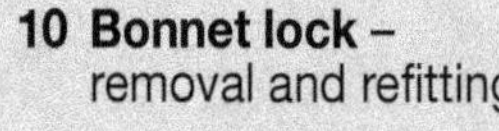

10 Bonnet lock – removal and refitting

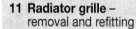

Removal

1 If required, to make access easier, remove the front bumper as described in Section 6.

2 Make alignment marks around the bonnet lock to aid refitting, then undo the two retaining screws **(see illustration 8.10)**.

3 Disengage the outer cable and end fitting from the lock **(see illustration 9.5)**.

Refitting

4 Refitting is a reversal of removal, using the alignment marks. Check that the mechanism functions correctly before closing the bonnet.

11 Radiator grille – removal and refitting

Note: *The following procedure is on early models, pre-facelift.*

Removal

1 Open the bonnet, and remove the front bumper as described in Section 6.

2 Unclip the grille from the bumper, taking care not to damage the retaining clips **(see illustration)**.

Refitting

3 Refitting is a reversal of removal.

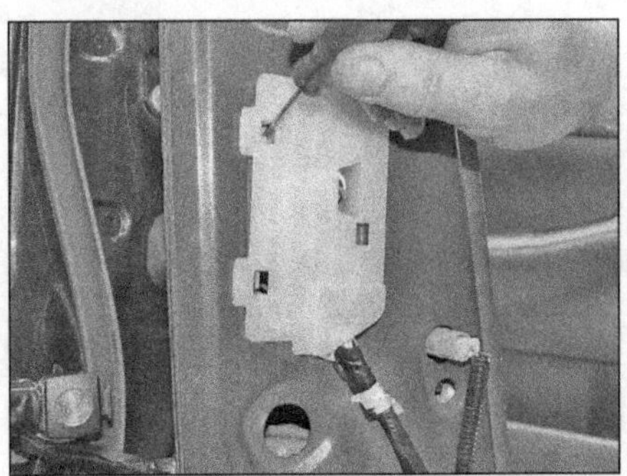

12.2a Release the securing clips . . .

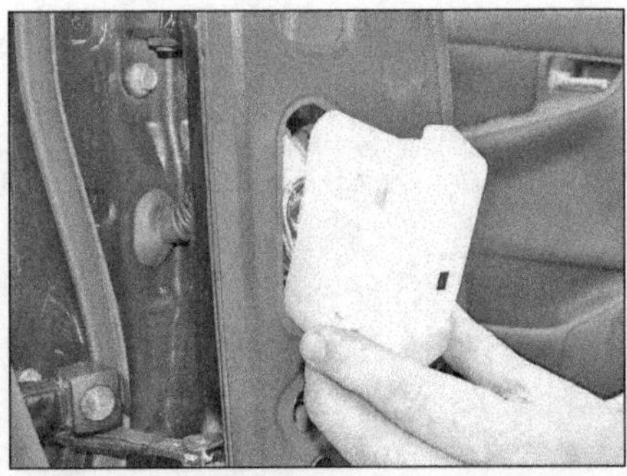

12.2b . . . remove the plastic trim panel . . .

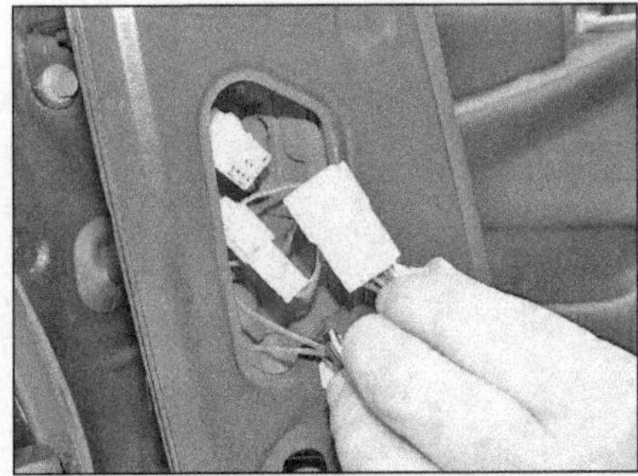

12.2c . . . and then disconnect the wiring block connectors

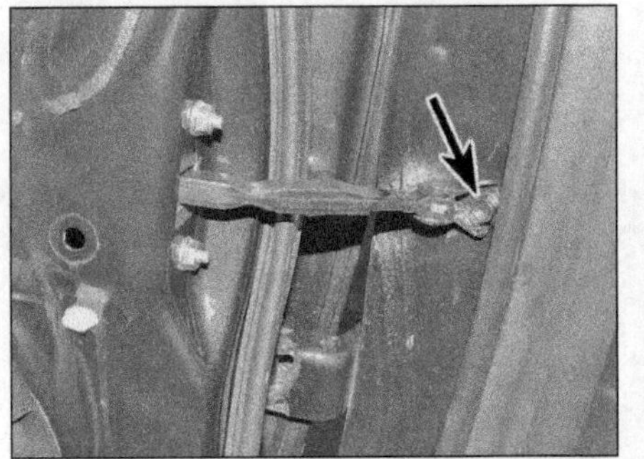

12.4 Check strap retaining bolt (arrowed)

12.6 Door hinge retaining bolts (arrowed)

12.7 Adjust the lock striker by slackening the mounting screws and tapping the striker

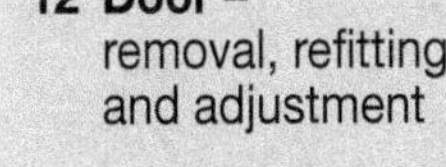

12 Door – removal, refitting and adjustment

Removal and refitting

1 Remove the door trim panel (see Section 13). Disconnect any electrical connectors and push them through the door opening so they won't interfere with removal.

2 Alternatively, remove the inner pillar trim panels, and disconnect the wiring block connectors from inside the pillar and withdraw the wiring from the door pillar **(see illustrations)**.

3 Position a jack or axle stand under the door or have an assistant on hand to support the door when the hinge bolts are removed. **Note:** *If a jack or stand is used, place a rag between it and the door to protect the door's paint.*

4 Remove the door check strap bolt **(see illustration)**.

5 Scribe around the door bolts to aid refitting.

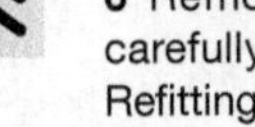

6 Remove the hinge-to-door bolts and carefully detach the door **(see illustration)**. Refitting is the reverse of removal.

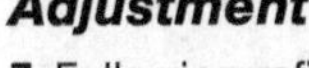

Adjustment

7 Following refitting, make sure the door is aligned properly. Adjust it if necessary as follows:

a) Up-and-down and forward-and-backward adjustments are made by loosening the hinge-to-body bolts and moving the door as necessary.

b) In-and-out and up-and-down adjustments are made by loosening the door side hinge bolts and moving the door as necessary.

c) The door lock striker can also be adjusted both up-and-down and sideways to provide a positive engagement with the locking mechanism. This is done by loosening the screws and moving the striker as necessary ***(see illustration)****.*

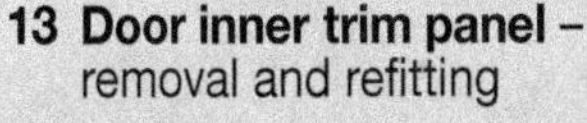

13 Door inner trim panel – removal and refitting

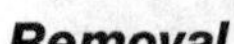

Removal

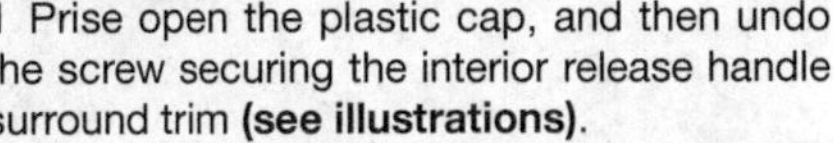

1 Prise open the plastic cap, and then undo the screw securing the interior release handle surround trim **(see illustrations)**.

2 Carefully unclip the armrest cover from the door trim panel and undo the two retaining screws **(see illustrations)**.

3 On manual window regulator-equipped models, remove the window crank by working a cloth back-and-forth behind the handle to dislodge the retaining clip. A special tool is

13.1a Unclip the plastic trim . . .

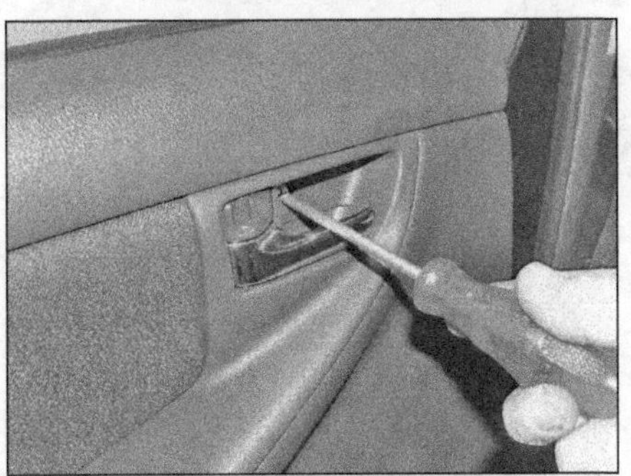

13.1b . . . and undo the retaining screw

13.2a Unclip the armrest trim . . .

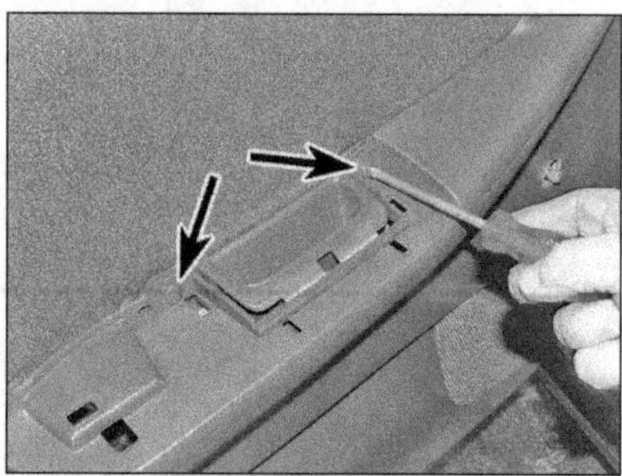
13.2b . . . and undo the retaining screws (arrowed)

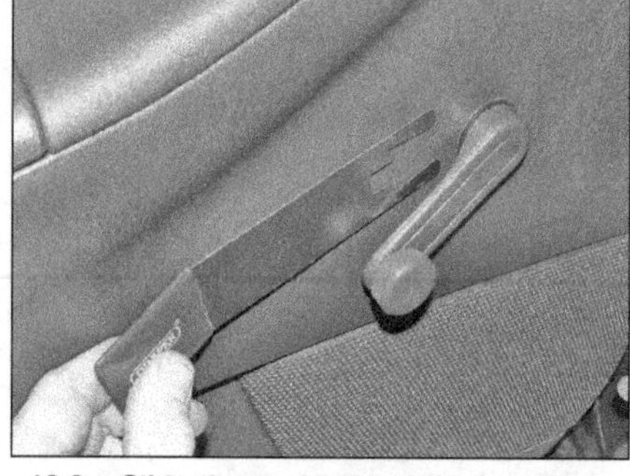
13.3a Slide the tool behind the handle to release the clip . . .

13.3b . . . and remove the winder handle and washer

13.6 Carefully unclip the door trim panel

13.7 Remove the weathershield/ soundproofing

available for this purpose but it's not essential. With the retaining clip released, pull off the handle, and recover the plastic washer behind the handle **(see illustrations)**.

4 On power window models, pry out the switch assembly to remove, and then unplug the electrical connector.

5 Work around the outer edge of the door and release the retaining clips, taking care not to damage them.

6 Once all of the clips are disengaged, detach the trim panel, unplug any electrical connectors and remove the trim panel from the vehicle by gently pulling it up and out **(see illustration)**.

7 For access to the inner door remove the plastic weathershield and soundproofing **(see illustration)**. Peel back the plastic cover, taking care not to tear it.

Refitting

8 To refit the trim panel, first press the weathershield back into place. If necessary, add more sealant to hold it in place.

9 Prior to refitment of the door panel, be sure to refit any clips in the panel which may have come out during the removal procedure and stayed in the door.

10 Plug in any electrical connectors and place the panel in position. Press it into place until the clips are seated and install any retaining screws and armrest/door pulls. Refit the manual regulator window handle or power switch assembly.

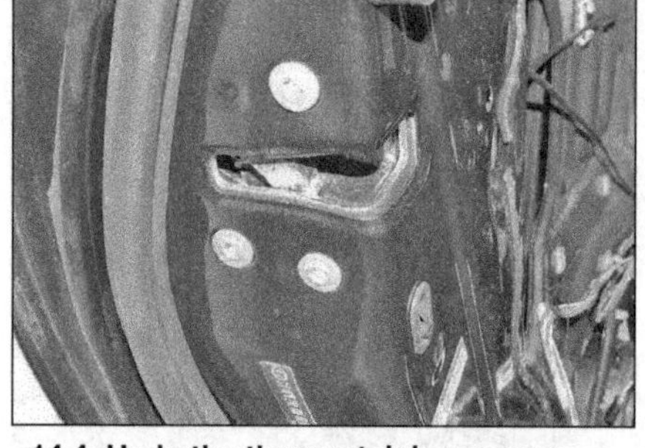
14.4 Undo the three retaining screws . . .

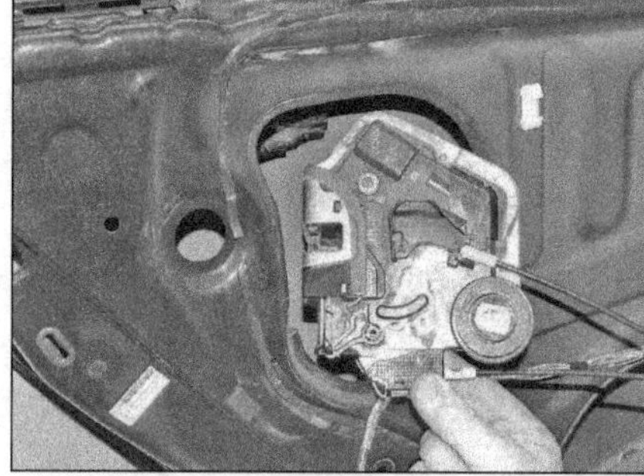
14.5 . . . and remove the door lock assembly

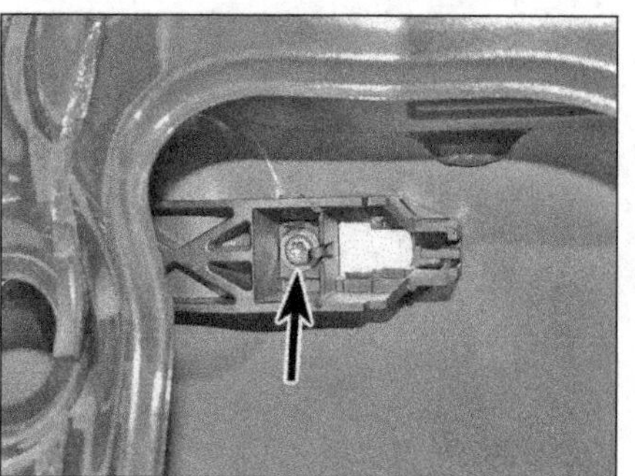
14.6a Undo the retaining screw (arrowed) . . .

14.6b . . . and remove the outer handle mounting frame

14 Door handle and lock components – removal and refitting

1 Remove the door trim panel and the plastic weathershield (Section 13).

Door latch

Removal

2 Undo the bolt and remove the window guide from rear of the door. On rear doors, remove the guide as described in Section 15.

3 Remove the lock cylinder and outside handle as described in paragraphs 8 to 11.

4 Remove the latch retaining Torx screws from the end of the door **(see illustration)**.

5 Withdraw the door latch and door lock solenoid – disconnect the wiring plugs as the assembly is withdrawn **(see illustration)**.

6 Reaching inside the door panel, undo the retaining screws and remove the outer handle mounting frame **(see illustrations)**.

Refitting

7 Refitting is the reverse of removal.

Lock cylinder and outside handle

Removal

8 Working at the edge of the door in alignment to the door lock cylinder, remove the rubber grommet from the edge of the door. On rear doors, remove the grommet from inside the door panel and undo the retaining screw to remove the outer handle end cap **(see illustration)**.

9 Insert screwdriver through the hole to access the side of the lock cylinder.

10 Slacken the securing screw and withdraw the lock cylinder from the handle assembly – front doors only.

11 To remove the outer handle, slide it to the rear of the door and withdraw it from the door panel. Remove the rubber gaskets and check them for damage **(see illustrations)**.

Refitting

12 Refitting is the reverse of removal.

Inside handle

Removal

13 Unclip the inner handle from the door panel, and then disconnect the operating cable from inside the handle control lever **(see illustration)**.

Refitting

14 Refitting is the reverse of removal.

14.8 Remove the outer end cap

14.11a Slide the handle out from the door panel

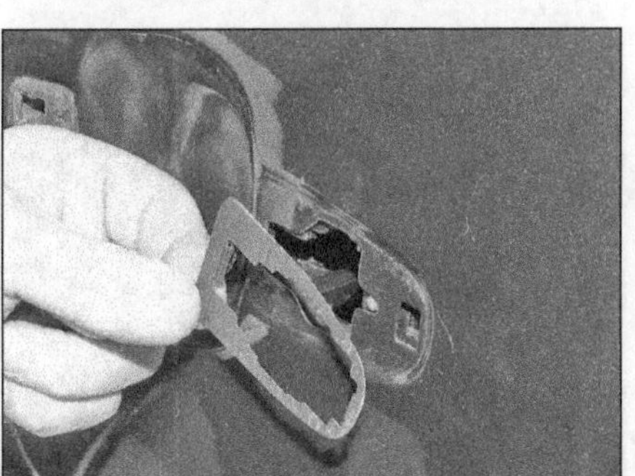

14.11b Check the condition of the door handle seals

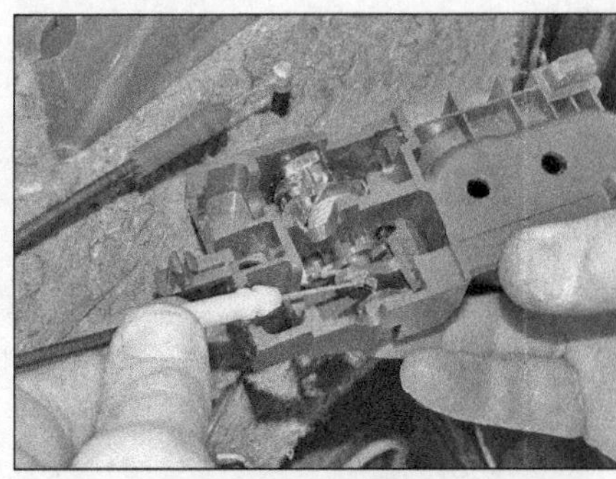

14.13 Release the operating cables from the handle

15 Door glass and regulator – removal and refitting

Removal

Front door window

1 Lower the window glass approximately 1/2 of full travel.

2 Remove the door trim panel and the plastic weathershield (Section 13).

3 Place a rag inside the door panel to help prevent scratching the glass and remove the two glass mounting bolts **(see illustration)**.

4 Remove the glass by pulling it up.

Front door window regulator

5 Remove the door inner trim panel and the plastic weathershield (Section 13).

6 Undo the two bolts securing the window to the regulator, then lift the window upwards and secure it at the top of the door using tape.

7 Disconnect the window regulator wiring plug (where applicable).

8 The regulator is retained by 4 bolts and one nut (manual windows) or 5 bolts and one nut (power windows). Undo the bolts/nut and manoeuvre the regulator from the door **(see illustration)**.

9 Manoeuvre the regulator from the door. At the time of writing, it would appear that the electric motor is integral with the regulator, and must be renewed as an assembly. Check with your Toyota dealer or specialist.

Rear door window glass

10 Lower the window completely, then carefully prise out and remove the window rubber guide from the door frame **(see illustration)**.

11 Undo the screws securing the window

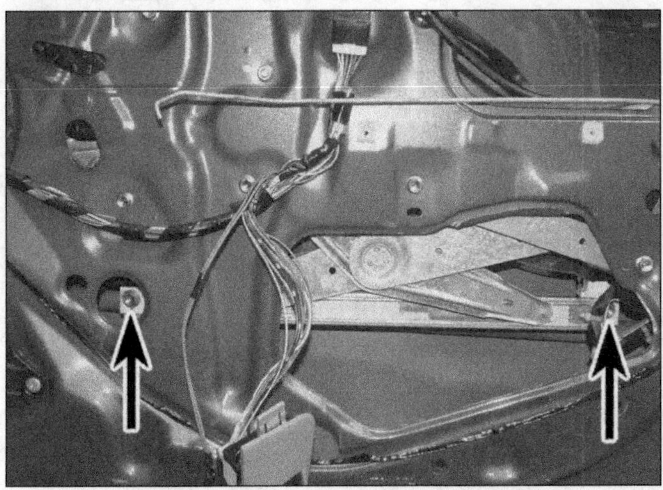

15.3 Undo the glass mounting bolts (arrowed)

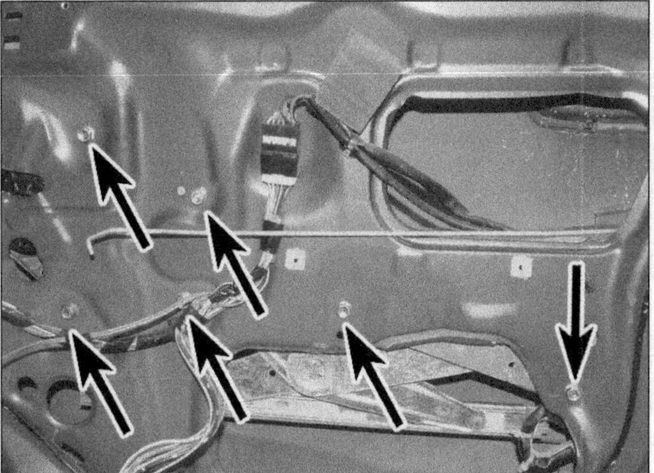

15.8 Window regulator bolts (arrowed – models with electric windows)

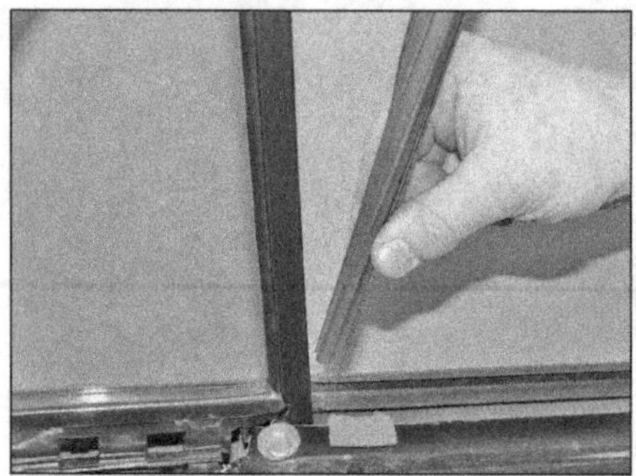
15.10 Slide out the rubber guide from the door frame

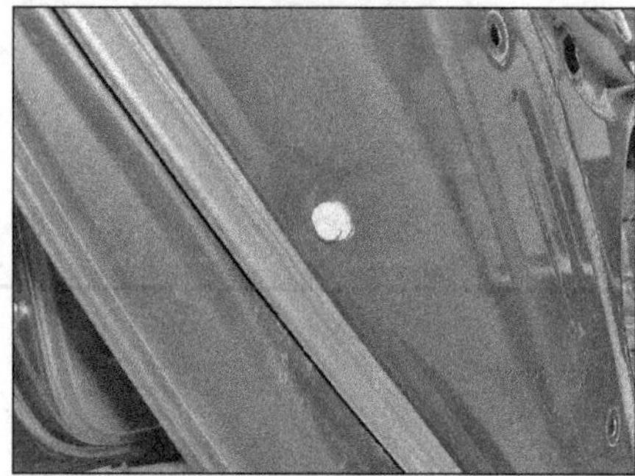
15.11a Undo the window guide lower bolt . . .

15.11b . . . the centre window guide bolt . . .

15.11c . . . and the upper screw . . .

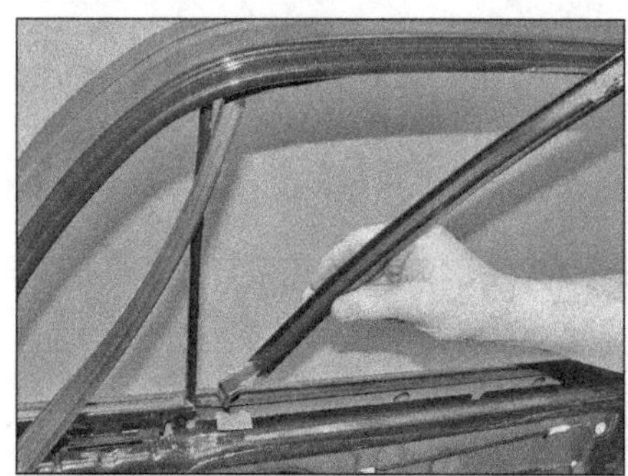
15.11d . . . and withdraw the window guide

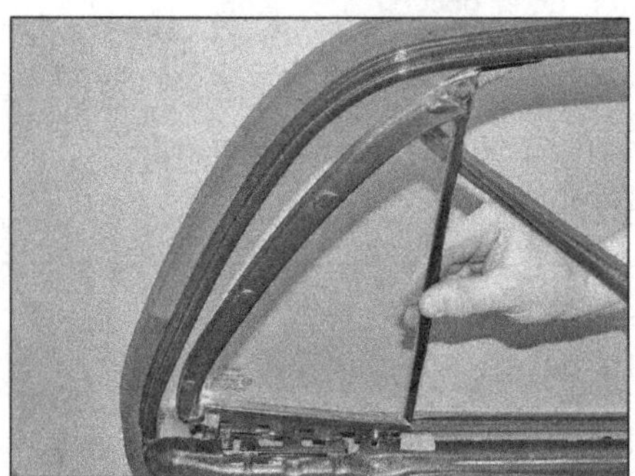
15.12 Slide the rear fixed glass out from the frame

guide in place, and remove the guide **(see illustrations)**.

12 Withdraw the rear fixed quarter glass from the door frame **(see illustration)**.

13 Manoeuvre the window sideways to disengage the lift channel at the base of the window from the regulator arm roller and remove it from the window **(see illustration)**.

Rear door window regulator

14 Undo the bolts and remove the regulator assembly, disengaging it from the guide on the bottom of the window glass **(see illustrations)**. On models with power windows, disconnect the motor wiring plug, as the assembly is withdrawn.

15 At the time of writing, it would appear that the electric motor is integral with the regulator, and must be renewed as an assembly. Check with your Toyota dealer or specialist.

Refitting

16 Refitting is the reverse of removal, but prior to refitting the plastic weatherstrip check the window operates smoothly.

17 After refitting the window, it may be necessary to manually operate the power window switch to fully close the window. This allows the system to 'learn' the fully closed position.

16 Boot lid and lock components – removal and refitting

Removal

Boot lid

1 Open the boot, and paint alignment marks around the hinges on the underside of the boot lid.

2 Undo the four bolts and remove the boot lid.

Boot lock

3 Release the clips and remove the boot lid trim panel.

4 Undo the two retaining bolts, disconnect the control link and remove the lock assembly. Disconnect any wiring plugs as the assembly is removed (where applicable).

Boot lock cylinder

5 Release the clips and remove the boot lid trim panel.

6 Undo the two retaining bolts, disconnect the control link and remove the cylinder assembly. Disconnect any wiring plugs as the assembly is removed.

15.13 Tilt the window glass and lift it out from the door

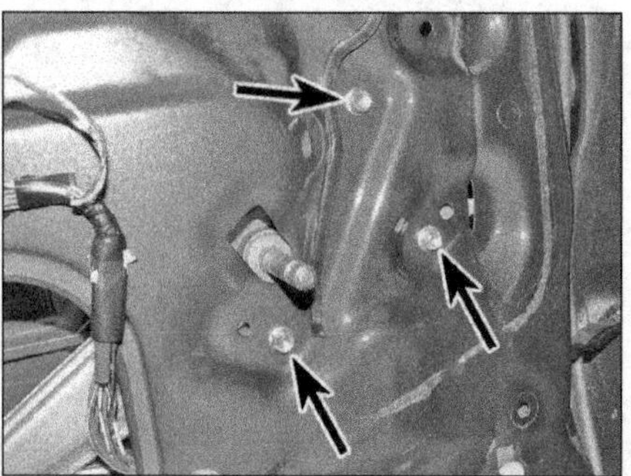
15.14a Undo the three retaining bolts (arrowed – manual window shown) . . .

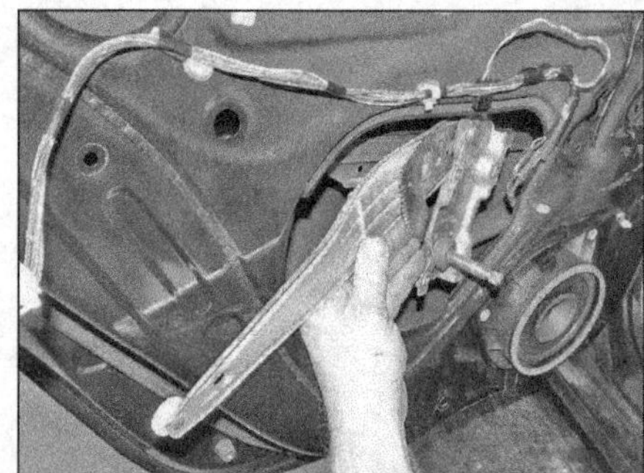
15.14b . . . and withdraw the window regulator out from the door aperture

Refitting

7 Refitting is a reversal of removal. If necessary, the position of the lock striker plate can be adjusted by prising out the clips and removing the plastic trim panels behind the rear light units each side, followed by the boot sill inner trim panel. Slacken the two retaining bolts and reposition the striker plate.

17 Tailgate, lock components and support struts – removal and refitting

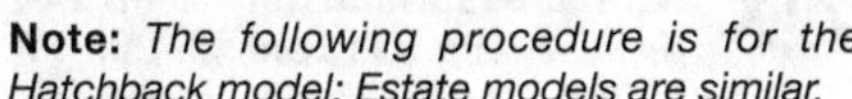

Note: *The following procedure is for the Hatchback model; Estate models are similar.*

Tailgate

Removal

1 Open the tailgate and cover the edges of the compartment with pads or cloths to protect the painted surfaces when the tailgate is removed.

2 Insert a flat-bladed tool between the inner trim panel and the tailgate. Work around the edge of the panel and release the retaining clips **(see illustration)**. Note that the panel may be secured by plastic expansion rivets. With these, push in the centre pin and prise the rivet from place. Remove the panel.

3 Disconnect any cables or wire harness connectors attached to the tailgate that would interfere with removal. The wiring will need to be removed from the tailgate **(see illustrations)**.

4 Use a marking pen to make alignment marks around the hinge mounting flanges **(see illustration)**.

5 Have an assistant support the tailgate and detach the support struts as described in this Section.

6 While an assistant supports the tailgate, remove the tailgate-to-hinge bolts on both sides and lift it off.

Refitting and adjustment

7 Refitting is the reverse of removal. **Note:** *When refitting the tailgate, align the hinges with the marks made during removal.*

8 After refitting, close the tailgate and make sure it's in proper alignment with the surrounding panels.

9 Adjustments to the tailgate position are made by loosening the hinge-to-tailgate bolts or nuts and gently moving the tailgate into correct alignment.

10 The tailgate latch position can be adjusted by loosening the adjusting bolts and moving the latch. The latch striker can be adjusted by loosening the mounting screws and gently tapping it into position with a plastic hammer.

Tailgate lock assembly

11 Remove the tailgate inner trim panel as described in paragraph 2.

12 Undo the two retaining nuts and remove the handle from the tailgate, unclip the operating cable from the handle as it is removed **(see illustration)**.

13 Disconnect the lock wiring connectors from inside the tailgate **(see illustration)**.

14 Release the securing clip and disconnect the linkage rod from the lock cylinder **(see illustration)**.

15 Undo the three retaining bolts, and withdraw the lock assembly from the lower edge of the tailgate **(see illustrations)**.

17.2 Work around the edge of the tailgate trim panel and release the clips

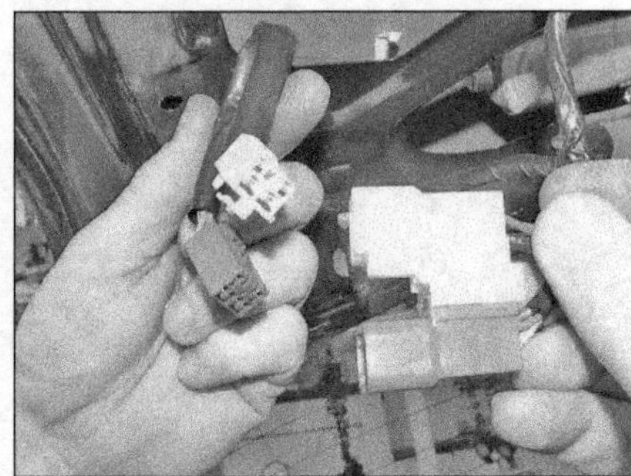

17.3a Disconnect the wiring block connectors . . .

17.3b . . . and disconnect the rubber gaiter from the top of the tailgate

17.4 Tailgate hinge bolts

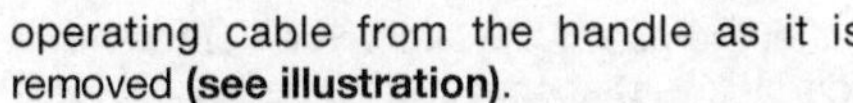

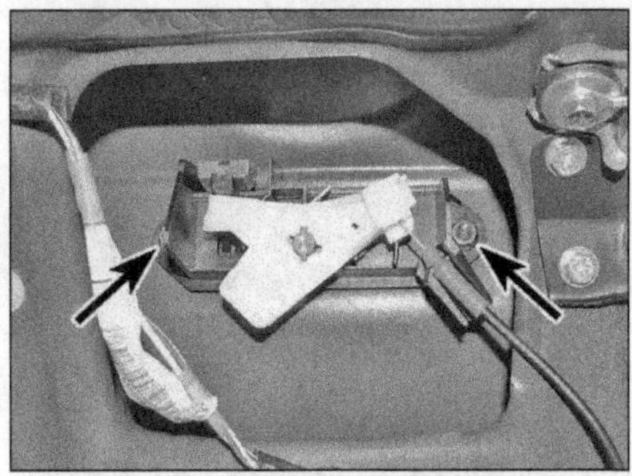

17.12a Undo the retaining nuts . . .

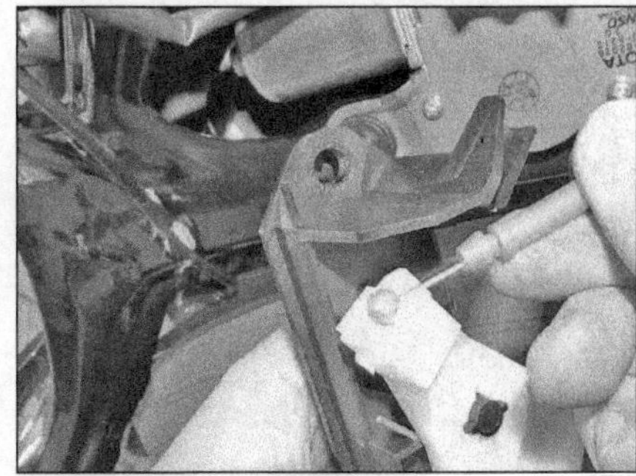

17.12b . . . and disconnect the operating cable

17.13 Disconnect the lock wiring connector

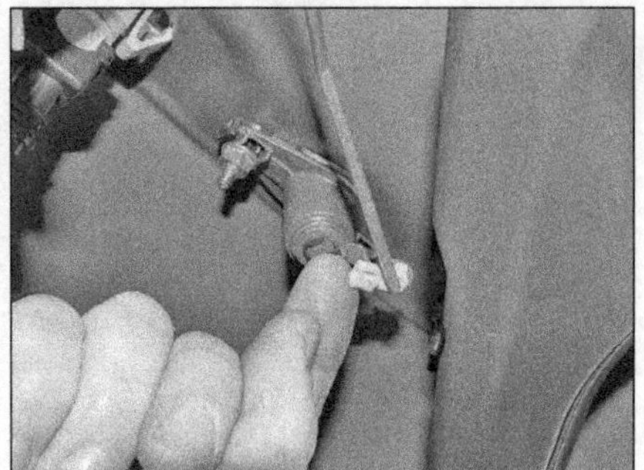

17.14 Release the locking clip on the operating rod

17.15a Undo the three retaining bolts . . .

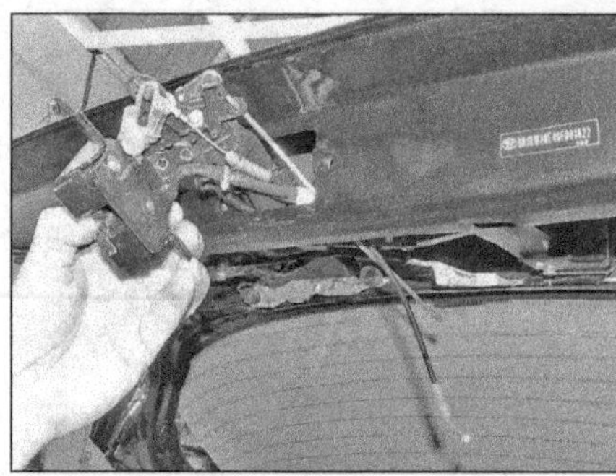
17.15b . . . and remove the lock assembly

17.16 Remove the rear trim panel

17.17 Tailgate lock striker

16 To remove the tailgate lock striker, open the tailgate, and remove the sill trim panel **(see illustration)**.

17 Make alignment marks around the striker plate, then undo the two screws and remove the striker. Disconnect the release cable as the striker is withdrawn **(see illustration)**.

18 Refitting is a reversal of removal.

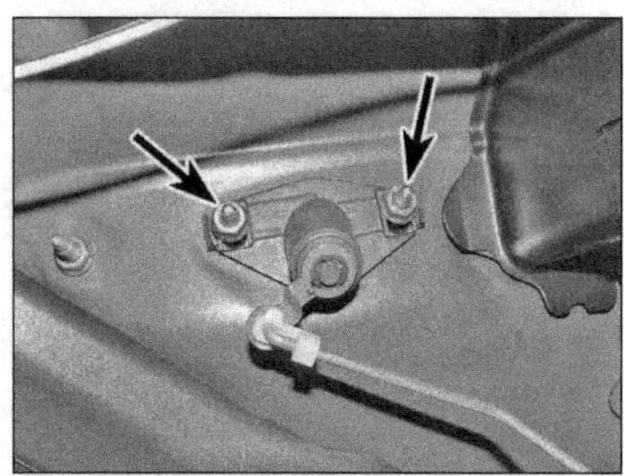
17.20 Undo the two retaining nuts

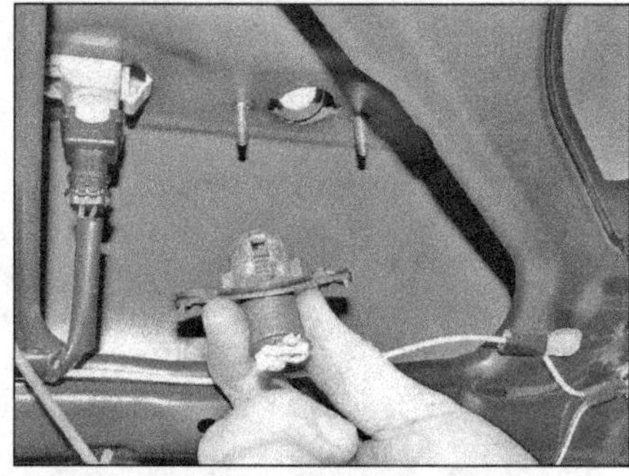
17.21 Disconnect the linkage rod and remove the lock

17.23a Undo the bolts from the lower part of the tailgate strut

17.23b Prise the clip (arrowed) and remove the upper part of the tailgate strut

Tailgate lock cylinder

19 Remove the tailgate inner trim panel as described in paragraph 2.

20 Release the securing clip and disconnect the link rod from the cylinder operating arm **(see illustration)**.

21 Undo the two retaining nuts and remove the lock cylinder bracket from the tailgate **(see illustration)**.

22 Refitting is a reversal of removal.

Tailgate support struts

Warning: The support strut is filled with pressurised gas – do not disassemble this component. If it is faulty renew it with a new one.

Note: *The rear tailgate is heavy and somewhat awkward to hold securely while renewing the struts – at least two people should perform this procedure.*

23 Open the tailgate and support it in the open position. Undo the bolts holding the bracket at the lower end of the strut, and then prise out the retaining clips and pull the struts from the upper mounting studs **(see illustrations)**.

24 Refitting is a reversal of removal.

18 Central locking components – removal and refitting

Note: *The central locking system is equipped with a sophisticated self-diagnosis capability. Before removing any of the central locking components, have the system interrogated by a Toyota dealer or suitably-equipped specialist to pinpoint the fault.*

Removal

Electronic control unit (ECU)

1 The central locking system is controlled by an ECU.

2 Release the retaining clips and lower the ECU out of position.

3 Disconnect the wiring connector(s) and remove the ECU from the vehicle. **Note:** *If the control unit is renewed, it may need to be programmed before use. Entrust this task to a Toyota dealer or specialist.*

Door lock actuator

4 Remove the door lock as described in Section 14. The central locking actuator is integral with the door lock assembly.

Boot lock actuator

5 Remove the boot lock as described in Section 16. The actuator is integral with the boot lock assembly.

Tailgate lock actuator

6 Refer to Section 17.

Refitting

7 Refitting is the reverse of removal. Prior to refitting any trim panels removed for access thoroughly check the operation of the central locking system.

20.3 Undo the three mounting nuts and remove the mirror assembly

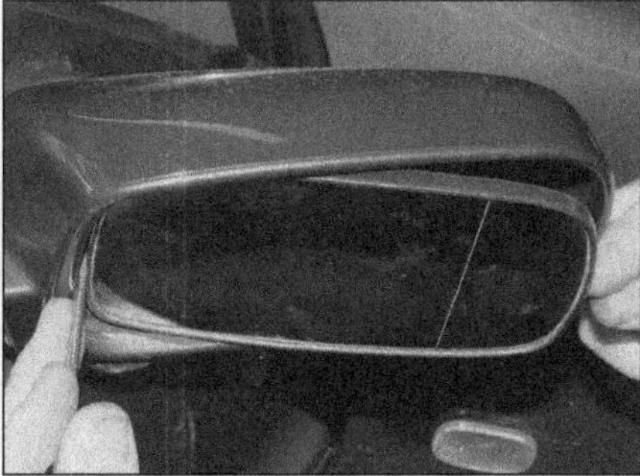

20.5 Slide the mirror glass to the outside, then pull it rearwards

20.10 Undo the three screws (arrowed) and remove the mirror motor

19 Electric window components – removal and refitting

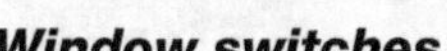

Window switches

1 Refer to Chapter 12, Section 4.

Window motors

2 At the time of writing, it would appear that the electric motor is integral with the regulator (see Section 15), and must be renewed as an assembly. Check with your Toyota dealer or specialist.

20 Mirrors and associated components – removal and refitting

Exterior mirror assembly

1 On models with manually-adjustable mirrors, carefully prise off the triangular plastic trim panel over the mirror mounting.

2 On models with electrically-adjustable mirrors, remove the door inner trim panel as described in Section 13, then disconnect the mirror wiring plug.

3 On all models, undo the three mounting nuts and remove the mirror assembly **(see illustration)**.

4 Refitting is the reverse of removal, tightening the mirror nuts securely.

Exterior mirror glass

5 Slide the mirror glass a little to the outside, then pull the outer edge rearwards and remove it **(see illustration)**.

6 Disconnect the mirror heater wiring plugs (where applicable) as the mirror is withdrawn.

7 Refitting is a reversal of removal.

Exterior mirror switch

8 Refer to Chapter 12, Section 4.

Exterior mirror motor

9 Remove the mirror glass as previously described.

10 Undo the three screws, and remove the motor **(see illustration)**. Note that it may be necessary to cut the wires to the mirror motor, as the plug is too large to pass through the cable guide. When refitting the motor, splice the new wires to the plug.

11 Refitting is a reversal of removal.

21 Windscreen, fixed windows and rear screen/tailgate glass – general information

1 These areas of glass are secured by the tight fit of the weatherstrip in the body aperture, and are bonded in position with a special adhesive. Renewal of such fixed glass is a difficult, messy and time-consuming task, which is beyond the scope of the home mechanic. It is difficult, unless one has plenty of practice, to obtain a secure, waterproof fit. Furthermore, the task carries a high risk of breakage; this applies especially to the laminated glass windscreen. In view of this, owners are strongly advised to have this sort of work carried out by one of the many specialist windscreen fitters.

22 Sunroof – general information and motor renewal

General information

1 Due to the complexity of the sunroof mechanism, considerable expertise is needed to repair, renew or adjust the sunroof components successfully. Removal of the roof first requires the headlining to be removed, which is a complex and tedious operation, and not a task to be undertaken lightly. Therefore, any problems with the sunroof (except sunroof motor renewal) should be referred to a Toyota dealer or specialist.

Renewal

Motor

2 Motor renewal required the front section of the headlining to be lowered (See paragraph 1). Once the headlining has been lowered, disconnect the wiring plug, undo the three retaining bolts, and remove the motor complete with relay. Once removed, do not attempt to rotate the motor spindle.

3 Refitting is a reversal of removal.

Switch

4 Remove the interior light lens as described in Chapter 12, Section 8, then undo the two switch retaining screws, disconnect the wiring plug and remove the switch.

5 Refitting is a reversal of removal.

23 Body exterior fittings – removal and refitting

Wheel arch liners and body underpanels

1 The various plastic covers fitted to the underside of the vehicle are secured in position by a mixture of screws, nuts and retaining clips, and removal will be fairly obvious on inspection. Work methodically around, removing its retaining screws and releasing its retaining clips until the panel is free and can be removed from the underside of the vehicle. Most clips used on the vehicle are simply prised out of position. Other clips can be released by unscrewing/prising out the centre pins and then removing the clip.

Body trim strips and badges

2 The various body trim strips and badges are held in position with a special adhesive tape. Removal requires the trim/badge to be heated, to soften the adhesive, and then cut away from the surface. Due to the high risk of damage to the vehicle's paintwork during this operation, it is recommended that this task should be entrusted to a Toyota dealer or suitably-equipped specialist.

24 Seats – removal and refitting

Front seat

Removal

Warning: The front seats may be fitted with side airbags. If they are, disconnect the battery negative lead (Chapter 5A), then wait at least 5 minutes before commencing work on any aspect of the seat.

24.1a Prise off the plastic covers . . .

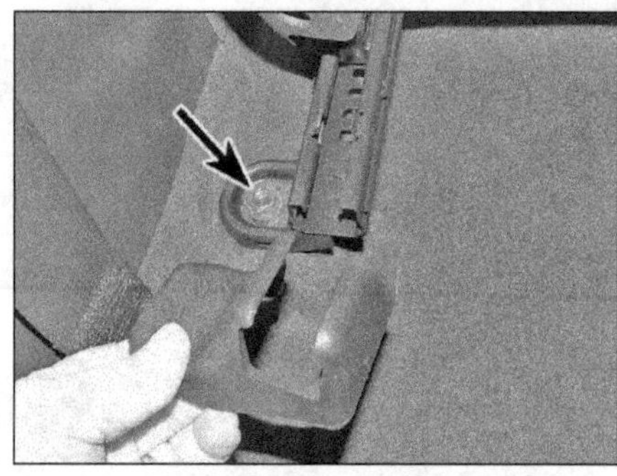

24.1b . . . and undo the front seat rail rear mounting bolts (arrowed)

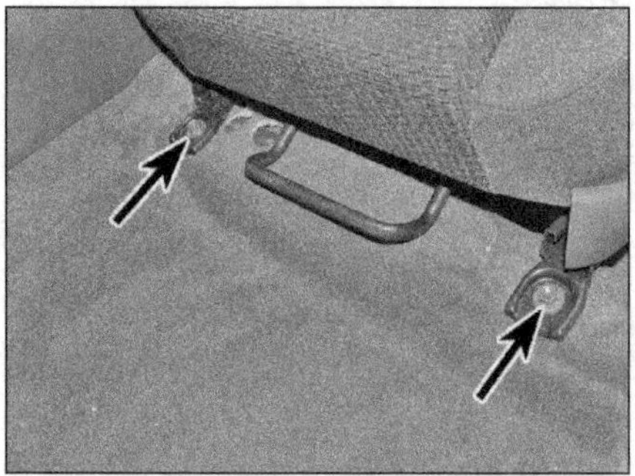

24.2 Seat rail front mounting bolts (arrowed)

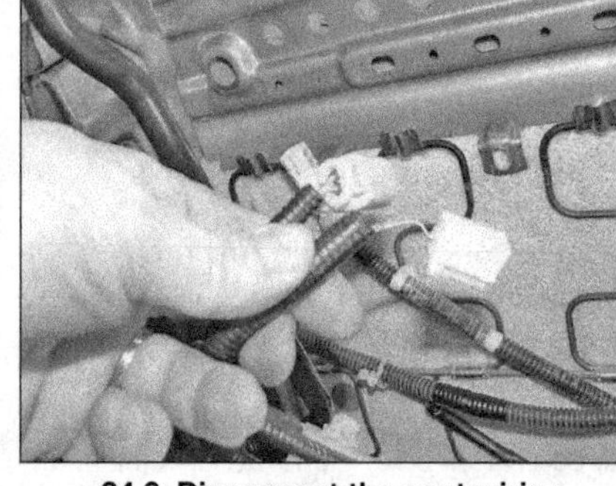

24.3 Disconnect the seat wiring connectors

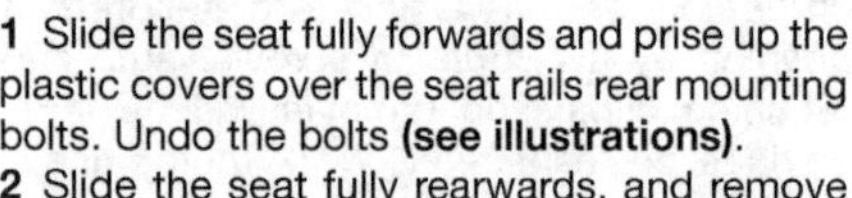

1 Slide the seat fully forwards and prise up the plastic covers over the seat rails rear mounting bolts. Undo the bolts **(see illustrations)**.

2 Slide the seat fully rearwards, and remove the front mounting bolts **(see illustration)**.

3 Tip the seat rearwards a little, then disconnect any wiring plug(s) and remove the seat from the passenger cabin **(see illustration)**.

Refitting

4 Refitting is the reverse of removal, noting the following points.

a) Fit the seat retaining bolts and tighten them by hand only. Slide the seat fully forwards and then slide it back by two stops of the seat locking mechanism. Rock the seat to ensure that the seat locking mechanism is correctly engaged then tighten the mounting bolts to the specified torque.

b) Ensure that the wiring is connected and correctly routed.

Saloon rear seat

Removal

5 Pull up on the front of the seat cushion to release the left- and right-hand retaining clips, and remove it forwards and out from the vehicle.

6 Undo the retaining bolts and remove the seat backrest from the passenger compartment.

Refitting

7 Refitting is the reverse of removal, making sure the seat back is located correctly, and the seat belt buckles and lap belt are fed through the intended openings.

Hatchback and Estate rear seat

Removal

8 Lift the front of the seat cushion upwards and then tilt the seat cushion forwards, Release the hinged locating rods from the floor panel, and then lift the cushion and remove it from the vehicle **(see illustrations)**.

9 Undo the centre seat belt anchorage point on the vehicle floor **(see illustration)**.

10 On estate models, undo the lower mounting bolts from the side rear seat cushions, and then lift them up to unclip them from the retaining clip. Remove side seat cushions from the vehicle.

11 Working in the luggage compartment at the rear of the rear seat backs, remove the retaining clip and pull back the carpet to access the rear seat securing bolts **(see illustrations)**.

12 Fold the seat backrests forwards, undo the bolt each side securing the seat to the hinges, and remove the seat backrest.

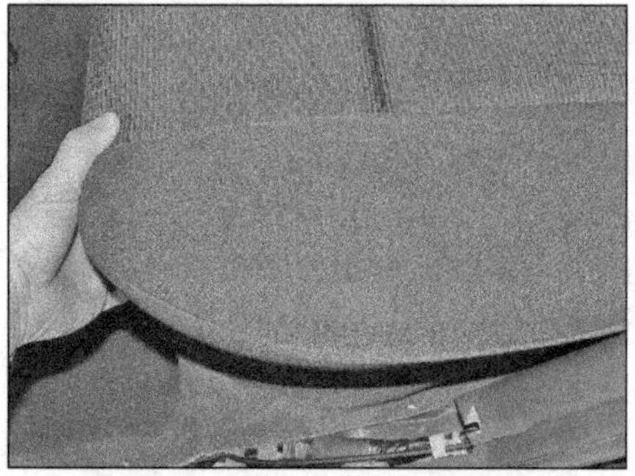

24.8a Lift the front of the rear seat . . .

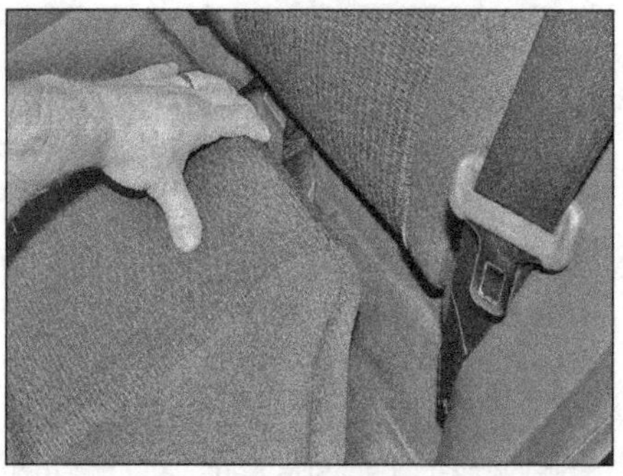

24.8b . . . and tilt the rear of the seat forward

24.8c Release the hinged rods from the floor panel . . .

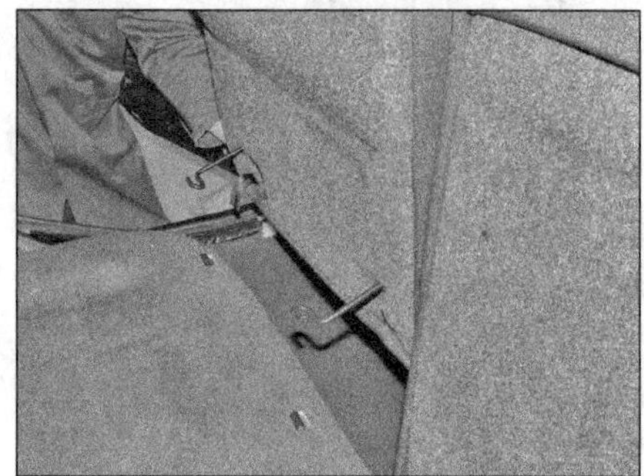

24.8d . . . and lift the rear seat cushion out from the vehicle

24.9 Centre seat belt anchorage bolt

24.11a Release the securing clip . . .

24.11b . . . pull back the carpet to access bolt

Refitting

13 Refitting is the reverse of removal, making sure the seat back is located correctly, and the seat belt buckles and lap belt are fed through the intended openings.

25 Front seat belt tensioning mechanism – general information

1 Most models are fitted with a front seat belt tensioner system. The system is designed to instantaneously take up any slack in the seat belt in the case of a sudden frontal impact, therefore reducing the possibility of injury to the front seat occupants. The tensioner is incorporated into the design of the inertia reels, located behind the B-pillar lower trim panels.

2 The seat belt tensioner is triggered by a frontal impact above a predetermined force. Lesser impacts, including impacts from behind, will not trigger the system.

3 When the system is triggered, a pyrotechnic device causes the inertia reel to retract. This prevents the seat belt moving and keeps the occupant in position in the seat. Once the tensioner has been triggered, the seat belt will be permanently locked and the assembly must be renewed.

4 There is a risk of injury if the system is triggered inadvertently when working on the vehicle. If any work is to be carried out on the seat belt disable, the tensioner by disconnecting the battery negative lead (see Chapter 5A), and waiting at least 5 minutes before proceeding.

5 Also note the following warnings before contemplating any work on the front seat belt inertia reel.

Warning: If the tensioner mechanism is dropped, it must be renewed, even it has suffered no apparent damage.

- ***Do not allow any solvents to come into contact with the tensioner mechanism.***
- ***Do not subject the inertia reel to any form of shock as this could accidentally trigger the seat belt tensioner.***

26 Seat belt components – removal and refitting

Warning: Read Section 25 before proceeding.

Removal

Front seat belts

1 Remove the front seat as described in Section 24.

2 Remove the front door sill trim panel and the lower B-pillar trim panel as described in Section 27.

3 Prise off the cap, and undo the bolt securing the front seat belt upper anchorage to the vehicle body **(see illustrations)**.

4 Pull the door seals back from inside the door aperture and then unclip the upper trim panel from the door pillar **(see illustrations)**.

5 Release the catch and disconnect the wiring plug from the inertia reel **(see illustrations)**.

6 Unscrew the inertia reel retaining bolt(s) and remove the seat belt from the door pillar **(see illustrations)**.

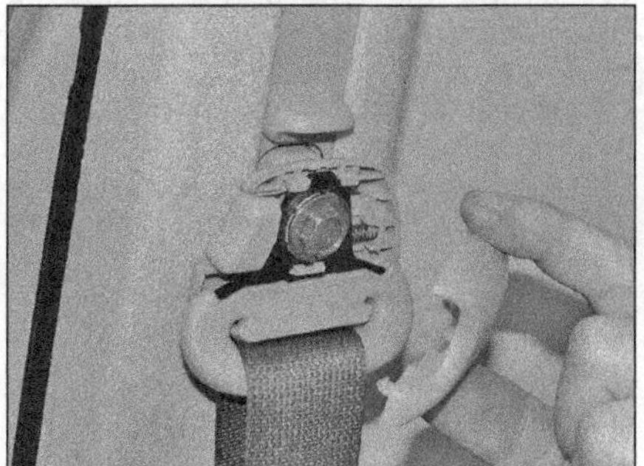
26.3a Prise off the cap . . .

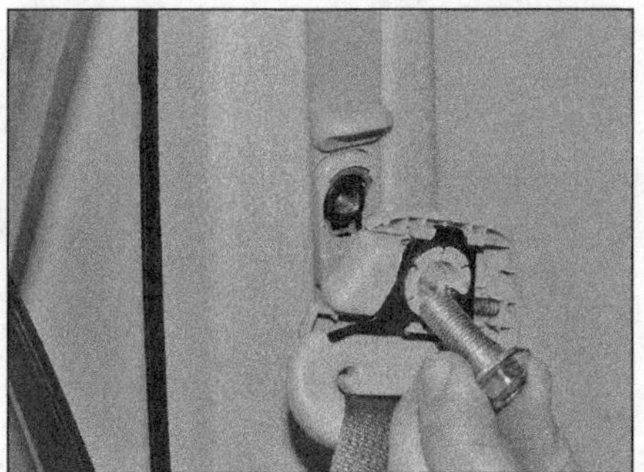
26.3b . . . and remove the seat belt upper anchorage bolt

26.4a Pull back the door seal . . .

26.4b . . . and unclip the upper pillar trim panel

26.5a Release the locking clip . . .

26.5b . . . and disconnect the wiring connector

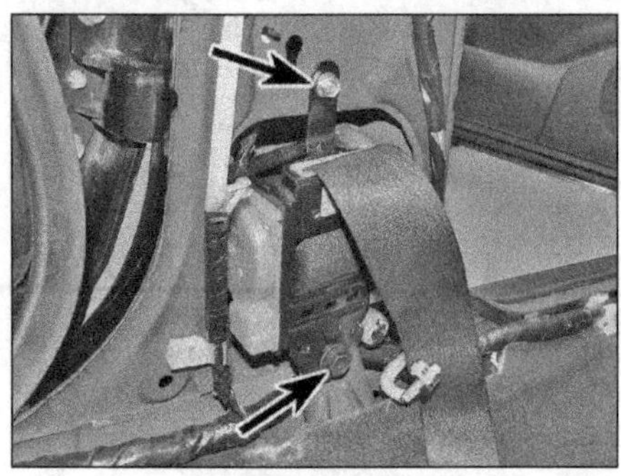
26.6a Undo the retaining bolts (arrowed) . . .

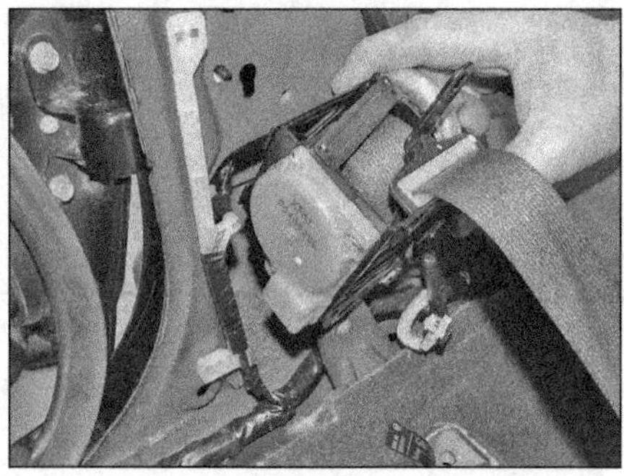
26.6b . . . and remove the inertia reel from the pillar

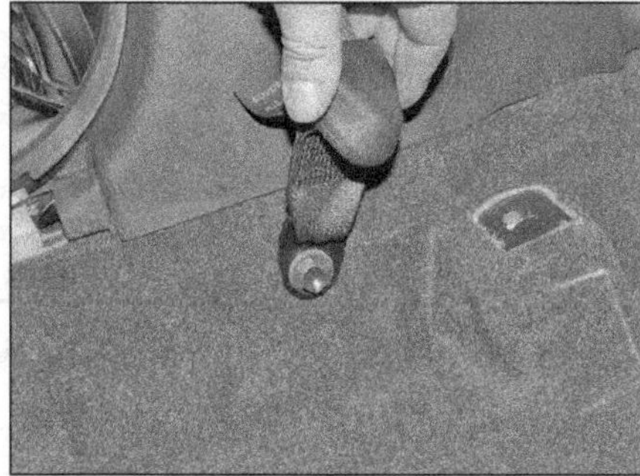
26.7 Unclip the cover and remove the lower anchorage bolt

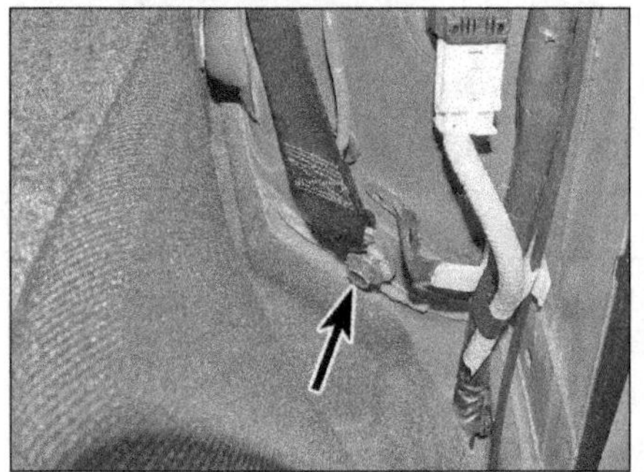
26.15 Rear side seat belt lower anchorage point

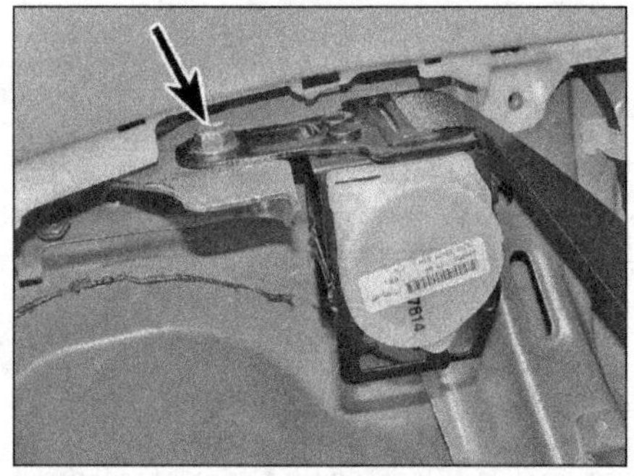
26.16 Rear side seat belt inertia reel bolt (arrowed)

26.19 Centre seat belt lower anchorage point

7 Unclip the plastic cover, and then undo the bolt securing the lower seat belt anchorage **(see illustration)**.

Fixed rear seat belts

8 Remove the rear seat (see Section 24).

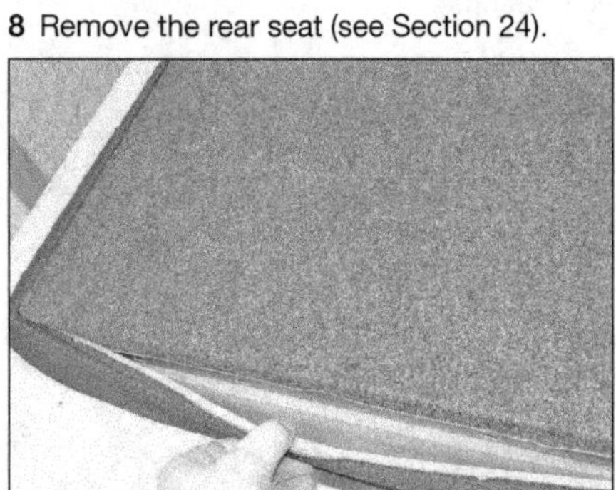
26.20 Unclip the trim from around the outer edge of the seat back

26.22a Release the securing clips (arrowed) – cover removed for clarity . . .

9 Remove the parcel shelf and C-pillar trims as described in Section 27.

10 Slacken and remove the bolts and washers securing the rear seat belts to the vehicle body and remove the centre belt and buckle.

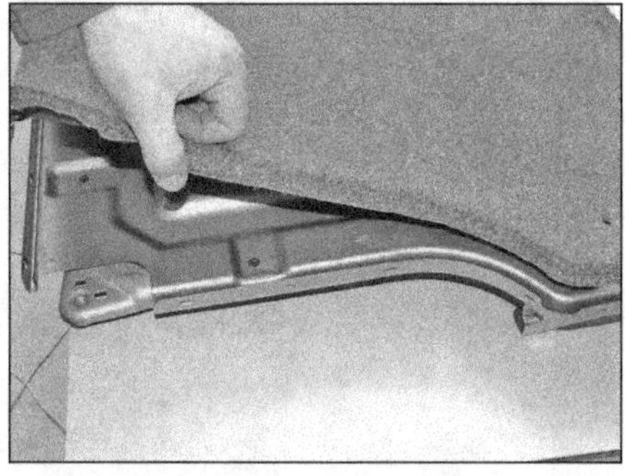
26.21 Pull the carpet from the back of the seat

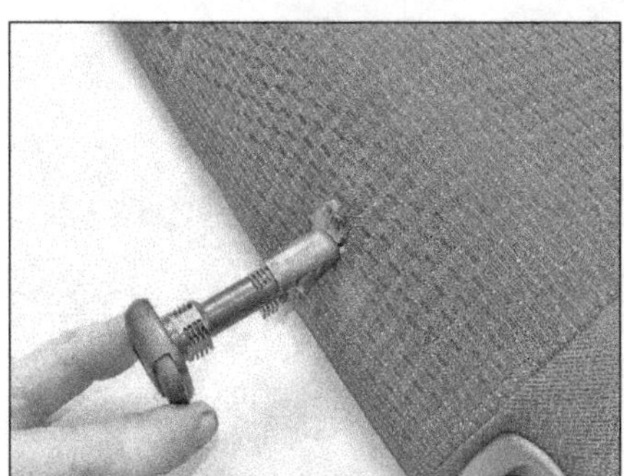
26.22b . . . and withdraw the headrest inserts

11 Unscrew the inertia reel retaining bolt and remove the seat belt(s).

Folding rear seat side belts

12 Fold the rear seats forward.

13 Remove the rear parcel shelf.

14 Remove the C-pillar lower trim as described in Section 27.

15 Slacken and remove the bolt securing the lower end of the belt to the body (if not already done) **(see illustration)**.

16 The inertia reel is secured by one bolt. Slacken and remove the bolt **(see illustration)**.

17 Manoeuvre the assembly from the vehicle, noting the routing of the seat belt.

Rear centre belt

18 Remove the rear seat cushion as described in Section 24.

19 Undo the bolts securing the seat belt anchorage to the floor. Note the positions of any washers/spacers fitted **(see illustration)**.

20 Fold the seat backrest forward, and then unclip the fabric cover from around the seat cushion **(see illustration)**. This will not be able to be completely removed until the headrest plastic inserts and other plastic covers have been removed from the top of the seat back.

21 Unclip the rear carpet covering from the rear of the seat **(see illustration)**.

22 If required, reach up inside the seat back and release the securing clips at the bottom of the headrest inserts and withdraw them from the seat back **(see illustrations)**.

23 Unclip the plastic trim from around the seat belt, and then remove the seat cover,

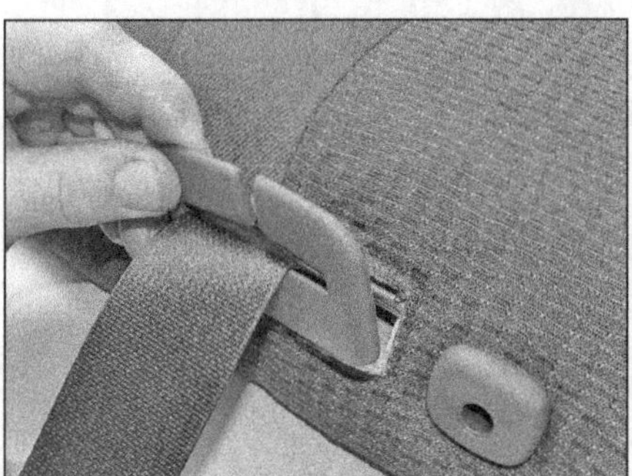
26.23a Unclip the plastic trim . . .

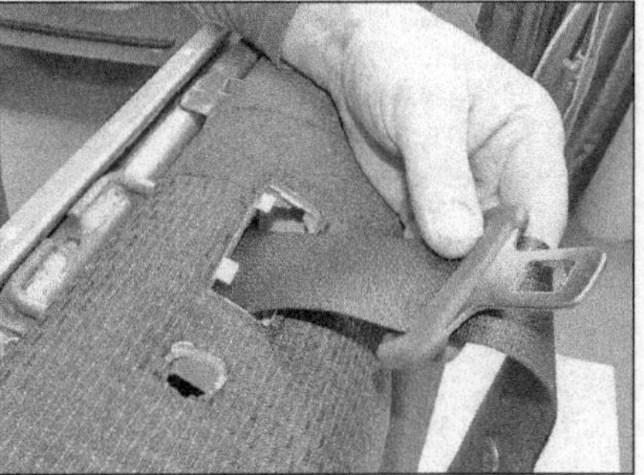
26.23b . . . and remove the seat cover over the seat belt

26.24 Centre inertia reel seat belt location in rear seat back

passing the seat belt through the slot in the cover **(see illustrations)**.

24 Undo the bolt and pull the inertia reel from its position in the rear seat back **(see illustration)**.

Refitting

25 Refitting is a reversal of the removal procedure, ensuring that all the seat belt mounting bolts are tightened to the specified torque, and all disturbed trim panels are securely retained by all the relevant retaining clips.

27 Interior trim – removal and refitting

Interior trim panels

1 The interior trim panels are secured using either screws or various types of trim fasteners, usually studs or clips.

2 Check that there are no other panels overlapping the one to be removed; usually there is a sequence that has to be followed that will become obvious on close inspection.

3 Remove all obvious fasteners, such as screws. If the panel will not come free, it is held by hidden clips or fasteners. These are usually situated around the edge of the panel and can be prised up to release them; note, however, that they can break quite easily so new ones should be available. The best way of releasing such clips, without the correct type of tool, is to use a large flat-bladed screwdriver. Note that some panels are secured by plastic expanding rivets, where the centre pin must be prised up before the rivet can be removed. Note in many cases that the adjacent sealing strip must be prised back to release a panel.

4 When removing a panel, never use excessive force or the panel may be damaged; always check carefully that all fasteners have been removed or released before attempting to withdraw a panel.

5 Refitting is the reverse of the removal procedure; secure the fasteners by pressing them firmly into place and ensure that all disturbed components are correctly secured to prevent rattles.

A-pillar trim

6 Using a wooden or plastic flat-bladed lever, starting at the top, carefully prise the trim away from the pillar **(see illustration)**.

7 Release the retaining strap from the rear of the trim and disengage the lower end from the facia **(see illustration)**.

8 Refitting is the reverse of the removal procedure; secure the fasteners by pressing them firmly into place.

B-pillar trim

9 Begin by carefully pulling the door seal from the door aperture at the B-pillar **(see illustration)**.

10 Carefully prise up the front and rear door sill trim panels, releasing them from their retaining clips **(see illustration)**.

11 Pull the bottom edge of the lower trim in towards the centre of the vehicle to release it from the retaining clips, and then carefully prise it out of the upper panel **(see illustration)**.

12 Refitting is the reverse of the removal procedure; secure the fasteners by pressing

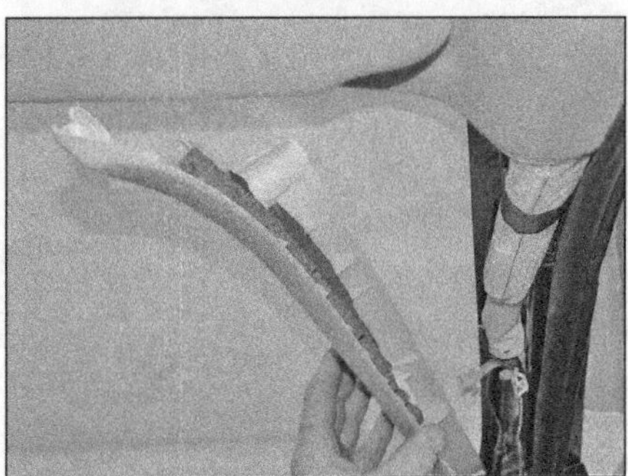
27.6 Pull away the top of the A-pillar trim . . .

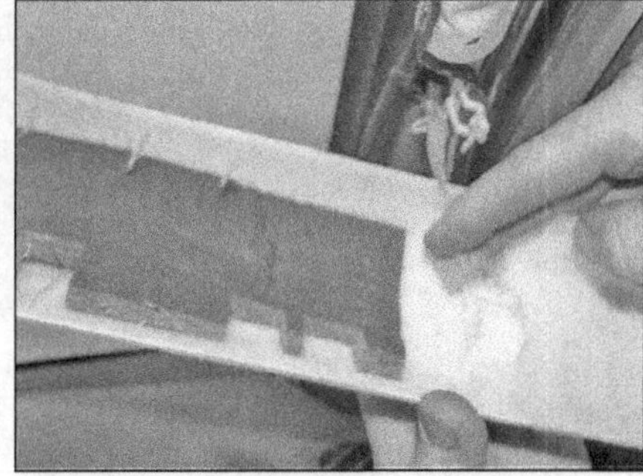
27.7 . . . and release the retaining strap

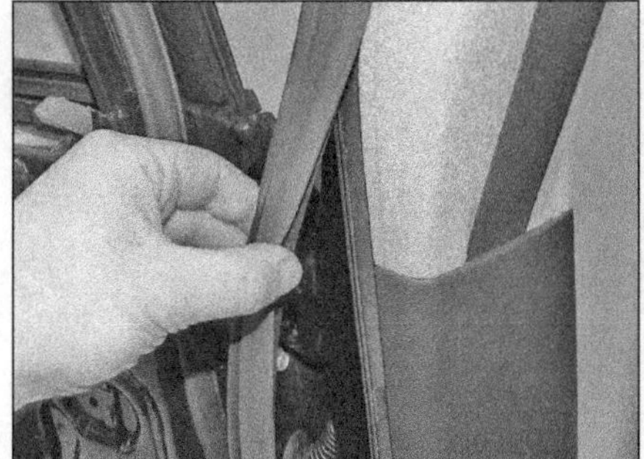
27.9 Pull back the rubber door seal

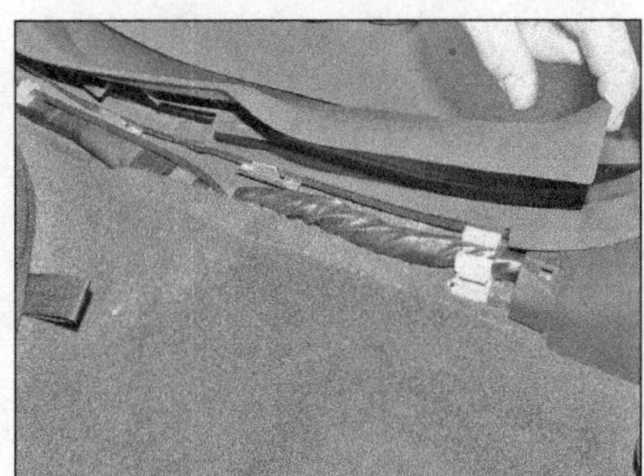
27.10 Unclip the door sill trim panels

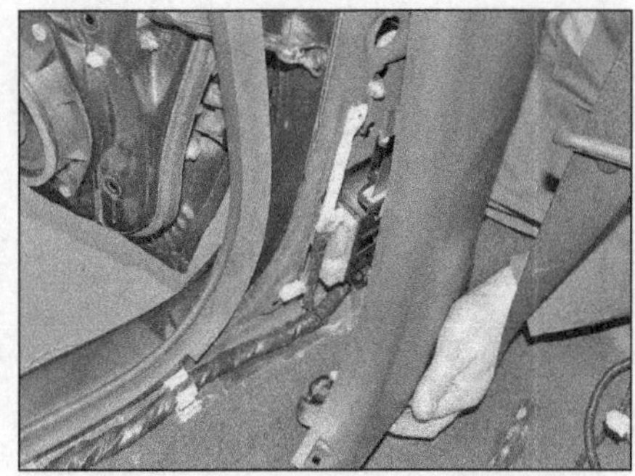
27.11 Pull the bottom of the B-pillar trim towards the centre of the vehicle

27.24 Remove the storage compartment

27.25 Unclip the luggage compartment light

27.26a Release the retaining clips . . .

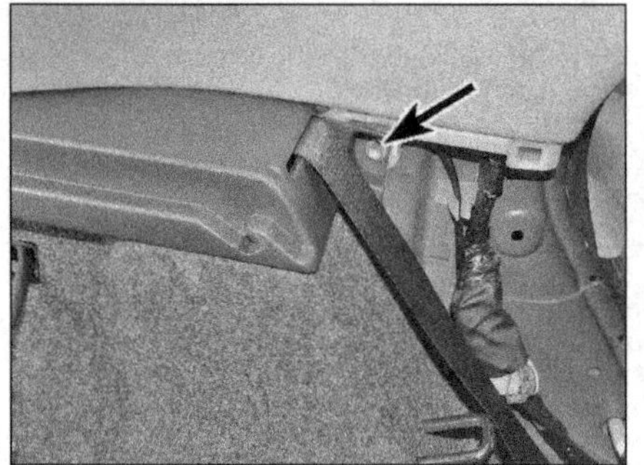
27.26b . . . undo the retaining bolts . . .

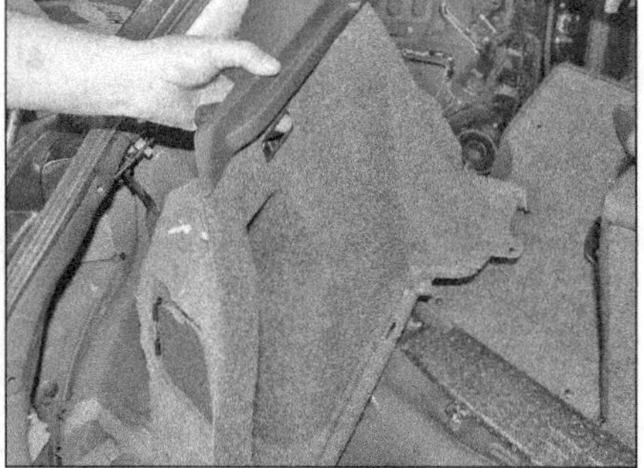
27.26c . . . and carefully remove the trim panel

them firmly into place and ensure that all disturbed components are correctly secured to prevent rattles.

B/C-pillar trim

3-door Hatchback models

13 Begin by carefully prising up the front door sill trim panel with its retaining clips.

14 Remove the rear seat backrest as described in Section 24.

15 Undo the rear side seat belt lower anchorage bolt, then prise off the cap and undo the upper seat belt anchorage bolt from the B-pillar.

16 Undo the screw, prise out the clip, and pull the lower B-pillar/side panel from place.

17 Remove the luggage compartment carpet, then unscrew the two plastic nuts and remove the tailgate sill trim panel.

18 Prise up and remove the plastic trim at the top of the luggage compartment side trim panel.

19 Undo the screws/prise out the clips and remove the luggage compartment side trim panel. Disconnect the speaker wiring plug as the panel is removed.

20 Undo the screws and pull the B/C pillar trim from place. Feed the seat belt through the slot in the panel.

21 Refitting is the reverse of the removal procedure; secure the fasteners by pressing them firmly into place and ensure that all disturbed components are correctly secured to prevent rattles.

C-pillar trim

Note: *The following procedure is for the Hatchback model; Estate and Saloon models are similar.*

22 Remove the rear seat cushion as described in Section 24.

23 Remove the rear parcel shelf.

24 Remove the carpet and storage tray from the luggage compartment **(see illustration)**.

25 Where applicable, unclip the luggage compartment light unit from the side cover **(see illustration)**.

26 Working your way around the lower side trim panel remove the retaining clips and bolts, then withdraw the panel from the vehicle **(see illustrations)**.

27 Pull the weatherstrip from the door aperture adjacent to the C-pillar trim and seat lower side panel.

28 Undo the retaining bolt and unclip the upper trim panel from the C-pillar **(see illustration)**.

29 Refitting is a reversal of removal.

Tailgate trim panel

30 Open the tailgate and insert a flat-bladed tool between the inner trim panel and the tailgate. Work around the edge of the panel and release the retaining clips **(see illustration)**. Remove the panel.

31 Refitting is a reversal of removal, ensuring any damaged clips are renewed.

Glovebox

32 Open the glovebox and undo the screw from the operating arm at the side of the glovebox. Disconnect the arm from the glovebox **(see illustrations)**.

33 Pull the glovebox downwards from its position in the facia, and then unclip the lower part from the facia **(see illustrations)**.

34 If required unclip the operating arm

27.28a Undo the retaining bolts . . .

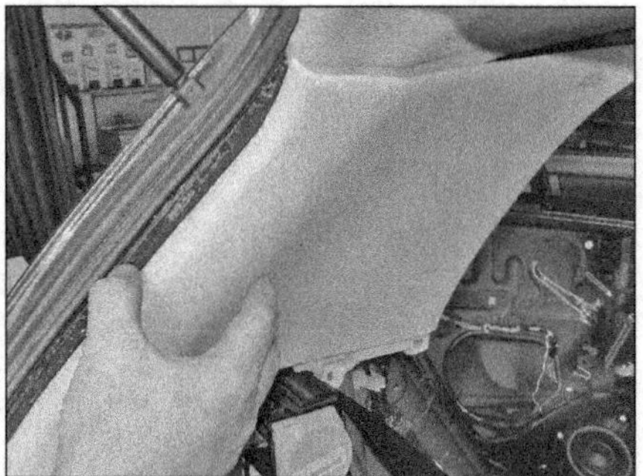
27.28b . . . and carefully unclip the trim panel

27.30 Carefully unclip the trim panel from the tailgate

27.32a Undo the retaining screw . . .

27.32b . . . and disconnect the operating arm

27.33a Unclip the glovebox . . .

from the side of the glovebox aperture **(see illustration)**.

35 Refitting is a reversal of removal.

Carpets

36 The passenger compartment floor carpet is in one piece, secured at its edges by screws or clips; usually the same fasteners used to secure the various adjoining trim panels.

37 Carpet removal and refitting is reasonably straightforward but very time-consuming because all adjoining trim panels must be removed first, as must components such as the seats, the centre console and seat belt lower anchorages.

Headlining

38 The headlining is clipped to the roof and can be withdrawn only once all fittings such as the grab handles, sunvisors, sunroof (if fitted), windscreen, rear quarter windows and related trim panels have been removed, and the door, tailgate and sunroof aperture sealing strips have been prised clear.

39 Note that headlining removal and refitting requires considerable skill and experience if it is to be carried out without damage and is therefore best entrusted to an expert.

Driver's side lower facia panels

40 Undo the retaining screws and remove the trim from under the facia panel **(see illustrations)**.

41 Open the storage pocket and unclip it from the facia panel **(see illustration)**.

27.33b . . . releasing it from the facia (arrowed)

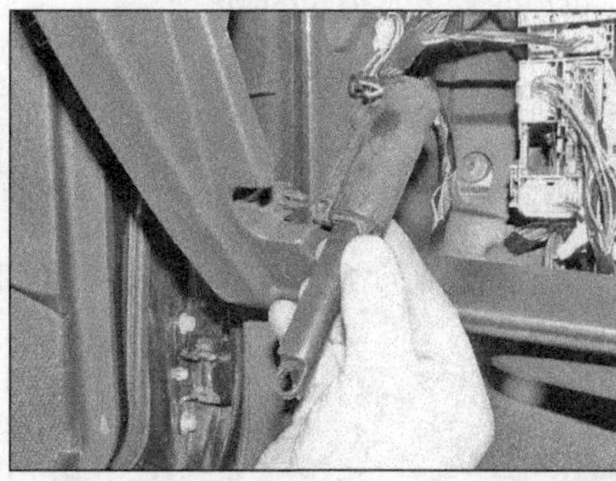
27.34 Unclip the operating arm from the facia

42 Pull down the centre section of the lower panel, undo the retaining screws and remove it from the facia panel **(see illustrations)**.

43 Refitting is a reversal of removal.

Sunvisors

44 Unclip the sunvisor from the inner mounting, then undo the screw(s) and remove the mounting **(see illustration)**.

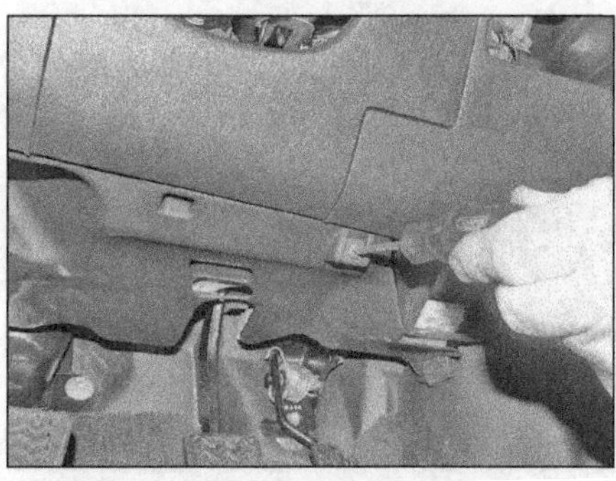
27.40a Undo the retaining screws . . .

27.40b . . . and remove the lower trim panel

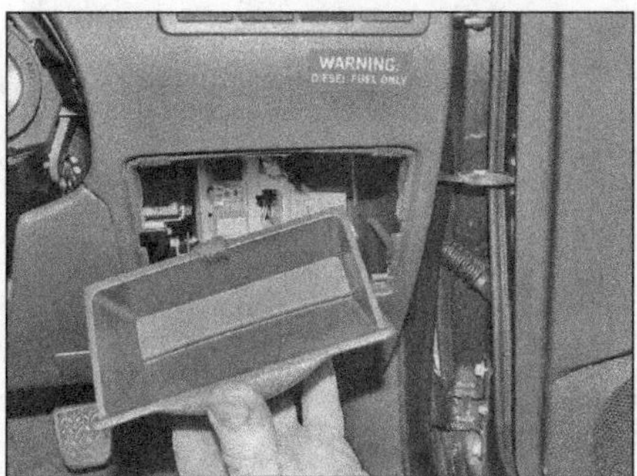

27.41 Unclip the storage pocket from the facia

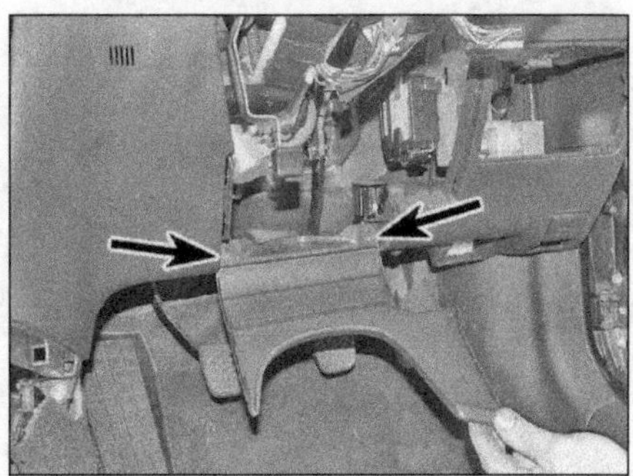
27.42a Open the trim panel and undo the retaining screws (arrowed)

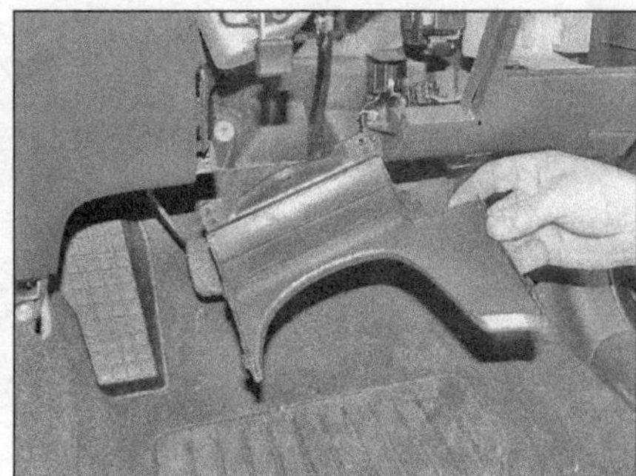
27.42b Remove the trim panel

45 To remove the locating clips, turn a quarter of a turn and pull out from the headlining **(see illustration)**.

46 Refitting is a reversal of removal.

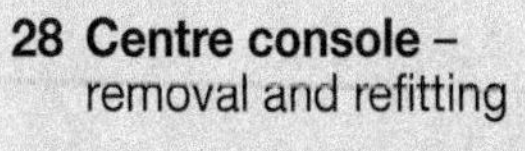

28 Centre console – removal and refitting

Removal

1 Lift the lid on the rear storage compartment and undo the two screws in the base of the compartment **(see illustration)**.

2 Unclip the trim panel from below the handbrake lever **(see illustration)**.

3 Unclip the ashtray and remove it from the front of the centre console **(see illustration)**.

4 Prise up the gear lever surround trim, and disconnect the wiring connector from the cigarette lighter **(see illustrations)**.

5 Unscrew the knob from the top of the gear lever and pull the gaiter and trim over the gear lever **(see illustrations)**.

6 Undo the two retaining screws from the front of the centre console **(see illustration)**.

7 Lift the console over the handbrake lever and remove it from the passenger compartment **(see illustration)**. Where applicable, disconnect any wiring plugs as the console is removed.

27.44 Sunvisor mounting screws

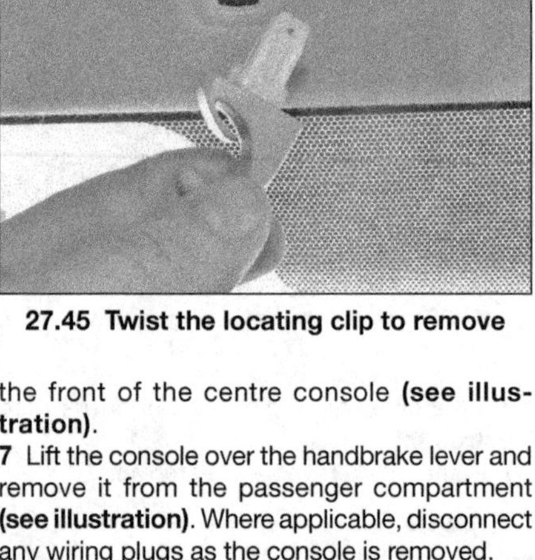

27.45 Twist the locating clip to remove

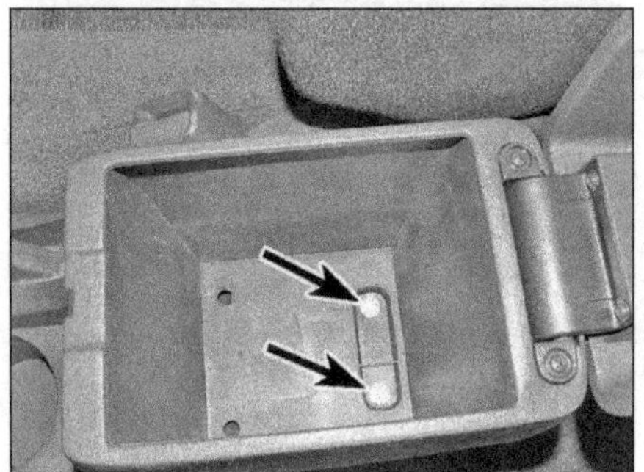

28.1 Lift the lid on the storage box, and undo the two screws (arrowed)

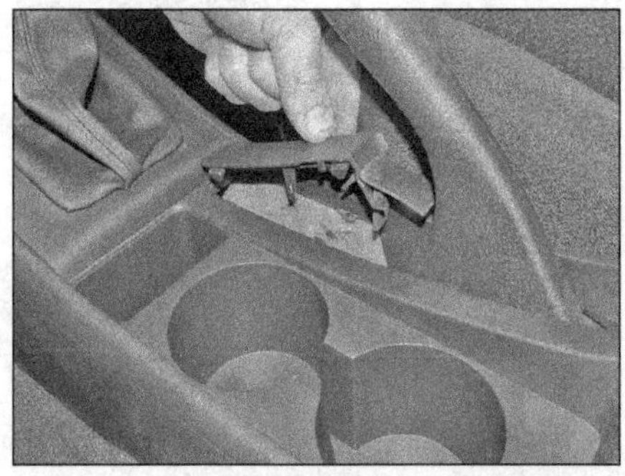

28.2 Unclip the handbrake trim panel

28.3 Remove the ashtray

28.4a Unclip the gear lever gaiter trim panel . . .

28.4b . . . and disconnect the cigar lighter

28.5a Unscrew the gear knob . . .

28.5b . . and slide the gaiter over the gear lever

28.6 Undo the two retaining screws (arrowed) at the front of the centre console

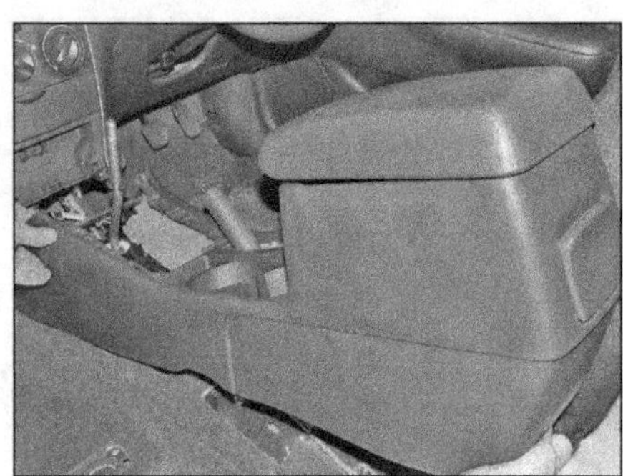

28.7 Lift the centre console over the handbrake lever to remove

29.8a Remove the lower shroud . . .

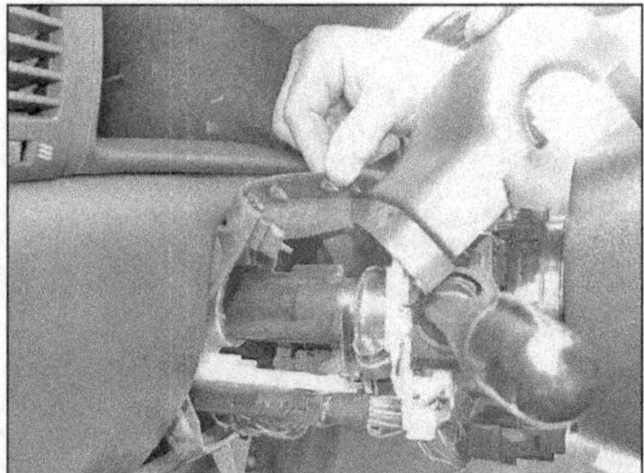
29.8b . . . and unclip the upper shroud

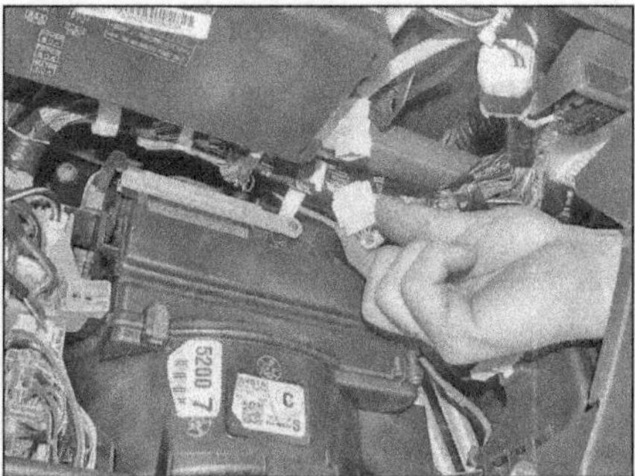
29.10 Disconnect the passenger airbag wiring connector

Refitting

8 Refitting is the reverse of removal, making sure all fasteners are securely tightened.

29 Facia panel assembly – removal and refitting

Note: *The facia panel is in two parts, first remove the upper part and then the lower part can be removed.*

Removal

1 Disconnect the battery negative lead as described in Chapter 5A.

2 Remove the centre console as described in Section 28.

3 Remove the driver's side facia lower trim panels as described in Section 27.

4 Remove the steering wheel as described in Chapter 10.

5 Remove the instrument cluster and central information/audio unit as described in Chapter 12.

6 Remove the A-pillar trims as described in Section 27.

7 Remove the heater control panel as described in Chapter 3.

8 Undo the three screws and remove the steering column lower shroud, then unclip the upper shroud from the retaining clips along the trim on the facia panel **(see illustrations)**.

9 Remove the steering column combination switches and facia panel switches as described in Chapter 12.

10 Reach through the glovebox aperture in the facia and disconnect the passenger airbag wiring connector **(see illustration)**.

11 Release the retaining clips and unclip the air vents from each side of the facia panel **(see illustrations)**.

12 Undo the retaining screws from inside the air vent apertures **(see illustration)**.

13 The upper part of the facia panel can now be removed from inside the passenger compartment **(see illustration)**.

14 Unclip the bonnet release lever from the driver's side lower facia panel **(see illustration)**.

15 Release the securing clips from each side of the lower facia panel **(see illustration)**.

16 Undo the retaining bolts from along the upper edge of the lower facia panel **(see illustration)**.

17 Working your way along the top of the lower facia panel, release the retaining clips from the air ducts **(see illustration)**.

18 Undo the plastic securing nut and

29.11a Carefully lever the air vents . . .

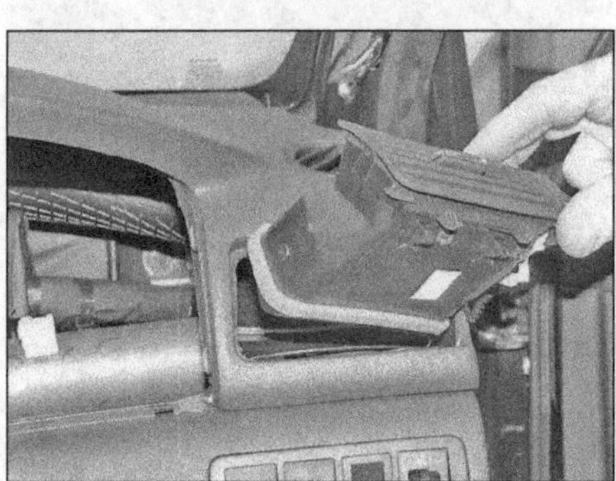
29.11b . . . out from the facia panel

29.12 Undo the retaining screws (arrowed) from inside the air vent aperture

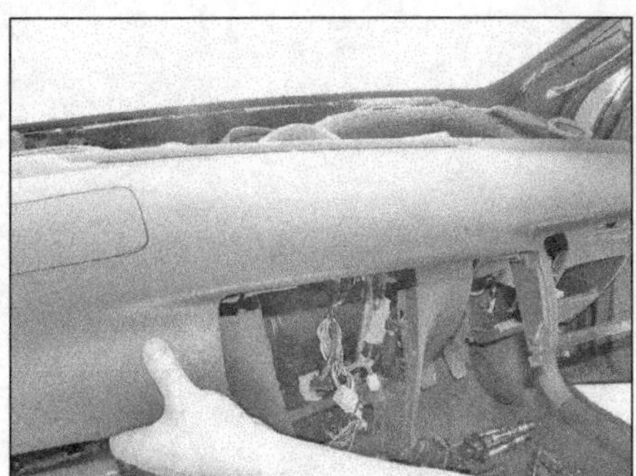
29.13 Removing the upper part of the facia panel

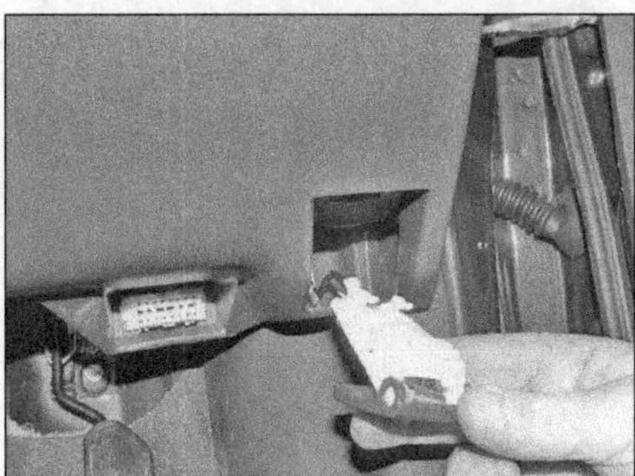
29.14 Unclip the bonnet release lever from the facia

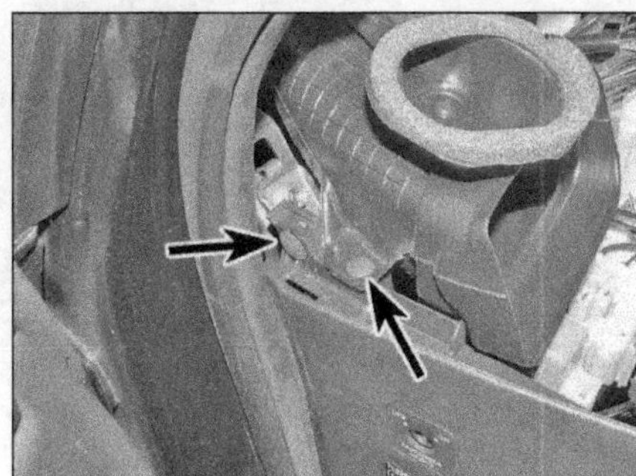
29.15 Release the securing clips (arrowed) at each end of the facia

29.16 Undo the retaining bolts across the top of the crossbrace

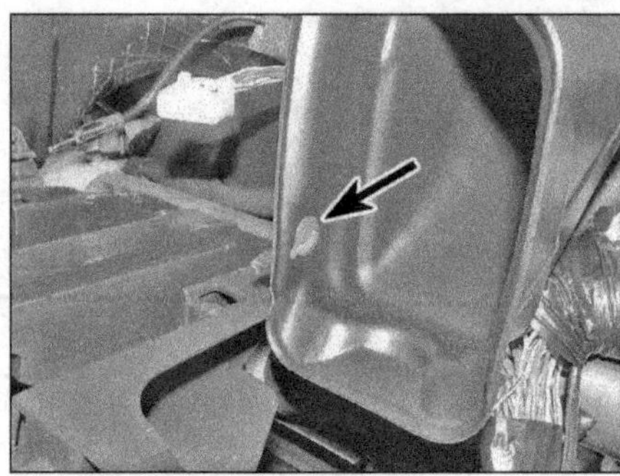

29.17 Release the securing clips (arrowed) in the centre air ducts

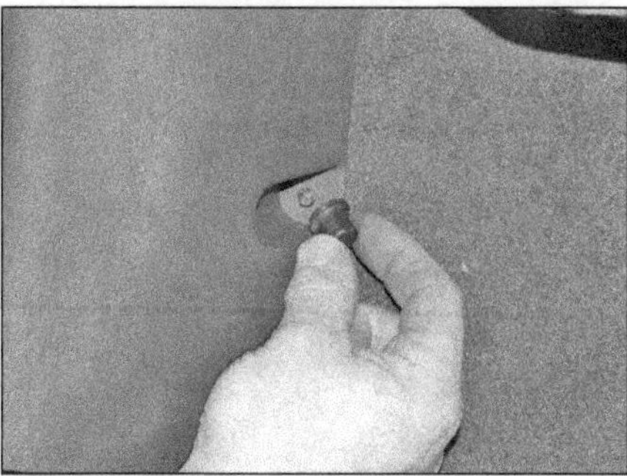

29.18a Undo the plastic securing nut . . .

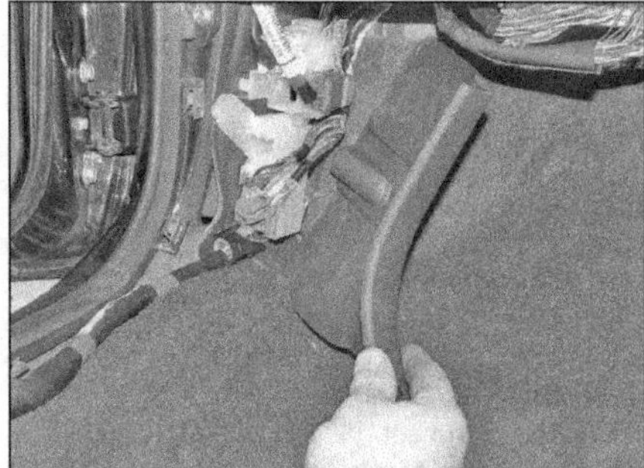

29.18b . . . and remove the kick panels from both sides

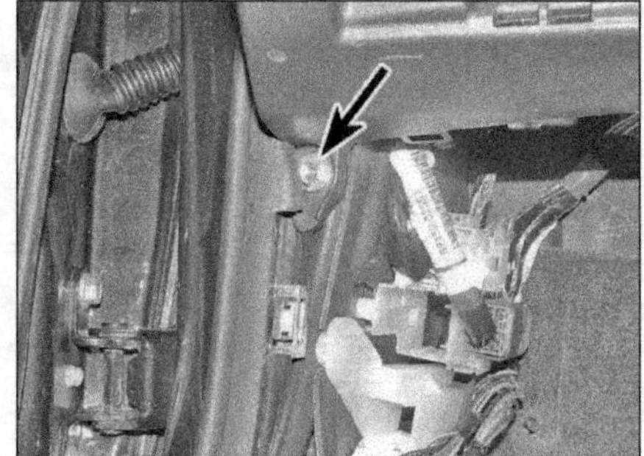

29.18c Undo the lower facia panel retaining bolts – one side shown

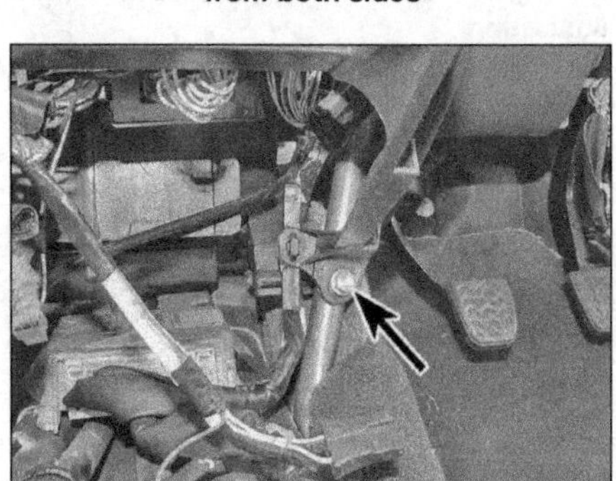

29.19 Undo the retaining bolt (arrowed) from the strengthening brace

29.20 Undo the bolt from inside the glovebox aperture

remove the both front kick panels and then remove the lower facia retaining bolts **(see illustrations)**.

19 Remove the lower facia retaining bolt from the strengthening brace **(see illustration)**.

20 Undo the retaining bolt from inside the glovebox aperture **(see illustration)**.

21 Undo the screws/clips securing the the wiring loom to the inside of the lower facia panel, make a note of the fitted positions and routing of any wiring looms before releasing the cable ties attached to the facia, then manoeuvre the lower facia panel from the vehicle.

Refitting

22 Refitting is a reversal of the removal procedure, noting the following points:

a) Manoeuvre the facia into position and ensure that the wiring is correctly routed and securely retained by its facia clips.

b) Clip the facia back into position, ensure the locating lugs at the front edge of the facia engage correctly, making sure all the wiring connectors are fed through their respective apertures, then refit all the facia fasteners and tighten them securely.

c) On completion, reconnect the battery and check that all the electrical components and switches function correctly.

Chapter 12
Body electrical system

Contents

Degrees of difficulty

Easy, suitable for novice with little experience 	**Fairly easy,** suitable for beginner with some experience	**Fairly difficult,** suitable for competent DIY mechanic	**Difficult,** suitable for experienced DIY mechanic	**Very difficult,** suitable for expert DIY or professional

Specifications

General

System type	12 volt, negative earth
Fuses	See wiring diagrams at end of Chapter and stickers on fusebox lids for specific vehicle details

Bulbs

	Wattage
Brake/tail light:	
Hatchback and Saloon	21/5 bayonet
Estate	21/5 wedge
Foglight:	
Front (halogen):	
Hatchback	42 H10
Saloon and Estate	51 HB4
Rear:	
Hatchback and Saloon	21 bayonet
Estate	21 wedge
Headlight (halogen):	
Main beam:	
Hatchback	55 H7
Saloon and Estate	60 HB3
Dipped beam	55 H7
High-level brake light	16 wedge
Indicator side repeater lights	5 wedge (amber)
Indicators:	
Front	21 bayonet (amber)
Rear:	
Hatchback	21 bayonet
Saloon	21 bayonet (amber)
Estate	21 wedge (amber)
Luggage compartment light:	
Hatchback and Estate	5 festoon
Saloon	3.8 bayonet
Number plate light	5 wedge
Reversing light:	
Hatchback and Saloon	21 bayonet
Estate	21 wedge
Sidelights	5 wedge

Torque wrench settings

	Nm	lbf ft
Driver's airbag fasteners	9	7
Driver's airbag sensor lock release bolt	9	7
SRS control module	20	15
SRS front crash sensors	20	15
SRS side crash sensors	20	15
Windscreen/tailgate wiper arm nuts	20	15

1 General information

The electrical system is of 12 volt negative earth type. Power for the lights and all electrical accessories is supplied by a lead-acid type battery, which is charged by the belt-driven alternator.

This Chapter covers repair and service procedures for the various electrical components not associated with the engine. Information on the battery, alternator and starter motor can be found in Chapter 5A.

Warning: Before carrying out any work on the electrical system, read through the precautions given in 'Safety first!' at the beginning of this manual and in Chapter 5A.

2 Electrical fault finding – general information

Note: *Refer to the precautions given in 'Safety first!' and in Section 1 of this Chapter before starting work. The following tests relate to testing of the main electrical circuits, and should not be used to test delicate electronic circuits, particularly where an electronic control unit is used.*

General

1 A typical electrical circuit consists of an electrical component; any switches, relays, motors, fuses, fusible links or circuit breakers related to that component, and the wiring and connectors which link the component to both the battery and the chassis. To help to pinpoint a problem in an electrical circuit, wiring diagrams are included at the end of this Chapter.

2 Before attempting to diagnose an electrical fault, first study the appropriate wiring diagram to obtain a complete understanding of the components included in the particular circuit concerned. The possible sources of a fault can be narrowed down by noting if other components related to the circuit are operating properly. If several components or circuits fail at one time, the problem is likely to be related to a shared fuse or earth connection.

3 Electrical problems usually stem from simple causes, such as loose or corroded connections, a faulty earth connection, a blown fuse, a melted fusible link, or a faulty relay. Visually inspect the condition of all fuses, wires and connections in a problem circuit before testing the components. Use the wiring diagrams to determine which terminal connections will need to be checked in order to pinpoint the trouble spot.

4 The basic tools required for electrical fault finding include a circuit tester or voltmeter (a 12 volt bulb with a set of test leads can also be used for certain tests); an ohmmeter (to measure resistance and check for continuity); a battery and set of test leads; and a jumper wire, preferably with a circuit breaker or fuse incorporated, which can be used to bypass suspect wires or electrical components. Before attempting to locate a problem with test instruments, use the wiring diagram to determine where to make the connections.

Warning: Under no circumstances may live measuring instruments such as ohmmeters, voltmeters or a bulb and test leads be used to test any of the SRS airbag, SIPS bag, or pyrotechnical seat belt circuitry. Any testing of these components must be left to a Toyota dealer, as there is a danger of activating the system if the correct procedures are not followed.

5 To find the source of an intermittent wiring fault (usually due to a poor or dirty connection, or damaged wiring insulation), a wiggle test can be performed on the wiring. This involves wiggling the wiring by hand to see if the fault occurs as the wiring is moved. It should be possible to narrow down the source of the fault to a particular section of wiring. This method of testing can be used in conjunction with any of the tests described in the following sub-Sections.

6 Apart from problems due to poor connections, two basic types of fault can occur in an electrical circuit – open-circuit, or short-circuit.

7 Open-circuit faults are caused by a break somewhere in the circuit, which prevents current from flowing. An open-circuit fault will prevent a component from working.

8 Short-circuit faults are caused by a short somewhere in the circuit, which allows the current flowing in the circuit to escape along an alternative route, usually to earth. Short-circuit faults are normally caused by a breakdown in wiring insulation, which allows a feed wire to touch either another wire, or an earthed component such as the bodyshell. A short-circuit fault will normally cause the relevant circuit fuse to blow.

Finding an open-circuit

9 To check for an open-circuit, connect one lead of a circuit tester or the negative lead of a voltmeter either to the battery negative terminal or to a known good earth.

10 Connect the other lead to a connector in the circuit being tested, preferably nearest to the battery or fuse. At this point, battery voltage should be present, unless the lead from the battery or the fuse itself is faulty (bearing in mind that some circuits are live only when the ignition switch is moved to a particular position).

11 Switch on the circuit, then connect the tester lead to the connector nearest the circuit switch on the component side.

12 If voltage is present (indicated either by the tester bulb lighting or a voltmeter reading, as applicable), this means that the section of the circuit between the relevant connector and the switch is problem-free.

13 Continue to check the remainder of the circuit in the same fashion.

14 When a point is reached at which no voltage is present, the problem must lie between that point and the previous test point with voltage. Most problems can be traced to a broken, corroded or loose connection.

Finding a short-circuit

15 To check for a short-circuit; first disconnect the load(s) from the circuit (loads are the components which draw current from a circuit, such as bulbs, motors, heating elements, etc).

16 Remove the relevant fuse from the circuit, and connect a circuit tester or voltmeter to the fuse connections.

17 Switch on the circuit; bearing in mind that some circuits are live only when the ignition switch is in a particular position.

18 If voltage is present (indicated either by the tester bulb lighting or a voltmeter reading, as applicable), this means that there is a short-circuit.

19 If no voltage is present during this test, but the fuse still blows with the load(s) reconnected, this indicates an internal fault in the load(s).

Finding an earth fault

20 The battery negative terminal is connected to earth – the metal of the engine/transmission and the vehicle body – and many systems are wired so that they only receive a positive feed, the current returning via the metal of the car body. This means that the component mounting and the body form part of that circuit. Loose or corroded mountings can therefore cause a range of electrical faults, ranging from total failure of a circuit, to a puzzling partial failure. In particular, lights may shine dimly (especially when another circuit sharing the same earth point is in operation), motors (eg, wiper motors or the radiator cooling fan motor) may run slowly, and the operation of one circuit may have an apparently unrelated effect on another.

21 Note that on many vehicles, earth straps are used between certain components, such as the engine/transmission and the body, usually where there is no metal-to-metal contact between components, due to flexible rubber mountings, etc.

22 To check whether a component is properly earthed, disconnect the battery and connect one lead of an ohmmeter to a known good earth point. Connect the other lead to the wire or earth connection being tested. The resistance reading should be zero; if not, check the connection as follows.

23 If an earth connection is thought to be faulty, dismantle the connection, and clean both the bodyshell and the wire terminal (or the component earth connection mating surface) back to bare metal. Be careful to remove all traces of dirt and corrosion, and then use a knife to trim away any paint, so that a clean metal-to-metal joint is made. On reassembly, tighten the joint fasteners securely; if a wire terminal is being refitted, use serrated washers between the terminal and the bodyshell, to ensure a clean and secure connection.

24 When the connection is remade, prevent the onset of corrosion in the future by applying a coat of petroleum jelly or silicone-based grease, or by spraying on (at regular intervals) a proprietary ignition sealer, or a water-dispersant lubricant.

3 Fuses and relays – general information

Fuses

1 The fuses are located in the fuseboxes situated in the engine compartment on the passenger's side, just in front of the suspension turret, in the passenger cabin fusebox behind the glovebox on the left-hand side of the facia (RHD models), and the relays are behind the driver's side storage compartment in the facia panel **(see illustrations)**.

2 If a fuse blows, the electrical circuit(s) protected by that fuse will cease to operate. The fuse positions and the circuits protected depends on vehicle specification, model year and country. Refer to the wiring diagrams at the end of this Chapter, and the sticker on the fusebox lid, which gives details for the particular vehicle.

3 To remove a fuse, first switch off the ignition. Using the plastic removal tool provided, pull the fuse out of its terminals **(see illustrations)**. The wire within the fuse should be visible; if the fuse is blown, the wire will be broken or melted.

4 Always renew a fuse with one of an identical rating; never use a fuse with a different rating from the original, or substitute anything else, as it may lead to a fire. Never renew a fuse more than once without tracing the source of the trouble. The fuse rating is stamped on top of the fuse; note that fuses are also colour-coded for easy recognition. Spare fuses are provided in the fusebox.

5 Persistent blowing of a particular fuse indicates a fault in the circuit(s) protected.

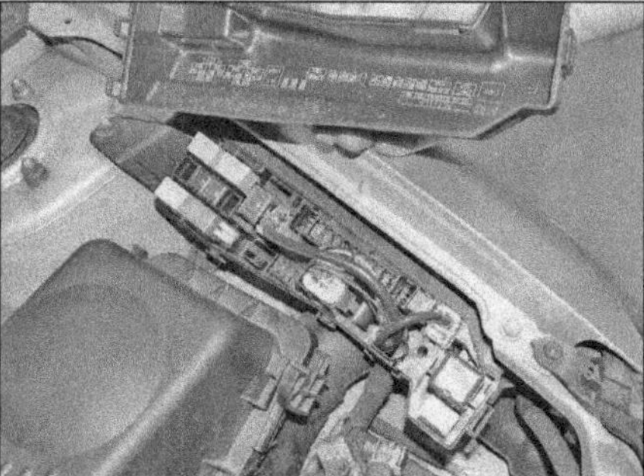

3.1a Underbonnet main fusebox

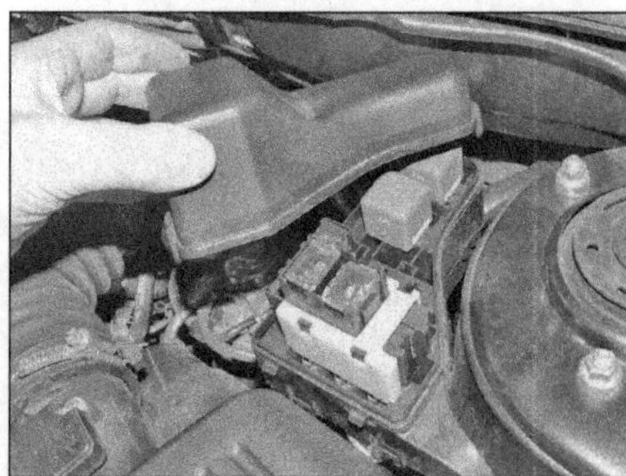

3.1b Underbonnet relay box – diesel models

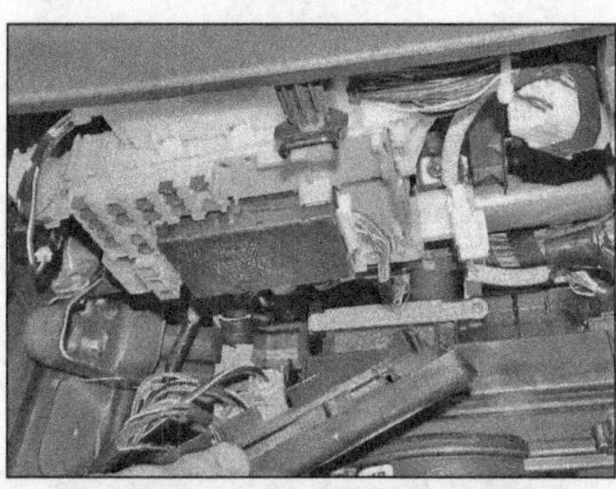

3.1c Main fusebox inside passenger compartment behind glovebox

3.1d Relays behind storage compartment in facia

Where more than one circuit is involved, switch on one item at a time until the fuse blows, so showing in which circuit the fault lies.

6 Besides a fault in the electrical component concerned, a blown fuse can also be caused by a short-circuit in the wiring to the component. Look for trapped or frayed wires allowing a live wire to touch vehicle metal, and for loose or damaged connectors.

7 Note that **only** the blade-type fuses should ever be renewed by the DIY mechanic. If one of the large fusible links in the main fusebox blows, this indicates a serious electrical fault which should be diagnosed by a Toyota dealer or automotive electrical specialist.

Relays

8 A relay is an electrically operated switch, which is used for the following reasons:

a) A relay can switch a heavy current remotely from the circuit in which the current is flowing, allowing the use of lighter-gauge wiring and switch contacts.

b) A relay can receive more than one control input, unlike a mechanical switch.

c) A relay can have a timer function ñ for example an intermittent wiper delay.

9 If a circuit that includes a relay develops a fault, remember that the relay itself could be faulty. A basic test of relay operation is to have an assistant switch on the item concerned, while you listen for a click from the relay. This would at least determine whether the relay is switching or not, but is not conclusive proof that a relay is working.

10 Most relays have four or five terminals – two terminals supplying current to its solenoid winding to provide the switching, a main current input and either one or two outputs to either supply or isolate the component concerned (depending on its configuration). Using the wiring diagrams at the end of this

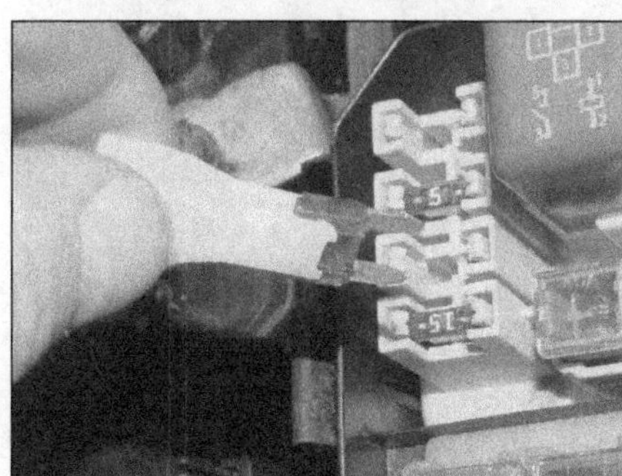

3.3a Use the plastic tweezers provided to pull a fuse from its terminals

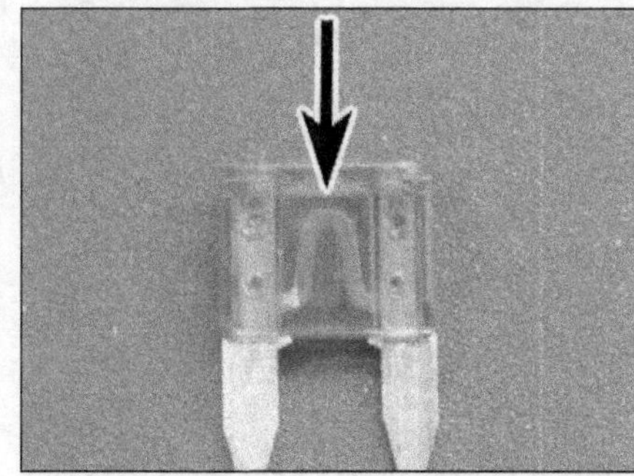

3.3b The wire within the fuse (arrowed) should be visible

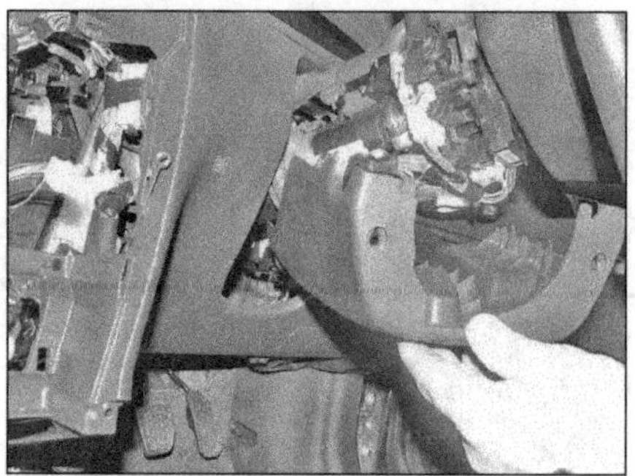
4.2a Remove the lower steering column shroud . . .

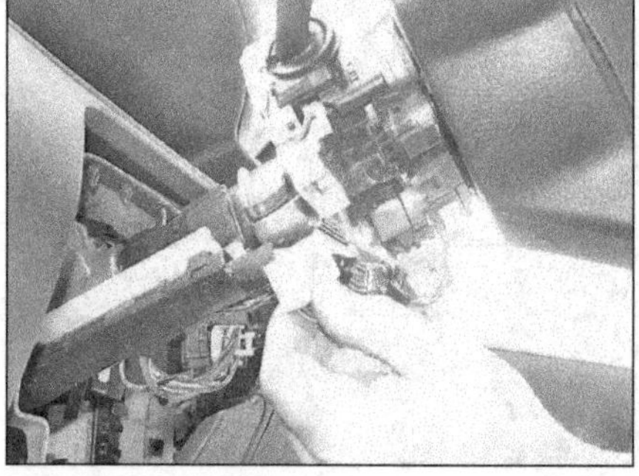
4.3a Disconnect the wiring connector from the light switch . . .

Chapter, test to ensure that all connections deliver the expected voltage or good earth.

11 Ultimately, testing is by substitution of a known good relay, but be careful – relays that look similar are not necessarily identical for purposes of substitution.

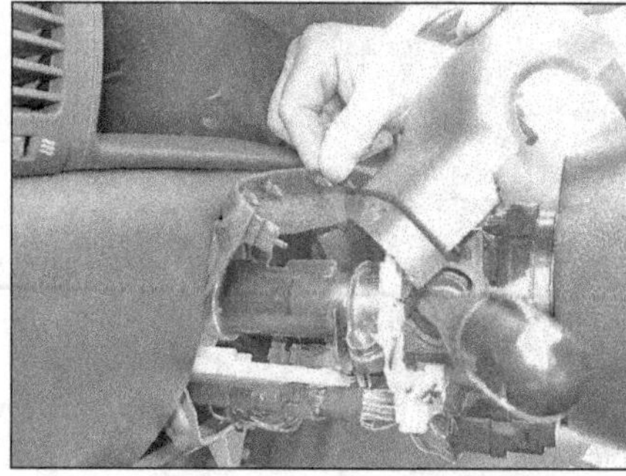
4.2b . . . and unclip the upper shroud

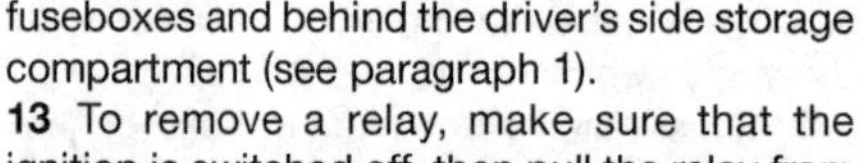
4.3b . . . and the wiper switch

12 The relays are found in the all the fuseboxes and behind the driver's side storage compartment (see paragraph 1).

13 To remove a relay, make sure that the ignition is switched off, then pull the relay from its socket. Push the new relay firmly in to refit.

4 Switches – removal and refitting

Steering column switches

1 Release the steering column height adjuster, and move the steering wheel downwards from the facia as far as possible.

2 Undo the three retaining screws and remove the steering column lower shroud, then release the upper shroud from the retaining clips along the facia panel **(see illustrations)**.

3 Disconnect the wiring plugs, from both the light switch and wiper switch **(see illustrations)**.

4 Each switch is secured by a securing clip, release the securing clips and withdraw the switch out to the side carefully **(see illustrations)**.

5 Refit the switches using a reversal of removal.

Ignition/key lock cylinder

6 Release the steering column height adjuster, and move the steering wheel downwards from the facia as far as possible.

7 Undo the three retaining screws and remove the steering column lower shroud, then release the upper shroud from the retaining clips along the facia panel **(see illustrations 4.2a and 4.2b)**.

8 Disconnect the wiring connector from the transponder, and then carefully unclip it from the ignition lock housing **(see illustrations)**.

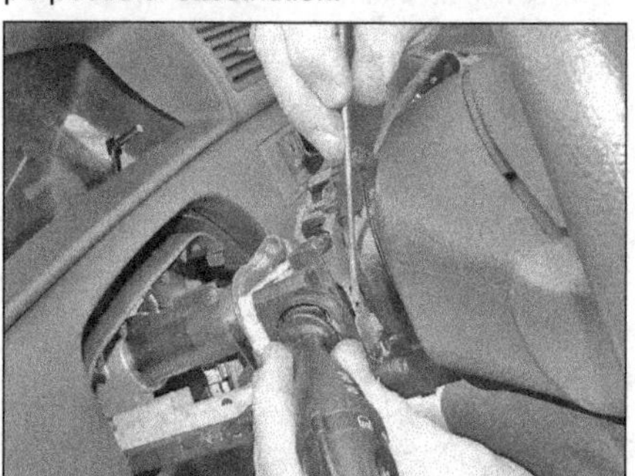
4.4a Release the securing clip . . .

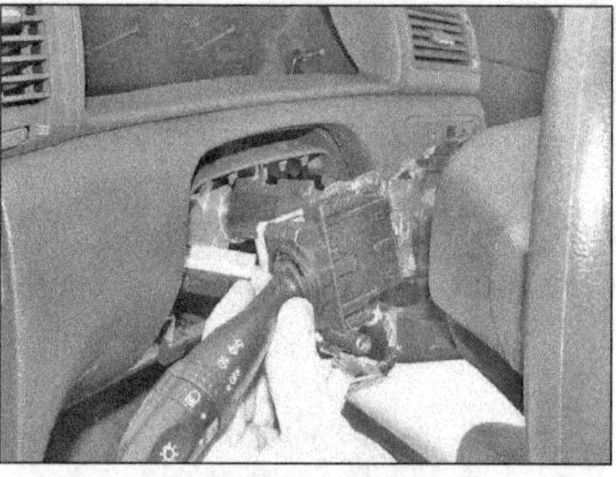
4.4b . . . and slide the light switch out from the bracket

4.4c Release the securing clip . . .

4.4d . . . and slide the wiper switch out from the bracket

4.8a Disconnect the wiring connector . . .

4.8b . . . and unclip the transponder from the switch

4.9a Release the locking peg (arrowed) . . .

4.9b . . . and slide out the lock cylinder

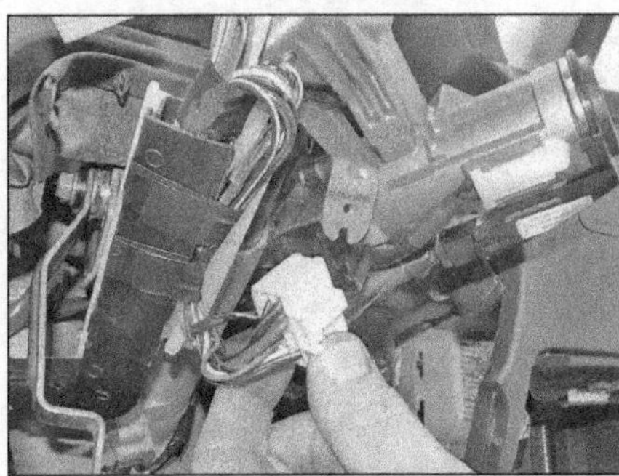

4.13 Disconnect the wiring connector from the ignition switch

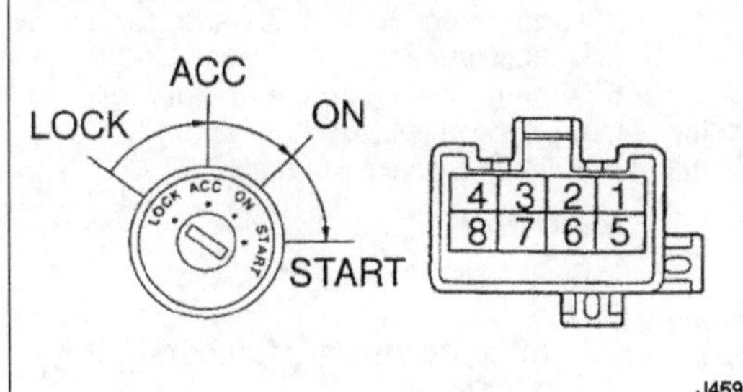

Switch position	Tester connection	Specified condition
LOCK	–	No continuity
ACC	5 – 6	Continuity
ON	1 – 4 5 – 6 – 8	Continuity
START	1 – 3 – 4 5 – 7 – 8	Continuity

4.14 Ignition switch terminal guide and continuity table

9 With the key in the Accessory position, insert a small screwdriver or punch in the hole in the casting and press the release button while pulling the lock cylinder straight out. Remove it from the steering column **(see illustrations)**.

10 Refitting is the reverse of removal.

Ignition/starter switch

11 Release the steering column height adjuster, and move the steering wheel downwards from the facia as far as possible.

12 Undo the three retaining screws and remove the steering column lower shroud, then release the upper shroud from the retaining clips along the facia panel **(see illustrations 4.2a and 4.2b)**.

13 Disconnect the wiring connector to the rear of the ignition switch **(see illustration)**.

14 Use an ohmmeter to check for continuity at the indicated terminals with the switch in each indicated position **(see illustration).**

15 Renew the switch if continuity is not as specified.

16 Remove the screws retaining the switch to the rear of the lock cylinder housing and remove the switch **(see illustration)**.

17 Refitting is the reverse of removal.

Hazard warning light switch

18 Remove the heater control panel as described in Chapter 3.

19 Release the retaining clips and withdraw the switch assembly from the rear of the heater control panel **(see illustration)**.

20 Refitting is a reversal of removal.

Door panel switches

21 Prise up the switch panel from the door trim. Disconnect the wiring plugs as the panel is withdrawn.

22 Undo the screws and remove the switch assembly from the panel.

23 Refitting is a reversal of removal.

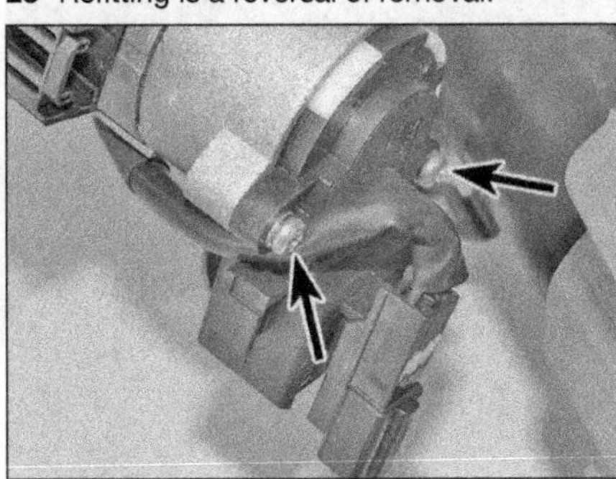

4.16 Switch retaining screws (arrowed)

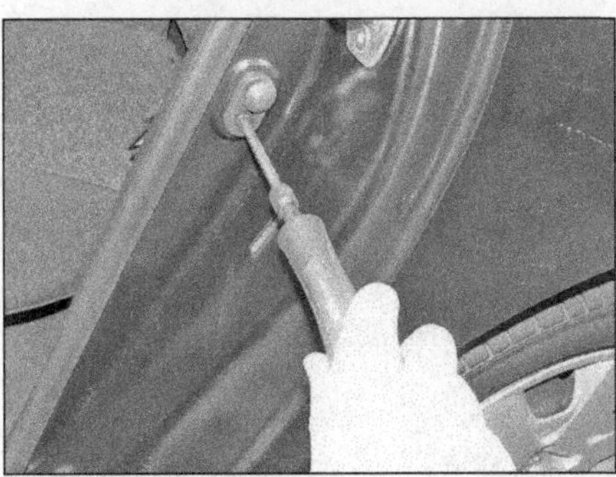

4.24a Undo the retaining screw . . .

Door courtesy light switches

24 Undo the screw and pull the switch from the door aperture **(see illustrations)**.

25 Disconnect the wiring plug and remove the switch.

26 Refitting is a reversal of removal.

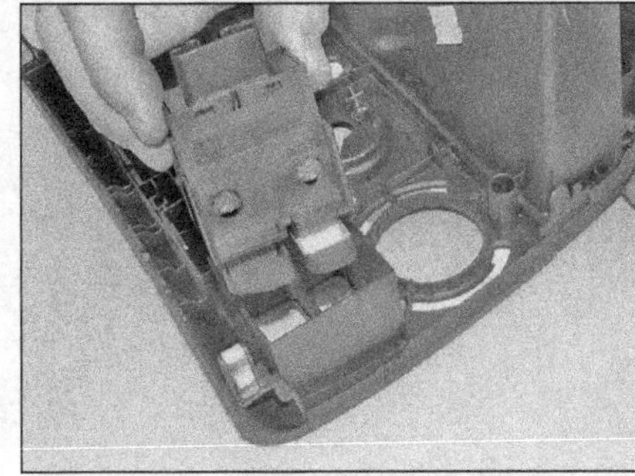

4.19 Unclip the switch from the trim panel

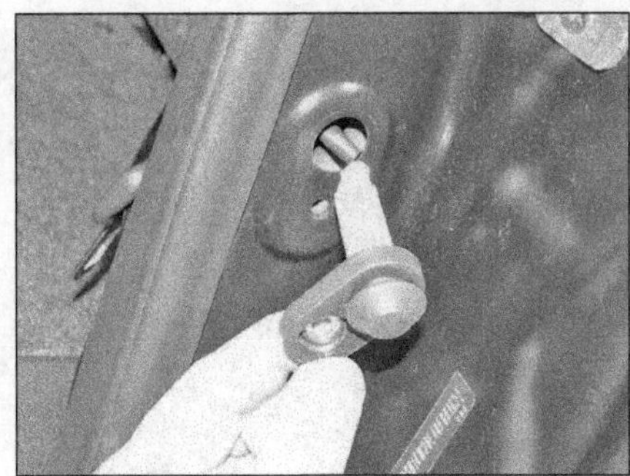

4.24b . . . and remove the light switch

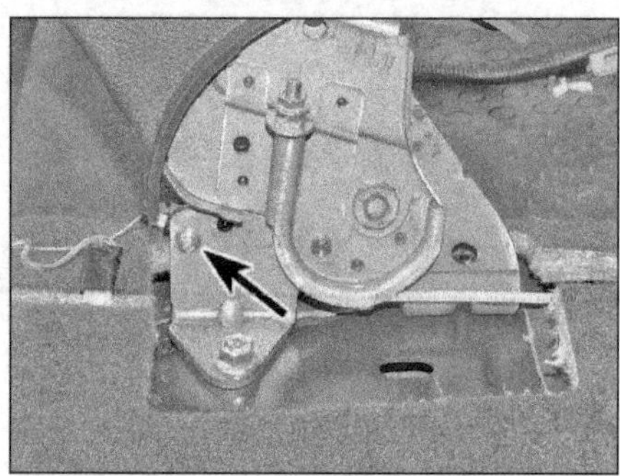

4.29 Handbrake warning light switch retaining screw – arrowed

Stop-light switch

27 Refer to Chapter 9.

Handbrake warning light switch

28 Remove the centre console as described in Chapter 11.

29 Undo the screw securing the switch to the handbrake bracket **(see illustration)**.

30 Lift out the switch, disconnect the spade connector and remove it.

31 Refitting is a reversal of removal. Check for correct operation of the switch before refitting the console.

Headlight beam level control

32 Release the clips and pull the switch from the facia panel, disconnect the wiring connector as it is removed **(see illustration)**.

33 Refitting is a reversal of removal.

Heated rear window switch

34 The procedure for the heated rear window switch is identical to that described for the hazard warning light switch.

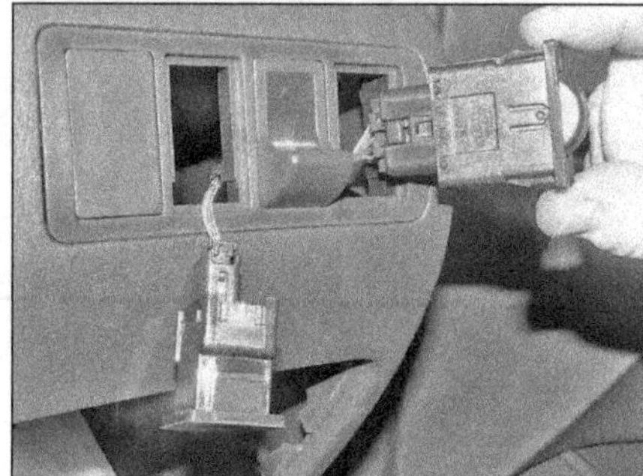

4.32 Unclip the switches from the facia trim panel

Air conditioning switch

35 The procedure for the air conditioning switch is identical to that described for the hazard warning light switch.

Passenger airbag off switch

36 The procedure for the passenger airbag off switch is identical to that described for the heated rear window switch.

Sunroof switch

37 Undo the screw and remove the interior light lens.

38 Undo the two screws and remove the switch. Undo the light unit retaining screw, turn the light unit over and undo the two wiring connections for the switch.

39 Refitting is a reversal of removal.

5 Instrument panel – removal and refitting

Removal

1 Disconnect the cable from the negative battery terminal (Chapter 5A).

2 Move the steering wheel to its lowest position, and fully extended the column (where possible).

3 Undo the two retaining clips/screws and pull the instrument panel surround from the facia **(see illustrations)**.

4 Remove the upper retaining screw and tilt the instrument panel rearwards to remove **(see illustrations)**.

5 Unplug the electrical connectors and remove the panel **(see illustration)**.

6 Refitting is reversal of removal.

Refitting

7 Refitting is a reversal of removal.

6 Indicator/hazard flasher unit – renewal

1 The indicator/hazard flasher unit is responsible for controlling the flow of power to directional indicators. The indicators should flash at a rate of 60 to 120 times per minute. The flasher unit is fitted to the relay board behind the driver's side storage compartment. Unclip the storage compartment from the facia panel.

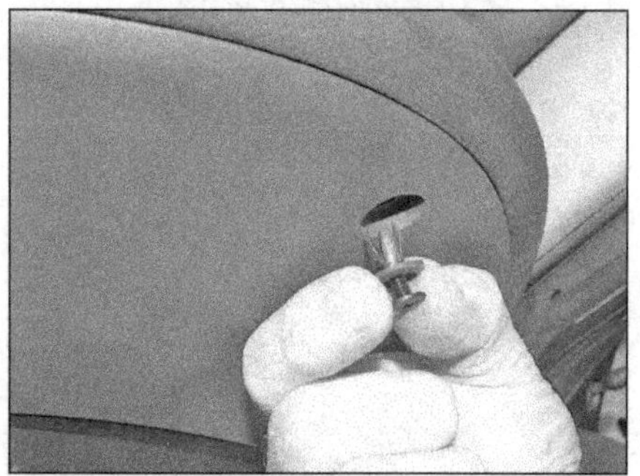

5.3a Remove the retaining screw/clip . . .

5.3b . . . and remove the instrument surround panel

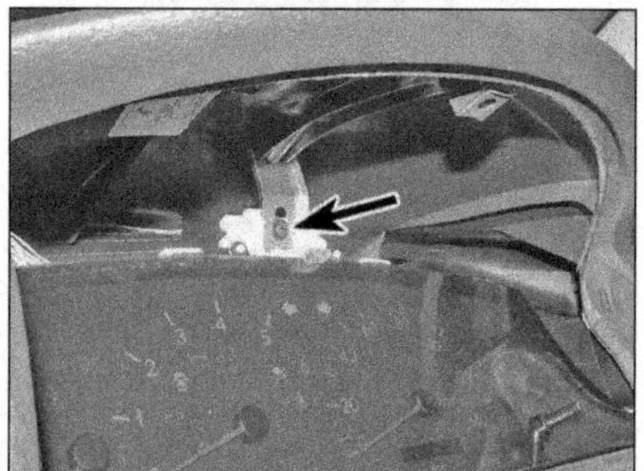

5.4a Remove the retaining screw (arrowed) . . .

5.4b . . . and remove the instrument panel

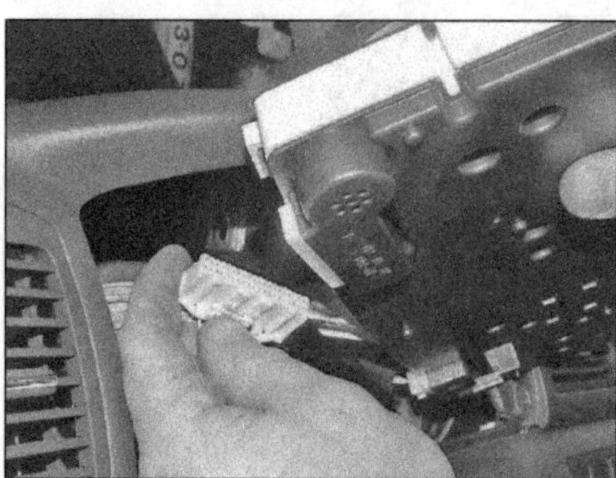

5.5 Disconnect the wiring connectors from the rear of the panel

6.2 Flasher relay (arrowed)

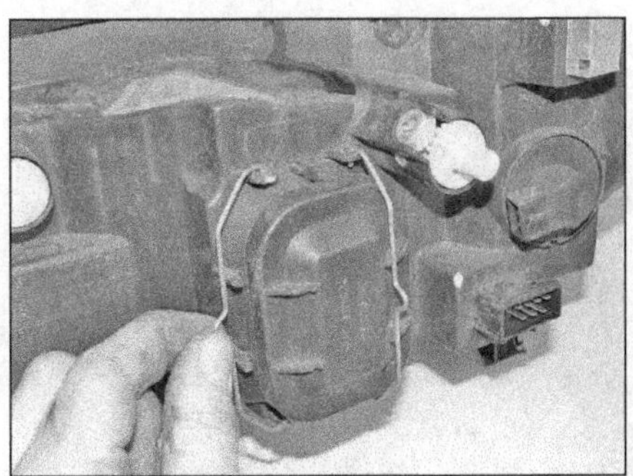
7.2a Release the retaining clips . . .

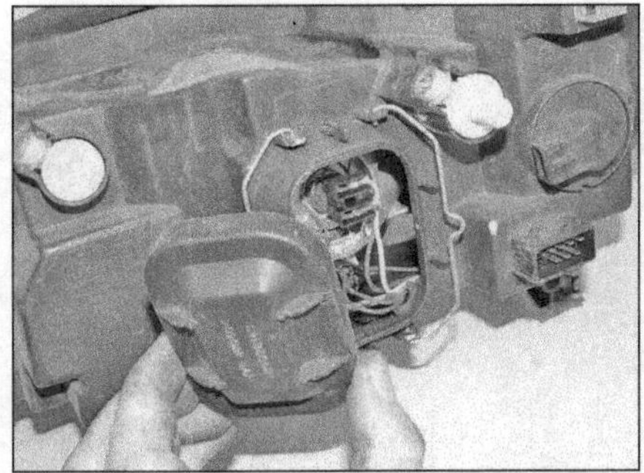
7.2b . . . and remove the plastic cover

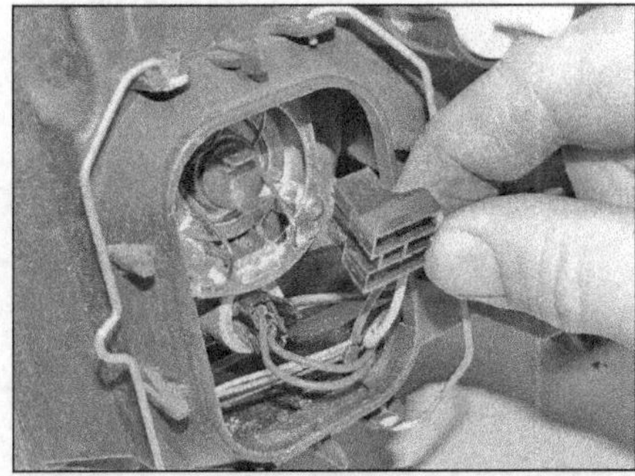
7.3a Disconnect the wiring connector . . .

2 Pull the relay out from the side of the housing **(see illustration)**.

3 Push the new relay into place, and refit the storage compartment.

7 Bulbs (exterior lights) – renewal

General

1 Whenever a bulb is renewed, note the following points:

a) Remember that if the light has just been in use, the bulb may be extremely hot.

b) Always check the bulb contacts and holder, ensuring that there is clean metal-to-metal contact between the bulb and its live(s) and earth. Clean off any corrosion or dirt before fitting a new bulb.

c) Wherever bayonet-type bulbs are fitted, ensure that the live contact(s) bear firmly against the bulb contact.

d) Always ensure that the new bulb is of the correct rating and that it is completely clean before fitting it; this applies particularly to headlight/foglight bulbs (see below).

e) With quartz halogen bulbs (headlights and similar applications), use a tissue or clean cloth when handling the bulb; do not touch the bulb glass with the fingers. Even small quantities of grease from the fingers will cause blackening and premature failure. If a bulb is accidentally touched, clean it with methylated spirit and a clean rag.

Headlight dipped beam

2 Release the retaining clips and remove the plastic cover from the rear of the light unit **(see illustrations)**.

3 Pull the wiring plug off the rear of the bulb, release the securing clip and withdraw the bulb from the headlight unit **(see illustrations)**.

4 When fitting the new bulb, do not touch the glass (paragraph 1). Make sure that the lugs on the bulb flange engage with the slots in the holder.

5 Refitting is a reversal of removal.

Headlight main beam

6 Unclip the rubber cover from the rear of the light unit **(see illustration)**.

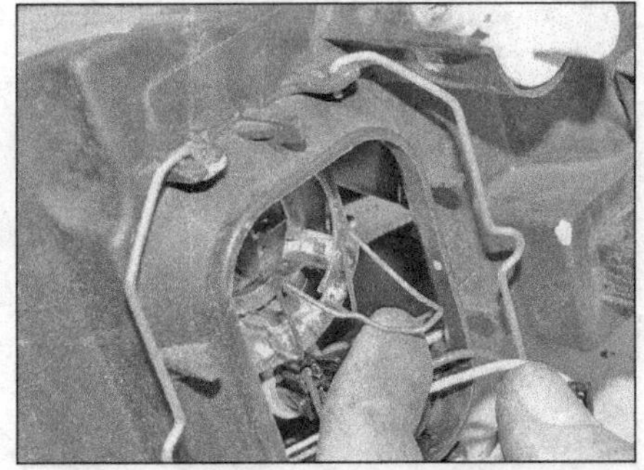
7.3b . . . release the retaining clip . . .

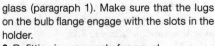

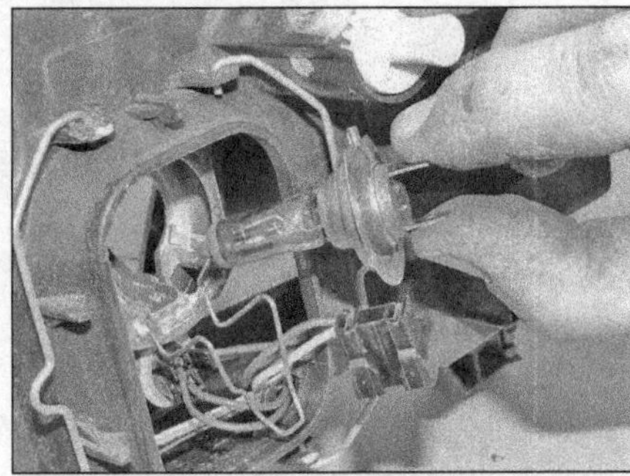
7.3c . . . and remove the bulb

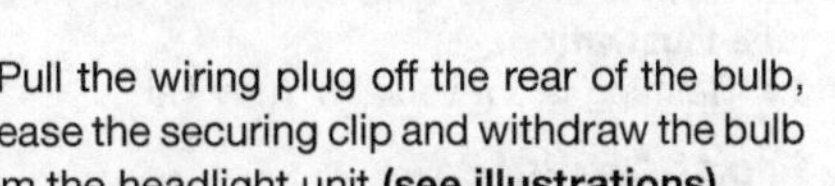

7 Pull the wiring plug off the rear of the bulb, release the securing clip and withdraw the bulb from the headlight unit **(see illustrations)**.

8 When fitting the new bulb, do not touch the glass (paragraph 1). Make sure that the lugs on the bulb flange engage with the slots in the holder.

9 Refitting is a reversal of removal.

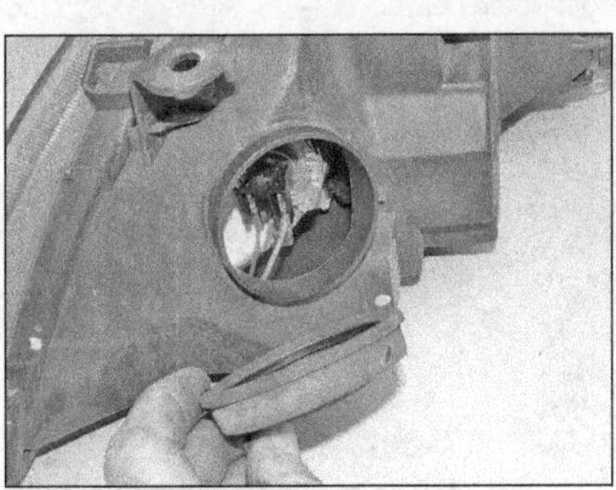
7.6 Unclip the rubber cover

7.7a Disconnect the wiring connector . . .

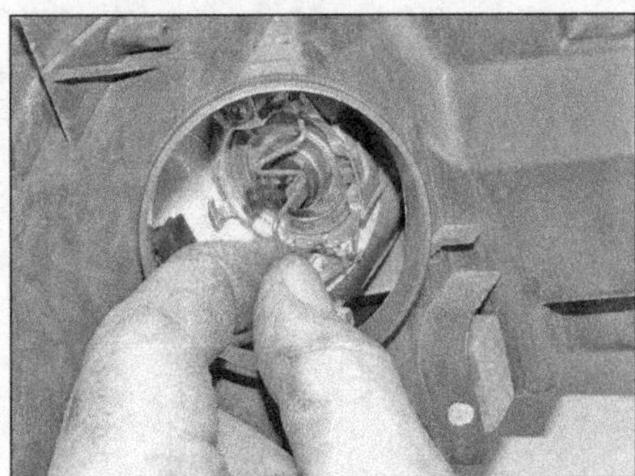
7.7b . . . release the retaining clip . . .

7.7c . . . and remove the bulb

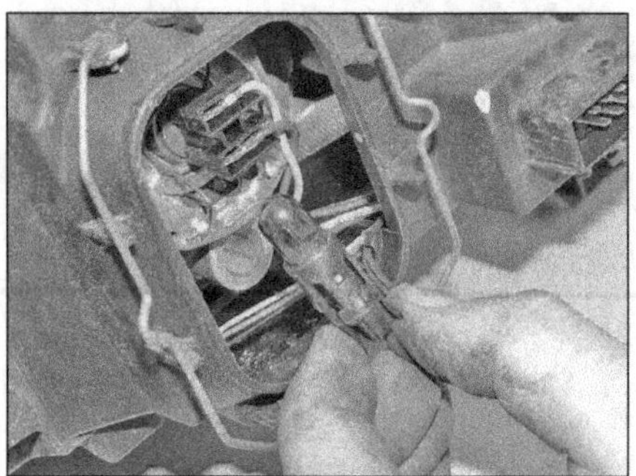
7.11 Pull the bulbholder out from the headlight

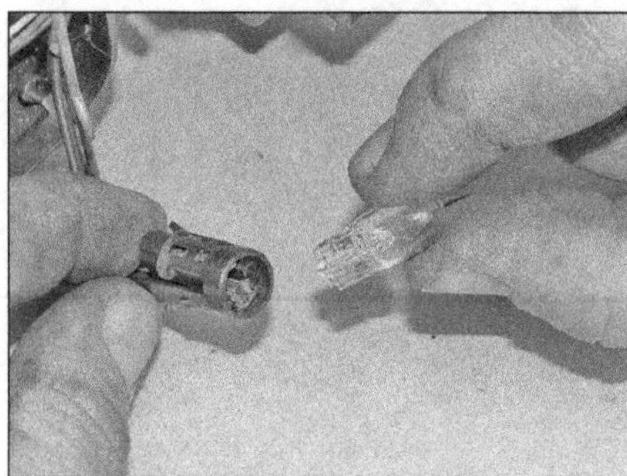
7.12 Wedge type bulb fitted

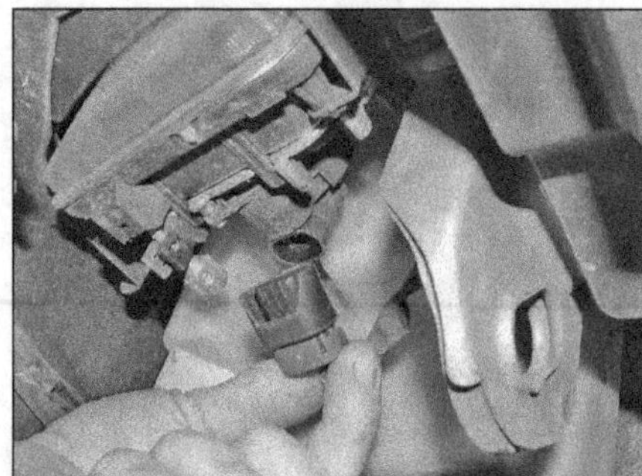
7.15 Disconnect the wiring connector

7.16 Twist the bulbholder to remove

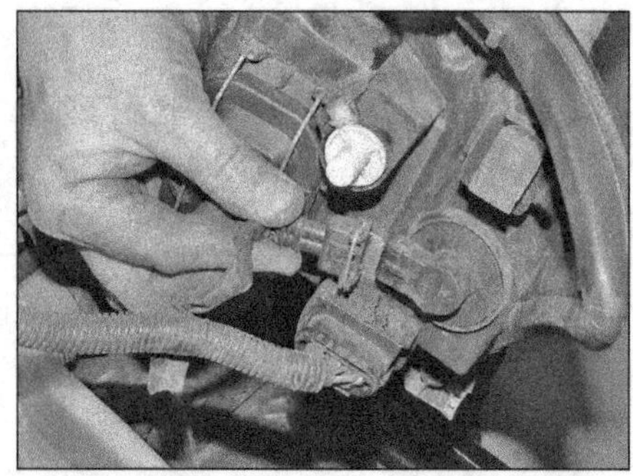
7.19 Disconnect the wiring connector

7.20 Twist the bulb holder to remove

Front sidelight

10 Release the retaining clips and remove the plastic cover from the rear of the light unit **(see illustrations 7.2a and 7.2b)**.

11 Pull the bulbholder out from the headlight unit **(see illustration)**.

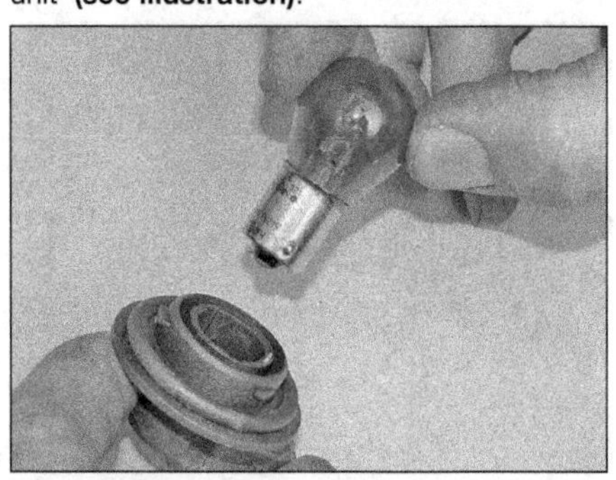
7.21 Push the bulb in and twist, to remove it from the holder

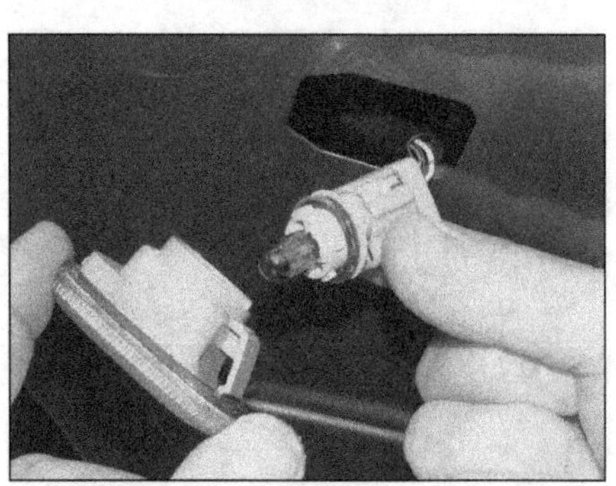
7.24 Twist the side repeater bulbholder anti-clockwise and pull it from place

12 Pull the wedge type bulb from the holder **(see illustration)**.

13 Refitting is a reversal of removal.

Front foglight

14 Unclip the splash shield from under the front of the bumper.

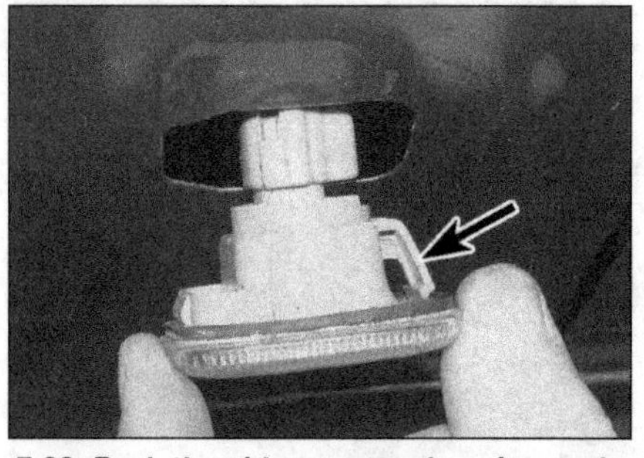
7.23 Push the side repeater lens forwards to compress the clip (arrowed), then pull the other end of the lens from the wing

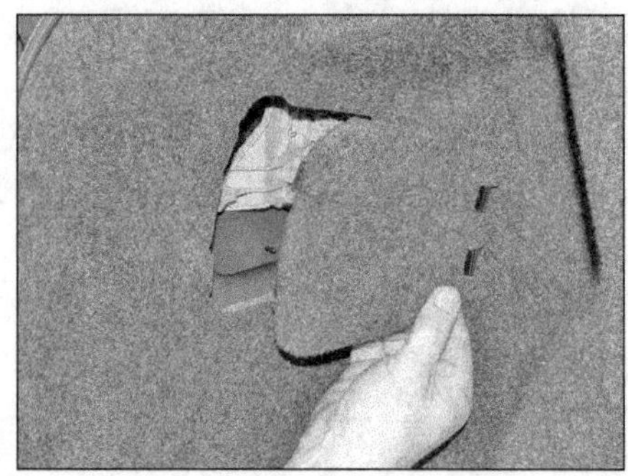
7.27 Open the access panel

15 Disconnect the wiring connector from the rear of the bulbholder **(see illustration)**.

16 Rotate the bulbholder and remove it from the rear of the light unit **(see illustration)**. Note the bulb is part of the bulbholder.

17 Insert the new bulb and holder, making sure it is located securely.

18 The remainder of refitting is a reversal of removal.

Front direction indicator

19 Disconnect the wiring connector from the rear of the light unit **(see illustration)**.

20 Rotate the bulbholder anti-clockwise and pull it from the light unit **(see illustration)**.

21 The bulb is a bayonet fitting. Push it in a little, rotate it anti-clockwise and pull it from the bulbholder **(see illustration)**.

22 Refitting is a reversal of removal.

Direction indicator side repeater

23 Use a flat-bladed screwdriver to push the lens forward, and lever the rear edge of the lens from the wing **(see illustration)**. Take great care not to damage the vehicle bodywork – use a piece of card between the screwdriver and the wing.

24 Twist the bulbholder through a quarter-turn anti-clockwise to release it from the light unit, and withdraw the holder **(see illustration)**.

25 Pull the bulb from its holder, and press the new one into position.

26 Refitting is a reversal of removal.

Rear light cluster

Hatchback

27 From within the luggage compartment,

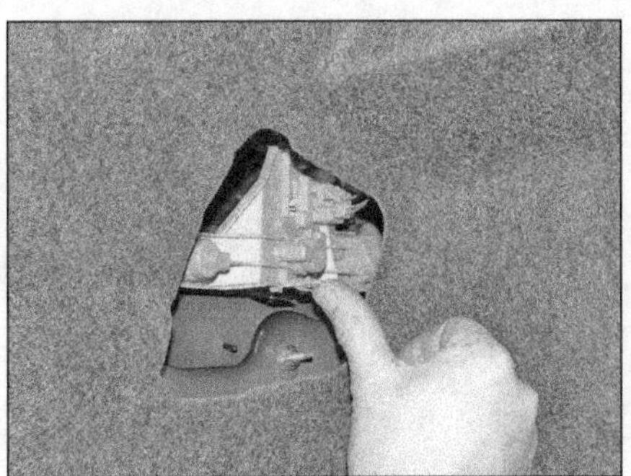

7.28a Release the retaining clip . . .

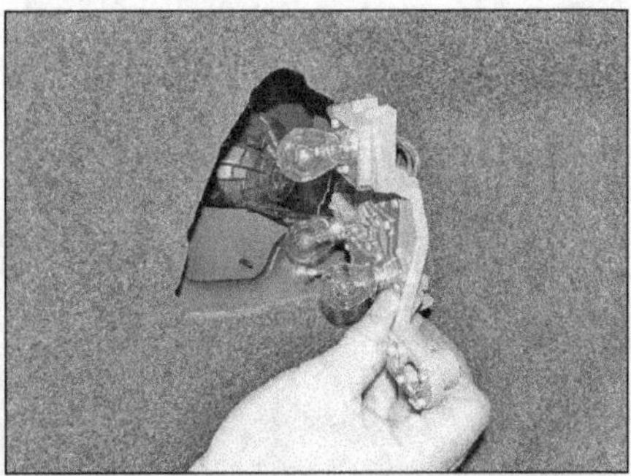

7.28b . . . and withdraw the bulbholder

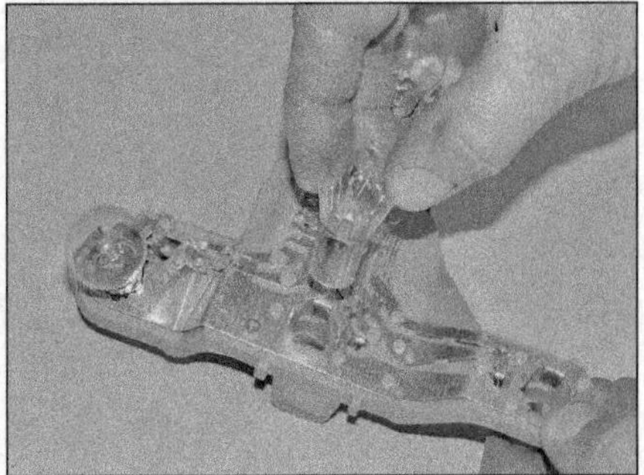

7.29 Push the bulb in and twist, to remove it from the holder

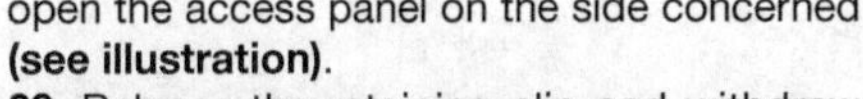

open the access panel on the side concerned **(see illustration)**.

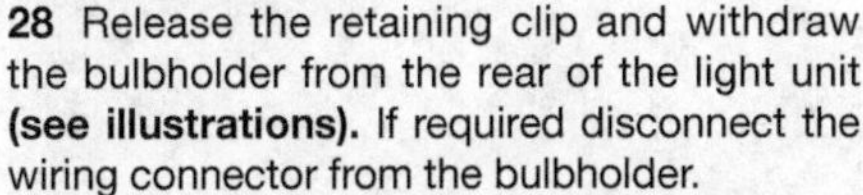

28 Release the retaining clip and withdraw the bulbholder from the rear of the light unit **(see illustrations).** If required disconnect the wiring connector from the bulbholder.

29 Push in and twist the bulb anti-clockwise to remove it from the bulbholder **(see illustration)**.

30 Refitting is a reversal of removal.

Saloon and Estate models

31 Open the boot. Two different types of access cover are fitted. Either prise open the cover with a screwdriver, or undo the nuts and pull the cover from place.

32 Twist the bulbholder anti-clockwise and pull it from the light unit. Push in and twist the bulb anti-clockwise to remove it from the bulbholder.

33 Refitting is a reversal of removal.

High-level stop-light

Hatchback models

34 Remove the high-level brake light unit as described in Section 9.

35 Twist the bulbholder anti-clockwise and pull it from the light unit **(see illustration)**.

36 Pull the wedge type bulb(s) from the holder **(see illustration)**.

37 Refitting is a reversal of removal.

Saloon models

38 Prise up the front edge of the light cover from the parcel shelf, then pull the cover forward.

39 Twist the bulbholder anti-clockwise, and pull it from the light unit. Pull the wedge bulb from the holder.

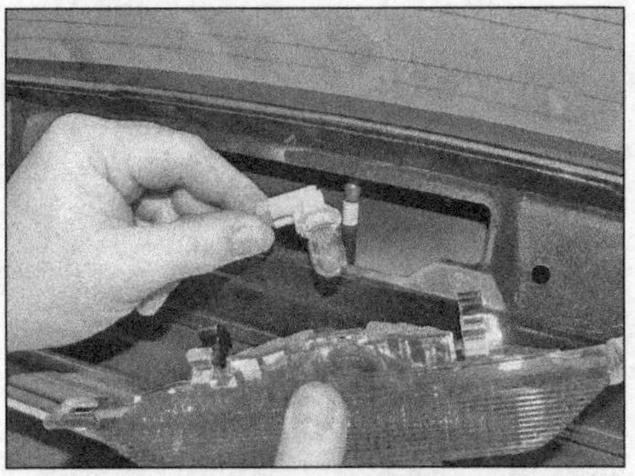

7.35 Twist the bulbholder to remove from the light unit

40 Refitting is a reversal of removal.

Estate models

41 Pull the access cover downwards.

42 Rotate the bulbholder anti-clockwise and remove it from the light unit. Pull the wedge bulb from the holder.

43 Refitting is a reversal of removal.

Number plate light

Hatchback models

44 Carefully prise open the access cover in the tailgate trim panel **(see illustration).**

45 Rotate the bulbholder anti-clockwise and pull it from the light unit **(see illustration).**

46 Pull the wedge bulb from the holder **(see illustration)**.

47 Refitting is a reversal of removal.

Saloon models

48 Remove the boot lid inner trim panel.

7.36 Pull the wedge type bulb out from the holder

49 Rotate the bulbholder anti-clockwise and pull it from the light unit. Pull the wedge bulb from the holder.

50 Refitting is a reversal of removal.

Estate models

51 Undo the two screws securing the light unit to the tailgate.

52 Rotate the bulbholder anti-clockwise and pull it from the light unit. Pull the wedge bulb from the holder.

53 Refitting is a reversal of removal.

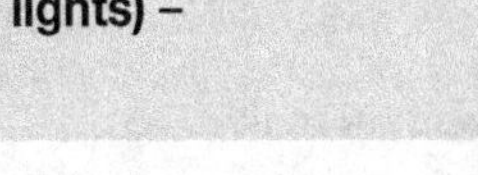

8 Bulbs (interior lights) – renewal

General

1 Whenever a bulb is renewed, note the following points:

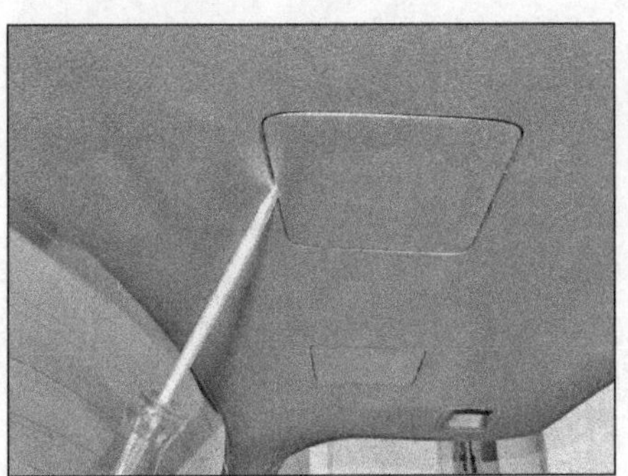

7.44 Open the access panel

7.45 remove the bulb holder

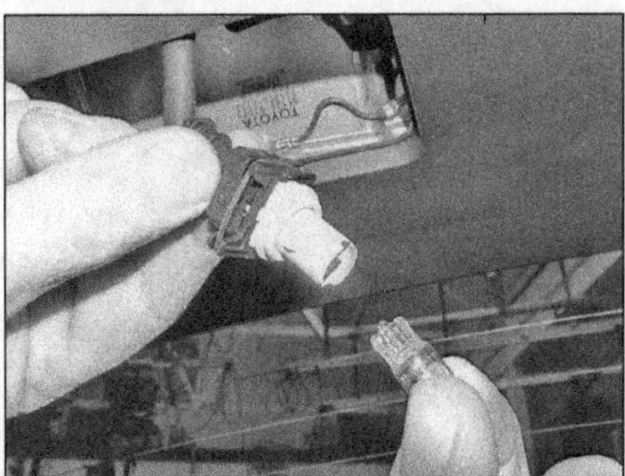

7.46 Pull the wedge type bulb out from the holder

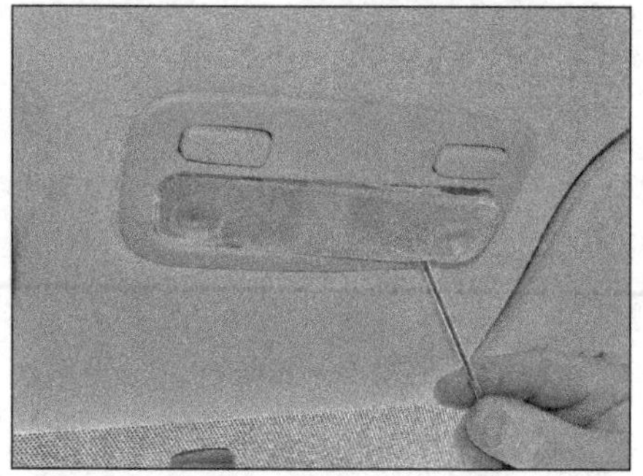
8.3a Unclip the front interior light lens

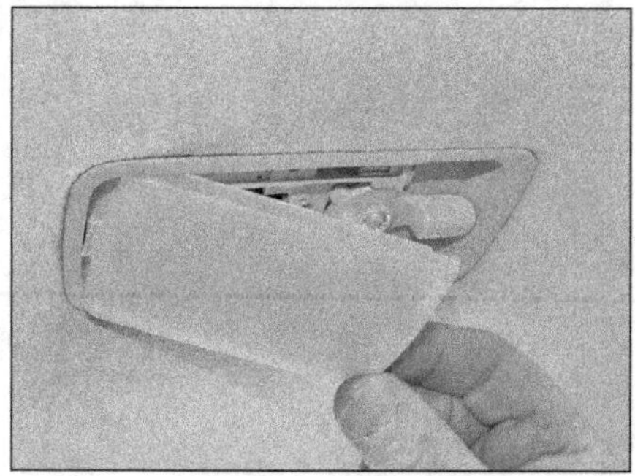
8.3b Unclip the rear interior light lens

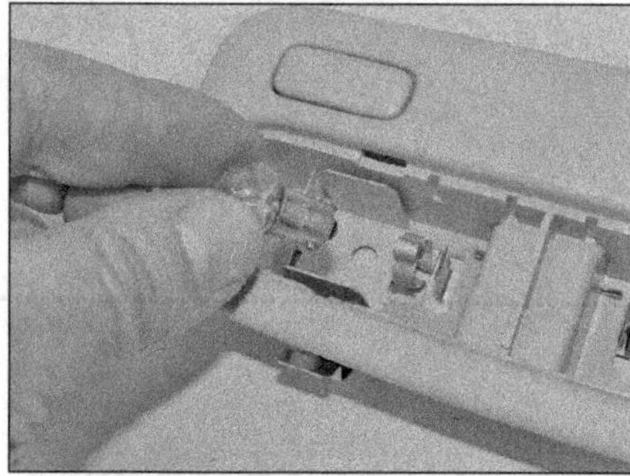
8.4a Twist and remove the front light unit bulb

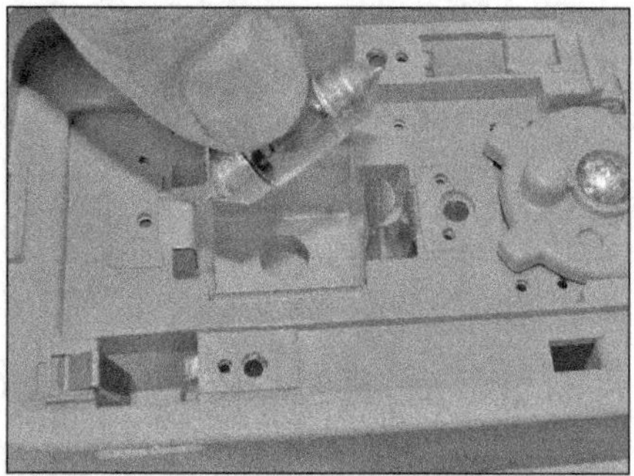
8.4b Pull the festoon bulb out from the rear light unit

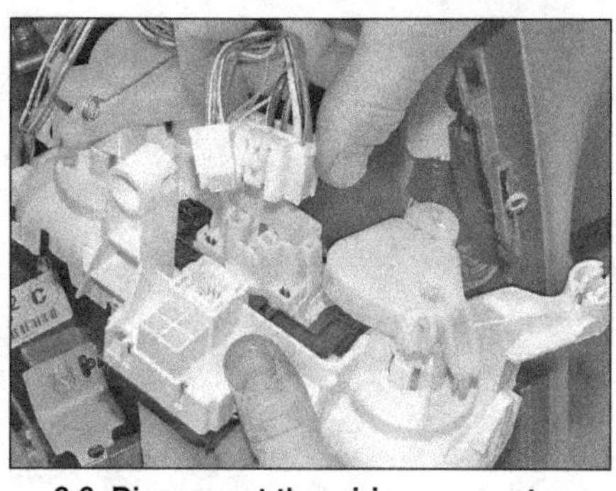
8.6 Disconnect the wiring connector

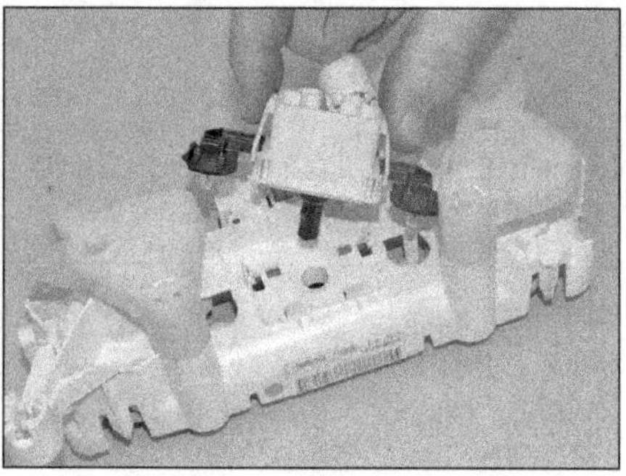
8.7 Unclip the centre switch assembly

a) *Remember that if the light has just been in use, the bulb may be extremely hot.*
b) *Always check the bulb contacts and holder, ensuring that there is clean metal-to-metal contact between the bulb and its live(s) and earth. Clean off any corrosion or dirt before fitting a new bulb.*
c) *Wherever bayonet-type bulbs are fitted, ensure that the live contact(s) bear firmly against the bulb contact.*
d) *Always ensure that the new bulb is of the correct rating and that it is completely clean before fitting it.*

2 Some switch illumination/pilot bulbs are integral with their switches, and cannot be renewed separately.

Courtesy/interior light

3 Using a small flat-bladed screwdriver, carefully prise the lens from place **(see illustrations)**. **Note:** *On some models, the lens may be retained by a screw*

4 On the front light unit, twist the bayonet type bulb to release it from the light unit. On rear light unit, pull the festoon bulb from the contacts **(see illustrations)**.

5 Refitting is a reversal of removal.

Heater control panel illumination

6 Remove the heater control panel as described in Chapter 3. Disconnect the wiring plugs as the panel is removed **(see illustration)**.

7 Carefully prise the centre control switch assembly complete with illumination light bulbs from the rear of the heater control panel **(see illustration)**.

8 The wedge-type bulbs simply pull from place **(see illustration)**.

9 Refitting is a reversal of removal.

Automatic transmission selector panel illumination

10 Unclip the trim from around the gear lever.

11 Twist the bulbholder anti-clockwise and then pull it from the selector housing **(see illustration)**.

12 Pull the wedge type bulb from the holder.

13 Refitting is a reversal of removal.

Instrument panel lights

14 Remove the instrument panel as described in Section 5.

15 Where possible, rotate the bulbholder anti-clockwise and pull it from the rear of the panel **(see illustration)**. The bulbs are integral with the holders.

16 Refitting is a reversal of removal.

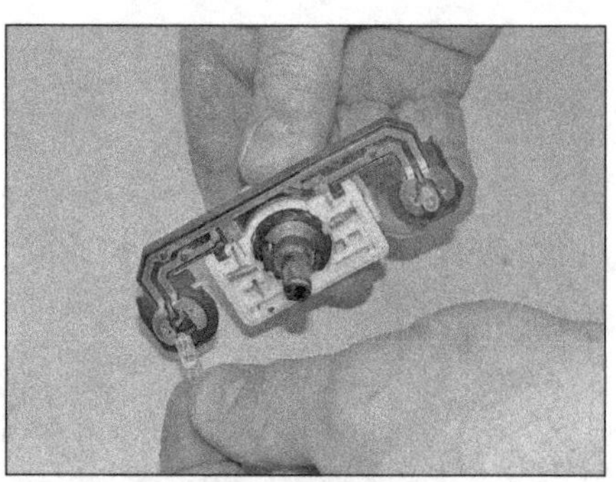
8.8 Pull the wedge type bulb out from the holder

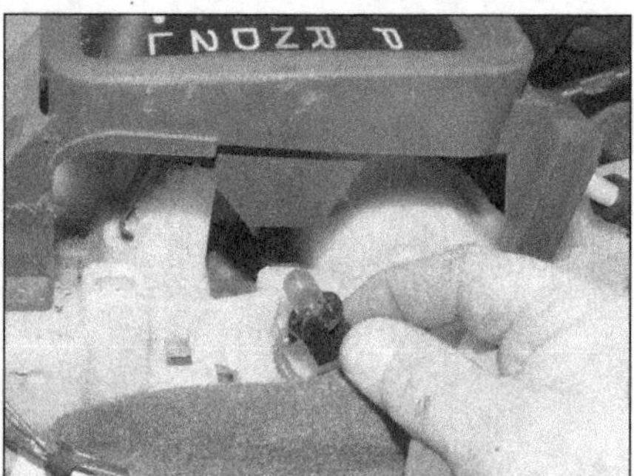
8.11 Twist the bulbholder anti-clockwise, and pull it from the selector lever panel

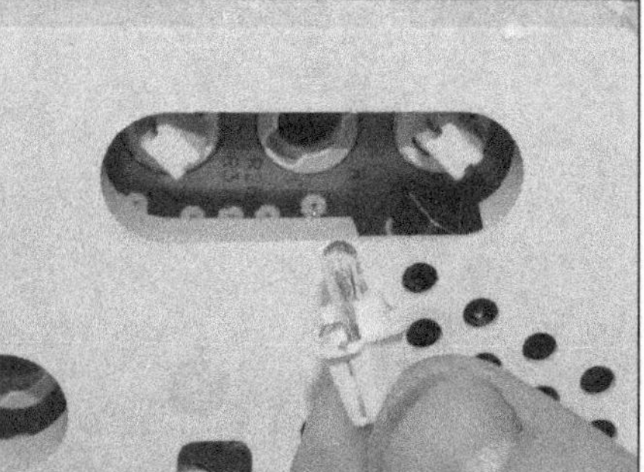
8.15 The instrument panel illumination bulbs are integral with the bulbholders

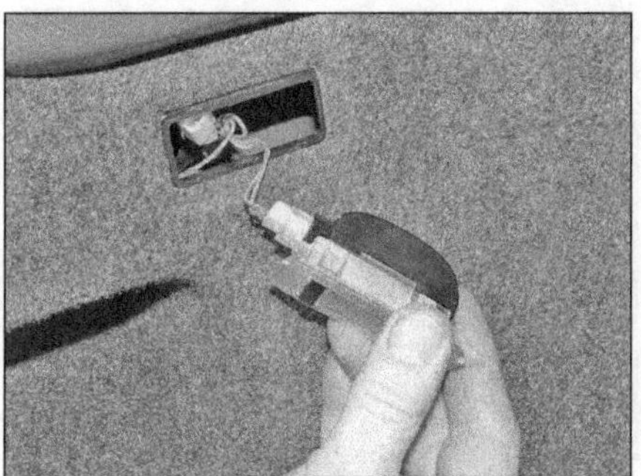
8.17 Unclip the luggage compartment light unit

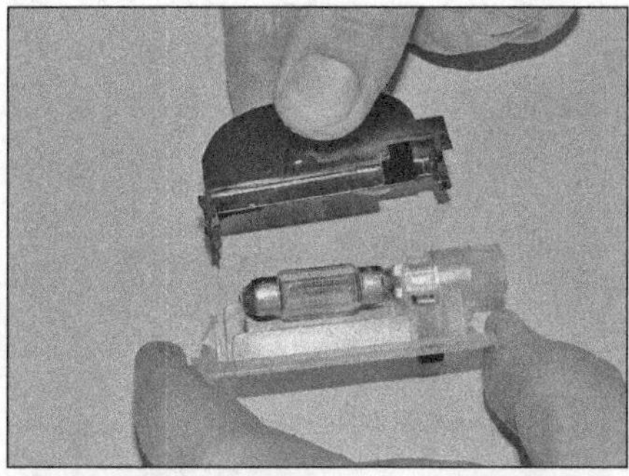
8.18a Unclip the cover from the rear of the light . . .

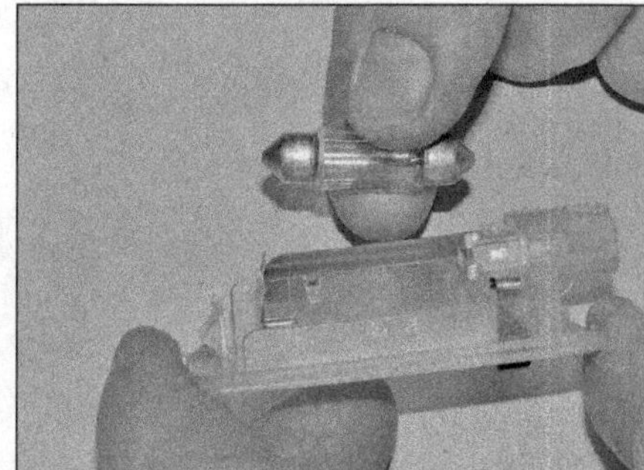
8.18b . . . and pull the festoon bulb out from the light unit

8.21a Unclip the switch from the trim panel . . .

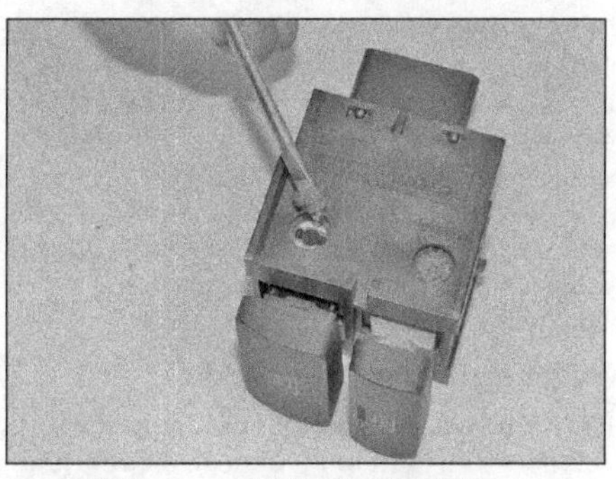
8.21b . . . twist the bulbholder . . .

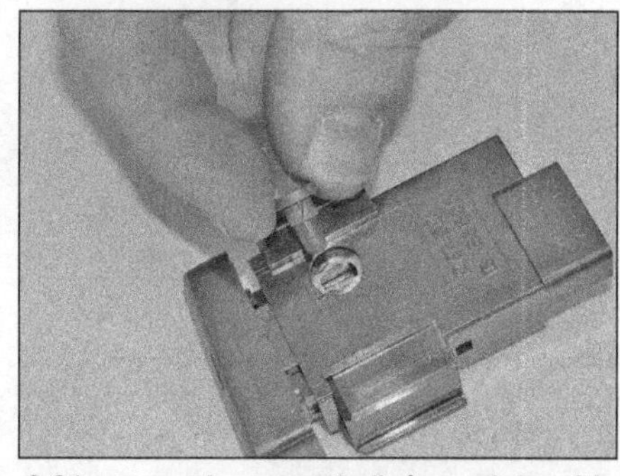
8.21c . . . and remove bulb (complete with holder)

Luggage area illumination

17 Carefully prise the light unit from the side of the luggage compartment **(see illustration)**.

18 Remove the cover from the rear of the light unit and unclip the bulb from the holder **(see illustrations)**.

19 Refitting is a reversal of removal.

Facia panel switch/lights

20 Remove the relevant switch (see Section 4).

21 Use a screwdriver to rotate the bulbholder anti-clockwise, and remove it **(see illustrations)**. The bulb is integral with the holder.

22 Refitting is a reversal of removal.

9 Exterior light units – removal and refitting

Caution: Ensure the ignition is turned off before proceeding.

Headlight

1 Open the bonnet, release the screws and retaining clips and remove the plastic cover from across the front of the engine compartment **(see illustration)**.

2 Remove the front bumper as described in Chapter 11.

3 Undo the two retaining bolts from the top of the headlight unit **(see illustration)**.

4 Undo the retaining bolt from the lower outer edge of the headlight unit **(see illustration)**.

5 Pull the headlight forward releasing it from the lower securing bracket **(see illustration)**.

6 Disconnect the wiring plugs and remove the headlight **(see illustration)**.

7 Refitting is a reversal of removal. Have the headlight beam alignment checked on completion (see Section 10).

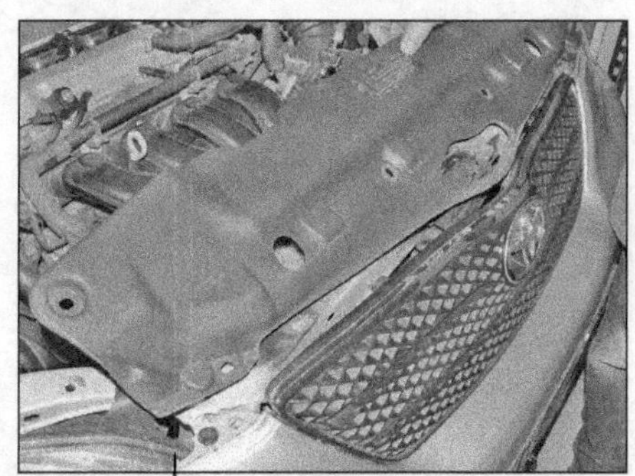
9.1 Remove the trim panel from across the front of the engine compartment

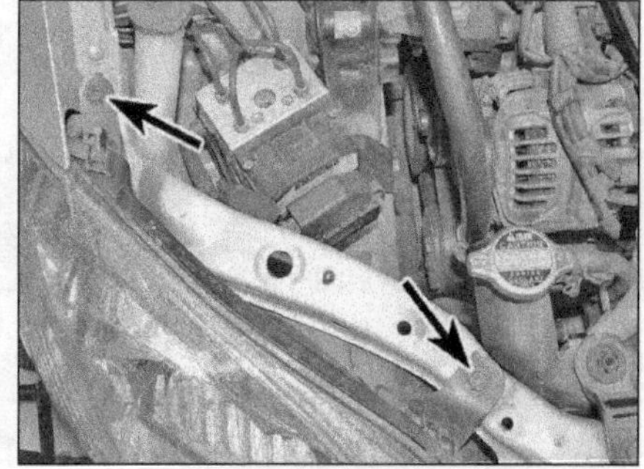
9.3 Undo the two upper retaining screws (arrowed)

9.4 Undo the lower retaining bolt (arrowed)

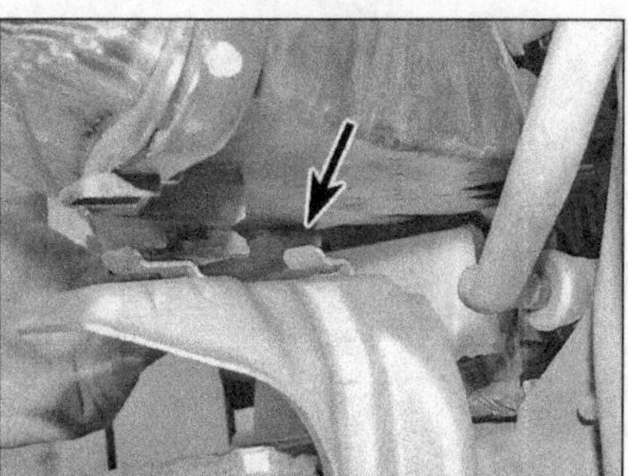
9.5 Release the headlight from the securing clip (arrowed)

9.6 Disconnect the wiring connectors as the headlight is removed

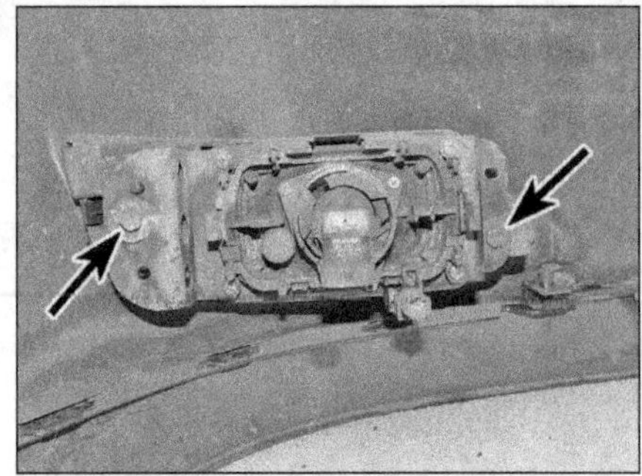
9.10 Foglight retaining bolts (arrowed)

9.12 Foglight adjusting screw (arrowed)

Front foglight

8 Unclip the splash shield from under the front of the bumper.

9 Disconnect the wiring connector from the rear of the bulbholder.

10 Undo the two retaining bolts and pull the foglight from its position in the rear of the bumper **(see illustration)**.

11 Refitting is a reversal of removal.

12 To adjust the foglight aim, rotate the adjusting screw to the desired position **(see illustration).**

Front direction indicator

13 The front indicator is part of the headlight unit, see paragraphs 1 to 7 to remove the headlight unit.

Front indicator side repeater

14 Use a flat-bladed screwdriver to push the lens forward, and lever the rear edge of the lens from the wing **(see illustration 7.23)**. Take great care no to damage the vehicle bodywork – use a piece of card between the screwdriver and the wing.

15 Twist the bulbholder through a quarter-turn anti-clockwise to release it from the light unit, and withdraw the holder.

16 Refitting is a reversal of removal.

Rear light clusters

17 From within the luggage compartment, release the light unit access cover **(see illustration)**. If required, pull back the carpet from the side of the luggage compartment.

18 Disconnected the rear light cluster wiring plugs(s).

19 Undo the nuts and remove the cluster from the vehicle **(see illustrations)**.

20 Refitting is a reversal of removal.

High-level brake light

Hatchback models

21 Carefully unclip the trim panel from inside the tailgate **(see illustration)**.

22 Release the retaining clips and withdraw the light from the tailgate **(see illustrations)**.

23 Disconnect the light unit wiring plug, as the light unit is removed.

24 Refitting is a reversal of removal.

Saloon and Estate models

25 No information was available at the time of writing.

Number plate light

Hatchback models

26 Remove the tailgate trim panel as described in Chapter 11, Section 27.

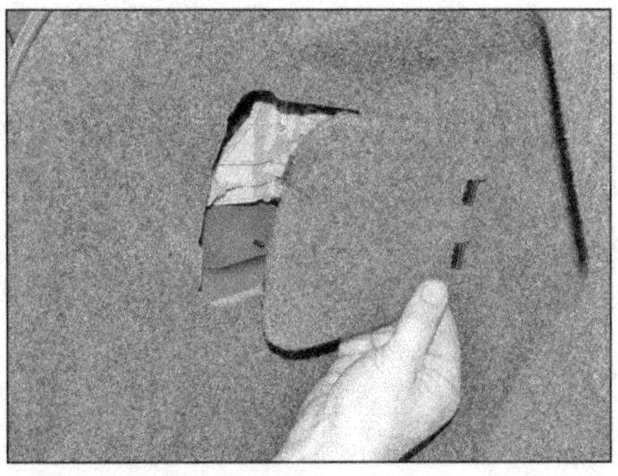
9.17 Open the access panel

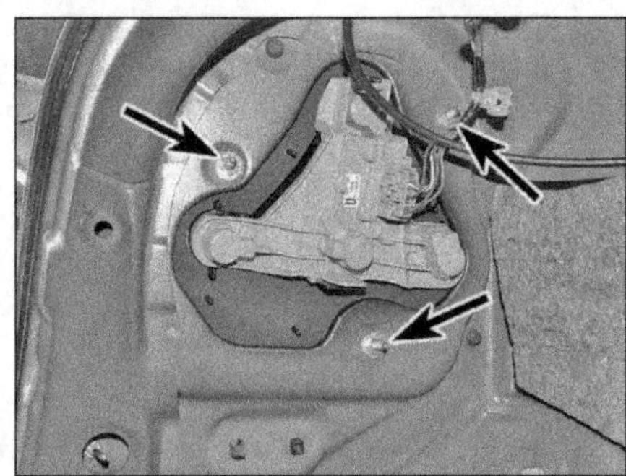
9.19a Undo the retaining nuts (arrowed) . . .

9.19b . . . and remove the rear light unit

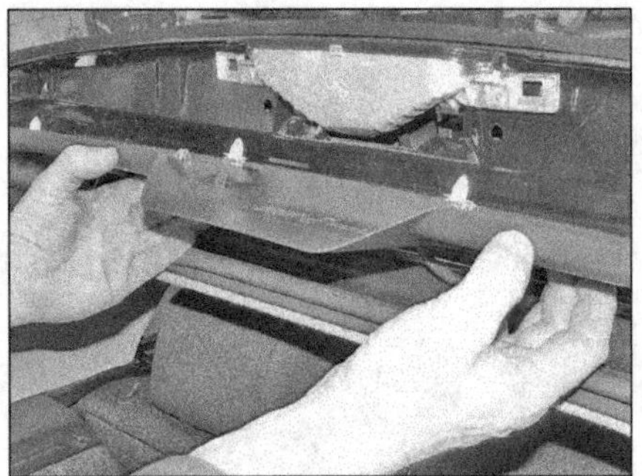
9.21 Unclip the trim panel

9.22a Release the securing clips (arrowed) . . .

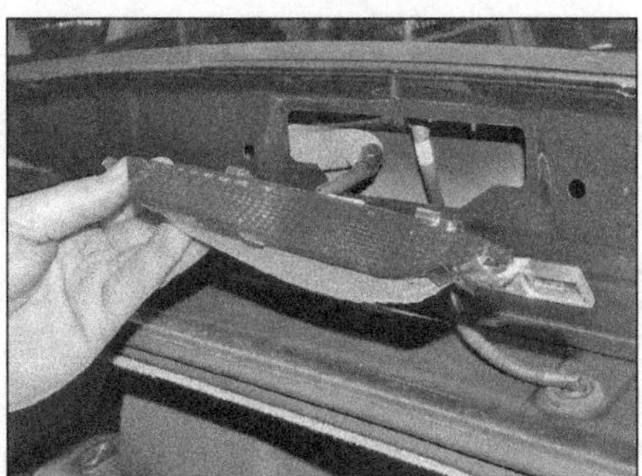
9.22b . . . and remove the light unit

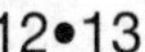

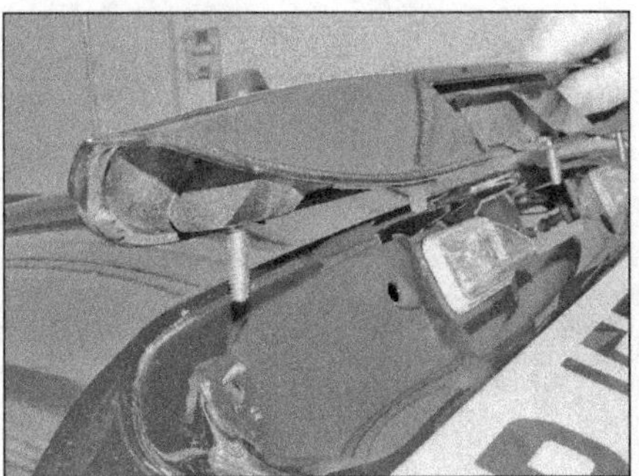

9.27 Remove the number plate trim panel

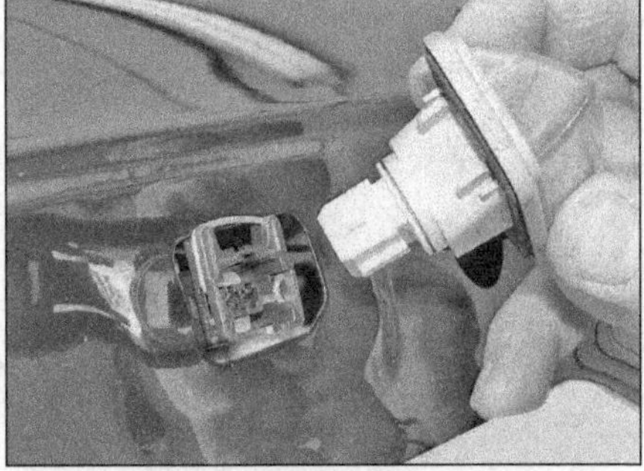

9.28 Remove the number plate light

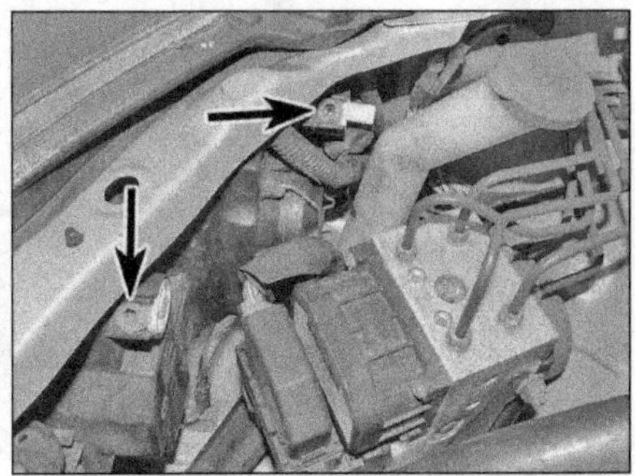

10.2 Headlight aim adjusting screws (arrowed)

27 Release the fasteners and remove the exterior trim from over the number plate lights **(see illustration)**.

28 Release the clips and withdraw the number plate light from the tailgate **(see illustration)**.

29 Refitting is a reversal of removal.

Saloon and Estate models

30 No information was available at the time of writing.

10 Headlight beam alignment – checking and adjusting

1 Beam alignment should be carried out by a Toyota dealer or other specialist having the necessary optical alignment equipment.

2 For reference, the headlights can be adjusted by means of the vertical and horizontal adjuster controls at the back of the headlight unit **(see illustration)**.

3 Some models are equipped with an electrically-operated headlight beam adjustment system, which is controlled through the switch on the facia. On these models, ensure that the switch is set to the off position before adjusting the headlight aim.

11 Headlight beam control motor – removal and refitting

At the time of writing, then beam control motor appears not to be available as a separate part. If faulty, the entire headlamp unit must be renewed as described in Section 9. Check with your Toyota dealer or parts specialist.

12 Horn – renewal

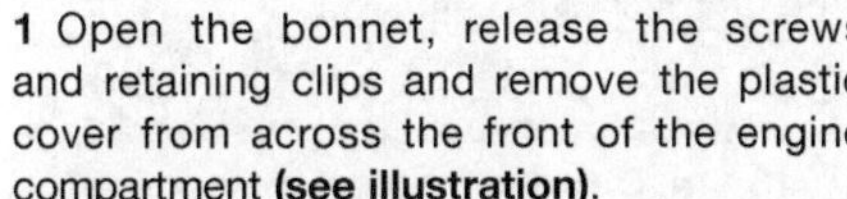

1 Open the bonnet, release the screws and retaining clips and remove the plastic cover from across the front of the engine compartment **(see illustration)**.

2 Working behind the grille panel, undo the bolt from the horn bracket and withdraw it from behind the radiator **(see illustration)**. Disconnect the wiring plug as the horn is removed.

3 Refitting is a reversal of removal.

12.1 Remove the trim panel from across the front of the engine compartment

12.2 Horn bracket retaining bolt (arrowed)

13 Washer system components – removal and refitting

Washer reservoir

1 Remove the front bumper as described in Chapter 11.

2 Disconnect the washer tubes and wiring plugs from the washer pumps **(see illustration)**.

3 Working from the outside of the washer reservoir, undo the three mounting bolts **(see illustrations)**.

4 Undo the inner mounting bolt, release the filler neck from the inner wing panel and remove the reservoir from under the wing panel **(see illustration)**.

5 Refitting is a reversal of removal.

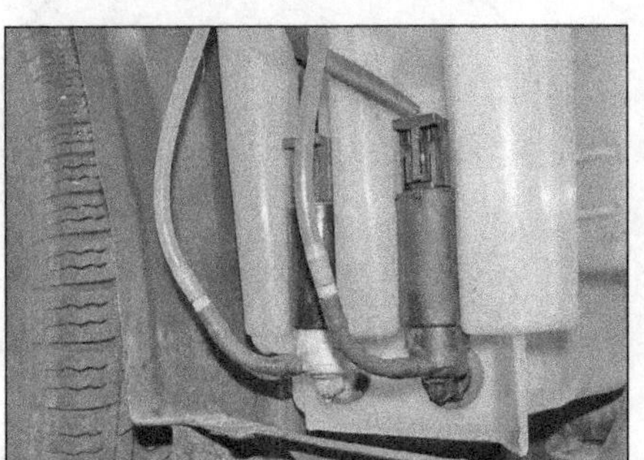

13.2 Washer pumps in reservoir

13.3a Undo the outer two bolts (arrowed) . . .

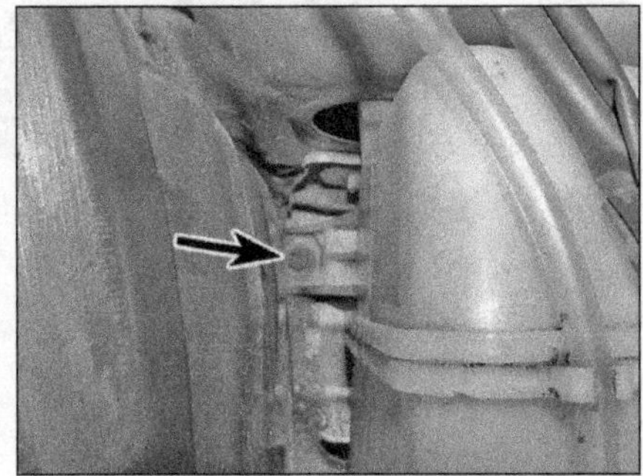

13.3b . . . and the inner bolt (arrowed)

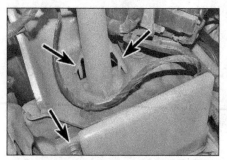

13.4 Undo the mounting bolt (arrowed) and release the filler neck retaining clips (arrowed)

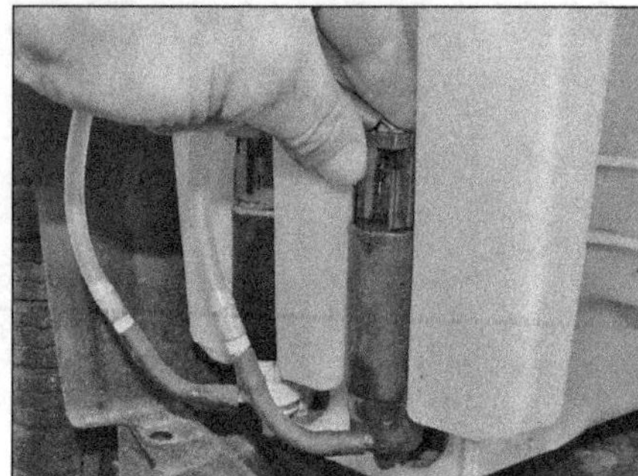

13.7 Disconnect the wiring connectors

13.9 Pull the pump from the grommet in the washer fluid reservoir

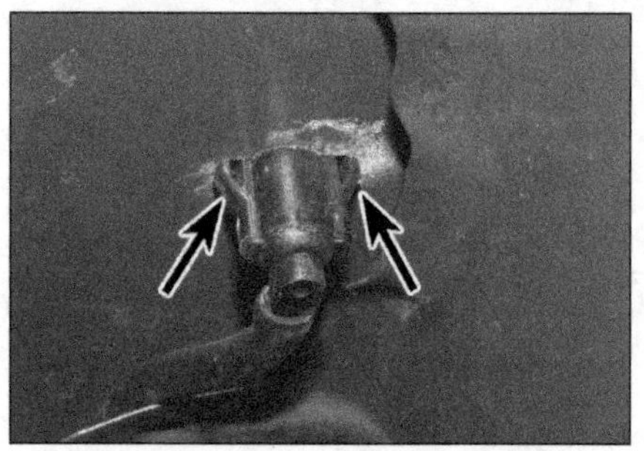

13.13 Squeeze together the clips (arrowed) and pull the windscreen washer jet from the bonnet

13.17a Disconnect the washer hose (arrowed) . . .

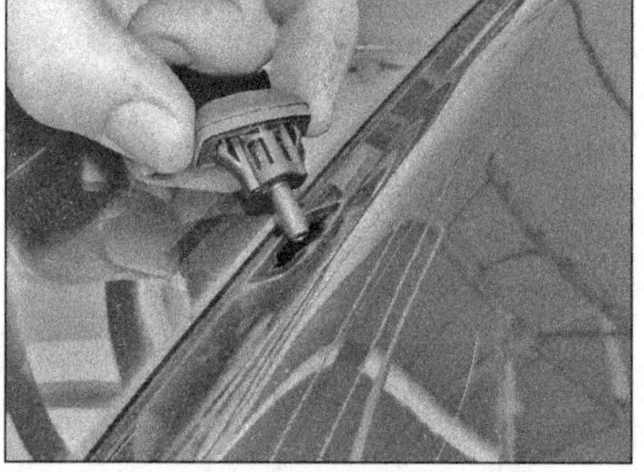

13.17b . . . and unclip the washer jet

Washer pump

6 Remove the front bumper as described in Chapter 11.

7 Note their fitted locations, then pull the hose(s) from the motor, and disconnect the motor wiring plug(s) **(see illustration)**.

8 Place a container under the reservoir, and be prepared for spillage.

9 Grip the washer pump and pull it out of the reservoir **(see illustration)**.

10 Refitting is a reversal of removal.

Washer jets

Windscreen jet

11 Open the bonnet.

12 Disconnect the jet wiring plug (where applicable) and disconnect the washer hose.

13 Squeeze together the two retaining clips on the underside of the jet using pliers, and remove the jet from the bonnet **(see illustration)**.

14 Push the jet into its location until the clips spring out to lock. Reconnect the fluid hose and wiring plug (where applicable)

15 If required, adjust the jet nozzle(s) using a pin so that liquid is sprayed onto the centre of the glass.

Rear screen jet

16 Open the tailgate, and remove the high-level rear brake light as described in Section 9, of this Chapter.

17 Disconnect the fluid hose from the washer jet, and then release the retaining clips and withdraw the washer jet from the top of the tailgate **(see illustrations)**.

18 Push the jet into its location until the clips spring out to lock, and then reconnect the fluid hose.

19 Refitting is a reversal of removal.

20 If required, adjust the jet nozzle(s) using a pin so that liquid is sprayed onto the top of the glass.

Non-return check valve

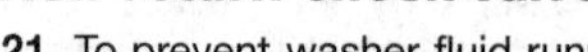

21 To prevent washer fluid running back into the reservoir, a non-return valve is fitted into the supply hose to each washer jet. Open the bonnet, and release the washer hose from the retaining clips.

22 Carefully pull the hoses from the non-return valve, noting the direction of flow marking on the valve.

23 It should only be possible to blow through the valve in one direction. If faulty, the valve must be renewed.

24 Refitting is a reversal of removal.

14 Wiper arms – removal and refitting

Removal

1 Before removing the wiper arm, make a mark on the screen for the position of the wiper blade. Note some screens may already be marked with a line or a dot, to aid refitting.

2 Prise off the cover (where applicable) then slacken the nut at the base of the wiper arm **(see illustrations)**.

3 Using a rocking motion, pull the arms off the splines **(see illustration)**. If necessary, use a puller to remove the arms.

4 On the tailgate wiper, fold up or remove

14.2a Unclip the plastic cover . . .

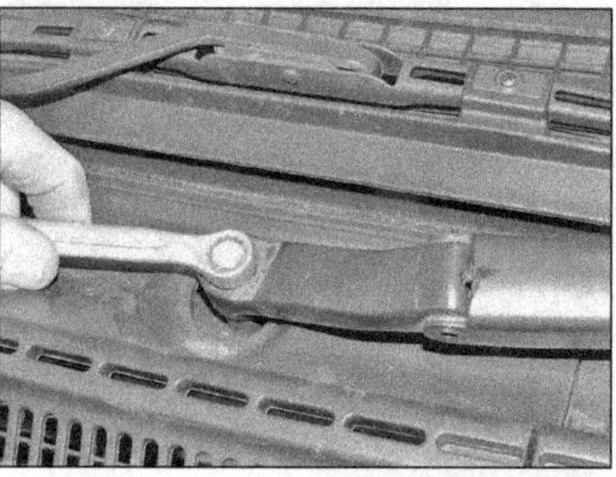

14.2b . . . and slacken the retaining nut

14.3 Remove the wiper arm from the spindle

the cover, and undo the nut securing the arm to the spindle. Pull the arm from the spindle using a rocking motion **(see illustration)**.

Refitting

5 Switch the relevant wiper on, and then switch it off again to ensure that the motor and linkage are parked. Position the windscreen wiper arm on the spindle, so that the wiper blade is in the correct position on the screen, as noted on removal. Tighten the wiper arm retaining bolt and refit the plastic cover.

15 Windscreen wiper motor and linkage – removal and refitting

Removal

1 Switch the wipers on, then off again to ensure that the motor and linkage are parked.

15.4a Release the securing clips . . .

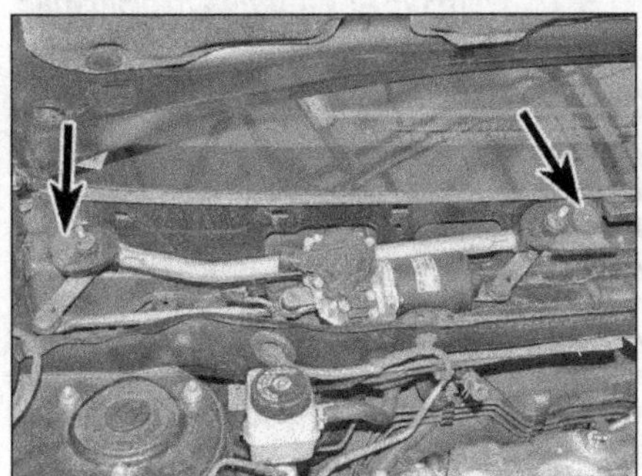

15.5b . . . and undo the wiper assembly retaining bolts (arrowed)

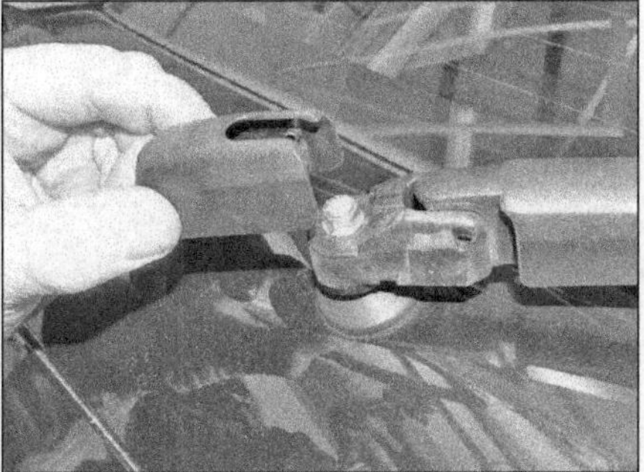

14.4 Unclip the cover from the rear wiper arm

2 Remove the windscreen wiper arms as described in Section 14.

3 Working your way along the rear of the engine compartment unclip the rubber seal from the scuttle panel **(see illustration)**.

4 Undo the retaining screws/clips and remove the scuttle trim panel from the top of the wiper motor and linkage **(see illustrations)**.

5 Disconnect the wiper motor wiring plug, then undo the mounting bolts and remove the motor, complete with linkage **(see illustrations)**.

6 If required, disconnect the linkage or remove the motor, as required.

Refitting

7 If removed, refit the linkage or motor, and tighten the retaining bolts securely

8 Refit the motor assembly and tighten the mounting bolts securely. Reconnect the wiring plug.

15.4b . . . and remove the scuttle panel trim

16.4 Disconnect the wiring connector

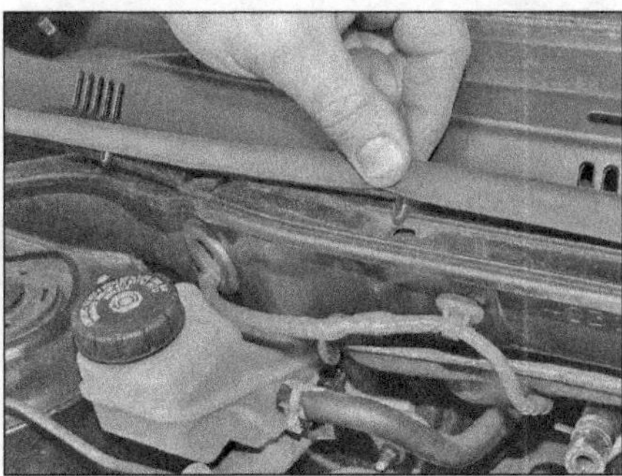

15.3 unclip the seal from the rear of the engine compartment

9 The remainder of refitting is a reversal of removal.

16 Tailgate wiper motor – removal and refitting

Removal

1 Switch the wiper on then off again to ensure that the motor and linkage are parked.

2 Remove the tailgate wiper arm as described in Section 14. On Estate models, undo the spindle nut.

3 Remove the tailgate interior trim panel as described in Chapter 11, Section 27.

4 Disconnect the motor wiring plug **(see illustration)**.

5 Undo the motor retaining bolts and withdraw it from the tailgate **(see illustration)**.

15.5a Disconnect the wiring connector . . .

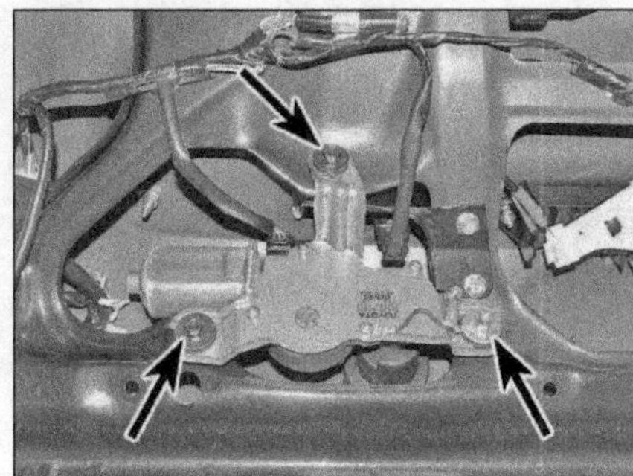

16.5 Wiper motor securing bolts (arrowed)

17.2a Undo the audio unit securing bolts (arrowed) . . .

17.2c . . . and withdraw the unit from the facia

Refitting

6 Refit the motor to the tailgate and securely tighten the mounting bolts.

7 If a new motor is being fitted, temporarily connect the wiring connector, switch on the motor then switch it off again to ensure that it is parked.

8 Refitting is a reversal of removal.

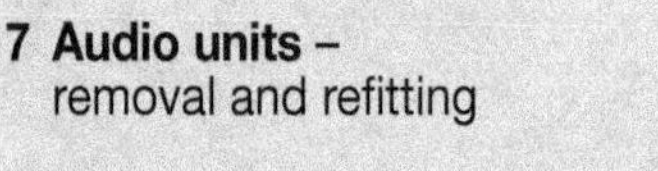

17 Audio units – removal and refitting

Removal

1 Remove the heater control panel from the facia as described in Chapter 3.

2 Undo the four mounting bolts and carefully withdraw the unit from its position in the facia **(see illustrations)**.

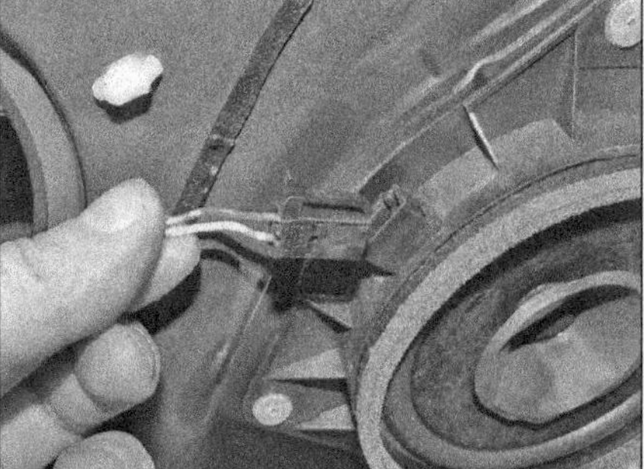

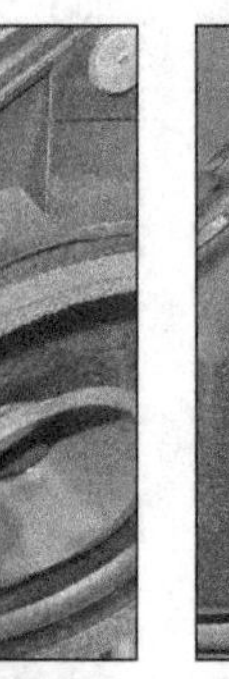

18.2 Disconnect the wiring connector

17.2b . . . carefully lever . . .

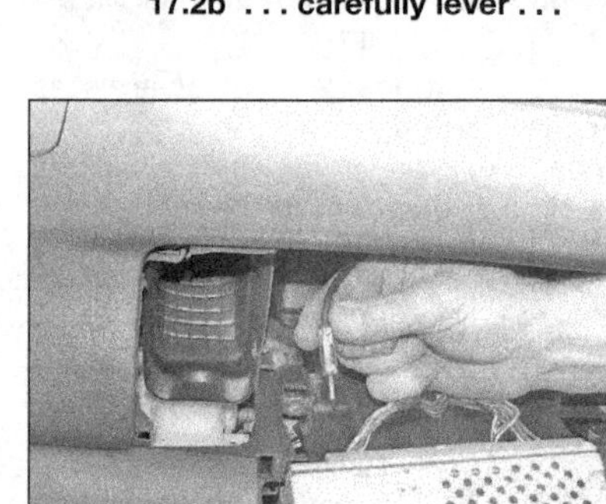

17.3 Disconnect the aerial lead and wiring connectors

3 Disconnect the wiring plugs and aerial lead, as the unit is withdrawn **(see illustration)**.

Refitting

4 Refitting is a reversal of removal.

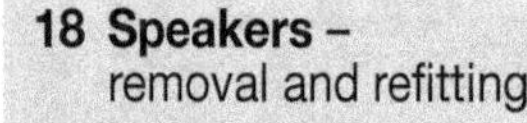

18 Speakers – removal and refitting

Door speaker

1 Remove the door trim panel as described in Chapter 11.

2 Disconnect the wiring connector from the speaker **(see illustration)**

3 Drill out the rivets securing the speaker to the door frame **(see illustration)**.

4 Remove the speaker and clean out the old rivets from the door panel.

5 Refitting is a reversal of removal.

18.3 Rivets (arrowed) securing speaker to door panel

Parcel shelf speaker

6 Remove the parcel shelf

7 Prise up the trim panel above the speaker.

8 Disconnect the speaker wiring plug.

9 Undo the screws, and then lift the speaker from position.

10 Refitting is a reversal of removal.

19 Supplemental Restraint System (SRS) – general information and precautions

General information

A supplemental restraint system is fitted in various forms as standard or optional equipment depending on model and territory.

The main system component is a driver's airbag, which is designed to prevent serious chest and head injuries to the driver during an accident. There are also airbags for the front seat passenger and side airbags (built into the side of the front seats). Side impact crash sensors are located on the B-pillars and/or C-pillars of the vehicle, with two frontal sensors fitted on the left- and right-hand side of the engine compartment. A control module is fitted under the front section of the centre console. The module incorporates a deceleration sensor, and a microprocessor ECM to monitor the severity of the impact and trigger the airbag where necessary. The airbag is inflated by a gas generator, which forces the bag out of the module cover in the centre of the steering wheel, or out of a cover on the passenger's side of the facia/seat cover/headlining. A contact reel behind the steering wheel at the top of the steering column ensures that a good electrical connection is maintained with the airbag at all times, as the steering wheel is turned in each direction.

In addition to the airbag units, the supplemental restraint system also incorporates pyrotechnical seat belt tensioners fitted in the belt inertia reel assembly. The pyrotechnical units are also triggered by the crash sensors, in conjunction with the airbags, to tighten the seat belts and provide additional collision protection.

Precautions

Warning: Any attempt to dismantle the airbag module, SIPS bag, crash sensors, contact reel, seat belt tensioners or any associated wiring or components without dedicated equipment, and the specialist knowledge needed to use it correctly, could result in severe personal injury and/or malfunction of the system.

- ***Before carrying out any work on the SRS components, disconnect the battery and wait for at least 5 minutes for any residual electrical energy to dissipate before proceeding.***
- ***Handle the airbag unit with extreme care as a precaution against personal injury, and always hold it with the cover facing***

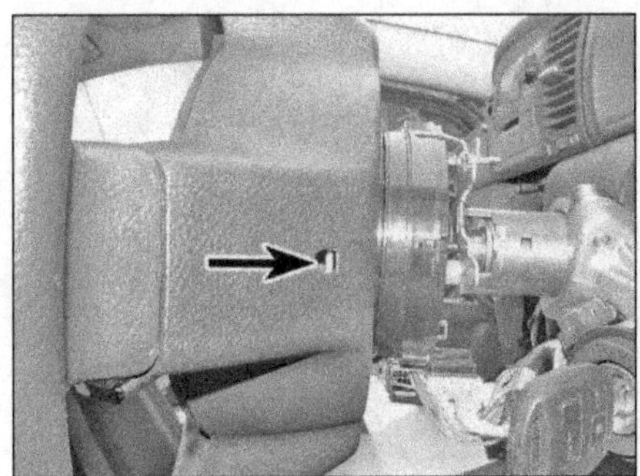
20.2a Use a screwdriver . . .

20.2b . . . to release the securing spring clip (arrowed)

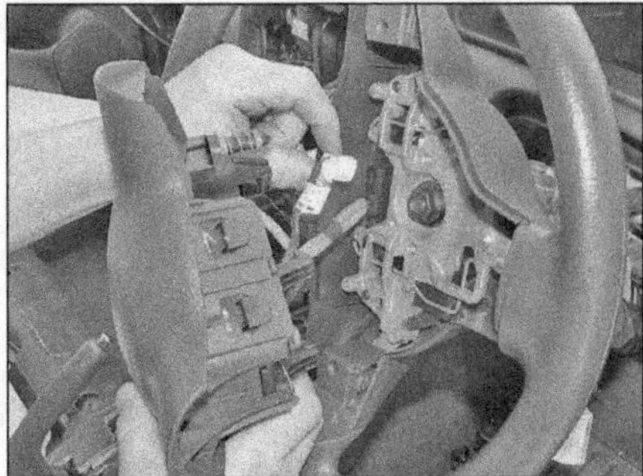
20.3 Disconnect the wiring connectors

away from the body. If in doubt concerning any proposed work involving the airbag unit or its control circuitry, consult a Toyota dealer.

- ***Note that the airbag(s) must not be subjected to temperatures in excess of 90°C. When the airbag is removed, ensure that it is stored with the pad facing up to prevent possible inflation.***
- ***Do not allow any solvents or cleaning agents to contact the airbag assemblies. They must be cleaned using only a damp cloth.***
- ***The airbag(s) and control unit are both sensitive to impact. If either is dropped or damaged they should be renewed.***
- ***Disconnect the airbag control unit wiring plug prior to using arc-welding equipment on the vehicle.***

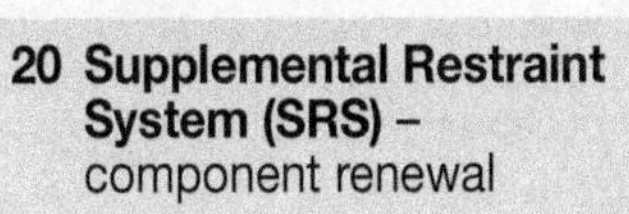

20 Supplemental Restraint System (SRS) – component renewal

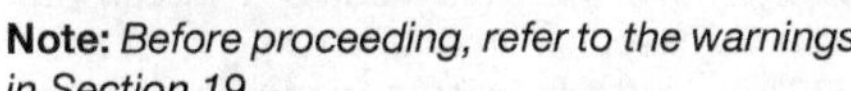
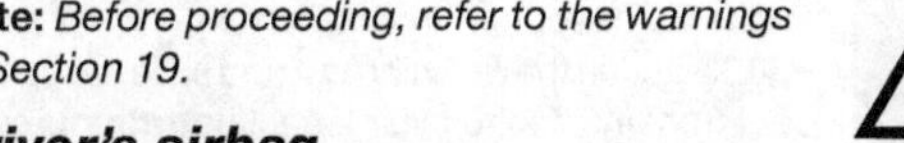

Note: *Before proceeding, refer to the warnings in Section 19.*

Driver's airbag

Removal

1 Turn the ignition key to off, then disconnect the cable from the negative terminal of the battery (see Chapter 5A), then wait at least 5 minutes before proceeding.

2 From the straight-ahead position, turn the steering wheel a quarter of a turn anti-clockwise. Insert a screwdriver into the hole in the rear of the steering wheel on the right-hand side, to release the locking clip **(see illustrations)**.

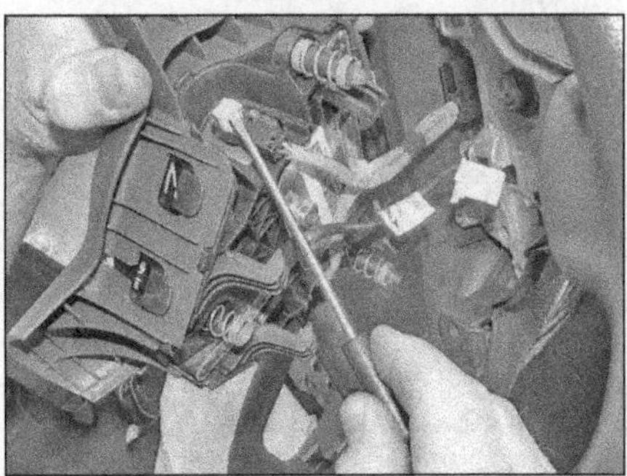
20.4a Release the locking clip . . .

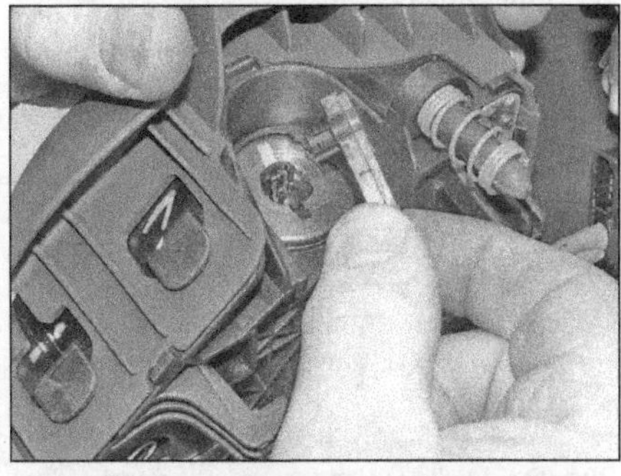
20.4b . . . and disconnect the wiring connector from the airbag

3 With the clip released withdraw the airbag module off the steering wheel **(see illustration)**.

4 Release the locking clips and disconnect the module electrical connectors **(see illustrations)**.

Warning: Set the airbag module down with the trim side facing up.

Refitting

5 Plug in the electrical connectors for the airbag module and fit the locking clips **(see illustration)**.

6 Make sure the airbag module electrical connector is positioned correctly and that the wires don't interfere with anything, then press the airbag module onto the steering wheel, making sure retaining clip secures the airbag.

7 Make sure that no one is inside the car, and then reconnect the battery negative lead.

Driver's airbag contact reel

Removal

8 Remove the airbag unit as described above, and the steering wheel and column shrouds as described in Chapter 10.

9 Remove the steering column switches as described in Section 4 of this Chapter.

10 Withdraw the unit from the steering column and disconnect the wiring plug **(see illustrations)**. Noting its fitted position for refitting.

Refitting

11 Refit the unit to the steering column in the position noted on removal and connect the wiring connector.

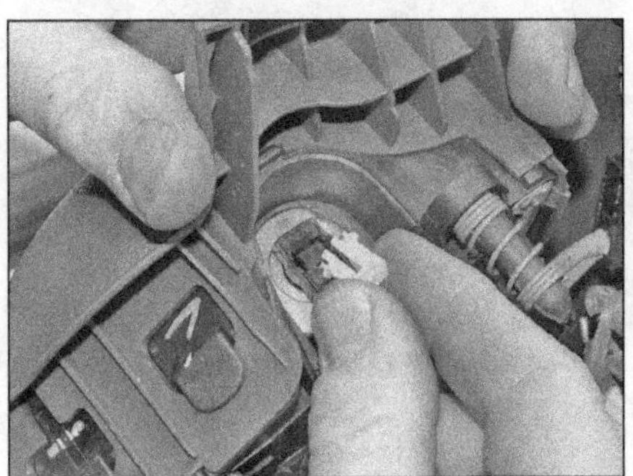
20.5 Make sure the locking clip is secure

20.10a Withdraw the contact reel from the steering column . . .

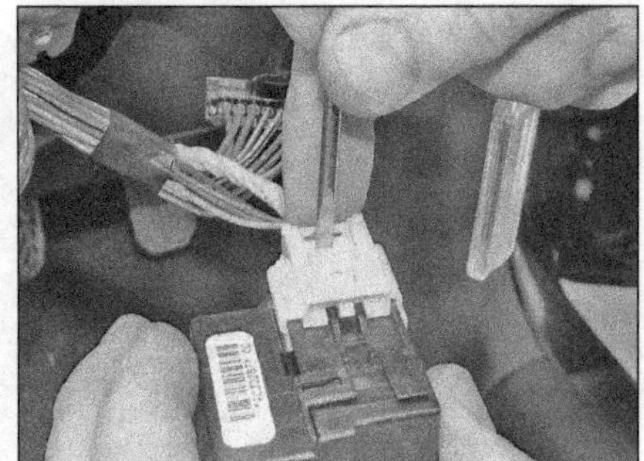
20.10b . . . and disconnect the wiring connectors

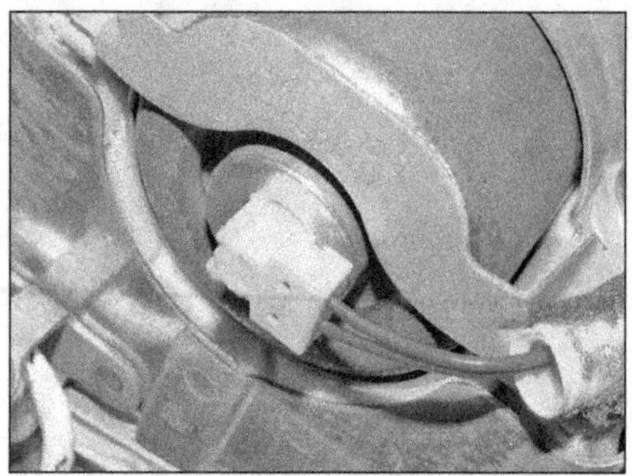
20.16 Airbag wiring connector

12 Refit the steering column switches as described in Section 4.

13 Refit the steering wheel as described in Chapter 10, and the airbag unit as described above.

Passenger's airbag

Removal

14 Disconnect the battery negative lead (see Chapter 5A), and wait 5 minutes before proceeding.

15 Remove the upper facia as described in Chapter 11. The airbag unit is bolted to the underside of the upper facia panel.

16 If required, disconnect the wiring connectors from each side of the airbag unit **(see illustration)**.

17 Undo the retaining nuts/bolts, and then remove the airbag from the facia **(see illustration)**.

20.17 Passenger airbag securing nuts/ bolts

Refitting

18 Refitting is a reversal of removal.

19 On completion, make sure that no one is inside the car, and then reconnect the battery negative lead.

Airbag control module

Removal

20 Disconnect the battery negative lead as described in Chapter 5A. Wait at least 5 minutes before proceeding, to allow any residual electrical energy to dissipate.

21 Remove the centre console as described in Chapter 11.

22 Unclip the carpet at each side, then undo the module mounting bolts **(see illustration)**. The airbag control module is situated under the heater housing in front of the gear lever assembly.

23 Depress the retaining clips and disconnect the module wiring plugs **(see illustration)**.

20.22 Location of airbag control module

Refitting

24 Refitting is a reversal of removal, ensuring the module is fitted with the arrow on its top surface facing forwards.

25 On completion, make sure that no one is inside the car, and then reconnect the battery negative lead.

Side airbags

26 The side airbag units are built into the front seats, and their removal requires that the seat fabric be removed. This is not considered to be a DIY operation, and should be referred to a Toyota dealer or upholstery specialist.

Side crash sensors

27 Disconnect the battery negative lead as described in Chapter 5A. Wait at least 5 minutes before proceeding, to allow any residual electrical energy to dissipate.

28 On models equipped with side airbags, the side crash sensors are fitted to the vehicle's B-pillar and/or C-pillar (depending on model).

Removal from B-pillar

29 Remove the front seat belt inertia reel units as described in Chapter 11.

30 Slacken the retaining nut and slide the sensor out from inside the pillar **(see illustration)**.

31 Release the securing clip and disconnect the wiring plug from the sensor **(see illustration)**.

Removal from C-pillar

32 Lift up the rear seat cushion and drop the rear seat backs down.

33 Pull back the rubber door seal and unclip the inner C-pillar lower trim panel **(see illustrations)**.

20.23 Release the securing clip (arrowed) and disconnect the wiring connector

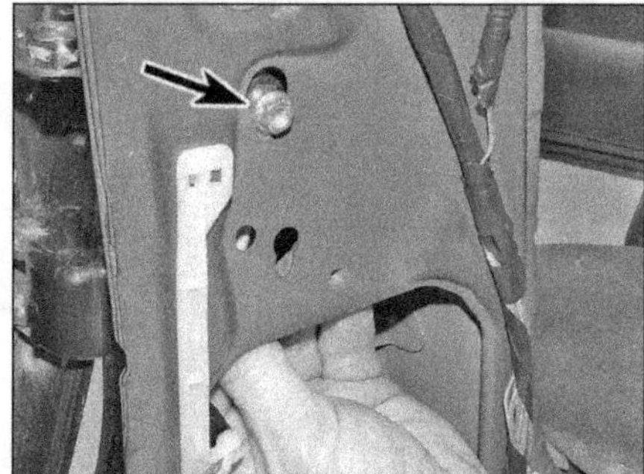
20.30 Slacken the securing nut (arrowed)

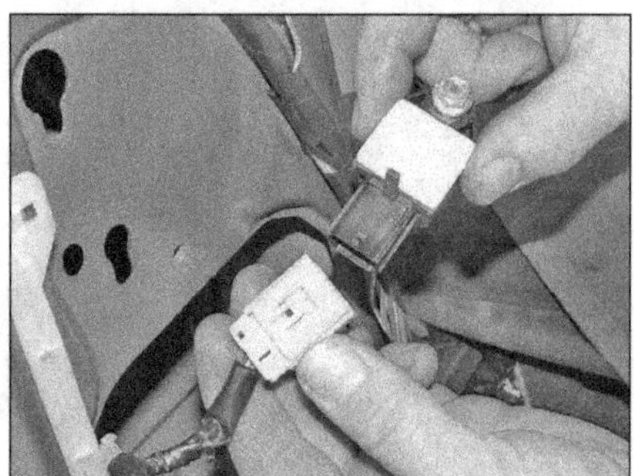
20.31 Disconnect the wiring connector

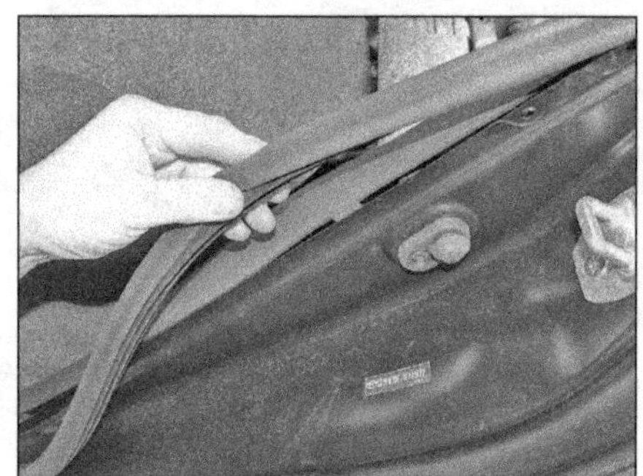
20.33a Pull back the door seal . . .

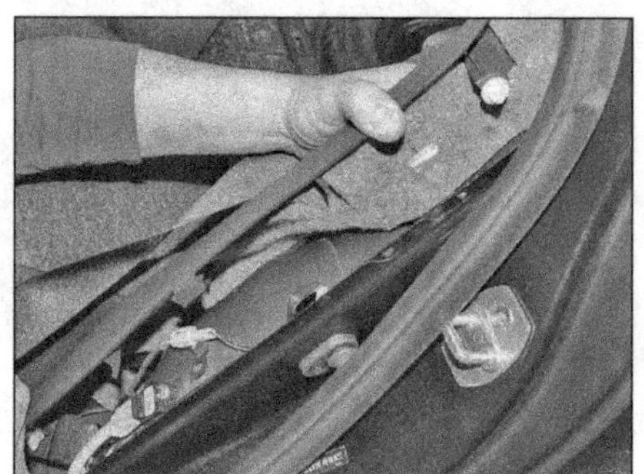
20.33b . . . and unclip the trim panel

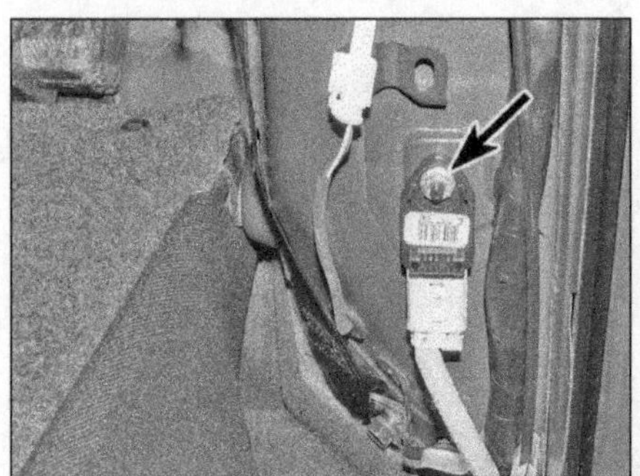
20.34 Crash sensor retaining nut (arrowed)

34 Slacken the retaining nut and remove the sensor from the pillar, and disconnect the wiring plug from the sensor **(see illustration)**.

Refitting

35 Refit the sensor(s) to the pillar(s) and tighten the retaining nuts to the specified torque. Reconnect the wiring plug.

36 The remainder of refitting is a reversal of removal.

37 On completion, make sure that no one is inside the car, and then reconnect the battery negative lead.

Front crash sensors

Removal

38 Disconnect the battery negative lead as described in Chapter 5A. Wait at least 5 minutes before proceeding, to allow any residual electrical energy to dissipate.

39 There are two front crash sensors, one at each side in the engine compartment on the front chassis leg.

40 Disconnect the sensor wiring plug, and undo the sensor mounting bolt to remove **(see illustration)**.

Refitting

41 Refitting is a reversal of removal, tightening the retaining bolts to the specified torque.

42 On completion, make sure that no one is inside the car, and then reconnect the battery negative lead.

21 Wiring diagrams – general information

Since it isn't possible to include all wiring diagrams for every year covered by this manual, the following diagrams are those that are typical and most commonly needed **(see illustration)**.

20.40 Location of front crash sensor (arrowed)

Prior to troubleshooting any circuits, check the fuse and circuit breakers (if equipped) to make sure they're in good condition. Make sure the battery is properly charged and check the cable connections.

When checking a circuit, make sure that all connectors are clean, with no broken or loose terminals. When unplugging a connector, do not pull on the wires. Pull only on the connector housings themselves.

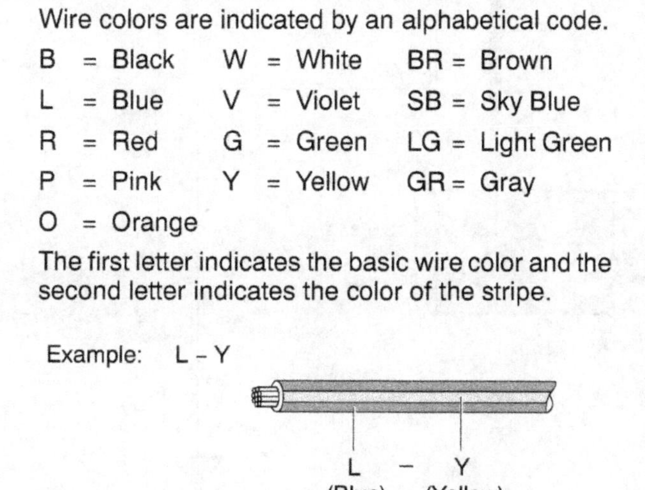

Wire colors are indicated by an alphabetical code.
B = Black W = White BR = Brown
L = Blue V = Violet SB = Sky Blue
R = Red G = Green LG = Light Green
P = Pink Y = Yellow GR = Gray
O = Orange
The first letter indicates the basic wire color and the second letter indicates the color of the stripe.
Example: L - Y
L – Y
(Blue) (Yellow)

21.1 Wiring diagram colour code chart

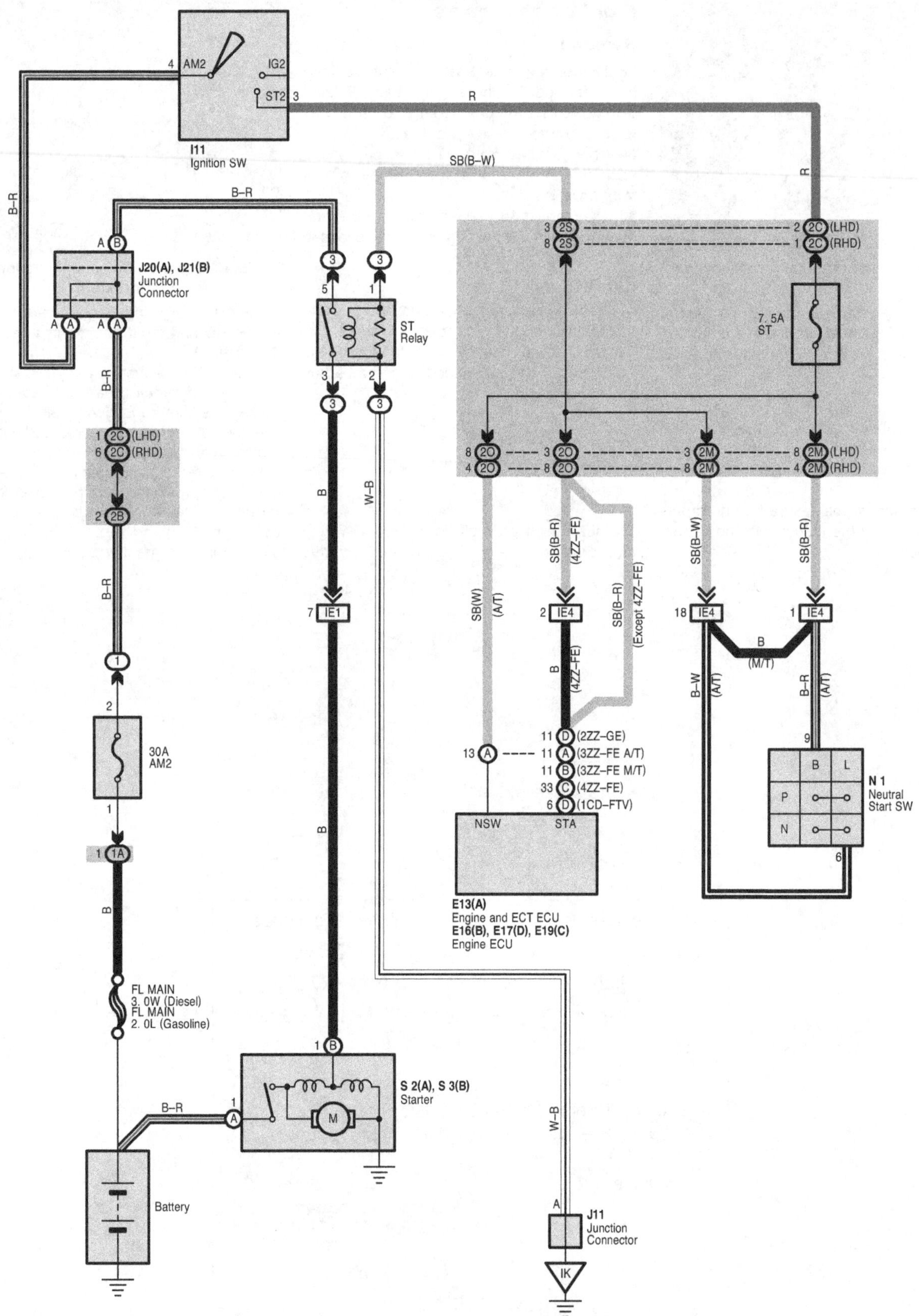

Diagram 1 - Starting system

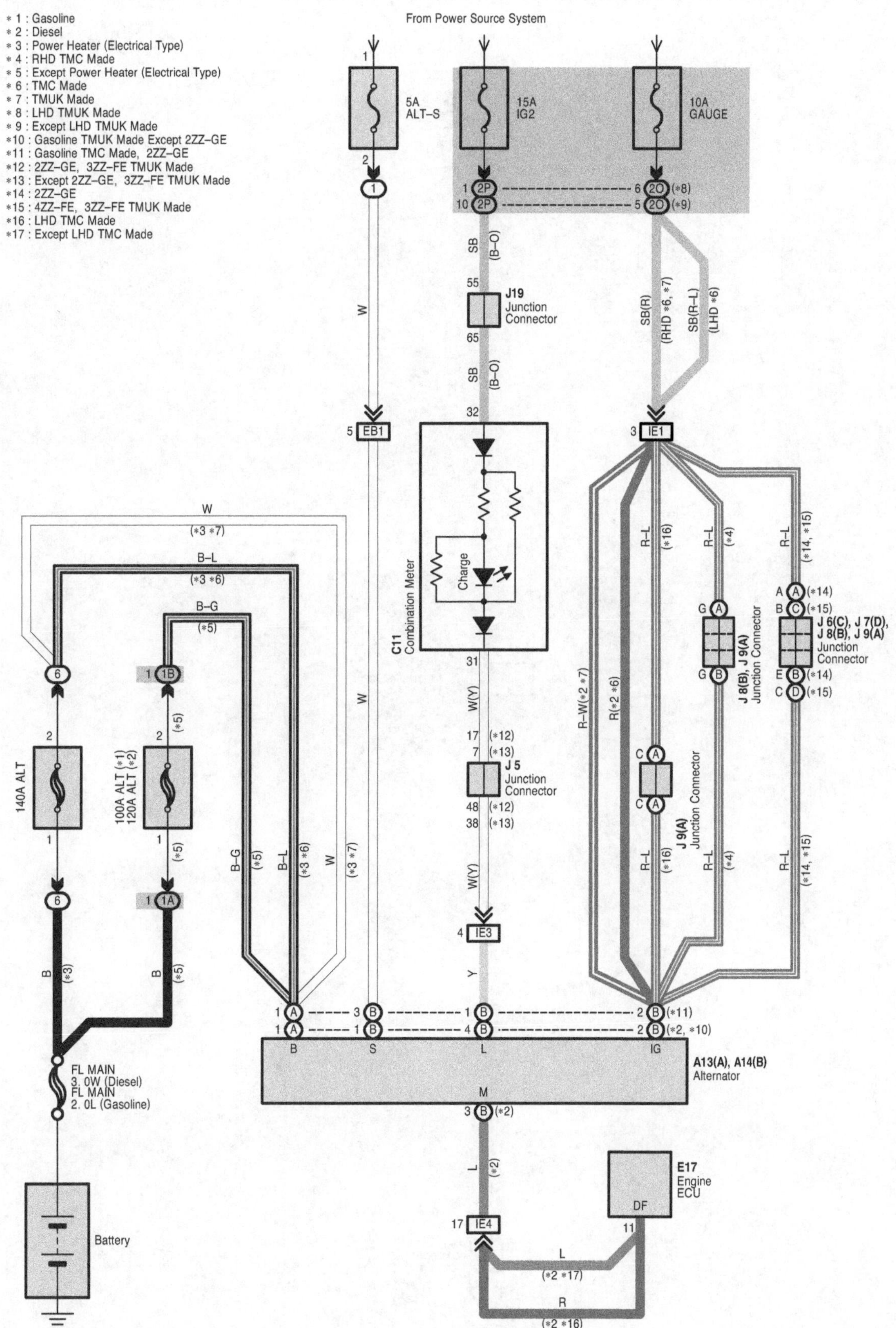

*1 : Gasoline
*2 : Diesel
*3 : Power Heater (Electrical Type)
*4 : RHD TMC Made
*5 : Except Power Heater (Electrical Type)
*6 : TMC Made
*7 : TMUK Made
*8 : LHD TMUK Made
*9 : Except LHD TMUK Made
*10 : Gasoline TMUK Made Except 2ZZ–GE
*11 : Gasoline TMC Made, 2ZZ–GE
*12 : 2ZZ–GE, 3ZZ–FE TMUK Made
*13 : Except 2ZZ–GE, 3ZZ–FE TMUK Made
*14 : 2ZZ–GE
*15 : 4ZZ–FE, 3ZZ–FE TMUK Made
*16 : LHD TMC Made
*17 : Except LHD TMC Made
From Power Source System
5A ALT–S
15A IG2
10A GAUGE
2P
2O (*8)
2O (*9)
SB (B–O)
J19 Junction Connector
SB(R) (RHD *6, *7)
SB(R–L) (LHD *6)
EB1
IE1
C11 Combination Meter
Charge
W (*3 *7)
B–L (*3 *6)
B–G (*5)
R–L (*16)
R–L (*4)
R–L (*14, *15)
J 6(C), J 7(D), J 8(B), J 9(A) Junction Connector
J 8(B), J 9(A) Junction Connector
J 9(A) Junction Connector
R–W(*2 *7)
R(*2 *6)
140A ALT
100A ALT (*1)
120A ALT (*2)
W(Y)
17 (*12)
7 (*13)
J 5 Junction Connector
48 (*12)
38 (*13)
IE3
B (*3)
B (*5)
Y
(*11)
(*2, *10)
B S L IG
A13(A), A14(B) Alternator
M
FL MAIN 3. 0W (Diesel)
FL MAIN 2. 0L (Gasoline)
L (*2)
E17 Engine ECU
DF
IE4
L (*2 *17)
R (*2 *16)
Battery

Diagram 2 - Charging system

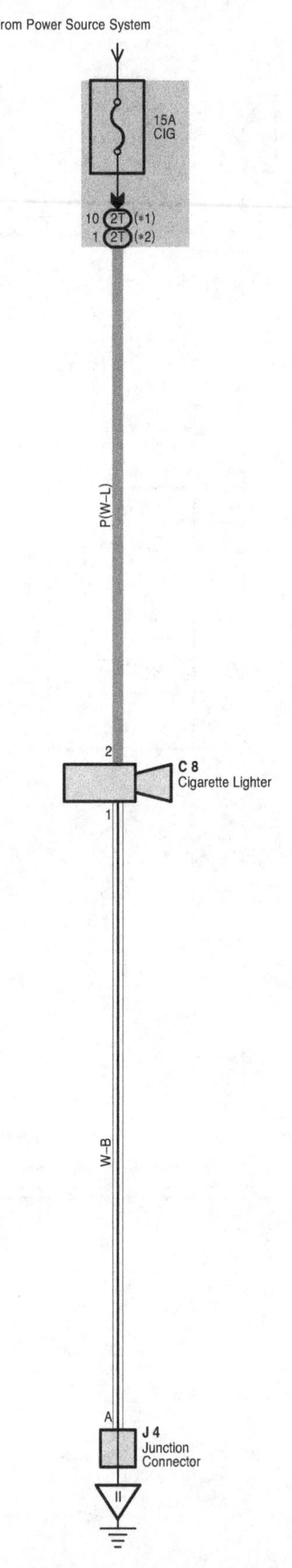

Diagram 3 - Cigarette lighter

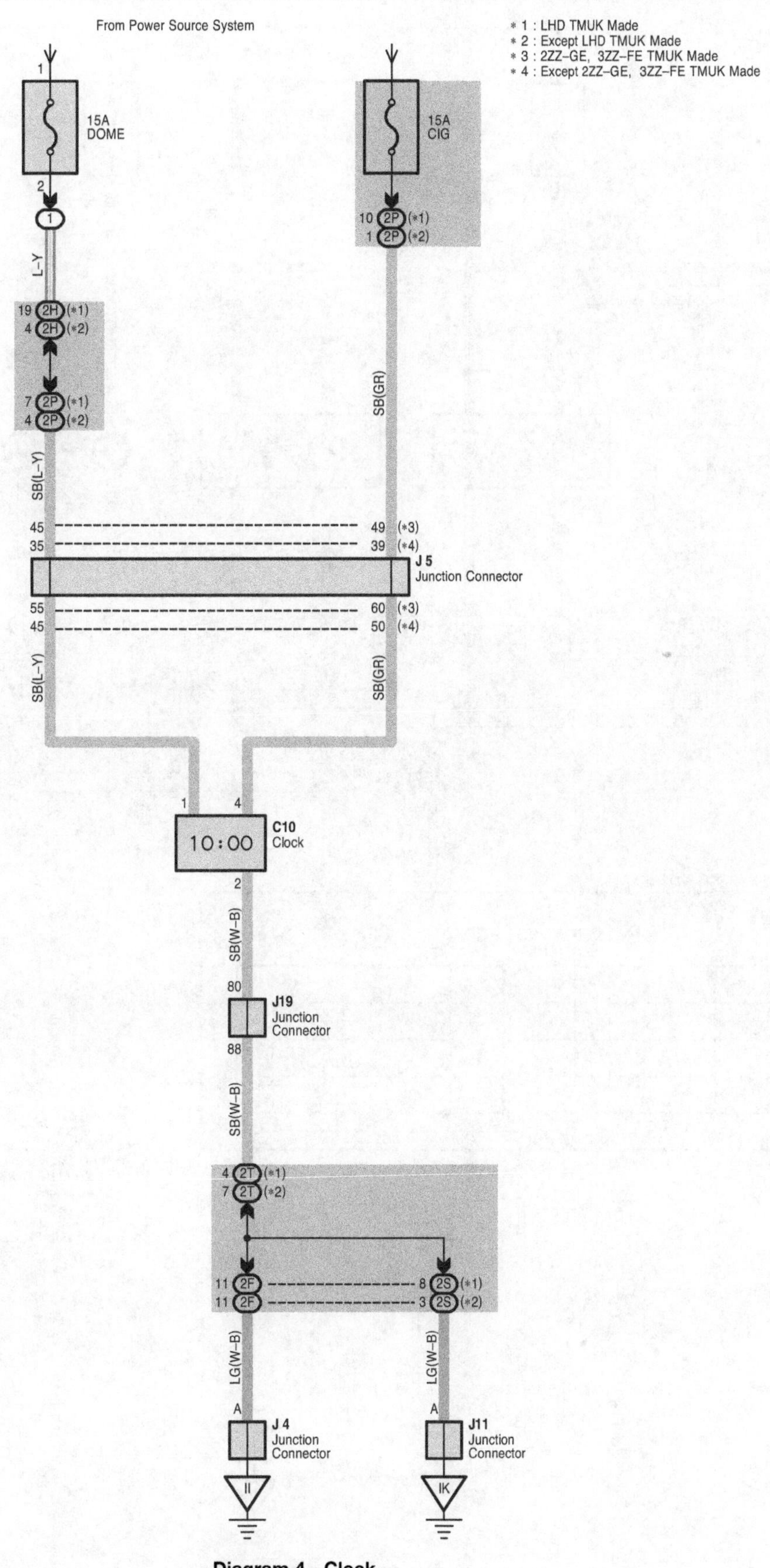

Diagram 4 - Clock

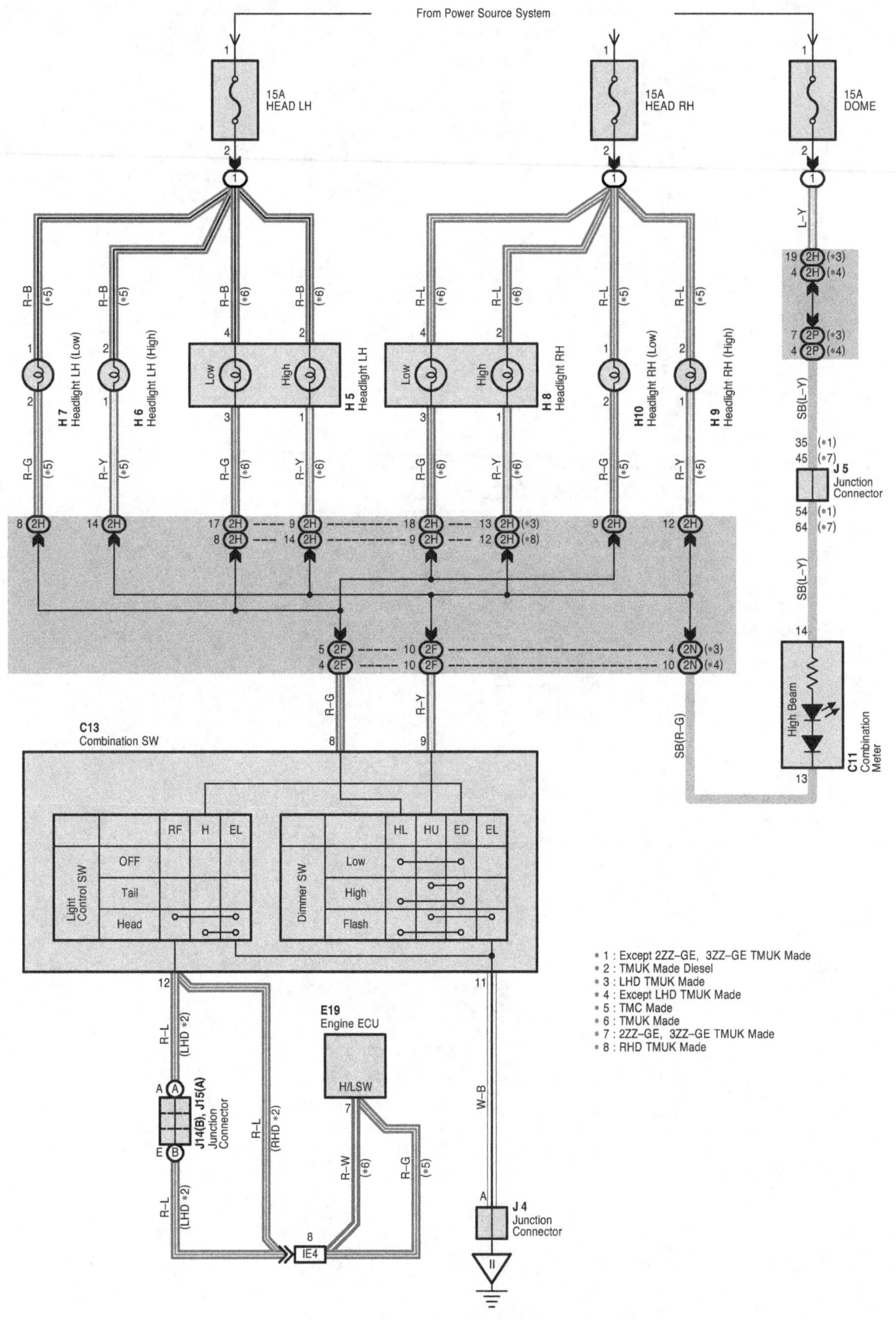

Diagram 5 - Headlights

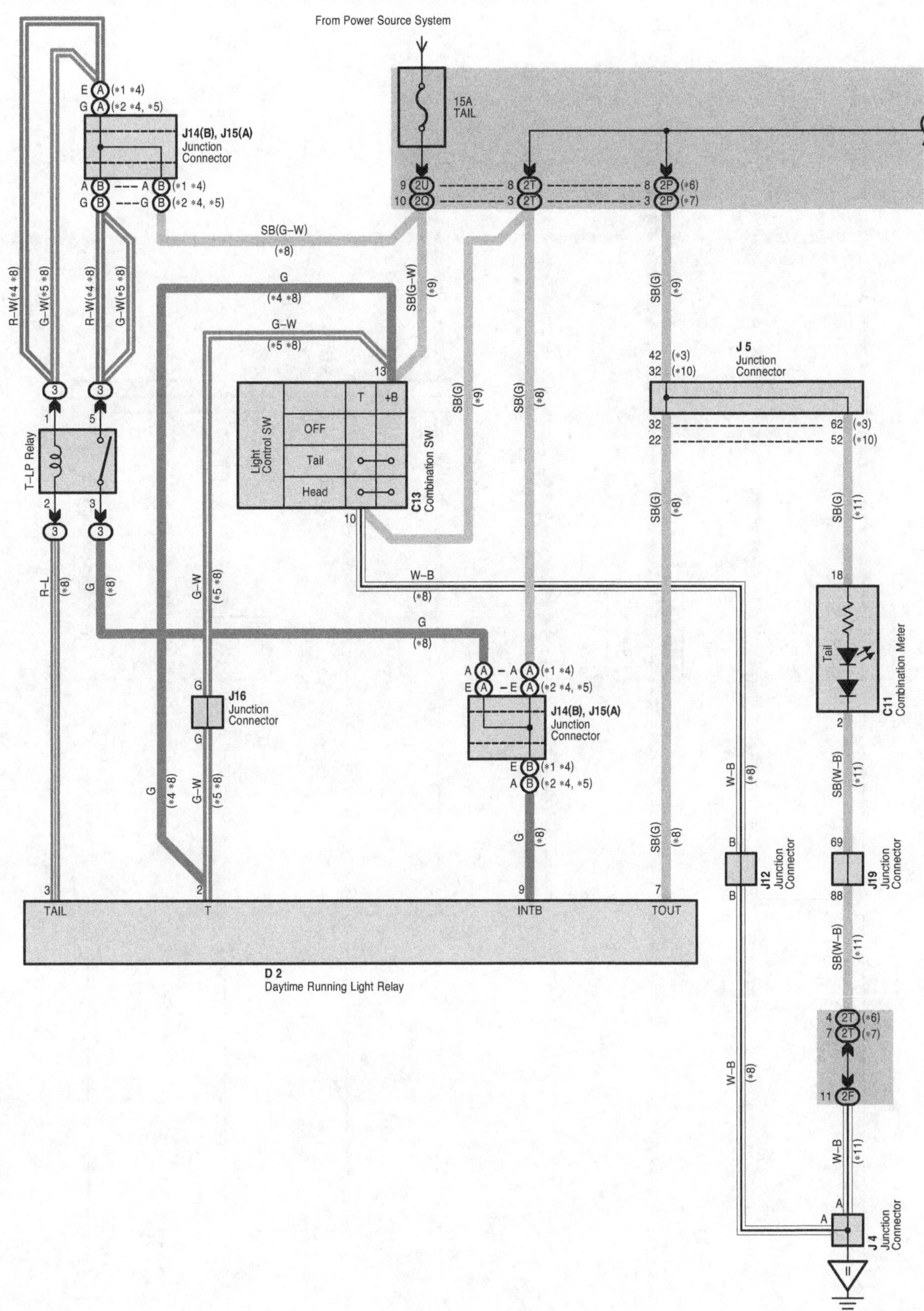

Diagram 6a - Tail lights

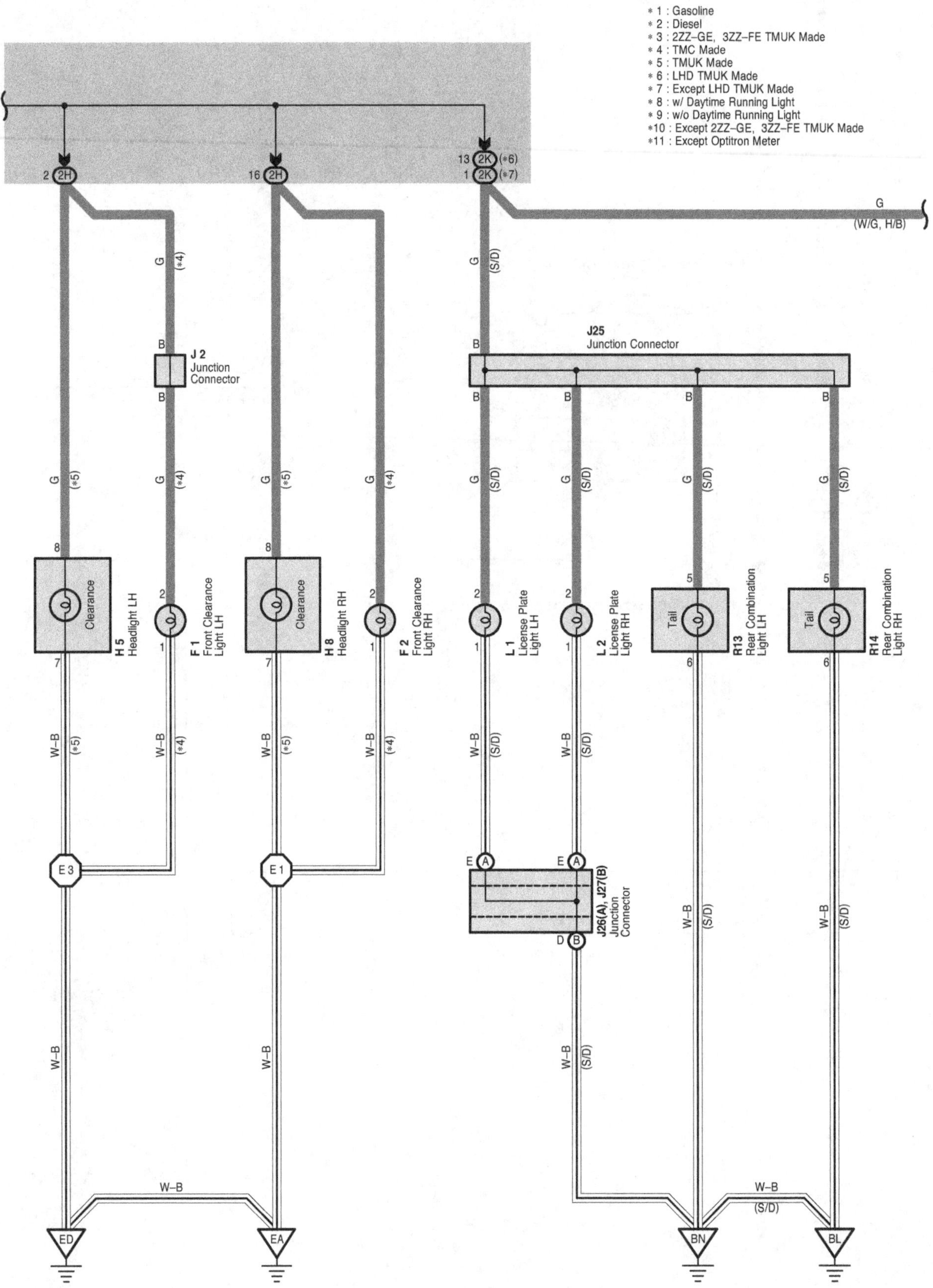

∗1 : Gasoline
∗2 : Diesel
∗3 : 2ZZ–GE, 3ZZ–FE TMUK Made
∗4 : TMC Made
∗5 : TMUK Made
∗6 : LHD TMUK Made
∗7 : Except LHD TMUK Made
∗8 : w/ Daytime Running Light
∗9 : w/o Daytime Running Light
∗10 : Except 2ZZ–GE, 3ZZ–FE TMUK Made
∗11 : Except Optitron Meter
J 2 Junction Connector
J25 Junction Connector
H 5 Headlight LH
Clearance
F 1 Front Clearance Light LH
H 8 Headlight RH
F 2 Front Clearance Light RH
L 1 License Plate Light LH
L 2 License Plate Light RH
R13 Rear Combination Light LH
Tail
R14 Rear Combination Light RH
J26(A), J27(B) Junction Connector
W–B
G
(W/G, H/B)
(S/D)

Diagram 6b - Tail lights (continued)

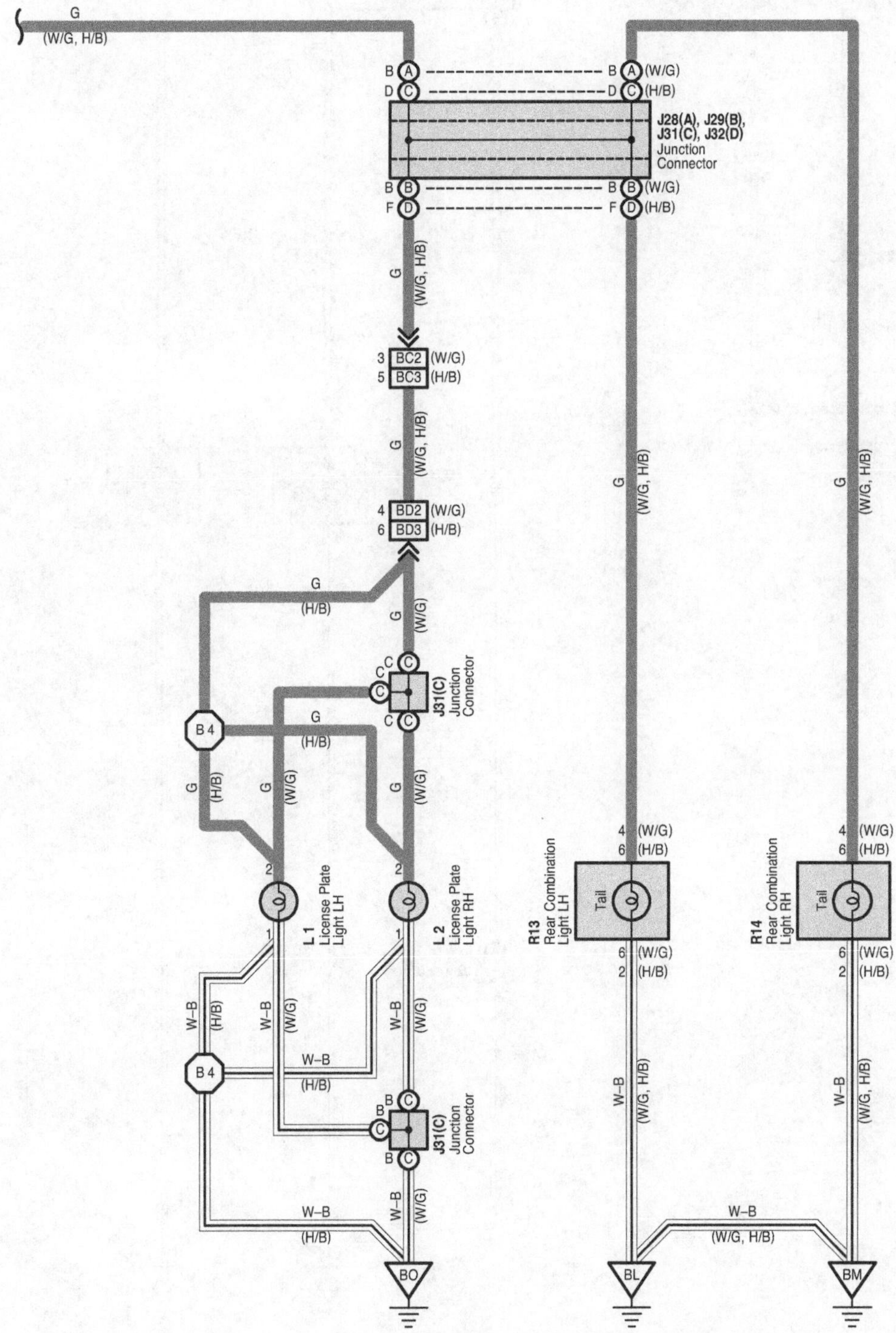

Diagram 6c - Tail lights (continued)

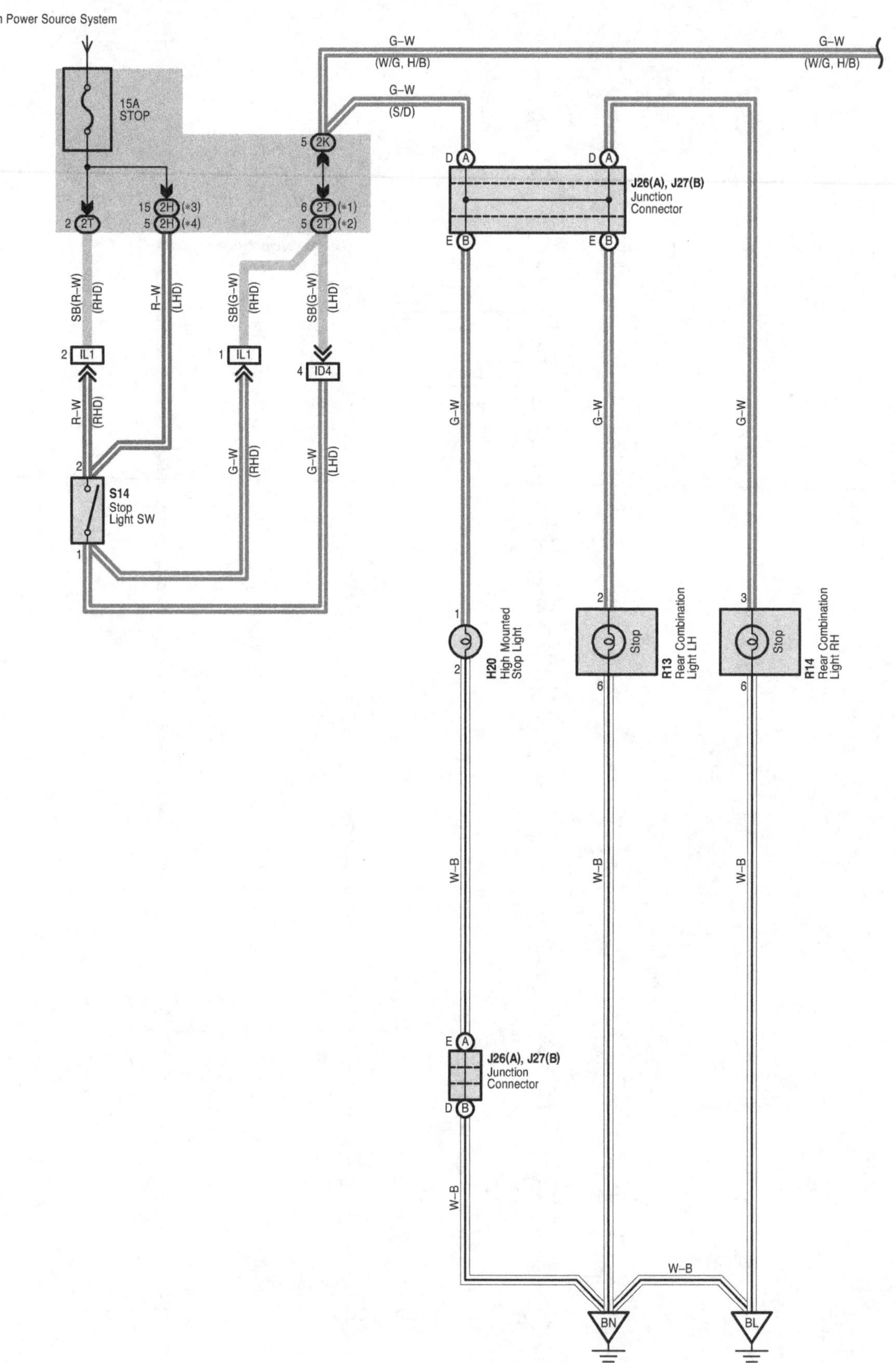

Diagram 7a - Stop lights

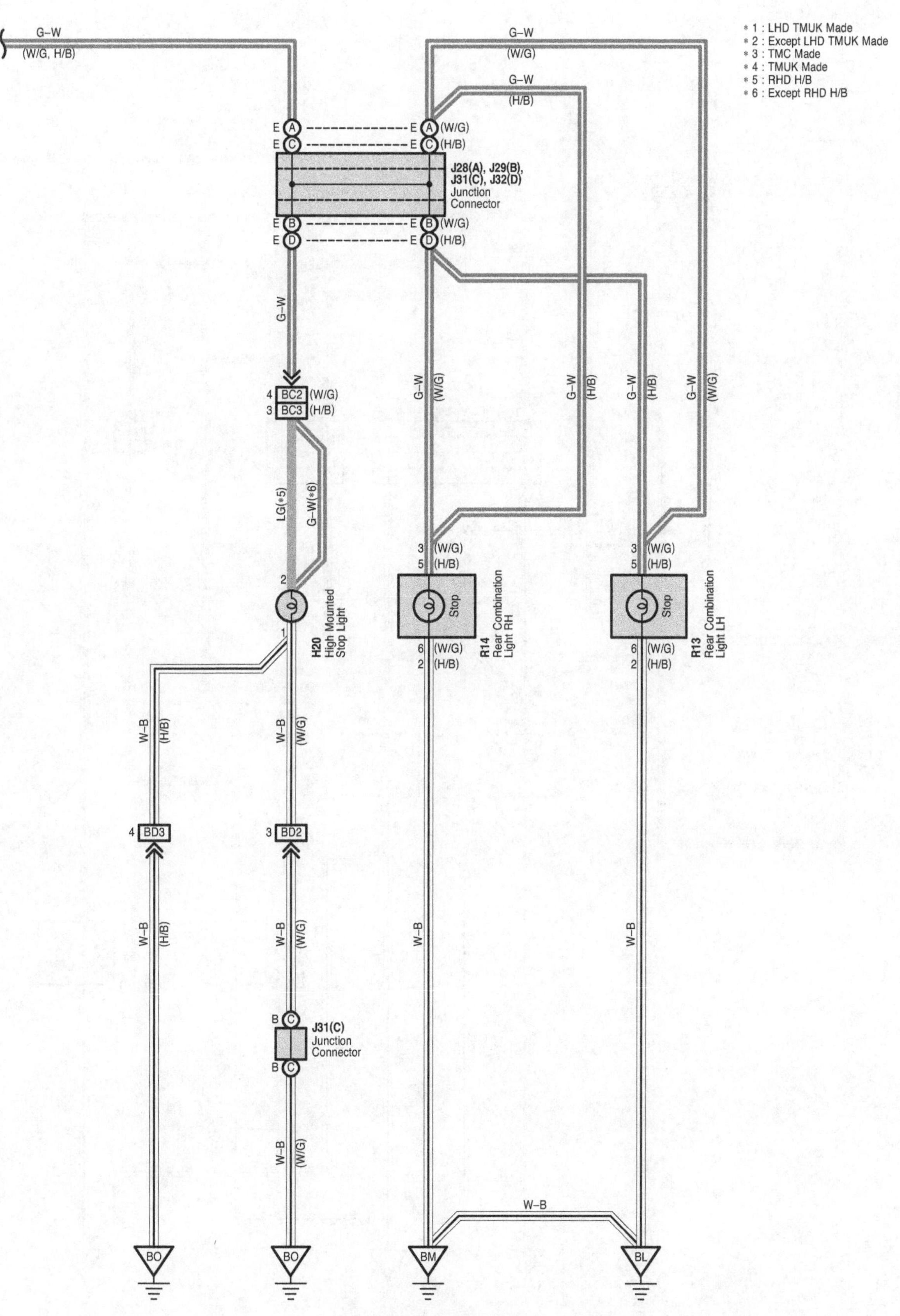

Diagram 7b – Stop lights (continued)

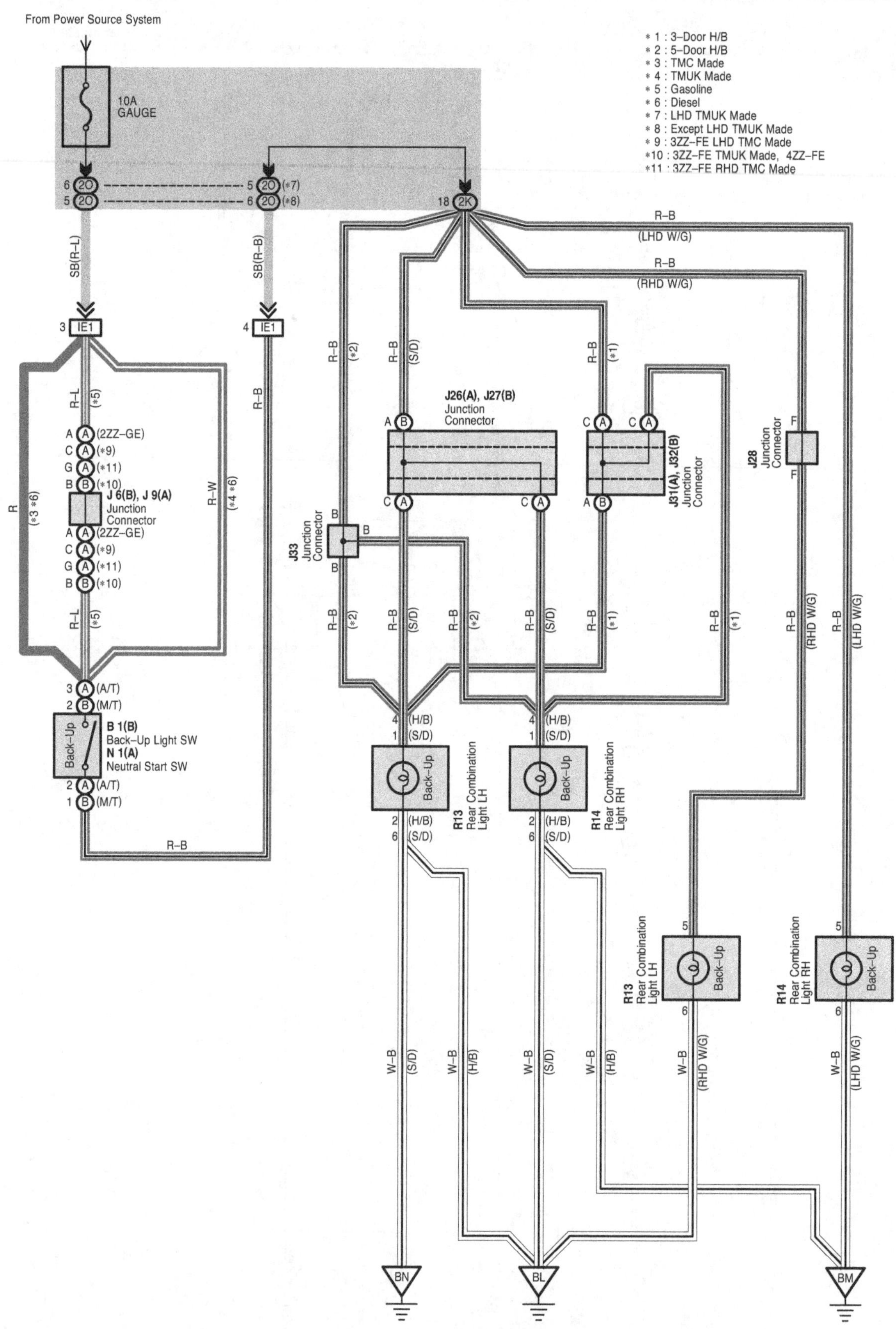

Diagram 8 – Reversing lights

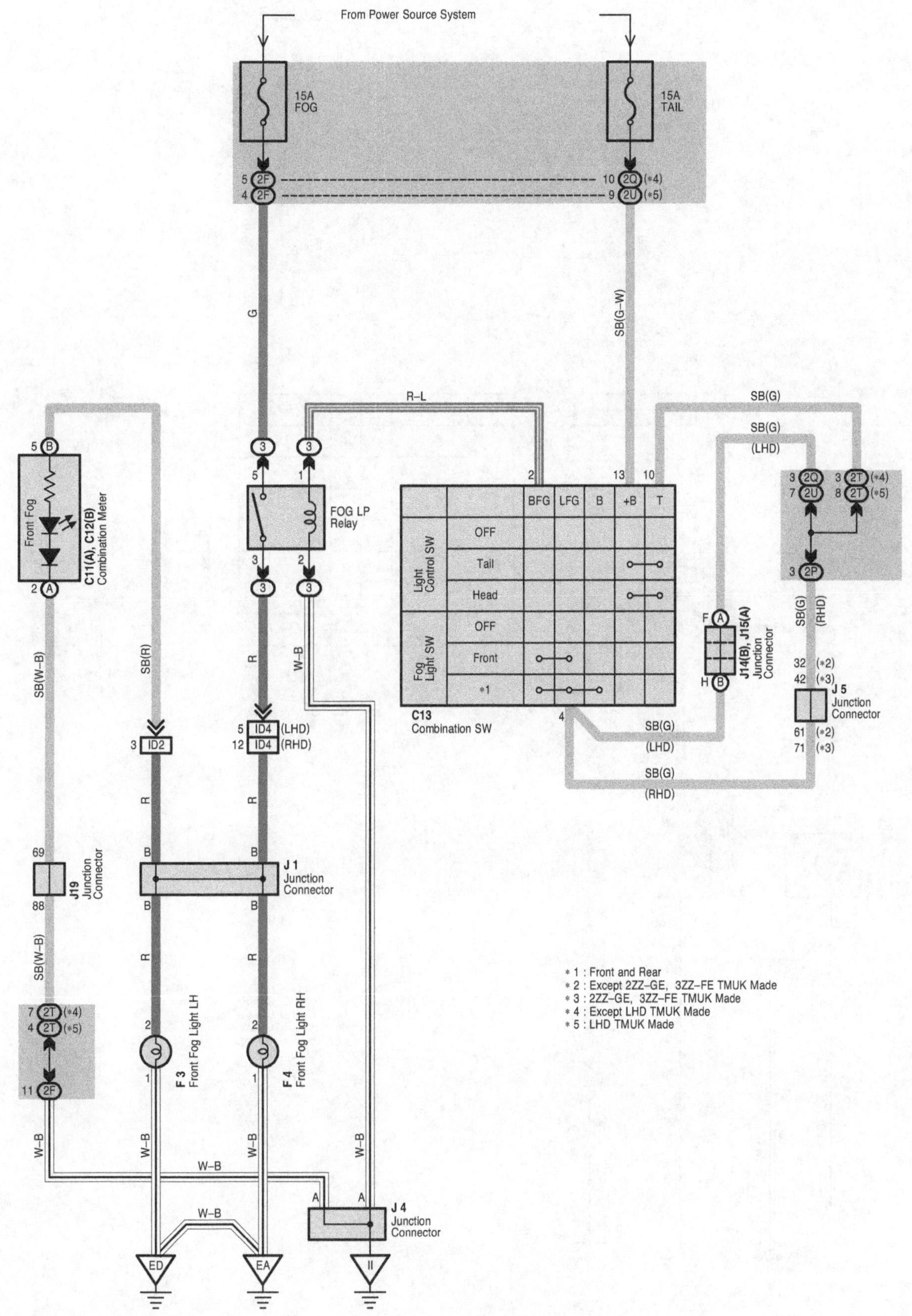

Diagram 9 – Front foglight

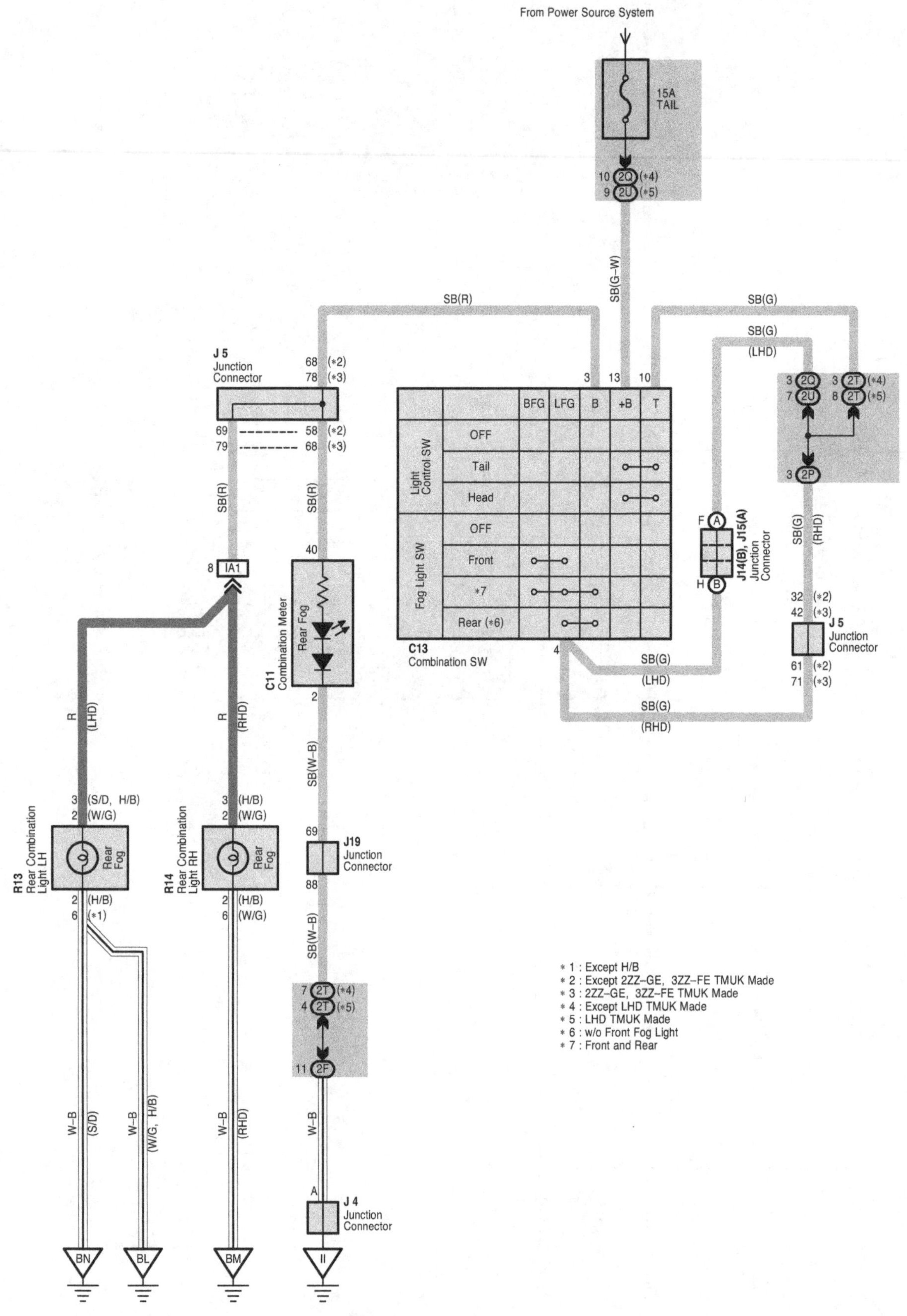

Diagram 10 – Rear foglight

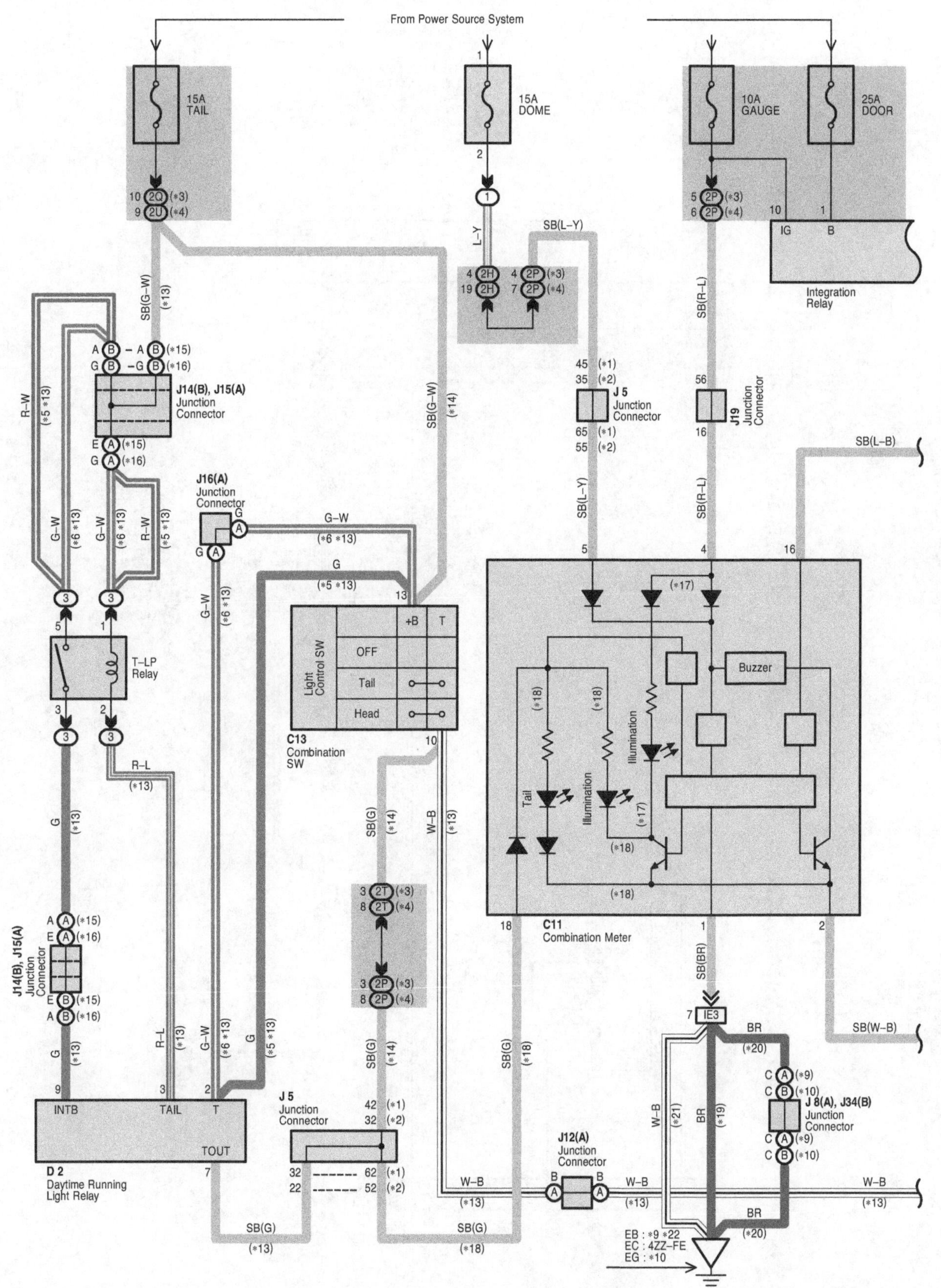

Diagram 11a - Key reminder and lights on buzzer

* 1 : 2ZZ–GE, 3ZZ–FE TMUK Made
* 2 : Except 2ZZ–GE, 3ZZ–FE TMUK Made
* 3 : Except LHD TMUK Made
* 4 : LHD TMUK Made
* 5 : TMC Made
* 6 : TMUK Made
* 7 : TMC Made LHD Diesel
* 8 : TMC Made Except LHD Diesel
* 9 : Gasoline
*10 : Diesel
*11 : RHD H/B
*12 : RHD Except H/B
*13 : w/ Daytime Running Light
*14 : w/o Daytime Running Light
*15 : TMC Made Gasoline
*16 : Except TMC Made Gasoline
*17 : Optitron Meter Type
*18 : Except Optitron Meter Type
*19 : TMC Made LHD 3ZZ–FE, TMUK Made 3ZZ–FE 4ZZ–FE 1CD–FTV
*20 : 2ZZ–GE, TMC Made 1CD–FTV RHD 3ZZ–FE
*21 : TMC Made 4ZZ–FE
*22 : Except 4ZZ–FE

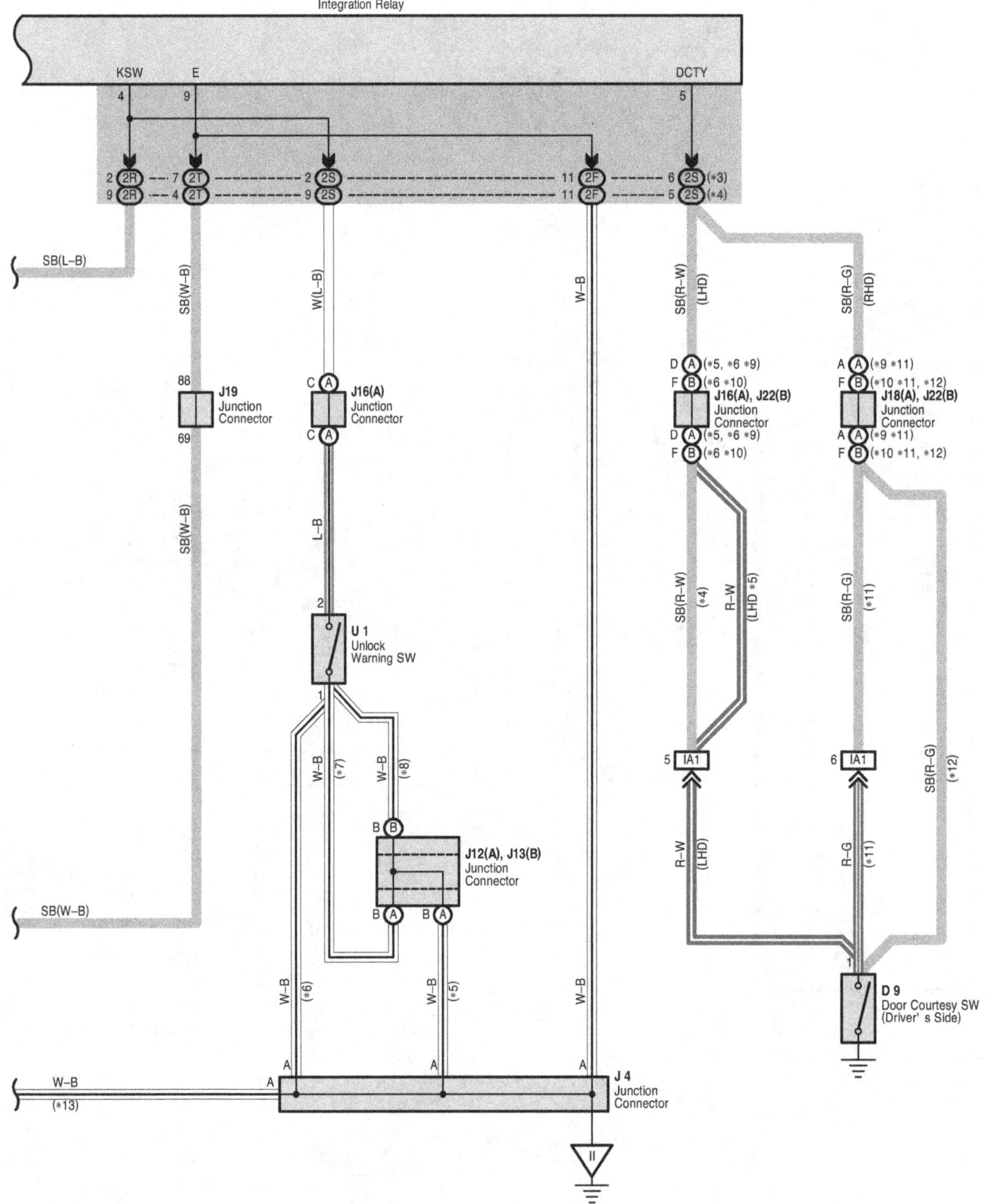

Diagram 11b - Key reminder and lights on buzzer (continued)

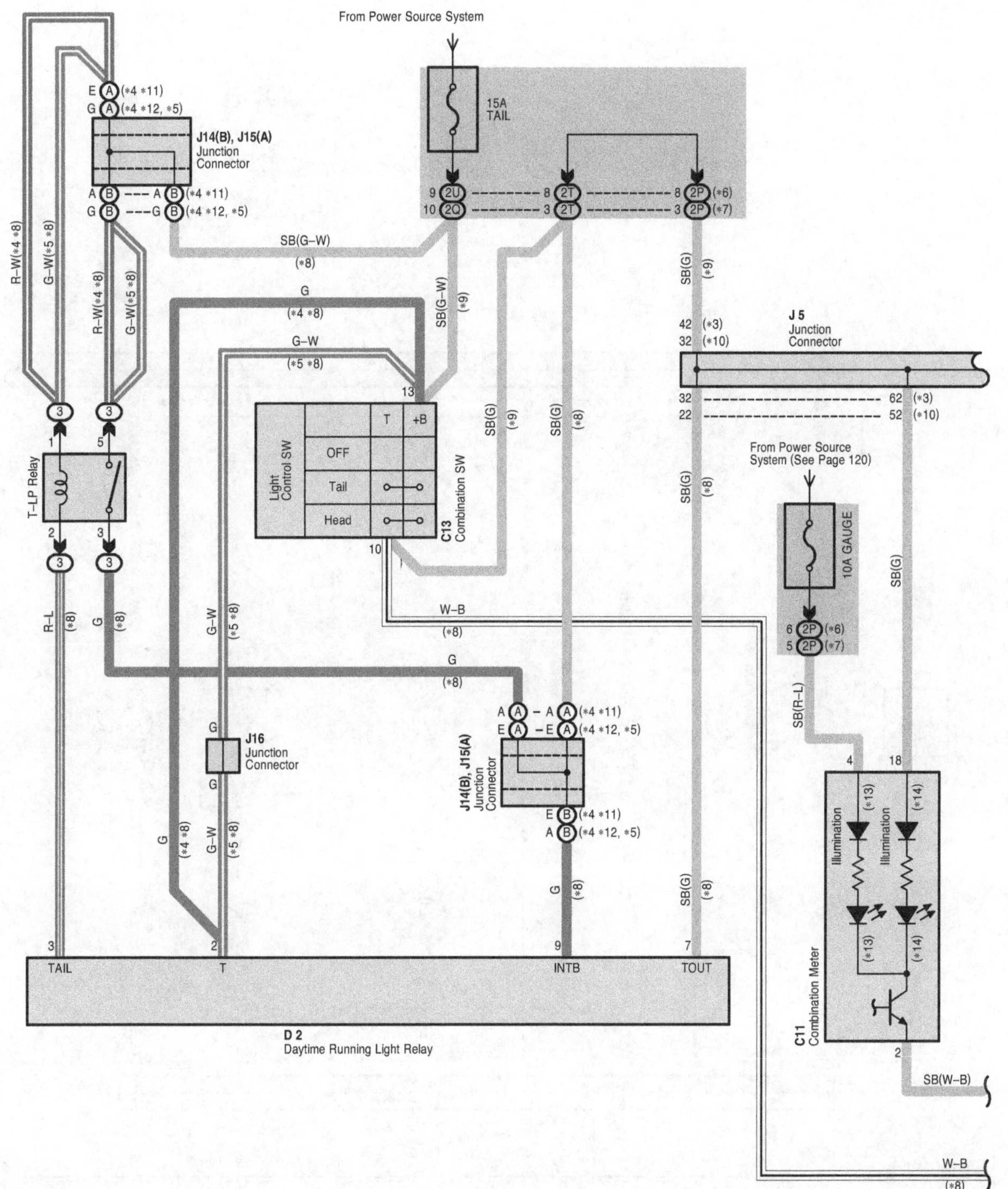

Diagram 12a - Interior illumination

* 1 : Automatic A/C
* 2 : Except Automatic A/C
* 3 : 2ZZ–GE, 3ZZ–FE TMUK Made
* 4 : TMC Made
* 5 : TMUK Made
* 6 : LHD TMUK Made
* 7 : Except LHD TMUK Made
* 8 : w/ Daytime Running Light
* 9 : w/o Daytime Running Light
*10 : Except 2ZZ–GE, 3ZZ–FE TMUK Made
*11 : Gasoline
*12 : Diesel
*13 : Optitron Meter
*14 : Except Optitron Meter

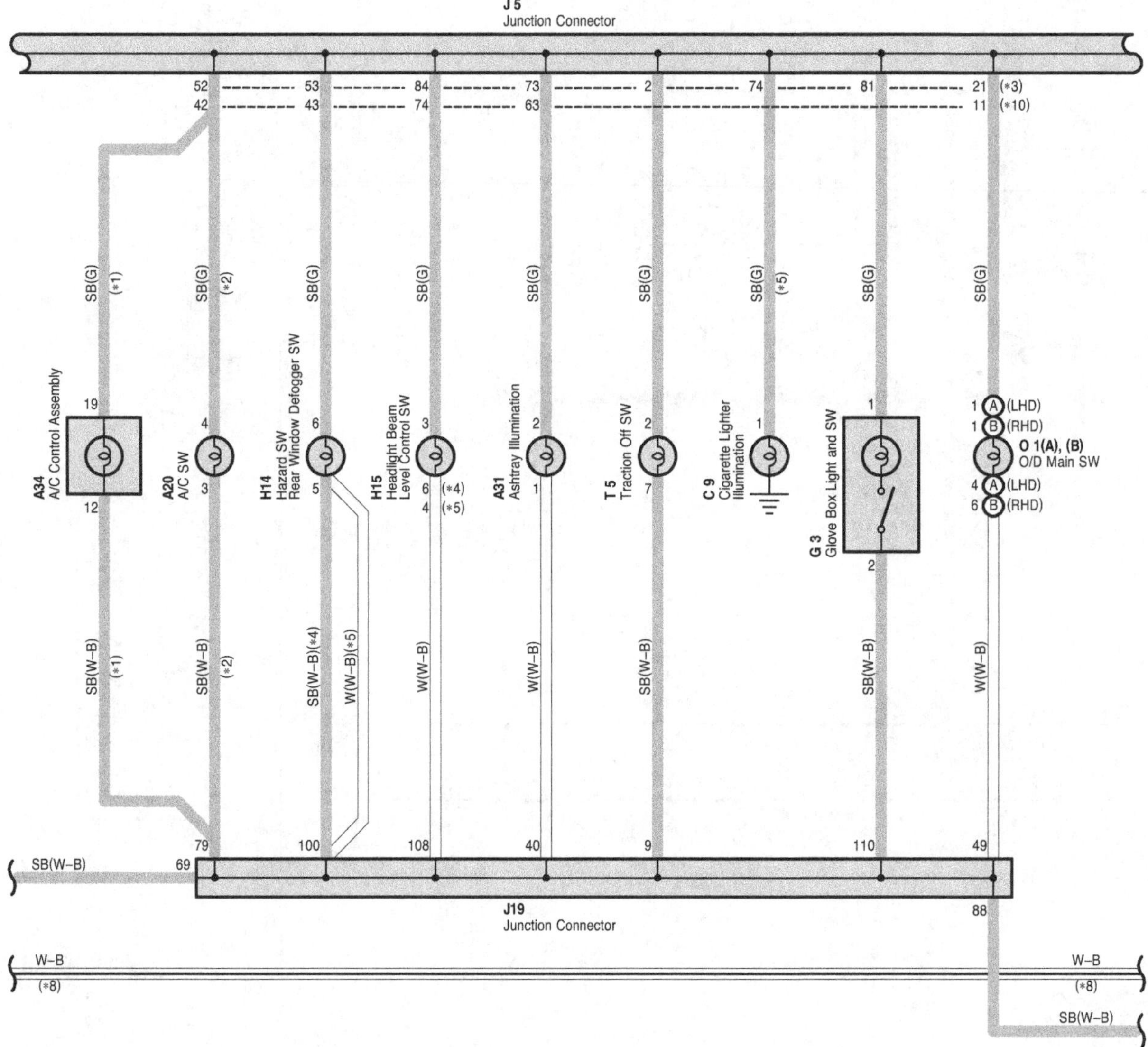

Diagram 12b - Interior illumination (continued)

* 3 : 2ZZ–GE, 3ZZ–FE TMUK Made
* 4 : TMC Made
* 5 : TMUK Made
* 6 : LHD TMUK Made
* 7 : Except LHD TMUK Made
* 8 : w/ Daytime Running Light
*10 : Except 2ZZ–GE, 3ZZ–FE TMUK Made
*11 : Gasoline
*12 : Diesel
*15 : w/ Navigation System Map Type
*16 : w/o Navigation System Map Type

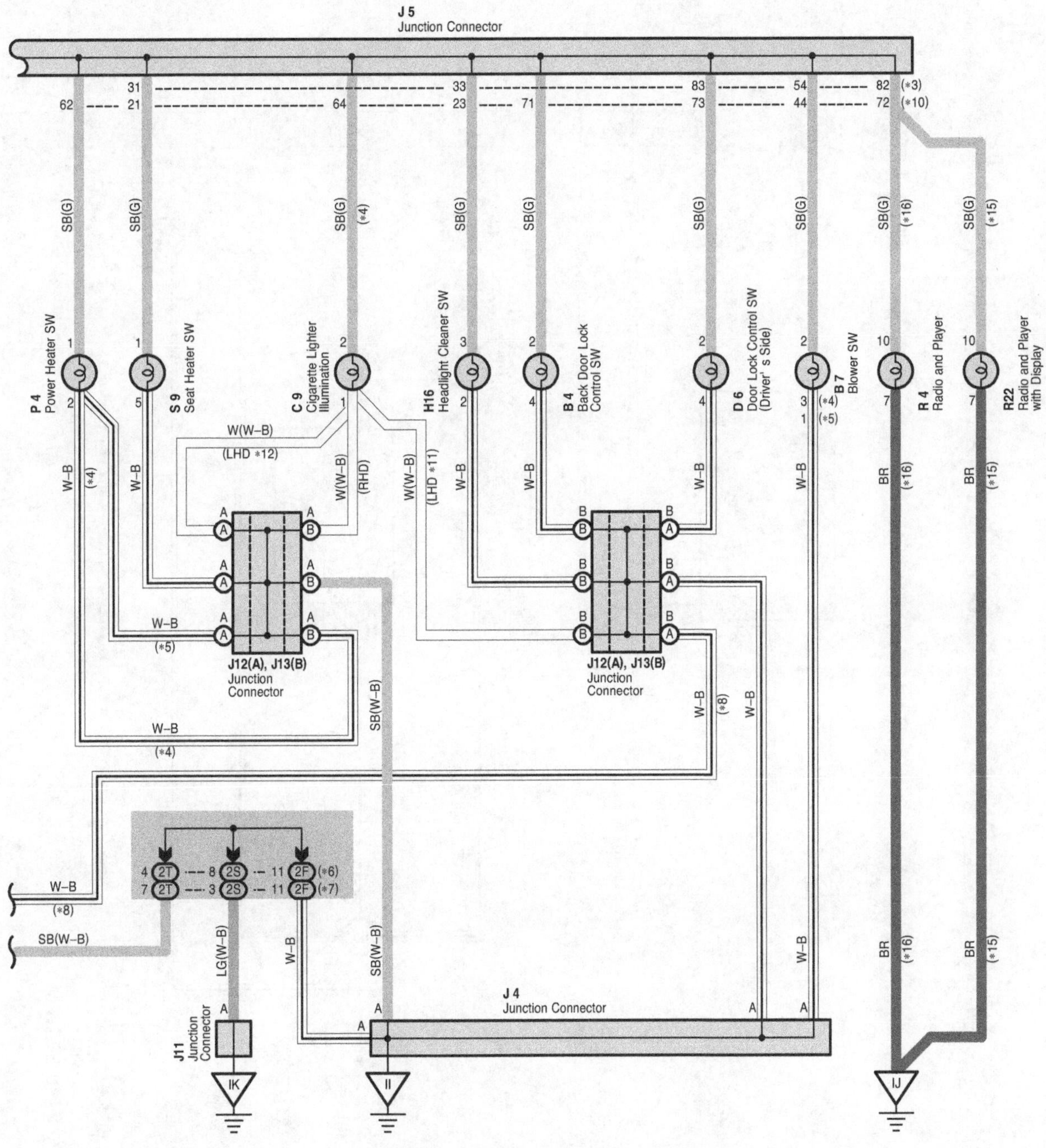

Diagram 12c - Interior illumination (continued)

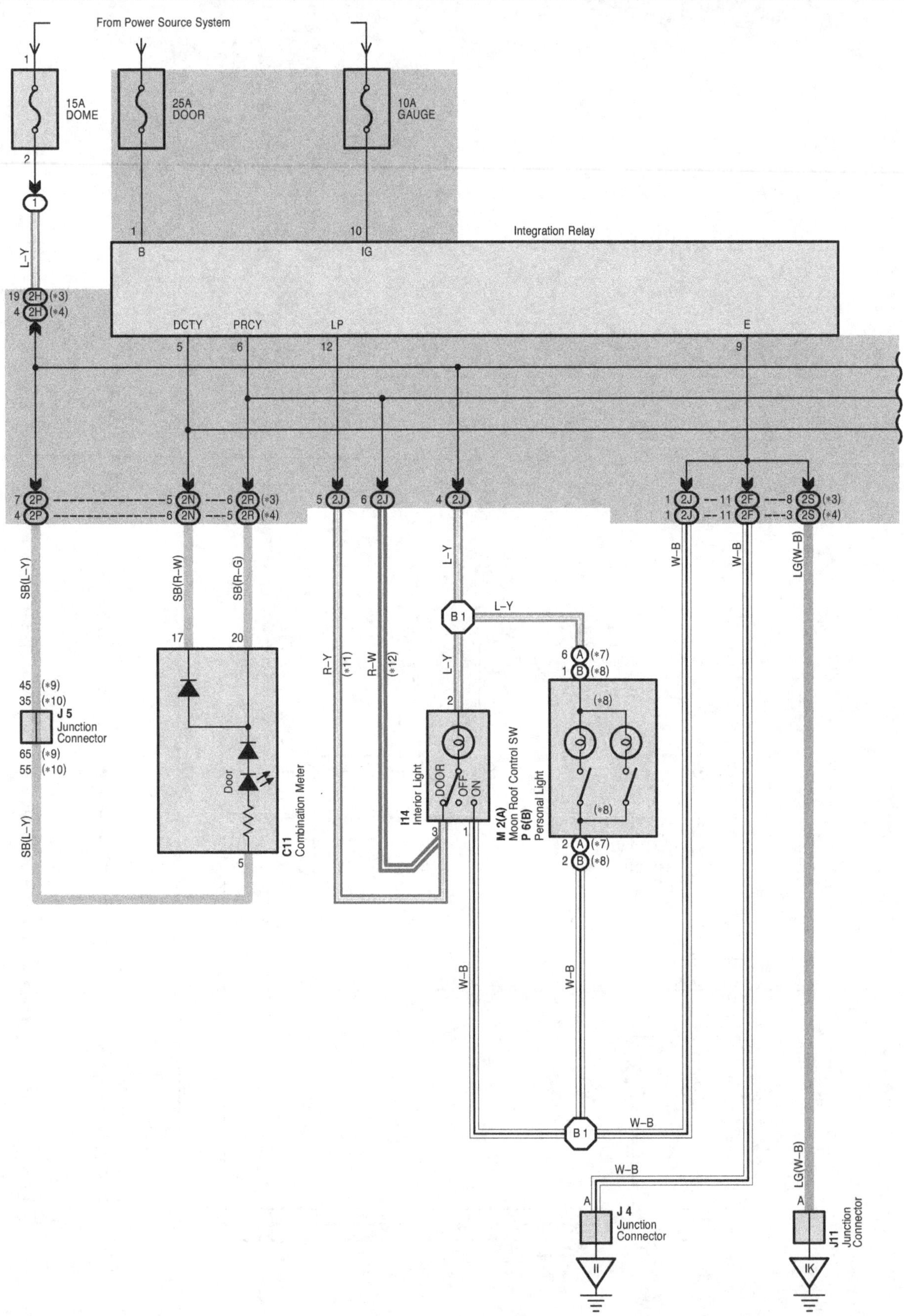

Diagram 13a - Interior lighting

∗ 1 : Gasoline
∗ 2 : Diesel
∗ 3 : LHD TMUK Made
∗ 4 : Except LHD TMUK Made
∗ 5 : H/B Gasoline
∗ 6 : W/G, H/B Diesel
∗ 7 : w/ Moon Roof
∗ 8 : w/o Moon Roof
∗ 9 : 2ZZ–GE, 3ZZ–FE TMC Made
∗10 : Except 2ZZ–GE, 3ZZ–FE TMC Made
∗11 : w/ Illuminated Entry
∗12 : w/o Illuminated Entry
∗13 : LHD TMC Made

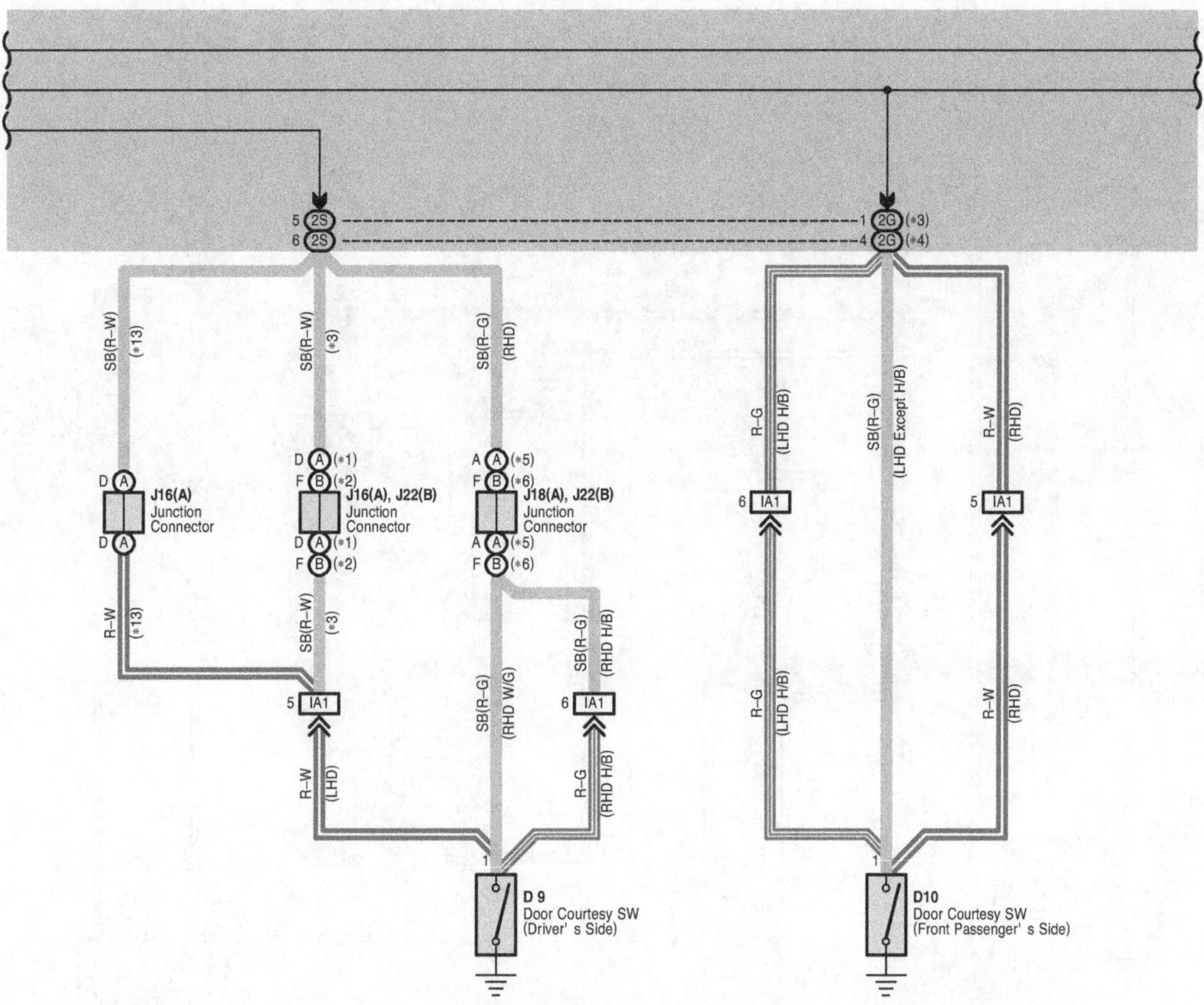

Diagram 13b - Interior lighting (continued)

* 3 : LHD TMUK Made
* 4 : Except LHD TMUK Made
*14 : 5-Door H/B
*15 : W/G, 3-Door H/B
*16 : 3-Door H/B

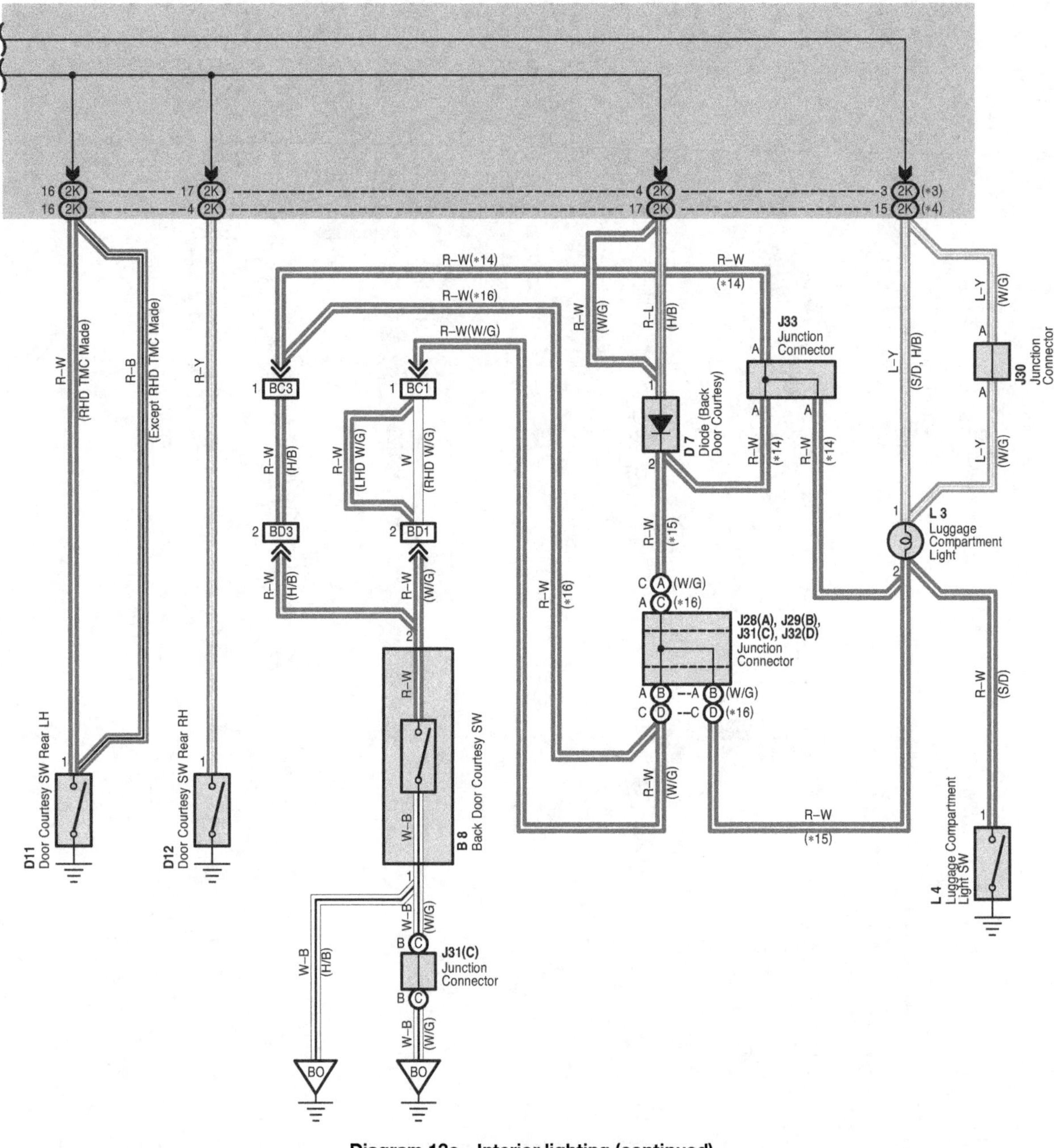

Diagram 13c - Interior lighting (continued)

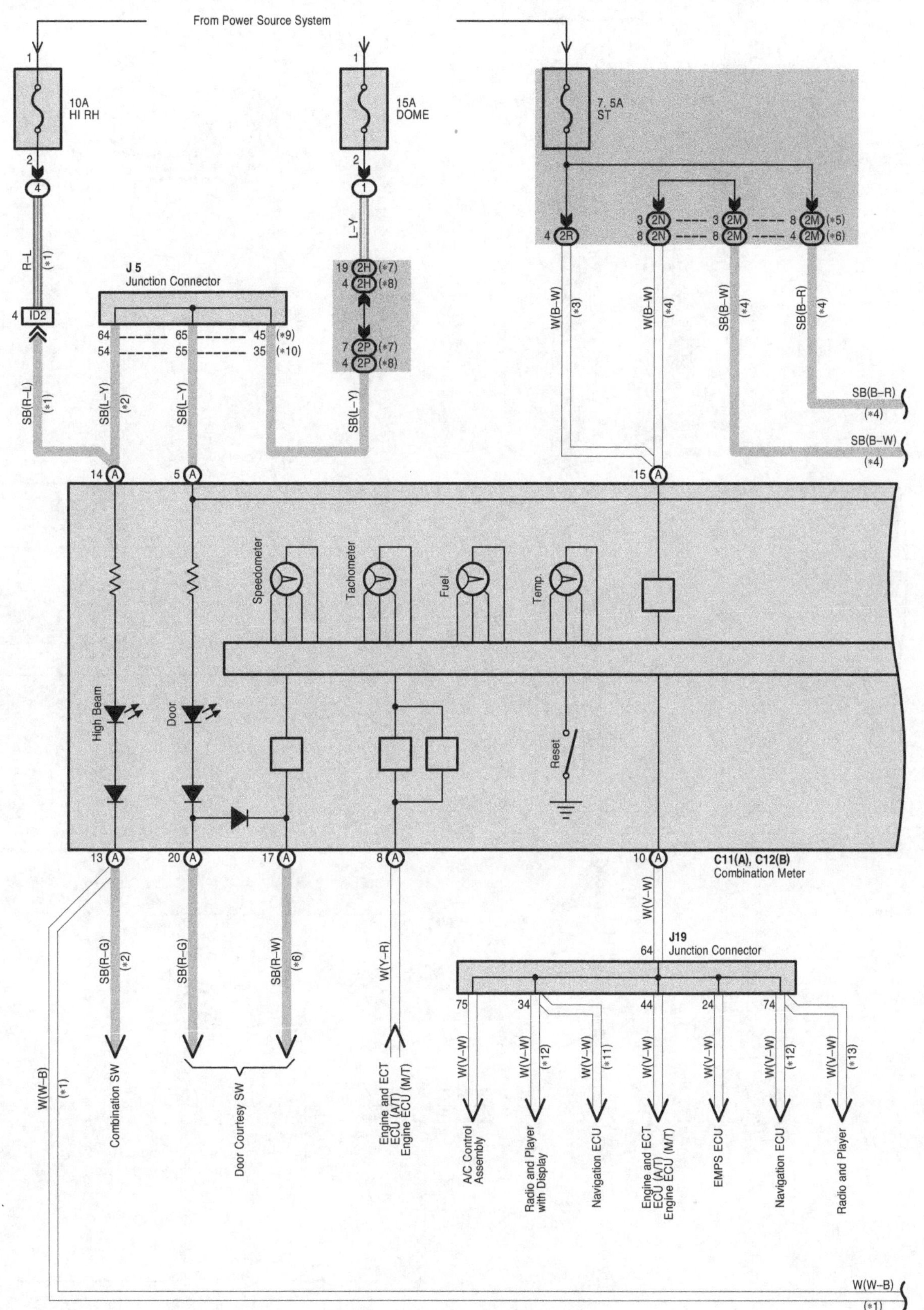

Diagram 14a - Instrument cluster

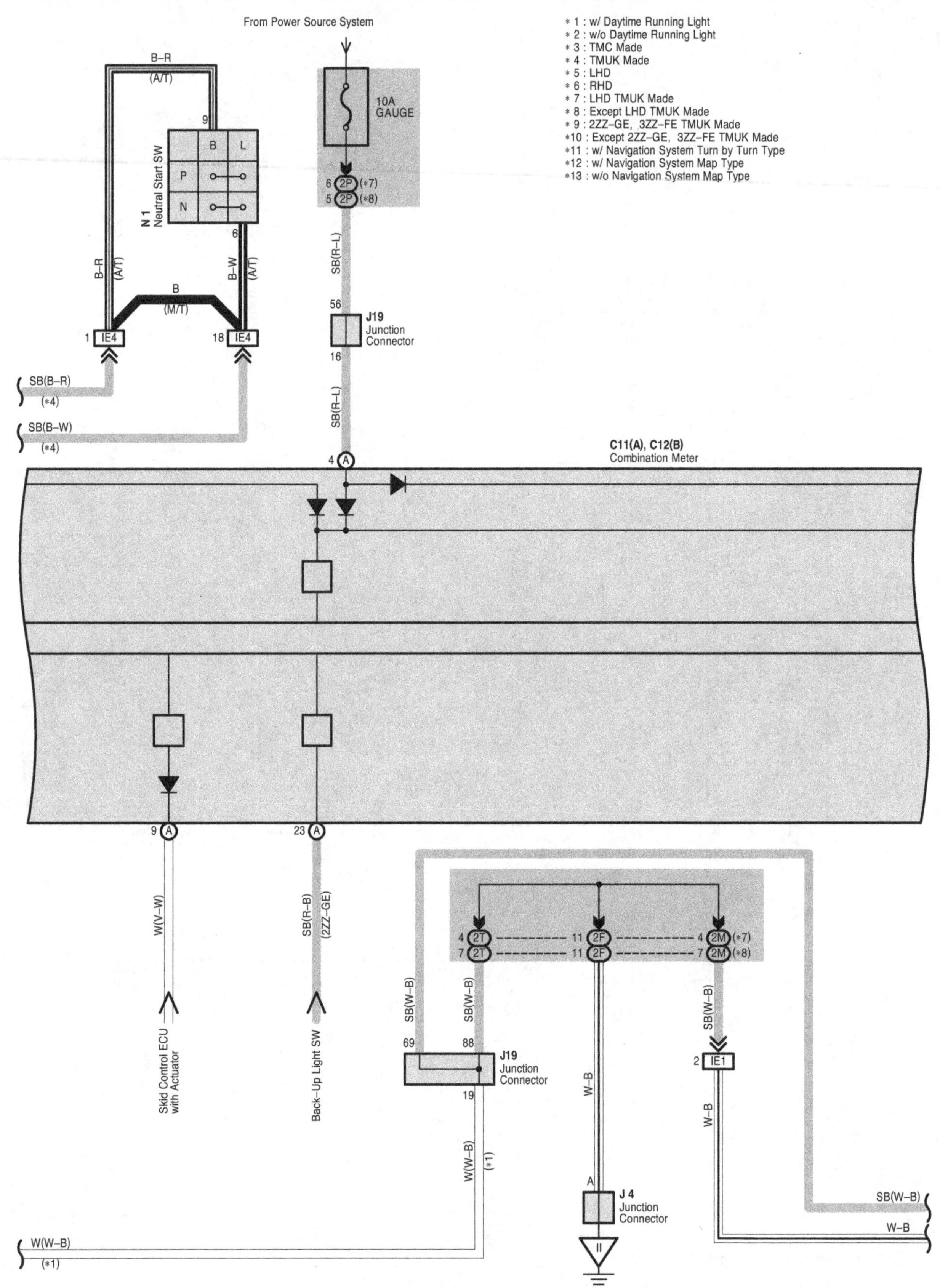

From Power Source System
* 1 : w/ Daytime Running Light
* 2 : w/o Daytime Running Light
* 3 : TMC Made
* 4 : TMUK Made
* 5 : LHD
* 6 : RHD
* 7 : LHD TMUK Made
* 8 : Except LHD TMUK Made
* 9 : 2ZZ–GE, 3ZZ–FE TMUK Made
*10 : Except 2ZZ–GE, 3ZZ–FE TMUK Made
*11 : w/ Navigation System Turn by Turn Type
*12 : w/ Navigation System Map Type
*13 : w/o Navigation System Map Type
B–R
(A/T)
10A
GAUGE
N 1
Neutral Start SW
B L
P
N
J19
Junction
Connector
SB(B–R)
(*4)
SB(B–W)
(*4)
C11(A), C12(B)
Combination Meter
W(V–W)
SB(R–B)
(2ZZ–GE)
Skid Control ECU
with Actuator
Back–Up Light SW
SB(W–B)
W–B
J 4
Junction
Connector
W(W–B)
(*1)

Diagram 14b - Instrument cluster (continued)

*1 : w/ Daytime Running Light
*2 : w/o Daytime Running Light
*3 : TMC Made
*4 : TMUK Made
*7 : LHD TMUK Made
*8 : Except LHD TMUK Made
*14 : Optitron Meter
*15 : Except Optitron Meter

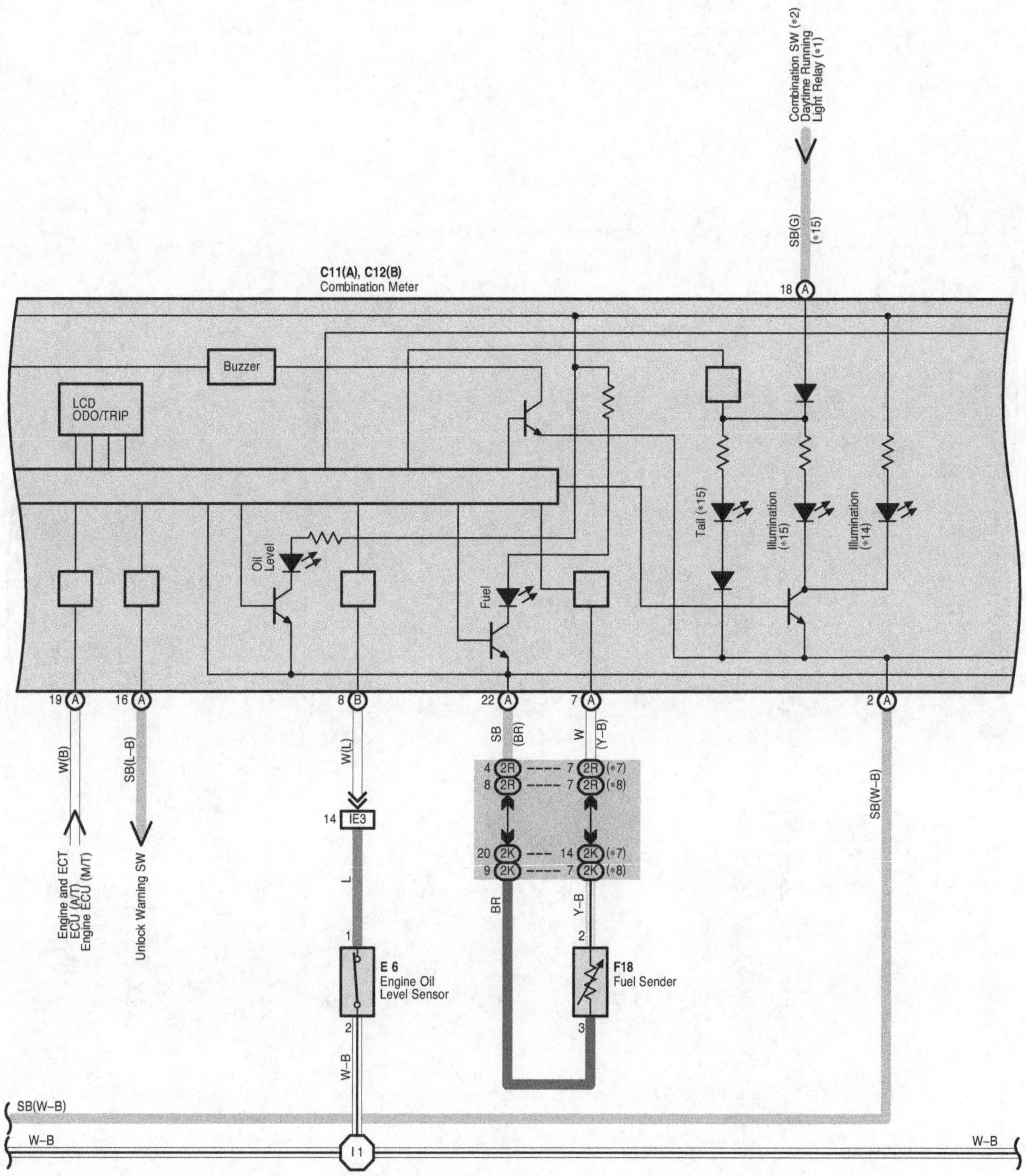

Diagram 14c - Instrument cluster (continued)

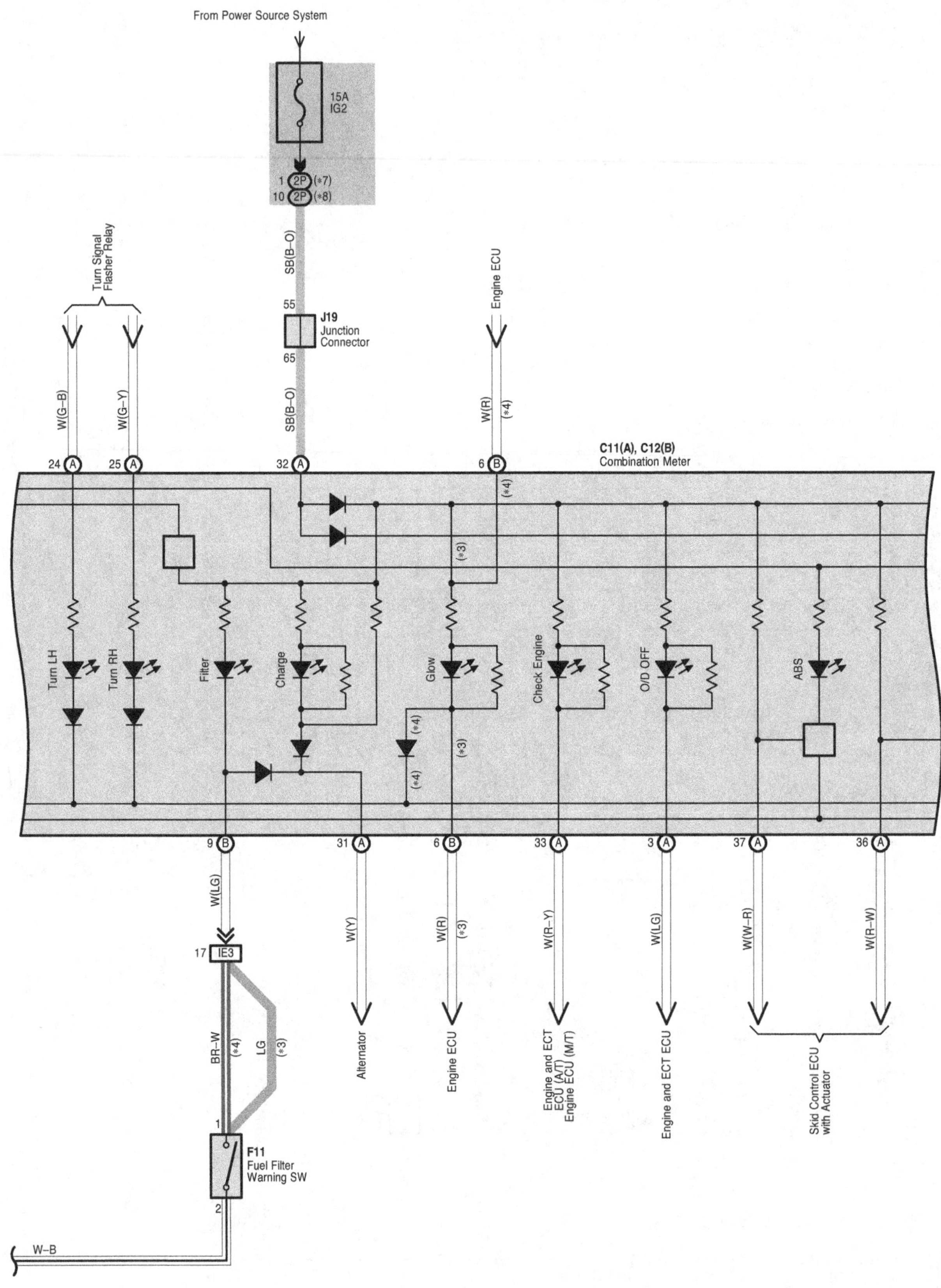

Diagram 14d - Instrument cluster (continued)

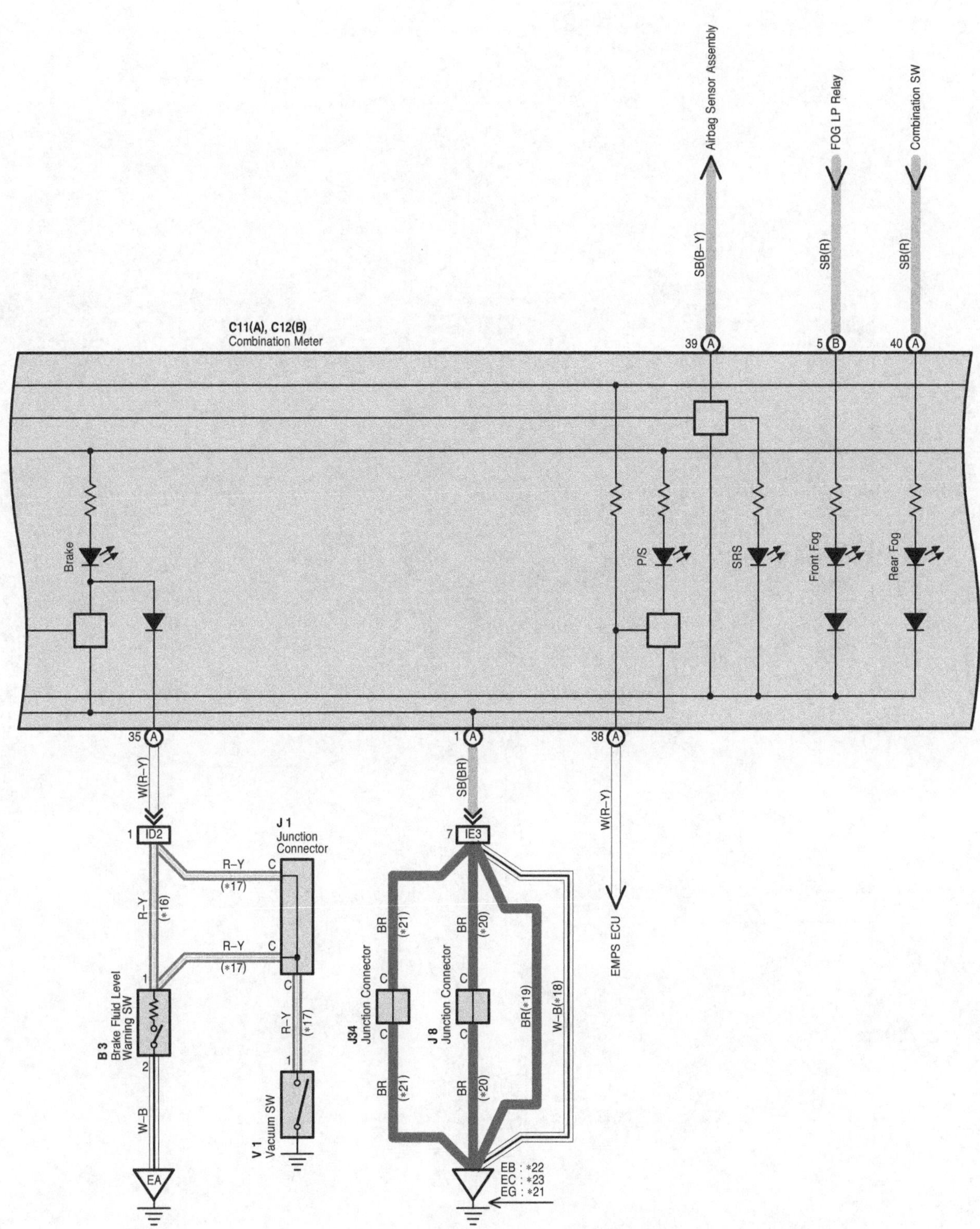

Diagram 14e - Instrument cluster (continued)

*16 : Gasoline
*17 : Diesel
*18 : 4ZZ–FE TMC Made
*19 : LHD TMC Made 3ZZ–FE, TMUK Made Except 2ZZ–GE 1CD–FTV
*20 : 2ZZ–GE, RHD TMC Made 3ZZ–FE
*21 : 1CD–FTV
*22 : Gasoline Except 4ZZ–FE
*23 : 4ZZ–FE

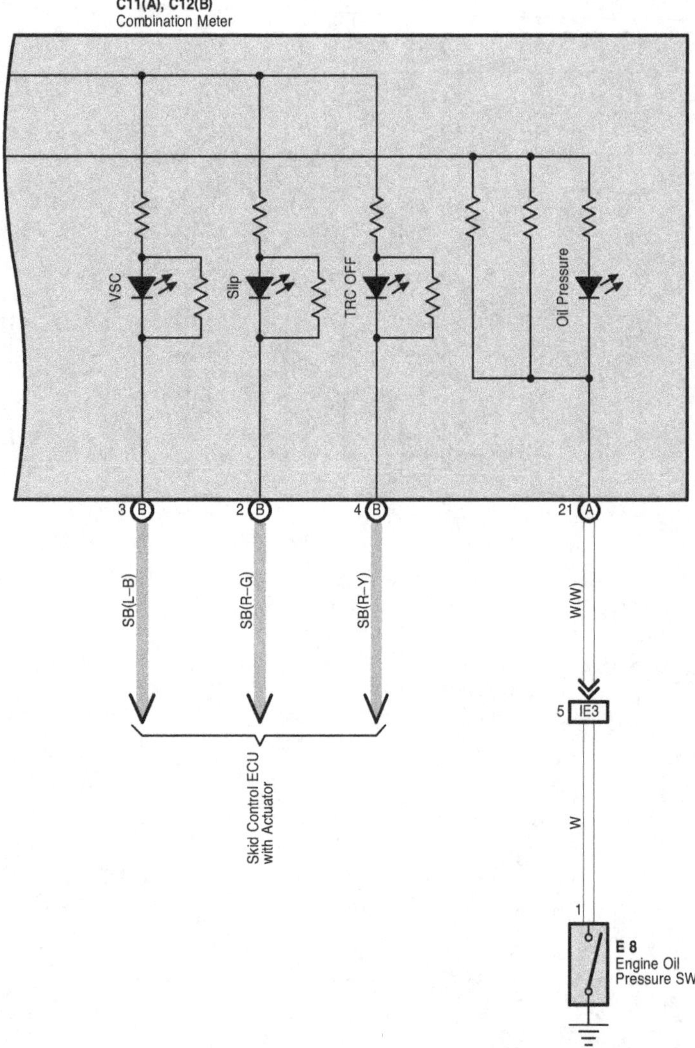

Diagram 14f - Instrument cluster (continued)

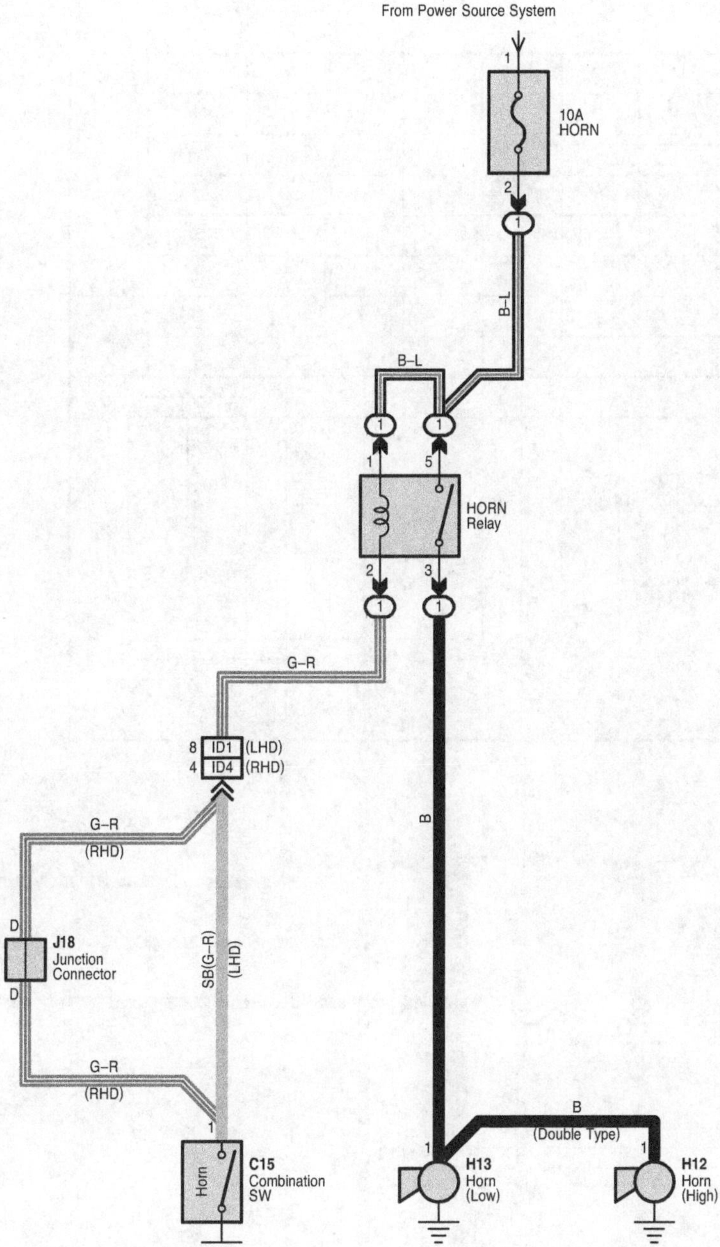
From Power Source System
1
10A
HORN
2
1
B–L
B–L
1
1
1
5
HORN
Relay
2
3
1
1
G–R
8 ID1 (LHD)
4 ID4 (RHD)
G–R
(RHD)
D
J18
Junction
Connector
D
SB(G–R)
(LHD)
B
G–R
(RHD)
1
Horn
C15
Combination
SW
B
(Double Type)
1
H13
Horn
(Low)
1
H12
Horn
(High)

Diagram 15 - Horn

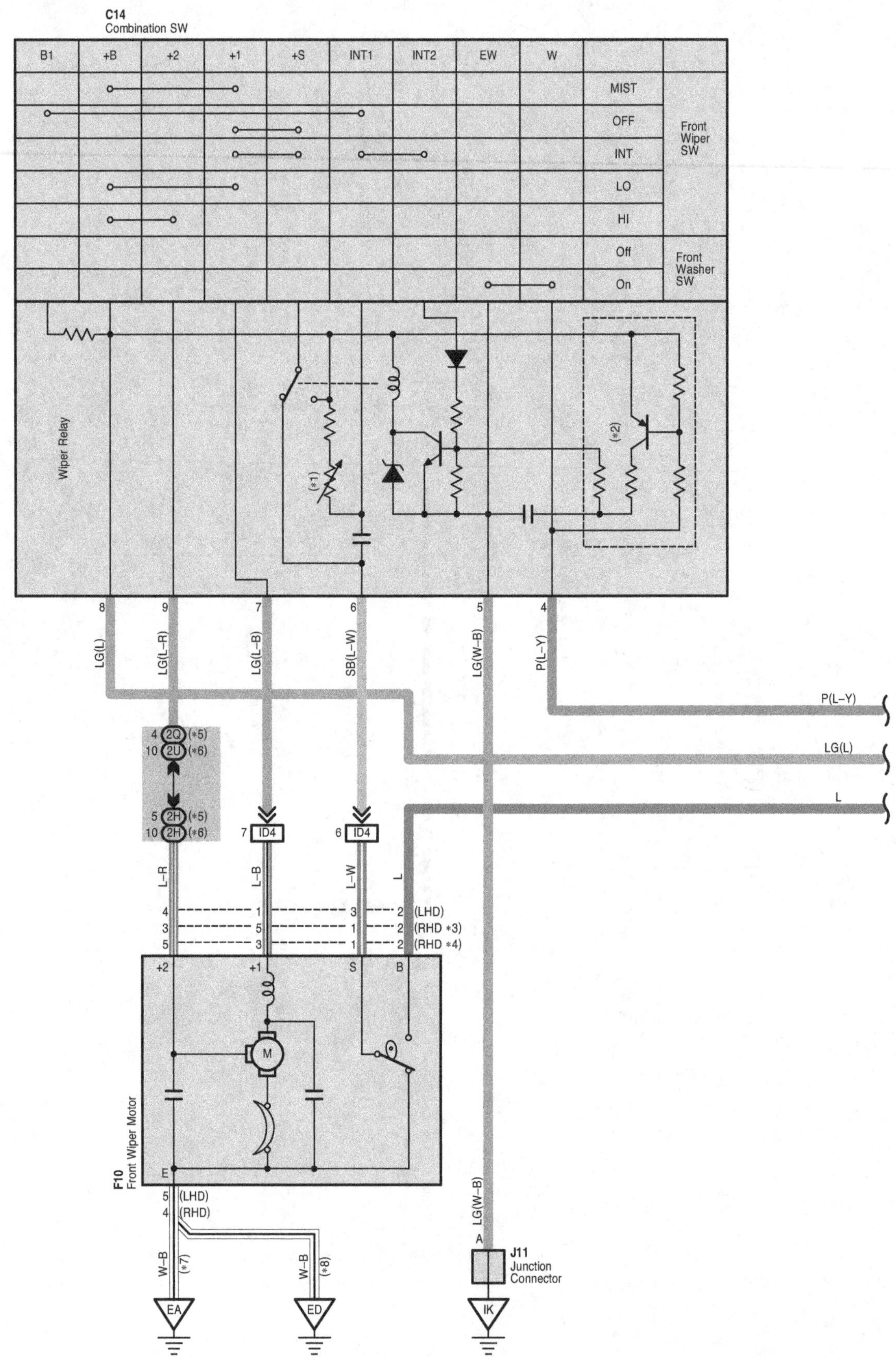

Diagram 16a - Front wash/wipe

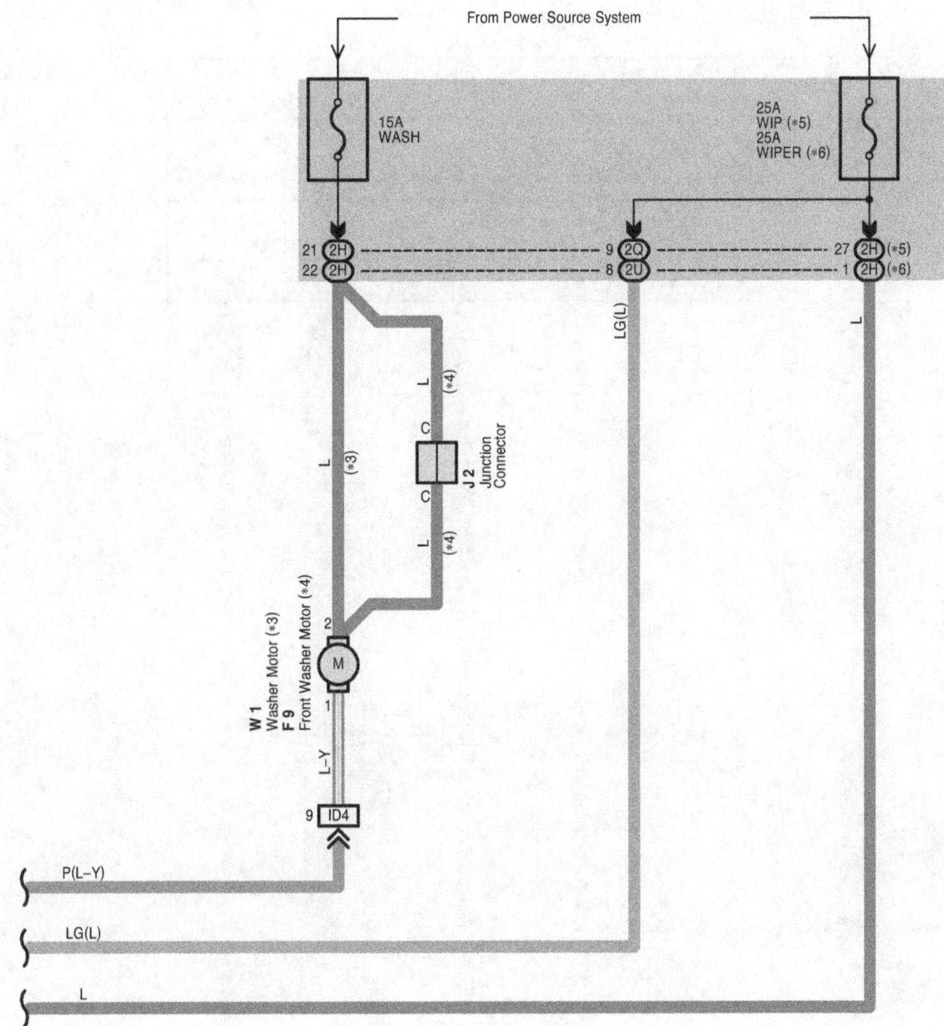

* 1 : Intermittent Volume SW
* 2 : w/ Washer Continuous
* 3 : TMC Made
* 4 : TMUK Made
* 5 : Except LHD TMUK Made
* 6 : LHD TMUK Made
* 7 : TMC Made RHD Gasoline
* 8 : Except TMC Made RHD Gasoline

Diagram 16b - Front wash/wipe (continued)

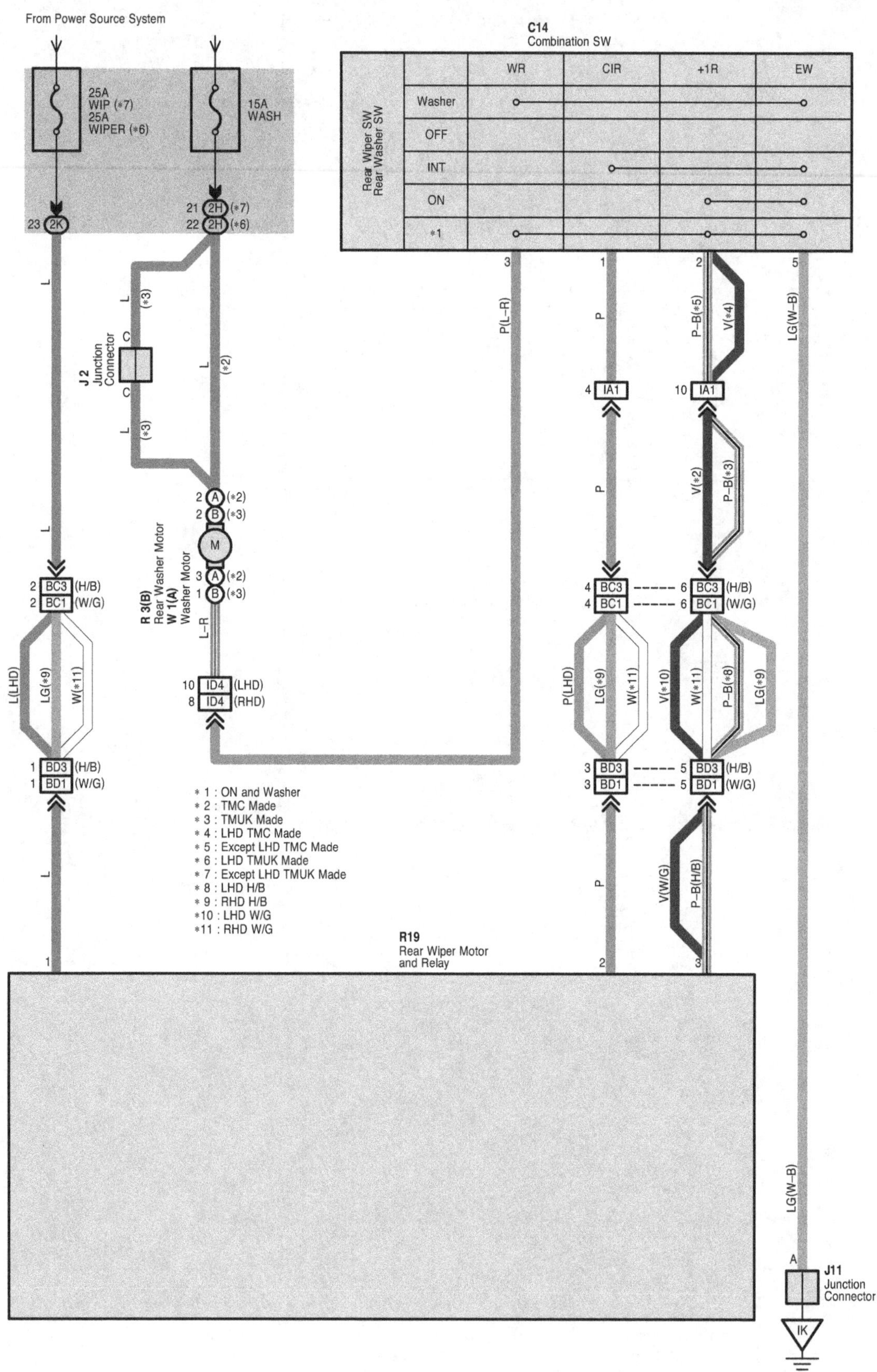

Diagram 17 – Rear wash/wipe

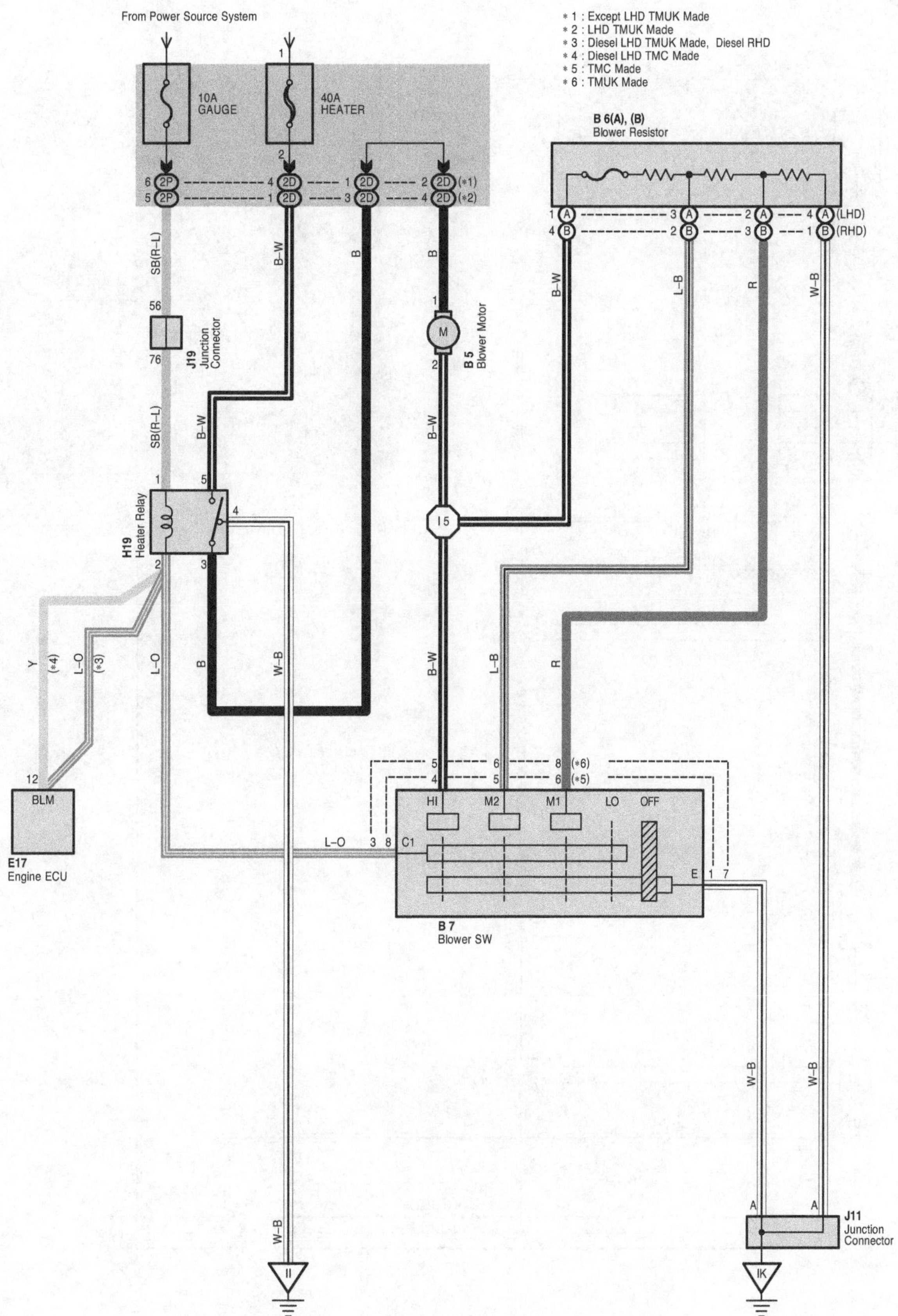

Diagram 18 – Heater

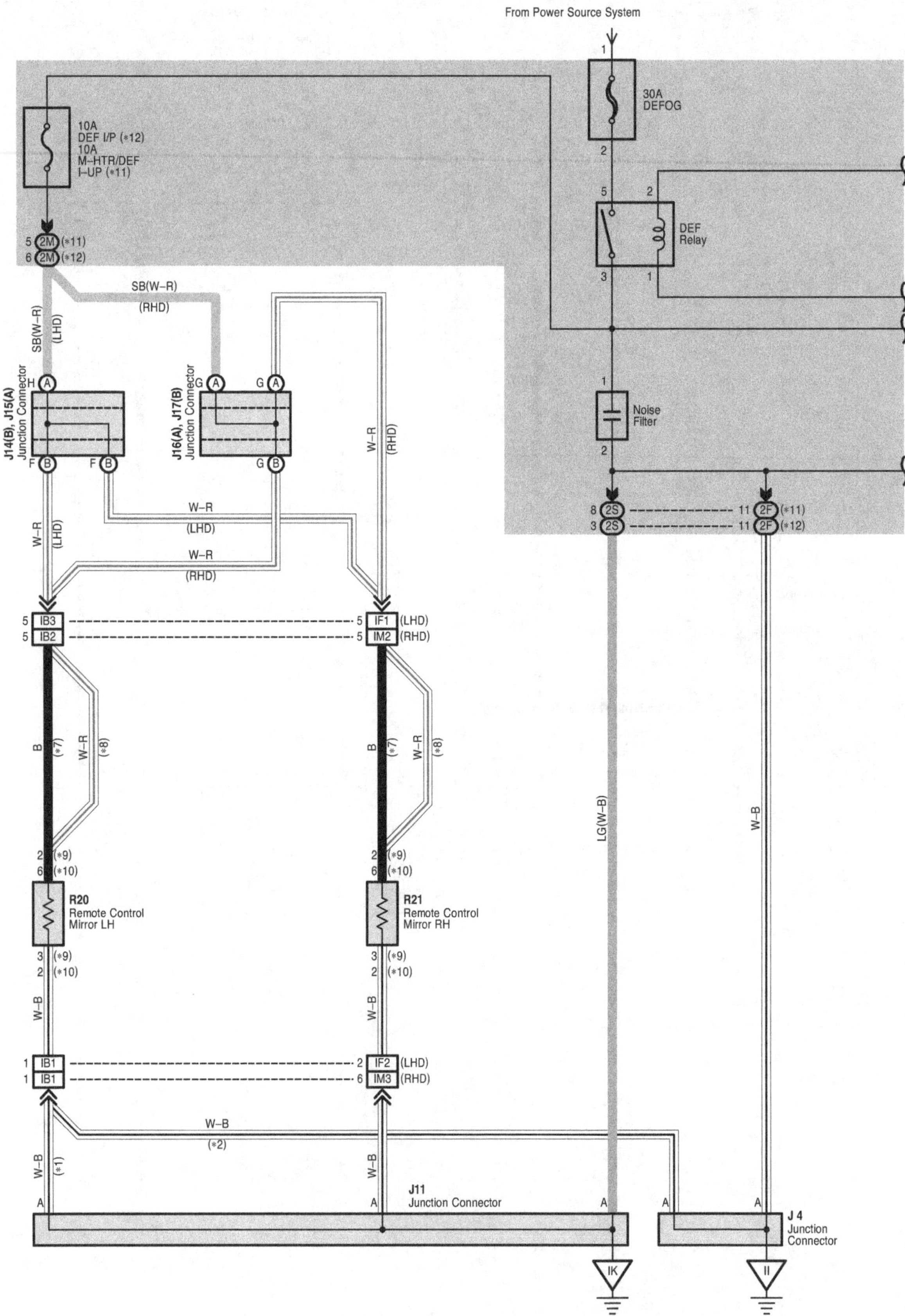

Diagram 19a - Heated rear window and heated mirrors

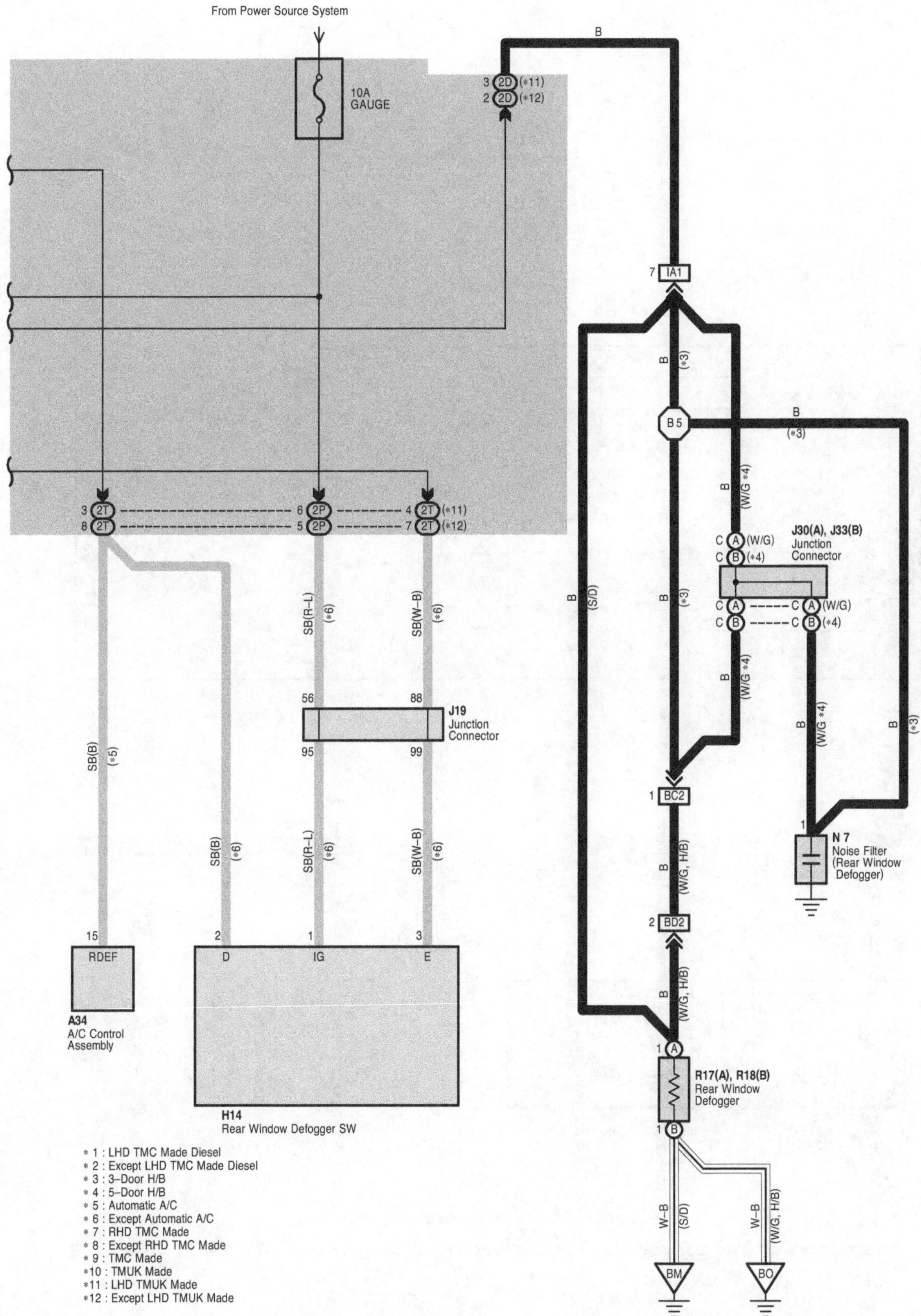

* 1 : LHD TMC Made Diesel
* 2 : Except LHD TMC Made Diesel
* 3 : 3–Door H/B
* 4 : 5–Door H/B
* 5 : Automatic A/C
* 6 : Except Automatic A/C
* 7 : RHD TMC Made
* 8 : Except RHD TMC Made
* 9 : TMC Made
*10 : TMUK Made
*11 : LHD TMUK Made
*12 : Except LHD TMUK Made

Diagram 19b - Heated rear window and heated mirrors (continued)

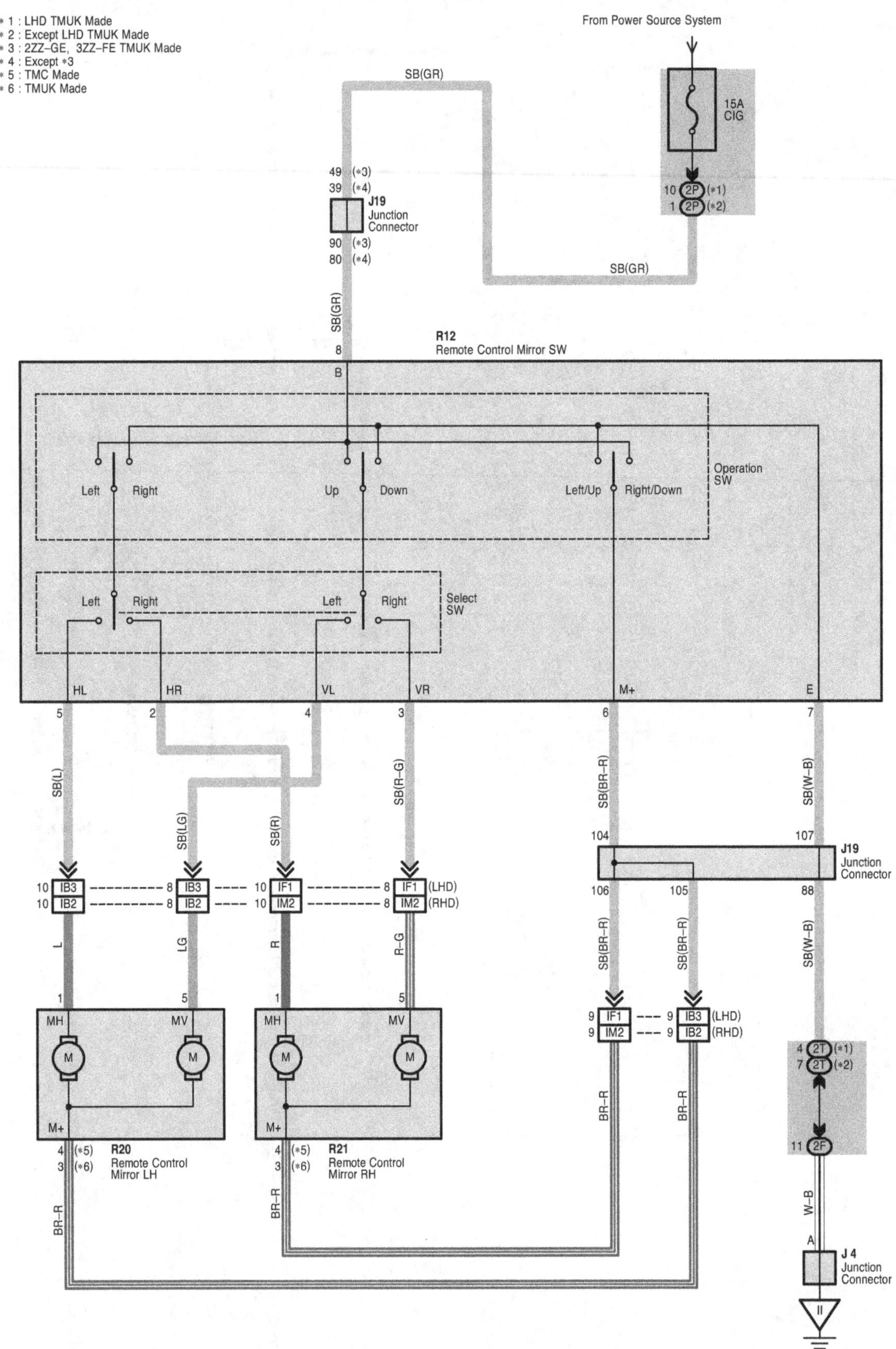

Diagram 20 - Electric mirrors

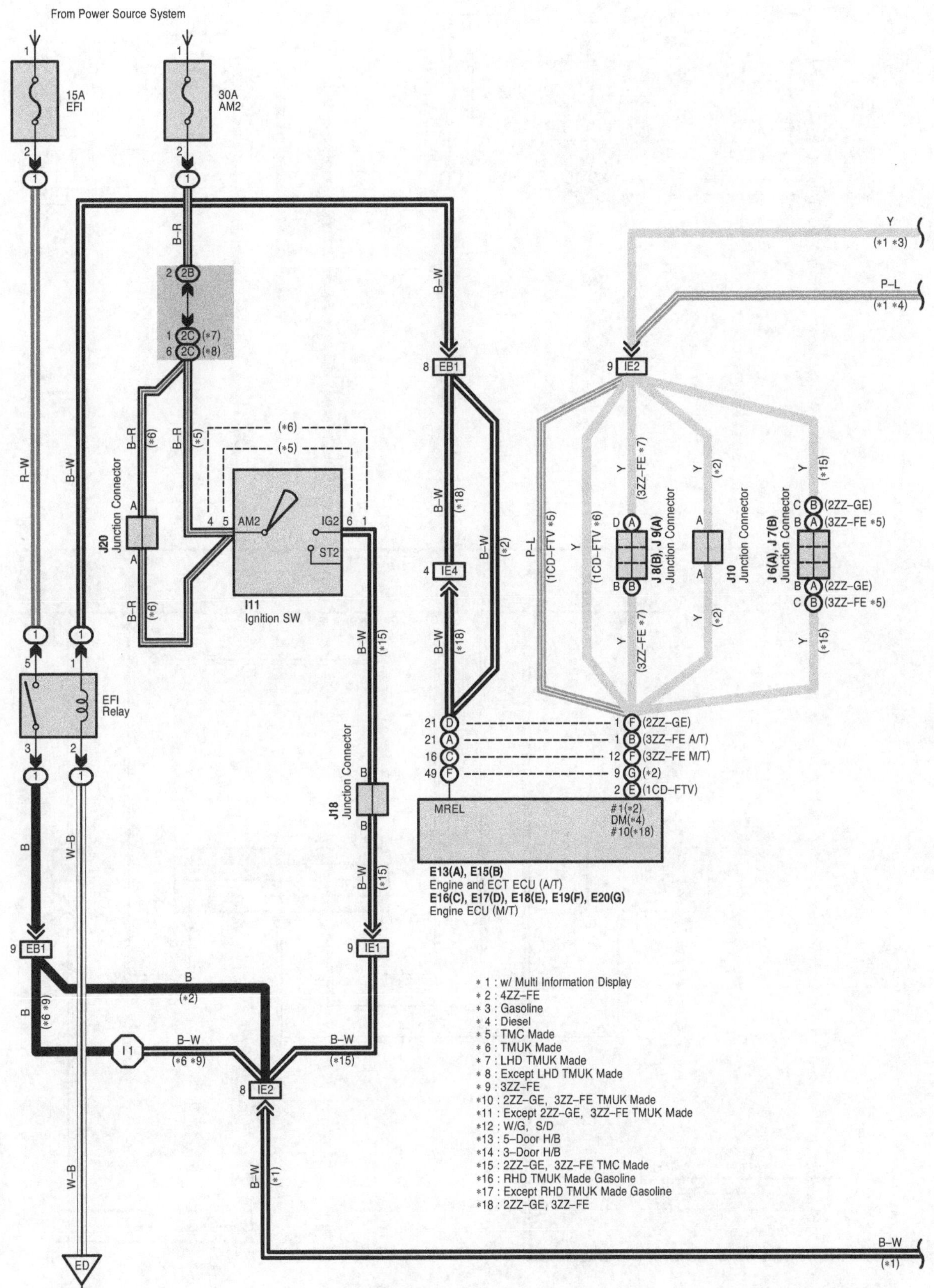

Diagram 21a - Audio system

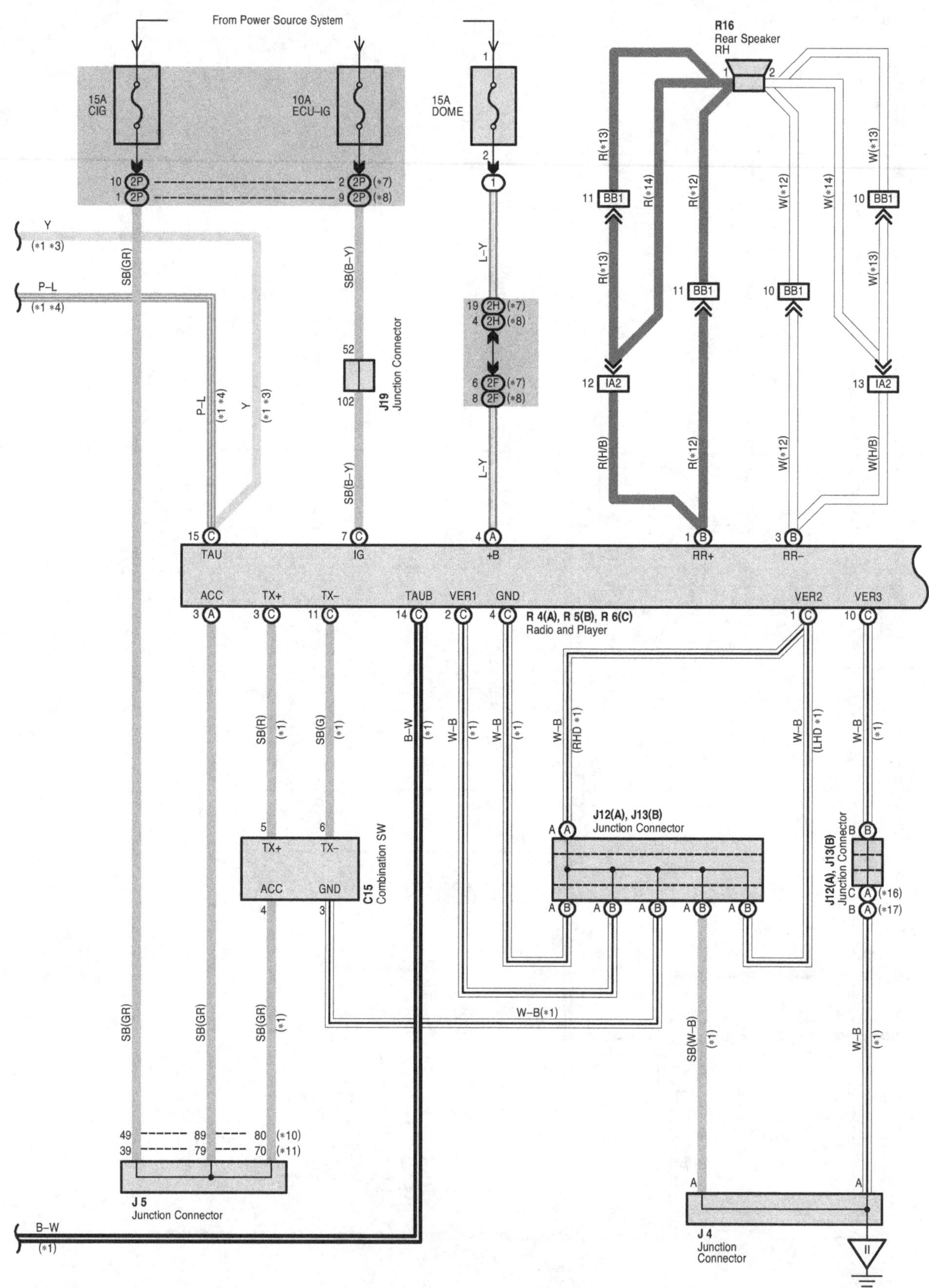

Diagram 21b - Audio system (continued)

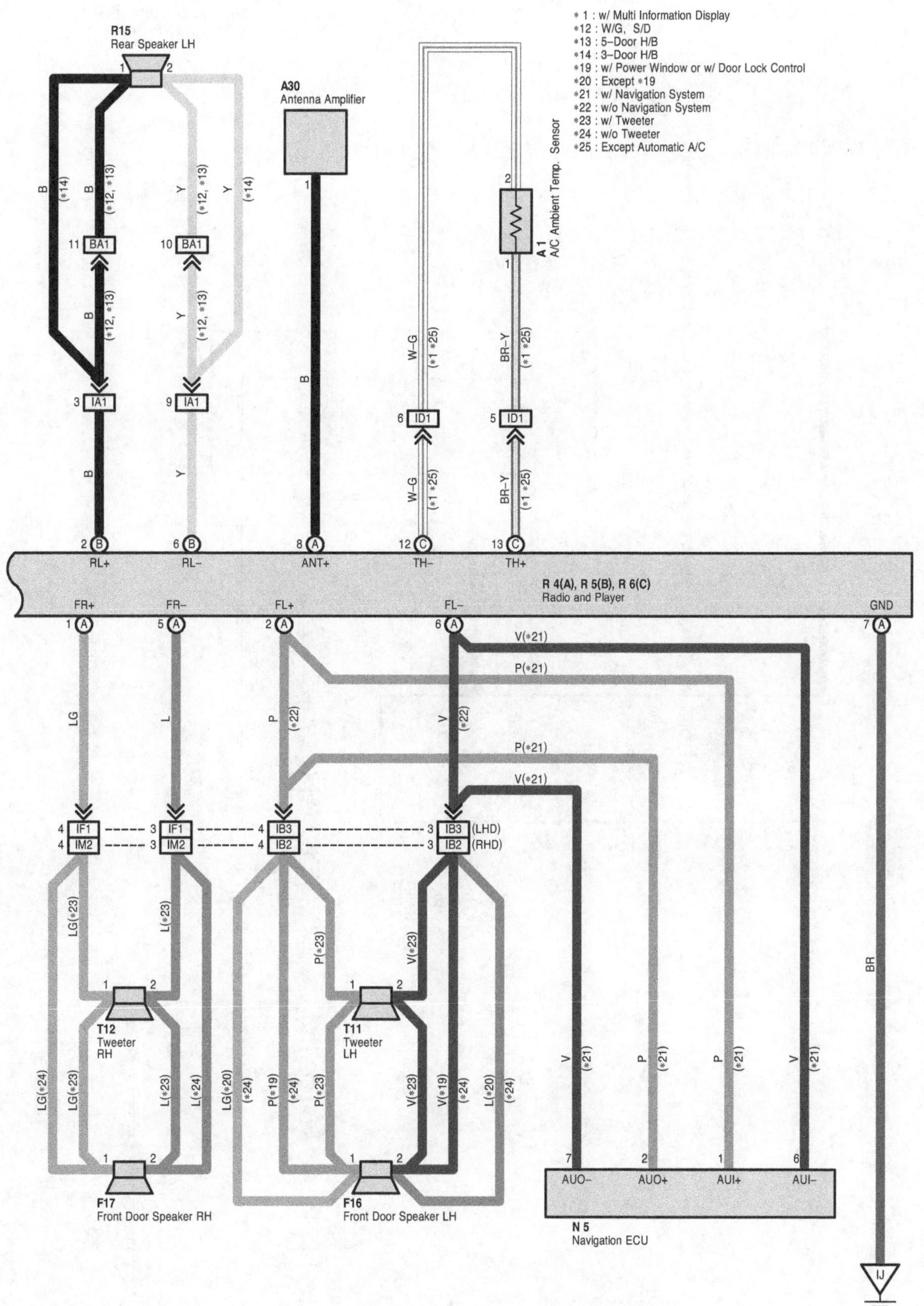

Diagram 21c - Audio system (continued)

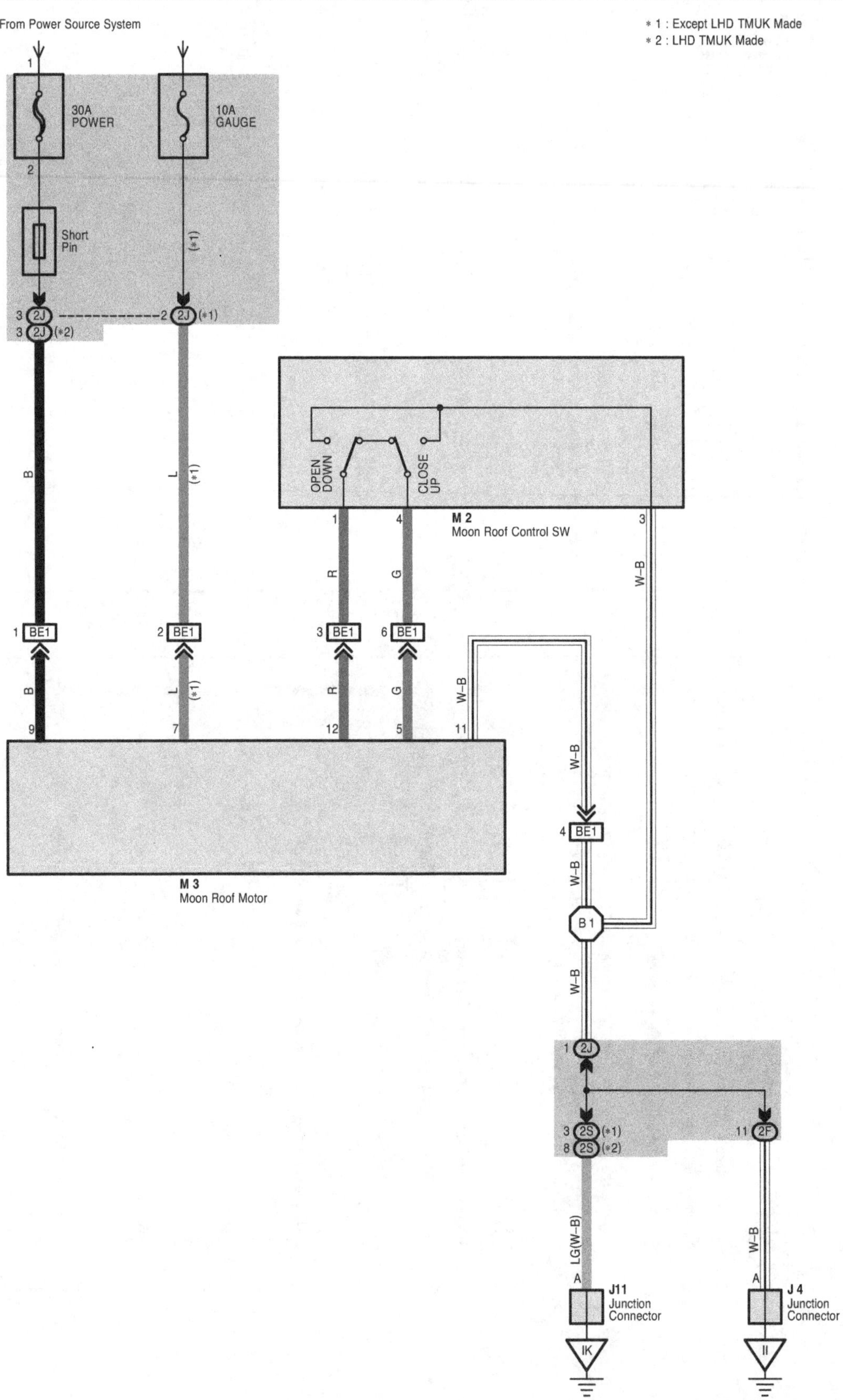

Diagram 22 - Sunroof

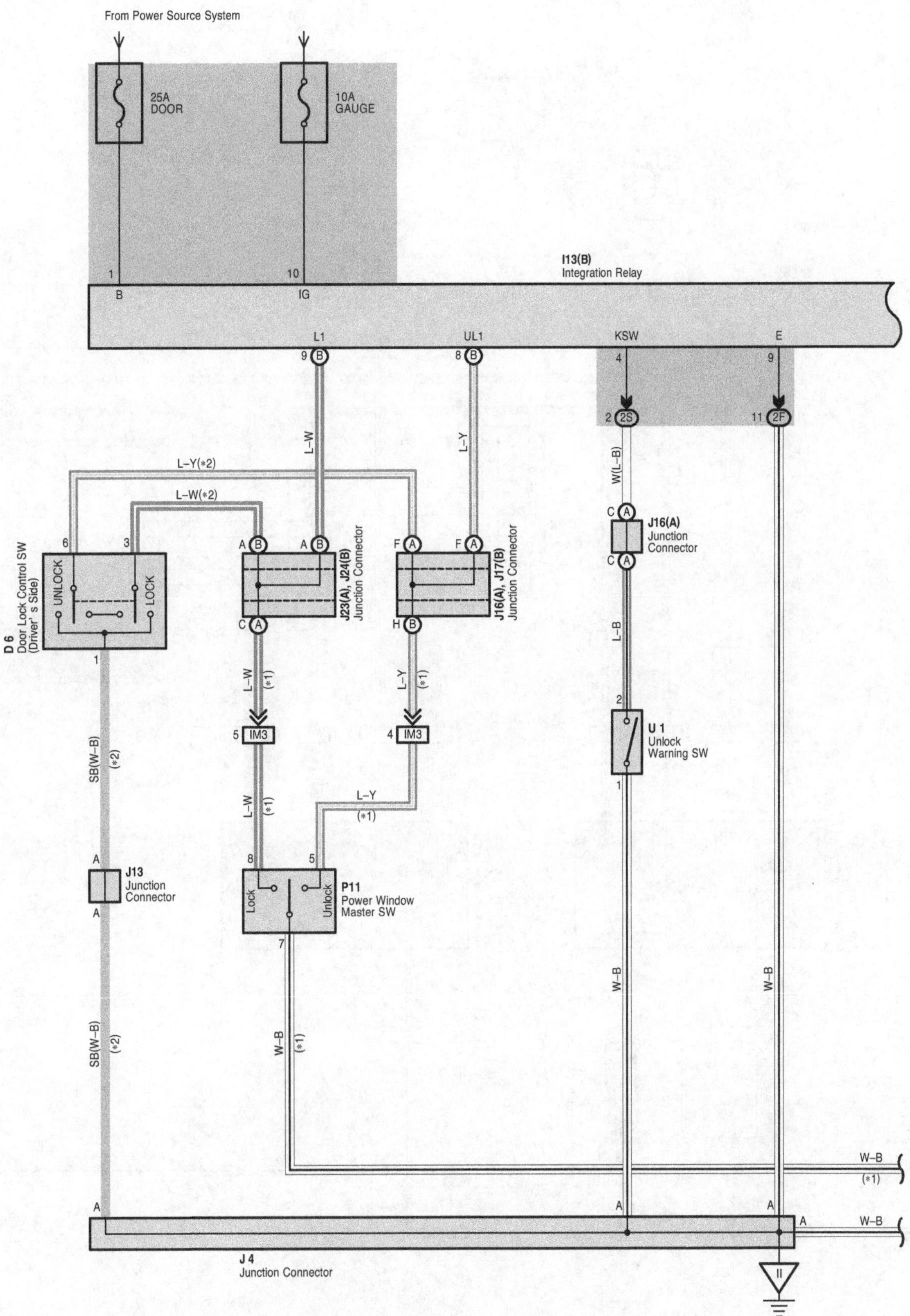

Diagram 23a - Central locking (double locking)

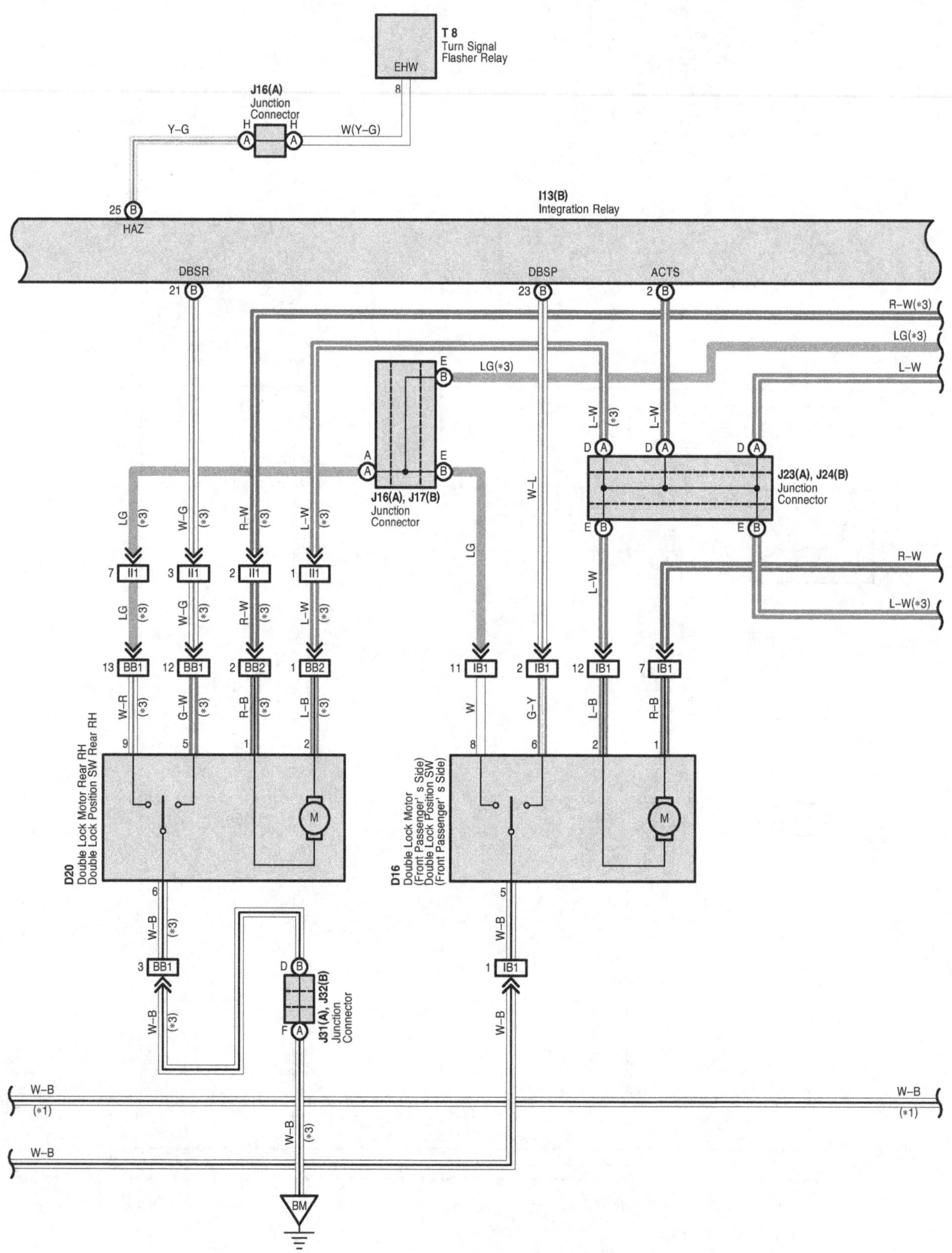

Diagram 23b - Central locking (double locking) (continued)

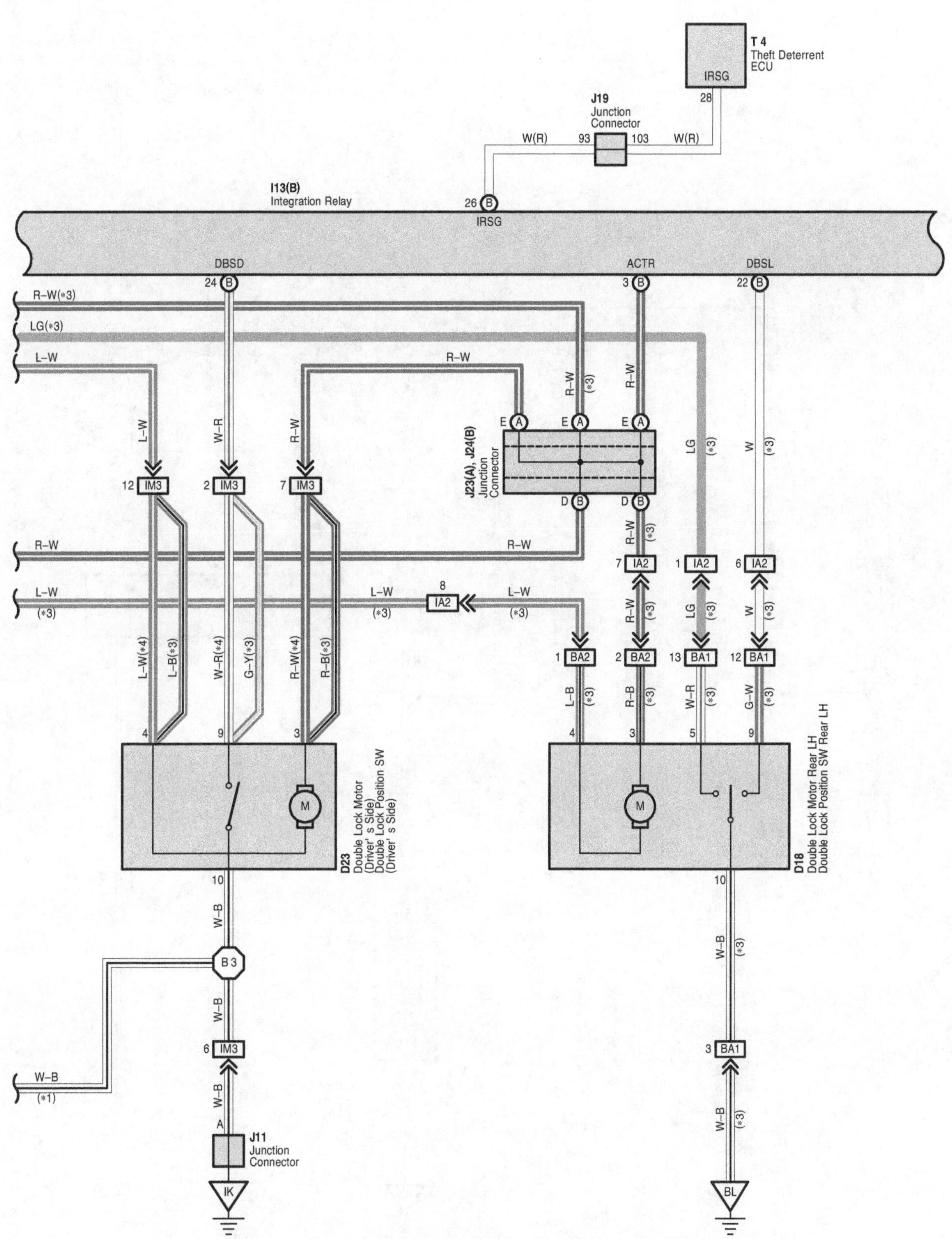

Diagram 23c - Central locking (double locking) (continued)

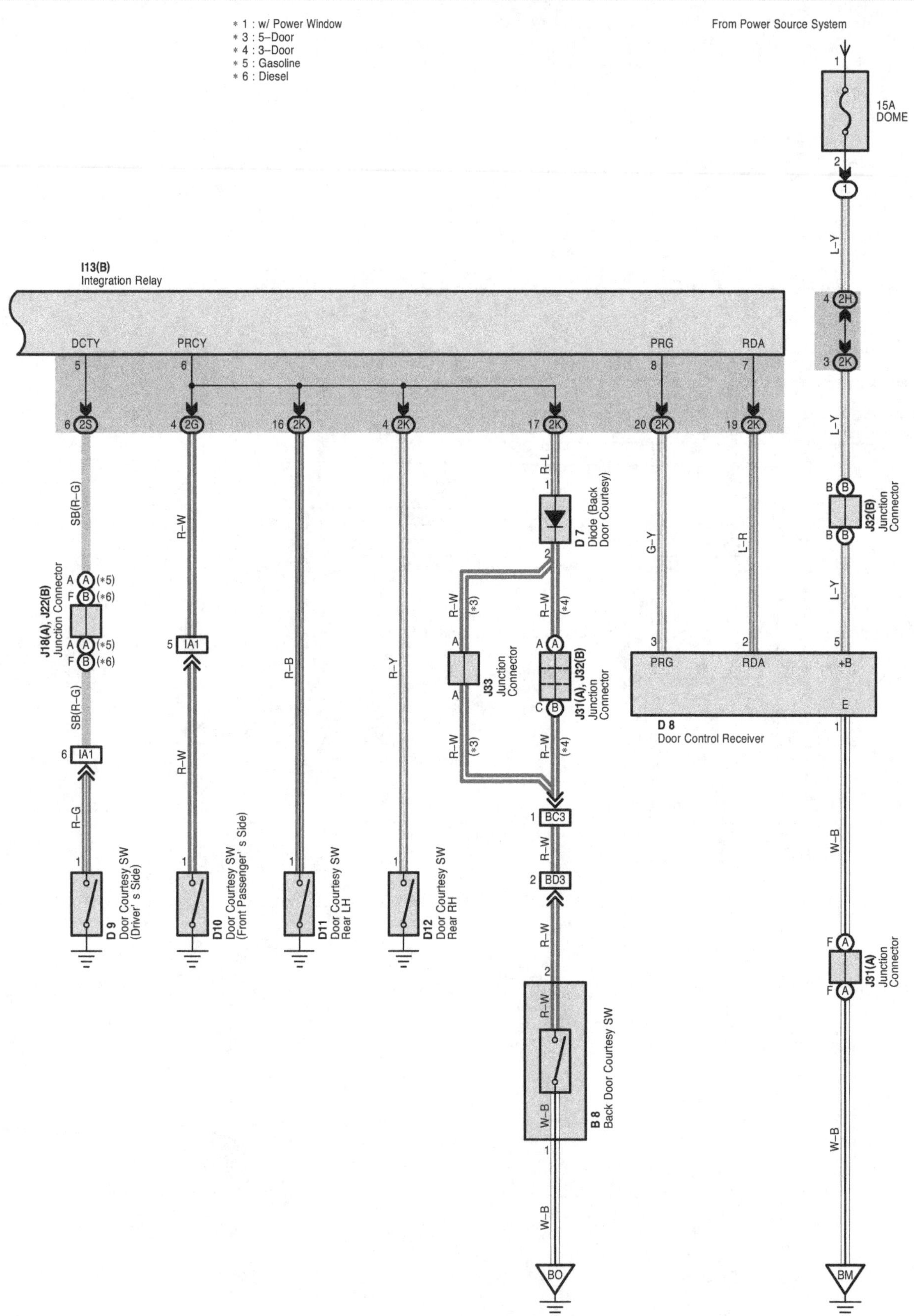

Diagram 23d - Central locking (double locking) (continued)

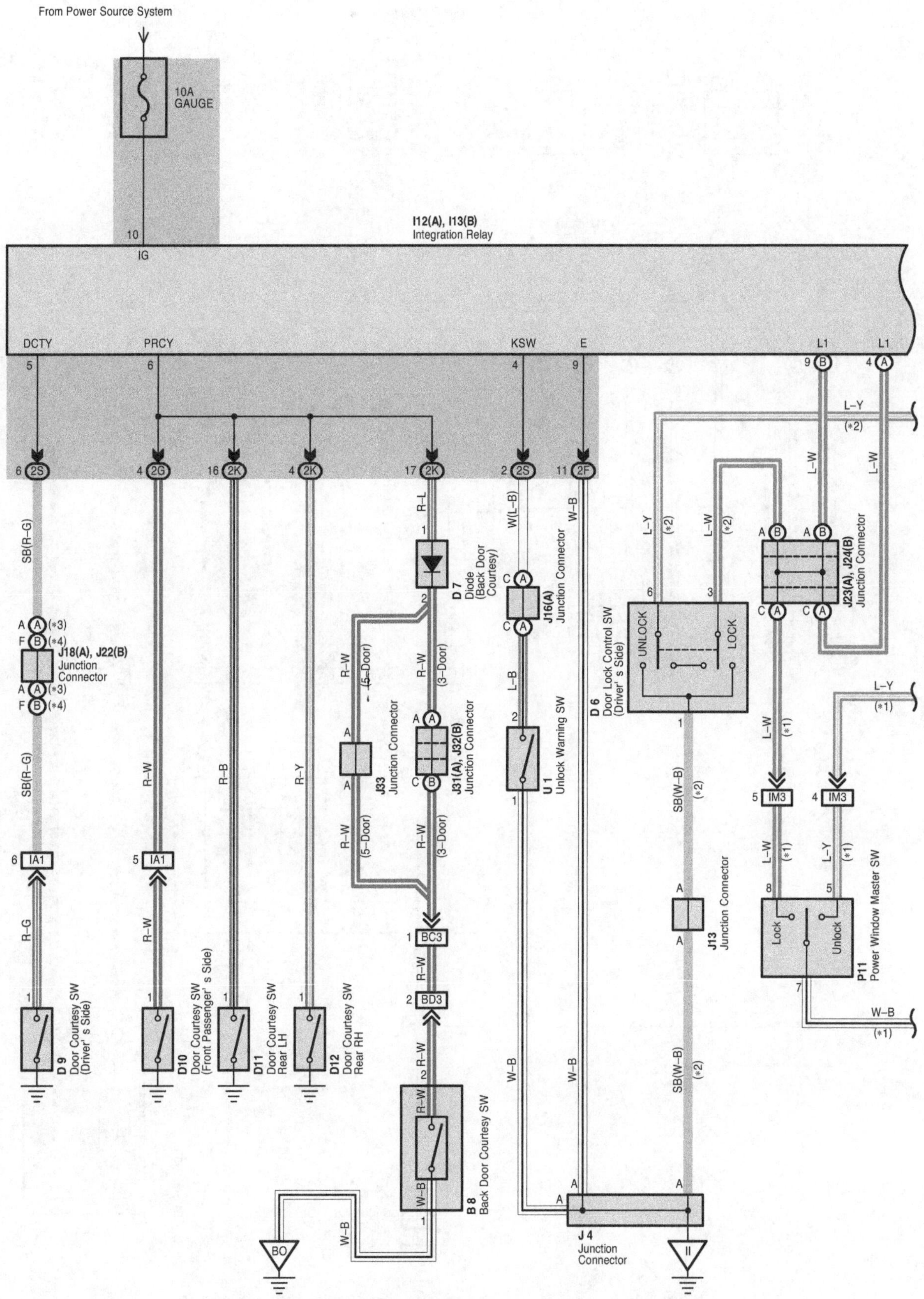

Diagram 24a - Remote central locking

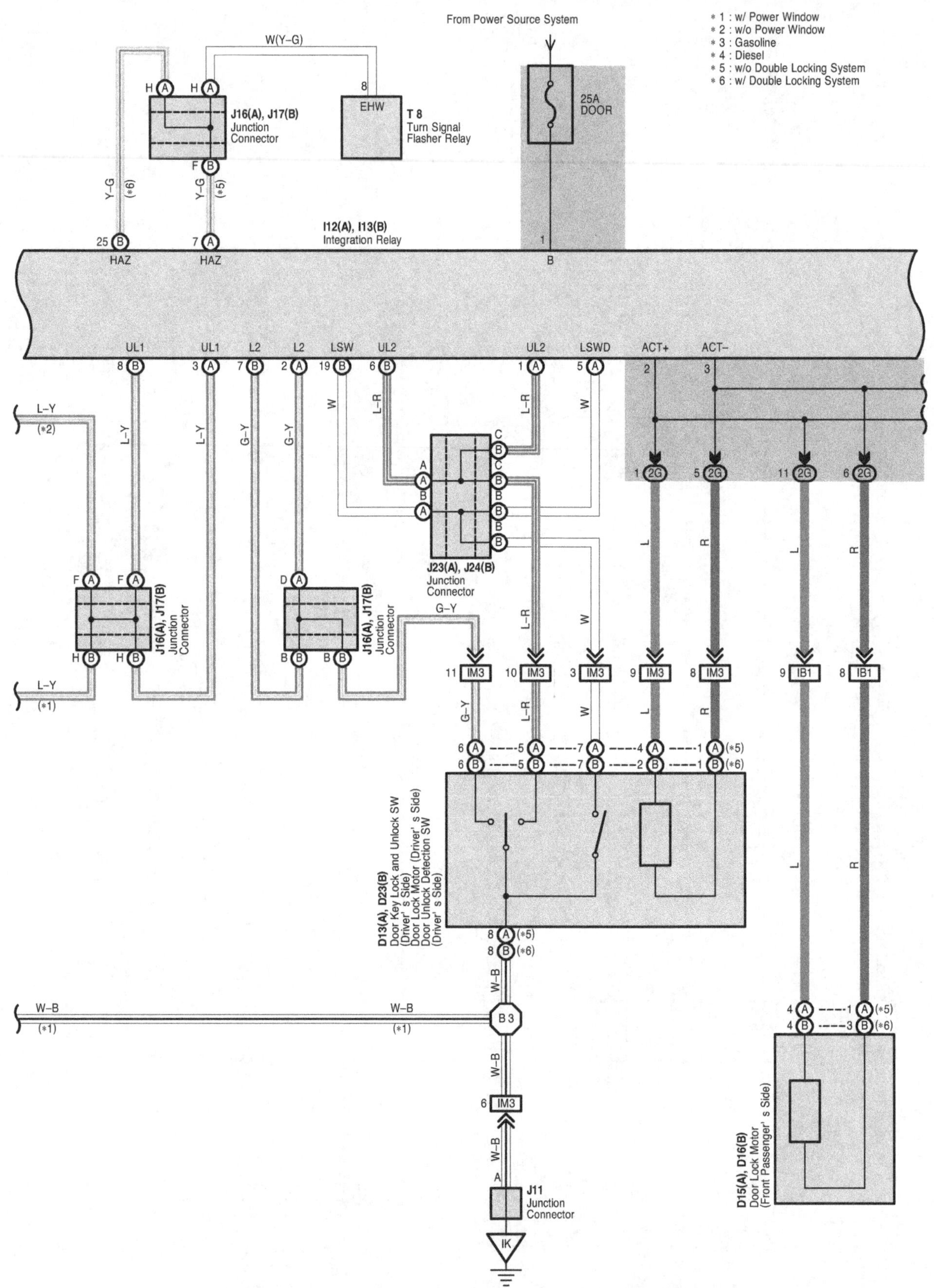

Diagram 24b - Remote central locking (continued)

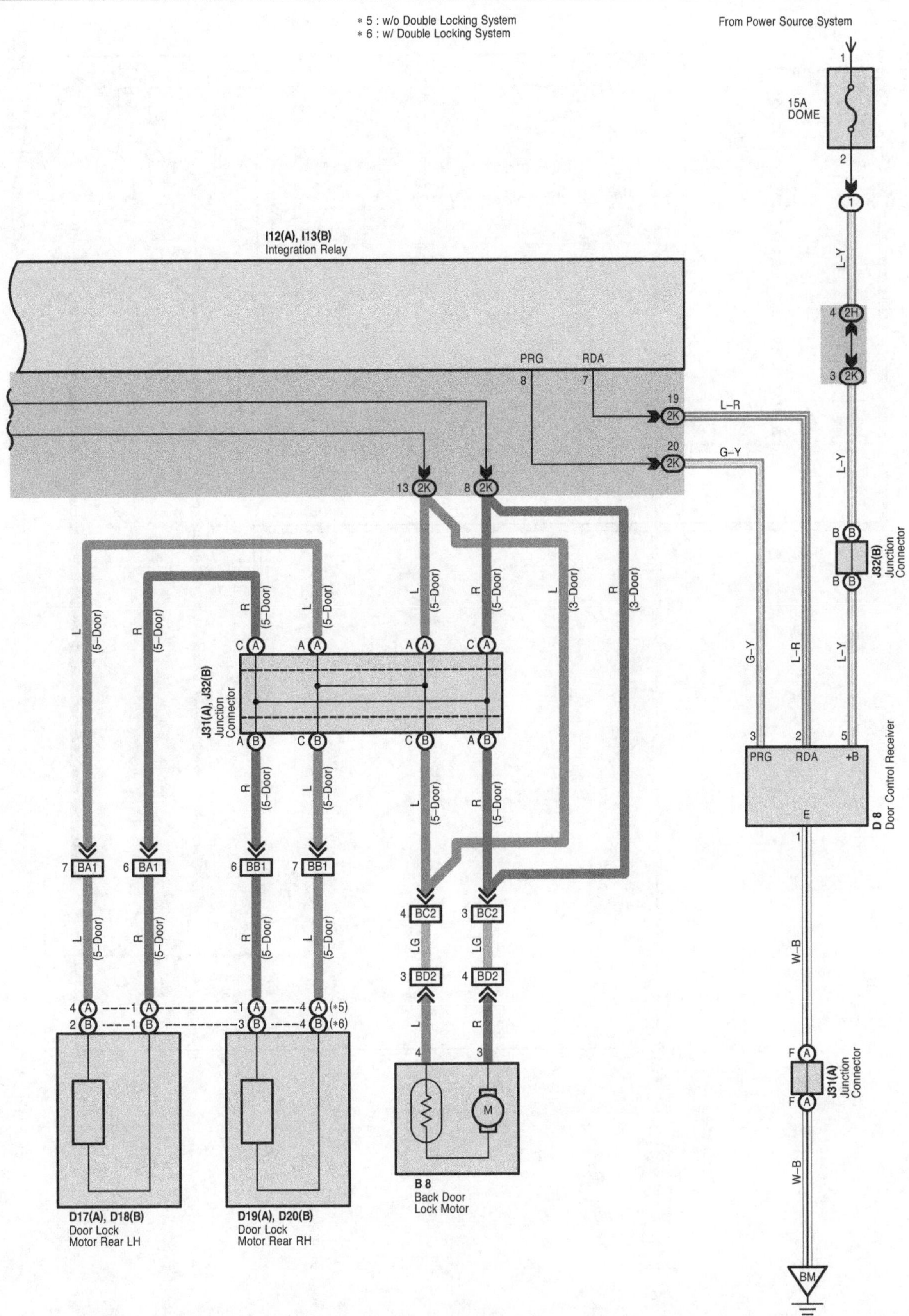

Diagram 24c - Remote central locking (continued)

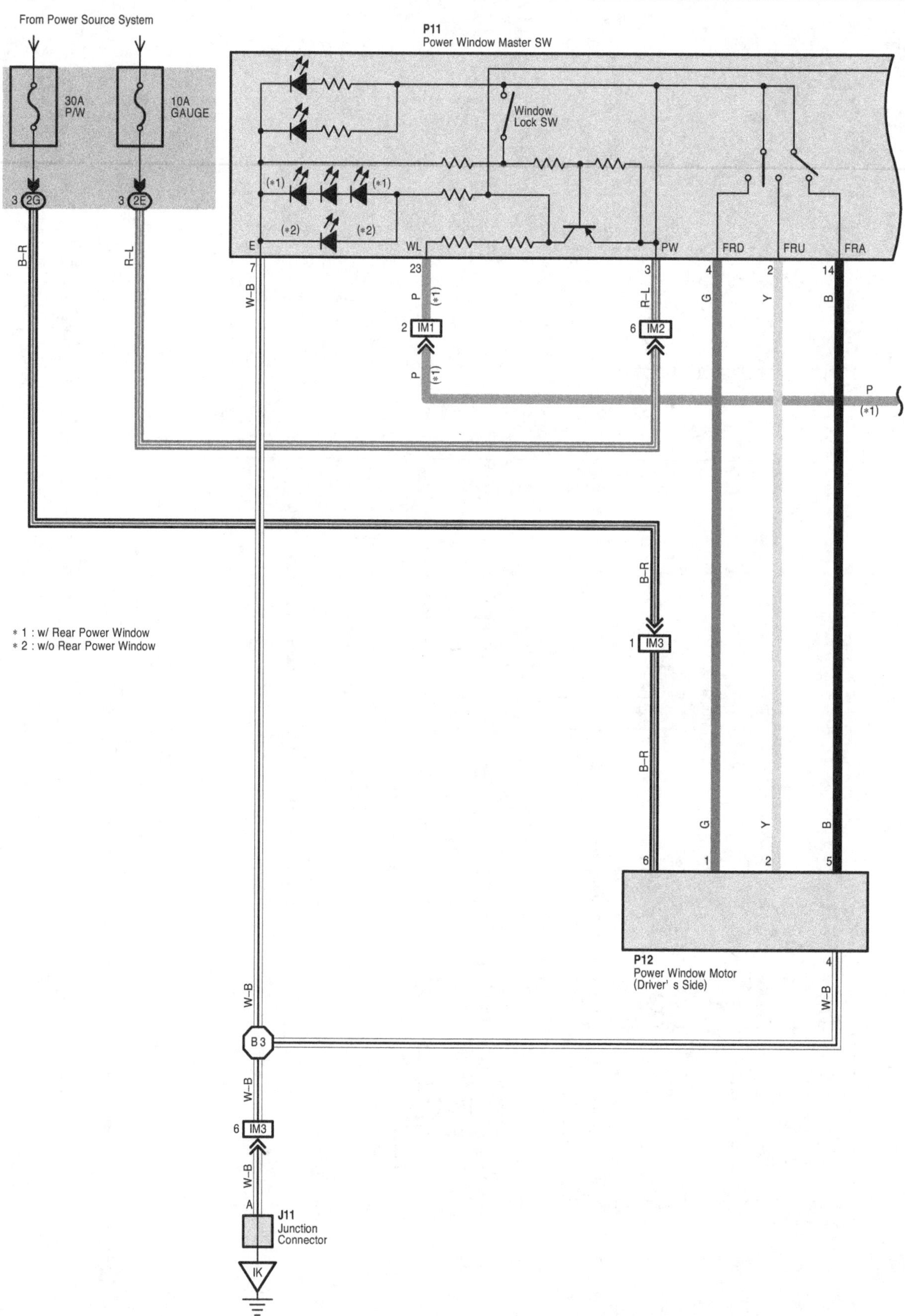

Diagram 25a - Electric windows

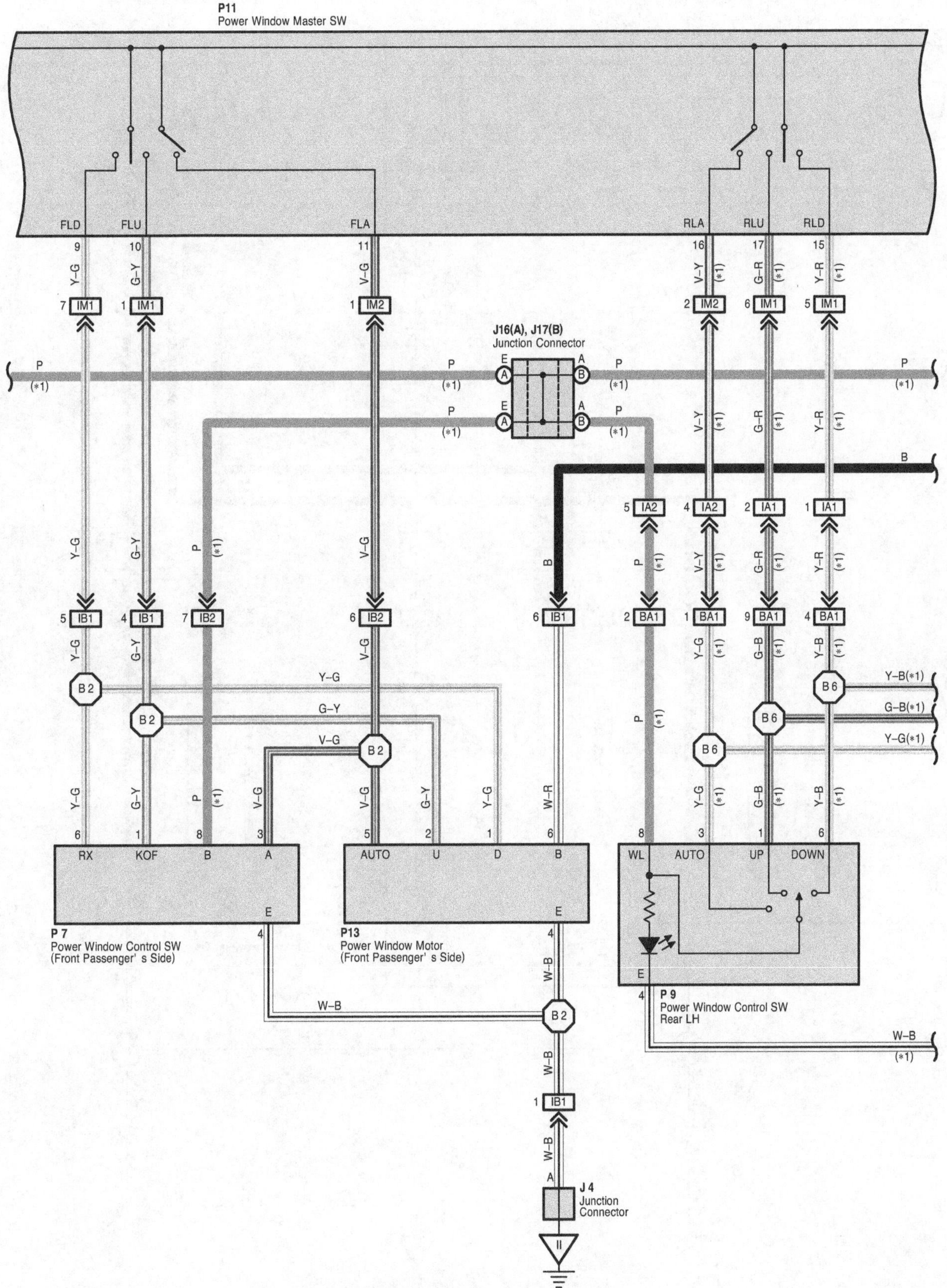

Diagram 25b - Electric windows (continued)

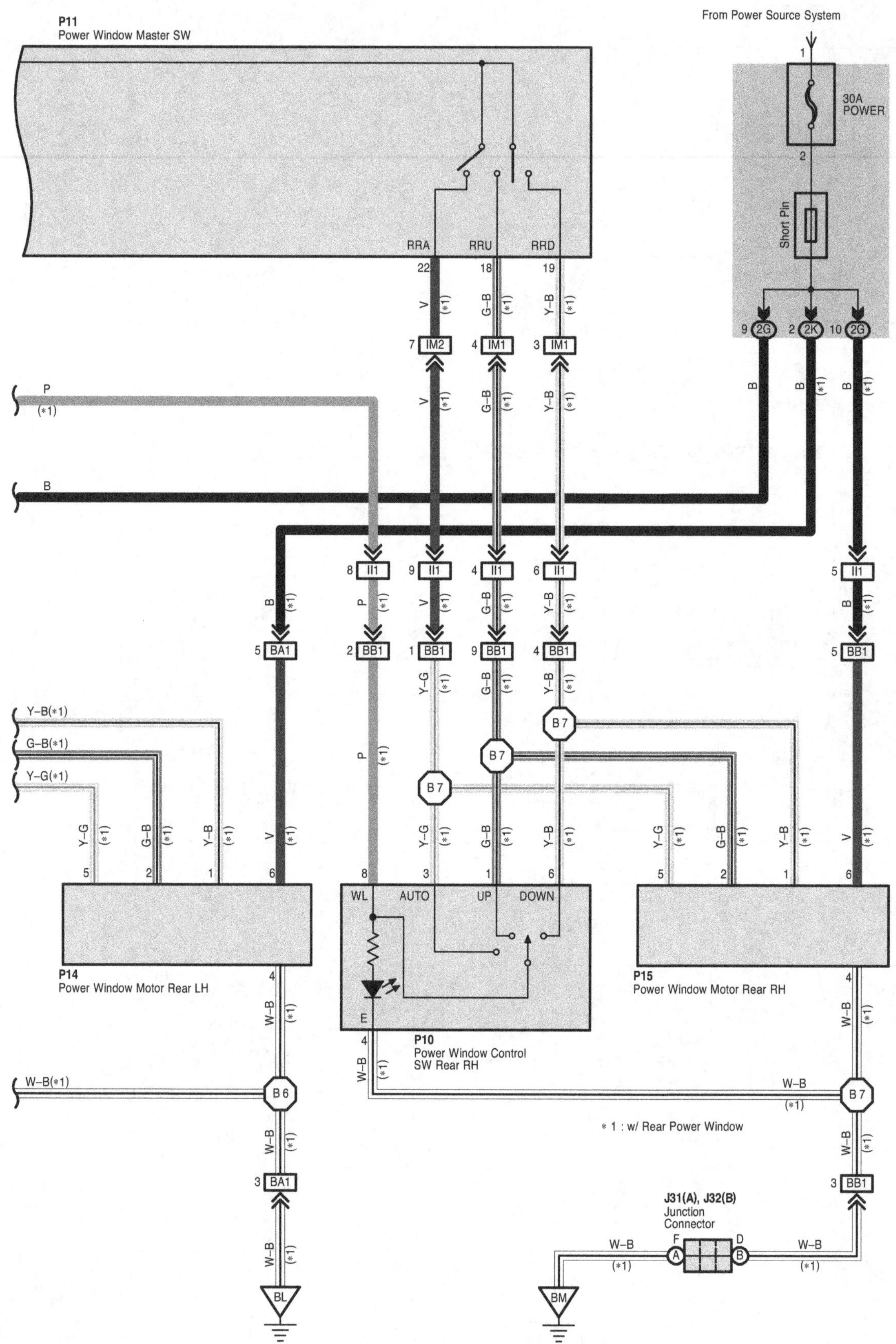

Diagram 25c - Electric windows (continued)

Dimensions and weights

Note: *All figures are approximate, and may vary according to model. Refer to manufacturer's data for exact figures.*

Dimensions

Overall length:	
Hatchback	4180 mm
Saloon	4410 mm
Estate	4410 mm
Overall width (excluding mirrors)	1710 mm
Overall height (unladen):	
Hatchback	1475 mm
Saloon	1470 mm
Estate (excluding roof rails)	1500 mm
Wheelbase	2600 mm

Weights

Maximum gross vehicle weight*:	
1.4 litre petrol engine	1655 kg
1.6 litre petrol engine:	
Manual transmission	1655 kg
Automatic transmission	1670 kg
2.0 litre diesel engine	1780 kg
Maximum towing weight*:	
Unbraked trailer :	
1.4 litre petrol engine	450 kg
1.6 litre petrol engine	450 kg
2.0 litre diesel engine	450 kg
Braked trailer:	
1.4 litre petrol engine	1000 kg
1.6 litre petrol engine	1300 kg
2.0 litre diesel engine	1300 kg

** Refer to the Vehicle Identification Plate for the exact figures for your vehicle (see Vehicle identification)*

Fuel economy

Although depreciation is still the biggest part of the cost of motoring for most car owners, the cost of fuel is more immediately noticeable. These pages give some tips on how to get the best fuel economy.

Working it out

Manufacturer's figures

Car manufacturers are required by law to provide fuel consumption information on all new vehicles sold. These 'official' figures are obtained by simulating various driving conditions on a rolling road or a test track. Real life conditions are different, so the fuel consumption actually achieved may not bear much resemblance to the quoted figures.

How to calculate it

Many cars now have trip computers which will display fuel consumption, both instantaneous and average. Refer to the owner's handbook for details of how to use these.

To calculate consumption yourself (and maybe to check that the trip computer is accurate), proceed as follows.

1. Fill up with fuel and note the mileage, or zero the trip recorder.
2. Drive as usual until you need to fill up again.
3. Note the amount of fuel required to refill the tank, and the mileage covered since the previous fill-up.
4. Divide the mileage by the amount of fuel used to obtain the consumption figure.

For example:

Mileage at first fill-up (a) = 27,903
Mileage at second fill-up (b) = 28,346
Mileage covered (b - a) = 443
Fuel required at second fill-up = 48.6 litres

The half-completed changeover to metric units in the UK means that we buy our fuel in litres, measure distances in miles and talk about fuel consumption in miles per gallon. There are two ways round this: the first is to convert the litres to gallons before doing the calculation (by dividing by 4.546, or see Table 1). So in the example:

48.6 litres ÷ 4.546 = 10.69 gallons
443 miles ÷ 10.69 gallons = 41.4 mpg

The second way is to calculate the consumption in miles per litre, then multiply that figure by 4.546 (or see Table 2).

So in the example, fuel consumption is:

443 miles ÷ 48.6 litres = 9.1 mpl
9.1 mpl x 4.546 = 41.4 mpg

The rest of Europe expresses fuel consumption in litres of fuel required to travel 100 km (l/100 km). For interest, the conversions are given in Table 3. In practice it doesn't matter what units you use, provided you know what your normal consumption is and can spot if it's getting better or worse.

Table 1: conversion of litres to Imperial gallons

litres	1	2	3	4	5	10	20	30	40	50	60	70
gallons	0.22	0.44	0.66	0.88	1.10	2.24	4.49	6.73	8.98	11.22	13.47	15.71

Table 2: conversion of miles per litre to miles per gallon

miles per litre	5	6	7	8	9	10	11	12	13	14
miles per gallon	23	27	32	36	41	46	50	55	59	64

Table 3: conversion of litres per 100 km to miles per gallon

litres per 100 km	4	4.5	5	5.5	6	6.5	7	8	9	10
miles per gallon	71	63	56	51	47	43	40	35	31	28

Maintenance

A well-maintained car uses less fuel and creates less pollution. In particular:

Filters

Change air and fuel filters at the specified intervals.

Oil

Use a good quality oil of the lowest viscosity specified by the vehicle manufacturer (see *Lubricants and fluids*). Check the level often and be careful not to overfill.

Spark plugs

When applicable, renew at the specified intervals.

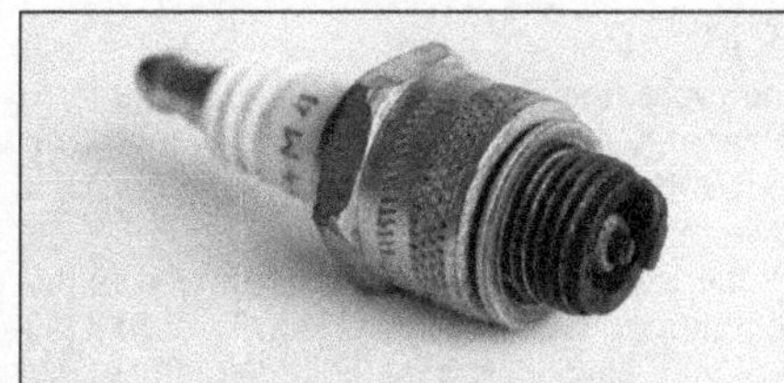

Tyres

Check tyre pressures regularly. Under-inflated tyres have an increased rolling resistance. It is generally safe to use the higher pressures specified for full load conditions even when not fully laden, but keep an eye on the centre band of tread for signs of wear due to over-inflation.

When buying new tyres, consider the 'fuel saving' models which most manufacturers include in their ranges.

Driving style

Acceleration

Acceleration uses more fuel than driving at a steady speed. The best technique with modern cars is to accelerate reasonably briskly to the desired speed, changing up through the gears as soon as possible without making the engine labour.

Air conditioning

Air conditioning absorbs quite a bit of energy from the engine – typically 3 kW (4 hp) or so. The effect on fuel consumption is at its worst in slow traffic. Switch it off when not required.

Anticipation

Drive smoothly and try to read the traffic flow so as to avoid unnecessary acceleration and braking.

Automatic transmission

When accelerating in an automatic, avoid depressing the throttle so far as to make the transmission hold onto lower gears at higher speeds. Don't use the 'Sport' setting, if applicable.

When stationary with the engine running, select 'N' or 'P'. When moving, keep your left foot away from the brake.

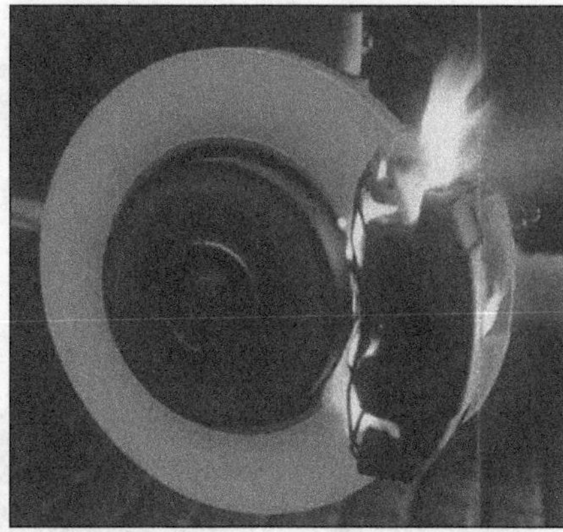

Braking

Braking converts the car's energy of motion into heat – essentially, it is wasted. Obviously some braking is always going to be necessary, but with good anticipation it is surprising how much can be avoided, especially on routes that you know well.

Carshare

Consider sharing lifts to work or to the shops. Even once a week will make a difference.

Electrical loads

Electricity is 'fuel' too; the alternator which charges the battery does so by converting some of the engine's energy of motion into electrical energy. The more electrical accessories are in use, the greater the load on the alternator. Switch off big consumers like the heated rear window when not required.

Freewheeling

Freewheeling (coasting) in neutral with the engine switched off is dangerous. The effort required to operate power-assisted brakes and steering increases when the engine is not running, with a potential lack of control in emergency situations.

In any case, modern fuel injection systems automatically cut off the engine's fuel supply on the overrun (moving and in gear, but with the accelerator pedal released).

Gadgets

Bolt-on devices claiming to save fuel have been around for nearly as long as the motor car itself. Those which worked were rapidly adopted as standard equipment by the vehicle manufacturers. Others worked only in certain situations, or saved fuel only at the expense of unacceptable effects on performance, driveability or the life of engine components.

The most effective fuel saving gadget is the driver's right foot.

Journey planning

Combine (eg) a trip to the supermarket with a visit to the recycling centre and the DIY store, rather than making separate journeys.

When possible choose a travelling time outside rush hours.

Load

The more heavily a car is laden, the greater the energy required to accelerate it to a given speed. Remove heavy items which you don't need to carry.

One load which is often overlooked is the contents of the fuel tank. A tankful of fuel (55 litres / 12 gallons) weighs 45 kg (100 lb) or so. Just half filling it may be worthwhile.

Lost?

At the risk of stating the obvious, if you're going somewhere new, have details of the route to hand. There's not much point in achieving record mpg if you also go miles out of your way.

Parking

If possible, carry out any reversing or turning manoeuvres when you arrive at a parking space so that you can drive straight out when you leave. Manoeuvering when the engine is cold uses a lot more fuel.

Driving around looking for free on-street parking may cost more in fuel than buying a car park ticket.

Premium fuel

Most major oil companies (and some supermarkets) have premium grades of fuel which are several pence a litre dearer than the standard grades. Reports vary, but the consensus seems to be that if these fuels improve economy at all, they do not do so by enough to justify their extra cost.

Roof rack

When loading a roof rack, try to produce a wedge shape with the narrow end at the front. Any cover should be securely fastened – if it flaps it's creating turbulence and absorbing energy.

Remove roof racks and boxes when not in use – they increase air resistance and can create a surprising amount of noise.

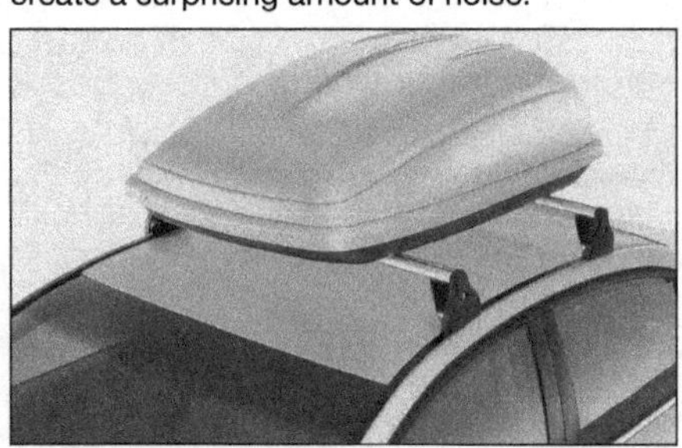

Short journeys

The engine is at its least efficient, and wear is highest, during the first few miles after a cold start. Consider walking, cycling or using public transport.

Speed

The engine is at its most efficient when running at a steady speed and load at the rpm where it develops maximum torque. (You can find this figure in the car's handbook.) For most cars this corresponds to between 55 and 65 mph in top gear.

Above the optimum cruising speed, fuel consumption starts to rise quite sharply. A car travelling at 80 mph will typically be using 30% more fuel than at 60 mph.

Supermarket fuel

It may be cheap but is it any good? In the UK all supermarket fuel must meet the relevant British Standard. The major oil companies will say that their branded fuels have better additive packages which may stop carbon and other deposits building up. A reasonable compromise might be to use one tank of branded fuel to three or four from the supermarket.

Switch off when stationary

Switch off the engine if you look like being stationary for more than 30 seconds or so. This is good for the environment as well as for your pocket. Be aware though that frequent restarts are hard on the battery and the starter motor.

Windows

Driving with the windows open increases air turbulence around the vehicle. Closing the windows promotes smooth airflow and reduced resistance. The faster you go, the more significant this is.

And finally . . .

Driving techniques associated with good fuel economy tend to involve moderate acceleration and low top speeds. Be considerate to the needs of other road users who may need to make brisker progress; even if you do not agree with them this is not an excuse to be obstructive.

Safety must always take precedence over economy, whether it is a question of accelerating hard to complete an overtaking manoeuvre, killing your speed when confronted with a potential hazard or switching the lights on when it starts to get dark.

Conversion factors

Length (distance)

Inches (in)	x 25.4	= Millimetres (mm)	x 0.0394	=	Inches (in)
Feet (ft)	x 0.305	= Metres (m)	x 3.281	=	Feet (ft)
Miles	x 1.609	= Kilometres (km)	x 0.621	=	Miles

Volume (capacity)

Cubic inches (cu in; in³)	x 16.387	= Cubic centimetres (cc; cm³)	x 0.061	=	Cubic inches (cu in; in³)
Imperial pints (Imp pt)	x 0.568	= Litres (l)	x 1.76	=	Imperial pints (Imp pt)
Imperial quarts (Imp qt)	x 1.137	= Litres (l)	x 0.88	=	Imperial quarts (Imp qt)
Imperial quarts (Imp qt)	x 1.201	= US quarts (US qt)	x 0.833	=	Imperial quarts (Imp qt)
US quarts (US qt)	x 0.946	= Litres (l)	x 1.057	=	US quarts (US qt)
Imperial gallons (Imp gal)	x 4.546	= Litres (l)	x 0.22	=	Imperial gallons (Imp gal)
Imperial gallons (Imp gal)	x 1.201	= US gallons (US gal)	x 0.833	=	Imperial gallons (Imp gal)
US gallons (US gal)	x 3.785	= Litres (l)	x 0.264	=	US gallons (US gal)

Mass (weight)

Ounces (oz)	x 28.35	= Grams (g)	x 0.035	=	Ounces (oz)
Pounds (lb)	x 0.454	= Kilograms (kg)	x 2.205	=	Pounds (lb)

Force

Ounces-force (ozf; oz)	x 0.278	= Newtons (N)	x 3.6	=	Ounces-force (ozf; oz)
Pounds-force (lbf; lb)	x 4.448	= Newtons (N)	x 0.225	=	Pounds-force (lbf; lb)
Newtons (N)	x 0.1	= Kilograms-force (kgf; kg)	x 9.81	=	Newtons (N)

Pressure

Pounds-force per square inch (psi; lbf/in²; lb/in²)	x 0.070	= Kilograms-force per square centimetre (kgf/cm²; kg/cm²)	x 14.223	=	Pounds-force per square inch (psi; lbf/in²; lb/in²)
Pounds-force per square inch (psi; lbf/in²; lb/in²)	x 0.068	= Atmospheres (atm)	x 14.696	=	Pounds-force per square inch (psi; lbf/in²; lb/in²)
Pounds-force per square inch (psi; lbf/in²; lb/in²)	x 0.069	= Bars	x 14.5	=	Pounds-force per square inch (psi; lbf/in²; lb/in²)
Pounds-force per square inch (psi; lbf/in²; lb/in²)	x 6.895	= Kilopascals (kPa)	x 0.145	=	Pounds-force per square inch (psi; lbf/in²; lb/in²)
Kilopascals (kPa)	x 0.01	= Kilograms-force per square centimetre (kgf/cm²; kg/cm²)	x 98.1	=	Kilopascals (kPa)
Millibar (mbar)	x 100	= Pascals (Pa)	x 0.01	=	Millibar (mbar)
Millibar (mbar)	x 0.0145	= Pounds-force per square inch (psi; lbf/in²; lb/in²)	x 68.947	=	Millibar (mbar)
Millibar (mbar)	x 0.75	= Millimetres of mercury (mmHg)	x 1.333	=	Millibar (mbar)
Millibar (mbar)	x 0.401	= Inches of water (inH$_2$O)	x 2.491	=	Millibar (mbar)
Millimetres of mercury (mmHg)	x 0.535	= Inches of water (inH$_2$O)	x 1.868	=	Millimetres of mercury (mmHg)
Inches of water (inH$_2$O)	x 0.036	= Pounds-force per square inch (psi; lbf/in²; lb/in²)	x 27.68	=	Inches of water (inH$_2$O)

Torque (moment of force)

Pounds-force inches (lbf in; lb in)	x 1.152	= Kilograms-force centimetre (kgf cm; kg cm)	x 0.868	=	Pounds-force inches (lbf in; lb in)
Pounds-force inches (lbf in; lb in)	x 0.113	= Newton metres (Nm)	x 8.85	=	Pounds-force inches (lbf in; lb in)
Pounds-force inches (lbf in; lb in)	x 0.083	= Pounds-force feet (lbf ft; lb ft)	x 12	=	Pounds-force inches (lbf in; lb in)
Pounds-force feet (lbf ft; lb ft)	x 0.138	= Kilograms-force metres (kgf m; kg m)	x 7.233	=	Pounds-force feet (lbf ft; lb ft)
Pounds-force feet (lbf ft; lb ft)	x 1.356	= Newton metres (Nm)	x 0.738	=	Pounds-force feet (lbf ft; lb ft)
Newton metres (Nm)	x 0.102	= Kilograms-force metres (kgf m; kg m)	x 9.804	=	Newton metres (Nm)

Power

Horsepower (hp)	x 745.7	= Watts (W)	x 0.0013	=	Horsepower (hp)

Velocity (speed)

Miles per hour (miles/hr; mph)	x 1.609	= Kilometres per hour (km/hr; kph)	x 0.621	=	Miles per hour (miles/hr; mph)

Fuel consumption*

Miles per gallon, Imperial (mpg)	x 0.354	= Kilometres per litre (km/l)	x 2.825	=	Miles per gallon, Imperial (mpg)
Miles per gallon, US (mpg)	x 0.425	= Kilometres per litre (km/l)	x 2.352	=	Miles per gallon, US (mpg)

Temperature

Degrees Fahrenheit = (°C x 1.8) + 32

Degrees Celsius (Degrees Centigrade; °C) = (°F - 32) x 0.56

** It is common practice to convert from miles per gallon (mpg) to litres/100 kilometres (l/100km), where mpg x l/100 km = 282*

Spare parts are available from many sources, including maker's appointed garages, accessory shops, and motor factors. To be sure of obtaining the correct parts, it may sometimes be necessary to quote the vehicle identification number. If possible, it can also be useful to take the old parts along for positive identification. Items such as starter motors and alternators maybe available under a service exchange scheme – any parts returned should be clean.

Our advice regarding spare part sources is:

Officially appointed garages

This is the best source of parts, which are peculiar to your car, and are not otherwise generally available (eg, badges, interior trim, certain body panels, etc). It is also the only place at which you should buy parts if the vehicle is still under warranty.

Accessory shops

These are very good places to buy materials and components needed for the maintenance of your car (oil, air and fuel filters, spark plugs, light bulbs, drivebelts, oils and greases, brake pads, touch-up paint, etc). Components of this nature sold by a reputable shop are of the same standard as those used by the car manufacturer.

Besides components, these shops will also sell tools and general accessories, usually have convenient opening hours, charge lower prices, and can often be found close to home. Some accessory shops also have parts counters where components needed for almost any repair job can be purchased or ordered.

Motor factors

Good factors will stock all the more important components, which wear out comparatively quickly and can sometimes supply individual components needed for the overhaul of a larger assembly. They may also handle work such as cylinder block reboring, crankshaft regrinding and balancing, etc.

Tyre and exhaust specialists

These outlets may be independent or members of a local or national chain. They frequently offer competitive prices when compared with a main dealer or local garage, but it will pay to obtain several quotes before making a decision. Also ask what 'extras' may be added to the quote – for instance, fitting a new valve and balancing the wheel are both often charged on top of the price of a new tyre.

Other sources

Beware of parts or materials obtained from market stalls, car boot sales or similar outlets. Such items are not invariably sub-standard, but there is little chance of compensation if they do prove unsatisfactory. In the case of safety-critical components such as brake pads there is the risk not only of financial loss but also of an accident causing injury or death.

Vehicle identification

Modifications are a continuing and unpublicised process in vehicle manufacture, quite apart from major model changes. Spare parts manuals and lists are compiled upon a numerical basis, the individual vehicle identification numbers being essential for correct identification of the part concerned.

When ordering spare parts, always give as much information as possible. Quote the car model, year of manufacture, body and engine numbers.

The *vehicle identification number (VIN) plate* is fitted to the bulkhead in the engine compartment. The plate carries the vehicle identification number (VIN) and vehicle weight information **(see illustration)**.

The engine number is situated on the front face of the cylinder block on diesel engines, and on the left-hand end (transmission end) of the cylinder block on petrol models **(see illustration)**

The VIN number is stamped into the bulkhead at the rear of the engine compartment

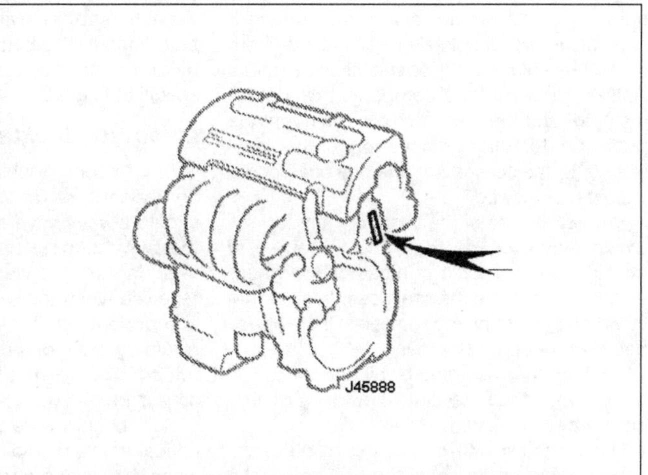

Engine number location – petrol engines

Whenever servicing, repair or overhaul work is carried out on the car or its components, observe the following procedures and instructions. This will assist in carrying out the operation efficiently and to a professional standard of workmanship.

Joint mating faces and gaskets

When separating components at their mating faces, never insert screwdrivers or similar implements into the joint between the faces in order to prise them apart. This can cause severe damage which results in oil leaks, coolant leaks, etc upon reassembly. Separation is usually achieved by tapping along the joint with a soft-faced hammer in order to break the seal. However, note that this method may not be suitable where dowels are used for component location.

Where a gasket is used between the mating faces of two components, a new one must be fitted on reassembly; fit it dry unless otherwise stated in the repair procedure. Make sure that the mating faces are clean and dry, with all traces of old gasket removed. When cleaning a joint face, use a tool which is unlikely to score or damage the face, and remove any burrs or nicks with an oilstone or fine file.

Make sure that tapped holes are cleaned with a pipe cleaner, and keep them free of jointing compound, if this is being used, unless specifically instructed otherwise.

Ensure that all orifices, channels or pipes are clear, and blow through them, preferably using compressed air.

Oil seals

Oil seals can be removed by levering them out with a wide flat-bladed screwdriver or similar implement. Alternatively, a number of self-tapping screws may be screwed into the seal, and these used as a purchase for pliers or some similar device in order to pull the seal free.

Whenever an oil seal is removed from its working location, either individually or as part of an assembly, it should be renewed.

The very fine sealing lip of the seal is easily damaged, and will not seal if the surface it contacts is not completely clean and free from scratches, nicks or grooves. If the original sealing surface of the component cannot be restored, and the manufacturer has not made provision for slight relocation of the seal relative to the sealing surface, the component should be renewed.

Protect the lips of the seal from any surface which may damage them in the course of fitting. Use tape or a conical sleeve where possible. Lubricate the seal lips with oil before fitting and, on dual-lipped seals, fill the space between the lips with grease.

Unless otherwise stated, oil seals must be fitted with their sealing lips toward the lubricant to be sealed.

Use a tubular drift or block of wood of the appropriate size to install the seal and, if the seal housing is shouldered, drive the seal down to the shoulder. If the seal housing is unshouldered, the seal should be fitted with its face flush with the housing top face (unless otherwise instructed).

Screw threads and fastenings

Seized nuts, bolts and screws are quite a common occurrence where corrosion has set in, and the use of penetrating oil or releasing fluid will often overcome this problem if the offending item is soaked for a while before attempting to release it. The use of an impact driver may also provide a means of releasing such stubborn fastening devices, when used in conjunction with the appropriate screwdriver bit or socket. If none of these methods works, it may be necessary to resort to the careful application of heat, or the use of a hacksaw or nut splitter device.

Studs are usually removed by locking two nuts together on the threaded part, and then using a spanner on the lower nut to unscrew the stud. Studs or bolts which have broken off below the surface of the component in which they are mounted can sometimes be removed using a stud extractor. Always ensure that a blind tapped hole is completely free from oil, grease, water or other fluid before installing the bolt or stud. Failure to do this could cause the housing to crack due to the hydraulic action of the bolt or stud as it is screwed in.

When tightening a castellated nut to accept a split pin, tighten the nut to the specified torque, where applicable, and then tighten further to the next split pin hole. Never slacken the nut to align the split pin hole, unless stated in the repair procedure.

When checking or retightening a nut or bolt to a specified torque setting, slacken the nut or bolt by a quarter of a turn, and then retighten to the specified setting. However, this should not be attempted where angular tightening has been used.

For some screw fastenings, notably cylinder head bolts or nuts, torque wrench settings are no longer specified for the latter stages of tightening, "angle-tightening" being called up instead. Typically, a fairly low torque wrench setting will be applied to the bolts/nuts in the correct sequence, followed by one or more stages of tightening through specified angles.

Locknuts, locktabs and washers

Any fastening which will rotate against a component or housing during tightening should always have a washer between it and the relevant component or housing.

Spring or split washers should always be renewed when they are used to lock a critical component such as a big-end bearing retaining bolt or nut. Locktabs which are folded over to retain a nut or bolt should always be renewed.

Self-locking nuts can be re-used in non-critical areas, providing resistance can be felt when the locking portion passes over the bolt or stud thread. However, it should be noted that self-locking stiffnuts tend to lose their effectiveness after long periods of use, and should then be renewed as a matter of course.

Split pins must always be replaced with new ones of the correct size for the hole.

When thread-locking compound is found on the threads of a fastener which is to be re-used, it should be cleaned off with a wire brush and solvent, and fresh compound applied on reassembly.

Special tools

Some repair procedures in this manual entail the use of special tools such as a press, two or three-legged pullers, spring compressors, etc. Wherever possible, suitable readily-available alternatives to the manufacturer's special tools are described, and are shown in use. In some instances, where no alternative is possible, it has been necessary to resort to the use of a manufacturer's tool, and this has been done for reasons of safety as well as the efficient completion of the repair operation. Unless you are highly-skilled and have a thorough understanding of the procedures described, never attempt to bypass the use of any special tool when the procedure described specifies its use. Not only is there a very great risk of personal injury, but expensive damage could be caused to the components involved.

Environmental considerations

When disposing of used engine oil, brake fluid, antifreeze, etc, give due consideration to any detrimental environmental effects. Do not, for instance, pour any of the above liquids down drains into the general sewage system, or onto the ground to soak away. Many local council refuse tips provide a facility for waste oil disposal, as do some garages. If none of these facilities are available, consult your local Environmental Health Department, or the National Rivers Authority, for further advice.

With the universal tightening-up of legislation regarding the emission of environmentally-harmful substances from motor vehicles, most vehicles have tamperproof devices fitted to the main adjustment points of the fuel system. These devices are primarily designed to prevent unqualified persons from adjusting the fuel/air mixture, with the chance of a consequent increase in toxic emissions. If such devices are found during servicing or overhaul, they should, wherever possible, be renewed or refitted in accordance with the manufacturer's requirements or current legislation.

OIL CARE
FOLLOW THE CODE
OIL BANK LINE
0800 66 33 66
www.oilbankline.org.uk

Note: It is antisocial and illegal to dump oil down the drain. To find the location of your local oil recycling bank, call this number free.

The jack supplied with the vehicle should only be used for changing the roadwheels – see *Wheel changing* at the front of this manual. When carrying out any other kind of work, raise the vehicle using a hydraulic (or 'trolley') jack, and always supplement the jack with axle stands at the vehicle jacking points.

When using a hydraulic jack or axle stands, always position the jack head or axle stand head under one of the relevant jacking points; the jacking point is the area marked by two cut-outs in the sill **(see illustration)**. Use a block of wood between a trolley jack or axle stand and the sill – the block of wood should have a groove cut into it, into which the welded flange of the sill will locate.

Do not attempt to jack the vehicle under the front crossmember, the sump, or any of the suspension components.

The jack supplied with the vehicle locates in the jacking points on the underside of the sills – see *Wheel changing*. Ensure that the jack head is correctly engaged before attempting to raise the vehicle.

Warning: Never work under, around, or near a raised vehicle, unless it is adequately supported in at least two places.

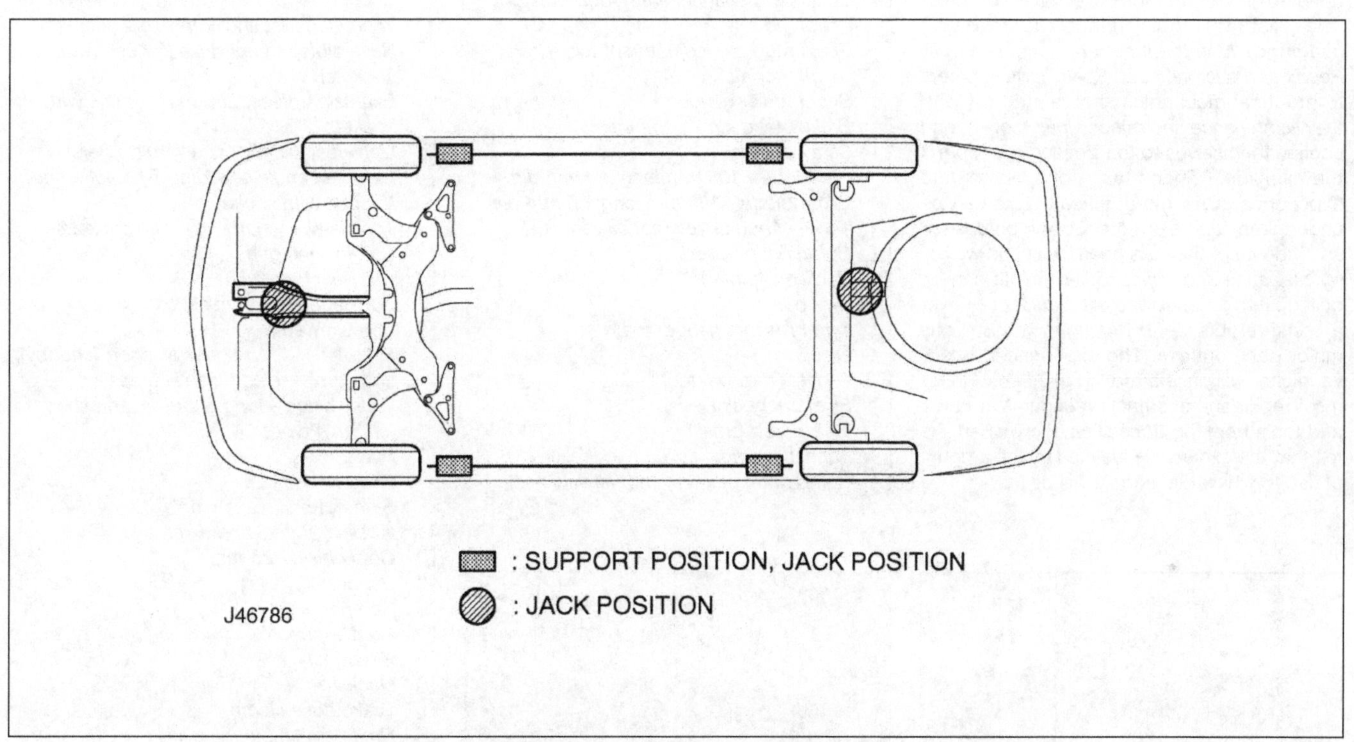

Underside of the vehicle showing the jacking points and axle stand support positions

Introduction

A selection of good tools is a fundamental requirement for anyone contemplating the maintenance and repair of a motor vehicle. For the owner who does not possess any, their purchase will prove a considerable expense, offsetting some of the savings made by doing-it-yourself. However, provided that the tools purchased meet the relevant national safety standards and are of good quality, they will last for many years and prove an extremely worthwhile investment.

To help the average owner to decide which tools are needed to carry out the various tasks detailed in this manual, we have compiled three lists of tools under the following headings: *Maintenance and minor repair*, *Repair and overhaul*, and *Special*. Newcomers to practical mechanics should start off with the *Maintenance and minor repair* tool kit, and confine themselves to the simpler jobs around the vehicle. Then, as confidence and experience grow, more difficult tasks can be undertaken, with extra tools being purchased as, and when, they are needed. In this way, a *Maintenance and minor repair* tool kit can be built up into a *Repair and overhaul* tool kit over a considerable period of time, without any major cash outlays. The experienced do-it-yourselfer will have a tool kit good enough for most repair and overhaul procedures, and will add tools from the *Special* category when it is felt that the expense is justified by the amount of use to which these tools will be put.

Maintenance and minor repair tool kit

The tools given in this list should be considered as a minimum requirement if routine maintenance, servicing and minor repair operations are to be undertaken. We recommend the purchase of combination spanners (ring one end, open-ended the other); although more expensive than open-ended ones, they do give the advantages of both types of spanner.

- ☐ *Combination spanners:*
  Metric - 8 to 19 mm inclusive
- ☐ *Adjustable spanner - 35 mm jaw (approx.)*
- ☐ *Spark plug spanner (with rubber insert) - petrol models*
- ☐ *Spark plug gap adjustment tool - petrol models*
- ☐ *Set of feeler gauges*
- ☐ *Brake bleed nipple spanner*
- ☐ *Screwdrivers:*
  Flat blade - 100 mm long x 6 mm dia
  Cross blade - 100 mm long x 6 mm dia
  Torx - various sizes (not all vehicles)
- ☐ *Combination pliers*
- ☐ *Hacksaw (junior)*
- ☐ *Tyre pump*
- ☐ *Tyre pressure gauge*
- ☐ *Oil can*
- ☐ *Oil filter removal tool*
- ☐ *Fine emery cloth*
- ☐ *Wire brush (small)*
- ☐ *Funnel (medium size)*
- ☐ *Sump drain plug key (not all vehicles)*

Repair and overhaul tool kit

These tools are virtually essential for anyone undertaking any major repairs to a motor vehicle, and are additional to those given in the *Maintenance and minor repair* list. Included in this list is a comprehensive set of sockets. Although these are expensive, they will be found invaluable as they are so versatile - particularly if various drives are included in the set. We recommend the half-inch square-drive type, as this can be used with most proprietary torque wrenches.

The tools in this list will sometimes need to be supplemented by tools from the *Special* list:

- ☐ *Sockets (or box spanners) to cover range in previous list (including Torx sockets)*
- ☐ *Reversible ratchet drive (for use with sockets)*
- ☐ *Extension piece, 250 mm (for use with sockets)*
- ☐ *Universal joint (for use with sockets)*
- ☐ *Flexible handle or sliding T "breaker bar" (for use with sockets)*
- ☐ *Torque wrench (for use with sockets)*
- ☐ *Self-locking grips*
- ☐ *Ball pein hammer*
- ☐ *Soft-faced mallet (plastic or rubber)*
- ☐ *Screwdrivers:*
  Flat blade - long & sturdy, short (chubby), and narrow (electrician's) types
  Cross blade – long & sturdy, and short (chubby) types
- ☐ *Pliers:*
  Long-nosed
  Side cutters (electrician's)
  Circlip (internal and external)
- ☐ *Cold chisel - 25 mm*
- ☐ *Scriber*
- ☐ *Scraper*
- ☐ *Centre-punch*
- ☐ *Pin punch*
- ☐ *Hacksaw*
- ☐ *Brake hose clamp*
- ☐ *Brake/clutch bleeding kit*
- ☐ *Selection of twist drills*
- ☐ *Steel rule/straight-edge*
- ☐ *Allen keys (inc. splined/Torx type)*
- ☐ *Selection of files*
- ☐ *Wire brush*
- ☐ *Axle stands*
- ☐ *Jack (strong trolley or hydraulic type)*
- ☐ *Light with extension lead*
- ☐ *Universal electrical multi-meter*

Sockets and reversible ratchet drive

Brake bleeding kit

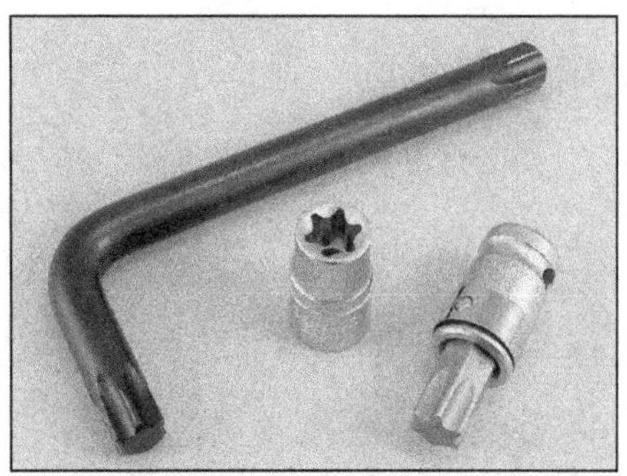
Torx key, socket and bit

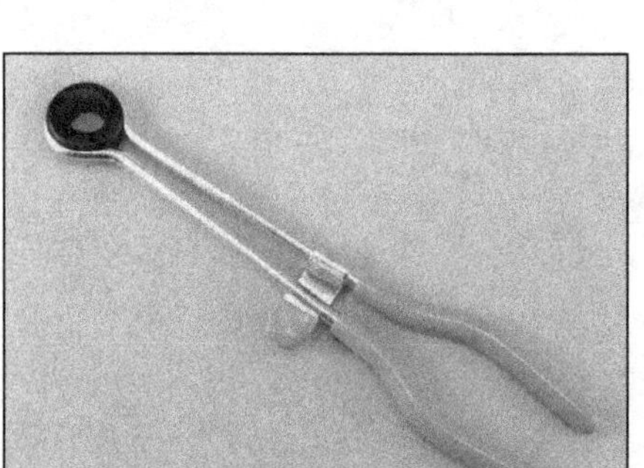
Hose clamp

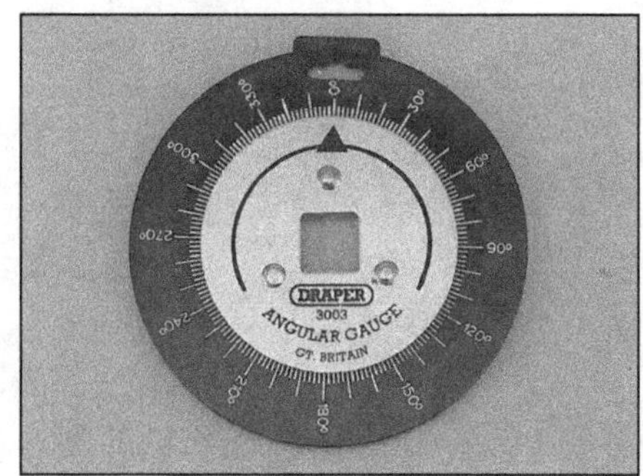

Angular-tightening gauge

Special tools

The tools in this list are those which are not used regularly, are expensive to buy, or which need to be used in accordance with their manufacturers' instructions. Unless relatively difficult mechanical jobs are undertaken frequently, it will not be economic to buy many of these tools. Where this is the case, you could consider clubbing together with friends (or joining a motorists' club) to make a joint purchase, or borrowing the tools against a deposit from a local garage or tool hire specialist. It is worth noting that many of the larger DIY superstores now carry a large range of special tools for hire at modest rates.

The following list contains only those tools and instruments freely available to the public, and not those special tools produced by the vehicle manufacturer specifically for its dealer network. You will find occasional references to these manufacturers' special tools in the text of this manual. Generally, an alternative method of doing the job without the vehicle manufacturers' special tool is given. However, sometimes there is no alternative to using them. Where this is the case and the relevant tool cannot be bought or borrowed, you will have to entrust the work to a dealer.

- ☐ *Angular-tightening gauge*
- ☐ *Valve spring compressor*
- ☐ *Valve grinding tool*
- ☐ *Piston ring compressor*
- ☐ *Piston ring removal/installation tool*
- ☐ *Cylinder bore hone*
- ☐ *Balljoint separator*
- ☐ *Coil spring compressors (where applicable)*
- ☐ *Two/three-legged hub and bearing puller*
- ☐ *Impact screwdriver*
- ☐ *Micrometer and/or vernier calipers*
- ☐ *Dial gauge*
- ☐ *Stroboscopic timing light*
- ☐ *Dwell angle meter/tachometer*
- ☐ *Fault code reader*
- ☐ *Cylinder compression gauge*
- ☐ *Hand-operated vacuum pump and gauge*
- ☐ *Clutch plate alignment set*
- ☐ *Brake shoe steady spring cup removal tool*
- ☐ *Bush and bearing removal/installation set*
- ☐ *Stud extractors*
- ☐ *Tap and die set*
- ☐ *Lifting tackle*
- ☐ *Trolley jack*

Buying tools

Reputable motor accessory shops and superstores often offer excellent quality tools at discount prices, so it pays to shop around.

Remember, you don't have to buy the most expensive items on the shelf, but it is always advisable to steer clear of the very cheap tools. Beware of 'bargains' offered on market stalls or at car boot sales. There are plenty of good tools around at reasonable prices, but always aim to purchase items which meet the relevant national safety standards. If in doubt, ask the proprietor or manager of the shop for advice before making a purchase.

Care and maintenance of tools

Having purchased a reasonable tool kit, it is necessary to keep the tools in a clean and serviceable condition. After use, always wipe off any dirt, grease and metal particles using a clean, dry cloth, before putting the tools away. Never leave them lying around after they have been used. A simple tool rack on the garage or workshop wall for items such as screwdrivers and pliers is a good idea. Store all normal spanners and sockets in a metal box. Any measuring instruments, gauges, meters, etc, must be carefully stored where they cannot be damaged or become rusty.

Take a little care when tools are used. Hammer heads inevitably become marked, and screwdrivers lose the keen edge on their blades from time to time. A little timely attention with emery cloth or a file will soon restore items like this to a good finish.

Working facilities

Not to be forgotten when discussing tools is the workshop itself. If anything more than routine maintenance is to be carried out, a suitable working area becomes essential.

It is appreciated that many an owner-mechanic is forced by circumstances to remove an engine or similar item without the benefit of a garage or workshop. Having done this, any repairs should always be done under the cover of a roof.

Wherever possible, any dismantling should be done on a clean, flat workbench or table at a suitable working height.

Any workbench needs a vice; one with a jaw opening of 100 mm is suitable for most jobs. As mentioned previously, some clean dry storage space is also required for tools, as well as for any lubricants, cleaning fluids, touch-up paints etc, which become necessary.

Another item which may be required, and which has a much more general usage, is an electric drill with a chuck capacity of at least 8 mm. This, together with a good range of twist drills, is virtually essential for fitting accessories.

Last, but not least, always keep a supply of old newspapers and clean, lint-free rags available, and try to keep any working area as clean as possible.

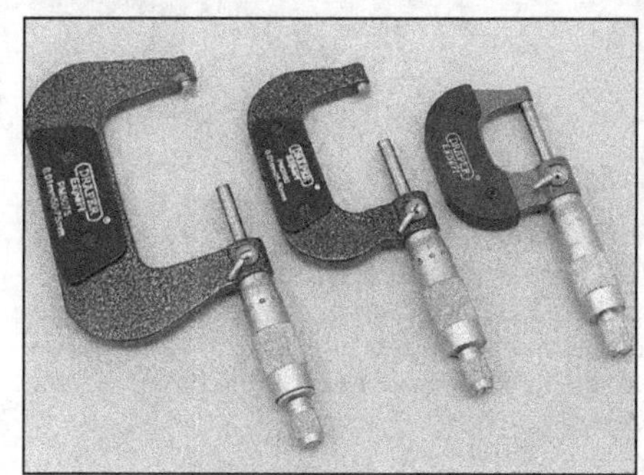

Micrometers

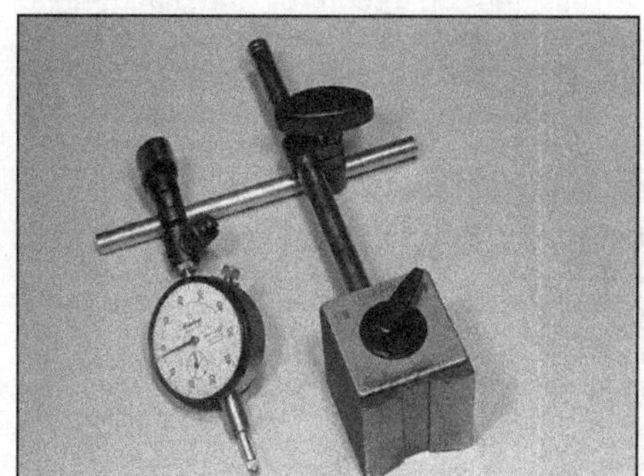

Dial test indicator ("dial gauge")

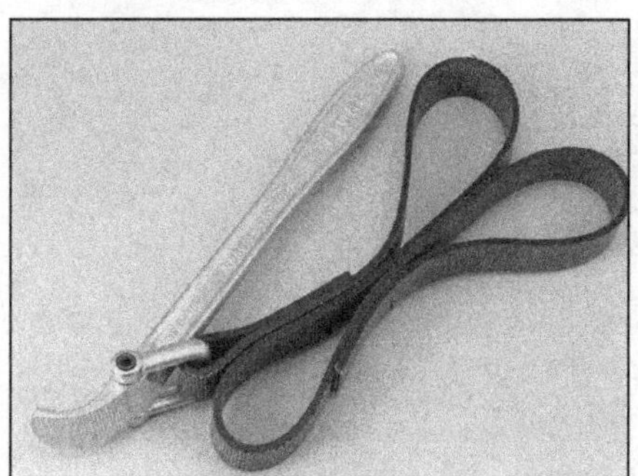

Strap wrench

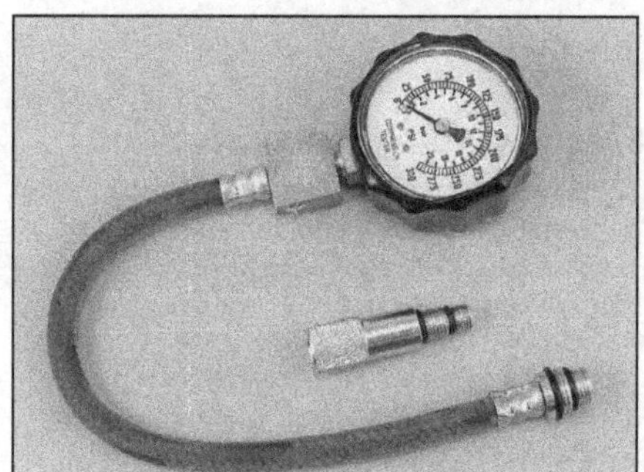

Compression tester

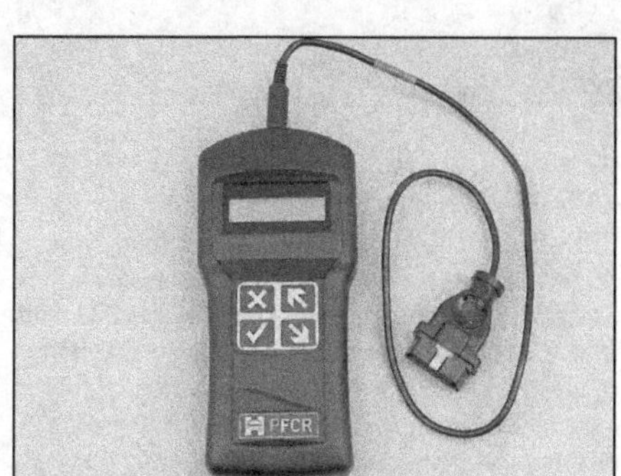

Fault code reader

MOT test checks

This is a guide to getting your vehicle through the MOT test. Obviously it will not be possible to examine the vehicle to the same standard as the professional MOT tester. However, working through the following checks will enable you to identify any problem areas before submitting the vehicle for the test.

It has only been possible to summarise the test requirements here, based on the regulations in force at the time of printing. Test standards are becoming increasingly stringent, although there are some exemptions for older vehicles.

An assistant will be needed to help carry out some of these checks.

The checks have been sub-divided into four categories, as follows:

1 Checks carried out **FROM THE DRIVER'S SEAT**

2 Checks carried out **WITH THE VEHICLE ON THE GROUND**

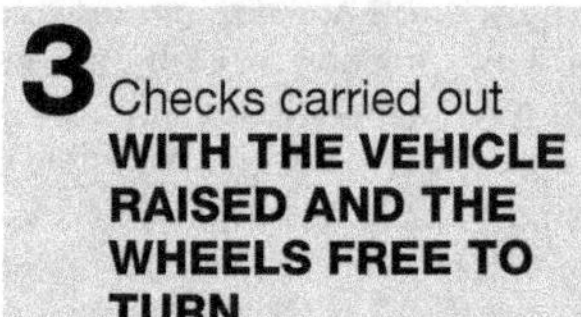

3 Checks carried out **WITH THE VEHICLE RAISED AND THE WHEELS FREE TO TURN**

4 Checks carried out on **YOUR VEHICLE'S EXHAUST EMISSION SYSTEM**

1 Checks carried out FROM THE DRIVER'S SEAT

Handbrake

☐ Test the operation of the handbrake. Excessive travel (too many clicks) indicates incorrect brake or cable adjustment.

☐ Check that the handbrake cannot be released by tapping the lever sideways. Check the security of the lever mountings.

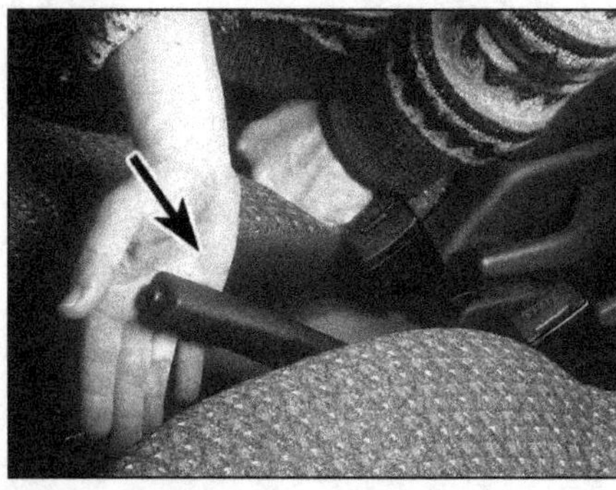

Footbrake

☐ Depress the brake pedal and check that it does not creep down to the floor, indicating a master cylinder fault. Release the pedal, wait a few seconds, then depress it again. If the pedal travels nearly to the floor before firm resistance is felt, brake adjustment or repair is necessary. If the pedal feels spongy, there is air in the hydraulic system which must be removed by bleeding.

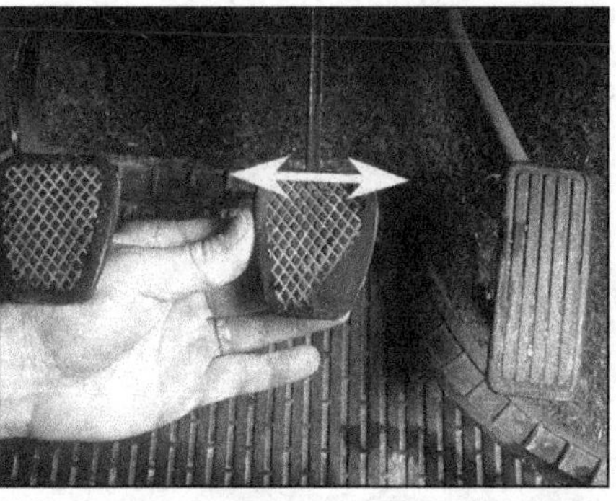

☐ Check that the brake pedal is secure and in good condition. Check also for signs of fluid leaks on the pedal, floor or carpets, which would indicate failed seals in the brake master cylinder.

☐ Check the servo unit (when applicable) by operating the brake pedal several times, then keeping the pedal depressed and starting the engine. As the engine starts, the pedal will move down slightly. If not, the vacuum hose or the servo itself may be faulty.

Steering wheel and column

☐ Examine the steering wheel for fractures or looseness of the hub, spokes or rim.

☐ Move the steering wheel from side to side and then up and down. Check that the steering wheel is not loose on the column, indicating wear or a loose retaining nut. Continue moving the steering wheel as before, but also turn it slightly from left to right.

☐ Check that the steering wheel is not loose on the column, and that there is no abnormal

movement of the steering wheel, indicating wear in the column support bearings or couplings.

Windscreen, mirrors and sunvisor

☐ The windscreen must be free of cracks or other significant damage within the driver's field of view. (Small stone chips are acceptable.) Rear view mirrors must be secure, intact, and capable of being adjusted.

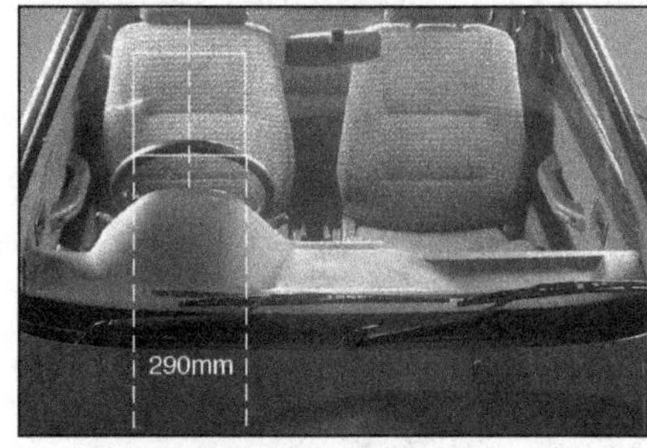

☐ The driver's sunvisor must be capable of being stored in the "up" position.

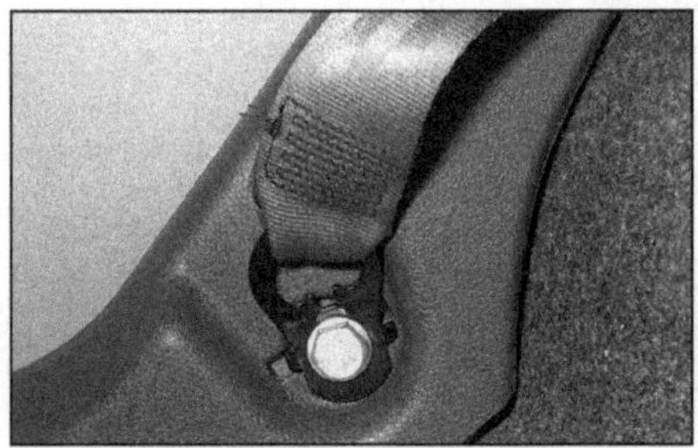

Seat belts and seats

Note: *The following checks are applicable to all seat belts, front and rear.*

☐ Examine the webbing of all the belts (including rear belts if fitted) for cuts, serious fraying or deterioration. Fasten and unfasten each belt to check the buckles. If applicable, check the retracting mechanism. Check the security of all seat belt mountings accessible from inside the vehicle.

☐ Seat belts with pre-tensioners, once activated, have a "flag" or similar showing on the seat belt stalk. This, in itself, is not a reason for test failure.

☐ The front seats themselves must be securely attached and the backrests must lock in the upright position.

Doors

☐ Both front doors must be able to be opened and closed from outside and inside, and must latch securely when closed.

2 Checks carried out WITH THE VEHICLE ON THE GROUND

Vehicle identification

☐ Number plates must be in good condition, secure and legible, with letters and numbers correctly spaced – spacing at (A) should be at least twice that at (B).

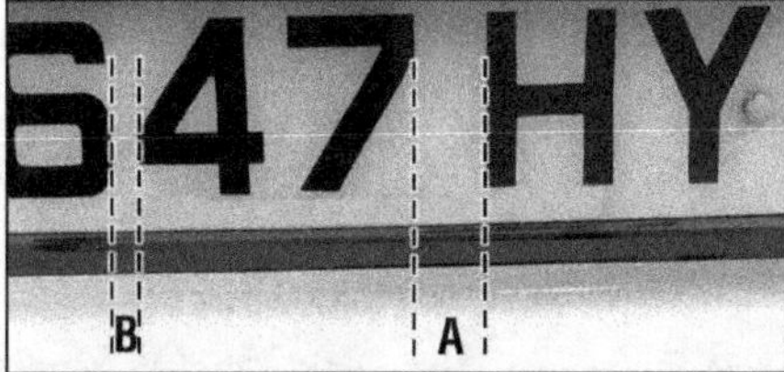

☐ The VIN plate and/or homologation plate must be legible.

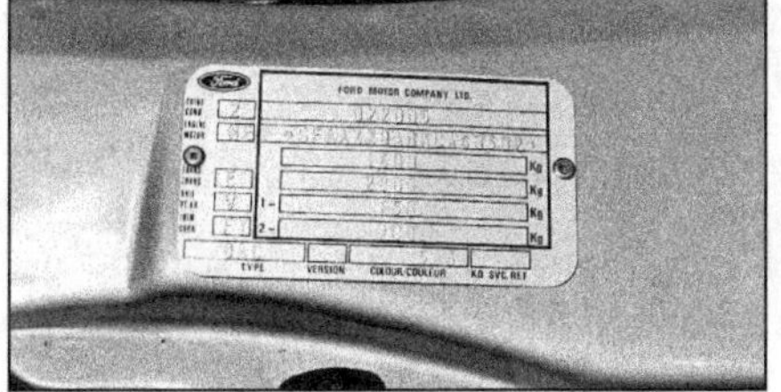

Electrical equipment

☐ Switch on the ignition and check the operation of the horn.

☐ Check the windscreen washers and wipers, examining the wiper blades; renew damaged or perished blades. Also check the operation of the stop-lights.

☐ Check the operation of the sidelights and number plate lights. The lenses and reflectors must be secure, clean and undamaged.

☐ Check the operation and alignment of the headlights. The headlight reflectors must not be tarnished and the lenses must be undamaged.

☐ Switch on the ignition and check the operation of the direction indicators (including the instrument panel tell-tale) and the hazard warning lights. Operation of the sidelights and stop-lights must not affect the indicators - if it does, the cause is usually a bad earth at the rear light cluster.

☐ Check the operation of the rear foglight(s), including the warning light on the instrument panel or in the switch.

☐ The ABS warning light must illuminate in accordance with the manufacturers' design. For most vehicles, the ABS warning light should illuminate when the ignition is switched on, and (if the system is operating properly) extinguish after a few seconds. Refer to the owner's handbook.

Footbrake

☐ Examine the master cylinder, brake pipes and servo unit for leaks, loose mountings, corrosion or other damage.

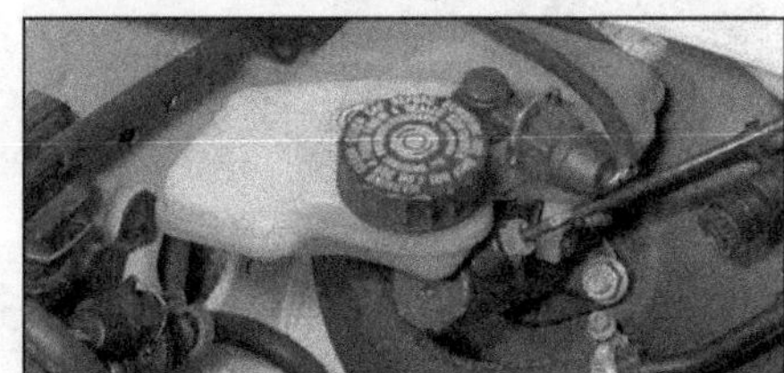

☐ The fluid reservoir must be secure and the fluid level must be between the upper (**A**) and lower (**B**) markings.

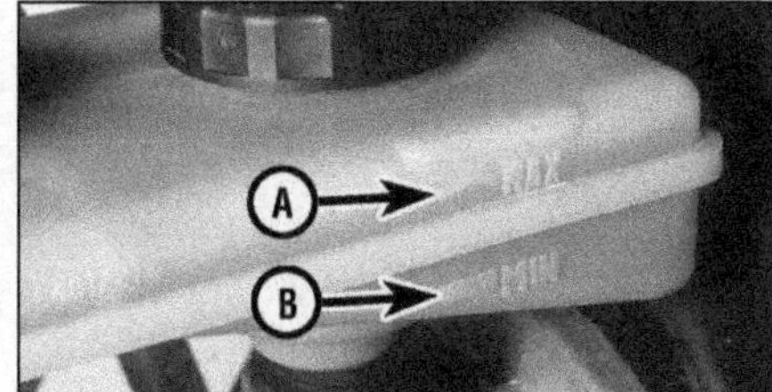

☐ Inspect both front brake flexible hoses for cracks or deterioration of the rubber. Turn the steering from lock to lock, and ensure that the hoses do not contact the wheel, tyre, or any part of the steering or suspension mechanism. With the brake pedal firmly depressed, check the hoses for bulges or leaks under pressure.

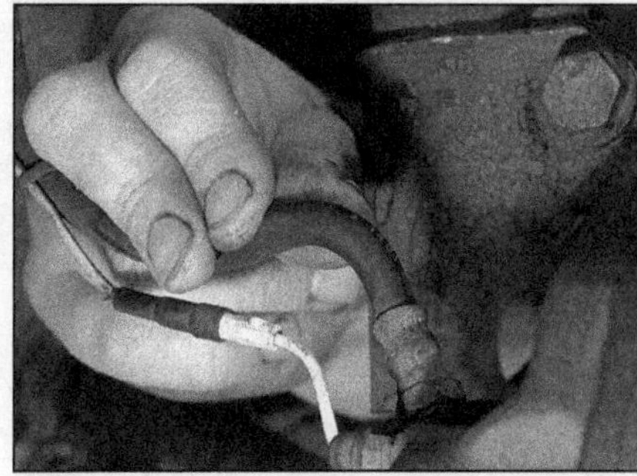

Steering and suspension

☐ Have your assistant turn the steering wheel from side to side slightly, up to the point where the steering gear just begins to transmit this movement to the roadwheels. Check for excessive free play between the steering wheel and the steering gear, indicating wear or insecurity of the steering column joints, the column-to-steering gear coupling, or the steering gear itself.

☐ Have your assistant turn the steering wheel more vigorously in each direction, so that the roadwheels just begin to turn. As this is done, examine all the steering joints, linkages, fittings and attachments. Renew any component that shows signs of wear or damage. On vehicles with power steering, check the security and condition of the steering pump, drivebelt and hoses.

☐ Check that the vehicle is standing level, and at approximately the correct ride height.

Shock absorbers

☐ Depress each corner of the vehicle in turn, then release it. The vehicle should rise and then settle in its normal position. If the vehicle continues to rise and fall, the shock absorber is defective. A shock absorber which has seized will also cause the vehicle to fail.

Exhaust system

☐ Start the engine. With your assistant holding a rag over the tailpipe, check the entire system for leaks. Repair or renew leaking sections.

3 Checks carried out WITH THE VEHICLE RAISED AND THE WHEELS FREE TO TURN

Jack up the front and rear of the vehicle, and securely support it on axle stands. Position the stands clear of the suspension assemblies. Ensure that the wheels are clear of the ground and that the steering can be turned from lock to lock.

Steering mechanism

☐ Have your assistant turn the steering from lock to lock. Check that the steering turns smoothly, and that no part of the steering mechanism, including a wheel or tyre, fouls any brake hose or pipe or any part of the body structure.

☐ Examine the steering rack rubber gaiters for damage or insecurity of the retaining clips. If power steering is fitted, check for signs of damage or leakage of the fluid hoses, pipes or connections. Also check for excessive stiffness or binding of the steering, a missing split pin or locking device, or severe corrosion of the body structure within 30 cm of any steering component attachment point.

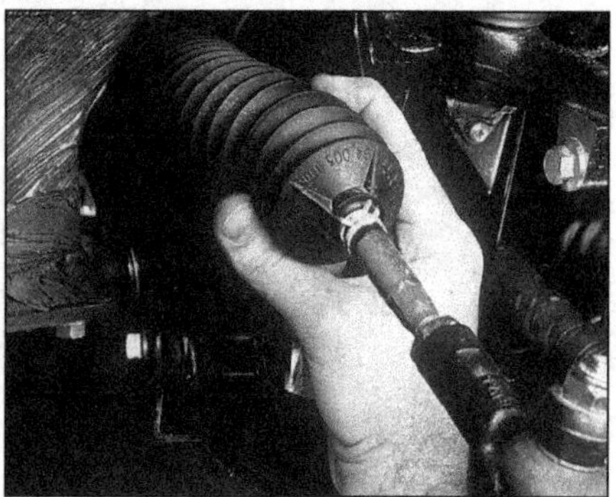

Front and rear suspension and wheel bearings

☐ Starting at the front right-hand side, grasp the roadwheel at the 3 o'clock and 9 o'clock positions and rock gently but firmly. Check for free play or insecurity at the wheel bearings, suspension balljoints, or suspension mountings, pivots and attachments.

☐ Now grasp the wheel at the 12 o'clock and 6 o'clock positions and repeat the previous inspection. Spin the wheel, and check for roughness or tightness of the front wheel bearing.

☐ If excess free play is suspected at a component pivot point, this can be confirmed by using a large screwdriver or similar tool and levering between the mounting and the component attachment. This will confirm whether the wear is in the pivot bush, its retaining bolt, or in the mounting itself (the bolt holes can often become elongated).

☐ Carry out all the above checks at the other front wheel, and then at both rear wheels.

Springs and shock absorbers

☐ Examine the suspension struts (when applicable) for serious fluid leakage, corrosion, or damage to the casing. Also check the security of the mounting points.

☐ If coil springs are fitted, check that the spring ends locate in their seats, and that the spring is not corroded, cracked or broken.

☐ If leaf springs are fitted, check that all leaves are intact, that the axle is securely attached to each spring, and that there is no deterioration of the spring eye mountings, bushes, and shackles.

☐ The same general checks apply to vehicles fitted with other suspension types, such as torsion bars, hydraulic displacer units, etc. Ensure that all mountings and attachments are secure, that there are no signs of excessive wear, corrosion or damage, and (on hydraulic types) that there are no fluid leaks or damaged pipes.

☐ Inspect the shock absorbers for signs of serious fluid leakage. Check for wear of the mounting bushes or attachments, or damage to the body of the unit.

Driveshafts (fwd vehicles only)

☐ Rotate each front wheel in turn and inspect the constant velocity joint gaiters for splits or damage. Also check that each driveshaft is straight and undamaged.

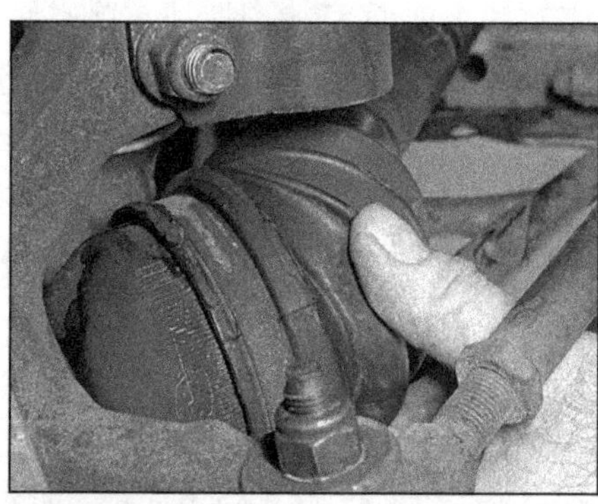

Braking system

☐ If possible without dismantling, check brake pad wear and disc condition. Ensure that the friction lining material has not worn excessively, (A) and that the discs are not fractured, pitted, scored or badly worn (B).

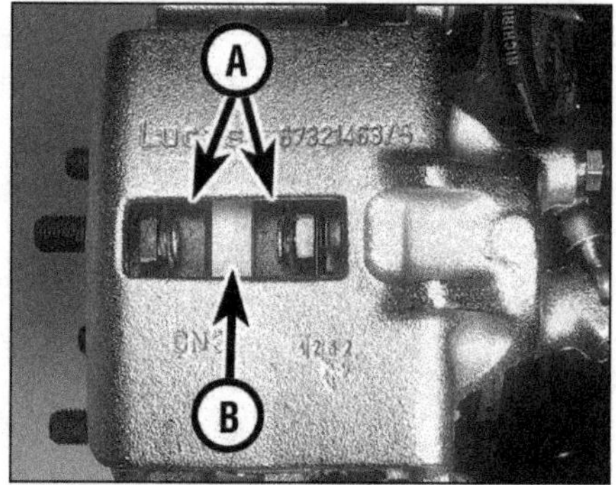

☐ Examine all the rigid brake pipes underneath the vehicle, and the flexible hose(s) at the rear. Look for corrosion, chafing or insecurity of the pipes, and for signs of bulging under pressure, chafing, splits or deterioration of the flexible hoses.

☐ Look for signs of fluid leaks at the brake calipers or on the brake backplates. Repair or renew leaking components.

☐ Slowly spin each wheel, while your assistant depresses and releases the footbrake. Ensure that each brake is operating and does not bind when the pedal is released.

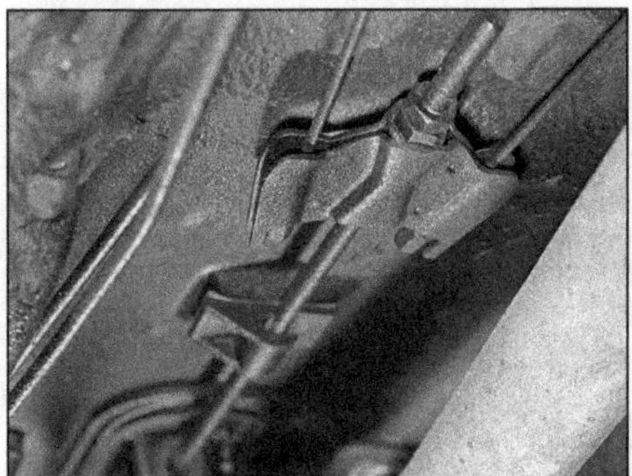

☐ Examine the handbrake mechanism, checking for frayed or broken cables, excessive corrosion, or wear or insecurity of the linkage. Check that the mechanism works on each relevant wheel, and releases fully, without binding.

☐ It is not possible to test brake efficiency without special equipment, but a road test can be carried out later to check that the vehicle pulls up in a straight line.

Fuel and exhaust systems

☐ Inspect the fuel tank (including the filler cap), fuel pipes, hoses and unions. All components must be secure and free from leaks.

☐ Examine the exhaust system over its entire length, checking for any damaged, broken or missing mountings, security of the retaining clamps and rust or corrosion.

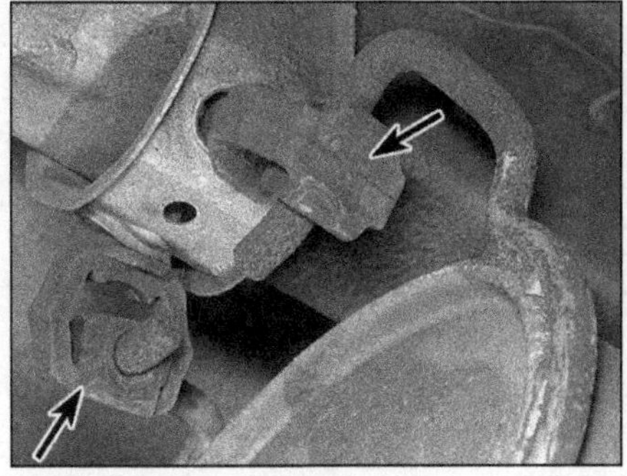

Wheels and tyres

☐ Examine the sidewalls and tread area of each tyre in turn. Check for cuts, tears, lumps, bulges, separation of the tread, and exposure of the ply or cord due to wear or damage. Check that the tyre bead is correctly seated on the wheel rim, that the valve is sound and properly seated, and that the wheel is not distorted or damaged.

☐ Check that the tyres are of the correct size for the vehicle, that they are of the same size and type on each axle, and that the pressures are correct.

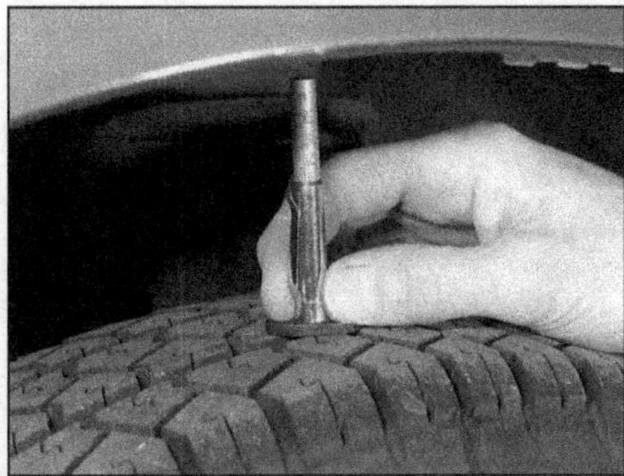

☐ Check the tyre tread depth. The legal minimum at the time of writing is 1.6 mm over at least three-quarters of the tread width. Abnormal tread wear may indicate incorrect front wheel alignment.

Body corrosion

☐ Check the condition of the entire vehicle structure for signs of corrosion in load-bearing areas. (These include chassis box sections, side sills, cross-members, pillars, and all suspension, steering, braking system and seat belt mountings and anchorages.) Any corrosion which has seriously reduced the thickness of a load-bearing area is likely to cause the vehicle to fail. In this case professional repairs are likely to be needed.

☐ Damage or corrosion which causes sharp or otherwise dangerous edges to be exposed will also cause the vehicle to fail.

4 Checks carried out on **YOUR VEHICLE'S EXHAUST EMISSION SYSTEM**

Petrol models

☐ The engine should be warmed up, and running well (ignition system in good order, air filter element clean, etc).

☐ Before testing, run the engine at around 2500 rpm for 20 seconds. Let the engine drop to idle, and watch for smoke from the exhaust. If the idle speed is too high, or if dense blue or black smoke emerges for more than 5 seconds, the vehicle will fail. Typically, blue smoke signifies oil burning (engine wear); black smoke means unburnt fuel (dirty air cleaner element, or other fuel system fault).

☐ An exhaust gas analyser for measuring carbon monoxide (CO) and hydrocarbons (HC) is now needed. If one cannot be hired or borrowed, have a local garage perform the check.

CO emissions (mixture)

☐ The MOT tester has access to the CO limits for all vehicles. The CO level is measured at idle speed, and at 'fast idle' (2500 to 3000 rpm). The following limits are given as a general guide:

At idle speed – Less than 0.5% CO
At 'fast idle' – Less than 0.3% CO
Lambda reading – 0.97 to 1.03

☐ If the CO level is too high, this may point to poor maintenance, a fuel injection system problem, faulty lambda (oxygen) sensor or catalytic converter. Try an injector cleaning treatment, and check the vehicle's ECU for fault codes.

HC emissions

☐ The MOT tester has access to HC limits for all vehicles. The HC level is measured at 'fast idle' (2500 to 3000 rpm). The following limits are given as a general guide:

At 'fast idle' – Less then 200 ppm

☐ Excessive HC emissions are typically caused by oil being burnt (worn engine), or by a blocked crankcase ventilation system ('breather'). If the engine oil is old and thin, an oil change may help. If the engine is running badly, check the vehicle's ECU for fault codes.

Diesel models

☐ The only emission test for diesel engines is measuring exhaust smoke density, using a calibrated smoke meter. The test involves accelerating the engine at least 3 times to its maximum unloaded speed.

Note: *On engines with a timing belt, it is VITAL that the belt is in good condition before the test is carried out.*

☐ With the engine warmed up, it is first purged by running at around 2500 rpm for 20 seconds. A governor check is then carried out, by slowly accelerating the engine to its maximum speed. After this, the smoke meter is connected, and the engine is accelerated quickly to maximum speed three times. If the smoke density is less than the limits given below, the vehicle will pass:

Non-turbo vehicles: 2.5m-1
Turbocharged vehicles: 3.0m-1

☐ If excess smoke is produced, try fitting a new air cleaner element, or using an injector cleaning treatment. If the engine is running badly, where applicable, check the vehicle's ECU for fault codes. Also check the vehicle's EGR system, where applicable. At high mileages, the injectors may require professional attention.

Engine

- ☐ Engine fails to rotate when attempting to start
- ☐ Engine rotates, but will not start
- ☐ Engine difficult to start when cold
- ☐ Engine difficult to start when hot
- ☐ Starter motor noisy or excessively-rough in engagement
- ☐ Engine starts, but stops immediately
- ☐ Engine idles erratically
- ☐ Engine misfires at idle speed
- ☐ Engine misfires throughout the driving speed range
- ☐ Engine hesitates on acceleration
- ☐ Engine stalls
- ☐ Engine lacks power
- ☐ Engine backfires
- ☐ Oil pressure warning light on with engine running
- ☐ Engine runs-on after switching off
- ☐ Engine noises

Cooling system

- ☐ Overheating
- ☐ Overcooling
- ☐ External coolant leakage
- ☐ Internal coolant leakage
- ☐ Corrosion

Fuel and exhaust systems

- ☐ Excessive fuel consumption
- ☐ Fuel leakage and/or fuel odour
- ☐ Excessive noise or fumes from exhaust system

Clutch

- ☐ Pedal travels to floor – no pressure or very little resistance
- ☐ Clutch fails to disengage (unable to select gears)
- ☐ Clutch slips (engine speed rises, with no increase in vehicle speed)
- ☐ Judder as clutch is engaged
- ☐ Noise when depressing or releasing clutch pedal

Manual transmission

- ☐ Noisy in neutral with engine running
- ☐ Noisy in one particular gear
- ☐ Difficulty engaging gears
- ☐ Jumps out of gear
- ☐ Vibration
- ☐ Lubricant leaks

Automatic transmission

- ☐ Fluid leakage
- ☐ Transmission fluid brown, or has burned smell
- ☐ General gear selection problems
- ☐ Transmission will not downshift (kickdown) on full throttle
- ☐ Engine won't start in any gear, or starts in gears other than P or N
- ☐ Transmission slips, shifts roughly, is noisy, or has no drive in forward or reverse gears

Driveshafts

- ☐ Clicking or knocking noise on turns (at slow speed on full-lock)
- ☐ Vibration when accelerating or decelerating

Braking system

- ☐ Vehicle pulls to one side under braking
- ☐ Noise (grinding or high-pitched squeal) when brakes applied
- ☐ Excessive brake pedal travel
- ☐ Brake pedal feels spongy when depressed
- ☐ Excessive brake pedal effort required to stop vehicle
- ☐ Judder felt through brake pedal or steering wheel when braking
- ☐ Brakes binding
- ☐ Rear wheels locking under normal braking

Suspension and steering systems

- ☐ Vehicle pulls to one side
- ☐ Wheel wobble and vibration
- ☐ Excessive pitching and/or rolling around corners, or during braking
- ☐ Wandering or general instability
- ☐ Excessively-stiff steering
- ☐ Excessive play in steering
- ☐ Lack of power assistance
- ☐ Tyre wear excessive

Electrical system

- ☐ Battery will not hold a charge for more than a few days
- ☐ Ignition/no-charge warning light stays on with engine running
- ☐ Ignition/no-charge warning light fails to come on
- ☐ Lights inoperative
- ☐ Instrument readings inaccurate or erratic
- ☐ Horn inoperative, or unsatisfactory in operation
- ☐ Windscreen/tailgate wipers failed, or unsatisfactory in operation
- ☐ Windscreen/tailgate washers failed, or unsatisfactory in operation
- ☐ Electric windows inoperative, or unsatisfactory in operation
- ☐ Central locking system inoperative, or unsatisfactory in operation

Introduction

The vehicle owner who does his or her own maintenance according to the recommended service schedules should not have to use this section of the manual very often. Modern component reliability is such that, provided those items subject to wear or deterioration are inspected or renewed at the specified intervals, sudden failure is comparatively rare. Faults do not usually just happen as a result of sudden failure, but develop over a period of time. Major mechanical failures in particular are usually preceded by characteristic symptoms over hundreds or even thousands of miles. Those components, which do occasionally fail without warning, are often small and easily carried in the vehicle.

With any fault-finding, the first step is to decide where to begin investigations. Sometimes this is obvious, but on other occasions, a little detective work will be necessary. The owner who makes half a dozen haphazard adjustments or replacements may be successful in curing a fault (or its symptoms), but will be none the wiser if the fault recurs, and ultimately may have spent more time and money than was necessary. A calm and logical approach will be found to be more satisfactory in the long run. Always take into account any warning signs or abnormalities that may have been noticed in the period preceding the fault – power loss, high or low gauge readings, unusual smells, etc – and remember that failure of components such as fuses or spark plugs may only be pointers to some underlying fault.

The pages which follow provide an easy-reference guide to the more common problems which may occur during the operation of the vehicle. These problems and their possible causes are grouped under headings denoting various components or systems, such as Engine, Cooling system, etc. The general Chapter which deals with the problem is also shown in brackets; refer to the relevant part of that Chapter for system-specific information. Whatever the fault, certain basic principles apply. These are as follows:

Verify the fault. This is simply a matter of

being sure that you know what the symptoms are before starting work. This is particularly important if you are investigating a fault for someone else, who may not have described it very accurately.

Don't overlook the obvious. For example, if the vehicle won't start, is there fuel in the tank? (Don't take anyone else's word on this particular point, and don't trust the fuel gauge either!) If an electrical fault is indicated, look for loose or broken wires before digging out the test gear.

Cure the disease, not the symptom. Substituting a flat battery with a fully-charged one will get you off the hard shoulder, but if the underlying cause is not attended to, the new battery will go the same way. Similarly, changing oil-fouled spark plugs (petrol models) for a new set will get you moving again, but remember that the reason for the fouling (if it wasn't simply an incorrect grade of plug) will have to be found and corrected.

Don't take anything for granted. Particularly, don't forget that a 'new' component may itself be defective (especially if it's been rattling around in the boot for months), and don't leave components out of a fault diagnosis sequence just because they are new or recently fitted. When you do finally diagnose a difficult fault, you'll probably realise that all the evidence was there from the start.

Diesel fault diagnosis

The majority of starting problems on small diesel engines are electrical in origin. The mechanic who is familiar with petrol engines but less so with diesel may be inclined to view the diesel's injectors and pump in the same light as the spark plugs and distributor, but this is generally a mistake.

When investigating complaints of difficult starting for someone else, make sure that the correct starting procedure is understood and is being followed. Some drivers are unaware of the significance of the preheating warning light – many modern engines are sufficiently forgiving for this not to matter in mild weather, but with the onset of winter, problems begin. Glow plugs in particular are often neglected – just one faulty plug will make cold-weather starting very difficult.

As a rule of thumb, if the engine is difficult to start but runs well when it has finally got going, the problem is electrical (battery, starter motor or preheating system). If poor performance is combined with difficult starting, the problem is likely to be in the fuel system. The low-pressure (supply) side of the fuel system should be checked before suspecting the injectors and high-pressure pump. The most common fuel supply problem is air getting into the system, and any pipe from the fuel tank forwards must be scrutinised if air leakage is suspected.

Engine

Engine fails to rotate when attempting to start

- ☐ Battery terminal connections loose or corroded (*Weekly checks*).
- ☐ Battery discharged or faulty (Chapter 5A).
- ☐ Broken, loose or disconnected wiring in the starting circuit (Chapter 5A).
- ☐ Defective starter motor (Chapter 5A).
- ☐ Starter pinion or flywheel/driveplate ring gear teeth loose or broken (Chapter 2A, 2B and 5A).
- ☐ Engine earth strap broken or disconnected (Chapter 12).

Engine rotates, but will not start

- ☐ Fuel tank empty.
- ☐ Battery discharged (engine rotates slowly) (Chapter 5A).
- ☐ Battery terminal connections loose or corroded (*Weekly checks*).
- ☐ Worn, faulty or incorrectly-gapped spark plugs – petrol models (Chapter 1A).
- ☐ Air in fuel system – diesel models (Chapter 1B).
- ☐ Engine management system fault (Chapter 4A or 4B).
- ☐ Low cylinder compressions (Chapter 2A or 2B).
- ☐ Major mechanical failure (eg camshaft drive) (Chapter 2A or 2B).

Engine difficult to start when cold

- ☐ Battery discharged (Chapter 5A).
- ☐ Battery terminal connections loose or corroded (*Weekly checks*).
- ☐ Worn, faulty or incorrectly-gapped spark plugs – petrol models (Chapter 1A).
- ☐ Preheating system fault – diesel models (Chapter 5A).
- ☐ Engine management system fault (Chapter 4A or 4B).

Engine difficult to start when hot

- ☐ Air filter element dirty or clogged (Chapter 1A or 1B).
- ☐ Engine management system fault (Chapter 4A or 4B).
- ☐ Low cylinder compressions (Chapter 2A).

Starter motor noisy or excessively rough in engagement

- ☐ Starter pinion or flywheel/driveplate ring gear teeth loose or broken (Chapters 2A, 2B and 5A).
- ☐ Starter motor mounting bolts loose or missing (Chapter 5A).
- ☐ Defective starter motor (Chapter 5A).

Engine starts, but stops immediately

- ☐ Vacuum leak at the throttle housing/inlet manifold – petrol models (Chapter 4A).
- ☐ Engine management system fault (Chapter 4A or 4B).
- ☐ Blocked injector/fuel injection system fault (Chapter 4A or 4B).
- ☐ Faulty injectors – diesel models (Chapter 4B).
- ☐ Air in fuel system – diesel models (Chapter 4B).

Engine idles erratically

- ☐ Vacuum leak at the throttle housing/inlet manifold – petrol models (Chapter 4A).
- ☐ Worn, faulty or incorrectly-gapped spark plugs – petrol models (Chapter 1A).
- ☐ Engine management system fault (Chapter 4A or 4B).
- ☐ Uneven or low cylinder compressions (Chapter 2A).
- ☐ Camshaft lobes worn (Chapter 2A or 2B).
- ☐ Timing belt/chain incorrectly fitted (Chapter 2A or 2B).
- ☐ Faulty injectors – diesel models (Chapter 4B).

Engine misfires at idle speed

- ☐ Worn, faulty or incorrectly-gapped spark plugs (Chapter 1A).
- ☐ Vacuum leak at the throttle housing/inlet manifold (Chapter 4A).
- ☐ Blocked injector/fuel injection system fault (Chapter 4A or 4B).
- ☐ Faulty injectors – diesel models (Chapter 4B).
- ☐ Engine management system fault (Chapter 4A or 4B).
- ☐ Uneven or low cylinder compressions (Chapter 2A).
- ☐ Disconnected, leaking, or perished crankcase ventilation hoses (Chapter 4B).

Engine misfires throughout the driving speed range

- ☐ Fuel filter blocked (Chapter 1A or 1B).
- ☐ Fuel pump faulty (Chapter 4A or 4B).
- ☐ Fuel tank vent blocked, or fuel pipes restricted (Chapter 4A or 4B).
- ☐ Worn, faulty or incorrectly-gapped spark plugs – petrol models (Chapter 1A).
- ☐ Vacuum leak at the throttle housing/inlet manifold – petrol models (Chapter 4A).
- ☐ Engine management system fault (Chapter 4A or 4B).
- ☐ Faulty ignition HT coil (Chapter 5B).
- ☐ Faulty injectors – diesel models (Chapter 4B).
- ☐ Uneven or low cylinder compressions (Chapter 2A or 2B).
- ☐ Blocked injector/fuel injection system fault (Chapter 4A or 4B).

Engine (continued)

Engine hesitates on acceleration

- ☐ Worn, faulty or incorrectly-gapped spark plugs – petrol models (Chapter 1A).
- ☐ Vacuum leak at the throttle housing/inlet manifold – petrol models (Chapter 4A).
- ☐ Engine management system fault (Chapter 4A or 4B).
- ☐ Faulty injectors – diesel models (Chapter 4B).

Engine stalls

- ☐ Fuel filter blocked – diesel models (Chapter 1B).
- ☐ Fuel pump faulty (Chapter 4A or 4B).
- ☐ Fuel tank vent blocked, or fuel pipes restricted (Chapter 4A).
- ☐ Worn, faulty or incorrectly-gapped spark plugs – petrol models (Chapter 1A).
- ☐ Vacuum leak at the throttle housing/inlet manifold – petrol models (Chapter 4A).
- ☐ Engine management system fault (Chapter 4A or 4B).
- ☐ Blocked injector/fuel injection system fault (Chapter 4A or 4B).
- ☐ Faulty injectors – diesel models (Chapter 4B).

Engine lacks power

- ☐ Timing belt/chain incorrectly fitted (Chapter 2A or 2B).
- ☐ Fuel filter blocked – diesel models (Chapter 1B).
- ☐ Fuel pump faulty (Chapter 4A or 4B).
- ☐ Uneven or low cylinder compressions (Chapter 2A).
- ☐ Worn, faulty or incorrectly-gapped spark plugs – petrol models (Chapter 1A).
- ☐ Vacuum leak at the throttle housing/inlet manifold – petrol models (Chapter 4A).
- ☐ Engine management system fault (Chapter 4A or 4B).
- ☐ Brakes binding (Chapters 1A, 1B and 9).
- ☐ Clutch slipping (Chapter 6).

Engine backfires

- ☐ Timing belt/chain incorrectly fitted (Chapter 2A or 2B).
- ☐ Vacuum leak at the throttle housing/inlet manifold – petrol models (Chapter 4A).
- ☐ Engine management system fault (Chapter 4A or 4B).
- ☐ Blocked injector/fuel injection system fault (Chapter 4A or 4B).

Oil pressure warning light on with engine running

- ☐ Low oil level, or incorrect oil grade (*Weekly checks*).
- ☐ Faulty oil pressure warning light switch (Chapter 2A).
- ☐ Worn engine bearings and/or oil pump (Chapter 2C).
- ☐ High engine operating temperature (Chapter 3).
- ☐ Oil pressure relief valve defective (Chapter 2A or 2B).
- ☐ Oil pick-up strainer clogged (Chapter 2A or 2B).

Engine runs-on after switching off

- ☐ Excessive carbon build-up in engine (Chapter 2C).
- ☐ High engine operating temperature (Chapter 3).
- ☐ Engine management system fault (Chapter 4A or 4B).
- ☐ Faulty shut-off valve faulty – diesel models (Chapter 4B).

Engine noises

Pre-ignition (pinking) or knocking during acceleration or under load

- ☐ Engine management system fault (Chapter 4A or 4B).
- ☐ Incorrect grade of spark plug – petrol models (Chapter 1A).
- ☐ Incorrect grade of fuel (Chapter 4A or 4B).
- ☐ Vacuum leak at the throttle housing/inlet manifold – petrol models (Chapter 4A).
- ☐ Excessive carbon build-up in engine (Chapter 2C).

Whistling or wheezing noises

- ☐ Leaking inlet manifold or throttle housing gasket (Chapter 4A).
- ☐ Leaking vacuum hose (Chapters 4A, 4B and 9).
- ☐ Blowing cylinder head gasket (Chapter 2A or 2B).

Tapping or rattling noises

- ☐ Worn valve gear or camshaft (Chapter 2A, 2B or 2C).
- ☐ Ancillary component fault (coolant pump, alternator, etc) (Chapters 3, 5A, etc).

Knocking or thumping noises

- ☐ Worn big-end bearings (regular heavy knocking, perhaps less under load) (Chapter 2C).
- ☐ Worn main bearings (rumbling and knocking, perhaps worsening under load) (Chapter 2C).
- ☐ Piston slap (most noticeable when cold) (Chapter 2C).
- ☐ Ancillary component fault (coolant pump, alternator, etc) (Chapters 3, 5A, etc).

Cooling system

Overheating

- ☐ Insufficient coolant in system (*Weekly checks*).
- ☐ Thermostat faulty (stuck closed) (Chapter 3).
- ☐ Radiator core blocked, or grille restricted (Chapter 3).
- ☐ Electric cooling fan or sensor faulty (Chapter 3).
- ☐ Pressure cap faulty (Chapter 3).
- ☐ Inaccurate temperature gauge/sensor (Chapter 3).
- ☐ Airlock in cooling system (Chapter 1A or 1B).
- ☐ Engine management system fault (Chapter 4A or 4B).

Overcooling

- ☐ Thermostat faulty (stuck open) (Chapter 3).
- ☐ Inaccurate temperature gauge/sensor (Chapter 3).

External coolant leakage

- ☐ Deteriorated or damaged hoses or hose clips (Chapter 1A or 1B).
- ☐ Radiator core or heater matrix leaking (Chapter 3).
- ☐ Pressure cap faulty (Chapter 3).
- ☐ Coolant pump leaking (Chapter 3).
- ☐ Boiling due to overheating (Chapter 3).
- ☐ Core plug leaking (Chapter 2C).

Internal coolant leakage

- ☐ Leaking cylinder head gasket (Chapter 2A or 2B).
- ☐ Cracked cylinder head or cylinder bore (Chapter 2A, 2B or 2C).

Corrosion

- ☐ Infrequent draining and flushing (Chapter 1A or 1B).
- ☐ Incorrect coolant mixture or inappropriate coolant type (Chapter 1A or 1B).

Fuel and exhaust systems

Excessive fuel consumption

- ☐ Air filter element dirty or clogged (Chapter 1A or 1B).
- ☐ Engine management system fault (Chapter 4A or 4B).
- ☐ Faulty injector(s) (Chapter 4A or 4B).
- ☐ Tyres under-inflated (*Weekly checks*).
- ☐ Brakes binding (Chapters 1A, 1B and 9).

Fuel leakage and/or fuel odour

- ☐ Damaged or corroded fuel tank, pipes or connections (Chapter 4A).
- ☐ Faulty fuel injection system (Chapter 4A or 4B).

Excessive noise or fumes from exhaust system

- ☐ Leaking exhaust system or manifold joints (Chapters 1 and 4A).
- ☐ Leaking, corroded or damaged silencers or pipe (Chapters 1A, 1B and 4A).
- ☐ Broken mountings causing body or suspension contact (Chapters 1A, 1B and 4A).

Clutch

Pedal travels to floor – no pressure or very little resistance

- ☐ Air in hydraulic system/faulty master or slave cylinder (Chapter 6).
- ☐ Broken clutch release bearing or fork (Chapter 6).
- ☐ Broken diaphragm spring in clutch pressure plate (Chapter 6).

Clutch fails to disengage (unable to select gears)

- ☐ Air in hydraulic system/faulty master or slave cylinder (Chapter 6).
- ☐ Clutch disc sticking on gearbox input shaft splines (Chapter 6).
- ☐ Clutch disc sticking to flywheel or pressure plate (Chapter 6).
- ☐ Faulty pressure plate assembly (Chapter 6).
- ☐ Clutch release mechanism worn or incorrectly assembled (Chapter 6).

Clutch slips (engine speed rises, with no increase in vehicle speed)

- ☐ Faulty hydraulic release system (Chapter 6).
- ☐ Clutch disc linings excessively worn (Chapter 6).
- ☐ Clutch disc linings contaminated with oil or grease (Chapter 6).
- ☐ Faulty pressure plate or weak diaphragm spring (Chapter 6).

Judder as clutch is engaged

- ☐ Clutch disc linings contaminated with oil or grease (Chapter 6).
- ☐ Clutch disc linings excessively worn (Chapter 6).
- ☐ Faulty or distorted pressure plate or diaphragm spring (Chapter 6).
- ☐ Worn or loose engine or gearbox mountings (Chapter 2A, 2B or 2C).
- ☐ Clutch disc hub or gearbox input shaft splines worn (Chapter 6).

Noise when depressing or releasing clutch pedal

- ☐ Worn clutch release bearing (Chapter 6).
- ☐ Worn or dry clutch pedal bushes (Chapter 6).
- ☐ Faulty pressure plate assembly (Chapter 6).
- ☐ Pressure plate diaphragm spring broken (Chapter 6).
- ☐ Broken clutch disc cushioning springs (Chapter 6).

Manual transmission

Noisy in neutral with engine running

- ☐ Input shaft bearings worn (noise apparent with clutch pedal released, but not when depressed) (Chapter 7A).*
- ☐ Clutch release bearing worn (noise apparent with clutch pedal depressed, possibly less when released) (Chapter 6).

Noisy in one particular gear

- ☐ Worn, damaged or chipped gear teeth (Chapter 7A).*

Difficulty engaging gears

- ☐ Clutch fault (Chapter 6).
- ☐ Worn or damaged gear selection cables (Chapter 7A).
- ☐ Worn synchroniser units (Chapter 7A).*

Jumps out of gear

- ☐ Worn or damaged gear selection cables (Chapter 7A).
- ☐ Worn synchroniser units (Chapter 7A).*
- ☐ Worn selector forks (Chapter 7A).*

Vibration

- ☐ Lack of oil (Chapters 1A and 1B).
- ☐ Worn bearings (Chapter 7A).*

Lubricant leaks

- ☐ Leaking differential output oil seal (Chapter 7A).
- ☐ Leaking housing joint (Chapter 7A).*
- ☐ Leaking input shaft oil seal (Chapter 7A).

** Although the corrective action necessary to remedy the symptoms described is beyond the scope of the home mechanic, the above information should be helpful in isolating the cause of the condition, so that the owner can communicate clearly with a professional mechanic.*

Automatic transmission

Note: *Due to the complexity of the automatic transmission, it is difficult for the home mechanic to properly diagnose and service this unit. For problems other than the following, the vehicle should be taken to a Toyota dealer service department or suitably equipped specialist.*

Fluid leakage

- ☐ Automatic transmission fluid is usually dark in colour. Fluid leaks should not be confused with engine oil, which can easily be blown onto the transmission by airflow.
- ☐ To determine the source of a leak, first remove all built-up dirt and grime from the transmission housing and surrounding areas using a degreasing agent, or by steam-cleaning. Drive the vehicle at low speed, so airflow will not blow the leak far from its source. Raise and support the vehicle, and determine where the leak is coming from.

Transmission fluid brown, or has burned smell

- ☐ Transmission fluid level low, or fluid in need of renewal (Chapter 1A).

General gear selection problems

- ☐ Chapter 7B deals with checking and adjusting the selector cable on automatic transmissions. The following are common problems which may be caused by a poorly-adjusted cable:
  - a) *Engine starting in gears other than Park or Neutral.*
  - b) *Indicator panel showing a gear other than that being used.*
  - c) *Vehicle moves when in Park or Neutral.*
  - d) *Poor gear shift quality or erratic gearchanges.*
- ☐ Refer to Chapter 7B for the selector cable adjustment procedure.

Transmission will not downshift (kickdown) at full throttle

- ☐ Low transmission fluid level (Chapter 1A).
- ☐ Incorrect selector cable adjustment (Chapter 7B).

Engine won't start in any gear, or starts in gears other than Park or Neutral

- ☐ Incorrect park/neutral position switch adjustment (Chapter 7B).
- ☐ Incorrect selector cable adjustment (Chapter 7B).

Transmission slips, shifts roughly, is noisy, or has no drive in forward or reverse gears

- ☐ There are many probable causes for the above problems, but the home mechanic should be concerned with only one possibility – fluid level. Before taking the vehicle to a dealer or transmission specialist, check the fluid level as described in Chapter 1A. Correct the fluid level as necessary, or change the fluid. If the problem persists, professional help will be necessary.

Driveshafts

Clicking or knocking noise on turns (at slow speed on full-lock)

- ☐ Lack of constant velocity joint lubricant, possibly due to damaged gaiter (Chapter 8).
- ☐ Worn outer constant velocity joint (Chapter 8).

Vibration when accelerating or decelerating

- ☐ Worn inner constant velocity joint (Chapter 8).
- ☐ Bent or distorted driveshaft (Chapter 8).

Braking system

Note: *Before assuming that a brake problem exists, make sure that the tyres are in good condition and correctly inflated, that the front wheel alignment is correct, and that the vehicle is not loaded with weight in an unequal manner. Apart from checking the condition of all pipe and hose connections, any faults occurring on the anti-lock braking system should be referred to a Toyota dealer for diagnosis.*

Vehicle pulls to one side under braking

- ☐ Worn, defective, damaged or contaminated brake pads/shoes on one side (Chapter 9).
- ☐ Seized or partially-seized brake caliper (Chapter 9).
- ☐ A mixture of brake pad materials fitted between sides (Chapter 9).
- ☐ Brake caliper mounting bolts loose (Chapter 9).
- ☐ Worn or damaged steering or suspension components (Chapters 1A, 1B and 10).

Noise (grinding or high-pitched squeal) when brakes applied

- ☐ Brake pad material worn down to metal backing (Chapters 1A, 1B and 9).
- ☐ Excessive corrosion of brake disc. May be apparent after the vehicle has been standing for some time (Chapter 9).
- ☐ Foreign object (stone chipping, etc) trapped between brake disc and shield (Chapter 9).

Excessive brake pedal travel

- ☐ Faulty master cylinder (Chapter 9).
- ☐ Air in hydraulic system (Chapter 9).
- ☐ Faulty vacuum servo unit (Chapter 9).

Brake pedal feels spongy when depressed

- ☐ Air in hydraulic system (Chapter 9).
- ☐ Deteriorated flexible rubber brake hoses (Chapters 1A, 1B and 9).
- ☐ Master cylinder mounting nuts loose (Chapter 9).
- ☐ Faulty master cylinder (Chapter 9).

Excessive brake pedal effort required to stop vehicle

- ☐ Faulty vacuum servo unit (Chapter 9).
- ☐ Disconnected, damaged or insecure brake servo vacuum hose (Chapter 9).
- ☐ Primary or secondary hydraulic circuit failure (Chapter 9).
- ☐ Seized brake caliper (Chapter 9).
- ☐ Brake pads incorrectly fitted (Chapter 9).
- ☐ Incorrect grade of brake pads fitted (Chapter 9).
- ☐ Brake pads contaminated (Chapter 9).

Judder felt through brake pedal or steering wheel when braking

Note: *This is normal when braking hard in ABS-equipped vehicles.*

- ☐ Excessive run-out or distortion of discs (Chapters 9).
- ☐ Brake pads worn (Chapters 1 and 9).
- ☐ Brake caliper mounting bolts loose (Chapter 9).
- ☐ Wear in suspension or steering components or mountings (Chapters 1A, 1B and 10).

Brakes binding

- ☐ Seized brake caliper (Chapter 9).
- ☐ Incorrectly-adjusted handbrake mechanism (Chapter 9).
- ☐ Faulty master cylinder (Chapter 9).

Rear wheels locking under normal braking

- ☐ Rear brake pads contaminated (Chapters 1A, 1B and 9).
- ☐ ABS system fault (Chapter 9).

Suspension and steering

Note: *Before diagnosing suspension or steering faults, be sure that the trouble is not due to incorrect tyre pressures, mixtures of tyre types, or binding brakes.*

Vehicle pulls to one side

- ☐ Defective tyre (*Weekly checks*).
- ☐ Excessive wear in suspension or steering components (Chapters 1A, 1B and 10).
- ☐ Incorrect front wheel alignment (Chapter 10).
- ☐ Damage to steering or suspension components (Chapter 1A or 1B).

Wheel wobble and vibration

- ☐ Front roadwheels out of balance (vibration felt mainly through the steering wheel) (Chapters 1A, 1B and 10).
- ☐ Rear roadwheels out of balance (vibration felt throughout the vehicle) (Chapters 1A, 1B and 10).
- ☐ Roadwheels damaged or distorted (Chapters 1A, 1B and 10).
- ☐ Faulty or damaged tyre (*Weekly checks*).
- ☐ Worn steering or suspension joints, bushes or components (Chapters 1A, 1B and 10).
- ☐ Wheel nuts loose (Chapters 1A, 1B and 10).

Excessive pitching and/or rolling around corners, or during braking

- ☐ Defective shock absorbers (Chapters 1A, 1B and 10).
- ☐ Broken or weak spring and/or suspension part (Chapters 1A, 1B and 10).
- ☐ Worn or damaged anti-roll bar or mountings (Chapter 10).

Wandering or general instability

- ☐ Incorrect front wheel alignment (Chapter 10).
- ☐ Worn steering or suspension joints, bushes or components (Chapters 1A, 1B and 10).
- ☐ Roadwheels out of balance (Chapters 1A, 1B and 10).
- ☐ Faulty or damaged tyre (*Weekly checks*).
- ☐ Wheel nuts loose (Chapters 1A, 1B and 10).
- ☐ Defective shock absorbers (Chapters 1A, 1B and 10).

Excessively-stiff steering

- ☐ Seized track rod end balljoint or suspension balljoint (Chapters 1A, 1B and 10).
- ☐ Incorrect front wheel alignment (Chapter 10).
- ☐ Steering rack or column bent or damaged (Chapter 10).
- ☐ Power steering fault (Chapter 10).

Excessive play in steering

- ☐ Worn steering column universal joint (Chapter 10).
- ☐ Worn steering track rod end balljoints (Chapters 1A, 1B and 10).
- ☐ Worn steering rack (Chapter 10).
- ☐ Worn steering or suspension joints, bushes or components (Chapters 1A, 1B and 10).

Lack of power assistance

- ☐ Faulty power steering motor (Chapter 10).
- ☐ Faulty steering rack (Chapter 10).

Tyre wear excessive

Tyre treads exhibit feathered edges

- ☐ Incorrect toe setting (Chapter 10).

Tyres worn in centre of tread

- ☐ Tyres over-inflated (*Weekly checks*).

Tyres worn on inside and outside edges

- ☐ Tyres under-inflated (*Weekly checks*).

Tyres worn on inside or outside edges

- ☐ Incorrect camber/castor angles (wear on one edge only) – (Chapter 10).
- ☐ Worn steering or suspension joints, bushes or components (Chapters 1A, 1B and 10).
- ☐ Excessively-hard cornering.
- ☐ Accident damage.

Tyres worn unevenly

- ☐ Tyres/wheels out of balance (*Weekly checks*).
- ☐ Excessive wheel or tyre run-out (Chapter 1A or 1B).
- ☐ Worn shock absorbers (Chapters 1A, 1B and 10).
- ☐ Faulty tyre (*Weekly checks*).

Electrical system

Note: *For problems associated with the starting system, refer to the faults listed under 'Engine' earlier in this Section.*

Battery won't hold a charge for more than a few days

- ☐ Battery defective internally (Chapter 5A).
- ☐ Battery terminal connections loose or corroded (*Weekly checks*).
- ☐ Auxiliary drivebelt broken, worn or incorrectly adjusted (Chapter 1A or 1B).
- ☐ Alternator not charging at correct output (Chapter 5A).
- ☐ Alternator or voltage regulator faulty (Chapter 5A).
- ☐ Short-circuit causing continual battery drain (Chapters 5A and 12).

Ignition/no-charge warning light stays on with engine running

- ☐ Auxiliary drivebelt broken, worn, or incorrectly adjusted (Chapter 1A or 1B).
- ☐ Internal fault in alternator or voltage regulator (Chapter 5A).
- ☐ Broken, disconnected, or loose wiring in charging circuit (Chapter 5A).

Ignition/no-charge warning light fails to come on

- ☐ Warning light bulb blown (Chapter 12).
- ☐ Broken, disconnected, or loose wiring in warning light circuit (Chapter 12).
- ☐ Alternator faulty (Chapter 5A).

Electrical system (continued)

Lights inoperative

- ☐ Bulb blown (Chapter 12).
- ☐ Corrosion of bulb or bulbholder contacts (Chapter 12).
- ☐ Blown fuse (Chapter 12).
- ☐ Faulty relay (Chapter 12).
- ☐ Broken, loose, or disconnected wiring (Chapter 12).
- ☐ Faulty switch (Chapter 12).

Instrument readings inaccurate or erratic

Fuel or temperature gauges give no reading

- ☐ Faulty gauge sensor unit (Chapter 3 or 4).
- ☐ Wiring open-circuit (Chapter 12).
- ☐ Faulty gauge (Chapter 12).

Fuel or temperature gauges give continuous maximum reading

- ☐ Faulty gauge sensor unit (Chapter 3 or 4).
- ☐ Wiring short-circuit (Chapter 12).
- ☐ Faulty gauge (Chapter 12).

Horn inoperative, or unsatisfactory in operation

Horn operates all the time

- ☐ Horn push either earthed or stuck down (Chapter 12).
- ☐ Horn cable-to-horn push earthed (Chapter 12).

Horn fails to operate

- ☐ Blown fuse (Chapter 12).
- ☐ Cable or cable connections loose, broken or disconnected (Chapter 12).
- ☐ Faulty horn (Chapter 12).

Horn emits intermittent or unsatisfactory sound

- ☐ Cable connections loose (Chapter 12).
- ☐ Horn mountings loose (Chapter 12).
- ☐ Faulty horn (Chapter 12).

Windscreen/tailgate wipers failed, or unsatisfactory in operation

Wipers fail to operate, or operate very slowly

- ☐ Wiper blades stuck to screen, or linkage seized or binding (Chapters 1 and 12).
- ☐ Blown fuse (Chapter 12).
- ☐ Cable or cable connections loose, broken or disconnected (Chapter 12).
- ☐ Faulty built-in system interface (BSI) unit (Chapter 12).
- ☐ Faulty wiper motor (Chapter 12).

Wiper blades sweep over too large or too small an area of the glass

- ☐ Wiper arms incorrectly positioned on spindles (Chapter 12).
- ☐ Excessive wear of wiper linkage (Chapter 12).
- ☐ Wiper motor or linkage mountings loose or insecure (Chapter 12).

Wiper blades fail to clean the glass effectively

- ☐ Wiper blade rubbers worn or perished (*Weekly checks*).
- ☐ Wiper arm tension springs broken, or arm pivots seized (Chapter 12).
- ☐ Insufficient windscreen washer additive to adequately remove road film (*Weekly checks*).

Windscreen/tailgate washers failed, or unsatisfactory in operation

One or more washer jets inoperative

- ☐ Blocked washer jet (*Weekly checks*).
- ☐ Disconnected, kinked or restricted fluid hose (Chapter 12).
- ☐ Insufficient fluid in washer reservoir (*Weekly checks*).

Washer pump fails to operate

- ☐ Broken or disconnected wiring or connections (Chapter 12).
- ☐ Blown fuse (Chapter 12).
- ☐ Faulty washer switch (Chapter 12).
- ☐ Faulty washer pump (Chapter 12).

Electric windows inoperative, or unsatisfactory in operation

Window glass will only move in one direction

- ☐ Faulty switch (Chapter 12).

Window glass slow to move

- ☐ Regulator seized or damaged, or in need of lubricant (Chapter 11).
- ☐ Door internal components or trim fouling regulator (Chapter 11).
- ☐ Faulty motor (Chapter 11).

Window glass fails to move

- ☐ Blown fuse (Chapter 12).
- ☐ Broken or disconnected wiring or connections (Chapter 12).
- ☐ Faulty motor (Chapter 11).

Central locking system inoperative, or unsatisfactory in operation

Complete system failure

- ☐ Blown fuse (Chapter 12).
- ☐ Broken or disconnected wiring or connections (Chapter 12).

Door/tailgate locks but will not unlock, or unlocks but will not lock

- ☐ Broken or disconnected link rod(s) (Chapter 11).
- ☐ Faulty lock motor (Chapter 11).

One lock fails to operate

- ☐ Broken or disconnected wiring or connections (Chapter 12).
- ☐ Faulty lock motor (Chapter 11).
- ☐ Broken, binding or disconnected link rod(s) (Chapter 11).

A

ABS (Anti-lock brake system) A system, usually electronically controlled, that senses incipient wheel lockup during braking and relieves hydraulic pressure at wheels that are about to skid.
Air bag An inflatable bag hidden in the steering wheel (driver's side) or the dash or glovebox (passenger side). In a head-on collision, the bags inflate, preventing the driver and front passenger from being thrown forward into the steering wheel or windscreen.
Air cleaner A metal or plastic housing, containing a filter element, which removes dust and dirt from the air being drawn into the engine.
Air filter element The actual filter in an air cleaner system, usually manufactured from pleated paper and requiring renewal at regular intervals.

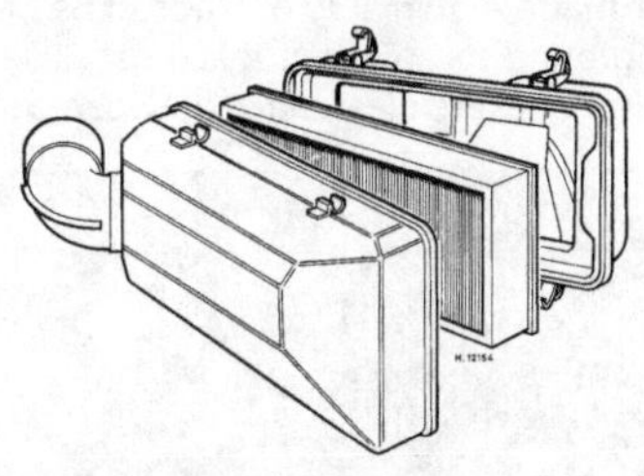

Air filter

Allen key A hexagonal wrench which fits into a recessed hexagonal hole.
Alligator clip A long-nosed spring-loaded metal clip with meshing teeth. Used to make temporary electrical connections.
Alternator A component in the electrical system which converts mechanical energy from a drivebelt into electrical energy to charge the battery and to operate the starting system, ignition system and electrical accessories.
Ampere (amp) A unit of measurement for the flow of electric current. One amp is the amount of current produced by one volt acting through a resistance of one ohm.
Anaerobic sealer A substance used to prevent bolts and screws from loosening. Anaerobic means that it does not require oxygen for activation. The Loctite brand is widely used.
Antifreeze A substance (usually ethylene glycol) mixed with water, and added to a vehicle's cooling system, to prevent freezing of the coolant in winter. Antifreeze also contains chemicals to inhibit corrosion and the formation of rust and other deposits that would tend to clog the radiator and coolant passages and reduce cooling efficiency.
Anti-seize compound A coating that reduces the risk of seizing on fasteners that are subjected to high temperatures, such as exhaust manifold bolts and nuts.
Asbestos A natural fibrous mineral with great heat resistance, commonly used in the composition of brake friction materials. Asbestos is a health hazard and the dust created by brake systems should never be inhaled or ingested.
Axle A shaft on which a wheel revolves, or which revolves with a wheel. Also, a solid beam that connects the two wheels at one end of the vehicle. An axle which also transmits power to the wheels is known as a live axle.
Axleshaft A single rotating shaft, on either side of the differential, which delivers power from the final drive assembly to the drive wheels. Also called a driveshaft or a halfshaft.

B

Ball bearing An anti-friction bearing consisting of a hardened inner and outer race with hardened steel balls between two races.
Bearing The curved surface on a shaft or in a bore, or the part assembled into either, that permits relative motion between them with minimum wear and friction.

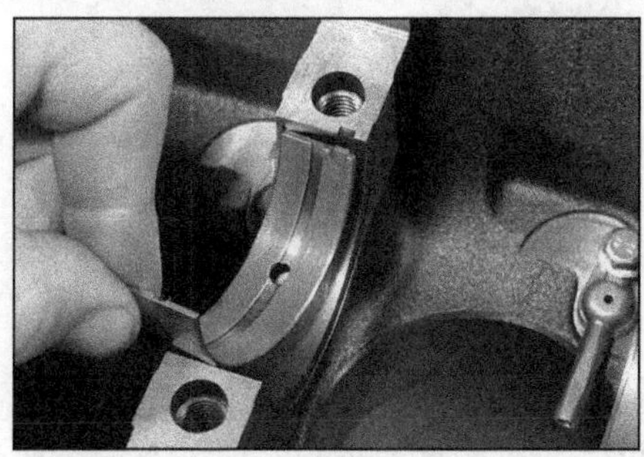

Bearing

Big-end bearing The bearing in the end of the connecting rod that's attached to the crankshaft.
Bleed nipple A valve on a brake wheel cylinder, caliper or other hydraulic component that is opened to purge the hydraulic system of air. Also called a bleed screw.
Brake bleeding Procedure for removing air from lines of a hydraulic brake system.

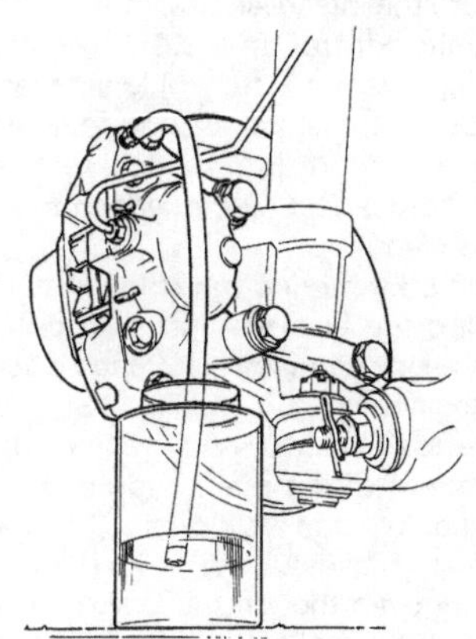

Brake bleeding

Brake disc The component of a disc brake that rotates with the wheels.
Brake drum The component of a drum brake that rotates with the wheels.
Brake linings The friction material which contacts the brake disc or drum to retard the vehicle's speed. The linings are bonded or riveted to the brake pads or shoes.
Brake pads The replaceable friction pads that pinch the brake disc when the brakes are applied. Brake pads consist of a friction material bonded or riveted to a rigid backing plate.
Brake shoe The crescent-shaped carrier to which the brake linings are mounted and which forces the lining against the rotating drum during braking.
Braking systems For more information on braking systems, consult the *Haynes Automotive Brake Manual*.
Breaker bar A long socket wrench handle providing greater leverage.
Bulkhead The insulated partition between the engine and the passenger compartment.

C

Caliper The non-rotating part of a disc-brake assembly that straddles the disc and carries the brake pads. The caliper also contains the hydraulic components that cause the pads to pinch the disc when the brakes are applied. A caliper is also a measuring tool that can be set to measure inside or outside dimensions of an object.
Camshaft A rotating shaft on which a series of cam lobes operate the valve mechanisms. The camshaft may be driven by gears, by sprockets and chain or by sprockets and a belt.
Canister A container in an evaporative emission control system; contains activated charcoal granules to trap vapours from the fuel system.

Canister

Carburettor A device which mixes fuel with air in the proper proportions to provide a desired power output from a spark ignition internal combustion engine.
Castellated Resembling the parapets along the top of a castle wall. For example, a castellated balljoint stud nut.
Castor In wheel alignment, the backward or forward tilt of the steering axis. Castor is positive when the steering axis is inclined rearward at the top.

Catalytic converter A silencer-like device in the exhaust system which converts certain pollutants in the exhaust gases into less harmful substances.

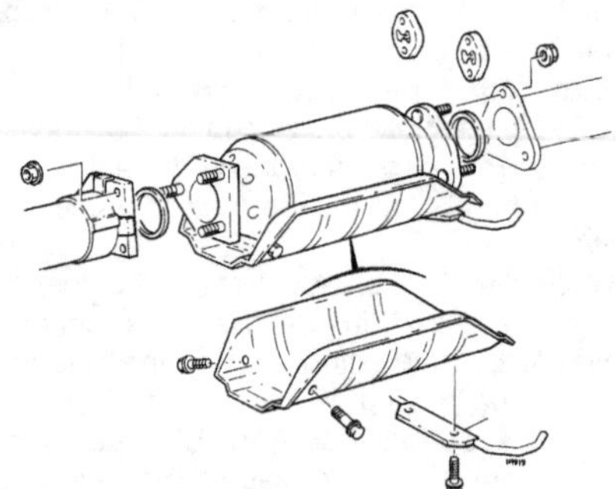

Catalytic converter

Circlip A ring-shaped clip used to prevent endwise movement of cylindrical parts and shafts. An internal circlip is installed in a groove in a housing; an external circlip fits into a groove on the outside of a cylindrical piece such as a shaft.

Clearance The amount of space between two parts. For example, between a piston and a cylinder, between a bearing and a journal, etc.

Coil spring A spiral of elastic steel found in various sizes throughout a vehicle, for example as a springing medium in the suspension and in the valve train.

Compression Reduction in volume, and increase in pressure and temperature, of a gas, caused by squeezing it into a smaller space.

Compression ratio The relationship between cylinder volume when the piston is at top dead centre and cylinder volume when the piston is at bottom dead centre.

Constant velocity (CV) joint A type of universal joint that cancels out vibrations caused by driving power being transmitted through an angle.

Core plug A disc or cup-shaped metal device inserted in a hole in a casting through which core was removed when the casting was formed. Also known as a freeze plug or expansion plug.

Crankcase The lower part of the engine block in which the crankshaft rotates.

Crankshaft The main rotating member, or shaft, running the length of the crankcase, with offset "throws" to which the connecting rods are attached.

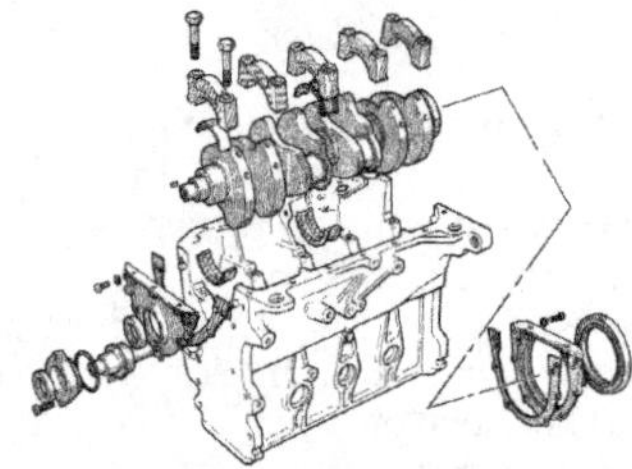

Crankshaft assembly

Crocodile clip See Alligator clip

D

Diagnostic code Code numbers obtained by accessing the diagnostic mode of an engine management computer. This code can be used to determine the area in the system where a malfunction may be located.

Disc brake A brake design incorporating a rotating disc onto which brake pads are squeezed. The resulting friction converts the energy of a moving vehicle into heat.

Double-overhead cam (DOHC) An engine that uses two overhead camshafts, usually one for the intake valves and one for the exhaust valves.

Drivebelt(s) The belt(s) used to drive accessories such as the alternator, water pump, power steering pump, air conditioning compressor, etc. off the crankshaft pulley.

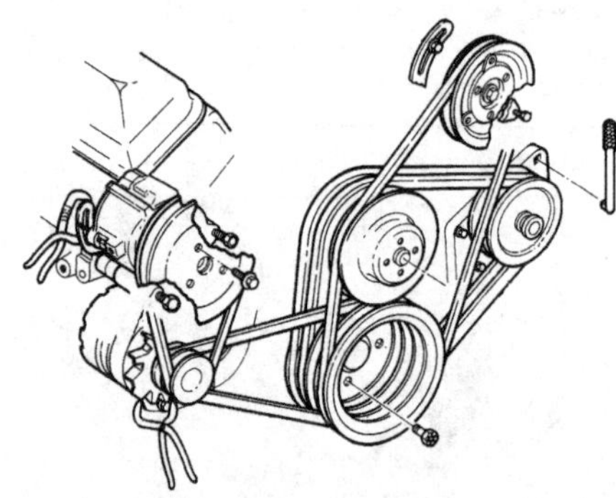

Accessory drivebelts

Driveshaft Any shaft used to transmit motion. Commonly used when referring to the axleshafts on a front wheel drive vehicle.

Drum brake A type of brake using a drum-shaped metal cylinder attached to the inner surface of the wheel. When the brake pedal is pressed, curved brake shoes with friction linings press against the inside of the drum to slow or stop the vehicle.

E

EGR valve A valve used to introduce exhaust gases into the intake air stream.

Electronic control unit (ECU) A computer which controls (for instance) ignition and fuel injection systems, or an anti-lock braking system. For more information refer to the *Haynes Automotive Electrical and Electronic Systems Manual.*

Electronic Fuel Injection (EFI) A computer controlled fuel system that distributes fuel through an injector located in each intake port of the engine.

Emergency brake A braking system, independent of the main hydraulic system, that can be used to slow or stop the vehicle if the primary brakes fail, or to hold the vehicle stationary even though the brake pedal isn't depressed. It usually consists of a hand lever that actuates either front or rear brakes mechanically through a series of cables and linkages. Also known as a handbrake or parking brake.

Endfloat The amount of lengthwise movement between two parts. As applied to a crankshaft, the distance that the crankshaft can move forward and back in the cylinder block.

Engine management system (EMS) A computer controlled system which manages the fuel injection and the ignition systems in an integrated fashion.

Exhaust manifold A part with several passages through which exhaust gases leave the engine combustion chambers and enter the exhaust pipe.

F

Fan clutch A viscous (fluid) drive coupling device which permits variable engine fan speeds in relation to engine speeds.

Feeler blade A thin strip or blade of hardened steel, ground to an exact thickness, used to check or measure clearances between parts.

Feeler blade

Firing order The order in which the engine cylinders fire, or deliver their power strokes, beginning with the number one cylinder.

Flywheel A heavy spinning wheel in which energy is absorbed and stored by means of momentum. On cars, the flywheel is attached to the crankshaft to smooth out firing impulses.

Free play The amount of travel before any action takes place. The "looseness" in a linkage, or an assembly of parts, between the initial application of force and actual movement. For example, the distance the brake pedal moves before the pistons in the master cylinder are actuated.

Fuse An electrical device which protects a circuit against accidental overload. The typical fuse contains a soft piece of metal which is calibrated to melt at a predetermined current flow (expressed as amps) and break the circuit.

Fusible link A circuit protection device consisting of a conductor surrounded by heat-resistant insulation. The conductor is smaller than the wire it protects, so it acts as the weakest link in the circuit. Unlike a blown fuse, a failed fusible link must frequently be cut from the wire for replacement.

G

Gap The distance the spark must travel in jumping from the centre electrode to the side electrode in a spark plug. Also refers to the spacing between the points in a contact breaker assembly in a conventional points-type ignition, or to the distance between the reluctor or rotor and the pickup coil in an electronic ignition.

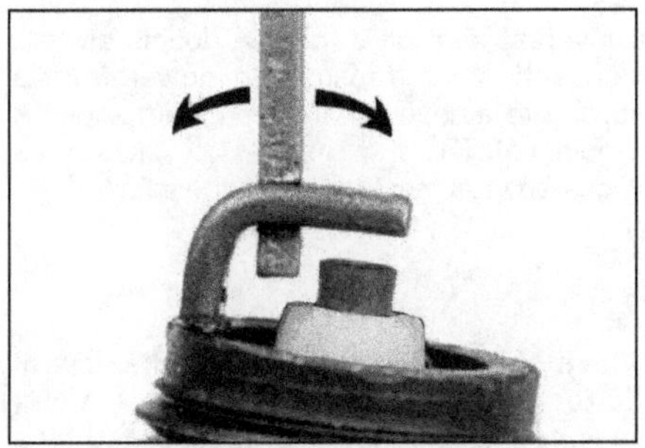

Adjusting spark plug gap

Gasket Any thin, soft material - usually cork, cardboard, asbestos or soft metal - installed between two metal surfaces to ensure a good seal. For instance, the cylinder head gasket seals the joint between the block and the cylinder head.

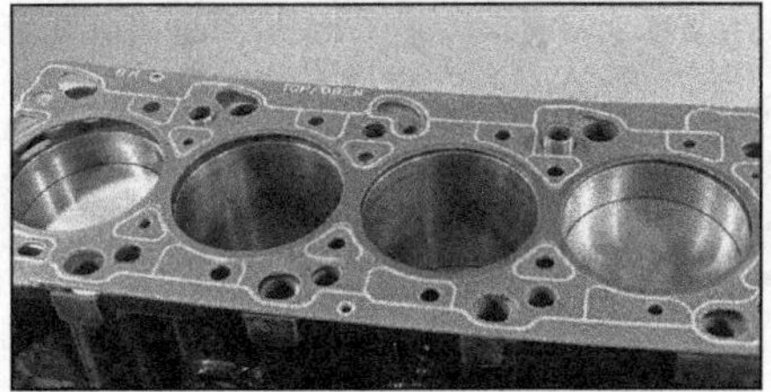

Gasket

Gauge An instrument panel display used to monitor engine conditions. A gauge with a movable pointer on a dial or a fixed scale is an analogue gauge. A gauge with a numerical readout is called a digital gauge.

H

Halfshaft A rotating shaft that transmits power from the final drive unit to a drive wheel, usually when referring to a live rear axle.

Harmonic balancer A device designed to reduce torsion or twisting vibration in the crankshaft. May be incorporated in the crankshaft pulley. Also known as a vibration damper.

Hone An abrasive tool for correcting small irregularities or differences in diameter in an engine cylinder, brake cylinder, etc.

Hydraulic tappet A tappet that utilises hydraulic pressure from the engine's lubrication system to maintain zero clearance (constant contact with both camshaft and valve stem). Automatically adjusts to variation in valve stem length. Hydraulic tappets also reduce valve noise.

I

Ignition timing The moment at which the spark plug fires, usually expressed in the number of crankshaft degrees before the piston reaches the top of its stroke.

Inlet manifold A tube or housing with passages through which flows the air-fuel mixture (carburettor vehicles and vehicles with throttle body injection) or air only (port fuel-injected vehicles) to the port openings in the cylinder head.

J

Jump start Starting the engine of a vehicle with a discharged or weak battery by attaching jump leads from the weak battery to a charged or helper battery.

L

Load Sensing Proportioning Valve (LSPV) A brake hydraulic system control valve that works like a proportioning valve, but also takes into consideration the amount of weight carried by the rear axle.

Locknut A nut used to lock an adjustment nut, or other threaded component, in place. For example, a locknut is employed to keep the adjusting nut on the rocker arm in position.

Lockwasher A form of washer designed to prevent an attaching nut from working loose.

M

MacPherson strut A type of front suspension system devised by Earle MacPherson at Ford of England. In its original form, a simple lateral link with the anti-roll bar creates the lower control arm. A long strut - an integral coil spring and shock absorber - is mounted between the body and the steering knuckle. Many modern so-called MacPherson strut systems use a conventional lower A-arm and don't rely on the anti-roll bar for location.

Multimeter An electrical test instrument with the capability to measure voltage, current and resistance.

N

NOx Oxides of Nitrogen. A common toxic pollutant emitted by petrol and diesel engines at higher temperatures.

O

Ohm The unit of electrical resistance. One volt applied to a resistance of one ohm will produce a current of one amp.

Ohmmeter An instrument for measuring electrical resistance.

O-ring A type of sealing ring made of a special rubber-like material; in use, the O-ring is compressed into a groove to provide the sealing action.

Overhead cam (ohc) engine An engine with the camshaft(s) located on top of the cylinder head(s).

Overhead valve (ohv) engine An engine with the valves located in the cylinder head, but with the camshaft located in the engine block.

Oxygen sensor A device installed in the engine exhaust manifold, which senses the oxygen content in the exhaust and converts this information into an electric current. Also called a Lambda sensor.

P

Phillips screw A type of screw head having a cross instead of a slot for a corresponding type of screwdriver.

Plastigage A thin strip of plastic thread, available in different sizes, used for measuring clearances. For example, a strip of Plastigage is laid across a bearing journal. The parts are assembled and dismantled; the width of the crushed strip indicates the clearance between journal and bearing.

Plastigage

Propeller shaft The long hollow tube with universal joints at both ends that carries power from the transmission to the differential on front-engined rear wheel drive vehicles.

Proportioning valve A hydraulic control valve which limits the amount of pressure to the rear brakes during panic stops to prevent wheel lock-up.

R

Rack-and-pinion steering A steering system with a pinion gear on the end of the steering shaft that mates with a rack (think of a geared wheel opened up and laid flat). When the steering wheel is turned, the pinion turns, moving the rack to the left or right. This movement is transmitted through the track rods to the steering arms at the wheels.

Radiator A liquid-to-air heat transfer device designed to reduce the temperature of the coolant in an internal combustion engine cooling system.

Refrigerant Any substance used as a heat transfer agent in an air-conditioning system. R-12 has been the principle refrigerant for many years; recently, however, manufacturers have begun using R-134a, a non-CFC substance that is considered less harmful to the ozone in the upper atmosphere.

Rocker arm A lever arm that rocks on a shaft or pivots on a stud. In an overhead valve engine, the rocker arm converts the upward movement of the pushrod into a downward movement to open a valve.

Rotor In a distributor, the rotating device inside the cap that connects the centre electrode and the outer terminals as it turns, distributing the high voltage from the coil secondary winding to the proper spark plug. Also, that part of an alternator which rotates inside the stator. Also, the rotating assembly of a turbocharger, including the compressor wheel, shaft and turbine wheel.

Runout The amount of wobble (in-and-out movement) of a gear or wheel as it's rotated. The amount a shaft rotates "out-of-true." The out-of-round condition of a rotating part.

S

Sealant A liquid or paste used to prevent leakage at a joint. Sometimes used in conjunction with a gasket.

Sealed beam lamp An older headlight design which integrates the reflector, lens and filaments into a hermetically-sealed one-piece unit. When a filament burns out or the lens cracks, the entire unit is simply replaced.

Serpentine drivebelt A single, long, wide accessory drivebelt that's used on some newer vehicles to drive all the accessories, instead of a series of smaller, shorter belts. Serpentine drivebelts are usually tensioned by an automatic tensioner.

Serpentine drivebelt

Shim Thin spacer, commonly used to adjust the clearance or relative positions between two parts. For example, shims inserted into or under bucket tappets control valve clearances. Clearance is adjusted by changing the thickness of the shim.

Slide hammer A special puller that screws into or hooks onto a component such as a shaft or bearing; a heavy sliding handle on the shaft bottoms against the end of the shaft to knock the component free.

Sprocket A tooth or projection on the periphery of a wheel, shaped to engage with a chain or drivebelt. Commonly used to refer to the sprocket wheel itself.

Starter inhibitor switch On vehicles with an automatic transmission, a switch that prevents starting if the vehicle is not in Neutral or Park.

Strut See MacPherson strut.

T

Tappet A cylindrical component which transmits motion from the cam to the valve stem, either directly or via a pushrod and rocker arm. Also called a cam follower.

Thermostat A heat-controlled valve that regulates the flow of coolant between the cylinder block and the radiator, so maintaining optimum engine operating temperature. A thermostat is also used in some air cleaners in which the temperature is regulated.

Thrust bearing The bearing in the clutch assembly that is moved in to the release levers by clutch pedal action to disengage the clutch. Also referred to as a release bearing.

Timing belt A toothed belt which drives the camshaft. Serious engine damage may result if it breaks in service.

Timing chain A chain which drives the camshaft.

Toe-in The amount the front wheels are closer together at the front than at the rear. On rear wheel drive vehicles, a slight amount of toe-in is usually specified to keep the front wheels running parallel on the road by offsetting other forces that tend to spread the wheels apart.

Toe-out The amount the front wheels are closer together at the rear than at the front. On front wheel drive vehicles, a slight amount of toe-out is usually specified.

Tools For full information on choosing and using tools, refer to the *Haynes Automotive Tools Manual.*

Tracer A stripe of a second colour applied to a wire insulator to distinguish that wire from another one with the same colour insulator.

Tune-up A process of accurate and careful adjustments and parts replacement to obtain the best possible engine performance.

Turbocharger A centrifugal device, driven by exhaust gases, that pressurises the intake air. Normally used to increase the power output from a given engine displacement, but can also be used primarily to reduce exhaust emissions (as on VW's "Umwelt" Diesel engine).

U

Universal joint or U-joint A double-pivoted connection for transmitting power from a driving to a driven shaft through an angle. A U-joint consists of two Y-shaped yokes and a cross-shaped member called the spider.

V

Valve A device through which the flow of liquid, gas, vacuum, or loose material in bulk may be started, stopped, or regulated by a movable part that opens, shuts, or partially obstructs one or more ports or passageways. A valve is also the movable part of such a device.

Valve clearance The clearance between the valve tip (the end of the valve stem) and the rocker arm or tappet. The valve clearance is measured when the valve is closed.

Vernier caliper A precision measuring instrument that measures inside and outside dimensions. Not quite as accurate as a micrometer, but more convenient.

Viscosity The thickness of a liquid or its resistance to flow.

Volt A unit for expressing electrical "pressure" in a circuit. One volt that will produce a current of one ampere through a resistance of one ohm.

W

Welding Various processes used to join metal items by heating the areas to be joined to a molten state and fusing them together. For more information refer to the *Haynes Automotive Welding Manual.*

Wiring diagram A drawing portraying the components and wires in a vehicle's electrical system, using standardised symbols. For more information refer to the *Haynes Automotive Electrical and Electronic Systems Manual.*

Note: *References throughout this index are in the form* "**Chapter number**" • "**Page number**". *So, for example, 2C•15 refers to page 15 of Chapter 2C.*

Note: *References throughout this index are in the form* **"Chapter number" • "Page number"**. *So, for example, 2C•15 refers to page 15 of Chapter 2C.*

Note: *References throughout this index are in the form* **"Chapter number" • "Page number"**. *So, for example, 2C•15 refers to page 15 of Chapter 2C.*

Preserving Our Motoring Heritage

<
The Model J Duesenberg Derham Tourster. Only eight of these magnificent cars were ever built – this is the only example to be found outside the United States of America

Almost every car you've ever loved, loathed or desired is gathered under one roof at the Haynes Motor Museum. Over 300 immaculately presented cars and motorbikes represent every aspect of our motoring heritage, from elegant reminders of bygone days, such as the superb Model J Duesenberg to curiosities like the bug-eyed BMW Isetta. There are also many old friends and flames. Perhaps you remember the 1959 Ford Popular that you did your courting in? The magnificent 'Red Collection' is a spectacle of classic sports cars including AC, Alfa Romeo, Austin Healey, Ferrari, Lamborghini, Maserati, MG, Riley, Porsche and Triumph.

A Perfect Day Out

Each and every vehicle at the Haynes Motor Museum has played its part in the history and culture of Motoring. Today, they make a wonderful spectacle and a great day out for all the family. Bring the kids, bring Mum and Dad, but above all bring your camera to capture those golden memories for ever. You will also find an impressive array of motoring memorabilia, a comfortable 70 seat video cinema and one of the most extensive transport book shops in Britain. The Pit Stop Cafe serves everything from a cup of tea to wholesome, home-made meals or, if you prefer, you can enjoy the large picnic area nestled in the beautiful rural surroundings of Somerset.

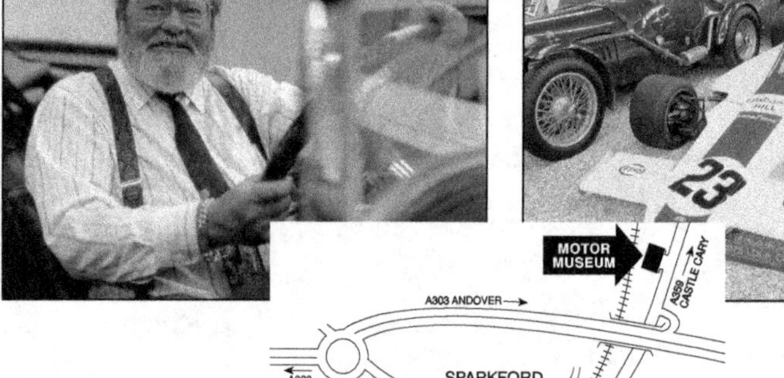

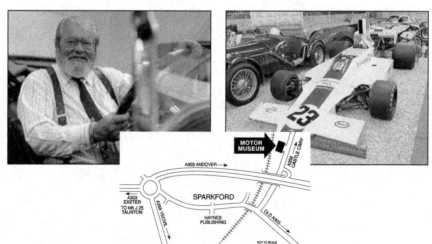

>
John Haynes O.B.E., Founder and Chairman of the museum at the wheel of a Haynes Light 12.

<
Graham Hill's Lola Cosworth Formula 1 car next to a 1934 Riley Sports.

The Museum is situated on the A359 Yeovil to Frome road at Sparkford, just off the A303 in Somerset. It is about 40 miles south of Bristol, and 25 minutes drive from the M5 intersection at Taunton.

Open 9.30am - 5.30pm (10.00am - 4.00pm Winter) 7 days a week, *except Christmas Day, Boxing Day and New Years Day*

Special rates available for schools, coach parties and outings Charitable Trust No. 292048